"Beyond the Blue Mountain"

Bartholomew Pastoral Records

Baptisms, Births, Marriages, Funerals

Carbon County
Lehigh County
Schuylkill County and
Northampton County, Pennsylvania

Carolyn Zimmerman Johns

HERITAGE BOOKS
2008

HERITAGE BOOKS
AN IMPRINT OF HERITAGE BOOKS, INC.

Books, CDs, and more—Worldwide

For our listing of thousands of titles see our website
at
www.HeritageBooks.com

Published 2008 by
HERITAGE BOOKS, INC.
Publishing Division
100 Railroad Ave. #104
Westminster, Maryland 21157

Copyright © 2001 Carolyn Zimmerman Johns

Other books by the author:
Beyond the Blue Mountain: Mahoning Township, Carbon County, Pennsylvania

All rights reserved. No part of this book may be reproduced or transmitted in any form or by any means, electronic or mechanical, including photocopying, recording or by any information storage and retrieval system without written permission from the author, except for the inclusion of brief quotations in a review.

International Standard Book Number: 978-0-7884-1892-1

Table Of Contents

<u>Description</u>	<u>Page</u>
Preface	*V*
Reverend Bartholomew and the churches he served	*VII*
Notes about Reverend Bartholomew's career	*VIII*
Letters of resignation	*IX*
Obituary: "The Reformed Church Messenger	*X*
Births and baptisms: November 4, 1869 to June 22, 1903	*7*
Marriages: February 28, 1864 to July 2, 1903	*54*
Funerals: June 9, 1861 to September 9, 1895	*88*
Combined index	*113*

Carolyn Zimmerman Johns is also the author of:

"Beyond the Blue Mountain": Mahoning Township

Contains transcribed text of the following reports:

Tax List of Towamensing Township, Northampton County, PA: 1761 & 1764
Tax Lists: Penn Township Northampton County, PA: 1773 & 1784
Federal census: Penn Township, Northampton County, PA: 1790 & 1800
Federal Census: East Penn Township, Northampton County, PA: 1810; 1820; 1830; & 1840
Federal Census: Mahoning Township, Carbon County, PA: 1850 to 1920
Federal Agricultural Census: Mahoning Township, Carbon County, PA: 1850 to 1880
Federal Mortality Census: Mahoning Township, Carbon County, PA: 1850 to 1880
Federal Veterans Census: Mahoning Township, Carbon County, PA
Civil War Soldiers, Patriotism
Strauss Cemetery Listing
St John's Cemetery Listing
Zimmerman Cemetery Listing
Nothstein Cemetery Listing

 This research aid provides a detailed resource for anyone doing research about the people who passed through or who stayed in Mahoning Township, Carbon County, PA. Usually information of the kind contained in this book is available through a variety of sometimes hard to obtain sources. This book contains all the listed sources in one volume and then supplies a full name index to the <u>complete</u> book of records. Finally the introduction to each section of the book also contains a complete reference to the source documents that were used. Cross referencing, alternative spellings and the search for family ties can be a truly rewarding experience

Carolyn Zimmerman Johns was born and raised in Mahoning Township.

Preface:

January 2001

Dear Reverend Bartholomew,

I found the record of my mother's baptism that took place in April of 1896, in the handwriting of the man who performed the ceremony. Ecstasy! Your records were in front of me, day-by-day, month-by-month, and year-by-year from 1861 to 1903. Baptisms, marriages and funerals were surely the most important events in the lives of your parishioners. I noticed some funerals coming sadly, soon after the birth and baptisms of children. Others came only after marriage, and after more births and baptisms were recorded with the individual as a parent.

I recognized other names from my family and finally started marking the names from Mahoning Valley that I knew so well. I found that many people were using your records to look for their families that came from lower Carbon and Schuylkill Counties, and that they were having difficulty understanding your script. Transcribing the earliest records, which were the hardest to read without intent study, seemed the most important first step for easier access.

I felt myself drawn into the transcription routine and kept going page after page. I deciphered your handwriting, done over a forty-two-year span requiring the spelling of names, that I am sure many times were unfamiliar to you. This is not a complaint, dear man, but instead it is a heart-felt thank you for your help. Many times your presence and strength helped me through the long hours of comparing names and the way you made different letters. Most amazing was that these hints came to me in Pennsylvania Dutch, which is what the German you spoke has come to be called.

Handwritten script has changed quite a bit in the last one hundred years and many of us now have machines on which to print information such as your records in our homes. These papers that I have been transcribing were but copies of words written by you up to one hundred and forty years ago with instruments quite different than those to which we have become accustomed to today.

The curator of the library at Franklin and Marshall College in Lancaster, Pennsylvania, where the original books in which you wrote are housed allowed me to use them to check some entries that were blurred on my copy. I can report to you that in the year 2001, your records are still being carefully preserved.

I hope I understood all of the clues you gave me and that I have interpreted your work to your satisfaction. In behalf of all the people who will use this transcription to identify not only their ancestors but the important events in their lives, thank you for your care in noting this information. In the name of all those ancestors, thank you for being a strong pillar upon which they could depend for strength and guidance in the very hard times in which they lived.

Yours truly,

Carolyn Zimmerman Johns

The Reverend Abraham Bartholomew
(March 17, 1833 – August15, 1903)

Charges as recorded by Reverend Bartholomew:

Nazareth Church	Nazareth	May 1861 to 1894
St. Paul's Church	Big Creek	May 1, 1863 to 1876
St. Jacob's Church	Weissport	September 7, 1863 to 1876
St. John's Church	Mahoning Township	May 1, 1864 to 1894
St. John's Church	Towamensing Township	March 26, 1865 to 1876
Dinkey Church	Pennsville	November 19, 1871 to 1894
Ben Salem Church	East Penn Township	March 14, 1875 to 1894
Zion's Church	West Penn Township	March 14, 1875 to 1894
St. Peter's Church	Mantzville	February 15, 1875 to 1894

Notes:

The Reverend Charles Beck at Stone Church, near Kreidersville, Pa, confirmed him as a member of the Reformed Church at the age of 16.

The territory that was his parish (December 1950) now enjoys the services of six pastors.

In addition to his brothers, two sisters survived him: Mrs. Jonathan Krauss, of Bath, and Mrs. W. J. Evans, of Slatington.

The funeral took place from his late residence at the corner of South 3rd and Bridge Streets on Thursday afternoon at 1:30. The services were held at the Lehighton Zion Reformed Church. Interment was made at the family plot at Lehighton Cemetery.

To the Reverend Abraham Bartholomew:

At an election for Pastor, held in the St. Peter's Congregation on the 18th day of July, 1880 you were duly elected to that office; and in accordance with the instructions given us, we the elders and deacons of aforesaid congregation do hereby unite in solemn calling you to the pastoral office as above mentioned and affectionately urge upon you the acceptance of our call. The duties, which will be required of you, are those, which usually belong to pastoral office, specifically set forth in the constitution of the Synod of the Reformed Church in the United States. To encourage you in the discharge of the duties of your important office, we promise you in the name of the members of the congregation all proper attention, love and obedience in the Lord, and in consideration of services we do obligate you in their behalf to pay you for your support, the sum of one hundred annually so long as you continue to be out pastor. In witness of the above transaction and obligation we do hereunto subscribe our names this 3rd day of April A. D. 1881

Daniel M. Dreisbach; Wm H. Wehr, Deacons; Jacob Mantz, Elder

Abraham Bartholomew served from April 3rd 1881 until August 13, 1894.

The first step taken to organize the present Reformed congregation (which became The Zion Reformed Church in Lehighton) appears on the records of East Pennsylvania Classis. At an adjourned meeting held in Catasauqua, May 20, 1872, Rev. Abraham Bartholomew was authorized to organize a congregation at Lehighton." (Historical sketch prepared by Rev. David A. Winter to mark the 35th anniversary)

Paid, S. E. Ayers, MD, and $25.00 on July 30, 1888, being one half of the $50.00, which I promised to pay him in case he could cure my rectal trouble.... Abraham Bartholomew. (This entry was included because it may give a clue to the physical disabilities that resulted in his retirement from churchly duties.)

There are 1,968 births and baptisms, 1,191 marriages, and 1,360 funerals reported in his records. When witnesses are included there are references to 10, 832 people

A microfilm copy of Abraham Bartholomew's original records was made at library of the Evangelical and Reformed Church Historical Society located in the Lancaster Theological Seminary at 555 West James Street in Lancaster, Pa. 17603 on the 30th of June 1973. The Church of the Latter Day Saints has assigned film Number 0940437 to the microfilm containing his records.

Letters of Resignation: Lehighton, Pa, October 1st, 1887

To the Consistories of the Mahoning Charge:

My Dear Brother

In the providence of God, a painful duty devolves upon me as your pastor. It is well known amongst you that during the past three months, I have not been able to discharge the duties of my sacred calling My sickness is of such a lingering nature, that no one can tell, how soon, if ever I may minister in spiritual things again. As I do not wish to hinder the work of the Lord, nor keep you from calling another pastor, I hereby affectionately tender you my resignation to take effect, November 1st, 1887, with the request that you unite with me in petitioning the classis of Lehigh, to dissolve the pastoral relations.

Believe me, I take this step with feelings of deep sorrow. It is not that I love you less, but that the cause of Christ may not suffer through the illness of one of his servants. I most cheerfully bear testimony to your constant and hearty cooperation in advancing the kingdom of our dear Redeemer. Let us then tenderly dissolve the bond of loving fellowship which has held us together during many years of earnest, and I trust, faithful service. And now, may the peace of God which passeth all understanding keep your hearts and minds in Christ Jesus. Amen-

Your affectionate pastor,

Abraham Bartholomew

To the Reverend Classis of Lehigh

Dear Brother
At a meeting of the consistories of the Mahoning Charge, held at Lehighton, Pa. In October 1887, the resignation of the Pastor Rev. A. Bartholomew was read. In view of the facts set forth in the call, we, the elders and deacons of the Mahoning Charge, do hereby join our pastor in petitioning your Reverend body to dissolve the pastoral relations

Yours respectfully,

To the Reverend Classis of Lehigh,

Dear Brother,

I have a sad report to submit to your reverend body. The present condition of my health compels me, at least for a season, to lay down the pastoral staff. I deeply regret this step, but we know that all things shall work together for good for them that love the Lord.

In view of my resignation as pastor of the Mahoning Charge, I respectively ask you to appoint another supply for the St. Peter's congregation.

Yours in the Lord,
A. B.

Reverend Abraham Bartholomew

Reprinted from:

The Reformed Church Messenger; Vol. LXXII, No. 37
Dated September 10, 1903

"If we were to write the epitaph on the monument of this servant of God, who died in the triumphs of the faith, it would be, 'magnified his office'. His whole heart was spent in the up building of the kingdom of grace in the hearts of men. The Church would wield a greater influence in the world if all her office bearers had more of his mind and spirit. At the funeral service, the Rev. J. G. Dengler read the obituary, in which he paid a just tribute to the life and work of one who labored much and suffered more for over forty years as a minister of Christ, and from which we have quoted freely in this sketch.

Rev. Abraham Bartholomew was born in Dannersville, Northampton County, on March 17th, 1833. He was a son of George H. and Hannah Bartholomew, and was the oldest of eight children. We are assured that the parental home was one of positive Christian nature. His first educational training he received in the public schools. Later on he entered the Classical Academy at Easton where he came under the molding influence of Dr. Van Deveer, and the Rev. Dr. Apple, men known for their strong intellectual ability and positive Christian characters. Liberally prepared according to the facilities of the day, he then entered the Theological Seminary at Mercersburg, where he was brought, among others, under the tuition of two men whose names are familiar, not only to the Church, but even to the entire theological world, Rev. Drs. Philip Schaff and Bernard C. Wolff. He was licensed to preach by East Pennsylvania Classis at a meeting held in Fogelsville, in May 1861, and in November of the same year he was solemnly ordained to the holy ministry, and installed as pastor of the congregation at Nazareth. The committee consisted of Revs. D. V. Heisler and E. W. Reinicke. This congregation was at that time small, and mostly made up of retired farmers. Before he had entered the ministry he had successfully taught school ten years, and now, because his congregation was small and support insufficient, he again taught two terms more. In the spring of 1862, in addition to serving at Nazareth, he began to preach at Big Creek, Carbon County, and in 1864 he moved to Lehighton, where he lived for almost forty years.

From this time on he must, indeed, have been a busy man, for he served no less than nine congregations. In 1876 Big Creek, Weissport and Towamensing were separated from his large and growing field, and Rev. J. E. Freeman was elected as pastor. It was his oft-expressed wish that the five congregations up to the time of his resignation, should be divided into two pastoral charges, because they constituted too large a field for one man to serve. He knew the demands of the field and he had a clear conscientious sense also of the demands of a pastor. This charge he served faithfully, oft times under conditions and endurances of which the people generally knew little, or nothing, until his physical disability forced him to resign, which took place August 14th, 1894.

Time does not allow us to dwell on the significance of his pastorate, much as we feel like paying a proper tribute to a revered father, who has left such a distinct impress, and whom we learned to love for his noble record and his sterling qualities of character. Think as best you can of the state of things thirty to forty years ago. Think of the vast field he traversed, the roads, the weather. Think of humanity as it is, as it was. Think of a mortal man standing up and moving among men, bidding them for thirty-three years to lead Christian lives. Here are a few statistics that are full of meaning for those who reflect: Married 1,191 couples, baptized 1,968, confirmed 1,569, had alone 1360 funerals, and assisted at many others. This same territory is now occupied by five self-supporting pastoral charges—namely, Weissport, Towamensing, Lehighton, Mauch Chunk, and Mahoning.

Our brief sojourn in this section, our frequent contact and conversation with many former parishioners and friends of the departed, and our social fellowship, has confirmed us in our conclusion concerning these leading official qualities of Father Bartholomew. In the pulpit a man of very ready and forceful powers commanding attention and sustaining it. His preaching was teaching or doctrinal, needing no reinforcement outside of the clear thinking of the Bible and the standards of the Church. For him, the Word, the Sacraments, the Holy Office were divine institutions, all sufficient to sustain themselves, but to save the world, and to advance the kingdom of God among men. He was pronouncedly churchly in personnel appearance, in the pulpit, among his people; in his home to the very end of his life there was no mistake in a man who was clearly conscious that he was a minister of the Gospel. No wonder people generally speak so well of him. He was a positive powerful preacher, a dignified, but very cordial and approachable pastor, tactful in practical affairs of is official life.

He was married to Miss Sarah Newhard, of Pennsville, Northampton County, on December 7th, 1861, who so shared all the sorrows and trials of which others did not dream. Three sons survive him—viz., Rev. Calvin E. of Cressona; Eugene U. of Wilkes-Barre, and Rev. Dr, Allen R. Bartholomew, Secretary of the Board of Foreign Missions, his brother.

Nine years ago Brother Bartholomew was forced to retire from active official work, not because of a waning of the powers of mind, heart, or will or even of general bodily health. Chain an eagle by one foot and his lofty flight is hindered. Do we reflect upon the trials this brother endured, constituted as he was, mind so active, spirit so cheerful, will so resolute, heart so loyal to office and Church and even a body generally so healthful and vigorous, yet during all these years of forced retirement? There is much to reflect upon: the trial, and inner trials, he had to pass through. Who in all those years has visited him and not found him the cheerful Christian gentleman, ready to talk far rather about the things of the Church than about his trials and hindrances, or to find him despondent, careless, unhappy. He kept in touch with the movements of the Church and the world. His mind never ran empty. More than once we found on Mondays that he had read and reflected upon the Gospel and Epistle. His Bible and other works of solid worth lay at easy reach. In a word, he kept his heart and mind from sinking into the slough of despair, and so with quiet resignation to the will of God who orders all in his wisdom and love, he met the last and severest period of his sufferings, until his spirit was released from it's bondage, and entered into rest and blessedness on Saturday, August 15th, at 2 p.m., aged 70 years, 4 months, and 28 days. 'And I heard a voice from heaven saying unto me, Write, blessed are the dead which die in the Lord from henceforth: yea, saith the Spirit, that they may rest from their labors and their works do follow them'"

Author's Note

Several date conflicts require explanation:

a. Rev. Bartholomew started his ministry in May of 1861. He was formally ordained as Pastor of the Nazareth Church in November of 1861.
b. Rev. Bartholomew completed his ministry on August 13, 1894 and handed in his resignation on August 14, 1894.
c. Rev. Bartholomew served several churches at the same time. Church services were held at different times on a Sunday to allow him to go from church to church. Some times the church services were held every other week.
d. After the "formal" completion of his pastoral duties Rev. Bartholomew was frequently called upon to participate in baptisms marriages and funerals. He preformed Baptisms until June 22, 1903, Marriages until July 2, 1903, and Funerals until September 9, 1895.
e. Rev. Bartholomew has recorded 41 more funerals and one less birth than listed by the author of his obituary.

Carolyn Zimmerman Johns

Births, Baptisms, Marriages, and Funerals

Recorded by:

Reverend Abraham Bartholomew

Beyond the Blue Mountain, Vol. II

Bartholomew's Births and Baptism's

Births and Baptisms

April 4, 1866 to June 22, 1903

Line #	Surname	Child Given	Middle	Birth Day	Birth Mth	Birth Year	Baptism Day	Baptism Mth	Baptism Year	Father Given	Mother Given	Nee	Witness Given	Witness Surname	Witness Given	Witness Surname
B-1	Solomon	Anna	Elizabeth	4	April	1866	4	Nov	1869	George	Anna Eliza	Taglehner	-	-	-	-
B-2	Solomon	John		4	June	1868	4	Nov	1869	George	Anna Eliza	Taglehner	-	-	-	-
B-3	Meinhard	Charles	Augustus	25	June	1869	6	Nov	1869	Charles	Elizabeth B	Voelker	Charles	May	Alavesta	Thomas
B-4	Beltz	Estella	Amanda	25	Feb	1869	7	Nov	1869	Isaac	Caroline	Ebert				
B-5	Ruch	Emma	Louisa	5	Sept	1869	7	Nov	1869	Christopher	Amelia	Daring	Adolph	Darring	Emma	Boll
B-6	Leibenguth	Edward	Franklin	17	Sept	1869	7	Nov	1869	Franklin	Mary	Scheckler				
B-7	Beltz	Laura	Martina	6	Sept	1869	7	Nov	1869	Harrison	Emma	Neitzel	Rebecca	Neitzel		
B-8	Dunbar	Sarah	Elizabeth	12	July	1869	13	Nov	1869	Robert	Sarah	Fritzinger	Lafayette	Brown	Mary Ann	Helder
B-9	Green	James	Franklin	4	Oct	1869	14	Nov	1869	Aaron	Lucy Ann	Knappenberger				
B-10	Kromer	Martin	Alfred	10	Sept	1869	14	Nov	1869	John	Hannah	Saeger	Alfred	Kromer	Priscilla	Roth
B-11	Moyer	Charles	Wilson	17	Oct	1869	23	Nov	1869	Franklin	Fianna	Bartholomew	Wilson	German	Ellen	Bartholomew
B-12	Bowman	Lee	Hudders	13	Oct	1869	28	Nov	1869	Rodger	Sarah	Jones	Henry	Bowman	Lewina	Peter
B-13	Schnell	Emma	Elizabeth	17	Oct	1869	28	Nov	1869	Reuben	Louisa	Dengler				
B-14	Brown	Ellen	Elmira	19	Sept	1869	28	Nov	1869	Lewis	Mary Amanda	Cope	P.	Buck	Eva Ann	Eckhart
B-15	Arner	Calvin	Elijah	7	Oct	1869	1	Dec	1869	John H	Mary	Wehr				
B-16	Bechtel	Francis	Elizabeth	4	Nov	1869	5	Dec	1869	Aaron	Jarrusa	Frantz			Susan	Beck
B-17	Zone	Charles	Joseph	14	Nov	1869	12	Dec	1869	Joseph	Johannah	Kaiser	Franz	Ludwig		
B-18	Gommery	Harrison	Nelson	25	Oct	1869	12	Dec	1869	William	Mary Ann	Kreitz				
B-19	Fulmer	Carrie		24	Nov	1869	14	Dec	1869	Edwin	Catharine	Breifogel				
B-20	Dotter	Irwin	Ellsworth	16	Sept	1869	19	Dec	1869	Lazarus	Angelina	Ziegenfuss	Thomas	Fink	Sarah Ann	Walck
B-21	Rape	Harry		15	Nov	1869	19	Dec	1869	Jonas	Rachel	Ruth	Henry	Franz		
B-22	Nanstiel	John	Adolph	10	Nov	1869	19	Dec	1869	John A	Anna Christianna	Hoffman				
B-23	Kauffman	William	Henry	19	Dec	1869	21	Dec	1869	William	Louisa Sarah	Sterner	Henry	Sterner	Mary	Hahn
B-24	Behler	Wilson		27	Sept	1869	26	Dec	1869	Levi	Matilda	Peter	William	Peter	Harriet	Stroup
B-25	Lerch	Morris	William	12	Dec	1869	29	Dec	1869	Peter A	Mary Ann	Romig				
B-26	Rappe	George	John	1	Oct	1869	1	Jan	1870	Christian	Catherine	Lauber	Charles	Miller		
B-27	Rappe	William	Christian	4	Dec	1867	1	Jan	1870	Christian	Catherine	Lauber				
B-28	Pettit	Robert	Harry	21	Dec	1869	1	Jan	1870	Robert	Amanda	Rinker	William	Rinker	Sarah	Lower (Anewalt)
B-29	Bower	Louisa		11	Sept	1869	9	Jan	1870	John	Lydia	(Bower)	Elias	Anewalt	Eliza	(Brown)
B-30	Kern	Jacob	Milton	9	Dec	1869	9	Jan	1870	Peter	Jane	Brotzman	Jacob	Brown	Matilda	
B-31	Arner	Quintin	David	6	Nov	1869	9	Jan	1870	Thomas	Eliza_	(Arner)	David	Schaefer	Sally Ann	(Schaefer)
B-32	Kunkle	Eugene	Albert	26	May	1869	10	Jan	1870	Joel	Susanna	Boyer	Tobias	Greenzweig	Elizabeth	Roth
B-33	Reger	Ida	Rebecca	11	Nov	1869	16	Jan	1870	William E	Sophia	Pfleider				
B-34	Balliet	Sarah	Jenetta	18	Jan	1870	21	Jan	1870	Nathan	Sarah Ann	Meinhart				
B-35	Blose	Dianna	Rebecca	6	Nov	1869	23	Jan	1870	Simon	Harrietta	Wagner	Daniel	Beer	Rebecca	Blose
B-36	Kindt	Howard	Andrew	12	Dec	1869	25	Jan	1870	Francis	Susan	Boyer				
B-37	Hontz	John	Franklin	10	Dec	1869	30	Jan	1870	John	Matilda	Dreisbach	Gideon	Nothstein	Leah	Steigerwalt
B-38	Field	William	Samuel	3	Jan	1870	3	Feb	1870	Samuel F	Elvina	Kern	Nathan	Kern	Sally	Rex
B-39	Kunsman	Oliver	Pearce	13	Dec	1870	6	Feb	1870	Jacob	Mary	Peter	William	Remaly	Minnie	Blose

Beyonnd the Blue Mountain, Vol. II   Births and Baptisms

Line #	Surname	Child Given	Middle	Birth Day	Birth Mth	Birth Year	Baptism Day	Baptism Mth	Baptism Year	Father Given	Mother Given	Nee	Witness Given	Witness Surname	Witness Given	Witness Surname
B-40	Lichtenwalder	Anna	Maria Elizabeth	24	Sept	1869	6	Feb	1870	Daniel	Sally Ann	(Lichtenwalter)	Reuben	Green	Mary	(Green)
B-41	Milherin	Robert	Edwin	10	Jan	1870	6	Feb	1870	William	Louisa	Solt	John	Beltz	Manda	Solt
B-42	Wanamacher	Charles	Harrison	8	Dec	1870	6	Feb	1870	Franklin W	Emaline	Lower	Rebecca	Bennett		
B-43	Heiny	Franklin		3	Nov	1861	9	Feb	1870	Levi	Sarah	Bergy				
B-44	Heiny	Louisa		16	Sept	1865	9	Feb	1870	Levi	Sarah	Bergy				
B-45	Heiny	Minnie		15	Dec	1866	9	Feb	1870	Levi	Sarah	Bergy				
B-46	Heiny	Mary	Eliza	6	Sept	1869	9	Feb	1870	Levi	Sarah	Bergy				
B-47	Spoonheimer	Mary	Lucetta	7	July	1869	13	Feb	1870	William H	Amanda	Hontz				
B-48	Rohrbach	William	Henry	19	Dec	1869	14	Feb	1870	Abel	Rebecca	Seitz				
B-49	Serfass	Priscilla	Jane	20	Nov	1869	15	Feb	1870	Josiah	Eliza	Marecome				
B-50	Hahn	Elmira		2	Sept	1869	15	Feb	1870	Edwin H	Elizabeth Jane	Dunlap	Lucinda	Hand		
B-51	Beninger	James		25	Dec	1869	16	Feb	1870	Adam	Sally	Moser				
B-52	Ahner	Emma	Alice	31	Dec	1869	18	Feb	1870	Reuben	Elizabeth	Hartman	William	Ziegenfuss	Kate	Haid
B-53	Berger	Mary	Jane	11	July	1869	18	Feb	1870	William	Amanda	Fisher	Sally	Haid		
B-54	Bennyhoof	John	Henry	8	Dec	1869	27	Feb	1870	John	Elizabeth	Krum				
B-55	Knecht	William	Franklin	10	Jan	1870	28	Feb	1870	Francis	Emma	Adams	Elizabeth	Gaumer		
B-56	Bowman	Alton		16	Jan	1870	1	Mar	1870	Josiah	Louisa	Berkemeyer				
B-57	Arner	Emma	Lily	25	Dec	1869	5	Mar	1870	Ammon	Anna	Beltz				
B-58	Ramaly	Ellen	Zarena	11	Jan	1870	6	Mar	1870	Moses	Sarah	Arner	Henry	Ramaly	Lydia	Miller
B-59	Fogel	Alavesta		1	Nov	1869	15	Mar	1870	Christian	Cassian	Reppert				
B-60	Nicholous	Irwin	Franklin	29	Oct	1869	20	Mar	1870	Benjamin	Catherine	Heiny	Sarah	Markley		
B-61	Kostenbader	Calvin	Henry	7	Sept	1869	20	Mar	1870	Josiah	Fayetta	Walck	John A	Boyer	Elizabeth	Christman
B-62	Walck	Mary	Agnes	21	Jan	1870	20	Mar	1870	John E	Eva Ann	Greenzweig	George	Walck	Mary	Dottery
B-63	Farren	Thomas	Richard	2	Feb	1870	20	Mar	1870	Daniel	Harriet	O'Brian				
B-64	Muschlitz	Sylvester		23	Nov	1869	22	Mar	1870	William	Susanna Amanda	Brotzman				
B-65	Newhard	Allen	Albert	20	Jan	1870	24	Mar	1870	John	Elizabeth Ann	Schaefer				
B-66	Seiler	Emma	Leah	3	Mar	1870	26	Mar	1870	Samuel	Elizabeth	Graver	Lewis	Graver	Leah	Lauchnor
B-67	Walck	Alice	Tewilia	2	Jan	1870	27	Mar	1870	Philip	Mary	(Walck)	Solomon	Walck	Elizabeth	(Walck)
B-68	Ziegenfuss	Ida		19	Mar	1870	27	Mar	1870	Nathan	Emmaline	Sensinger	Daniel	Sensinger	Caroline	Kneff
B-69	Bartholomew	Minerva	Mantinia	6	Mar	1870	28	Mar	1870	Henry	Euphenia	Gross				
B-70	Xander	Wilson	Edwin	14	Mar	1870	3	April	1870	Charles Wm.	Catherine	Graver				
B-71	Trumbore	Elsie	Agnes	11	Dec	1869	3	April	1870	Nathan	Ellen	Dreher				
B-72	Stolmacher	Mary	Wilhelmina	11	Nov	1867	4	April	1870	John	Agata	Hundshammer				
B-73	Stolmacher	Helga	Matilida	12	Dec	1869	4	April	1870	John	Agata	Hundshammer				
B-74	Waterbaer	Emma	Henrietta	23	Apr	1869	15	April	1870	William	Henrietta	Kaiser	Johannah	Kaiser		
B-75	Kemery	Kate	Lovenia	10	Jan	1870	15	April	1870	Nathan	Lucinda	Patterson	Maria	Patterson		
B-76	Souders	Charles	Francis	9	Nov	1869	17	April	1870	Joseph	Mary Ann	Kiefer	Jacob	Scherer	Susan	Kelchner
B-77	Blose	Lovina		17	Jan	1870	17	April	1870	Peter	Mary	Buck	John	Beltz	Lovina	Buck
B-78	Solt	Agnes	Pauline	7	Mar	1870	17	April	1870	Paul	Pauline Barta	Nitsche	William	Nitsche	Pauline	Barta
B-79	Romig	Lucy	Jane	5	Mar	1870	17	April	1870	Ephraim	Mary Ann	Polsgrofe	Mary Ann	Kolb		
B-80	Romig	Clara	Irena	5	Mar	1870	17	April	1870	Ephraim	Mary Ann	Polsgrafe	Lucy Ann	Polsgrafe		
B-81	Gombert	Ellen	Louisa	20	Jan	1870	22	April	1870	Jonathan	Anna	Hontz	Nathan	Gombert	Medina	Krum

Births and Baptisms

Line #	Surname	Child Given	Child Middle	Birth Day	Birth Mth	Birth Year	Baptism Day	Baptism Mth	Baptism Year	Father Given	Mother Given	Nee	Witness Given	Witness Surname	Witness Given	Witness Surname
B-82	Mertz	Ellamanda		3	Feb	1870	22	April	1870	Nathan	Sally Ann	Freyman	—	—		
B-83	Smith	Mary	Ann	8	Mar	1870	30	April	1870	Samuel	Levinia	Gale		Grow		Frederic
B-84	Solt	Emma	Elizabeth	16	Mar	1870	1	May	1870	Josiah	Christianna	Snyder				
B-85	Musselman	Ida	Minerva	5	May	1870	8	May	1870	Harrison	Anna	Kessler				
B-86	Bachman	Emaline		13	Dec	1869	8	May	1870	Daniel	Ellen	Balliet				
B-87	Leffler	Ellen	Elizabeth	25	Feb	1869	8	May	1870	Aaron	Leanna	Rehrig	Henry	Beinemman	Margaret	Zundle
B-88	Tinny	Harry	Oscar	10	Feb	1870	8	May	1870	Newton H	Alvina	Bennyhoof	Aaron	Leffler	Leanna	Rehrig
B-89	Steiner	William	Robert	27	Mar	1869	8	May	1870	Nelson David	Emaline	Bennyhoof	Jonas	Bennyhoof	Elizabeth	Wasem
B-90	Fickweiler	John		29	April	1869	8	May	1870	Christian	Anna Margeret	Voegel	John	Schumacher	Anna Margeret	Fickweiler
B-91	Buss	Matilda		3	Mar	1870	15	May	1870	John Tobias	Eva	Maute	Enos	Reiser	Matilda	Bundly
B-92	Solt	William	James	13	Feb	1870	15	May	1870	Solomon	Eliza	Esch				
B-93	Beer	Rosanna		10	April	1870	15	May	1870	Alfred	Rosanna	Hagenbuch	John	Goodheil	Mary	Steinheisser
B-94	Fogel	John	Elmer	13	Feb	1870	15	May	1870	Stephen	Catherine	Kuntzman	John A	Boyer	Elizabeth	Christman
B-95	Frederick	Anna	Sevilla	30	Mar	1870	22	May	1870	Wm. Frederick	Eliza	Grow	William	Grow	Anna Maria	Mertz
B-96	Lackawuck	Mary	Jane	24	Jan	1870	22	May	1870	Frederic	Catherine	Schleicher				
B-97	Kauffman	Emma	Sarah	4	May	1870	29	May	1870	Charles	Maria	Walb	David	Walb	Sarah	Eckhart
B-98	Beer	Mary Jane	Pruella	1	Mar	1870	29	May	1870	Isaiah	Catherine	Olenwine				
B-99	Kleintopp	Charles	Valentine	6	April	1870	12	June	1870	Charles	Harriet	Kratz				
B-100	Hartman	Sarah	Amelia	17	April	1870	12	June	1870	Charles	Matilda	Herman	Jacob	Scherer	Lucy	Strassburger
B-101	Levan	Elmer	Stephen	18	Mar	1870	12	June	1870	Hiram	Maria	Dreisbach				
B-102	Wehr	Alvin	Adam	10	April	1870	19	June	1870	Nathan	Mary	Gombert	David	Wehr	Carolina	Ebert
B-103	Schaeffer	Mary	Ellen Jane	31	Mar	1870	19	June	1870	Dav d	Celestia Jane	Acker	Mary Ann	Acker		
B-104	Hagenbuch	John	Amroe	12	May	1870	26	June	1870	John	Eliza	Schwartz	Elias	Anewalt	Eliza	Reichert
B-105	Noll	Alvin	Thomas	24	May	1870	26	June	1870	William	Molly	Graver				
B-106	Kuntz	Francis	Edgar	22	April	1870	26	June	1870	Richard	Selinda	Schwartz				
B-107	Webb	Nathan	Nathaniel	15	Feb	1870	26	June	1870	Samuel	Mary	Blose	Henrietta	Weiss	Mary	Webb
B-108	Leffler	Edward	Franklin	2	Mar	1870	26	June	1870	Nathan	Ellen	Weiss				
B-109	Heilman	Pearcy	Oscar	7	May	1870	3	July	1870	Geo. Washington	Mary	Dreher				
B-110	Hoffman	Emma	Sophia	21	May	1870	3	July	1870	David	Harriet	Kretz	William	Gommery	Mary	Kreitz
B-111	Becker	Edwin	Sopherus	22	April	1870	10	July	1870	Edwin	Cassenta	Beer				
B-112	Stemmler	Quinton		19	April	1870	10	July	1870	Reuben	Louisa	Schmidt	Solomon	Stemmler	Lucy	Green
B-113	Walck	Henry	Sylvester	18	May	1870	10	July	1870	Willia m	Harriet	Selzer	Henry	Selzer	Maria	Walck
B-114	Kreiser	Amelia	Lucetta	6	Mar	1870	10	July	1870	Jacob	Catherine	Wirkley	William	Nitschie	Paulina	Barta
B-115	Fisher	Katelei	Sarah Jeanetta	6	Aug	1869	7	July	1870	Thomas	Hannah	Rabenold	John	Confer	Elizabeth	Guldner
B-116	Schaefer	Thomas	Franklin	20	Jan	1870	20	July	1870	Peter	Catherine	Heiland			Maria	Heiland
B-117	Baumgarten	Mary	Jane	9	Mar	1870	24	July	1870	Antho'y	Sarah	Schaefer			Lydia	Beltz
B-118	Strohl	Carry	June	21	June	1870	24	July	1870	William H	Mary Ann	Strohl	Aaron	Strohl	Eva	(Strohl)
B-119	Grill	Elmira	Elizabeth	26	June	1870	24	July	1870	Samuel	Carolina	(Grill)	Robert	McDaniel	Elizabeth	(McDaniel)
B-120	Graver	Hannah	Virginia	1	April	1870	24	July	1870	Samuel	Hannah	Horn	William	Seaboldt	Susan	Horn
B-121	Weida	William	Franklin	15	April	1870	31	July	1870	Aaron	Henrietta	Adams				
B-122	Weiss	George	William	11	Jan	1870	20	Aug	1870	Nero	Louisa	Hontz				
B-123	Horn	Oscar	Edwin	12	July	1870	21	Aug	1870	Thomas J	Refena	Stroup	Jacob B	Stroup	Anna Eliza	Stroup

Beyond the Blue Mountain, Vol. II

Births and Baptisms

Line #	Surname	Child Given	Middle	Birth Day	Mth	Year	Baptism Day	Mth	Year	Father Given	Mother Given	Nee	Witness Given	Surname	Witness Given	Surname
B-124	Kuebler	Henry	Franklin	29	June	1870	20	Aug	1870	Aaron	Louisa	Blose	Henry	Kuebler	Elizabeth	Moyer
B-125	Behler	Harry	Valentine	26	June	1870	21	Aug	1870	William	Matilda	Blose	John	Goodheil	Wilhelmina	(Blose)
B-126	Anthony	Elmira	Lucetta	30	June	1870	21	Aug	1870	John	Esther	Dorwort				Hill
B-127	Buss	Mary		26	Mar	1870	21	Aug	1870	Jacob	Josephina	Hill	Christian	Sandherr	Maria	Hill
B-128	Sandherr	Charles	William	27	July	1870	21	Aug	1870	Christian	Magdalena	Hill	John	Schatzlein	Frederica	Sandherr
B-129	Koons	Zacharias		2	May	1870	26	Aug	1870	Jeremiah	Kitty	Fenstermaker	Isaac	Moyer	Elizabeth	Leiby
B-130	McFarland	Wesley	Victor	4	Aug	1870	10	Sept	1870	Henry	Rebecca	(McFarland)				
B-131	Strohl	Mary	Alice	27	July	1870	10	Sept	1870	Harrison	Sarah	(Strohl)	Aaron	Strohl	Eva	(Strohl)
B-132	Mulhearn	Charles	Franklin	16	Feb	1869	6	Sept	1870	Edward	Anna Maria	Bachman	Rosa Ann	Malhearn		
B-133	Beltz	Aquilla	Jane	3	Aug	1870	11	Sept	1870	David	Louisa	Snyder				
B-134	Dreisbach	Alwena	Louisa	2	July	1870	11	Sept	1870	Dennis	Sarah	Walck	David	Walck	Selinda	Solt
B-135	Nothstein	Henry	Ammon	9	Aug	1870	20	Sept	1870	Ammon	Rosa Ann	Moser				
B-136	Schwab	William	Henry	1	May	1870	21	Sept	1870	Charles H	Matilda	Wilkraut				
B-137	Boyer	Pearce	Wilson	12	Aug	1870	25	Sept	1870	Owen H	Mary Jane	Kolb				
B-138	Hontz	Henry	Pearce	17	Aug	1870	25	Sept	1870	Nathan	Lucy Ann	Walck				
B-139	Boyer	Lora	Olivia	25	June	1870	2	Oct	1870	John F	Anny	Scherer				
B-140	Weida	Nelson		15	July	1869	3	Oct	1870	William	Ellen	Strohm				
B-141	Schmidt	Maehlon	Richard	28	July	1870	6	Oct	1870	Franklin	Elizabeth	Haid				
B-142	Hartman	Samuel		23	June	1870	8	Oct	1870	Lewis	Mary	Boyer	Daniel	Arner	Amelia	Hahn
B-143	Held	Alwin	William	2	Sept	1870	9	Oct	1870	Franklin	Amelia	Nitche	William	Nitche	Paulina	Barta
B-144	Foster	Sophia	Cecilia	2	Aug	1870	9	Oct	1870	Adam	Manda	Kunkle				
B-145	Kuhns	Louisa	Lucetta	13	Sept	1870	9	Oct	1870	David	Sarah	Gilbert				
B-146	Wissner	Catherine		15	Aug	1870	16	Oct	1870	John	Anna Elizabeth	Gross				
B-147	Giggle	William		9	Feb	1870	16	Oct	1870	Oliver	Margaretha	Kaiser				
B-148	Graver	Luelue	Irena	13	July	1870	16	Oct	1870	Andrew	Catherine	Henry	Reuben	Musselman	Sarah	Henny
B-149	Klotz	Charles	Warren	4	Aug	1870	16	Oct	1870	William F	Lizzie B	Henny				
B-150	Frantz	Charles	Edwin	13	Sept	1870	23	Oct	1870	Godfrey	Anna	Rex	John	Scherer	Hetty	Frantz
B-151	Kromer	Mary	Elizabeth	29	Sept	1870	27	Oct	1870	Irwin	Martha	Hartman			Elizabeth	Hartman
B-152	David	Albert	Milton	10	Aug	1870	29	Oct	1870	Charles	Emaline	Nothstein				
B-153	Steinheiser	Thomas	Wilson	8	Oct	1870	30	Oct	1870	Charles	Anna Maria	Walter				
B-154	Goodheil	Amelia		15	Mar	1870	30	Oct	1870	John	Mary Ann	Schneider				
B-155	Fenstermache	Emma	Arabella	12	July	1870	30	Oct	1870	John	Mary Ann	Mantz	Manasseh	Acker	Catherine	Anthony
B-156	Webb	Ida		24	Sept	1870	2	Nov	1870	James	Sarah	Shoemaker				
B-157	Grow	Emma	Amelia	20	Sept	1870	6	Nov	1870	Henry	Sally Ann	Cochran	William	Frederic	Eliza	Grow
B-158	Kunkle	Mary	Agnes	24	Aug	1870	13	Nov	1870	George	Sarah	(Kunkle)				
B-159	Stout	Araminda	Catherine	17	Sept	1870	13	Nov	1870	David	Mary Ann	Walck				
B-160	Brong	William	Albert	13	Nov	1870	13	Nov	1870	Jacob	Anna Maria	Graver	Joseph	Feist	Sarah Ann	Graver
B-161	Frederici	Charles	John	26	Aug	1870	16	Nov	1870	W.C.	Christianna	Behler				
B-162	Wentz	Clara	Amelia	21	Oct	1870	4	Dec	1870	Harrison	Selinda	Hand	Daniel	Arner	Amelia	Hahn
B-163	Borhor	Mary	Jane	31	Oct	1870	4	Dec	1870	James	Leah	Kemerer				
B-164	Geggus	Mary	Alice	1	Oct	1870	8	Dec	1870	Lewis	Salome	Delp				
B-165	Blose	Jacob	Fulton	12	Oct	1870	11	Dec	1870	Jacob	Selinda	Peter				

Beyond the Blue Mountain, Vol. II

Births and Baptisms

Line #	Surname	Child Given	Child Middle	Birth Day	Birth Mth	Birth Year	Baptism Day	Baptism Mth	Baptism Year	Father Given	Mother Given	Nee	Witness Given	Witness Surname	Witness Given	Witness Surname
B-166	Lower	Eva	Emma Jane	14	Oct	1870	11	Dec	1870	William	Amanda	Anewalt	Lewis	Anewalt	Sarah	Schneck
B-167	Blose	Sally	Ann	27	Oct	1870	11	Dec	1870	Thomas	Sarah	Lower	Elias	Anewalt	Eliza	Reichert
B-168	Solt	James	Granville	11	July	1870	19	Dec	1870	Isaiah	Lucy Ann	Zimmerman				
B-169	Beltz	Joseph	Franklin	10	Sept	1870	25	Dec	1870	Joseph	Lydia	(Betz)				
B-170	Dorwort	Jannie	Augusta	2	Oct	1870	25	Dec	1870	William	Harriet	Scherer				
B-171	Strohl	Elmira	Agnes	1	Sept	1870	25	Dec	1870	Levi	Susanna	(Strohl)	Daniel	Behler	Christianna	(Behler)
B-172	McGinlay	Robert	Fremont	11	Oct	1870	1	Jan	1871	Henry	Abby	Rheinsmith				
B-173	Haintz	Luther	Dallas	14	Nov	1870	5	Jan	1871	Henry	Mary Ann	Schwartz			Rachel	Haintz
B-174	Haintz	Harry	Albert	14	Nov	1870	5	Jan	1871	Henry	Mary Ann	Schwartz			Carolina	Bowman
B-175	Bowman	Emma	Carolina	22	Dec	1870	5	Jan	1871	W'lson	Carolina	Arner			Abbey	Bowman
B-176	Mertz	Irwin	Oscar	19	Dec	1870	5	Jan	1871	William	Joannah	Mertz	James		Anna	Mertz
B-177	Sabbach	George	William	6	Oct	1870	6	Jan	1871	Philip Frederich	Anna S	Campton				
B-178	Hauck	Charles	Gustav	11	April	1870	8	Jan	1871	John	Sarah	Islem	Charles	Armbruster	Mary Ann	Armbruster
B-179	Muschlitz	Elizabeth	Levina	28	Nov	1870	10	Jan	1871	Robert	Levina	Boyer				
B-180	Green	John	Richard	7	Oct	1870	10	Jan	1871	William	Mary	Eckhart				
B-181	Kleintopp	Lily	Aravesta	5	Dec	1870	15	Jan	1871	James W	Amanda	Walck	Thomas	Fink	Sarah Ann	Walck
B-182	Acker	Howard	William	1	Aug	1870	22	Jan	1871	John	Mary	Rehrig	George W	Fulmer	Ellen	Acker
B-183	Leibenguth	Bessie	Emma	27	Dec	1870	25	Jan	1871	Fra'klin	Mary	Scheckler				
B-184	Guth	Emma	Maria	9	Jan	1871	25	Jan	1871	Paul	Mary	Lambes				
B-185	Snyder	Jefferson	Franklin	7	Dec	1870	5	Feb	1871	David	Henrietta	Berkemeyer				
B-186	Bachman	Edgar	Uriah	28	Dec	1870	15	Feb	1871	William	Sarah C	Miller				
B-187	Silfies	Mary	Elizabeth	21	July	1870	15	Feb	1871	Reuben	Lucinda	Schmidt				
B-188	Mencke	Louisa		18	Jan	1871	19	Feb	1871	Friederich	Anna Eliza	Schmidt				
B-189	O'Brian	Ellen	Minerva	31	Jan	1871	20	Feb	1871	Samuel	Anzonetta	Kast	William A	Erwin	Ellamantina	Kast
B-190	Eberts	Emma	Missouri	5	Feb	1871	21	Feb	1871	Natr'an	Lydia Ann	Heintzelman	Daniel	Heintzelman	Polly	Stroup
B-191	Arner	Minnie	Dora	23	Jan	1871	25	Feb	1871	John H	Mary	Wher				
B-192	Schaefer	Wilson	Lewis	6	Jan	1871	26	Feb	1871	Thomas	Sarah Amanda	Moyer				
B-193	Wher	Emma	Louisa	20	Jan	1871	28	Feb	1871	David	Carolina	Ebert	Nathan	Wher	Mary Ann	Gombert
B-194	Fritzinger	Emma	Jane	21	Jan	1871	28	Feb	1871	Francis	Melinda	Bartholomew	Stephen	Fritzinger	Catherine	Sensinger
B-195	Leffler	Joseph	Wilson	23	Oct	1870	5	Mar	1871	Jacob	Catherine	Sleicher	Joseph	Kunkle	Amelia	Herman
B-196	Reinerd	Anna	Catherine	10	Jan	1871	5	Mar	1871	Peter	Anna	Lower	Nathan	Green	Catherine	(Green)
B-197	Kunkle	Korah	Matilda	17	Dec	1870	5	Mar	1871	Joseph	Amelia	Herman	Charles	Hartman	Matilida	(Hartman)
B-198	O'Brian	David	Warren	18	Oct	1870	8	Mar	1871	Benjamin	Rosa	Green	John	Gommery	Anna M	Horn
B-199	Bolsgrofe	Kate	Irena	25	Jan	1871	13	Mar	1871	Charles Jacob	Anna Maria	Kolb	Sarah	Kast		
B-200	Strohl	Purey	Edwin	2	Mar	1871	14	Mar	1871	Conrad	Florando	Correll				
B-201	Schindler	Ida	Alavesta	25	Jan	1871	14	Mar	1871	Christian	Mary Ann	Blose	Simeon	Blose	Harriet	Wagner
B-202	Serfass	Joseph	Willoughby	16	Mar	1870	16	Mar	1871	Mandes	Maria	Schmidt				
B-203	Kern	Henry	Adam	27	Jan	1871	19	Mar	1871	Peter	Jane	Brotzman	Henry	Smith	Catherine	(Smith)
B-204	Green	Emma	Jane	21	Jan	1871	19	Mar	1871	Thomas	Mary Ann	Christman	George	Schuck	Emma	Snyder
B-205	Mangold	Amelia		2	Feb	1871	19	Mar	1871	Friederick	Frederica	Weisset				
B-206	Rehrig	Lillie	Amasda	27	Sept	1870	19	Mar	1871	Charles	Mary	Acker	Susan	Seaboldt		
B-207	Miller	Caroline	Elburtha	9	Dec	1870	21	Mar	1871	Mahlor	Alice	Hollenbach				

Beyond the Blue Mountain, Vol. II Births and Baptisms

Line #	Surname	Child Given	Child Middle	Birth Day	Birth Mth	Birth Year	Baptism Day	Baptism Mth	Baptism Year	Father Given	Mother Given	Nee	Witness Given	Witness Surname	Witness Given	Witness Surname
B-208	Ziegenfuss	Irwin	Edwin	3	Feb	1871	26	Mar	1871	Nathan	Emaline	Sensinger	Edwin	Sensinger	Caroline	Geiger
B-209	Walck	Sylvester	Ulysses	15	Jan	1871	26	Mar	1871	Augustus	Sebilla	Kunkle	Thomas	Hahn	Mary	Boyer
B-210	Kunkle	Mary	Etta	1	Jan	1871	26	Mar	1871	Hilovius	Lucy	Walck				
B-211	Bartholomew	Ida		18	Feb	1871	2	April	1871	Elias	Rebecca	Henry				
B-212	Schaefer	Elmira	Agnes	26	Feb	1871	3	April	1871	Charles	Amelia	Stroup	David	Schaefer	Sally Ann	Kern
B-213	Sleider	John	Franklin	13	Jan	1871	15	April	1871	Edwin	Mary	Beltz	James E	Beltz	Julia	Remaly
B-214	Peter	Matilda	Esther	11	Mar	1871	15	April	1871	William	Esther	Stroup				
B-215	Behler	John	Milton	21	Jan	1871	15	April	1871	Levi	Matilda	Peter	Kate	Herb		
B-216	Scheckler	Lydia	Ann Selinda	13	Nov	1870	16	April	1871	William	Lydia Ann	Beltz	James E	Beltz	Selinda	Scheckler
B-217	Merkley	Martha	Elizabeth	7	Dec	1870	22	April	1871	Thomas	Elizabeth	Savitz	Edward	Walck	Maria	Montz
B-218	Graver	Caroline		7	Mar	1869	22	April	1871	Joshua	Catherine	Herman				
B-219	Graver	Harvey		1	Nov	1870	22	April	1871	Joshua	Catherine	Herman				
B-220	Beck	Emma	Laura	18	Mar	1871	22	April	1871	Alfred	Amanda	Moser	Owen	Klotz	Emaline	Flick
B-221	Becker	Emma	Elizabeth	25	Mar	1871	23	April	1871	Peter	July Ann	Freyman	Henry	Grow	Sally Ann	Cochran
B-222	Moulthrop	Henry	Christopher	15	Mar	1871	29	April	1871	William H	Priscilla	Trumbore				
B-223	Klotz	Agnes	Rebecca	21	Jan	1871	30	April	1871	Josiah	Rebecca	(Klotz)	Albert	Kunkle	Elizabeth	(Kunkle)
B-224	Benninger	Isola Anna	Matilda	27	Jan	1871	30	April	1871	Wilson	Lucy	Wher				
B-225	Spoonheimer	Martha		1	Mar	1871	2	May	1871	Reuben	Lydia	Kline				
B-226	Remaley	Albert	Franklin	13	April	1871	9	May	1871	Charles	Emma Elizabth	Rabenold	John	Confer	Elizabeth	Guldner
B-227	Reed	Carrie	Ellen	24	Mar	1871	10	May	1871	Aquila E	Maria L	Fritzinger				
B-228	Nothstein	Mary	Alice	12	Mar	1871	14	May	1871	Alwin	Susanna	Lauchnor				
B-229	Romig	Charles	Ephraim	2	April	1871	14	May	1871	Ephraim	Mary Ann	Polsgrove				
B-230	Berger	John	Alavesta	24	Oct	1870	21	May	1871	George	Catherine	Kemerer				
B-231	Shive	Mary	Alice	27	Oct	1870	21	May	1871	Alfred	Harriet	Steigerwalt				
B-232	O'Brian	Franklin		22	Feb	1871	21	May	1871	Joseph	Lizzie	Haid				
B-233	Koons	Minnie	Amanda	19	Mar	1871	21	May	1871	Willoughby	Sarah	Kistler	Joseph	Kistler	Polly	Hontz
B-234	Walck	Wilson	Walter	23	Mar	1871	21	May	1871	David	Selinda	Solt	Solomon	Walck	Elizabeth	(Walck)
B-235	Markley	Elmer	Stephen	20	Mar	1871	21	May	1871	Stephen	Zeniah	(Markley)	Cassius	Montz	Cassanta	Montz
B-236	Walck	Lilie	Alavesta	10	May	1871	22	May	1871	Edward	Maria	Montz	Joseph	Robert	Sarah	Walck
B-237	O'Niel	Lilie	Tewilia Louisa	2	April	1871	28	May	1871	William	Louisa	Krum	Levi	Krum	Elizabeth	Miller
B-238	Campbell	Martin	Lewis	15	Dec	1870	2	June	1871	Archibald	Sarah	Frohnheiser				
B-239	Mulhearn	Lilie	May	14	April	1871	9	June	1871	Edward	Anna Maria	Bachman				
B-240	Snyder	Charles	Franklin	23	May	1871	11	June	1871	Phaon	Emma	Kemerer	Harvey	Scherer	Anna Maria	Weiss
B-241	Kromer	Martha	Ann Agnes	12	Jan	1871	11	June	1871	Alfred	Ellen Jane	Weiss	Harvey	Scherer	Anna Maria	Weiss
B-242	Wolf	Henry	Palmer	10	Mar	1871	18	June	1871	John	Rebecca	Ziegenfuss				
B-243	Solt	Elva	Estilla	24	May	1871	18	June	1871	Henry	Amelia	Hahn				
B-244	Trumbore	Laura	Gertrude	8	May	1871	18	June	1871	Joseph	Julia	Derr				
B-245	Kelchner	Ellen	Korah	29	May	1871	25	June	1871	Edward	Lydia	Remaly	Robert	Walp	Eliza	Remaly
B-246	Ziegenfuss	Samuel		18	Mar	1871	25	June	1871	James	Mary	(Ziegenfuss)	Samuel	Chirstman	Catherine	(Chirstman)
B-247	Shive	Emma	Elmira	1	May	1871	25	June	1871	Ephraim	Mary Amanda	Green	Reuben	Green	Mary	(Green)
B-248	Peter	Ambrose	Franklin	16	May	1871	9	July	1871	Wallace	Hannah	Fritz				
B-249	Gower	George	Albert	1	Nov	1870	10	July	1871	Frederic	Susanna	(Gower)				

Beyond the Blue Mountain, Vol. II   Births and Baptisms   13

Line #	Surname	Child Given	Child Middle	Birth Day	Birth Mth	Birth Year	Baptism Day	Baptism Mth	Baptism Year	Father Given	Mother Given	Nee	Witness Given	Witness Surname	Witness Given	Witness Surname
B-250	Weida	Laura	Agnes	16	Jan	1871	15	July	1871	William	Ellen	Strohm				
B-251	Markley	Hattie	Elizabeth	8	May	1871	16	July	1871	Tilghman	Elizabeth	Dorwort	Thomas	Dorwart	Sarah	Newhart
B-252	Berger (?)	Frederic	Oscar	3	Nov	1854	23	July	1871				Alwin	Berger		
B-253	Berger (?)	Emmanuel	Arthur	19	May	1871	23	July	1871				Frederic	Berger	Matilda	Berger
B-254	Flickinger	Milton	Albert	19	Jul	1871	4	Aug	1871	Nathan	Louisa	Kerschner	Isaac	Beltz	Maria	Guldner
B-255	Miller	Anna	Laura	23	June	1871	9	Aug	1871	Frederic	Ellen	Webb			Mary	Webb
B-256	Hartman	Elmira		25	June	1871	10	Aug	1871	Joseph	Pauline	Fisher			Elizabeth	Hartman
B-257	Haron	Edwin	Alexander	20	July	1871	11	Aug	1871	Jonathan	Sarah	Math			Matilda	Weiss
B-258	Wehr	Emma	Alavesta	13	July	1871	18	Aug	1871	Owen	Ellen	Zimmerman				
B-259	Gable	Irwin	Aaron	24	June	1871	19	Aug	1871	Mandes	Sabina	Bartholomew				
B-260	Beidelman	Theodosia		2	Apr	1871	20	Aug	1871	Elias	Sarah	Knappenberger				
B-261	Fritzinger	Robert	Elmer	16	May	1871	20	Aug	1871	John	Henrietta	Fisher	Robert	Dunbar	Sarah	Fritzinger
B-262	Moran	Mary	Ellen	24	Dec	1870	20	Aug	1871	William	Elizabeth	Bollsgrofe				
B-263	Evans	Henry	Robert	26	Jan	1870	20	Aug	1871	James	Sarah	Bollsgrofe				
B-264	Trine	William	Eugene	26	Jun	1871	27	Aug	1871	John	Polly	Peter	William H	Rex	Catherine	Kemerer
B-265	Heffelfinger	Catherine	Alice	19	Jul	1871	28	Aug	1871	John	Sarah	Fisher	John	Schwab	Susanna	Schmitt
B-266	Kromer	William	Lee	23	Mar	1871	2	Sep	1871	Alfred	Lydia	Seiley	W. Lee	Stiles	Maria	Smith
B-267	Patterson	Levi	Preston	31	May	1871	2	Sep	1871	Charles A	Sarah	Dieterline	W. Lee	Stiles	Maria M	Smith
B-268	Schuck	Pearcy	Franklin	7	Aug	1871	10	Sep	1871	Charles	Sophia	Lentz				
B-269	Riegel	Clemen	Daniel	29	July	1871	16	Sep	1871	Joseph	Hermena	Horn				
B-270	Fritzinger	Henry	Wilson	23	July	1871	17	Sep	1871	Tilghman	Anzonetta	Goodheil				
B-271	Klotz	Laura	Taney	16	Aug	1871	17	Sep	1871	Owen	Emaline	Flick	Joseph	Nothstein	Abby	Hill
B-272	Rehrig	Charles	Henry	18	June	1871	1	Oct	1871	Lewis H	Jane	Bridelman				
B-273	Beltz	Thomas	Franklin	1	July	1871	1	Oct	1871	Herry	Lavina	Buck	Jonas	Buck	Catherine	(Buck)
B-274	Ferber	Ida	Clendora	16	Aug	1871	1	Oct	1871	Reuben	Henrietta	Stroup	Joseph	Strohl	Kate	Strohl
B-275	Eberts	Emma	Messera	18	Aug	1871	5	Oct	1871	Owen	Polly	Heintzelman	William	Wertman	Carolina	Krumm
B-276	McDaniel	Emma	Martha	25	Aug	1871	8	Oct	1871	John Thomson	Lucy Ann	Rheinsmith	Nathan	Wehr	Mary	Gombert
B-277	Leffler	George	AlBurtis	13	Oct	1870	5	Oct	1871	Aaron	Leanna	Rehrig	David	Auge	Sarah	Rehrig
B-278	Bartholomew	William	Franklin	7	Aug	1871	8	Oct	1871	John	Catherine	Serfass	Robert	Bartholomew	Anna Maria	Ritz
B-279	Kresge	Ida	Clendora	8	Aug	1871	15	Oct	1871	Paul	Mary Ann	Stemmler	Solomon	Stemmler	Lucy	Green
B-280	Sleider	Anna	Matilda	16	Sep	1871	15	Oct	1871	William	Alvena	(Sleider)			Carolina	Maury
B-281	Fogel	Lafenns		13	Jul	1871	15	Oct	1871	Stephen	Catherine	(Fogel)	Joel	Ziegenfuss	Lucetta	(Ziegenfuss)
B-282	Blose	Albert	Milton	6	Sep	1871	15	Oct	1871	Lewis	Isabella	(Blose)	Thomas	Brown	Rebecca	(Brown)
B-283	Nanstiel	Edward	Uriah	17	Sep	1871	15	Oct	1871	Henry	Anna Cristianna	Hoffman				
B-284	Sheiry	Catherine		23	Sep	1871	16	Oct	1871	George	Mandaleine	Kromer				
B-285	Walck	Eugene	Lewis	13	Aug	1871	28	Oct	1871	Lewis	Rebecca	Kuebler				
B-286	Fritzinger	Clara	Elizabeth	16	Aug	1871	28	Oct	1871	John W.	Lucy	Kuebler	Lewis	Walck	Rebecca	Kuebler
B-287	Kuehner	Ellen	Dianna	15	Sep	1871	29	Oct	1871	August	Christianna	(Kuehner)	Joel	Ziegenfuss	Lucetta	(Ziegenfuss)
B-288	Kauffman	Robert	Sylvester	10	Oct	1871	29	Oct	1871	Charles	Maria	Walp				
B-289	Graver	Jennie	Irena	11	Aug	1871	29	Oct	1871	Owen	Fianna	Solt				
B-290	Heilman	Oscar	Eugene	29	Sep	1871	29	Oct	1871	Nathan	Amanda	Balliet				
B-291	Heilman	Ida	Agnes	1	Sep	1871	31	Oct	1871	George W	Mary	Dreher				

Beyond the Blue Mountain, Vol. II

Births and Baptisms

Line #	Surname	Child Given	Child Middle	Birth Day	Birth Mth	Birth Year	Baptism Day	Baptism Mth	Baptism Year	Father Given	Mother Given	Nee	Witness Given	Witness Surname	Witness Given	Witness Surname
B-292	Frederic	Calvin	Elwin	3	Sep	1871	5	Nov	1871	William	Eliza	Grow	Tilghman		Catharine	Frederic
B-293	Hunsicker	Alfred	Leslie	15	June	1871	6	Nov	1871	Reuben	Lucy ann	Bauer		Rabenold		
B-294	Houser	Amelia	Rebecca	22	Jun	1871	10	Nov	1871	Joseph T	Elizabeth	Berthol				
B-295	Arner	William	Franklin	26	Sep	1871	12	Nov	1871	John	Amanda	Horn				
B-296	Zone	Rosa	Louisa	2	Nov	1871	16	Nov	1871	Joseph	Johannah	Kaiser				
B-297	McFarland	Emma	Louisa	8	Sep	1871	19	Nov	1871	Joseph	Mary	Hemler	Jacob	Gottshall	Eliza	(Gottshall)
B-298	Knerr	Milton	Edward	7	July	1871	19	Nov	1871	Joseph	Josephina	Houser	Abraham	Greenewalt	Mary	Lentz
B-299	Dreisbach	Sarah	Emma	6	Oct	1871	23	Nov	1871	William	Sarah	Walck				
B-300	Schnell	Ambrose	Walter	30	Aug	1871	26	Nov	1871	Dennis	Louisa	Dengler				
B-301	Eisenhower	Eugene	Edwin	29	Sep	1871	26	Nov	1871	Reuben	Mary Alice	Flick				
B-302	Hough	Carolina		8	Oct	1871	3	Dec	1871	Edwin	Bregitta	Kirschner	Nathan	Gombert	Medina	Krum
B-303	Grow	Surie	Lousia	8	Oct	1871	3	Dec	1871	Oliver	Elizabeth	Frederic	Adam	Faust	Sarah	Cunfer
B-304	Spoonheimer	Edward	Pearce	12	July	1871	10	Dec	1871	Jonathan	Amanda	Hontz				
B-305	Schafer	William	Henry	13	Oct	1871	10	Dec	1871	Henry	Catherine	(Schafer)			Mary	Sleider
B-306	Stroup	Messina	Alavesta	15	Nov	1871	10	Dec	1871	Solomon	Caroline	Long				
B-307	Kunsman	Mary	Luella	23	Oct	1871	10	Dec	1871	Moses	Mary	Peter				
B-308	Moyer	Clara		19	May	1871	10	Dec	1871	Jacob	Abigail	Kuntz				
B-309	Giggle	Alwies		26	June	1871	10	Dec	1871	Lafayette	Margeret	Kaiser				
B-310	Berg	Charles	William	6	Nov	1871	10	Dec	1871	Peter	Emma	Moyer	George	Rapp	Hannah	(Rapp)
B-311	Billy	Helena		15	Sept	1871	10	Dec	1871	James	Mary Ann	Moyer			Hannah	Miller
B-312	Hunsicker	Clara	Eliza	7	Sep	1871	10	Dec	1871	Edwin	Eliza	Esch				
B-313	Boehmler	Daniel		11	Oct	1871	10	Dec	1871	Frederich	Fransisca	Kerner			Carolina	Kerner
B-314	Brown	Palmer	Jacob	17	Oct	1871	21	Dec	1871	Jacob	Matilda	Green	Ephraim	Shive	Amanda	Green
B-315	Waterbaer	Franklin	Thomas	6	Jun	1871	22	Dec	1871	William	Henrietta	Kaiser				
B-316	Wert	Rosa	Alwenia	28	Nov	1871	22	Dec	1871	Willoughby	Maria	Hartranft				
B-317	Webb	Rosanna		31	Oct	1871	25	Dec	1871	James	Sarah	Shoemaker	Frederic	Miller	Ellen	Webb
B-318	Riegel	John		13	Oct	1871	25	Dec	1871	Joshua	Sarah	Leiby				
B-319	Ruch	Harry	Edgar	8	Dec	1871	25	Dec	1871	Elias	Mary	Sendel				
B-320	Yenser	Charles	Elmer	5	Nov	1871	25	Dec	1871	Charles	Mary	Bartholomew	Charles A	Beck	Sophia	Frantz
B-321	Lutz	Christianna		11	Oct	1871	26	Dec	1871	Isaac B	Annetta	Kleintopp	Samuel	Meckes	Anna F	Kleintopp
B-322	Hontz	Ira		6	Nov	1871	31	Dec	1871	Ammon	Elizabeth	Montz	Boaz	Hontz	Kitty	Ehle
B-323	Leukle	Charles	Henry	30	Sep	1871	1	Jan	1872	William	Priscilla	Walck	Moses	Hough	Anna Maria	Walck
B-324	Schuck	Charles	Lovene	15	Nov	1871	9	Jan	1872	George	Emma	Snyder				
B-325	Finkler	Charles	Peter	28	Dec	1871	9	Jan	1872	Peter	Carolina	Kuehner				
B-326	Stein	Emma	Ellemanda	18	Nov	1871	9	Jan	1872	George	Carolina	Hauck				
B-327	Metzger	Ellemanda		3	Oct	1871	9	Jan	1872	Christopher	Eliza	Heffelfinger				
B-328	Whiteman	Abraham		14	Mar	1871	13	Jan	1872	Daniel	Carolina	Schwartzwood	Mary	Pfeifer		
B-329	Heffelfinger	Alwin	Oscar	18	Nov	1871	14	Jan	1872	Freeman	Lenah	(Heffelfinger)				
B-330	Trainer	Ellen	Matilda	18	Oct	1871	14	Jan	1872	Charles	Elizabeth	Platt				
B-331	Weida	Lily	Ann	9	July	1868	15	Jan	1872	Peter	Lucy Ann	Ruch				
B-332	Brotzman	Stewart	Abraham	31	Oct	1871	21	Jan	1872	Charles	Christianna	Boyer				
B-333	Dotter	Harry	Elsworth	19	Dec	1871	24	Jan	1872	Lewis	Sally Ann	Weiss				

Beyomnd the Blue Mountain, Vol. II

Births and Baptisms

Line #	Surname	Child Given	Child Middle	Birth Day	Birth Mth	Birth Year	Baptism Day	Baptism Mth	Baptism Year	Father Given	Mother Given	Nee	Witness Given	Witness Surname	Witness Given	Witness Surname
B-334	Chardon	Emma	Matten	26	Oct	1871	28	Jan	1872	Daniel	Sarah	Rackawack	William	Shipe	Ella	Mertz
B-335	Rackawack	Anna	Maria	21	Aug	1862	28	Jan	1872	Frederic	Catherine	Schleicher				
B-336	Weida	Charles		15	Jan	1872	30	Jan	1872	Aaron	Henrietta	Adams				
B-337	Merkel	Lewis	Theodore	4	Nov	1871	6	Feb	1872	Theodore	Amelia	Pehle				
B-338	Smith	Alfred		29	Dec	1871	11	Feb	1872	Owen	Selinda	Andrews	Jacob	Behler	Sabina	Andrews
B-339	Arner	Emanuel		20	Dec	1871	11	Feb	1872	John	Jane	Batman	Elias	George	Elizabeth	Evans
B-340	Schnell	Tilghman	Eugene	25	Dec	1871	11	Feb	1872	Oliver	Priscilla	Rhoad	Tilghman	Schnell	Mary Ann	Fath
B-341	Reichard	Sulie	Ann	4	Jan	1872	12	Feb	1872	Aaron	Ellen	Nothstein	Daniel	Nothstein	Anna	Heilman
B-342	O Brian	Scott		21	Dec	1871	14	Feb	1872	David O	Catherine	Walker				
B-343	Frey	Emma	Susanna	31	Jan	1872	15	Feb	1872	Samuel	Sabrina	Kemerer				
B-344	Walck	George	Ammon	21	Sep	1871	18	Feb	1872	John	Eva Ann	Green	John A	Boyer	Elizabeth	(Boyer)
B-345	Kostenbader	Mary Ann		12	Nov	1871	18	Feb	1872	Josiah	Fayette	Walck				
B-346	Wolkermuth	Emma	Bertha	4	Jan	1872	18	Feb	1872	Otto	Anna	Wuerstler				
B-347	Koons	Emma	Estilla	7	Oct	1871	24	Feb	1872	Richard	Selinda	Schwartz				
B-348	Fisher	Adam	Francis	14	Jan	1872	25	Feb	1872	John	Elizabeth	Kunkle	Adam	Foster	Amanda	Kunkle
B-349	Remely	Amelia	Alice	21	Nov	1871	25	Feb	1872	Moses	Sarah Amanda	Arner	Daniel	Arner	Amelia	Hahn
B-350	Gumbert	Mary	Alice	4	Jan	1872	25	Feb	1872	James	Ellen	Mertz	Nathan	Wher	Mary	Gumbert
B-351	Hoffman	Juliann		26	Dec	1871	3	Mar	1872	David	Harriet	Kreitz	Sarah	Kast		
B-352	Rex	Charles	Martin	5	Feb	1872	3	Mar	1872	Alfred	Sally Elmira	Freyman	William H	Rex	Catharine	Kemerer
B-353	Zellner	William	Franklin	11	Feb	1872	3	Mar	1872	Franklin	Mary Ann	Blose				
B-354	Young	George		5	May	1869	7	Mar	1872	James	Mary Ann	Freyman				
B-355	Young	Esta		11	April	1871	7	Mar	1872	James	Mary Ann	Freyman				
B-356	Gommery	John	Edgar	2	Feb	1872	8	Mar	1872	John	Anna	Horn	Thomas	Horn	Dianna	Frey
B-357	Weida	Priscilla		31	Jan	1872	10	Mar	1872	Benjamin	Elizabeth	Knecht				
B-358	Rex	Charles	William	4	Jan	1872	10	Mar	1872	William	Mary Cassia	Eck				
B-359	Strong	Willmer		27	Dec	1871	11	Mar	1872	James C	Margaret	Houseworth	Maehlon	Leichliter		
B-360	Heberling	John	Edward	12	Feb	1872	12	Mar	1872	Samuel G	Angeline	Ruch				
B-361	Neier	George	Henry	24	Sep	1871	12	Mar	1872	Isaac	Harriet	Shell				
B-362	Geiger	Jane	Irena	12	Dec	1871	13	Mar	1872	Joseph	Rebecca	Wertman	Isaac	Moyer	Elizabeth	Leiby
B-363	Weiss	John	Charles Gustav	17	Oct	1871	18	Mar	1872	Charles August	Eva	Kliefer				
B-364	Hill	Emma	Rebecca	7	Jan	1872	19	Mar	1872	Abraham	July Ann	Walck	John	Ruch	Lenah	Bartholomew
B-365	Zimmerman	William	Martin	2	Nov	1857	19	Mar	1872	Gideon	Mary Ann	Waters				
B-366	Zimmerman	Catherine	Ellen	14	April	1854	19	Mar	1872	Gideon	Mary Ann	Waters				
B-367	Beer	Henry	Francis	24	Jan	1872	22	Mar	1872	Francis	Wilmina	Blose	Simon	Blose	Herinetta	Wagner
B-368	Green	Emma	Araminda	30	Jan	1872	22	Mar	1872	Aaron	Lucy	Knappenberger				
B-369	Greenewalt	Ida	Catherine	6	Jan	1872	23	Mar	1872	Danie	Sarah Jane	Beltz				
B-370	Beninger	Clara	Jane Elizabeth	11	Mar	1872	23	Mar	1872	Wilson	Lucy	Wehr				
B-371	Mertz	Agnew		6	Jan	1872	24	Mar	1872	Nathan	Sally Ann	Freyman	Tilghman	Rabenold	Catherine	Frederic
B-372	Albright	Enos	B				22	Mar	1872							
B-373	Ziegenfuss	Ida	Agnes	22	Feb	1872	24	Mar	1872	Lyman	Amanda	(Ziegenfuss)	Daniel	Sensinger	Caroline	(Sensinger)
B-374	Becker	Sarah	Tany	23	Dec	1871	28	Mar	1872	Edward	Cassenda	Beer				
B-375	Kemery	Urilla	Elizabeth	2	April	1872	12	April	1872	Nathan	Lucinda	Patterson	John	Patterson	Susan	Schmehl

Beyond the Blue Mountain, Vol. II

Births and Baptisms

Line #	Surname	Child Given	Middle	Birth Day	Mth	Year	Baptism Day	Mth	Year	Father Given	Mother Given	Nee	Witness Given	Surname	Witness Given	Surname
B-376	Gross	Theresa	Catherine	9	Dec	1871	12	April	1872	Henry	Selinda	Armbruster	George	Miller		
B-377	Kleintopp	Emma	Elmira	14	Dec	1871	14	April	1872	David	Emaline	Klein	Robert	McDaniel	Matilda	Herman
B-378	Strassburger	David	Matthias	29	Feb	1872	14	April	1872	Matthias	Hannah	Hartman	Charles	Hartman	Babet	Scheirer
B-379	Rapp	William	Frederic	19	Dec	1871	14	April	1872	Christian C	Catherine	Lauber	Charles	Miller	Catherine	Wells
B-380	Trumbore	Eugene		12	Mar	1872	14	April	1872	Henry	Rebecca	Cleaver	Wilson	Peter	Catherine	Dreisbach
B-381	Arner	William	John	23	Jan	1872	20	April	1872	Henry	Harriet	(Arner)	Amos	Miller	Catherine	Lechleiter
B-382	Gombert	Ira	Irena	6	Mar	1872	21	April	1872	Jonathan	Anna	Hontz	Joseph	Gombert	July Ann	Miller
B-383	Gombert	Alice	Sevilla	6	Nov	1871	21	April	1872	Stephen	Lydia	Hontz	Ephraim	Rehrig		
B-384	Levan	Ameda	Louisa	8	Mar	1872	21	April	1872	Isaac	Louisa	Dreisbach				
B-385	Stolle	Elizabeth		4	Jan	1872	21	April	1872	Albien	Caroline	Buhl			Anna	Stolle
B-386	Farren	Hattie	Elesta	27	Mar	1872	21	April	1872	Daniel	Harriet	O'Brian				
B-387	Stenner	Charles	Adam	8	Mar	1872	24	April	1872	Henry	Mary	Hahn				
B-388	Schwartz	Franklin	Alexander	29	Feb	1872	24	April	1872	John	Magdalene	Fillhower				
B-389	Moser	Edward	Wilson	31	Dec	1867	26	April	1872	Joseph David	Susanna	Barwick			Hester	Barwick
B-390	Moser	Hester	Estella	1	Aug	1869	26	April	1872	Joseph David	Susanna	Barwick				
B-391	Moser	William	Howard	20	Sep	1871	26	April	1872	Joseph David	Susanna	Barwick				
B-392	Johnson	Korah	Agnes	22	Sep	1868	26	April	1872	M. L	Dianna	Houser				
B-393	Koons	Jeremiah	Samuel	6	Mar	1872	28	April	1872	Jeremiah	Kitty	Fenstermacher	Hannah	Rapp	Sarah	Christman
B-394	Unangst	Henry	P	24	Dec	1872	5	May	1872	Henry	Sarah	Yenser	Isaac	Dengler		
B-395	Leffler	William	Andrew	3	Sep	1871	7	May	1872	Nathan	Ellen	Weiss				
B-396	Hontz	Silbie	Irena	12	Oct	1871	12	May	1872	Josiah	Sarah	Jenkins	Lewis	Schwab	Elizabeth	Hontz
B-397	Schwab	Ida	Rebecca	17	Mar	1872	12	May	1872	Lewis	Sevilla	Barwick	Martin	Barwick	Esther	Root
B-398	Rabe	William	Michael	18	Mar	1872	12	May	1872	Michael	Anna Maria	Rootman	Peter	Rootman	Elizabeth	Andrews
B-399	Hassel	Lewis	Henry	11	Jan	1872	12	May	1872	Jacob	Mary	Armbruster	Henry	Gross	Selinda	Armbruster
B-400	Schwenk	John	Alfred				12	May	1872	Henry	Susanna	Kramer			Sarah	Hartman
B-401	Moyer	Mary	Lizzie	19	Jan	1872	12	May	1872	John	Elmira	Jones				
B-402	Gruber	Hester	Irena	6	Aug	1871	12	May	1872	Henry	Rebecca	Rabe			Rachel	Rabe
B-403	Sibbach	Anna	Wilhelmina	21	Feb	1872	12	May	1872	Philip Frederich	Anna Salinda	Campton				
B-404	Arner	Laura	Agnes	2	May	1872	12	May	1872	William Harrison	Adeline Louisa	Snyder				
B-405	Tucker	May	Ellen	1	Sep	1871	12	May	1872	Henry	Mary Ann	Shive				
B-406	Haupt	Thomas	Jefferson	7	Apr	1872	12	May	1872	Nathan	Alavesta	Klotz	Owen	Klotz	Emaline	Flick
B-407	Beck	William	Albert	18	Mar	1872	12	May	1872	Charles A	Sophia	Frantz				
B-408	Nothstein	Wallace	Peter	28	Mar	1872	19	May	1872	Maehlon	Eliza Amanda	Dengler	Lewis	Dengler	Angeline	Herring
B-409	Rex	Charles	Augustus	3	Mar	1872	19	May	1872	Moses	Sarah Ann	Freyman				
B-410	Smith	Quinton	Harvey	15	Sep	1872	24	May	1872	William	Catherine	Knappenberg	Lewis	Anewalt	Sarah	(Anewalt)
B-411	Snyder	Eugene	Calvin	15	Dec	1871	26	May	1872	Washington	Sarah Ann	Schwartz	John	Esch	Fietta	Keller
B-412	Bollsgrofe	Hattie	Minerva	10	Mar	1872	26	May	1872	Charles	Anna Marie	Kolb				
B-413	Houser	Oscar	Eugene	25	Mar	1872	26	May	1872	Jonas	Susan	Remely				
B-414	Knecht	Susan		30	Apr	1872	2	June	1872	Samuel	Sarah	Schultz				
B-415	Reinheimer	Sarah	Francisca	7	Feb	1872	2	June	1872	John	Rachel	Ruth			Maria	Miller
B-416	Klotz	Leanna	Sevilla	9	Apr	1872	5	June	1872	Franklin	Sarah	Solt			Catherine E	Heilman
B-417	Noll	Charles	Edgar	11	Mar	1872	6	June	1872	William	Molly	Graver				

Beyonnd the Blue Mountain, Vol. II

Births and Baptisms

Line #	Surname	Child Given	Middle	Birth Day Mth Year	Baptism Day Mth Year	Father Given	Mother Given	Nee	Witness Given	Surname	Witness Given	Surname
B-418	Bachman	Emma	Rebecca	23 Jan 1872	8 June 1872	Joseph	Messina	Frohnheiser	Edward	Petzel	Sarah	(Petzel)
B-419	Stansberry	Edward	Daniel	20 May 1872	8 June 1872	Lorence	Susan	Reinard	Joseph	Geiger	Rebecca	Wertman
B-420	Faust	Mary	Ellen	12 May 1872	16 June 1872	Adam	Sarah	Confer	Rudolph	Rumble	Mary	Harris
B-421	Meinhart	Conrad	Alvin	25 Aug 1871	16 June 1872	Charles	Barbara	Felker	John	Otto	Cresencia	Biek
B-422	Solt	Isabella		20 April 1872	16 June 1872	Reuben	Juliann	Lentz				
B-423	Klotz	Sylvester		2 Feb 1872	9 June 1872	John F	Bregitta	Schnell				
B-424	Rehrig	Lester	Byron	7 April 1872	9 June 1872	Owen	Mary Ann	Rehrig				
B-425	Roberts	Luella		31 Mar 1872	23 June 1872	J M	Sarah	Walck	James W	Kleintopp	Manda	Walck
B-426	Nothstein	Leah		9 July 1872	23 June 1872	Dennis	Amanda Elizabeth	German	Elias	Nothstein	Leah	Hobbes
B-427	Longaker	Sarah	Ann	22 June 1872	10 July 1872	David	Polly	Hobbes				
B-428	Hontz	Thomas	Wison	2 Dec 1870	13 July 1872	Wison	Mary	Walck				
B-429	Lechliter	John		2 Feb 1871	13 July 1872	John	Liberia	Strong				
B-430	Berlin	William	Oscar	28 May 1872	14 July 1872	Henry F	Anjuline	Arner	George	Arner	Sarah	Snyder
B-431	Knauss	William	Elmer	3 July 1872	14 July 1872	Lewis	Eliza	Arner	Charles	Arner	Ellen	Solt
B-432	Miller	Jacob	Franklin	1 Apr 1872	14 July 1872	Alexander	Mary	Haid				
B-433	Brown	Mary	Jane	9 Jun 1872	21 July 1872	Levi	Belinda	Dieter	Simon	Brown	Catherine	(Brown)
B-434	Souders	David	Wilson	1 Mar 1872	21 July 1872	Joseph	Mary Ann	(Souders)	Charles	Brotzman	Christiana	Boyer
B-435	Techiaschky	Gustav	Henry	11 Apr 1872	21 July 1872	Frederich	Paulina	Schinke	Wentzel	Schinke	Maria Anna	(Schinke)
B-436	Paul	Mary	Ellen	28 Apr 1872	21 July 1872	John	Jarrettie	Schock	Frederick	Schock	Mary	Lewis
B-437	Remely	Almer	Eugene	7 May 1872	27 July 1872	Tilghman	Emma	Hankey				
B-438	Auge	William	Herbert	19 Apr 1872	28 July 1872	Dav d	Sarah Susanna	Rehrig				
B-439	Reiner	Elizabeth	Christianna	28 June 1872	4 Aug 1872	Simon	Christianna	Beer				
B-440	Weiss	John	Lewis	20 Jan 1872	4 Aug 1872	Nero	Louisa	Hontz				
B-441	Remaley	Sarah	Elizabeth	28 June 1872	11 Aug 1872	Charles	Emma	Rabenold	Tilghman	Rabenold	Catherine	Frederic
B-442	Wertman	Eli	Jefferson	19 Jun 1872	11 Aug 1872	Samuel	Sally Ann	Miller				
B-443	Sendel	Clara	Eva Jane	29 Jun 1872	11 Aug 1872	William	Sarah	Confer				
B-444	Mimm	Katie	Emaline	8 June 1872	11 Aug 1872	Levi	Elizabeth	Remaley	E. S.	Heintzelman	Polly	George
B-445	Fuehrer	Emma	Jane	4 Mar 1872	14 Aug 1872	William	Susanna	Haupt				
B-446	Frederic	Steven	Franklin	20 June 1872	18 Aug 1872	Stephen	Elizabeth	Lower	William	Schmidt	Catherine	Knappenberge
B-447	Bechtel	Ellen	Rachel	16 Jul 1872	19 Aug 1872	William	Elizabeth	Rabe				
B-448	Fisher	Clara	Ellen	28 June 1872	23 Aug 1872	William	Mary	Hahn				
B-449	Schuyler	Mary	Ellen Jane	16 July 1872	24 Aug 1872	Hiram	Angeline	Flickinger	William	Schultz	Mary	Young
B-450	Miller	John	Iasiah	7 July 1872	25 Aug 1872	William	Elizabeth	Rex				
B-451	Eslinger	Henry	William	14 June 1872	25 Aug 1872	John	Amelia	Willman	John	Walck	Louisa	Ernst
B-452	Noll	Harrison	Benjamin	19 June 1872	25 Aug 1872	Aaron	Eliza	Rehrig	Benjamin	Weida	Elizabeth	(Weida)
B-453	Moulthrop	Edgar	Ulysses	22 July 1872	25 Aug 1872	John F	Ellen	Shoemaker	Alfred	Rex	Sally Elmira	Freyman
B-454	Schleicher	Ellemina		10 Aug 1872	25 Aug 1872	Paul	Hannah	Ackerman				
B-455	Geggus	Mary	Etta	1 Aug 1872	25 Aug 1872	John	Louisa	Haid				
B-456	Geggus	Anna	Elizabeth	1 Aug 1872	25 Aug 1872	John	Louisa	Haid				
B-457	Geggus	Clara	Bella	7 Aug 1872	25 Aug 1872	Lewis	Salome	Delp				
B-458	Eck	Oliver	Granville	28 July 1872	26 Aug 1872	John	Mary Ann	Whiteman	Daniel	Kolb	Polly	Hartman
B-459	Meckes	Henry		13 July 1872	30 Aug 1872	Joseph	Mary Ann	Schaefer				

Beyonnd the Blue Mountain, Vol. II

Births and Baptisms

Line #	Surname	Child Given	Middle	Birth Day	Birth Mth	Birth Year	Baptism Day	Baptism Mth	Baptism Year	Father Given	Mother Given	Nee	Witness Given	Witness Surname	Witness Given	Witness Surname
B-460	Meckes	Annetta	Caroline	13	July	1872	30	Aug	1872	Joseph	Mary Ann	Schaefer	Samuel	Meckes	Fayetta	Kleintopp
B-461	Beer	Emma	Estella	4	July	1872	1	Sept	1872	Daniel	Rebecca	Walck	George	Walck	Mary	Dotterer
B-462	Wolf	Lillie		19	Apr	1870	1	Sept	1872	William M	Mary Jane	Kratzer				
B-463	Wolf	Frank		16	Aug	1872	1	Sept	1872	William	Mary Jane	Kratzer				
B-464	Nothstein	William	Penn	16	July	1872	1	Sept	1872	Conrad H	Elizabeth	Ackerman				
B-465	Guldner	Charles	Lewis	20	June	1871	3	Sept	1872	Henry	Sarah	Rehrig	Charles	Rehrig	Mary	Buck
B-466	Kromer	George	Alfred	16	Apr	1872	3	Sept	1872	Irwin	Martha	Hartman				
B-467	Baumgartner	Sarah	Ellen Catherine	17	July	1872	10	Sept	1872	Anthony	Sarah	Shaefer			Catherine	Shaefer
B-468	Ruch	Francis		15	Aug	1872	11	Sept	1872	Henry	Eva	Andreas				
B-469	Behler	Henry	Washington	27	July	1872	15	Sept	1872	William	Matilda	(Behler)	Oliwer	Blose	Emma Rebeccc	Stroup
B-470	Follweiler	Oliver W	Herbit	21	July	1872	18	Sept	1872	J.B.	Josephine	Schwartz	Wendel	Schafer	Eliza	(Schwartz)
B-471	Fisher	Charles	Walter	2	June	1872	18	Sept	1872	Newton B	Mary Ann	Rehrig	Lewis	Rehrig	Catherine	Beitelman
B-472	Walck	Loretta		17	Aug	1872	22	Sept	1872	William	Harriet	Selzer	Simon	Walck		
B-473	Andreas	Ellen	Minerva	20	July	1872	22	Sept	1872	Josiah	Matilda	Strohl				
B-474	Snyder	Laura	Anna Maria	10	Aug	1872	22	Sept	1872	Elias	Manda	Eck				
B-475	Rohrbach	Harriet	Ellenah	17	Aug	1872	27	Sept	1872	Abel	Rebecca	Green				
B-476	Beltz	Korah	Agnes	26	Aug	1872	29	Sept	1872	Joseph	Lydia	Gruber				
B-477	Rhoads	Ida	Clarenda	4	July	1872	2	Oct	1872	William	Annetta	Kuntz				
B-478	Nothstein	Nathan	Willliam	22	June	1872	5	Oct	1872	Charles	Catherine	Rabenold	John	Nothstein	Kitty	Freyman
B-479	Dreisbach	Valera	Alavesta	1	Sept	1872	6	Oct	1872	Aaron	Louisa	Wher	Daniel	Schafer	Sarah	Sendel
B-480	Hontz	Kitty	Ann Minerva	7	Aug	1872	6	Oct	1872	Moses	Zeniah	Rex	Henry	Gombert	Emaline	Hontz
B-481	Evert	Silas	Ambrose	22	Aug	1872	6	Oct	1872	John	Mary Jane	Fulton				
B-482	Mertz	Harrieta		2	Aug	1872	6	Oct	1872	Alfred	Mary Ann	Evert	Franklin	Zellner	Mary Ann	Blose
B-483	Frantz	Minnie	Marella	18	Aug	1872	10	Oct	1872	Godfrey	Anna	Rex	Aaron	Reichard	Ellen	Nothstein
B-484	Philhower	Maria	Magdalene	27	Sep	1872	10	Oct	1872	John	Anna	Fritz	Maria Magdalen	Schwartz		
B-485	Rex	Harriet	Susanna	17	July	1872	12	Oct	1872	Layfayette	Sarah	(Rex)				
B-486	Peter	Ida	Amelia	3	Sep	1872	12	Oct	1872	William	Esther	Stroup				
B-487	Feist	Laura	Lillie	9	Aug	1872	13	Oct	1872	Joseph	Sarah Ann	Graver				
B-488	Brong	Charles	Andrew	27	July	1872	13	Oct	1872	Jacob	Anna	Graver	Andrew	Graver	Elizabeth	Whitehead
B-489	Sensinger	Mary	Clarissa	10	Sep	1872	13	Oct	1872	William F	Mary Maria	Ziegenfuss				
B-490	Webb	Lizzie	Malvenia	26	Sep	1872	13	Oct	1872	Joseph S	Catherine	Miller	Malvenia	Miller	Polly	Hartman
B-491	Hartranft	Edwin	Peter	13	Jan	1872	20	Oct	1872	David	Matilida	Kolb	Daniel	Kolb		
B-492	Stemler	Wilson		27	July	1872	27	Oct	1872	Reuben	Louisa	(Stemler)	David	Beltz	Louisa	Snyder
B-493	Berger	Ida	Edilla	26	Sep	1872	27	Oct	1872	Elias	Emaline	Hunsicker				
B-494	Hagenbuch	Malton	Esther	8	Aug	1872	30	Oct	1872	John	Eliza ___	Schwartz				
B-495	Montz	Alwenia	Louisa	21	Sep	1872	3	Nov	1872	Cassius	Cassanda	Rinker	Jacob	Montz	Leah	(Montz)
B-496	Reinsmith	Lister	Emlen	26	Sept	1872	3	Nov	1872	Nathan	Messina	Kerschner	John	Nothstein	Kitty Ann	Freyman
B-497	Graver	Sarah	Jane	12	Sept	1872	9	Nov	1872	Adam Monroe	Isabella	Rhoads				
B-498	Evert	Ellen	Messina	10	Oct	1872	17	Nov	1872	Nathan	Sarah	Moyer				
B-499	Strohl	Ulysses	Grant	6	Sept	1872	24	Nov	1872	William H	Mary Ann	Grill	Henry	Mcfarland	Rebecca	Strohl
B-500	Rice	Etna	Josephena	7	Oct	1872	24	Nov	1872	Tilghman	Savenna	Strohl				
B-501	Frohnheiser	Harry	Winfield	22	Sept	1872	22	Sept	1872	Lewis	Anzonetta	Miller	Edward	Pethsel	Sarah	Pethsel

Births and Baptisms

Line #	Surname	Child Given	Child Middle	Birth Day	Birth Mth	Birth Year	Baptism Day	Baptism Mth	Baptism Year	Father Given	Mother Given	Née	Witness Given	Witness Surname	Witness Given	Witness Surname
B-502	Smith	Emma	Jane	12	June	1872	24	Nov	1872	Franklin	Elizabeth	Haid				
B-503	Grow	Carolina	Sevilla	25	Oct	1872	1	Dec	1872	Henry	Sally Ann	Cochran	John	Nothstein	KittyAnn	Freyman
B-504	Keiffly	Sabilla	Louisa	20	Oct	1872	1	Dec	1872	Adam	Manda	Kunkel	Augustus	Walck	Sabilla	Walck
B-505	Schaeffer	Lizzie	Agnes	10	Oct	1872	1	Dec	1872	Thomas	Sarah Amanda	Moyer	William	Schweibens	Louisa	(Schweibens)
B-506	Trainer	Thomas	Edward	24	Oct	1872	1	Dec	1872	Charles	Lenah	Platt				
B-507	Greenzweig	James	Alfred	4	July	1872	2	Dec	1872	William	Mary Ann	Eckhart				
B-508	Boyer	Oscar	Franklin	24	Sep	1872	2	Dec	1872	Franklin	July Ann	Grill	Nicholas	Grill	Elizabeth	(Grill)
B-509	Freyman	Kitty		24	Sep	1872	5	Dec	1872	Thomas	Susanna	Hobbes	John	Nothstein	Kitty Ann	Nothstein
B-510	Moyer	Erastes	Elmer	23	Sep	1872	5	Dec	1872	B J	Catherine	(Moyer)				
B-511	Engelman	Julius		20	Mar	1868	8	Dec	1872	Sylvester	Mary	Hauser				
B-512	Engelman	George		29	Mar	1870	8	Dec	1872	Syvester	Mary	Hauser				
B-513	Wher	Ida	Valieria	15	Sep	1872	14	Dec	1872	Owen	Ellen	Zimmerman				
B-514	Rauch	Osville		22	Oct	1872	15	Dec	1872	Peter	Polly	Miller	Levi	Weiss	Rebecca	Miller
B-515	Fenstermaker	Jacob	Daniel	11	Nov	1872	26	Dec	1872	John	Mary Ann	Montz	Phillip	German	Polly	Clauss
B-516	Graver	Carrie	May	1	May	1872	2	Jan	1873	William A	Isabella Jane	Roth				
B-517	Hoffman	Sally	Ann	20	Sept	1872	12	Jan	1873	Nathan	Catherine	Ackerman				
B-518	Balliet	Sarah	Leah	21	Nov	1872	12	Jan	1873	James D	Sophia	Albright			Sarah Ann	Schaefer
B-519	Hiskey	Carrie	Floyd	13	Oct	1872	14	Jan	1873	Herry	Angeline	Stettler				
B-520	Stroup	Fayetta	Rebecca	1	Dec	1872	19	Jan	1873	Josiah	Polly	Snyder				
B-521	Snyder	Jennie		8	Dec	1872	19	Jan	1873	Stephen	Susan	Scherer				
B-522	Kunkle	Ellen	Christianna	13	Aug	1872	19	Jan	1873	Joseph	Amelia	Herman	Daniel	Behler	Christianna	(Behler)
B-523	Washbon	Charles	Eugene	23	Sept	1872	19	Jan	1873	John Joseph	Emma Louisa	Weiss				
B-524	Reed	Elmer	Edgar	5	Oct	1872	19	Jan	1873	Aquilla E	Maria L	Fritzinger				
B-525	Strassburger	Warren	Herby	28	Oct	1872	19	Jan	1873	Jacob	Elphina	Moyer				
B-526	Anewalt	Eva	Anna	29	Nov	1872	22	Jan	1873	Lewis	Sarah Ann	Schneck	Harrison	Wertz	Mary	Schultz
B-527	Solt	Sarah	Jane	3	Sept	1872	23	Jan	1873	Henry	Amelia	Hahn				
B-528	Hartman	Elwin	Lewis	12	Oct	1872	26	Jan	1873	Lewis	Mary	Boyer	Lynford	Beer	July Ann	(Beer)
B-529	Solt	Sitna		14	Oct	1872	26	Jan	1873	Amos	Alavesta	Thomas	Reuben	Solt	Eliza	(Solt)
B-530	Kunkel	Paul	Edwin				26	Jan	1873	Hilorus	Lucy	Walck	Paul	Schweibens	Leah	Mangold
B-531	Hoffman	Elmira		4	Nov	1872	2	Feb	1873	Jacob D	July Ann	Troxel	Solomon D	Hoffman	Henrietta	Billman
B-532	Rehrig	Priscilla	Louisa	8	Dec	1872	2	Feb	1873	Reuben	Emaline	Ruch				
B-533	Kemmerer	Katie	Sevilla	1	Nov	1872	2	Feb	1873	Charles	Elizabeth	Gilbert				
B-534	Horn	Elmira	Agnes	14	Nov	1872	2	Feb	1873	Alfie P	Mary Ann	Fink				
B-535	Trine	Meta	Ida	31	Oct	1872	16	Feb	1873	John	Polly	Peter				
B-536	Zahn	Minnie	Clara	3	Feb	1872	16	Feb	1873	Joseph	Johannah	Kaiser				
B-537	Sleider	Mary	Ann Elizabeth	16	Nov	1872	17	Feb	1873	Edward	Mary Ann	Beltz	Lydia	Beltz		
B-538	Klotz	Charles	Daniel	5	Jan	1873	17	Feb	1873	Josiah	Rebecca	Beltz				
B-539	Smith	Lizzie	Anna	12	Dec	1872	22	Feb	1873	Emil	Matilda	Kop	Alfred	Haupt	Anna Matilda	Houser
B-540	Borhor	Elmira	Elizabeth	19	May	1872	28	Feb	1873	Lewis	Leah	Kemerer				
B-541	Gombert	Polly	Welesta	5	Jan	1873	1	Mar	1873	Jonas	Sarah	Riegel				
B-542	Mertz	Alwin	Edgar	26	Dec	1872	7	Mar	1873	William	Joannah	Mertz	Isaac	Beltz	Maria	Guldner
B-543	Lapp	Emma		28	Sept	1872	7	Mar	1873	John	Anna	Beltz				

Beyonnd the Blue Mountain, Vol. II

Births and Baptisms

Line #	Surname	Child Given	Middle	Birth Day Mth	Birth Year	Baptism Day Mth	Baptism Year	Father Given	Mother Given	Nee	Witness Given	Witness Surname	Witness Given	Witness Surname
B-544	Rehrig	Maggie	Jane	28 Jan	1873	7 Mar	1873	Lewis	Catherine	Beitelman				
B-545	Shabel	Milton	Arthur	28 Dec	1872	9 Mar	1873	Milton T	Catherine	Frohnheiser				
B-546	Moyer	Daniel		27 Nov	1872	9 Mar	1873	Abraham	Rebecca	Wertman				
B-547	Noll	Ambrose	Edgar	18 Jan	1873	9 Mar	1873	Augustus	Catherine	Barrel				
B-548	Schwab	George	Albert	23 Oct	1872	9 Mar	1873	Charles H	Matilda	Wilkraut			Lucy	Whitmer
B-549	Whiteman	Thomas		10 Feb	1873	9 Mar	1873	Daniel	Caroline	Schwartwood			Sarah	Schwartwood
B-550	Bowman	Glyde	Alexes	1 Feb	1873	15 Mar	1873	Victor	Isabella	Balliet	Henry	Bowman	Lewina	Peter
B-551	Beer	Sally	Rebecca	24 Jan	1873	16 Mar	1873	Alfred	Rosanna	Hagenbuch				
B-552	Reichard	Maehlon	Edmond	30 Sept	1872	16 Mar	1873	Maehlon	Lucy Ann	Rehrig				
B-553	Kuntz	William	Irwin	11 Mar	1873	17 Mar	1873	Richard	Selinda	Schwartz				
B-554	Rabenold	Sevilla	Isabella	14 Feb	1873	17 Mar	1873	Tighman	Catherine	Frederic	Charles	Remaley	Emma Elizabeti	Rabenold
B-555	Dreisbach	Elwin	Henry	1 Jan	1873	23 Mar	1873	Dennis	Sarah	Walck	Isaac	Levan	Louisa	Dreisbach
B-556	Fritzinger	Ellen	Louisa	9 Jan	1873	23 Mar	1873	John	Henrietta	Fisher	Stephen H	Fritzinger	Anna Maria	Fritzinger
B-557	Nothstein	William	Franklin	3 Jan	1873	23 Mar	1873	Alwin	Susanna	Lauchnor				
B-558	Fritzinger	Mary	Ellen	9 Jan	1873	23 Mar	1873	Joseph M	Sarah	Bartholomew				
B-559	Hartman	Milton	Elmer	5 Feb	1873	28 Mar	1873	Joseph	Pauline	Fisher	Columbus	Long	Louisa	Fisher
B-560	Rex	Tuwitta	Lucy Ann	3 Feb	1873	28 Mar	1873	Lewis A	Sarah	Strohl	Aaron	Strohl	Eva	(Strohl)
B-561	Maurer	Emma	Elizabeth	30 Jan	1873	30 Mar	1873	Franklin	Alice	Kern				
B-562	Peter	Charles	Admarill	10 Jan	1873	6 April	1873	Wallace I	Hannah	Fritz				
B-563	Knecht	Freddie	Anderson	23 Feb	1873	7 April	1873	Reuben	Catherine	Moyer	Priscilla	Weida		
B-564	Flickinger	Elizabeth	Anna	4 Mar	1867	14 April	1873	Elias	Catherine	Steigerwalt	Peter	Flickinger		
B-565	Helmers	Charles	William	24 Nov	1871	14 April	1873	Charles	Elwina Jane	Flickinger	Charles	Frehley	Matilida	Minnich
B-566	Strohm	George		16 April	1872	14 April	1873	Joseph	Levina	Scheekler				
B-567	Reed	Willie	Hunsicker	20 Jan	1873	20 April	1873	Franklin	Ellemanda	Bartholomew	Owen	Hunsicker	Sarah E	Kistler
B-568	Diehl	Alavesta	Elizabeth	1 Dec	1872	21 April	1873	Alwin	Sarah C	Peter				
B-569	Bartholomew	Albert	Orlando	12 April	1873	24 April	1873	Abraham	Sarah	Newhart				
B-570	Kern	William	Gustav	7 Feb	1873	26 April	1873	Peter	Jane	Brotzman	Adam	Anders	Maria	Settenfeld
B-571	O'Brian	Mary	Elizabeth	29 Mar	1873	26 April	1873	Joseph	Lizzie	Haid				
B-572	Boyer	Mary	Matilda	5 Feb	1873	26 April	1873	Alexander	Elizabeth	Remaly	Oliver	Blose	Emma	Stroup
B-573	Kauffman	Milton	Oliver	20 Mar	1873	27 April	1873	Charles	Maria	Walp				
B-574	Beidelman	John	Harrison	10 Jan	1873	27 April	1873	Jacob H	Elizabeth	Kansman				
B-575	Ruch	Charles	Franklin	14 Dec	1872	4 May	1873	William	Louisa	Arner	Catherine	Ruch		
B-576	Schultz	Asaba		24 Feb	1873	4 May	1873	Henry	Susanna	Hoffman				
B-577	Schock	Ellen	Susanna	13 Feb	1873	4 May	1873	John	Lucinda	Beck	Nathan	Hoffman	Kate	Ackerman
B-578	Scherer	Alice	Laura	15 April	1873	5 May	1873	John	Rosa Ann	Moser				
B-579	Trumbore	William	Henry	12 May	1870	5 May	1873	Alfred	Elizabeth	Lintz				
B-580	Trumbore	John	Alfred	5 Aug	1872	5 May	1873	Alfred	Elizabeth	Lintz				
B-581	Christman	George	Jacob	20 Feb	1873	7 May	1873	Joel	Lizzie	Musselman				
B-582	Lower	Ellen	Korah	12 Mar	1873	11 May	1873	William	Manda	Anewalt	Elias	Anewalt	Eliza	Reichard
B-583	Lower	Sally	Ann	18 Jan	1873	11 May	1873	Tilghman	Susanna	Reppert	Rebecca	Reppert		
B-584	Smith	Lesta	Eugene	3 April	1873	11 May	1873	Charles	Manda	Lentz				
B-585	Haupt	George	Frederic	14 Mar	1873	18 May	1873	Frederic	Mary Ann	Mertz	William	Mertz	Joannah	(Mertz)

Beyonnd the Blue Mountain, Vol. II

Births and Baptisms

Line #	Surname	Child Given	Child Middle	Birth Day	Birth Mth	Birth Year	Baptism Day	Baptism Mth	Baptism Year	Father Given	Mother Given	Nee	Witness Given	Witness Surname	Witness Given	Witness Surname
B-586	Gombert	Elmer	Sylvester	28	Mar	1873	18	May	1873	Nathan	Medina	Krum				
B-587	Koons	George	Henry	10	April	1873	18	May	1873	Willoughby	Sarah	Kistler	Henry	Werstein	Elizabeth	Beltz
B-588	Dorwart	Emma		24	Mar	1873	18	May	1873	Francis	Abby Ann	Walck	Thomas	Dorwort	Sarah	Newhart
B-589	Lerch	Charles	Henry	28	Mar	1873	25	May	1873	Owen	Catherine	Kuntzman	Joel	Ziegenfuss	Luzetta	Kuehner
B-590	Geiger	Korah	Lydiann	10	Apr	1873	25	May	1873	David	Louisa	Peter				
B-591	Webb	Thomas	Joseph	6	April	1873	25	May	1873	James	Sarah Ann	Shoemaker	Thomas M	Webb	Lucinda	Lentz
B-592	Dieterlein	Amelia	Christianna	6	Mar	1873	29	May	1873	Timothy	Sally Ann	Frantz	Lewis	Fisher	Mary	Frantz
B-593	Mangold	Caroline	Elizabeth	24	April	1873	1	June	1873	Frederic	Fredrica	Wieser	John	Mangold	Caroline	Neunstiel
B-594	Walck	Susan	Sophia	15	April	1873	15	June	1873	Augustus	Sabilla	Kunkle	Adam	Foster	Amanda	Kunkle
B-595	Gombert	Addie	Estella	9	Apr	1873	15	June	1873	James	Ellen	Mertz				
B-596	Frederic	Oscar	Elandes	18	Mar	1873	15	June	1873	William	Eliza	Grow	William	Grow	Anna Maria	Mertz
B-597	Simon	Harrison	William	30	Mar	1873	15	June	1873	Michael	Maria	Werth	Philip	Hartman	Sarah Amelia	Fenstermaker
B-598	Finkler	Flory	Ann	4	May	1873	22	June	1873	Peter	Caroline	Kuehner	Henry	Smith	Catherine	(Smith)
B-599	Lentz	Elmira		5	Apr	1873	22	June	1873	Stephen	Sarah	Muschlitz				
B-600	Kelchner	Lilie	Alice	-	-	-	22	June	1873	Edward	Lydia	Remaly	Henry	Remaley	Lydia	Miller
B-601	Kunsman	Emma	Catherine	14	Mar	1873	22	June	1873	Jacob	Mary	Peter				
B-602	Muthhart	William	Henry Elmer	28	June	1872	25	June	1873	Lewi	Emma	Moser				
B-603	Rehrig	Mandes	Nathaniel	30	Apr	1873	29	June	1873	William B	Amelia	Peter				
B-604	Balliet	Benjamin	Cyrus	28	Apr	1873	29	June	1873	John	Amanda	Rehrig	Hiram	Hankee	Elizabeth	Clause
B-605	Bowman	Ellen	Korah	13	Mar	1873	6	July	1873	Wilson D	Caroline	Arner	John	Hagenbuch	Eliza	Schwartz
B-606	Laux	Benjamin	Franklin	27	Aug	1867	6	July	1873	Maehlon B	Kate	Seller				
B-607	Laux	Edwin	Harrison	1	Dec	1868	6	July	1873	Maehlon B	Kate	Seller				
B-608	Laux	Amour	Addison	12	June	1871	6	July	1873	Maehlon B	Kate	Seller				
B-609	Laux	Robert	Arthur	5	Feb	1873	6	July	1873	Maehlon B	Kate	Sendel	Andrew (Sr)	Graver	Elizabeth	Whitehead
B-610	Ruch	Moulton	Webster	11	June	1873	9	July	1873	Elias	Mary	Wertman				
B-611	Geiger	Susanna	Catherine	8	May	1873	11	July	1873	Joseph	Rebecca	Sensinger	L. S.	Stansberry	Susanna	Reiner
B-612	Ziegenfuss	Korah	Emaline	16	June	1873	13	July	1873	William A	Sally Ann	Hartman	Nathan	Ziegenfuss	Emaline	Sensinger
B-613	Milherin	Harrison	Eugene	7	June	1873	13	July	1873	William	Mary Ann	Kaiser				
B-614	Snyder	Thomas	Jefferson	4	June	1873	20	July	1873	Paul	Eliza	Dotterer	Peter	Finkler	Caroline	Kuehner
B-615	Brown	Thomas	Oscar	14	May	1873	20	July	1873	James	Cassenda	Weiss	Jacob	Scheekler	Catherine	Remaly
B-616	Dreisbach	Mandes		12	April	1873	20	July	1873	Alexander	Ellen Jane	Bartholomew	Nero	Weiss	Louisa	Hontz
B-617	Gangware	Eliza	Harriet	29	Mar	1873	20	July	1873	John	Amand	Stroup	Francis	Fritzinger	Melinda	Bartholomew
B-618	Held	Wilmer	Franklin	18	May	1873	21	July	1873	Llewellynn	Sabina	Lambes				
B-619	Guth	Percy	Asa	30	May	1873	26	July	1873	Paul	Mary	Knecht				
B-620	Weida	James	Wilson	1	June	1873	27	July	1873	Benjamin	Elizabeth	Blose				
B-621	Dreher	Minnie	May	2	Feb	1873	30	July	1873	Frederic	Lucy	Smith				
B-622	Dreher	Harrie		22	June	1873	30	July	1873	Benoville	Lucy	Klose				
B-623	Shumacher	Ellen	Rebecca	23	Mar	1873	6	Aug	1873	John	Augustin	Strohm				
B-624	Weida	Wilson		9	Mar	1873	6	Aug	1873	William	Ellen	Dreisbach (Walck)				
B-625	Hontz	Ida	Savennah	24	May	1873	9	Aug	1873	John	Matilda	Dreisbach (Walck)	Daniel	Beltz	Elizabeth	Dreisbach (Walck)
B-626	Walck	Nelson	Ario	25	June	1873	10	Aug	1873	Philip	Mary	Sensinger	David	Walck	Salinda	(Walck)
B-627	Ziegenfuss	Edwin		1	July	1873	10	Aug	1873	Lyman	Ellemanda		Edwin	Sensinger	Caroline	Geiger

Beyond the Blue Mountain, Vol. II

Births and Baptisms

Line #	Surname	Child Given	Middle	Birth Day	Birth Mth	Birth Year	Baptism Day	Baptism Mth	Baptism Year	Father Given	Mother Given	Nee	Witness Given	Witness Surname	Witness Given	Witness Surname
B-628	Arner	Calvin	Eugene	3	July	1873	10	Aug	1873	Charles	Ellen Jane	Solt				
B-629	Beck	Edgar	Samuel	5	July	1873	16	Aug	1873	Alfred	Manda	Moser				
B-630	Youngkin	Charlie		13	June	1872	16	Aug	1873	Robert J	Barbara	Christman				
B-631	Blose	Henry	Edwin	12	July	1873	17	Aug	1873	David	Lucy Ann	Strassburger				
B-632	Strassburger	Hannah	Messina	20	July	1873	17	Aug	1873	Mathias	Hannah	Hartman				
B-633	Frederic	Charlie	Samuel	3	Mar	1873	17	Aug	1873	Lewis	Sarah Ann	Olenwine				
B-634	McFarland	Frank	Walter	18	July	1873	17	Aug	1873	Henry	Rebecca	Strohl				
B-635	Lower	Emma	Catherine	18	June	1873	17	Aug	1873	George D	Helenah	Krechel	George	Remaley	Sarah	Blose
B-636	Fenstermache	Irena	Deborah	25	May	1873	21	Aug	1873	Rueben	Levina	Frantz				
B-637	Rabe	Emma	Elizabeth	17	June	1873	22	Aug	1873	Franklin	Catherine	Traut				
B-638	Wolf	Henry	Harrison	16	June	1873	24	Aug	1873	Zacharias T	Lucette	Anthony	Owen	Wolf	Mary	Keiner
B-639	Stein	Harry	William	15	July	1873	31	Aug	1873	George	Caroline	Hauck	Charles	Steinheiser	Anna Maria	Walker
B-640	Dorword	Girdy	May	1	May	1873	31	Aug	1873	William	Harriet	Shary				
B-641	Riegel	Mary	Agnes	24	June	1873	31	Aug	1873	Joseph	Hermena	Horn				
B-642	Hollenbach	Ida	Elizabeth	1	July	1873	1	Sept	1873	Franklin	Catherine	Grasely			Angeline	Sherer
B-643	Sinyard	Jonathan		5	Aug	1873	2	Sept	1873	James	Sarah	Frantz				
B-644	Haintz	Bowman	William	15	Dec	1872	6	Sept	1873	William F	Adline	Stuckly	William	Schaefer	Mary	Deibert
B-645	Schnell	Charles	William	26	July	1873	6	Sept	1873	Oliver	Priscilla	Rhoad			Lydia	Schnell
B-646	Fenstermaker	Albert	Wilmington	23	July	1873	7	Sept	1873	Stephen	Catherine	Snyder	Dennis	Nothstein	Manda	German
B-647	Walck	Elwin	Jacob	24	June	1873	7	Sept	1873	Edward	Maria	Montz	James	Kleintopp	Ellemanda	Walck
B-648	Haupt	Mary	Elizabeth	14	July	1873	9	Sept	1873	George Frederick	Anna	Donehue				
B-649	Smith	Irwin	Gladen	16	Apr	1873	15	Sept	1873	Theodore	Elizabeth	Christman				
B-650	Ginder	Robert	Henry	5	Dec	1871	21	Sept	1873	Lewis	Maria	Walter				
B-651	Ginder	Isabella	Emaline	2	Aug	1873	21	Sept	1873	Lewis	Maria	Walter				
B-652	Heilman	Clara	Adline	24	June	1873	21	Sept	1873	George W	Mary	Dreher				
B-653	Walck	Sarah	Minnie Ann	20	June	1873	28	Sept	1873	John E	Eva Ann	Greenzweig				
B-654	Blose	Elmira	Susanna	22	July	1873	28	Sept	1873	Charles	Susanna	Solt	Oliver	Blose	Manda	Boyer
B-655	Kern	Anna	Korah	18	Aug	1873	28	Sept	1873	Francis	Amanda	Lehr	William	Behler	Matilda	Blose
B-656	Schnell	Alwin	Franklin	7	Aug	1873	5	Oct	1873	Aaron	Seniah	Sensinger	Daniel	Sensinger	Caroline	Neff
B-657	Bretney	Clemen	Henry	18	Sept	1873	5	Oct	1873	Thomas J	Mary Alice	Schaefer	Henry	Bretney	Salome	Beck
B-658	Markley	Eugene	Alexander	15	Aug	1873	10	Oct	1873	Tilghman	Elizabeth	Dorwort				
B-659	Fritzinger	Harrison	Hilbert	12	Aug	1873	12	Oct	1873	Joseph	Salinda	Scheekler	Jacob	Scheekler	Catherine	Remaley
B-660	Moulthrop	Aniza	Alonzo	15	Aug	1873	12	Oct	1873	William H H	Priscilla	Trumbore				
B-661	Pettit	Emma	Jane	5	Sep	1873	25	Oct	1873	George	Eliza	Remaly				
B-662	Ramely	Sallie	Messina	7	Aug	1873	25	Oct	1873	Moses	Sarah	Arner				
B-663	Krock	Howard	Milan	3	Oct	1873	26	Oct	1873	Daniel	Miranda Louisa	Newhart				
B-664	Hahn	William	Dennis	15	Sept	1873	2	Nov	1873	Edwin	Emma	Weber	Solomon	Webes	Ella	Shive
B-665	Zellner	Tilghman	Harrison	19	Sept	1873	2	Nov	1873	F Reuben	Mary Ann	Blose	Benjamin F	German	Mary	Miller
B-666	Grow	Carolina	Sevilla	29	Sept	1873	8	Nov	1873	Nathan	Sally Ann	Hobbes	Henry	Grow	Sally Ann	Cochran
B-667	Sifies	Lillie	Clendora	22	Aug	1873	9	Nov	1873	Jacob	Amanda	Zellner				
B-668	Sleider	Ida	Elizabeth	21	Sept	1873	9	Nov	1873	William Dennis	Elmina	Maury	Rebecca	Bennett		
B-669	Graver	Lillie	Telila	11	July	1873	9	Nov	1873	Owen	Fianna	Solt				

Beyonnd the Blue Mountain, Vol. II

Births and Baptisms

Line #	Surname	Child Given	Child Middle	Birth Day	Birth Mth	Birth Year	Baptism Day	Baptism Mth	Baptism Year	Father Given	Mother Given	Nee	Witness Given	Witness Surname	Witness Given	Witness Surname
B-670	Albright	Lizzie	Irena	8	Oct	1873	9	Nov	1873	Enos B	Emma	Geggus				
B-671	Noll	Angeline	Jeannetta	25	Sept	1873	16	Nov	1873	Aaron	Eliza	Rehrig				
B-672	Haintz	Charles	Franklin	10	Sept	1873	16	Nov	1873	Henry D	Mary Ann	Schwartz				
B-673	Beltz	Manda	Jane	27	Aug	1873	23	Nov	1873	Henry	Levina	Buck	James	Ziegenfuss	Polly	Eckhart
B-674	Snyder	George	Wesley	28	Oct	1873	24	Nov	1873	Pnaon	Emma	Kemerer				
B-675	Gombert	Harvey	Francis	7	Nov	1873	24	Nov	1873	Joseph	Sally Ann	Fenstermacher				
B-676	Fenstermache	Ellenora	May	16	Nov	1873	25	Nov	1873	Jchn	Mary Ann	Montz				
B-677	Faust	Sevilla	Isabella	27	Oct	1873	30	Nov	1873	Adam	Sarah	Confer	Lewis	Kemerer	Emma	Confer
B-678	Kressley	Korah	Elizabeth	15	Oct	1873	30	Nov	1873	Daniel	Mary Ann	Dilcher				
B-679	Scherer	Robert	Edwin	28	July	1873	7	Dec	1873	Ecwin	Elmina	Dreisbach	Lorenz	Zeiser	Harriet	Dreisbach
B-680	Bartholomew	Harrie	Nelson	5	Nov	1873	11	Dec	1873	Elias	Rebecca	Henry				
B-681	Sittler	Clairessa	Eulalia	10	Nov	1873	14	Dec	1873	John	Carrie	Seidel				
B-682	Krumn	John	Wilson	29	Apr	1873	17	Dec	1873	Nathan	Anna Maria	German	Wilson	German	Ellen	Bartholomew
B-683	Feist	Andrew	Joseph	4	Nov	1873	21	Dec	1873	Joseph	Sarah Ann	Graver				
B-684	Weiss	Carrie	Sevilla	8	Dec	1873	26	Dec	1873	William	Rosina	Steigerwalt				
B-685	Beer	Sarah	Agnes	15	Sept	1873	28	Dec	1873	Lynnford	July Ann	(Beer)				
B-686	Nace	Quincy	Llewellynn	28	Oct	1873	28	Dec	1873	Benjamin	Emma	Graver				
B-687	Kresgy	Charles	Henry	5	Nov	1873	4	Jan	1874	Paul	Mary Ann	Stemler	Nathan	Stemler	Rebecca	Snyder (Ziegenfuss)
B-688	Buck	Eliza		27	Oct	1873	4	Jan	1874	John	Mary Ann	Quin	Joel	Ziegenfuss	Luzetta	(Rabenold)
B-689	Rumble	Gordon	Ambrose	9	Dec	1873	9	Jan	1874	Rudolph	Eliza	Rabenold	Nathan	Rabenold	Mary	Rabenold
B-690	Heiser	Mary	Albertha	16	Aug	1873	20	Sept	1873	Morroe	Caroline	Rabenold	Rudolph	Rumble	Eliza	Rabenold
B-691	Stout	Milton	Osville	30	Nov	1873	11	Jan	1874	Zacharias	Sarah	Shoenberger	James	Kleintopp	Amanda	Walck
B-692	Weida	Harrison	Weido			1873	13	Jan	1874	Aaron	Henrietta	Adams				
B-693	Ferber	Ellen	Amelia	30	Nov	1873	13	Jan	1874	Reuben	Henrietta	Stroup				
B-694	Bechtel	Anna	Maria	30	Oct	1873	14	Jan	1874	Aaron	Jarrusa	Frantz	Andrea	Hamm	Zacilia	Graf
B-695	Bachman	Johnnie	Richard	1	Oct	1873	14	Jan	1874	Daniel	Hannah	Dengler				
B-696	Blose	Ellen	Rebecca	16	Nov	1873	18	Jan	1874	Lewis	Isabella	Brown	William	Kline	Ellen Jane	Blose
B-697	Mertz	Scottie	Albert	19	Jan	1874	19	Jan	1874	Alfred	Mary Ann	Everts	Samuel	Evert		
B-698	Mertz	Robert		19	Jan	1874	19	Jan	1874	Alfred	Mary Ann	Everts	John	Evert		
B-699	Grow	Albert	David Abraham	30	Dec	1873	25	Jan	1874	John	Elizabeth	Frederic	Josiah	Miller	Ella	Confer
B-700	Thomas	Zacharias	Robert	14	Apr	1872	27	Jan	1874	Zacharias	Sarah	Rabenold				
B-701	Rex	Asabey	Milton	20	Nov	1873	29	Jan	1874	William	Mary	Eck				
B-702	Kromer	Catherine	Manda	7	Dec	1873	8	Feb	1874	Irwin	Martha	Hartman	Franklin	Hahn	Catherine	Hartman
B-703	Lintz	Nora	Mantena	5	Nov	1873	8	Feb	1874	Charles	Adline	Klotz				
B-704	Metzger	Francis	Albert	30	Dec	1873	8	Feb	1874	Christoph	Elizabeth	Heffelfinger				
B-705	Kolb	Jonas	Henry	26	Dec	1873	8	Feb	1874	Reuben	Rebecca	Schaeffer	Jonas	Rehrig	Mary	Correll
B-706	Trainer	Sarah	Jane	26	Dec	1873	8	Feb	1874	Charles	Lena	Platt				
B-707	Ginder	Philip					10	Feb	1874	Isaac						
B-708	Yohe	Charles	Daniel	7	July	1873	15	Feb	1874	Alfred J	Elizabeth	Krum				
B-709	Johnston	Laura	Luella	26	June	1873	15	Feb	1874	M. L	Diana	Houser				
B-710	Schaefer	Herbert	Clayton	25	Nov	1873	15	Feb	1874	William	Ellevena	Fehr				
B-711	Borhor	Ada	Catherine	6	Jan	1874	16	Feb	1874	Lewis	Leah	Kemerer				

Births and Baptisms

Line #	Surname	Child Given	Middle	Birth Day	Mth	Year	Baptism Day	Mth	Year	Father Given	Mother Given	Nee	Witness Given	Surname	Witness Given	Surname
B-712	Britton	Manda	Isabella	27	Oct	1873	21	Feb	1874	Benoville	Mary	Hawk				
B-713	Arner	Joseph	Daniel				22	Feb	1874	Henry	Harriet	Henny	Henry	Bretney	Salome	Beck
B-714	Beck	Osville	Ulysses	10	Jan	1874	23	Feb	1874	Charles A	Sophia	Frantz				
B-715	Bartholomew	Anna	May	15	Oct	1873	26	Feb	1874	John	Catherine	Serfass			Anna	Hiller
B-716	Rolfink	William	Henry	28	Dec	1873	26	Feb	1874	John	Ellen	Rabe	Franklin	Rabe	Catherine	Trout
B-717	Moser	Sophia	Amelia	20	Oct	1873	26	Feb	1874	Joseph	Susan	Barwick			Suvilla	Schwab
B-718	Eisenhower	Lillie	Savannah	22	Feb	1874	26	Feb	1874	Edwin	Mary Alice	Flick				
B-719	Mantz	Carrie	Elizabeth	13	Feb	1874	1	Mar	1874	Francis	Sarah	Longacre	Lewis	Mantz	Kate	Dauber
B-720	Laub	Minerva	Estella	22	Jan	1874	1	Mar	1874	Aaron	Lucinda	Weber				
B-721	Ritz	Adlina	Sophia	5	Jan	1874	1	Mar	1874	James	Alavesta	Weber	Robert	Bartholomew	Anna Maria	Ritz
B-722	Wert	Ida	Amelia	8	Feb	1874	1	Mar	1874	Willoughby	Maria	Hartranft	Philip	Wertman	Sarah Amelia	Fenstermaker
B-723	Clewell	Martha	Magdalene	22	Dec	1873	1	Mar	1874	George	Sarah	Klotz	Owen	Klotz	Emaline	Flick
B-724	Lichtenwalter	Osville		12	Feb	1874	3	Mar	1874	Albert	Priscilla	Harleman				
B-725	Sheckler	Lillie	Agnes	20	Dec	1873	3	Mar	1874	William L	Ellen	Solt	Isaac	Moyer	Elizabeth	Leiby
B-726	Enzian	Henry		6	Feb	1874	3	Mar	1874	George	Anna Elizabeth	Hoffman				
B-727	Boyer	Robert	Andrew	3	Sept	1873	4	Mar	1874	Levi W	Amanda	Ash				
B-728	Feierich	Amelia	Henrietta	24	Sept	1873	6	Mar	1874	Henry	Catherine	Lichtenberger				
B-729	Riegel	George	Washington	22	Feb	1874	12	Mar	1874	Joshua	Sarah	Leiby				
B-730	Beltz	Minnie	Josephine	3	Oct	1873	12	Mar	1874	David	Mary	Kuntz				
B-731	Selzer	William	Henry	9	Feb	1874	15	Mar	1874	Henry	Catherine	Moyer				
B-732	Williamson	Ida	Pruella	15	Feb	1874	15	Mar	1874	James	---	Gombert				
B-733	Hontz	Delilah	Adlina	16	Dec	1873	19	Mar	1874	Josiah	Sarah	Jenkins			Hetty	Barwick
B-734	Klotz	Sarah	Irene Carrie	11	Sept	1873	22	Mar	1874	Franklin	Sarah	Solt			Amelia	Solt
B-735	Hahn	Jannie	Teliah	14	Feb	1874	22	Mar	1874	William	Mary	Klotz			Lucy Ann	Solt
B-736	Strohl	Quinton		24	Feb	1874	22	Mar	1874	Amos	Anna Maria	Schwab				
B-737	Strohl	Christianna	Estella	7	Mar	1874	22	Mar	1874	Josiah	Catherine Ellen	Zimmerman				
B-738	Arner	Laura	Estella	14	Feb	1874	22	Mar	1874	George	Rosa Ann	Scherer				
B-739	Moulthrop	Minnie	Rossville	11	Feb	1874	22	Mar	1874	John Francis	Ellen	Shoemaker				
B-740	Harron	Frankie	Henry	18	Jan	1874	24	Mar	1874	John	Sarah	Muth	Franklin	Winsland	Lucy Ann	Hontz
B-741	Beltz	William	May	8	May	1873	1	Apr	1874	Harrison	Emma	Neitzel				
B-742	Rhoad	Martha	Caroline	4	Feb	1874	5	Apr	1874	Reuben	Caroline	Hiskey			Augusta	Schumaker
B-743	Kunkel	Laura	Pernina	22	Nov	1873	11	Apr	1874	Joseph	Amelia	Herman	Simeon	Brown	Catherine	Greenzweig
B-744	Boyer	Purcy		18	Feb	1874	11	Apr	1874	John F	Anna	Scherer				
B-745	Eckhart	Emery	Estella	7	Oct	1873	13	Apr	1874	Daniel	Manda	Dotter	Joseph	Andrea	Kate	Bartholomew
B-746	Raber	Mary	Ann	3	Apr	1874	19	Apr	1874	John	Henrietta	Eaches	Edward	Reber	Mary	Anthony
B-747	Schaefer	David	James	12	May	1874	19	July	1874	Solomon	Catherine	Beltz			Lydia	Beltz
B-748	Kauffman	Sabina	Agnes	22	May	1874	19	July	1874	Charles	Maria	Walp				
B-749	Maurer	Charles	William	5	June	1874	19	July	1874	Franklin	Alice	Kern				
B-750	Meckes	Tillie		24	May	1874	29	July	1874	Samuel L	Anna Fayetta	Kleintopp				
B-751	Brown	Franklin	Walter	9	July	1874	2	Aug	1874	Levi	Belinda	Dieter	Nicholas	Grill	Elizabeth	(Grill)
B-752	Remaley	Sevilla	Maltilda	17	July	1874	2	Aug	1874	Charles	Emma E	Rabenold	Henry	Schwartz	Matilda	Remaley
B-753	Snyder	Robert	Elmer	21	Jan	1874	2	Aug	1874	Alexander	Rebecca	Shive				

Beyond the Blue Mountain, Vol. II   Births and Baptisms

Line #	Surname	Child Given	Middle	Birth Day Mth Year	Baptism Day Mth Year	Father Given	Mother Given	Nee	Witness Given	Witness Surname	Witness Given	Witness Surname
B-754	Kahn	Magdaline		7 Sept 1873	6 Aug 1874	Charles	Christiana	Ruben				
B-755	Moser	John	Anderson	21 June 1874	6 Aug 1874	Jacob	Susanna	Gilbert				
B-756	Hildebrand	Laura		23 June 1874	8 Aug 1874	Peter	Mary	Long				
B-757	Dreisbach	Mary	Jane	15 June 1874	9 Aug 1874	Dennis	Sarah	Walck				
B-758	Miller	George		18 July 1874	9 Aug 1874	Henry	Manda	Gromen				
B-759	Lynn	Korah	Mantana	3 Apr 1874	9 Aug 1874	Simon	Emeline	Rehrig				
B-760	Shive	Charles	Wilson	13 June 1874	15 Aug 1874	Alexander	Mary	Leiby	Levi	Weiss	Rebecca	Miller
B-761	Kleintopp	George	Walter	26 April 1874	16 Aug 1874	David	Emaline	Kline	Robert	McDaniel	Elizabeth	Green
B-762	Fuss	Mary	Elenora	30 June 1874	16 Aug 1874	Charles	Christianna	Smith	William	Rinker	Sarah	Lower
B-763	Dreisbach	William	Albert	3 July 1874	16 Aug 1874	Mandes	Balinda	Silfies				
B-764	Strohl	Ida	Sally	20 June 1874	24 Aug 1874	Levi	Susanna	Reiley	Manassas	Acker	Catherine	Anthony
B-765	Mulhearn	Rosalee		28 May 1873	25 Aug 1874	Edward	Anna Maria	Bachman				
B-766	Berger	Laura	Agnes	3 Aug 1874	28 Aug 1874	Elias	Emaline	Hunsicker				
B-767	Merkley	Frederick	Calvin F	3 Aug 1874	6 Sept 1874	Stephen	Zeniah	Montz	Frederick	Mangold	Frederica	Weiser
B-768	Mertz	Jefferson		30 June 1874	6 Sept 1874	Nathan	Sally	Freyman	Henry	Wehrstein	Elizabeth	Beltz
B-769	Gould	Hattie	Minerva	9 Aug 1874	12 Sept 1874	Jacob	Anna Catherine	Kleppinger				
B-770	Weiss	Louisa	Martha	20 May 1874	13 Sept 1874	Nero	Louisa	Hontz				
B-771	Sleider	William	Henry	1 Mar 1874	13 Sept 1874	Edward	Mary Ann	Beltz	William H	Sleider	Ellemena	Maury
B-772	Moyer	Amelia		10 Mar 1872	13 Sept 1874	John	Maria	Whiteman	Daniel	Sensinger	Caroline	Neff
B-773	Moyer	Mary	Elizabeth	28 Apr 1874	13 Sept 1874	John	Maria	Whiteman	Thomas	Hahn	Mary	Boyer
B-774	Schappel	Asaba	Jacob	20 Aug 1874	23 Sept 1874	Milton T	Catherine	Frohnheiser				
B-775	Gable	Meta	Agnes	1 Aug 1874	26 Sept 1874	Mandes	Sabina	Bartholomew				
B-776	Geiger	Mary	Rebecca	26 Mar 1874	26 Sept 1874	Joseph	Rebecca	Wertman	Robert	Bartholomew	Anna	Ritz
B-777	Greenzweig	Thomas	Franklin	27 Aug 1874	30 Sept 1874	William	Mary Ann	Eckhart				
B-778	Geggus	Hattie		3 Sept 1874	3 Oct 1874	John	Lucy	Haid				
B-779	Rabenold	Zurah		1 Sept 1874	4 Oct 1874	Tilghman	Catherine	Frederic	Nathan	Rabenold	Mary	Stoyer
B-780	German	Mary	Jane	8 Oct 1874	11 Oct 1874	Benjamin F	Mary	Miller	Reuben	Zellner	Mary Ann	Blose
B-781	Kaiser	Hannah	Agnes	6 Apr 1874	11 Oct 1874	William	Elizabeth	Wehr			Hannah	Zahn
B-782	Fritzinger	Edgar	Albert	26 Aug 1874	12 Oct 1874	Tilghman	Anzonetta	Goodheil				
B-783	Horn	Ida	Carolina	10 Jan 1874	17 Oct 1874	Alwin	Jane Amanda	Ross	William	Ross	Lewina	German
B-784	Moran	Frank	Aquila	12 Sept 1874	17 Oct 1874	William	Eliza	Bolsgrofe	Charles	Bolsgrafe	Anna Maria	Kolb
B-785	Warley	Mary	Amanda	24 Sept 1874	18 Oct 1874	Monroe	Eliza	Kuntz	Richard	Kuntz	Selinda	Schwartz
B-786	Ruch	Ira		19 Sept 1874	25 Oct 1874	Jacot	Lydia	Steigerwalt				
B-787	Stroup	Matilda	Harriet	12 Oct 1874	25 Oct 1874	Josiah	Polly	Snyder				
B-788	Frederici	Willie	Adams	19 Sept 1874	28 Oct 1874	W.C.	Christianna	Behler				
B-789	Peter	Abby	Catherine	19 Sept 1874	28 Oct 1874	William	Esther	Stroup	Jacob	Stroup	Catherine	Stroup
B-790	Kunsman	Alfred		26 July 1874	1 Nov 1874	Jacob	Mary	Peter				
B-791	Zimmerman	Nathan	Franklin	3 Sept 1874	1 Nov 1874	John	Susanna	Sensinger	Nathan	Ziegenfuss	Emaline	Sensinger
B-792	Sensinger	Calvin	Albert	29 June 1874	4 Nov 1874	Alfred	Alice	Miller				
B-793	Kuehner	Jemima	Amelia	2 Oct 1874	7 Nov 1874	Levi	Mary	Day				
B-794	Collins	Eugene	Alwin	30 Dec 1873	11 Nov 1874	John Henry	Belinda	Beer	Adam	Beer	Margaret	Strohl
B-795	Smith	Eliza	Maria			Edward	Maria	Dressel				

Beyond the Blue Mountain, Vol. II

Births and Baptisms

Line #	Surname	Child Given	Middle	Birth Day	Birth Mth	Birth Year	Baptism Day	Baptism Mth	Baptism Year	Father Given	Mother Given	Nee	Witness Given	Witness Surname	Witness Given	Witness Surname
B-796	Hills	George	Curtin	11	July	1874	11	Nov	1874	Abraham	July Ann	Walck				
B-797	Webb	Joseph	Stephen	26	Sept	1874	11	Nov	1874	Joseph S	Catherine	Miller				
B-798	Rehrig	Maggie	Jane	24	Feb	1874	11	Nov	1874	Alfred	Maria	Neff				
B-799	Trine	Elmer	Ellsworth	8	Oct	1874	19	Nov	1874	John	Polly	Peter				
B-800	Knecht	George	Pearce	3	Aug	1874	22	Nov	1874	Reuben	Catherine	Moyer	Amandus	Diehl	Jeanetta	Right
B-801	Walck	Mary	Alice	22	Oct	1874	29	Nov	1874	Augustus A	Sabilla	Kunkel	Philip	Walck	Mary	(Walck)
B-802	Dreher	Frederic		12	Sept	1874	10	Dec	1874	Frederic	Lucy	Blose				
B-803	Moyer	William	Frederic	23	June	1874	10	Dec	1874	Frederic	Mary	Koda				
B-804	Becker	Oliver		9	Sept	1874	12	Dec	1874	Peter	July Ann	Freyman	George H	Snyder	Mary Ann	Mertz
B-805	Miller	Lizzie	Henrietta	13	Sept	1874	13	Dec	1874	Lewis A	Sarah	Shive				
B-806	Gombert	Ida	Savannah	18	Sept	1874	26	Dec	1874	Jonathan	Anna	Hontz	John	Nothstein	Kitty Ann	Freyman
B-807	Green	Laura	Edna	10	Oct	1874	26	Dec	1874	Samuel	Sally Ann	Savitz	Peter	Mehrcam	Fayetta	Snyder
B-808	Arner	George	Franklin	3	Nov	1874	27	Dec	1874	Charles	Ellen	Solt				
B-809	Kemerer	Ida	Sophia	18	Dec	1874	28	Dec	1874	Lewis	Emma	Confer				
B-810	Cunfer	Michael		29	Sept	1874	28	Dec	1874	Jacob	Carolina	Rabenold				
B-811	Lerch	Ellen	Catherine	5	Nov	1874	3	Jan	1875	Owen	Catherine	Kuntz	Abraham	Harleman	Suanna	Kuehner
B-812	Strohl	Vinnie	Nora	26	Sept	1874	3	Jan	1875	William H	Mary	Krill	Jonas	Buck	Kate	Ziegenfus
B-813	Rex	Harriet		25	Dec	1874	9	Jan	1875	Moses	Sarah Ann	Freyman				
B-814	Weida	Alwin		19	Nov	1874	10	Jan	1875	Benjamin	Elizabeth	Knecht				
B-815	Fritzinger	Ida	Louisa	23	Dec	1874	10	Jan	1875	Levi	Leah	Miller				
B-816	Walck	Elmira	Luzetta	20	Feb	1874	11	Jan	1875	Lewis	Rebecca	Kuebler				
B-817	Balliet	Calvin	Joseph	11	Jan	1875	14	Jan	1875	Nathan	Sarah Ann	Meinhart				
B-818	Kolb	George	Griffith	23	July	1874	14	Jan	1875	Nathan	Anna	Whiteman				
B-819	Boyer	Edwin		24	Oct	1874	17	Jan	1875	Alexander	Elizabeth	Remaley				
B-820	Frederic	Puryetta		9	Sept	1874	17	Jan	1875	Stephen	Elizabeth	Lower	Alexander	Boyer	Elizabeth	Remaley
B-821	Becker	William	Henry	28	Oct	1874	17	Jan	1875	Samuel	Lydia	Breifogel	Jacob	Becker	Sussanna	Eckern
B-822	Berger	Franklin		19	Oct	1874	20	Jan	1875	George	Catherine	Kemerer				
B-823	Nothstein	Emma	Stella	25	Sept	1874	23	Jan	1875	Charles	Catherine	Rabenold	Monroe	Heyser	Caroline	Rabenold
B-824	Koons	Mary	Alice	20	Nov	1874	24	Jan	1875	Willoughby	Sarah	Kistler			Mary	Koons
B-825	Strohl	Josephine		22	Nov	1874	31	Jan	1875	Thomas Franklin	Anna Tewilia	Rice	Aaron	Strohl	Eve	Strohl
B-826	Rehrig	Victor	Calvin	5	Sept	1874	5	Feb	1875	Lewis	Catherine	Beidelman				
B-827	Long	Sarah	Jeanetta	27	Oct	1874	6	Feb	1875	Henry	Sarah	Haupt			Sarah	Haupt
B-828	Bechtel	George	Washington	14	Jan	1875	6	Feb	1875	William	Elizabeth	Rabe				
B-829	Rhoads	Hattie	Jane	15	Sept	1874	6	Feb	1875	William	Annetta	Koons				
B-830	Horn	Sallie	Melinda	6	Nov	1874	9	Feb	1875	Benjamin	Mary Ann	Werner				
B-831	Beer	Grant	Oscar	11	Jan	1875	14	Feb	1875	Francis	Wilmina	Blose	Jacob	Blose	Selinda	Peter
B-832	Kemerer	Harrie	Franklin	25	Dec	1874	15	Feb	1875	Charles	Anna	Gilbert				
B-833	Freyman	Emma	Emma Catherin	26	June	1874	17	Feb	1875	Daniel	Caroline	Forreider	John	Nothstein	Kitty Ann	Freyman
B-834	Wentz	Samuel	Purette	11	Nov	1874	21	Feb	1875	Harrison	Selinda	Haint	Charles	Blose	Susanna	Boyer
B-835	Weaver	Oscar	Franklin	7	Dec	1874	21	Feb	1875	Wilson	Henrietta	Gombert	Aaron	Gombert	Lucy Ann	Hontz
B-836	Auge	Edgar	Eugene	25	Oct	1874	21	Feb	1875	David	Sarah	Rehrig				
B-837	Stansberry	Wilmer	Amandus	11	Feb	1875	22	Feb	1875	Lorence	Susan	Reinard	Philip	Wertman		

Beyond the Blue Mountain, Vol. II

Births and Baptisms

Line #	Surname	Child Given	Middle	Birth Day	Mth	Year	Baptism Day	Mth	Year	Father Given	Mother Given	Nee	Witness Given	Surname	Witness Given	Surname
B-838	Smith	John	Franklin.	7	Oct	1874	28	Feb	1875	William	Catherine	Knappenberger				
B-839	Schultz	Nathan	Alwin	1	Dec	1874	7	Mar	1875	James	Sarah	Beck	Nathan	Hoffman	Kitty	Ackerman
B-840	Rex	Mahlon	Albert	1	July	1874	7	Mar	1875	Lafayette	Sarah	Rex				
B-841	Vogt	Sarah	Jane	21	Dec	1874	14	Mar	1875	Lenius	Mary	Snyder	John	Snyder	Rebecca	Leiby
B-842	Riegel	Anna	Lorraine	12	Feb	1875	19	Mar	1875	Joseph	Hermena	Strassberger				
B-843	Graver	Harrie	Elmer	25	Dec	1874	19	Mar	1875	Martin B	Regina	Hartranft				
B-844	Schumacher	William	Franklin	28	Feb	1875	21	Mar	1875	Owen	Mary Ellen	Thomas	Edwin	Sensinger	Caroline	Geiger
B-845	Solt	Sarah	Etna	15	Jan	1875	21	Mar	1875	Amos	Alavesta	Rehrig				
B-846	Reichard	Charles		11	Mar	1875	24	Mar	1875	Maehlon	Lucy Ann	Fritzinger	Edwin	Schultz	Savenna	Fritzinger
B-847	Bowman	Abby	Korah	9	Mar	1875	30	Mar	1875	Albert	Isabella	Longacre				
B-848	Montz	Sarah	Elmira	5	Feb	1875	4	Apr	1875	Francis	Sarah	Schumacher	John	Evert	Mary Jane	Fulton
B-849	Evert	Sarah	Jane	23	Feb	1875	27	Apr	1875	Lyman	Aquila	Ruth				
B-850	Reinheimer	Irwin	Eugene	10	June	1874	7	Apr	1875	John	Rachael	Shoemaker	Frederick	Miller	Ellen	Webb
B-851	Webb	Oliver		2	Feb	1875	9	Apr	1875	James	Sarah Ann	Klingemen	Jacob	Klingeman	Elizabeth	Kistler
B-852	Hobbes	Albert		9	Feb	1875	10	Apr	1875	Elias	Maria	Osenbach				
B-853	Hafer	Frederick	Edwin	21	Feb	1875	11	Apr	1875	Jarret	Kitty	Eckroth				
B-854	Correll	Laura	Minnie	29	Sept	1874	11	Apr	1875	Lewis	Matilda	Delp				
B-855	Geggus	Harrison	Lewis	24	Jan	1875	14	Apr	1875	Lewis	Salome	Miller				
B-856	Krumm	Lillie	Louisa	10	Mar	1875	15	Apr	1875	Levi	Elizabeth	Bartholomew				
B-857	Bretney	Emma	Minerva	10	Apr	1875	18	Apr	1875	Thomas J	Mary Alice	Shaefer	Daniel	Shaeffer	Sarah	Sendel
B-858	Faust	Charles	William	16	Mar	1875	18	Apr	1875	Adam	Sarah	Confer	Charles	Frohnheiser	Anna	Confer
B-859	Mertz	Mary	Alice	14	Feb	1875	18	Apr	1875	William	Johannah	Mertz				
B-860	Fritzinger	Francis	Eugene	1	Mar	1875	20	Apr	1875	Francis	Melinda	Solt				
B-861	Silfies	Laura	Estilla	22	Dec	1874	25	Apr	1875	Jacob	Amanda	Hartman	Charles	Hartman	Matilda	Herman
B-862	Dunbar	Matilda	Elizabeth	12	Mar	1875	25	Apr	1875	Calvin	Mary Jane	Fisher				
B-863	Hartman	James	Israel	19	Mar	1875	25	Apr	1875	Joseph	Pauline	Seily	Joseph	Klotz	Lydia	Kromer
B-864	Kromer	Estella	Viola	30	Oct	1874	25	Apr	1875	Alfred	Lydia Ann	Fisher	Thomas	Solt	Catherine	(Solt)
B-865	Fritzinger	John	Franklin	4	Feb	1875	25	Apr	1875	John	Henrietta	Boyer				
B-866	Boyer	Ida	Estella	10	Mar	1875	29	Apr	1875	Edward	Mary Ann	Greenzweig	Peter	Mehrcam	Fayette	(Mehrcam)
B-867	Walck	Lewis	Pearcie	2	Jan	1875	29	Apr	1875	John E	Eva	Ackerman				
B-868	Schleicher	Emma	Caroline	25	Mar	1875	2	May	1875	Paul	Hannah	Miller	Jonas	Gombert	Sarah	Riegel
B-869	Riegel	James	Daniel	22	Mar	1875	9	May	1875	John	Manda	Frohnheiser	Benjamin	Frohnheiser	Lucinda	McDaniel
B-870	Arner	Lizzie	Urila	22	Jan	1875	9	May	1875	Oscar	Caroline	Schaefer				
B-871	Snyder	Lydia	Elizabeth	17	Feb	1875	14	May	1875	Samuel	Kate	Mertz				
B-872	Gombert	James	Irwin	16	Feb	1875	16	May	1875	John E	Ellen	(Ziegenfuss)	Nathan	Ziegenfuss	Emma	(Ziegenfuss)
B-873	Ziegenfuss	Emma	Alavesta	27	Apr	1875	16	May	1875	Lyman	Ellamanda	(Smith)	Solomon	Stemmler	Lucy	(Stemmler)
B-874	Smith	Charles	Edwin	23	Feb	1875	16	May	1875	Harrison	Emma Jane	Fisher	Amos	Solt	Alavesta	Thomas
B-875	Emert	William	Sylvenus	25	Feb	1875	16	May	1875	William	Harriet	Frohnheiser				
B-876	Roeder	Alfred	Osborn Daniel	20	Feb	1875	22	May	1875	Herman A	Amanda	Horn	Alfred A	Walbert	Sabilla	Roeder
B-877	Heilman	Elmer	Ellsworth	9	Sept	1874	22	May	1875	John	Angeline	Smethers				
B-878	Beltz	Sarah	Emma	23	April	1875	23	May	1875	John	Leanda	Smith	Catherine	Smith		
B-879	Feist	Addie	Sarah	31	Jan	1875	23	May	1875	Joseph	Sarah	Graver				

27

Beyond the Blue Mountain, Vol. II

Births and Baptisms

Line #	Surname	Child Given	Middle	Birth Day	Birth Mth	Birth Year	Baptism Day	Baptism Mth	Baptism Year	Father Given	Mother Given	Nee	Witness Given	Witness Surname	Witness Given	Witness Surname
B-880	Neff	Henry	George	20	Nov	1874	1	June	1875	Paul	Sabina	Kolb			Eliza	Anewalt
B-881	Brown	Emma	Salinda	6	Mar	1875	1	June	1875	James	Catherine	Dotterer	Lafayette	Brown	Mary	Rabe
B-882	Anewalt	Lizzie	Korah	30	Apr	1875	1	June	1875	Lewis	Sarah	Schneck	John	Anewalt	Mary	Gruber
B-883	Heiser	William	Quinty	23	Nov	1874	6	June	1875	Joshua	Polly	Zettelmoyer				
B-884	Buss	Korah	Elmira	21	Feb	1875	12	June	1875	Solomon	Mary	Steinmetz				
B-885	Dorwort	Ida		24	Mar	1875	12	June	1875	Francis	Abby Ann	Walck	David	Stout	Mary	Walck
B-886	Clauss	George	Edward	13	Mar	1875	13	June	1875	Emanuel W	Ellen	Esch				
B-887	Newhart	Minnie	Irena	24	Mar	1875	13	June	1875	Derias William	Sarah	Scheckler				
B-888	Dreher	Franklin	Charles	5	May	1875	17	June	1875	Benoville	Lucy	Smith				
B-889	Fogel	Abraham	Robert	24	April	1875	20	June	1875	Stephen	Catherine	Kunsman	Abraham	Harleman	Susanna	Kuehner
B-890	Kunkle	Quinton		9	May	1875	20	June	1875	Hiloras	Louisa	Walck	Edward	Lentz	Rosa Ann	Mulhearn
B-891	Boyer	Hattie	May	17	Feb	1875	20	June	1875	Samuel	Adelaide	Ziegenfuss	Tilghman	Andreas	Polly	Harder
B-892	Schmidt	Wilson		20	June	1875	4	July	1875	Owen	Salinda	Andreas				
B-893	O'Brian	Harriet	Eva Angeline	5	May	1875	8	July	1875	Samuel	Susanna	Moser				
B-894	Simpson	Emma	Rebecca	13	May	1875	10	July	1875	John	Eliza	Blose	Ellen Jane	Blose		
B-895	Hahn	Mary	Elizabeth	5	May	1875	10	July	1875	Franklin	Catherine	Hartman	Manda	Foster		
B-896	Mertz	Ida	Jane	15	May	1875	10	July	1875	Wilford	Edith	Hough	Oliver	Hough	Bregitta	Kershner
B-897	Wolff	Philip	Robert	7	June	1875	11	July	1875	John	Rebecca	Ziegenfuss	Philip	Walck	Mary	(Walck)
B-898	Mangold	Mary	Alice	18	June	1875	11	July	1875	Frederick	Frederica	Weisch	Jacob	Meyer	Maria	(Meyer)
B-899	Koch	Emma	Jane	18	Dec	1874	11	July	1875	Franklin T	Mary Ann	Faht		Bartholomew		
B-900	Eisenhower	Herbert	Levi	19	Feb	1875	11	July	1875	Franklin	Christianna	Bartholomew	Ellen	Graver	Leah	Lauchnor
B-901	Brong	Harry	Elmer	25	May	1875	11	July	1875	Jacob	Anna	Graver	Lewis	Weiss	Fayette	Dreisbach
B-902	Dreisbach	Anna	Maria	9	June	1875	18	July	1875	Alexander	Ellen Jane	Weiss	Charles A			
B-903	Fenstermache	Ellemanda	Sovera	14	July	1875	19	July	1875	John	Mary	Montz				
B-904	Schwab	Lewis	Solomon	28	Mar	1875	19	July	1875	Charles H	Matilda	Willkraut				
B-905	Rieger	Emma	Alvenia	3	June	1875	23	July	1875	William	Sophia	Pfleiderer				
B-906	Onwalt	Adam	Oscar	23	June	1875	24	July	1875	Samuel	Mary	Knecht				
B-907	Bollsgrofe	Frankie	Jonathan	23	June	1875	25	July	1875	Charles	Anna	Kolb				
B-908	Kupfer	Emma		7	Apr	1875	27	July	1875	John	Pauline	Kneily	Pauline	Steitly		
B-909	Krotzer	Eliza	Jane	21	June	1875	28	July	1875	Ephraim W	Sarah Rebecca	Zimmerman				
B-910	Zellner	Ida	Alice	27	June	1875	1	Aug	1875	Reuben F	Mary Ann	Blose				
B-911	Hunsicker	Alfred	Daniel	7	July	1875	1	Aug	1875	Jeremiah D	Sarah	Flexer	Daniel H	Hartman	Polly	Snyder
B-912	Guth	Susan	Elizabeth	23	July	1875	1	Aug	1875	Paul	Mary	Lambes				
B-913	Stout	Amelia		12	Mar	1869	1	Aug	1875	Charles	Fanny	Meyers				
B-914	Stout	Isaac		1	June	1871	1	Aug	1875	Charles	Fanny	Meyers				
B-915	Stout	Ida		9	Oct	1873	1	Aug	1875	Charles	Fanny	Meyers				
B-916	Wolf	Annie	Flora	6	Feb	1875	6	Aug	1875	William M	Jane	Kratzer				
B-917	Kern	Elsie	May	28	July	1875	7	Aug	1875	Lafayette A	Rebecca	Farrel				
B-918	Solt	Emaline	Amelia	9	June	1875	8	Aug	1875	Reuben	July Ann	Lentz				
B-919	Frantz	Lewis		26	July	1875	13	Aug	1875	Lewis	Sarah Ann	Rex	Reuben	Wertman	Hannah	Steigerwalt
B-920	Stemler	Elmira		19	May	1875	15	Aug	1875	Reuben	Lucy	Smith	Charles	Schaefer	Amelia	Stroup
B-921	Snyder	Sitna	Albert	5	July	1875	15	Aug	1875	John	Harriet	Ziegenfuss	Alfred A	Walbert	Sybilla	Roeder

Beyond the Blue Mountain, Vol. II

Births and Baptisms

Line #	Surname	Child Given	Middle	Birth Day Mth Year	Baptism Day Mth Year	Father Given	Mother Given	Nee	Witness Given	Witness Surname	Witness Given	Witness Surname
B-922	Moser	Adaline	Elizabeth	4 Aug 1875	16 Aug 1875	Jacob	Susanna	Gilbert				
B-923	Weida	Peter		12 June 1875	17 Aug 1875	Aaron	Henrietta	Adams				
B-924	Weida	Irena	Serida	20 Oct 1874	21 Aug 1875	William	Ellen	Strohm				
B-925	Rex	Emanuel	Oscar	14 July 1875	24 Aug 1875	Gideon	Zeniah	Fritzinger				
B-926	Ruch	Mamie	Estella	12 Aug 1875	25 Aug 1875	Elias	Mary Ann	Sendel				
B-927	Gerber	Morris	Franklin	2 May 1875	28 Aug 1875	H. A.	Emma E	Heiser	Isaac	Gerber	Anna	Miller
B-928	Koenig	Elizabeth	Matilda	27 June 1875	28 Aug 1875	Solomon	Sarah	Houser	Edwin	Gerber	Sarah	Moyer
B-929	Smoyer	Sarah	Jane	18 July 1875	29 Aug 1875	James	Ellemina	Blose	Reuben Franklin	Zellner	Mary Ann	Blose
B-930	Ziegenfuss	Daniel	Elias	5 Aug 1875	5 Sep 1875	Wliam A	Sarah Ann	Sensinger				
B-931	Miller	Mary	Ann Jane	9 Aug 1875	5 Sep 1875	Richard	Elizabeth	Ziegenfuss	Justina	Pfahl		
B-932	Ziegenfuss	Edwin	Andrew	30 June 1875	12 Sep 1875	Lewis	Harriet	Wentz	James	Ziegenfuss	Mary	Eckhart
B-933	Frantz	William	Franklin	30 July 1875	12 Sep 1875	Gcdfrey	Anna	Rex	Joseph	Ruch	Jane Amanda	Snyder
B-934	Andrea	Emma	Lillie	25 Apr 1875	16 Sep 1875	Joseph	Catherine	Bartholomew				
B-935	Daniels	Robert	Charles	31 July 1875	23 Sep 1875	Jeremiah R	Mary Jane	Kleintopp				
B-936	Serfass	Sarah	Alice	15 July 1875	24 Sep 1875	Arrandus	Maria	Schmidt				
B-937	Sinyard	Matthew		26 July 1875	25 Sep 1875	James	Sarah Ann	Frantz				
B-938	Stark	Maria	Ottia	18 Sep 1875	26 Sep 1875	Henry	Catherine	Kranich				
B-939	Hontz	Sarah	Ellen	15 Apr 1875	9 Oct 1875	Nathan	Lucy Ann	Walck				
B-940	Spoonheimer	Lillie	Vesta	1 Sep 1875	9 Oct 1875	Henry	Manda	Hontz				
B-941	Dunlap	Ellen	Jane	20 Aug 1875	10 Oct 1875	Charles	Mary Ann	Hahn	Samuel	Dunlap	Salena	Shively
B-942	Reed	Acquilla	Elyard	13 Aug 1875	13 Oct 1875	Acquilla E	Maria L	Fritzinger				
B-943	Lintz	John	Allen	31 May 1875	17 Oct 1875	Charles	Adline	Klotz				
B-944	Schnell	Eliza	Jane	24 Aug 1875	21 Oct 1875	Oliver	Priscilla	Rhoad	Waldburg	Ruff		
B-945	Arner	Edwin	Webster	22 Sept 1875	3 Nov 1875	Moses	Wilmina	Lutz				
B-946	Geiger	Caroline	Arabella	16 Sept 1875	3 Nov 1875	Joseph	Rebecca	Wertman	Maria	Jones		
B-947	Kreamer	Charles	Henry	17 Aug 1875	6 Nov 1875	W.C.	Mary Ann	Muschlitz	Robert	Muschlitz	Lavina	Boyer
B-948	Bartholomew	William	Monroe	2 Oct 1875	7 Nov 1875	Elias	Rebecca	Henry				
B-949	Flickinger	Tillie	Minerva	13 Sept 1875	14 Nov 1875	George	Messina	Frohnheiser	Benjamin	Frohnheiser	Lucinda	McDaniel
B-950	Ginder	Amandes	Oliver	20 Mar 1873	19 Nov 1875	Alfred	Lydia	Lauchnor				
B-951	Ginder	Asaba	Milton	16 Oct 1875	19 Nov 1875	Alfred	Lydia	Lauchnor				
B-952	Hoffman	Amanda	Elizabeth	12 Aug 1875	21 Nov 1875	Jacob	July Ann	Troxell	Elias	Billmer	Polly	Right
B-953	Kromer	Savennah	Matilda	11 Sep 1875	21 Nov 1875	Irvin	Martha Ann	Hartman	Thomas	Hahn	Mary	Boyer
B-954	Dreisbach	Eva	Jane	2 Oct 1875	28 Nov 1875	Aaror	Louisa	Wher				
B-955	Rehrig	Pearcy	Franklin	19 Oct 1875	2 Dec 1875	Denn s	Julia Elizabeth	Lentz				
B-956	Green	John	Elvin	25 July 1875	5 Dec 1875	Lewis W	Emmaretha	Green	John E	Walck	Eve Ann	Green
B-957	Moyer	David		13 Sept 1875	12 Dec 1875	Abraham	Rebecca	Wertman				
B-958	Fisher	Joseph	C	5 Nov 1875	12 Dec 1875	John	Elizabeth	Connor	Joseph	Jackaway	Louisa	Kifley
B-959	Mantz	Lewis	Edwin	5 Nov 1875	19 Dec 1875	Lewis	Kate	Danber				
B-960	Remaley	Charles	Henry	2 Oct 1875	20 Dec 1875	William	Sarah	Hontz				
B-961	Frantz	Ida	Minerva	12 Nov 1875	25 Dec 1875	Francis F	Sally Ann	Kemerer				
B-962	Grim	Hattie	Maytana	5 Dec 1875	25 Dec 1875	Charles	Mary	Gerber				
B-963	Gerber	Charles	Daniel	2 Nov 1875	25 Dec 1875	Daniel	Emaline	Adams				

Beyond the Blue Mountain, Vol. II

Births and Baptisms

Line #	Surname	Child Given	Middle	Birth Day	Birth Mth	Birth Year	Baptism Day	Baptism Mth	Baptism Year	Father Given	Mother Given	Nee	Witness Given	Witness Surname	Witness Given	Witness Surname
B-964	Moulthrop	Lillie	May	7	Nov	1875	26	Dec	1875	John Francis	Ellen	Shoemaker				
B-965	Mulharen	Mary	Ann	24	Dec	1875	26	Dec	1875	Edward	Anna Maria	Bachman			Anna	Rehrig
B-966	Muschlitz	Robert	Lee	11	Sept	1875	28	Dec	1875	William	Susanna Amanda	Brotzman				
B-967	Seltzer	Milton	Lewis	5	Oct	1875	2	Jan	1876	Henry	Catherine	Moyer				
B-968	Ferber	Lillie	Venerva	13	Nov	1875	4	Jan	1876	Reuben	Harriet	Stroup	Harrison	Stroup	Amelia	(Stroup)
B-969	Lichtenwalter	Daisy	Louisa	16	Nov	1875	4	Jan	1876	Edwin	Amanda	Stenner	Mary Ann	Stenner		
B-970	Evans	George	Henry	29	Nov	1875	4	Jan	1876	William J	Amanda	Bartholomew				
B-971	Kolb	Harrison	Charonea	31	Oct	1875	6	Jan	1876	Nathan L B	Anna Maria	Whiteman				
B-972	Meyer	Frederick	Wilhelm	1	Jan	1876	16	Jan	1876	Frederick Wilhelm	Maria	Gorde	Frederick	Meyer		
B-973	Walck	Herby	Obadiah	21	Nov	1875	23	Jan	1876	Philip	Mary	Rose	Augustus	Walck	Sabilla	Kunkel
B-974	Remaly	Mary	Etta	20	Nov	1875	23	Jan	1876	Charles	Emma Elizabeth	Rabenold	Nathan	Rabenold	Mary	Stoyer
B-975	Rex	James	Forteis	20	Sep	1875	27	Jan	1876	William	Mary	Eck				
B-976	Weiss	Lilly	May	31	Dec	1875	28	Jan	1876	Nero	Louisa	Hontz				
B-977	Beck	Mary	Elizabeth	6	Jan	1876	29	Jan	1876	Charles A	Sophia	Frantz				
B-978	Graver	Ida	Alwenia	20	Nov	1875	30	Jan	1876	Owen	Fianna	Solt	Andrew	Graver	Elizabeth	Whitehead
B-979	Heller	William	Henry	21	July	1875	1	Feb	1876	Wilson	Mary Ann	Vogt	Lina	Redditz		
B-980	Hartinger	Letta	Jeanetta	31	Dec	1875	13	Feb	1876	Christian	Kate	Wertman	Mary	Hartinger		
B-981	Rolfink	John	Franklin	7	Oct	1875	26	Feb	1876	John	Ellen	Rabe				
B-982	Bechtel	Aaron	Franklin	21	Feb	1876	26	Feb	1876	William	Elizabeth	Rabe				
B-983	Schumacher	Minnie	Nora	17	Dec	1875	26	Feb	1876	Levi	Amanda	Rex	Godfrey	Frantz	Anna Maria	Rex
B-984	McDaniel	Puriette	Irwin	28	Dec	1875	27	Feb	1876	Thomas	Melinda	Brown	Robert	McDaniel	Elizabeth	Green
B-985	Buss	Josephena		27	May	1872	28	Feb	1876	Jacob	Josephena	Hills				
B-986	Buss	Amelia		2	Apr	1874	28	Feb	1876	Jacob	Josephena	Hills	Amelia	Rice		
B-987	Zehner	Jane	Alwenia	17	Jan	1876	8	Mar	1876	Levi	Elizabeth	Hauser				
B-988	Xander	Helenah	Catherine	20	Feb	1876	12	Mar	1876	Charles W	Catherine	Graver				
B-989	Nothstein	Sarah	Elmina	15	Feb	1876	12	Mar	1876	James H	Mary Ann	Fenstermache	David	Nothstein	Leah	Hunsicker
B-990	Mantz	Emma	Elizabeth	10	Feb	1876	12	Mar	1876	James	Henrietta	Hontz	Franklin	Steigerwalt	Harriet	Ohl
B-991	Hunsicker	Jane	Irena	7	Jan	1876	12	Mar	1876	Owen A	Sarah A	Reeser	Nathan	Steigerwalt	Rebecca	Krum
B-992	Andrew	Ellen	Mantanie	14	Jan	1876	14	Mar	1876	Levi	Jane	Green	John E	Walck	Eva Ann	Green
B-993	Shuck	Pearl	Summerfield	26	June	1876	15	Mar	1876	George D	Emma	Snyder				
B-994	Hartman	Mary	Jane	12	Jan	1876	19	Mar	1876	William H	Lydia Ann	Remaley	William	Milheim	Mary Ann	Hartman
B-995	Fenner	Adella	May	29	Aug	1875	20	Mar	1876	Erwin	Edna B	Anthony				
B-996	Beer	Leander	Henry	27	Feb	1876	22	Mar	1876	Amos	Louisa Cather	Smith				
B-997	Guth	Laura	Agnes	27	Feb	1876	2	Apr	1876	Albert J	Emma	Hawk				
B-998	Follweiler	Willoughby		15	Feb	1876	9	Apr	1876	George W	Louisa	Zellner				
B-999	Barrick	Mary	Ann	5	Feb	1876	9	Apr	1876	Joel	Elmina	Leininger	David	Rehrig	Maria	Leininger
B-1000	Stahler	Victorion		6	Dec	1875	9	Apr	1876	Stephen	Sally Ann	Weber				
B-1001	Ginder	William	Henry	3	Mar	1876	9	Apr	1876	James W	Flora Ann	Nothstein	Jonas	Nothstein	Elizabeth	Kemerer
B-1002	Pasch	Jacob	W.Aaron	7	Dec	1874	12	Apr	1876	Jacob	Melinda	Hill				
B-1003	Sensinger	Bertha	Elizabeth	1	Mar	1876	17	Apr	1876	William F	Mary	Ziegenfuss				
B-1004	Maurer	George	Adam	17	Apr	1876	18	Apr	1876	Franklin	Alice	Kern				
B-1005	Dieterline	Harry	Wesley	13	Feb	1876	21	Apr	1876	Timothy	Sarah	Frantz				

Beyond the Blue Mountain, Vol. II

Births and Baptisms

Line #	Surname	Child Given	Middle	Birth Day	Birth Mth	Birth Year	Baptism Day	Baptism Mth	Baptism Year	Father Given	Mother Given	Nee	Witness Given	Witness Surname	Witness Given	Witness Surname
B-1006	Kern	Korah	Estella	3	Mar	1876	23	Apr	1876	Jeremiah	Mary C	Odenwelder				
B-1007	Blose	Isabella	Manda	6	Mar	1876	23	Apr	1876	Lewis	Isabella	Brown	Lorentz		Harriet	Dreisbach
B-1008	Weiss	Stewart	Wilson	19	Jan	1876	24	Apr	1876	Samuel	Emaline	Brown				
B-1009	Blose	Carrie	Eliza	17	Mar	1876	24	Apr	1876	Robert	Lizzie	Stein				
B-1010	Fisher	Jennie	Lillie	24	Oct	1875	25	Apr	1876	William	Mary	Hahn				
B-1011	Gerber	Clinton	Uriah	1	Apr	1876	26	Apr	1876	Thomas	Flora Ann	Frantz				
B-1012	Fritzinger	Korah	Agnes	17	Mar	1876	26	Apr	1876	Tilghman	Anzonetta	Goodheil				
B-1013	Peter	Robert	Alfred	6	Mar	1876	30	Apr	1876	Lewis H	Ellen J	Gehl				
B-1014	Long	Katie	Alice	18	Apr	1876	3	May	1876	Jacob	Mary Jane	Zellner	William	Zellner	Molly	Stahl
B-1015	Kleintop	Charlie	Edwin	5	Jan	1876	5	May	1876	David	Emaline	Kline				
B-1016	Wher	Lillie	Attanie	12	Mar	1876	6	May	1876	Owen	Ellen	Zimmerman				
B-1017	Evert	Ida	Agnes	6	Apr	1876	6	May	1876	Lyman	Acquilla	Schumacher	Sarah	Haupt		
B-1018	Arndt	Levi	Oscar	29	Jan	1876	7	May	1876	Lennius	Ellen	Zettelmoyer				
B-1019	Remaley	Daniel	Webster	7	Feb	1876	14	May	1876	Moses	Sarah Manda	Arner				
B-1020	Dorwort	Bertha	Ann	12	Apr	1876	14	May	1876	James	Mary	Weber	Thomas	Dorwort	Sarah	Newhart
B-1021	Merkley	Homer	Ellsworth	21	Mar	1876	14	May	1876	Benjamin	Ellen	Dorwort	Jonas	Merkley	Catherine	Walck
B-1022	Miller	William		24	Feb	1876	14	May	1876	Henry	Manda	Groman				
B-1023	Mangold	John	Peter	4	Dec	1875	14	May	1876	Charles	Sarah	Solt				
B-1024	Kauffman	Charles	Amson	20	Apr	1876	21	May	1876	Charles	Maria Anna	Walp				
B-1025	Horn	Benjamin	William	22	Apr	1876	28	May	1876	Alwin	Manda	Ross	Benjamin	Horn	Caroline	Handwerk
B-1026	Schaefer	Howard	David	17	Apr	1876	29	May	1876	Charles	Amelia	Stroup	Paul	Kresge	Mary	Stemler
B-1027	Clewell	Franklin		14	Sept	1875	3	June	1876	George	Sarah	Klotz	Alvesta	Haupt		
B-1028	Maurer	Ida	Mantena Jane	23	May	1876	4	June	1876	Edwir	Sarah Jane	Miller				
B-1029	Scherer	Mary	Ellen	5	Sept	1875	10	June	1876	Harvey	Matilda	Snyder				
B-1030	Freeby	William	James	20	Apr	1876	25	June	1876	Joseph	Jane Amanda	Frohnheiser				
B-1031	Ritz	George	Aaron	15	June	1876	25	June	1876	James	Alvesta	Weber	Aaron	Laub		
B-1032	Haefer	Moses	William	13	May	1876	2	July	1876	Jared	Kitty	Osenbach				
B-1033	Moyer	Caroline		7	Mar	1876	2	July	1876	Jacob	Rebecca	Behler	John	Behler	Elizabeth	Moyer
B-1034	Peter	Emma	Lydia	2	June	1876	2	July	1876	John A	Emaline	Montz				
B-1035	Lynn	Harrison		5	June	1876	3	July	1876	Daniel	Catherine	Miller				
B-1036	Wert	Alice	Isabella	5	June	1876	8	July	1876	Willoughby	Maria	Hartranft				
B-1037	Walck	Granville	Alpheus	30	May	1876	9	July	1876	David	Salinda	Solt	William	Larose	Alice	Walck
B-1038	William	Charles	Edward	15	May	1876	11	July	1876	Jacob	Sabina	Schwab	Charles W	Schwab	Ellen	Solt
B-1039	Heilman	Mary	Jane	8	June	1876	13	July	1876	John	Angeline	Smutters				
B-1040	Long	William		15	June	1876	15	July	1876	Columbus	Louisa	Fisher	William	Leukle	Priscilla	Walck
B-1041	Kelchner	Mame	Elmira	13	May	1876	16	July	1876	Edward	Lydia	Remaley				
B-1042	Pettit	Buhla	Melinda	4	June	1876	16	July	1876	George	Eliza	Remaley	Lydia	Remaley		
B-1043	Schwartz	Harvey	Edgar	15	June	1876	20	July	1876	John F	Amelia	Hunsicker				
B-1044	Kemerer	Arthur	Eugene	24	May	1876	21	July	1876	Nathar	Lucinda	Patterson	Mary Ann	Miner		
B-1045	Ruch	Ida	Dowiah	18	June	1876	23	July	1876	Jacob	Lydia	Steigerwalt				
B-1046	Balliet	Lizzie		19	June	1876	29	July	1876	Stephen	Kate	Gerber				
B-1047	Billman	William	Henry	28	June	1876	30	July	1876	Eli	Polly	Rice	Solomon	Hoffman	Harriet	Billman

Beyonnd the Blue Mountain, Vol. II

Births and Baptisms

Line #	Surname	Child Given	Middle	Birth Day	Birth Mth	Birth Year	Baptism Day	Baptism Mth	Baptism Year	Father Given	Mother Given	Nee	Witness Given	Witness Surname	Witness Given	Witness Surname
B-1048	Rehrig	Rosa	Ann	6	May	1876	30	July	1876	Jonas	Polly	Loch				
B-1049	Rhoads	Korah	Jannie	3	June	1876	3	Aug	1876	Jeremiah J	Matilda	Miller				
B-1050	Wher	Charles	Albert	29	June	1876	6	Aug	1876	David	Caroline	Eberts	Nathan	Ebberts	Lydia	Heintzelman
B-1051	Hontz	Sarah	Alvesta	16	May	1876	6	Aug	1876	John	Matilda	Dreisbach	Jacob	Frantz	Denah	Lechleitner
B-1052	Dorwort	Estella		31	May	1876	6	Aug	1876	Francis	Abby Ann	Walck	Benjamin	Remaly	Sarah	Dorwort
B-1053	Rhoads	William	Henry	13	Apr	1876	9	Aug	1876	William	Annetta	Koons				
B-1054	Graver	Alburtis		18	June	1876	9	Aug	1876	Martin B	Regina E	Strassberger	Lewis	Graver	Leah	Lauchnor
B-1055	Kostenbader	Josiah	Lee	28	Feb	1876	13	Aug	1876	Josiah	Fayetta	Walck	Jacob	Swartz	Emaline	(Swartz)
B-1056	Walck	Emma	Missouri	28	Mar	1876	13	Aug	1876	Lewis	Rebecca	Kuebler				
B-1057	Snyder	Mary	Jane	30	July	1876	16	Aug	1876	Peter	Emma	Fehr	Daniel	Krock	Miranda	Newhart
B-1058	Quin	Alavesta		9	Aug	1876	17	Aug	1876	Monroe	Alavesta	Bowman	Eliza	Quin		
B-1059	Kolb	Kitty	Ann	25	July	1876	20	Aug	1876	Jonas	Sarah	Peter				
B-1060	Farren	Bertha	Pernetta	10	Jan	1876	20	Aug	1876	Daniel	Harriet	O'Brian				
B-1061	Youse	Emma	Elizabeth	10	Jan	1876	22	Aug	1876	Tobias	Maria	Schultz				
B-1062	Rackawack	Amelia		10	Aug	1876	9	Sept	1876	William	Lenah	Kremer	Henry	Kremer	Margeret	Thoma
B-1063	Knecht	Edgar	Elmer	24	June	1876	9	Sept	1876	Reuben	Kate	Moyer				
B-1064	Beer	Milton		5	Sept	1876	13	Sept	1876	Alexander	Sarah Catherine	Meensing	Charles	Meensing		
B-1065	Beer	Hattie		5	Sept	1876	13	Sept	1876	Alexander	Sarah Catherine	Meensing	Charles	Meensing		
B-1066	Meensing	William	Llewellynn	23	Aug	1876	13	Sept	1876	Ammon	Jane L	Schafer				
B-1067	Evert	Minnie	Jane	11	July	1876	16	Sept	1876	John	Mary Jane	Fulton				
B-1068	Snyder	Ellemanda	Priscilla	11	July	1876	17	Sept	1876	Tighman	Sarah S	Leiby	William	Knepper	Caroline	Leiby
B-1069	Eck	Franklin	Howard	13	July	1876	1	Oct	1876	John	Mary	Huntzberger				
B-1070	Reed	Ellen	Rebecca	29	Aug	1876	1	Oct	1876	Daniel	Elizabeth	Schoch				
B-1071	Stout	Elmira	Jane	18	Aug	1875	2	Oct	1876	John	Sarah	Snyder				
B-1072	Baer	Mary	Alice	13	Nov	1875	2	Oct	1876	Reuben	Susanna	Zimmerman				
B-1073	Anders	Charles	Henderson	3	Aug	1876	8	Oct	1876	Josiah	Matilda	Strohl				
B-1074	Gumbert	Korah	Elizabeth	27	Aug	1876	8	Oct	1876	Nathan	Medina	Krum				
B-1075	Walbert	Osbon	Frederic	1	Sept	1876	8	Oct	1876	Alfred A	Sibilla	Raeder	Owen	Klotz	Emaline	Flick
B-1076	Reinheimer	Albert	James	4	June	1876	12	Oct	1876	John	Rachel	Ruth				
B-1077	Reichard	Emma	Sevillia	22	Sept	1876	15	Oct	1876	Aaron	Ellen	Nothstein				
B-1078	Gombert	Lillie	Louisa	14	Sept	1876	15	Oct	1876	Joseph L	Sarah	Fenstermacher				
B-1079	Reinerd	Adam	Simon	6	Oct	1876	21	Oct	1876	Simon	Christiana	Beer				
B-1080	Fenstermache	Stephen	Oliver	29	Aug	1876	22	Oct	1876	Stephen	Catherine	Snyder	Nathan	Stemler	Rebecca	Snyder
B-1081	Kreitz	John	Edgar	3	Oct	1876	22	Oct	1876	George Henry	Harriet L	Miller	David	Ackerman	Maria	Miller
B-1082	Dauber	Sarah	Ellen	27	Aug	1876	24	Oct	1876	Isaac	Catherine	Kistler				
B-1083	Stahler	Isaac	Henry	12	July	1876	29	Oct	1876	Charles	Rebecca	Correll	David	Rex	Priscilla	Stahler
B-1084	Shoenberger	Harrison	Richard	6	Sept	1876	30	Oct	1876	Charles O	Matilda	Diehl				
B-1085	Krotzer	Sarah	Amelia	31	July	1876	30	Oct	1876	Walter V	Sarah R	Zimmerman				
B-1086	Everitt	Ellen	Gertrude	11	May	1876	5	Nov	1876	Lyman	Ellen	Barthold				
B-1087	Gregory	James	Edwin	11	Sept	1876	5	Nov	1876	Nathan Gregory	Christianna	Eckhart	William	Gregory	Elizabeth	Schafer
B-1088	Berger	Ira	Elmer	7	Oct	1876	5	Nov	1876	Elias	Emaline	Hunsicker				
B-1089	Snyder	Katie	Alvenia	11	June	1876	6	Nov	1876	Samuel	Kate	Schaefer				

Beyond the Blue Mountain, Vol. II

Births and Baptisms

Line #	Surname	Child Given	Middle	Birth Day	Birth Mth	Birth Year	Baptism Day	Baptism Mth	Baptism Year	Father Given	Mother Given	Nee	Witness Given	Witness Surname	Witness Given	Witness Surname
B-1090	Grow	Korah		13	Sept	1876	8	Nov	1876	John	Elizabeth	Frederic				
B-1091	Hill	Daniel	Tilden	16	Sept	1876	12	Nov	1876	Daniel M	Angeline	Lorah	Ephraim	Nothstein	Polly	Hill
B-1092	Miller	Livie	Urilla	12	July	1875	12	Nov	1876	Solomon	Mary Ann	Hill	Owen	Hunsicker	Sarah	Kistler
B-1093	Nothstein	Laura	Catherine	9	Oct	1876	12	Nov	1876	Benjamin	Emaline	Kreitz	John	Cunfer	Elizabeth	Guldner
B-1094	Faust	Ida	Jane	30	Sept	1876	12	Nov	1876	Jesse W	Matilda	Cunfer	Jonas	Knepper	Denah	Hauser
B-1095	Reedy	Alice	Jane	16	Oct	1876	26	Nov	1876	Harrison	Alwenia	Knepper	Aaron	Hauser	Maria	Follweiler
B-1096	Snyder	William	Tilden	21	Sept	1876	26	Nov	1876	John	Rebecca	Leiby	Maria	Patterson		
B-1097	Snyder	Abraham	Lewis	29	Oct	1876	27	Nov	1876	Phaon	Emaline	Kemerer				
B-1098	Laub	John	Enos	28	Nov	1876	29	Nov	1876	Aaron	Lucinda	Weber				
B-1099	Silfies	Namie	Evelin	8	Oct	1875	4	Dec	1876	Chester	Julia A	Shive				
B-1100	Silfies	Estella	May	30	Sept	1876	4	Dec	1876	Chester	Julia A	Shive				
B-1101	Mertz	Magdalene		22	Nov	1876	6	Dec	1876	Alfred	Mary Ann	Evert				
B-1102	Moser	Minnie	Mantena	3	Nov	1876	17	Dec	1876	Jacob	Susanna	Gilbert	Daniel	Hauser	Sarah	Gilbert
B-1103	Reed	Caroline		25	Aug	1876	17	Dec	1876	Frark	Ellen	Bartholomew	Joseph	Hunsicker	Caroline	Hauser
B-1104	Bennygouph	William	Franklin	22	Oct	1876	24	Dec	1876	Gideon	Christianna	Ohl	John	Nothstein	Sarah	Behler
B-1105	Mertz	Emma	Jane	14	Aug	1876	9	Jan	1877	Nathan	Sally Ann	Freyman	John	Steigerwalt	Kitty Ann	Freyman
B-1106	Ziegler	Clara	Luzetta	4	Dec	1876	10	Jan	1877	Ross	Elmira J	Steigerwalt	Nathan	Hess	Rebecca	Krum
B-1107	Schantz	Arabella	Cornelia	14	Nov	1876	10	Jan	1877	Esram S	Jane A B	Hess	Thomas	Balliet	Polly	Billig
B-1108	Hartinger	Aggie	Mantena	12	Dec	1876	10	Jan	1877	David	Kate	Balliet				
B-1109	Balliet	Martha	Sophia	22	Nov	1876	14	Jan	1877	John	Amanda	Rehrig	David D	Long	Maryetta	(Long)
B-1110	Bartholomew	Harry	Eugene	18	Oct	1876	20	Jan	1877	John	Catherine	Serfass				
B-1111	Fritzinger	Eva	Estella	22	Oct	1876	20	Jan	1877	Francis	Melinda	Bartholomew				
B-1112	Sensinger	Laura	Maria	20	Dec	1876	28	Jan	1877	Alfred	Alice	Miller				
B-1113	Williams	Norah	Udella	11	Dec	1876	29	Jan	1877	James	Kitty Ann	Gombert				
B-1114	Rehrig	Mary	Alice	15	Oct	1876	1	Feb	1877	James H	Anna	Mulharen				
B-1115	Ohl	Alwenia		2	Jan	1877	8	Feb	1877	Henry	Sabina	Gerber				
B-1116	Hill	Calvin	Francis	8	Jan	1877	8	Feb	1877	Levi	Lydia	Dengler				
B-1117	Nothstein	Mary	Alice	28	Dec	1876	11	Feb	1877	Lewis F	Angeline	Herring	Nathan	Eberts	Lydia	Heintzelman
B-1118	Gombert	Bertie	Eugene	24	Dec	1876	20	Feb	1877	James	Ellen	Mertz				
B-1119	O'Brian	Charles		16	Feb	1877	25	Feb	1877	Joseph	Elizabeth	Haid				
B-1120	Patterson	Lizzie	Jane	17	Feb	1876	28	Feb	1877	George	Mary	Chamberlain				
B-1121	Ohl	Albert		3	Feb	1877	4	Mar	1877	Elias	Lydia	Zettelmoyer	John	Zettelmoyer	Lydia	Schuman
B-1122	Houser	Clara	Elizabeth	9	Feb	1877	8	Mar	1877	Charles S	Kate	Miller				
B-1123	Smith	Ellen		20	Feb	1877	11	Mar	1877	Elias	Lewina	Herder				
B-1124	DeLong	William	Ira	4	Feb	1877	15	Mar	1877	James	Emma	Frantz				
B-1125	Smith	Owen	Franklin	4	Feb	1877	18	Mar	1877	Owen	Selinda	Andreas				
B-1126	Greasley	Mantana		2	Mar	1877	18	Mar	1877	William F	Lusanna	Steigerwalt				
B-1127	Schumacher	Minnie	Catherine	11	Feb	1877	25	Mar	1877	Owen	Mary	Hartranft				
B-1128	Mantz	Carrie	Elizabeth	20	Feb	1877	1	Apr	1877	Lewis	Emma	Daubenspeck				
B-1129	Troxel	Amelia		2	Jan	1877	1	Apr	1877	Charles	Kate	Steigerwalt				
B-1130	Schaefer	Calvin	Dennis	23	Dec	1876	3	Apr	1877	Solomon	Denah	Beltz	Henry	Werstein	Elizabeth	Beltz
B-1131	Rehrig	Charles	Asapa	16	Dec	1876	8	Apr	1877	Dennis	Julia	Lentz				

Beyond the Blue Mountain, Vol. II

Births and Baptisms

Line #	Surname	Child Given	Middle	Birth Day	Mth	Year	Baptism Day	Mth	Year	Father Given	Mother Given	Nee	Witness Given	Surname	Witness Given	Surname
B-1132	Bowman	Asapa	Milton	14	Mar	1877	8	Apr	1877	Albert	Isabella	Fritzinger				
B-1133	Rex	Ellenora		10	Feb	1877	9	Apr	1877	Tilghman R	Maria	Zettelmoyer				
B-1134	Reichard	William	Jacob	24	Mar	1877	15	Apr	1877	Samuel S	Fianna	Loch				
B-1135	Mantz	Francis	Joel	10	Mar	1877	15	Apr	1877	Francis G	Sarah	Longacre				
B-1136	Geiger	George	Abraham	23	Feb	1877	15	Apr	1877	Joseph	Rebecca	Wertman	Abraham L	Stout	Helenah	Anthony
B-1137	Kistler	Estella		3	Apr	1877	29	Apr	1877	David H	Lydia	Hobbes	Dennis	Nothstein	Amanda	German
B-1138	Houser	Minnie	Mantana	8	Mar	1877	29	Apr	1877	Lewis	Elmia	Kistler				
B-1139	Ruch	Richard	Daniel	10	Apr	1877	30	Apr	1877	Elias	Mary Ann	Sendel				
B-1140	Evert	Amos	Weston	26	Mar	1877	4	May	1877	Lyman	Aquila	Schumaker				
B-1141	Moser	Austin	Vincent	22	Mar	1877	6	May	1877	Benjamin F	Kate	Gombert			Mary Ann	Webb
B-1142	Webb	Ellen	Laura	17	Jan	1877	11	May	1877	James A	Sarah	Schumaker				
B-1143	Snyder	Andrew	Rutherford	11	June	1876	20	May	1877	Alexander	Rebecca	Shive				
B-1144	Haupt	Charles	Norman	28	Jan	1877	20	May	1877	Alfred	Anna	Hauser				
B-1145	Muthart	Willie	Mandes Edgar	3	Apr	1877	20	May	1877	Daniel	Rosa	Druckenmiller				
B-1146	Peter	Harrison	Ellsworth	27	Mar	1877	2	June	1877	Wallace I	Hannah	Fritz				
B-1147	Bennygouph	Nathan	Jonas	22	Apr	1877	3	June	1877	William	Adline	Hoffman	Nathan	Hoffman	Kitty	Ackerman
B-1148	Frantz	Calvin	Anderson	15	Apr	1877	3	June	1877	Godfrey	Anna Maria	Rex	Gideon	Peter	Hannah	Ruch
B-1149	Gerber	Anna	Rebecca	9	June	1877	12	June	1877	Isaac	Anna	Miller	Peter	Bachman	Maria	Miller
B-1150	Johnson	Alwin	Jimmie	13	May	1875	23	June	1877	M.L.	Dianna	Houser				
B-1151	Youngkin	Allen	Edgar	28	July	1876	23	June	1877	Robert J	Barbara	Christman				
B-1152	Zellner	Albert		29	May	1877	24	June	1877	Charles	Adaline	Wertman	William	Wertman	Caroline	Krumm
B-1153	Heilman	Wilson	Wesley	13	June	1877	28	June	1877	John	Angeline	Smutters				
B-1154	Noll	Bessie	Agnes	15	Apr	1877	30	June	1877	William	Molly Ann	Graver				
B-1155	Anthony	William	Henry	30	June	1877	7	July	1877	William H	Amanda	Miller				
B-1156	Bowman	Berthie	Amanda	23	May	1877	8	July	1877	Dallas	Emma	Noll				
B-1157	Rex	George	Washington	22	Feb	1877	15	July	1877	William	Mary Cassia	Eck				
B-1158	Yenser	Minnie	Elmira	7	June	1875	15	July	1877	Wilson	Sarah	Mengel				
B-1159	Bowman	Mary	Isabella	1	June	1877	15	July	1877	Francis	Amelia Isabella	Freyman				
B-1160	Grow	Minnie	Lucetta	25	Mar	1877	15	July	1877	Reuben	Mary	Schwartz	John F	Schwartz	Amelia	Hunsicker
B-1161	Kressley	Thomas	Marcus	25	Apr	1877	15	July	1877	Daniel	Mary	Dilcher				
B-1162	Dreisbach	Minnie	Attanie	5	May	1877	15	July	1877	Aaron	Louisa	Wher				
B-1163	Peter	Lillie	Mantanie	21	June	1877	22	July	1877	Edwin	Harriet	Rehrig	Gideon	Peter	Hannah	Ruch
B-1164	Sittler	George	Claudius	8	June	1877	22	July	1877	Tilghman E	Louisa	Hunsicker				
B-1165	Long	Villiera		3	July	1877	29	July	1877	David D	Margetta	Reber				
B-1166	Geggus	Anna	Elizabeth	24	May	1877	11	Aug	1877	Lewis	Salome	Delp				
B-1167	Kromer	Charles	Daniel	22	June	1877	18	Aug	1877	Irwin	Martha Ann	Hartman	Adam	Foster	Martha Ann	Kunkel
B-1168	Smawley	Ida	May	24	May	1877	19	Aug	1877	Wilson A	Francisco	Green				
B-1169	Wolf	Carrie	May	9	June	1877	30	Aug	1877	George	Lydia	Serfass				
B-1170	Bucks	Rosa	Rebecca	9	Feb	1877	1	Sept	1877	George	Lucy Ann	Sachs	William	Sassaman	Catherine	Kepner
B-1171	Houser	Alwenia		14	Aug	1877	4	Sept	1877	Jefferson	Rebecca	Miller	Catherine	Miller		
B-1172	Kuntz	Annie	Mary	30	July	1877	9	Sept	1877	David	Sarah	Gilbert				
B-1173	Trumbore	Robert	Wilbert	7	July	1877	9	Sept	1877	Elwin	July Ann	Klotz	Owen	Klotz	Emaline	Flick

Beyond the Blue Mountain, Vol. II

Births and Baptisms

Line #	Surname	Child Given	Middle	Birth Day	Birth Mth	Birth Year	Baptism Day	Baptism Mth	Baptism Year	Father Given	Mother Given	Nee	Witness Given	Witness Surname	Witness Given	Witness Surname
B-1174	Sinyard	Addie	Amelia	14	Aug	1877	14	Sept	1877	James	Sarah Ann	Frantz				
B-1175	Hauser	William	Benjamin	17	July	1877	16	Sept	1877	Franklin	Elizabeth	Keller	Aaron	Hauser	Maria	Follweiler
B-1176	Riegel	Ellen	Irena	30	June	1877	16	Sept	1877	Joseph	Hermena	Horn				
B-1177	Ebert	William	Wesley	19	May	1877	16	Sept	1877	Owen	Polly	Heintzelman	Daniel	Heintzelman	Mary Ann	Rex
B-1178	Schleicher	Milton	William	26	Aug	1877	23	Sept	1877	Paul	Hannah	Ackerman				
B-1179	Steigerwalt	Edgar	Calvin	11	Sept	1877	26	Sept	1877	Lewis	Emma	Walter				
B-1180	Frantz	Lizzie	Alice	21	Aug	1877	30	Sept	1877	William H	Amanda	Gerber				
B-1181	Reinhard	Katie	Polly Abisena	14	June	1877	30	Sept	1877	W. H	Anna Katella	Leininger	John	Berg	Emma	Handrisks
B-1182	Schlegel	Henry	Harrison	28	Aug	1877	30	Sept	1877	Tilghman	Dora	Morey				
B-1183	Hauser	Harry	Frank	14	Aug	1877	3	Oct	1877	Daniel	Sarah	Gilbert				
B-1184	Peter	Anna	Bel	31	Aug	1877	7	Oct	1877	Edwin	Catherine	Dotter				
B-1185	Hill	Manda	Sevilla	24	May	1877	9	Oct	1877	Jones	Rebecca	Billman				
B-1186	Hunsicker	Charles	David	9	Sept	1877	9	Oct	1877	Jeremiah D	Sarah	Flexer	David	Wertman	Lydia	Correll
B-1187	Rehrig	Lambert	Leander	26	Sept	1877	19	Oct	1877	Thomas	Codilia	Steigerwalt				
B-1188	Gombert	Meta	Clendora	27	Aug	1877	4	Nov	1877	Jonathan	Anna	Hontz	James	Williams	Kitty Ann	Gombert
B-1189	Lutz	Elmer		17	Apr	1877	6	Nov	1877	Jacob	Hannah	Miller				
B-1190	Schaefer	Anna	Christianna	14	Sept	1877	7	Nov	1877	JustLs	Anna	Reimold				
B-1191	Moyer	Maria	Minnie	22	Apr	1877	8	Nov	1877	Frederic W	Maria	Gordon	Frederic	Moyer	Maria	Sepman
B-1192	Lynn	Sarah	Elizabeth	22	Mar	1877	13	Nov	1877	Simon	Emaline	Rehrig				
B-1193	Ginder	Charles	Franklin	3	Nov	1877	24	Nov	1877	James W	Flora	Nothstein	Nathan	Semmel	Sophia	Nothstein
B-1194	Hontz	Valentine	Nathan	1	Apr	1877	29	Nov	1877	Nathan	Lucy	Walck				
B-1195	Hontz	Alavesta		22	Feb	1876	29	Nov	1877	Wilson	Mary	Walck				
B-1196	Lechleitner	Edward		30	July	1877	29	Nov	1877	John	Liberia	Strohm				
B-1197	Shindler	James	Edward	24	Sept	1877	2	Dec	1877	William	Priscilla	Nunemaker				
B-1198	Laub	Lizzie	Elmira	7	Nov	1877	7	Dec	1877	Aaron	Lucinda	Weber				
B-1199	Moulthrop	Lambert	Wesley	14	Oct	1877	8	Dec	1877	John Francis	Ellen	Shoemaker	Godfrey	Frantz	Anna Maria	Rex
B-1200	Hartinger	Jeannetta	Jane	27	Oct	1877	9	Dec	1877	Thomas	Mary	Wertman	Reuben	Wertman	Elizabeth	Britton
B-1201	Schoepe	Harry	Oscar	4	Sept	1877	15	Dec	1877	Albert	Maria	Reinhart	Henry	Beckendorf	Maria	(Beckendorf)
B-1202	Drier	Clemens		23	Nov	1877	20	Dec	1877	Charles Francis	Tewilia	Schleicher				
B-1203	Gerber	Alice	Mantena	6	Oct	1877	24	Dec	1877	Josiah	Amanda	Shellhammer	Gideon	Schumaker	Lewina	(Schumaker)
B-1204	Hill	Alavesta		4	Oct	1877	26	Dec	1877	Aaron	Alice	Sherry	Ephraim	Yostheimer	Polly	Hill
B-1205	Moulthrop	Annetta	May	13	Nov	1877	28	Dec	1877	William H H	Priscilla	Trumbore				
B-1206	Gombert	Zacharis		19	Nov	1877	30	Dec	1877	Henry	Emaline	Hontz	Zacharis	Wolf	Lucetta	Anthony
B-1207	Hartung	Ellen	Louisa	28	Mar	1877	5	Jan	1878	John	Catherine	Kneese	Christian	Hartung	Kate	Wertman
B-1208	Miller	Harvey	Robert	22	Nov	1877	18	Jan	1878	Solomcn	Mary	Hill	Sally	Bailey		
B-1209	Grim	Mary Ann	Henrietta	5	Jan	1878	3	Feb	1878	Charles Alfred	Mary Ann	Gerber				
B-1210	Steigerwalt	Emma	Ulena Alavesta	17	Nov	1877	3	Feb	1878	T W	Fanny C	Maury				
B-1211	Clewell	Ellen	Jane	9	Jan	1878	14	Feb	1878	George	Sarah	Klotz				
B-1212	Hartranft	Amanda	Emaline	29	Nov	1877	2	Mar	1878	David	Matilda	Kolb				
B-1213	Harter	Martha	Jane	7	Feb	1878	10	Mar	1878	John	Sarah	Smith				
B-1214	Hough	Franklin	Eugene	21	Dec	1877	10	Mar	1878	Oscar	Agnes	Dreher				
B-1215	Wertmam	Thura	Ellen	16	Feb	1878	12	Mar	1878	Owen Alfred	Rosa Ann	Peter				

Beyond the Blue Mountain, Vol. II

Births and Baptisms

Line #	Surname	Child Given	Middle	Birth Day	Birth Mth	Birth Year	Baptism Day	Baptism Mth	Baptism Year	Father Given	Mother Given	Nee	Witness Given	Witness Surname	Witness Given	Witness Surname
B-1216	Xander	John	Alwin	24	Feb	1878	17	Mar	1878	Charles W	Catherine	Graver				
B-1217	Anewalt	Ellen	Susanna	12	Feb	1878	23	Mar	1878	Samuel	Mary	Knecht				
B-1218	Nothstein	William	Jacob	12	Dec	1877	24	Mar	1878	Jacob	Matilda	Arner	Jacob	Hoffman	July Ann	Troxel
B-1219	Lentz	Alfred	Washington	27	Jan	1878	2	Apr	1878	Charles	Adline	Klotz				
B-1220	Zimmerman	Korah	Ada	2	Mar	1878	13	Apr	1878	Alfred	Kate	George				
B-1221	Kuntz	Daisy	Mae	4	Feb	1878	11	Apr	1878	William	Susanna	Kleintopp				
B-1222	Neff	Harry	Albert	6	Jan	1878	16	Apr	1878	John	Polly	Spengler				
B-1223	Bennygoff	George	Oiver	20	Feb	1878	21	Apr	1878	Phaon	Leah	Steigerwalt	Nathan	Frantz	Catherine	Gombert
B-1224	Horn	Garrett	Franklin	15	Jan	1878	5	May	1878	Zacharias H	Jane Amanda	Rex				
B-1225	Sandhers	Charles	Lewis	18	Mar	1878	9	May	1878	George	Sarah	Rehrig				
B-1226	Guldner	Mantana		10	Apr	1878	11	May	1878	Lewis H	Sophia	George	Nathan	Bear	Priscilla	Bacherd
B-1227	Arner	Howard	Llewellynn	7	Dec	1877	12	May	1878	Oscar	Jane Elizabeth	Anthony				
B-1228	Reinheimer	Harry	Sylvester	19	Apr	1878	19	May	1878	Joseph A	Sally Elmira	Freyman				
B-1229	Fritzinger	George	Richard	28	Apr	1878	19	May	1878	Lennius	Mary Ann	George				
B-1230	Wehr	Savilla	Eva	22	Apr	1878	26	May	1878	Cyrus	Mary Ann	Balliet	Thomas	Wehr	Catherine	Fritz
B-1231	Billman	Harry	Elias	6	May	1878	9	June	1878	Elias	Polly	Wright	David	Gerber	Manda	Zehner
B-1232	Leiby	Clinton Ell	Victor	22	Apr	1878	9	June	1878	Franklin	Sarah Ann Velare	Stout	Reuben F	Leiby	Lydia	Dreisbach
B-1233	Reed	George	Edward	9	Feb	1878	23	June	1878	Frank	Ellen	Bartholomew	George	Reed	Hetty	Bowers
B-1234	Koons	Lillie	Agnes	19	Feb	1878	30	June	1878	Willoughby	Sarah	Kistler	Owen	Hunsicker	Sarah Catherin	Kistler
B-1235	Miller	William	Franklin	5	June	1878	7	July	1878	Amos R	Kate	Reeser	Jacob	Leiby	Matilda	Gerber
B-1236	Gerber	Sarah	Agnes	7	June	1878	21	July	1878	Daniel	Emaline	Adams				
B-1237	Grasely	Asapa	Milton	21	May	1878	4	Aug	1878	Charles	Mary	Ginder	Isaac	Ginder	Leah	Rehrig
B-1238	Gerber	Martha	Arabella Anna	9	July	1878	6	Aug	1878	Thomas	Flora Ann	Frantz				
B-1239	Buss	Martha	Washington	22	Feb	1877	8	Aug	1878	Jacob	Josephena	Hills	Eva	Buss		
B-1240	Rehrig	Mary	Anna	26	July	1878	9	Aug	1878	Gideon	Susanna	Moyer				
B-1241	Balliet	James	Jacob	5	June	1878	11	Aug	1878	James	Sophia	Albright				
B-1242	Knecht	William	Franklin	21	June	1878	13	Aug	1878	James	Lucy Ann	Hontz				
B-1243	O'Brian	Minnie		23	July	1878	20	Aug	1878	Joseph	Elizabeth	Haid				
B-1244	Reichelderfer	William	Thomas	18	Apr	1878	17	Aug	1878	Rowland	Kate	Heil				
B-1245	Gerber	Jennie	Elizabeth	18	Jan	1878	17	Aug	1878	Henry A	Emma	Heiser				
B-1246	Schellhammer	Carrie	Alvinia	21	May	1878	24	Aug	1878	Monroe	Louisa	Sassaman	Wm	Sassaman	Catherine	Kepner
B-1247	Albright	Allen	Enos	9	July	1878	7	Sept	1878	Enos B	Emma	Geggus				
B-1248	Hontz	Matilda	Elmira	3	June	1878	22	Sept	1878	Moses	Zeniah	Rex	John H	Nothstein	Mira Ann	Rex
B-1249	Hartzell	Allie	Howard	9	Sept	1878	12	Oct	1878	Henry	Sarah	Zettelmoyer				
B-1250	Snyder	Luzetta	Maria	2	Aug	1878	13	Oct	1878	Franklin	Anna	Wanemacher				
B-1251	Heinbach	Ellenora	Clarrisa	3	Sept	1878	16	Oct	1878	Solomon	Catherine	Kern				
B-1252	Kolb	Harvey	Wesley	6	Sept	1878	24	Oct	1878	Nathan	Anna	Whiteman				
B-1253	Grow	Mary	Matilda	30	Sept	1878	5	Nov	1878	John	Elizabeth	Frederic				
B-1254	Leiby	Clara	Kate	13	Oct	1878	10	Nov	1878	Nathan	Kate	Wertman				
B-1255	Freeby	Ellen	Jane	16	Oct	1878	1	Dec	1878	Joseph	Jane Amanda	Frohnheiser				
B-1256	Rehrig	George	Benjamin	30	Aug	1878	1	Dec	1878	Lewis	Catherine	Beidelman				
B-1257	Farren	Kate	Elizabeth	11	Nov	1878	15	Jan	1879	Daniel	Harriet	O'Brian				

36

Births and Baptisms

Line #	Surname	Child Given	Middle	Birth Day	Mth	Year	Baptism Day	Mth	Year	Father Given	Mother Given	Nee	Witness Given	Witness Surname	Witness Given	Witness Surname
B-1258	Zehner	Benjamin		25	Oct	1878	15	Jan	1879	Timothy	Elizabeth	Kistler				
B-1259	Smawley	William	Henry	9	Dec	1878	23	Jan	1879	Wilson A	Franc-sco	Green				
B-1260	Nothstein	William	Alfred	14	Nov	1878	9	Feb	1879	Lewis F	Angeline	Herring				
B-1261	Williams	Lovetta	Anzonetta	3	Jan	1879	9	Feb	1879	James	Kitty Ann	Gombert				
B-1262	Gower	Elmira	Jane	30	Sept	1878	10	Feb	1879	Joseph	Elmire Jane	Holzer				
B-1263	Auge	Harvey	Esaias	15	Oct	1878	16	Feb	1879	David	Sarah Ann	Rehrig				
B-1264	Miller	Carrie	Louisa	26	Dec	1878	2	Mar	1879	James A	Louisa	Krum	Samuel	Balliet	Mary	Wertman
B-1265	Hauser	Claudius	Albert	10	Jan	1879	2	Mar	1879	Charles S	Kate	Miller				
B-1266	Troxell	Charles	Albert	6	Feb	1879	16	Mar	1879	Charles	Denah	Steigenwalt				
B-1267	Schumacher	Cyrus	Henry	14	Feb	1879	15	Mar	1879	Owen	Mary	Hartranft				
B-1268	Weber	Emma	Urane	4	Feb	1879	5	Apr	1879	Wilson	Henrietta	Gombert	Nathan	Gerber	Maria	Seidel
B-1269	Mertz	Emma	Estella	20	Mar	1879	7	Apr	1879	Alfred	Mary Ann	Evert				
B-1270	Kunkle	Emma	Ursulah	9	Feb	1879	21	Apr	1879	Dures	Susan	Walck				
B-1271	Stout	Alwin	Adam	13	Apr	1879	26	Apr	1879	John	Sarah	Snyder				
B-1272	Hoffman	Katie	Agnes	14	Mar	1879	27	Apr	1879	Jacob D	July Ann	Troxell	George	Reinhart	Sally Ann	Troxell
B-1273	Rehrig	Edgar	Milton	25	Feb	1879	30	Apr	1879	Thomas	Codelia	Steigenwalt				
B-1274	Kromer	Joseph	Irwin	7	Apr	1879	12	May	1879	Irwin	Martha Ann	Hartman	Harriet	Rehrig	Mary Etta	Fisher
B-1275	Peter	Emma	Louise	28	Apr	1879	22	May	1879	Edwin	Sarah	Smutters				
B-1276	Heilman	Orlando		23	Feb	1879	28	May	1879	John	Angeline	Serfass				
B-1277	Bartholomew	Carrie	May	4	Feb	1879	28	May	1879	John	Catherine	Snyder				
B-1278	Rehrig	Lizzie	Ann	6	Apr	1879	3	June	1879	Charles E	Viletta	Rex				
B-1279	Miller	Mary	Martha	21	Feb	1879	8	June	1879	William	Mary	Remaley	Benjamin	Nothstein	Emaline	Kreitz
B-1280	Kemerer	Thomas	Wesley	11	Feb	1879	8	June	1879	David	Sarah Ann	Fulton	Annetta	Rhoads		
B-1281	Evert	Gertrude	May	6	Apr	1879	13	June	1879	John	Mary Ann	Rex				
B-1282	Rex	David	Franklin	1	Nov	1878	15	June	1879	Lafayette	Sarah	Werly				
B-1283	Miller	Rosa	Ann	20	May	1879	22	June	1879	Henry	Sarah	Rhoad	Catherine	Ruff		
B-1284	Schnell	Emma	Laura	13	Jan	1879	26	June	1879	Oliver	Priscilla	Miller				
B-1285	Lynn	Mary	Matilda	12	Apr	1879	14	July	1879	Daniel	Kitty Ann	Mulharen				
B-1286	Rehrig	Maude	Elizabeth	21	Apr	1879	20	July	1879	James H	Anna	Anthony				
B-1287	Arner	Franklin	P	1	Feb	1879	20	July	1879	Oscar	Jane Elizabeth	Morey				
B-1288	Schlegel	Addie	Luellen	26	Apr	1879	20	July	1879	Tilghman	Dora	Fritz				
B-1289	Peter	Norton	Winfield	14	June	1879	27	July	1879	Wallace	Hannah	Rehrig				
B-1290	Noll	Sally	Ann Rebecca	24	Apr	1879	11	Aug	1879	Aaron	Eliza	Schumacher				
B-1291	Evert	Robert	James	8	July	1879	11	Aug	1879	Lyman	Aquila	Schwartz	Adam	Schray	Hannah	Kohl
B-1292	Grow	Robbie	Elsworth	4	Apr	1879	17	Aug	1879	Reuben	Mary Magdalene	Neitzel				
B-1293	Beltz	Harry	Adam	8	Apr	1879	19	Aug	1879	Harry	Emma	Ditcher				
B-1294	Kinsel	Lenah		18	Apr	1879	20	Aug	1879	Charles	Maria	Correll				
B-1295	Stahler	Emma	Henrietta	10	Apr	1879	23	Aug	1879	Charles	Rebecca	Hartinger				
B-1296	Hill	Ida	Irene	24	July	1879	23	Aug	1879	Thomas	Mary	Schultz				
B-1297	Youse	William	Elmer	19	May	1879	4	Sept	1879	Tobias	Maria	Beer				
B-1298	Steigerwalt	Sallie	May	14	Aug	1879	13	Sept	1879	Benjamin	Priscilla	Miller			Mary	Shively
B-1299	Rehr	John	Uriah	29	July	1879	15	Sept	1879	David	Maria		Franklin	Shively	Mary	Rehr

Beyond the Blue Mountain, Vol. II

Births and Baptisms

Line #	Surname	Child Given	Middle	Birth Day	Birth Mth	Birth Year	Baptism Day	Baptism Mth	Baptism Year	Father Given	Mother Given	Nee	Witness Given	Witness Surname	Witness Given	Witness Surname
B-1300	Kressley	Bessie	Clara	11	July	1879	21	Sept	1879	Daniel	Mary Ann	Dilcher				
B-1301	Mertz	Nathan		27	Mar	1879	21	Sept	1879	Nathan	Sally Ann	Freyman	Josiah	Miller	Amanda	Mertz
B-1302	Albright	Emma	Sophia	4	Aug	1879	21	Sept	1879	John FH	Rosa A	Klotz				
B-1303	Gombert	Lindney	Maurice	20	July	1879	21	Sept	1879	Joseph L	Sarah Ann	Fenstermacher				
B-1304	Spoonheimer	Charles	Andrew	21	Aug	1879	7	Oct	1879	Henry	Amanda	Hontz				
B-1305	Hill	Clara	Elizabeth	27	May	1879	11	Oct	1879	Jonas K	Rebecca	Billman				
B-1306	Balliet	Harry	Charles	4	Oct	1879	23	Oct	1879	John	Amanda	Rehrig				
B-1307	Frohnheiser	Charles	Henry	30	Aug	1879	1	Nov	1879	James	Emma E	Schappell	John F	Westen		
B-1308	Miller	Ulalia	Virgin	10	Sept	1879	9	Nov	1879	Aaron	Jeannetta	Frederici				
B-1309	Weidaw	Alice	Belle	6	Nov	1879	10	Nov	1879	Aaron	Sally Ann	Schappell				
B-1310	Snyder	William	David	29	Aug	1879	17	Nov	1879	Matthew R	Amanda	Milhouse				
B-1311	Ahner	Ida	Sevilla	27	July	1879	6	Nov	1879	Abraham	Mary	Remaly	Henry	Schwartz	Matilda	Remaley
B-1312	Henninger	Matilda	Viletta	1	Oct	1879	23	Nov	1879	Charles	Elizabeth	Gerber				
B-1313	Trainer	Martha	Susanna	23	Nov	1879	29	Nov	1879	Charles	Lenah	Platt				
B-1314	DeLong	Harry	Jacob	2	Nov	1879	30	Nov	1879	James	Emaline	Frantz	Jacob	Frantz	Christiana	Lechleiter
B-1315	Wher	Mapel	Graver	3	Nov	1879	30	Nov	1879	Lewis A	Adline	Graver	Alvenia	Lentz		
B-1316	Mantz	Charles	Martin	11	Nov	1879	7	Dec	1879	Lewis	Kate	Daubenspeck				
B-1317	Snyder	George	Washington	30	Oct	1879	7	Dec	1879	Samuel	Levina	Billman	John	Nothstein	Kitty Ann	Freyman
B-1318	Lapp	Mary Ann	Ellen	9	Oct	1879	18	Dec	1879	Franklin	Catherine	Everts				
B-1319	Ruch	Lizzie	Arabella	30	Nov	1879	21	Dec	1879	Lewis	Elizabeth	Mantz				
B-1320	Dreisbach	Martha	Lucetta	15	Sept	1879	28	Dec	1879	Lewis	Louisa	Wher				
B-1321	McWilliams	Thomas	Oliver	12	Oct	1879	29	Dec	1879	M.J.	Elizabeth	Musselman				
B-1322	Schappel	Oliver	Calvin	25	Nov	1879	14	Dec	1879	Milton T	Catherine	Frohnheiser				
B-1323	Hill	Robbie	Elias	2	Jan	1880	1	Feb	1880	Jonas	Harriet	Remaly				
B-1324	Schellhammer	James	Oscar	26	Jan	1880	2	Feb	1880	Franklin B	Sarah Ann	Houser	Gideon	Houser	Hannah	Rumple
B-1325	Schellhammer	Polly	Catherine	26	Jan	1880	2	Feb	1880	Franklin B	Sarah Ann	Houser	Rebecca	Follweiler		
B-1326	Gombert	Annie	Zenoba	21	Dec	1879	8	Feb	1880	Nathan	Medina	Krum				
B-1327	Walck	Minnie	Rebecca	23	Nov	1879	9	Feb	1880	Lewis	Rebecca	Kuebler				
B-1328	Rehrig	Ellen	Elizabeth	6	Dec	1879	15	Feb	1880	Dennis	Julia	Lentz				
B-1329	Mulhearn	Ida	Sevilla	24	Mar	1878	24	Feb	1880	Edward F	Anna Maria	Bachman				
B-1330	Reber	Oliver	William	16	Apr	1879	25	Feb	1880	W. W. (Dr)	Emma V	Graver	William	Sendel	Sarah Ann	Cunfer
B-1331	Hontz	Pearcy	Albert	15	Jan	1880	7	Mar	1880	Dennis	Matilda	Cunfer				
B-1332	Reinsmith	Meta	Sallie	12	Dec	1879	7	Mar	1880	Nathan	Messina	Kerschner				
B-1333	Meitzler	Jacob	Franklin	24	Feb	1880	4	Apr	1880	Josiah Benjamin	Ellen Jane	Kemerer	Thomas	Beltz	Sarah	Snyder
B-1334	Fenstermache	Minnie	Ellenora	18	Feb	1880	11	Apr	1880	Stephen	Catherine	Snyder				
B-1335	Heilman	Emma	Bell	31	Jan	1880	6	Apr	1880	John	Angeline	Smutters				
B-1336	Berger	George	Oliver	2	Feb	1880	17	Apr	1880	Elias	Emaline	Hunsicker				
B-1337	Bowman	Alwin	William	19	Mar	1880	18	Apr	1880	John	Fianna	Fritzinger	Susanna	Bowman		
B-1338	Leaser	Pearcy	Franklin	25	Mar	1880	26	Apr	1880	William F	Maria	Kolb				
B-1339	Knepper	Emma	Greena	7	May	1880	8	May	1880	Charles	Sarah Ann	Gerber				
B-1340	Kreitz	Charles	Asaba	21	Apr	1880	16	May	1880	George Henry	Harriet	Miller	John	Eberts	Lydia	Breiner
B-1341	Taylor	Emma	Elizabeth	16	Mar	1880	16	May	1880	Edward C	Susanna	Eberts				

Beyond the Blue Mountain, Vol. II

Births and Baptisms

Line #	Surname	Child Given	Middle	Birth Day	Birth Mth	Birth Year	Baptism Day	Baptism Mth	Baptism Year	Father Given	Mother Given	Nee	Witness Given	Witness Surname	Witness Given	Witness Surname
B-1342	Campbell	Charles	Henry	31	Mar	1880	20	May	1880	James	Emaline	Evert				
B-1343	Grim	Josephene	Endora	14	Apr	1880	23	May	1880	Charles Alfred	Mary Ann	Gerber				
B-1344	Xander	James	Harrison	23	May	1880	23	May	1880	Charles W	Catherine	Graver				
B-1345	Xander	Clifford	Franklin	12	April	1880	23	May	1880	Benjamin	Mary Ann	Martz				
B-1346	Smith	George	Alfred	22	April	1880	8	June	1880	James D	Alvena	Ruch				
B-1347	Anders	Ida	Victoria	16	Feb	1880	13	June	1880	Josiah	Matilda	Strohl				
B-1348	Blose	Geiden	Alfred	14	Dec	1879	26	June	1880	Alfred	Ellen Jane	Lynn				
B-1349	Rex	Lillie	Minerva	7	May	1880	27	June	1880	Emanuel	Susanna	Dreisbach	Tilghman	Rex	Emaline	Leiby
B-1350	Leiby	Luretta	Agnes	5	June	1880	3	July	1880	Franklin	Sarah Ann	Stout				
B-1351	Ebert	Lewis	Berdie	27	Nov	1878	3	July	1880	Owen	Polly	Heintzelman				
B-1352	Ebert	Charles	Albert	15	May	1880	3	July	1880	Owen	Polly	Heintzelman	Jonas	Rehrig	Polly	Loch
B-1353	Kressley	Andrew	Jackson	13	Mar	1880	18	July	1880	Charles	Mary Susanna	Ginder				
B-1354	Flickinger	Carrie	Sevilla	9	Apr	1880	21	July	1880	George	Messina	Frohnheiser				
B-1355	Snyder	John	Henry	22	Apr	1880	25	July	1880	Adam	Ellen	Beer	David	Beltz	Louisa	Snyder
B-1356	Frederick	Lean	Eugene	30	Apr	1880	31	July	1880	Walter	Rebecca	Houser				
B-1357	Brown	Clara	Minnie	25	June	1880	4	Aug	1880	John C	Mary	Hartung				
B-1358	Rehrig	Adam	Ephraim	24	June	1880	5	Aug	1880	Alexancer	Isabella	Diehl				
B-1359	Hoffman	Ida	Rebecca	14	July	1880	12	Aug	1880	Jerrane	Sallie	Frohnheiser				
B-1360	Hartung	Della	Viola	18	June	1880	14	Aug	1880	David	Kate	Balliet				
B-1361	Rhoads	Tilghman	Scott	20	May	1880	15	Aug	1880	Jeremiah J	Matilda	Miller				
B-1362	Koons	Savilla	Matilda	14	June	1880	22	Aug	1880	David	Sarah	Gilbert				
B-1363	Flickinger	Moses	William	12	June	1880	22	Aug	1880	Josiah	Clara	Hough				
B-1364	Ohl	Manda	Mantana	19	July	1880	29	Aug	1880	William	Emma	Houser	Nathan	Ziegler	Sally	Nothstein
B-1365	Ziegler	Oliver	Thomas	3	Aug	1880	29	Aug	1880	Henry	Susanna	Zehner	Daniel	Ohl	Mary	Daubenspeck
B-1366	Miller	Edwin	Oliver	28	Sept	1880	16	Oct	1880	Nathan	Kate	Beltz				
B-1367	Albright	Katie	Eveline	28	Sept	1880	17	Oct	1880	John F H	Rosa	Klotz				
B-1368	Ohl	Milton	Franklin	14	Sept	1880	24	Oct	1880	Owen	Rosa	Steigerwalt	Franklin	Steigerwalt	Harriet	Ohl
B-1369	Walck	George	Albert	27	Sept	1880	13	Nov	1880	George W	Mira Ann	Rex	Lewis	Walck	Rebecca	Kuebler
B-1370	Rehrig	Emma	Clinton	17	Oct	1880	27	Nov	1880	Charles E	Viletta	Snyder				
B-1371	Rehrig	Harrie	Edward	4	Sept	1880	2	Dec	1880	Thomas	Codilia	Steigerwalt				
B-1372	Freeby	Mandes	Henry	6	Dec	1880	23	Jan	1881	Joseph	Jane Amanda	Frohnheiser				
B-1373	Rex	Martin	Henry	24	Aug	1880	23	Jan	1881	Lafayette	Sarah	Rex				
B-1374	Steigerwalt	Buhla	Agnes	18	Dec	1880	27	Jan	1881	Benjamin F	Priscilla	Beer	Solomon	Steigerwalt	Judith	Lynn
B-1375	Mantz	Harrie	Edgar	8	Oct	1880	2	Feb	1881	Jacob	Henrietta	Briner				
B-1376	Markel	Emma	Rebecca	14	Dec	1880	26	Mar	1881	Charles F	Amelia Agnes	Walck				
B-1377	Hontz	Agnes	Louisa	14	Aug	1880	3	Apr	1881	Moses	Zeniah	Rex				
B-1378	Steigerwalt	Mary	Alvesta	11	Mar	1881	3	Apr	1881	A F	Maria	Bowman				
B-1379	Gerber	Mary	Alice	1	Apr	1881	18	Apr	1881	Daniel	Emaline	Addams				
B-1380	Ronemus	Samuel		18	Mar	1881	21	Apr	1881	William	Rebecca	Shaefer	Elias	Kantz	Mary	Yenser
B-1381	Taylor	William	Edward	1	Apr	1881	26	Apr	1881	Edward C	Susanna	Eberts				
B-1382	Turner	Clara	Mantana	28	Jan	1881	27	Apr	1881	William	Elizabeth	Wagner				
B-1383	Nunnamacher	Alice	Amia	3	Mar	1876	27	Apr	1881	Abraham	Mary Ann	Gottshall				

39

Beyond the Blue Mountain, Vol. II

Births and Baptisms

Line #	Surname	Child Given	Middle	Birth Day	Birth Mth	Birth Year	Baptism Day	Baptism Mth	Baptism Year	Father Given	Mother Given	Nee	Witness Given	Witness Surname	Witness Given	Witness Surname
B-1384	Nunnamacher	Kora	Addie	12	Apr	1878	27	Apr	1881	Abraham	Mary Ann	Gottshall				
B-1385	Dreher	Milton	Daniel	24	Dec	1880	27	Apr	1881	Benoville	Lucy	Smith				
B-1386	Levers	Anna	Agnes	31	Oct	1880	27	Apr	1881	Espen	Ida	Dreher				
B-1387	Schaefer	Mary	Matilda	11	Mar	1881	27	Apr	1881	Daniel	Polly Jane	Mantz				
B-1388	Hill	Gurdie	Irene	28	Mar	1881	2	May	1881	Sylvester	Emma Kate	Houser				
B-1389	Frantz	Mary	Ellen	9	Mar	1881	7	May	1881	William H	Amanda	Gerber				
B-1390	Mantz	Sabina	Deborah	3	Jan	1881	8	May	1881	Francis G	Sarah	Longacre				
B-1391	Mantz	Mary	Alvenia	28	Dec	1880	8	May	1881	James	Kate	Fenstermacher				
B-1392	Schumacher	Charlie	Wesley	16	Apr	1881	8	May	1881	Owen	Mary	Hartranft				
B-1393	Whitaker	William	James		Mar	1881	13	May	1881	James Franklin	Elemena	Ziegenfuss				
B-1394	Mertz	George	Oscar	15	Jan	1881	15	May	1881	Joseph	Alwilda	Lapp				
B-1395	Mertz	Harrie	Abel	29	Apr	1881	30	May	1881	Alfred	Mary	Eberts				
B-1396	Johnson	Anna	Irene	29	Oct	1879	30	May	1881	Claudious M	Emma	Rogers				
B-1397	Zehner	Ellemanda		11	May	1881	4	June	1881	Timothy	Elizabeth	Kistler				
B-1398	Sherry	Lillie	May	6	Apr	1881	5	June	1881	Elwood	Alice Louise	Glace				
B-1399	Shultz	William	Henry	18	Feb	1881	12	June	1881	James	Mary	Lower				
B-1400	Andreas	Addie	Eulibia	9	June	1881	19	June	1881	Levi	Sarah	Gombert				
B-1401	Clewell	Mary	Emaline	8	Oct	1880	9	July	1881	George	Sarah	Klotz	Maria	Bartholomew		
B-1402	Balliet	Eva	Jeanetta	14	June	1881	14	July	1881	Tilghman	Louisa	Eberts				
B-1403	Remaley	William	Henry	28	June	1881	24	July	1881	Charles	Emma E	Rabenold	William	Hartman	Matilda	Shirer
B-1404	Kolb	Leon		27	Feb	1881	25	July	1881	Nathan B	Anna Maria	Whiteman				
B-1405	Stout	Mary	Luella	13	June	1881	31	July	1881	Morris Lessly	Ellen C	Rex	David	Stout	Mary	Walck
B-1406	Hartranft	Sally	Ann Urana	11	Jan	1881	6	Aug	1881	David	Matilda	Kolb				
B-1407	Horn	Lilla	Belle	1	July	1881	6	Aug	1881	Zacharis H	Jane Amanda	Rex				
B-1408	Yeager	Josephine	Virginia	14	Oct	1880	8	Aug	1881	John H	Emma	Webb				
B-1409	Grasely	Louisa	Jane	3	July	1881	9	Aug	1881	Charles	Mary	Ginder				
B-1410	Smith	Richard	Charles	11	Dec	1880	13	Aug	1881	James	Amelia	Dotter				
B-1411	Bowman	Harvey	Albertie	9	July	1881	2	Aug	1881	Francis	Amelia	Freyman				
B-1412	Miller	Mamie	Velarie	29	July	1881	27	Aug	1881	David	Mary	Miller				
B-1413	Serfass	Owen	Sylvester	19	Oct	1880	27	Aug	1881	Mandes	Maria	Smith				
B-1414	Auge	Anna	Martha	9	Apr	1881	28	Aug	1881	David	Sarah Ann	Rehrig				
B-1415	Dreisbach	Carrie	May	18	May	1881	4	Sept	1881	Aaron	Louisa	Wehr				
B-1416	Dunn	Charles	Franklin	20	June	1881	13	Sept	1881	James H	Mary	Moyer	Gideon	Billman	Rebecca	Gerber
B-1417	McClean	Amacin	Virgin	2	Aug	1881	18	Sept	1881	Robert		Delong	James		Emma	Frantz
B-1418	Lutz	Irwin	Franklin	7	Sept	1881	4	Oct	1881	Jacob	Hannah	Miller				
B-1419	Smith	Korah	Maple	5	May	1881	14	Oct	1881	Franklin	Elizabeth	Haydt				
B-1420	Mantz	Minnie	Agnes	13	Sept	1881	16	Oct	1881	Elias	Sarah	Lecheitner				
B-1421	Reinheimer	George	Edgar	20	Sept	1881	20	Oct	1881	Joseph A	Sally Elmira	Freyman				
B-1422	Blose	Daisie	May	16	Mar	1881	5	Nov	1881	Afred	Ellen	Lynn				
B-1423	Brown	Lizzie	Viola	12	Oct	1881	20	Nov	1881	John C	Mary	Hartung				
B-1424	Zimmerman	Effie	Elizabeth	4	Sept	1881	27	Nov	1881	Nathan	Harriet	Gerber				
B-1425	Sittler	Wallace	Andrew	29	Nov	1881	10	Dec	1881	Wallace Ambrose	Harriet	Hunsicker				

40

Beyond the Blue Mountain, Vol. II

Births and Baptisms

Line #	Surname	Child Given	Middle	Birth Day	Mth	Year	Baptism Day	Mth	Year	Father Given	Mother Given	Nee	Witness Given	Surname	Witness Given	Surname
B-1426	Peter	Oliver	Stanley	9	Sept	1881	12	Dec	1881	Wallace	Hannah	Fritz				
B-1427	Reber	Charles	Alger	12	Sept	1881	13	Dec	1881	W.W	Sarah Louisa	Bowman	Catherine	Romig		
B-1428	Musselman	Mable	Rebecca	14	Nov	1881	25	Dec	1881	Thomas	Emaline E	Hunsicker				
B-1429	Nothstein	Claudius	John	9	Sept	1881	5	Jan	1882	John Henry	Sallie A	Muffley				
B-1430	Hontz	William	Franklin	24	Dec	1881	22	Jan	1882	Dennis	Matilda	Cunfer				
B-1431	Ohl	Oliver	Austin	1	Feb	1882	1	Mar	1882	Elias	Lydia	Zettelmoyer	Daniel	Ohl	Mary	Daubenspeck
B-1432	Snyder	William	May	4	Nov	1881	5	Mar	1882	Adam	Ellen	Beer	Thomas	Beltz	Sarah	Snyder
B-1433	Rex	Gertrude	Isabella	11	Jan	1882	12	Mar	1882	Alvin	Annie	Campbell	Joseph	Reinheimer	Sally Elmira	Freyman
B-1434	Rau	Mary	Mabel	1	Feb	1882	18	Mar	1882	Lewis W F	Emma Alice	Miller				
B-1435	Hamm	Lenah	Albert	28	feb	1882	30	Apr	1882	Andrew J	Laura A	Leibensperger				
B-1436	Wageman	Pearce	Louisa	27	Feb	1882	14	May	1882	Nathan	Sophia	Wertman				
B-1437	Rehrig	Ellen	Richard	22	Apr	1881	14	May	1882	Thomas J	Rachel	Belford				
B-1438	Drumbore	Charlie	Alger	4	May	1880	14	May	1882	Nathan	Ellen	Dreher				
B-1439	Rehrig	Henry	Adam	31	Mar	1882	14	May	1882	George	Mary	Knappenberger	Henry	Rehrig	Catherine	Bowman
B-1440	George	Charlie	Ellen	4	Mar	1882	28	May	1882	Penrose	Anna	Seibert				
B-1441	Weaver	William	Quintin	10	May	1882	4	June	1882	Wellington D	Fiana	Frohnheiser	Adam	Andreas	Mary	Steigerwalt
B-1442	Flickinger	Sarah	Albert	17	Mar	1882	17	June	1882	George	Messina	Beer				
B-1443	Steigerwalt	Ensebius	Estella	7	Apr	1882	17	June	1882	Benjamin F	Priscilla	Nothstein				
B-1444	Ginder	John	Mable	2	Apr	1882	17	June	1882	James W	Flora Ann	Hough	George	Kreitz	Harriet	Miller
B-1445	Flickinger	Hannah	Garfield	6	Mar	1882	25	June	1882	Josiah	Clara	Steigerwalt				
B-1446	Rehrig	Lillie	David	9	Apr	1882	1	July	1882	Thomas A	Cordelia	Riling				
B-1447	Moser	Edward	Clinton	1	Sept	1880	8	July	1882	Albert David	Anna Elizabeth	Riling				
B-1448	Moser	Wilson	Ellen	4	June	1882	8	July	1882	Albert David	Anna Elizabeth	Kratzer				
B-1449	Dreher	Robert	Howard	30	May	1882	22	July	1882	Charles	Anna M	Cunfer	John	Hunsicker	Mary Jane	Rubrecht
B-1450	Hunsicker	Elizabeth	Clayton	20	May	1882	31	July	1882	Jacob	Alvenia	Gumbert				
B-1451	Rex	Harry	Alvin	25	June	1882	13	Aug	1882	George	Matilda	Heor	Elias	Beltz	Abbey	Mantz
B-1452	Beltz	Franklin	Elmira	14	June	1882	15	Aug	1882	Franklin	Ida	Youse	Fianna	Youse		
B-1453	Smith	Alvin	Louisa	21	June	1882	16	Aug	1882	William	Ellen Lovina	Smutters				
B-1454	Heilman	Elsie	Edna	1	July	1881	28	Aug	1882	John	Angeline	Harpel				
B-1455	Krum	Katie	Winfield	4	May	1882	28	Aug	1882	Lewis	Meme	Zellner	Adopted parents			
B-1456	Scherer	Emma	Ida	6	June	1882	5	Sept	1882	Stephen	Mary	Schappell	Eli	Miller	Harriet	Zellner
B-1457	Frohnheiser	Sarah	Alvin	23	July	1882	9	Sept	1882	James	Emma	Evert				
B-1458	Lapp	Scott	Elnora	17	July	1882	9	Sept	1882	Charles Henry	Adline	Rex				
B-1459	Mertz	Ida	May	11	Aug	1882	9	Sept	1882	Edwin	Mary	Lauchnor				
B-1460	Nothstein	Pearce	Henry	22	June	1882	10	Sept	1882	Alvin	Susanna	Gilbert				
B-1461	Koons	Emma	Clinton	27	Aug	1882	16	Sept	1882	David	Sarah	Spengler				
B-1462	Fenstermache	Lizzie	Franklin	21	July	1882	16	Sept	1882	Franklin S	Vionetta C	Mertz				
B-1463	Schabo	William	Jefferson	6	July	1882	17	Sept	1882	Peter	Mary	Bochard				
B-1464	Smith	Irwin		4	Aug	1882	20	Sept	1882	Charles	Ellen	Bowman				
B-1465	Balliet	Benjamin		27	July	1882	1	Oct	1882	Lewis	Henrietta	Walter				
B-1466	Ginder	Thomas		8	July	1882	1	Oct	1882	Lewis	Sarah Maria	Walter				
B-1467	Ginder	Wallace		14	Feb	1881	1	Oct	1882	Lewis	Sarah Maria					

Beyond the Blue Mountain, Vol. II

Births and Baptisms

Line #	Surname	Child Given	Middle	Birth Day	Birth Mth	Birth Year	Baptism Day	Baptism Mth	Baptism Year	Father Given	Mother Given	Nee	Witness Given	Witness Surname	Witness Given	Witness Surname
B-1468	Ginder	Sally Ann	Harriet	19	Sept	1878	1	Oct	1882	Lewis	Sarah Maria	Walter				
B-1469	Ginder	William	Franklin	5	Nov	1876	1	Oct	1882	Lewis Franklin	Sarah Maria	Walter				
B-1470	Noll	Minerva	Catherine	28	June	1882	5	Oct	1882	Alvin Henry	Ellen	Breifogel				
B-1471	Hartung	Robbie		23	July	1881	7	Oct	1882	Christian	Kate	Wertman				
B-1472	Miller	Carrie	May	27	Aug	1882	15	Oct	1882	Albright Mahlon	Amanda Isabella	Green				
B-1473	Muthart	Katie	Alavesta	1	May	1882	4	Nov	1882	Levi	Emaline	Moser	Charles		Caroline	Wertman
B-1474	Rehrig	Maurice	Harrison	19	Oct	1882	13	Nov	1882	Thomas J	Rachel	Belford				
B-1475	Mertz	Anna	Matilda	20	Sept	1882	18	Nov	1882	Joseph	Alwilda	Lapp				
B-1476	Ruch	Adda	Sibilla	9	Mar	1882	25	Nov	1882	William	Louisa	Arner				
B-1477	Freeby	Sally	Lovina	18	Oct	1882	30	Nov	1882	George Edwin	Mary Ann	Shive				
B-1478	Harter	Oliver	Franklin	14	May	1882	11	Dec	1882	John	Sarah	Smith		Billman		
B-1479	Weber	Ida	Manilla	20	Aug	1882	24	Dec	1882	Wilson	Henrietta	Gombert				
B-1480	Walck	Robert	Sylvester	30	Sept	1882	1	Jan	1883	George W	Mira Ann	Rex				
B-1481	Benninghoff	Victor	James	29	May	1881	10	Jan	1883	William H	Adline	Hoffman				
B-1482	Smith	Korah		28	Dec	1882	21	Jan	1883	Elias	Lewina	Harter				
B-1483	Berger	George	Welles	9	Dec	1882	21	Jan	1883	Adam	Priscilla	Ruch				
B-1484	Williams	Katie	Elizabeth				28	Jan	1883	James	Kitty Ann	Gombert				
B-1485	Knepper	Odilla		2	Jan	1883	4	Feb	1883	Frank	Matilda	Eberts				
B-1486	Ohl	James	Franklin	10	Jan	1883	11	Feb	1883	Owen	Rosa	Steigerwalt				
B-1487	Eck	Emma	Mary Ann	30	Jan	1883	18	Feb	1883	Augustus	Tevilia	Kennel	James	Delong	Emma	Frantz
B-1488	Stout	Morris	David	27	Oct	1882	22	Feb	1883	Morris Lessly	Ellen C	Rex	John G	Rex	Eva Etta	Stout
B-1489	Mantz	Eugene	Albert	28	Dec	1882	25	Feb	1883	Francis G	Sarah	Longacre				
B-1490	Balliet	Savilla	Martie	—			4	Mar	1883	Stephen	Kate	Gerber				
B-1491	Rehrig	Estella	Mabel	31	Jan	1883	4	Mar	1883	Charles G	Catherine	Romig				
B-1492	Kreitz	William	Eugene	21	Jan	1883	19	Mar	1883	George Henry	Harriet L	Miller				
B-1493	Rehrig	Newton	Elias	21	June	1882	21	Mar	1883	Lewis F	Catherine	Beitelman				
B-1494	Balliet	Carrie	Ellen	7	Apr	1883	19	Apr	1883	Tilghman	Kate Louisa	Eberts				
B-1495	Schumacher	James	Albert	21	Mar	1883	21	Apr	1883	Owen	Mary	Hartranft				
B-1496	Hontz	Carolina	Martha	8	Nov	1882	22	Apr	1883	Moses	Zeniah	Rex				
B-1497	Peter	Lula	Jane	22	Mar	1883	3	May	1883	James F	Kitty Ann	Ruch				
B-1498	Schwab	Harrison	Granville	10	Oct	1882	5	May	1883	Charles H	Matilda	Willkraut				
B-1499	Sittler	Birdie	Ambrose	8	Mar	1883	6	May	1883	Wallace A	Harriet	Hunsicker				
B-1500	Krotzer	Laura	Ellen	8	Aug	1882	24	May	1883	Walter V	Sarah	Zimmerman				
B-1501	Cunfer	Robert	Josiah	20	Apr	1883	26	May	1883	Josiah	Fietta	Shoemaker				
B-1502	Shoemaker	Marvin	Oliver	17	Apr	1883	26	May	1883	Granville Addison	Elmira	Ruch				
B-1503	Dreisbach	Theresa	Bell	26	Mar	1883	27	May	1883	Aaron	Louisa	Wehr				
B-1504	Hartung	Hattie	Eva	2	Apr	1883	3	May	1883	David	Kate	Balliet				
B-1505	Zimmerman	Alwin		24	Mar	1883	10	June	1883	Nathan	Harriet	Gerber				
B-1506	Evert	Beula	Eva	6	Oct	1881	22	June	1883	John	Mary	Fulton				
B-1507	Grow	Sarah	Elmira	2	June	1883	24	June	1883	Nathan	Sarah	Hobbes				
B-1508	Remaley	Nathan	Tobias	5	June	1883	9	July	1883	Charles	Emma Eliza	Rabenold				
B-1509	Fritz	Clarence	Albert	20	Mar	1883	14	July	1883	Allen	Sabina	Gombert				

Beyond the Blue Mountain, Vol. II

Births and Baptisms

Line #	Surname	Child Given	Middle	Birth Day	Birth Mth	Birth Year	Baptism Day	Baptism Mth	Baptism Year	Father Given	Mother Given	Nee	Witness Given	Witness Surname	Witness Given	Witness Surname
B-1510	Ronamus	Robert		6	July	1883	5	Aug	1883	William	Rebecca	Schaeffer				
B-1511	Billman	Mary	Jane	9	July	1883	13	Aug	1883	Charles B	Harriet	Smith	Charles	Billman	Magdaline	Wertman
B-1512	Lentz	Anna	Irene	26	May	1883	18	Aug	1883	Edwin J	Ida	Moyer				
B-1513	Steigerwalt	Llewellyn	Osville	18	Sept	1883	26	Oct	1883	Benjamin F	Priscilla	Beer				
B-1514	Zimmerman	Wilmore	Edwin	6	Sept	1883	30	Oct	1883	Allen S	Lizzie	Klingaman				
B-1515	Dreher	Katie	Amelia	18	Oct	1883	19	Nov	1883	Benoville	Lucy	Smith				
B-1516	Levers	Harry	Edward	18	Apr	1883	19	Nov	1883	Espin	Ida	Dreher				
B-1517	Sherry	Ellwood	Henry	20	Oct	1883	2	Dec	1883	Ellwood	Alice Louisa	Glace				
B-1518	Schabo	Charles	Franklin	30	Sept	1883	29	Dec	1883	Peter	Mary	Mertz				
B-1519	Rex	John	Albert	14	Oct	1883	16	Jan	1884	William	Cassia	Eck	Manda	Barry	Matilda	Snyder
B-1520	Rex	Clara	Matilda	8	Apr	1883	16	Jan	1884	William	Cassia	Eck	Harvey	Sherry	Cassia	Eck
B-1521	Barry	George	Harvey	17	May	1884	16	Jan	1884	Theodore	Manda	Hontz	William	Rex		
B-1522	Rex	Agnes	Elnora	17	Dec	1883	2	Feb	1884	Lewis	Ellamanda	Silfies				
B-1523	Miller	George	Washington	16	Sept	1883	21	Feb	1884	David	Mary Ann	Miller				
B-1524	Frantz	Adella	Cordelia	14	Feb	1884	9	Mar	1884	Willoughby	Alavesta	Moser				
B-1525	Auge	Allen	Arthur	4	Oct	1883	1	Apr	1884	David	Sarah Ann	Rehrig				
B-1526	Graver	David	Howard	28	Feb	1883	10	Apr	1884	Martin B	Regina	Straussburger				
B-1527	Bowman	Robert	Levi	15	Apr	1884	26	Apr	1884	Francis	Amelia	Freyman				
B-1528	Mertz	Edwin	Allen	31	Mar	1884	3	May	1884	Granville	Emma	Freyman				
B-1529	Rehrig	Herbert	Charles	30	Apr	1884	8	June	1884	Charles G	Catherine	Romig				
B-1530	Stemler	Claude	Elmer	1	June	1884	16	July	1884	Olive` A	Emma J	Beer				
B-1531	Nunnemacher	George	Albert	24	Mar	1884	18	July	1884	Lewis	Hetty	Wertman	Caroline			
B-1532	Kleintop	Laura	May	6	Apr	1884	20	July	1884	James W	Amanda	Walck				
B-1533	Billman	Harry	Wilson	14	June	1884	20	July	1884	James W	Sarah Ann	Hartman	Charles	Billman	Caroline	Wertman
B-1534	Gombert	Carrie	May	22	June	1884	3	Aug	1884	Joseph L	Sarah Ann	Fenstermacher				
B-1535	Hough	William	Wilson	4	Apr	1884	3	Aug	1884	Edwin	Mary Ann	Horn				
B-1536	Lapp	Carrie	May	22	June	1884	5	Aug	1884	Charles Henry	Adline	Evert				
B-1537	Rabenold	Zacharias	Jonas	14	Feb	1884	6	Aug	1884	Charles B	Susan E	Moser				
B-1538	Evert	Ires	Sylvester	18	June	1884	8	Aug	1884	Charles	Mary	Sensinger				
B-1539	Fenstermache	Calvin	Osbon	27	July	1884	8	Sept	1884	Franklin S	Vionetta	Spengler				
B-1540	Schwartz	Jennie	May	13	Aug	1884	11	Sept	1884	Thomas A	Elmasia	Schwartz				
B-1541	Geiger	Jennie	May	28	May	1884	14	Sept	1884	Levi L	Ida A	Gombert	Joseph	Geiger	Rebecca	Wertman
B-1542	Ronemus	Robert	Roy	21	Aug	1884	21	Oct	1884	James S	Maria	Norwood				
B-1543	Mertz	Lillie	Jane	24	Sept	1884	1	Nov	1884	Joseph	Alwilda	Lapp				
B-1544	Trumbore	Edwin	Jacob	4	Oct	1884	3	Nov	1884	Elwin	July Ann	Klotz				
B-1545	Weaver	Clinton	Daniel Joseph	18	Nov	1884	24	Nov	1884	Jacob	Sarah Jane	Haberman	Joseph	Haberman	Sarah	Troxell
B-1546	Kemerer	Esther	Mary	10	Aug	1884	25	Nov	1884	George H	Ella Priscilla	Schwartz				
B-1547	Mertz	Lillie	Ellen	8	Nov	1884	20	Dec	1884	Edwin	Mary	Rex				
B-1548	Schmidt	Lillie	Amelia	1	Nov	1884	23	Dec	1884	Herman	Louisa	Schnell				
B-1549	Beck	Torence	C	23	May	1884	29	Dec	1884	Thomas J	Christiana	Bittner				
B-1550	Behen	Clara	Louisa	15	Nov	1884	14	Jan	1885	John H	Eurilla	Beuner				
B-1551	Diehl	Esther	May	28	Aug	1884	15	Jan	1885	Frank P	Mary	Strohrm				

Beyond the Blue Mountain, Vol. II

Births and Baptisms

Line #	Surname	Child Given	Middle	Birth Day	Birth Mth	Birth Year	Baptism Day	Baptism Mth	Baptism Year	Father Given	Mother Given	Nee	Witness Given	Witness Surname	Witness Given	Witness Surname
B-1552	Scheckler	Robert	Daniel	26	Aug	1884	30	Jan	1885	Daniel	Emma	Laubach				
B-1553	Spengler	Estella	May	30	Aug	1884	30	Jan	1885	James A	Ella	Hofford				
B-1554	Seila	Maple	Capitola	7	Nov	1884	9	Mar	1885	Charles	Alice	Kemerer				
B-1555	Dreher	Laura	May	15	July	1884	11	Mar	1885	Charles	Anna Maria	Krotzer				
B-1556	Gombert	Pearlie	Ada Aleina	6	Mar	1885	3	May	1885	Andrew J	Annie	Long				
B-1557	Lentz	Lillie Ann	Adline	8	Apr	1885	10	May	1885	Edwin J	Ida	Moyer				
B-1558	Moyer	Agnes	Elizabeth	13	Apr	1885	10	May	1885	Jonas Isaac	Anna Maria	Hoffman				
B-1559	Reichard	Carrie	Alice	10	Mar	1885	29	May	1885	James	Alice	Rehrig				
B-1560	Peter	Wilbur	Robison	16	Mar	1885	31	May	1885	Wallace I	Hannah	Fritz				
B-1561	Graver	Martin	Raymond	5	Mar	1885	9	June	1885	Martin B	Regina	Straussburger	Louisa	Blose		
B-1562	Mertz	Adam	Cleveland	16	May	1885	27	June	1885	Alfred	Mary Ann	Evert				
B-1563	Rex	Ida Anna	Estella	4	May	1885	1	July	1885	Elvin	Mary Ann	Bechtel				
B-1564	Buzzard	Miles	Lucius	29	Dec	1883	9	July	1885	George	Mary Anna	Xander				
B-1565	Sandherr	Estella	Irene	13	May	1885	9	July	1885	George	Alice	Rehrig				
B-1566	Evans	Flossy	Hannah May	5	Mar	1885	11	July	1885	William J	Amanda Eliza	Bartholomew				
B-1567	Ruch	William	Henry Wilson	28	May	1885	11	July	1885	Horace Greely	Hannah	Bachman	Manda	Fehnel		
B-1568	Hoffman	Clendora	Estella	20	June	1885	21	July	1885	Jerrane	Sallie	Frohnheiser	Rosa E	Young		
B-1569	Heintzelman	Estella	May	28	June	1885	26	July	1885	Osvil M	Libbie A	Benninghoff				
B-1570	Zimmerman	Mame	Estella	30	Apr	1885	16	Aug	1885	Nathan	Harriet	Gerber				
B-1571	Schaeffer	Charles	Edward	21	June	1885	19	Aug	1885	A H	Lilly Louisa	Godshall				
B-1572	Koons	Charles	Richard	26	Mar	1885	30	Aug	1885	Cornelius	Ellen	Young				
B-1573	Hill	Milton	Ernest	10	May	1885	5	Sept	1885	William	Emma A	Billman	Charles	Billman	Carolina	Wertman
B-1574	Steigerwalt	Emma	Lillie	16	Aug	1885	19	Sept	1885	Benjamin F	Priscilla	Beer				
B-1575	Frantz	Ellenora	Adline	22	Aug	1885	20	Sept	1885	Willoughby	Alavesta	Moser				
B-1576	Ginder	Clayton	Darwin	12	Aug	1885	2	Oct	1885	Philip	Francis	Dreisbach	William	Ronemus		
B-1577	Philips	Joanna	Stevens	1	Sept	1885	25	Oct	1885	Joseph	Mary Eva	Ronemus				Schaefer
B-1578	Rehrig	Ellen		28	Mar	1885	26	Oct	1885	Jonas	Polly	Loch				
B-1579	Embody	Lizzie	Ellamanda	9	Sept	1885	17	Nov	1885	Gideon	Levina	Kolb	Rueben	Fink	Maria	Rex
B-1580	Fenstermache	Ida	Augusta	6	Sept	1885	17	Nov	1885	Franklin S	Viletta	Spengler				
B-1581	Billman	George	Benjamin	3	Nov	1885	27	Nov	1885	Charles Benjamin	Harriet Adora	Smith				
B-1582	Hunsicker	Mary	Alice	16	Nov	1885	28	Nov	1885	John	Mary Ann	Rubrecht				
B-1583	Beck	Sarah	Estella	10	Dec	1885	6	Feb	1886	Thom. Washingto	Ellen	Bochard				
B-1584	Keegan	Irwin		14	July	1883	15	Feb	1886	Irwin	Eva Elizabeth	Harter				
B-1585	Rehrig	Clinton	Eugene	4	Jan	1886	6	Mar	1886	Reuben	Emaline	Ruch				
B-1586	Bartholomew	Lloyd	Anthony	28	Dec	1885	6	Mar	1886	Calvin E	Ella L	Anthony				
B-1587	Ronemus	Sarah		11	Feb	1886	11	Mar	1886	William	Rebecca	Schaefer				
B-1588	Reed	Edwin	Gilbert	8	Feb	1886	2	Apr	1886	Lewis	Sarah N	Reed				
B-1589	Eaches	Catherine		8	Feb	1886	4	Apr	1886	John	Ida	Robinson				
B-1590	Whiteneck	Ellemanda		21	Mar	1886	17	Apr	1886	Jefferson	Ida Priscilla	Keiser	Rebecca	Boyer		
B-1591	Peter	Cora	Hannah	16	Apr	1886	12	May	1886	Edwin C	Harriet	Rehrig				
B-1592	Kostenbader	Bulah		21	Feb	1886	15	May	1886	Samuel D	Matilda	Walck				
B-1593	Gombert	Ellanora		18	Feb	1886	17	May	1886	Joseph L	Sarah Ann	Fenstermacher				

Births and Baptisms

Line #	Surname	Child Given	Middle	Birth Day	Birth Mth	Birth Year	Baptism Day	Baptism Mth	Baptism Year	Father Given	Mother Given	Nee	Witness Given	Witness Surname	Witness Given	Witness Surname
B-1594	Nothstein	Josiah	Ellsworth	13	Jan	1886	25	May	1886	Lewis F	Angeline Eliz	Herring				
B-1595	Balliet	Estella	Louisa	15	Apr	1886	6	June	1886	Lewis Franklin	Henrietta	Bowman				
B-1596	Spengler	Harrison	Cleveland	9	Feb	1886	11	June	1886	James A	Ella May	Hofford				
B-1597	Mantz	Bula	Olivia	2	Feb	1886	27	June	1886	Francis G	Sarah	Longacre				
B-1598	Radcliff	Matilda	May	6	Apr	1886	8	July	1886	Justus	Eliza	Mehrhoff				
B-1600	Evert	Mamie	Florence	16	Feb	1886	2	Aug	1886	John	Mary Jane	Fulton				
B-1601	Gumbert	Mattie	Sarah	1	July	1886	15	Aug	1886	Andrew J	Annie D	Long				
B-1602	Peter	Cora	Esther	8	June	1886	22	Aug	1886	Wallace I	Hannah	Fritz				
B-1603	Rehrig	Luella	Minnie	8	June	1886	29	Aug	1886	Thomas A	Codilia	Steigerwalt	Mahoning			
B-1604	Eck	Charles	Edward	4	Aug	1886	29	Aug	1886	Augustus	Tewilia	Kennel	Clara	Eck	East Penn	
B-1605	Eck	Alice	Amelia	29	July	1886	29	Aug	1886	William	Matilda	Kolb	East Penn			
B-1606	Ginder	Irwin	Daniel	26	Aug	1886	4	Oct	1886	James	Flora Ann	Nothstein				
B-1607	Fritzinger	Allie	Edgar	6	Sept	1886	7	Oct	1886	Oscar	Mary Martha	Dutcher				
B-1608	Levers	Mary	Catherine	10	May	1885	28	Oct	1886	Espen	Ida	Dreher				
B-1609	Youse	Carrie	Adella	22	Aug	1886	11	Nov	1886	Milton A	Celesta	Beltz				
B-1610	Reinsmith	Mable	Estella	14	Nov	1886	2	Dec	1886	Nathan	Messina	Kerschner				
B-1611	Ruch	Clinton	Albert	25	Oct	1886	9	Dec	1886	William	Louisa	Arner				
B-1612	Wageman	Minnie	May	25	Oct	1886	21	Dec	1886	Nathan	Sophia	Wertman				
B-1613	Zellner	Emma	Harriet	20	Oct	1886	27	Dec	1886	Moses	Alice Ellen	Hoffman				
B-1614	Ginder	Rowlands	Albert	17	Feb	1886	1	Apr	1887	Philip	Francisca	Dreisbach				
B-1615	Ohl	Ida	Louisa	12	Apr	1887	8	May	1887	Owen	Rosa A	Steigerwalt				
B-1616	Mantz	Elias	Oliver	7	May	1887	22	May	1887	Elias	Sarah	Lechleitner				
B-1617	Dreher	George	Casper	18	Mar	1887	4	June	1887	Bencville	Lucy	Smith				
B-1618	Kistler	Oscar	Joseph	21	Apr	1887	5	June	1887	David Amandes	Alvena	Zimmerman				
B-1619	Reichard	Emma	Estella May	9	Apr	1887	15	June	1887	James	Clara Alice	Rehrig				
B-1620	Nothstein	Calvin	Walter	19	Feb	1887	3	July	1887	Milton	Emma J	Hoffman				
B-1621	Ronamus	Harriet		2	July	1887	17	July	1887	Peter	Rebecca	Schaeffer				
B-1622	Rehrig	William	Charles	8	June	1887	21	July	1887	James H	Anna	Mulharen				
B-1623	Hoffman	Emma	Manora	8	July	1887	27	July	1887	Jerrane	Sallie	Frohnheiser				
B-1624	Highland	William	Charles	15	Apr	1887	31	July	1887	Charles W	Emma E	Graver				
B-1625	Ohl	Mary	Jane	12	June	1887	2	Aug	1887	Henry	Sabina	Gerber				
B-1626	Fink	Myrtle	Edel Burga	7	July	1887	7	Aug	1887	William	Burga	(Fink)				
B-1627	Breiner	Elmer	Franklin	22	June	1887	7	Aug	1887	Benjamin Franklii	Janetta	(Breiner)				
B-1628	Ebberts	Walace	Ambrose	4	June	1887	14	Aug	1887	Amandus A	Emma E	Sitler	St. Peters			
B-1629	Fenstermache	Herman	John	23	May	1887	14	Aug	1887	Stephen	Kate	Snyder				
B-1630	Schabo	Minnie	Estella	18	July	1887	28	Aug	1887	Peter	Mary Ann	Mertz				
B-1631	Troxell	Harvey	Alvin	26	July	1887	30	Aug	1887	Frank Albert	Agnes M	Schock				
B-1632	Rehrig	Daisie	Isabella	25	June	1887	31	Aug	1887	Augustus	Ida E	Beltz				
B-1633	Kuntz	Mary	Catherine	27	Mar	1887	18	Sept	1887	Cornelius	Ellen	Young				
B-1634	Sherry	Mabel	Beers	23	Aug	1887	23	Oct	1887	Ellwood H	Alice	Glace				
B-1635	Andreas	Robert	Spencer	3	Sept	1887	13	Nov	1887	James Irwin	Fietta	George				
B-1636	Ginder	Oscar	Irwin	14	Oct	1887	23	Nov	1887	Charles Harrison	Mary Jane	Gumbert				

Beyond the Blue Mountain, Vol. II

Births and Baptisms

Line #	Surname	Child Given	Middle	Birth Day	Birth Mth	Birth Year	Baptism Day	Baptism Mth	Baptism Year	Father Given	Mother Given	Nee	Witness Given	Witness Surname	Witness Given	Witness Surname
B-1637	Freyman	Masie	Ada	7	Oct	1887	27	Nov	1887	William H	Kate M	Loch	Godfrey	Frantz	Anna Maria	Rex
B-1638	Miller	Ella	Minerva	15	Oct	1887	4	Dec	1887	Albright M	Isabella	Green	Oscar	Fritzinger	Mary Martha	Dutcher
B-1639	Heintzelman	Minnie	Aggierista	16	Aug	1887	11	Dec	1887	Osville M	Libbie A	Benninghoff				
B-1640	Gombert	Bertha	Ellen	7	Oct	1887	11	Dec	1887	Andrew J	Annie D	Long				
B-1641	Shoemaker	Victor	Allen	29	Oct	1887	11	Dec	1887	Charles M	Amanda E	McFarland	Godfrey	Frantz	Maria	Rex
B-1642	Ginder	Benjamin	Franklin	25	Aug	1887	14	Dec	1887	Charles A	Mary	Eck				
B-1643	Miller	Carrie	May	16	Nov	1887	27	Dec	1887	David	Mary	Miller				
B-1644	Bowman	Emma	Susanna	29	Nov	1887	19	Jan	1888	Harry James	Mary Alice	Schock	Susanna	Bowman		
B-1645	Zimmerman	Harvey	Edgar	29	Aug	1887	22	Jan	1888	Nathan	Harriet	Gerber				
B-1646	Dewerth	Norma	Elmira	19	July	1887	5	Feb	1888	Charles William	Elmira	Leeds				
B-1647	Wher	William	Webster	14	Jan	1888	19	Feb	1888	Lewis A	Adline	Graver				
B-1648	Steigerwalt	Oliver		6	Apr	1888	16	Apr	1888	Willoughby	Emma	Moyer				
B-1649	Gombert	Emma	Elnora	16	Dec	1887	22	Apr	1888	Nathan	Medina	Krum				
B-1650	Heim	Charles	Henry	23	Mar	1888	29	Apr	1888	Lewis F	Amanda	Beltz	Polly	Remaley		
B-1651	Albright	George	William	29	Dec	1887	5	May	1888	John F H	Rosa A	Klotz				
B-1652	Eck	Flossie	Amanda	15	Mar	1888	6	May	1888	William	Matilda	Kolb	Albert	Brown	Amanda	Freeby
B-1653	Ginder	Urias	Oscar	18	Apr	1888	10	May	1888	James W	Flora	Nothstein				
B-1654	Schleicher	George	Daniel	24	Apr	1888	19	May	1888	Charles Franklin	Emma Cather	Moyer				
B-1655	Mantz	Estella	Almeta	24	Apr	1888	20	May	1888	Lewis	Polly	Zehner	David	Gerber	Ellemanda	Zehner
B-1656	Noll	Harvey	Daniel	13	Feb	1888	20	May	1888	Alvin	Ellen	Breyfogel				
B-1657	Thomas	Ruth	Graver	18	Apr	1888	22	May	1888	Thomas D	Emma	Graver				
B-1658	Houser	Meinnie	Meay	4	Oct	1887	28	May	1888	Charles S	Kate	Miller				
B-1659	Hill	Flossie	Estella	-	-	-	5	June	1888	Adam	Mary	Green	Jane	Bachman		
B-1660	Hill	Willie	Alvin	-	-	-	5	June	1888	Adam	Mary	Green	Catherine	Bachert		
B-1661	Lauchnor	Clinton	Albert	11	May	1888	8	June	1888	Lewis	Louisa	Ohl				
B-1662	Snyder	James	Ferdinand R	25	Mar	1888	9	June	1888	M R	Amanda	Millhouse				
B-1663	Zimmerman	Ira	Lewis	10	May	1888	12	June	1888	Allen S	Lizzie	Klingaman				
B-1664	Remaley	Hattie	May	11	May	1888	24	June	1888	Wilson	Polly	Hunsicker	Joseph	Hunsicker	Caroline	Houser
B-1665	Hontz	baby					24	June	1888	Ammon						
B-1666	Nothstein	Eva	May	25	Apr	1888	30	June	1888	Milton	Emma	Hoffman				
B-1667	Cunfer	Lilia	Jemima	1	June	1888	1	July	1888	George Benjamin	Minerva	Ebberts				
B-1668	Smith	Ida	Luella	18	June	1888	8	July	1888	John	Ellen Manda	Ruch				
B-1669	Kistler	Mary	Emma	9	Mar	1888	9	July	1888	Jonathan	Alvena	Mantz				
B-1670	Bachman	Robbie	William	18	Aug	1887	21	July	1888	George James	Carrie	Buck	Louisa	Buck		
B-1671	Krauc	Odillon	Muffley	16	June	1888	21	July	1888	Edward	Lizzie	Muffley				
B-1672	Hobbes	Freddie	Elmer	21	Apr	1888	29	July	1888	Solomon	Levina	Zettelmoyer				
B-1673	Fritz	Emma	Estella	18	Apr	1888	16	Aug	1888	William A	Susarrna	Bowman				
B-1674	Kressley	John	Gottleib	2	June	1888	27	Aug	1888	Charles	Mary Ann	Ginder				
B-1675	Hunsicker	Jacob	Albert	2	Aug	1888	28	Aug	1888	Jacob	Alvena	Cunfer	Thomas	Remaley	Polly	Hobbes
B-1676	Mantz	Edna	Estella	23	July	1888	28	Aug	1888	J F	E L	Schaefer				
B-1677	Meitzler	Minnie	Jane	5	Aug	1888	2	Sept	1888	John Calvin	Emaline Jane	Gerber				
B-1678	Kistler	Oris	David	13	Aug	1888	2	Sept	1888	David Amandes	Alveria	Zimmerman				

Beyond the Blue Mountain, Vol. II

Births and Baptisms

Line #	Surname	Child Given	Middle	Birth Day	Birth Mth	Birth Year	Baptism Day	Baptism Mth	Baptism Year	Father Given	Mother Given	Nee	Witness Given	Witness Surname	Witness Given	Witness Surname
B-1679	Lentz	Sadie	Elizabeth	4	June	1888	4	Sept	1888	Edwin J	Ida	Moyer				
B-1680	Beer	John	Henry	1	Aug	1888	7	Sept	1888	Acam	Lucinda	Kleintop				
B-1681	Balliet	Katie	Fietta	3	Aug	1888	14	Sept	1888	Tilghman G	Lavina	Herring				
B-1682	Hontz	Lizzie	Alvenia	15	July	1887	23	Sept	1888	Moses	Zeniah	Rex				
B-1683	Beltz	Lottie	Magdalene	23	June	1887	26	Sept	1888	Elmer Ellsworth	Bel Lucretia	Strohm				
B-1684	Youse	Robert	Lee	7	July	1888	26	Sept	1888	Milton A	Celesta	Beltz				
B-1685	McLean	Lettie		27	Aug	1888	27	Sept	1888	Robert		Frantz				
B-1686	Grow	Lulu	May	3	Mar	1888	30	Sept	1888	Reuben	Mary	Schwartz				
B-1687	Fink	Willie	Oscar	8	July	1888	30	Sept	1888	Joseph W	Sarah	Fritzinger	Oscar	Fritzinger	Mary Martha	Dutcher
B-1688	Fenstermache	Jennva	Estella	15	Sept	1888	18	Oct	1888	Franklin S	Vinetta C	Spengler				
B-1689	Fenstermache	Walter	Leon	24	Sept	1888	23	Oct	1888	Stephen	Kate	Snyder				
B-1690	Beltz	Lizzie	Savilla	24	Oct	1888	4	Nov	1888	Thomas D	Susanna	Miller				
B-1691	Romig	Emma	Lovina	18	Sept	1888	13	Nov	1888	Maurice A	Emaline	Rehrig				
B-1692	Cunfer	Mandes	Ambrose	26	Oct	1888	29	Nov	1888	John C	Mary L	David				
B-1693	Brobst	Bessie	Emalina	16	Oct	1888	19	Dec	1888	James S	Regina	Mengel				
B-1694	Balliet	Harvey	Jacob	4	Dec	1888	25	Dec	1888	Stephen	Kate	Gerber	St. Peters			
B-1695	Arner	Henry	Raymond	20	Nov	1888	30	Dec	1888	Thomas J	Cora Alice	Mertz				
B-1696	Wageman	Hannah	Telina	11	Aug	1888	8	Jan	1888	Nathan	Sophia	Wertman				
B-1697	Dreher	Ida	Minerva	8	June	1888	11	Jan	1888	Charles	Anna	Kratzer				
B-1698	Trumbore	Laura	Tana	18	Nov	1888	13	Jan	1889	Elwin	July Ann	Klotz	Laura	Klotz		
B-1699	Ashner	Birdie	Irwin	29	Nov	1888	10	Feb	1889	James Franklin	Emma Jane	Schaeffer	Alexander	Schaeffer	Emma	Hayman
B-1700	Smith	—	—	—	—	—	17	Feb	1889	Henry	Harriet	Steigerwalt				Steigerwalt
B-1701	Hill	Estella	Luella	21	Feb	1889	3	Mar	1889	Edwin	Louisa	Andreas	Adam	Andreas	Flora Ann	
B-1702	Frantz	Raymond	Stanley Irwin	3	Mar	1889	30	Mar	1889	Wilson	Mary Ann	Neumayer				
B-1703	Sherry	Ida	Arsina	18	Jan	1889	14	Apr	1889	Ellwood H	Alice Louise	Glace				
B-1704	Moyer	Harrison	Morton	10	Mar	1889	3	May	1889		Emma	Moyer				
B-1705	Evert	Lizzie	Violet	11	Feb	1889	12	May	1889	John	Mary Jane	Fulton				
B-1706	Ratcliff	Elmer	Justus	27	Mar	1889	16	May	1889	Justus	Eliza	Mearhoff				
B-1707	Smith	Adam	Franklin	7	Mar	1889	18	May	1889	Franklin	Emma	Correll				
B-1708	Gombert	Mamie	Augusta	29	Feb	1889	2	June	1889	Andrew J	Annie D	Long	Mary	Haupt		
B-1709	Fritzinger	Curtie	Nelson	12	Apr	1889	15	June	1889	Oscar	Mary Martha	Dutcher				
B-1710	Zimmerman	Warren	Benjamin	21	Jan	1889	23	June	1889	Nathan	Harriet	Gerber				
B-1711	Rehrig	Aaron	Henry	2	Aug	1889	21	Sept	1889	Augustus	Ida E	Beltz				
B-1712	Andreas	Hannah	Mable	21	Aug	1889	3	Nov	1889	Thomas Franklin	Emma Louisa	Hunt				
B-1713	Freyman	Meta	Agnes	8	Sept	1889	3	Nov	1889	William H	Kate M	Loch				
B-1714	Schabo	Agnes	May	26	July	1889	16	Nov	1889	Peter	Mary Ann	Mertz				
B-1715	Smith	Mame	Sallie	3	Oct	1889	22	Nov	1889	John	Ellen	Ruch				
B-1716	Troxel	Amanda	Jennie	29	Oct	1889	3	Dec	1889	Frank A	Agnes M	Schock	William	Troxel	Mary	Miller
B-1717	Lentz	Estella	Amelia	12	Aug	1889	6	Jan	1890	Edwin J	Ida	Moyer				
B-1718	Mertz	Arthur	Clayton	19	Feb	1890	13	Apr	1890	John R	Ellen	Gombert				
B-1719	Miller	Hattie	Lovina	-	Dec	1889	18	Apr	1890	David	Mary	Miller				
B-1720	Klotz	Dora	Irene	20	Apr	1890	8	June	1890	Robert H	Fannie	Dentinger				

Beyond the Blue Mountain, Vol. II

Births and Baptisms

Line #	Surname	Child Given	Middle	Birth Day	Birth Mth	Birth Year	Baptism Day	Baptism Mth	Baptism Year	Father Given	Mother Given	Nee	Witness Given	Witness Surname	Witness Given	Witness Surname
B-1721	Ginder	Wesley	Raymond	7	May	1890	14	June	1890	Philip	Francis	Dreisbach				
B-1722	Ruch	Lizzie	Susanna	20	June	1890	15	July	1890	Charles	Fianna	Bowman				
B-1723	Andreas	Clara	Louisa	21	June	1890	17	July	1890	Levi	Sarah	Gombert				
B-1724	Hontz	Raymond	Jonas	2	Jan	1890	27	July	1890	Moses	Zeniah	Rex				
B-1725	Fritz	Laura	Clendora	4	June	1890	27	July	1890	William Amandes	Susanna V	Bowman	A F	Steigerwalt	Marie E	Bowman
B-1726	Hunsicker	Harry	Samuel	23	Feb	1890	5	Aug	1890	Jacob	Alvena	Cunfer				
B-1727	Gombert	George	Ira	28	June	1890	10	Aug	1890	Andrew J	Annie	Long	George	Rex	Tillie	Gombert
B-1728	McFarland	Rachel	Louisa	4	June	1890	18	Aug	1890	John J	Fietta	Rex				
B-1729	Hobbes	Mamie	Mesitta	3	May	1890	24	Aug	1890	Solomon D	Levina	Zettelmoyer				
B-1730	Roth	Willie	Ernest	17	June	1890	26	Aug	1890	Charles F	Ellen K	Arner				
B-1731	Bartholomew	Grace	Aldine	12	June	1890	3	Sept	1890	Calvin E	Ella L	Anthony				
B-1732	Leiby	William	Harrison	28	Aug	1890	19	Sept	1890	Daniel	Mary	Fritz				
B-1733	Moser	Luellen	Mary Jane	23	Apr	1890	20	Sept	1890	David M	Sallie C	Holtzer				
B-1734	Balliet	Raymond	Lewis	10	Aug	1890	29	Sept	1890	Lewis Franklin	Henrietta	Bowman				
B-1735	Andreas	Calvin	Albert	21	Sept	1890	31	Oct	1890	Rodger Elmer	Louisa	Sensinger				
B-1736	Fritzinger	Sally Ann	Amanda	12	Oct	1890	7	Nov	1890	Charles H	Kitty Ann	Ziegler				
B-1737	Geiger	Raymond	Adam	25	Sept	1890	15	Nov	1890	James A	Priscilla	Fritzinger				
B-1738	Bowman	George	James	3	Oct	1890	16	Nov	1890	Henry James	Alice	Schock	George	Schock	Angelina	Bierman
B-1739	Freeby	George	Edward	30	Nov	1890	10	Jan	1891	George E	Mary Ann	Shive				
B-1740	Fenstermaker	Daisie	Amelia	8	Nov	1890	16	Jan	1891	Franklin S	Vionetta C	Spengler				
B-1741	Fink	Robert	Harrison	27	Sept	1890	26	Jan	1891	Joseph W	Sarah Catherine	Fritzinger				
B-1742	Romig	Hattie	Estella	6	Jan	1891	14	Feb	1891	Maurice A	Emaline	Rehrig				
B-1743	Rehrig	Bertha	Adline	1	Nov	1890	26	Feb	1891	Dennis	Julia Elizabeth	Lentz				
B-1744	Zellner	Moses	Calvin	1	Feb	1891	12	Apr	1891	Moses	Alice Ellen	Hoffman				
B-1745	Bowman	James	---	28	Feb	1891	18	Apr	1891	John	Maria	Kolb				
B-1746	Mumbower	Harry	Josiah	3	Apr	1891	25	May	1891	Elmer	Emma Martha	McDaniel				
B-1747	Kistler	Clifford	Edgar	9	Apr	1891	4	June	1891	David Amandes	Alvena	Zimmerman				
B-1748	Winter	Harry	---	23	Mar	1891	20	June	1891	Daniel	Annetta	Geiger	Daniel	Hill	Angelina	(Hill)
B-1749	Weaver	Sadie	Luella	7	Mar	1891	20	June	1891	Wilson August	Henrietta	Gombert				
B-1750	Neff	Lewis	Edwin	17	Apr	1891	28	June	1891	Paul	Sabina	Kolb	Emma	Bachman		
B-1751	Shoemaker	Clendora	May	16	May	1891	28	June	1891	Charles M	Amanda Eliza	McFarland				
B-1752	Whitaker	Irwin	Isiah	10	Mar	1891	4	July	1891	James Franklin	Elemena	Ziegenfuss				
B-1753	Sherry	Cora	Jane	19	May	1891	12	July	1891	Ellwood	Alice Louisa	Glace				
B-1754	Gumbert	Flossie	Agnes	5	May	1891	28	Aug	1891	Frank	Caroline	Cunfer				
B-1755	Fritzinger	Charles	Oscar	26	June	1891	4	Oct	1891	Oscar	Mary Martha	Dutcher				
B-1756	Lentz	Robert	Franklin	30	May	1891	17	Oct	1891	Edwin J	Ida	Moyer				
B-1757	Oldt	Carrie	Edith	20	Sept	1891	25	Oct	1891	A F	Lizzie	Hunsicker				
B-1758	Horn	Clyde	Irwin	3	Oct	1891	15	Nov	1891	Oscar E	Alice Louisa	Sensinger				
B-1759	Fritzinger	John	Albert	16	Nov	1891	13	Dec	1891	Francis H	Mary N	Schott				
B-1760	Boyer	Florence	May	28	July	1888	1	Jan	1892	Milton C	Sarah A	Fenstermacher				
B-1761	Boyer	Ermie	Irene	19	Nov	1890	1	Jan	1892	Milton C	Sarah A	Fenstermacher				
B-1762	Semmel	Irwin	Clarence	10	Dec	1891	24	Jan	1892	Granville Henry	Sallie Lovenah	Andrews				

Beyond the Blue Mountain, Vol. II

Births and Baptisms

Line #	Surname	Child Given	Middle	Birth Day	Birth Mth	Birth Year	Baptism Day	Baptism Mth	Baptism Year	Father Given	Mother Given	Nee	Witness Given	Witness Surname	Witness Given	Witness Surname
B-1763	Gombert	Meta	Annie	14	Nov	1891	25	Jan	1892	Andrew J	Annie D	Long				
B-1764	McDaniel	Ella	Maud	27	Nov	1891	25	Jan	1892	James Erwin	Alice Cora	Miller				
B-1765	Freyman	Herbert	James	-	Dec	1891	14	Feb	1892	William H	Kate M	Loch				Bowman
B-1766	Rehrig	Eliza	Jane	16	Jan	1892	12	Mar	1892	Augustus	Ida E	Beltz	Aaron	Noll	Clara Ann	
B-1767	Lutz	Maud	May	4	Mar	1892	27	Mar	1892	Andrew D	Susanna	Leiby				Krum
B-1768	Leffler	Fred A	Dennis	8	Jan	1892	10	Apr	1892	Augustus	Elizabeth	Krum	Dennis	Rex	Emma	
B-1769	Flickinger	Lillie	Sophia	19	Feb	1892	22	Apr	1892	George W	Messina	Frohnheiser				
B-1770	Bartholomew	Carrie	May	26	Mar	1892	24	Apr	1892	Eugene M	Emma	Schuler				
B-1771	Hough	John	Allen	25	Feb	1890	23	Apr	1892	Martin A	Mary A	Miller				
B-1772	Eck	Calvin	Adam	26	Feb	1892	1	May	1892	William	Matilda	Kolb				
B-1773	Schappel			-	-	-	1	May	1892	Milton A	Sarah M	Rehrig		Rehrig		
B-1774	Ruch	Lillie	Messina	3	Apr	1892	15	May	1892	Charles	Fianna	Bowman	Messina			
B-1775	Steigerwalt	Emma	May	12	May	1892	12	June	1892	A F	Maria E	Bowman				
B-1776	Levan	William	Elmer	4	May	1892	23	June	1892	Frank	Lydia	Hill	Codilla	Saylor		
B-1777	Eberts	William	Walter	26	May	1892	26	June	1892	William	Lillie Missouri	Hontz	Frank	Sittler	Lydia	Eberts
B-1778	Ginder	Hannah	Meta	23	May	1892	10	July	1892	Charles A	Mary	Eck				
B-1779	Young	Elsie	May	6	June	1892	15	July	1892	Levi A	Emma Rebecca	Bachman				
B-1780	Nothstein	Etta	Luella	13	June	1892	17	July	1892	Milton	Emma J	Hoffman				
B-1781	Heintzelman	Alvin	Henry	18	Dec	1891	30	July	1892	Gideon	Ellen	Washburn				
B-1782	Heyser	Beuhla	Emily	23	May	1892	30	July	1892	Erwin	Hattie Estell	Gombert				
B-1783	Ruch	Freddie	Thomas	27	June	1892	7	Aug	1892	Harvey A	Ida E	Rex				
B-1784	Weidaw	Herby	Alvin	31	July	1892	10	Aug	1892	Samuel	Laura Matilda	Bamford				
B-1785	Solt	Arthur	Raymond	4	July	1892	14	Aug	1892	Jacob	Alice Savilla	Gombert				
B-1786	Nothstein	George	Henry	13	July	1892	20	Aug	1892	Henry Adam	Susanna Alvaretta	Miller				
B-1787	Andreas	Katie	Minerva	8	Aug	1892	4	Sept	1892	William Henry	Sussanna Elizabet	Ruch				
B-1788	Hoppes	Minnie	Louisa	17	July	1892	4	Sept	1892	Solomon D	Lovina	Zettelmoyer				
B-1789	Willman	Howard	Irwin	24	Aug	1892	15	Sept	1892	James Henry	Elmira	Miller				
B-1790	Rex	James	Daniel	4	Sept	1892	25	Sept	1892	Tighman F	Priscilla	Frantz				
B-1791	Rehrig	Catherine	Susanna	11	June	1892	25	Sept	1892	Lewis Henry	Catherine Jane	Beidelman	Catherine	Rehrig		
B-1792	Ratcliff	Myrtle	Virginia	4	Aug	1892	14	Oct	1892	Justus	Eliza	Mearhoff				
B-1793	Weaver	Minnie	Alvenia	28	June	1892	20	Oct	1892	Wilson August	Henrietta	Gombert				
B-1794	Bailey	Raymond	Clinton	-	-	-	20	Nov	1892	James S	Amanda	Neff				
B-1795	Romig	Isabella	May	22	Dec	1892	21	Jan	1893	Daniel F	Sally Ann	Schultz	Daniel L	Romig	Catherine	Hoffman
B-1796	Kremer	Essie	Laura	4	Feb	1893	7	Mar	1893	Tighman	Mary	Zehner				
B-1797	Gumbert	Welles	Penn	29	Jan	1893	7	Apr	1893	William P	Kate	Mertz				
B-1798	Gumbert	Sophia	-	25	Oct	1892	30	Apr	1893	Frank	Caroline	Cunfer				
B-1799	Gombert	Cecilia	May	27	Feb	1893	7	May	1893	Andrew J	Annie D	Long				
B-1800	Kistler	Bula	Polly	13	Apr	1893	14	May	1893	David Amandes	Alvena	Zimmerman				
B-1801	Gumbert	Daisie	Lillie May	24	Mar	1893	20	May	1893	Elmer	Alice Louisa	Beltz				
B-1802	Horn	Raymond	Edward	31	Oct	1892	21	Mar	1893	Oscar E	Alice Louisa	Sensinger				
B-1803	Fink	Lulu	Ada	31	Dec	1892	4	June	1893	Joseph W	Sarah	Fritzinger				
B-1804	Ashner	William	Raymond	3	May	1893	25	June	1893	James Franklin	Emma Jane	Schaeffer	William	Schaeffer	Sophia	Bourey

Beyond the Blue Mountain, Vol. II

Births and Baptisms

Line #	Surname	Child Given	Child Middle	Birth Day	Birth Mth	Birth Year	Baptism Day	Baptism Mth	Baptism Year	Father Given	Mother Given	Nee	Witness Given	Witness Surname	Witness Given	Witness Surname
B-1805	Rehrig	Mable	Jane	19	Feb	1893	8	July	1893	David	Anconetta	Webb				
B-1806	Shoemaker	Girtie	Estella	10	May	1893	9	July	1893	Charles M	Amanda Eliza	McFarland				
B-1807	Becker	Cassie	Valera	11	Feb	1893	9	July	1893	William Henry	Carolina Sewilla	Grow	Peter	Becker	July Ann	Freyman
B-1808	Geiger	Earl	Oliver	9	May	1893	18	July	1893	James A	Priscilla	Fritzinger				
B-1809	Lentz	Maud	Amanda	6	May	1893	22	July	1893	Edwin J	Ida	Moyer				
B-1810	Freyman	Girtie	Luella	13	May	1893	27	July	1893	Albertis J	Harriet	Freeby				
B-1811	Faust	Emma	Jane	22	Apr	1893	1	Aug	1893	Charles	Lizzie	Kunkle	Jacob	Arnold	Emma	Mclean
B-1812	Ohl	Harrison	Edgar	18	July	1893	13	Aug	1893	Jefferson	Malissa	Rex				
B-1813	Klotz	Emma	Rebecca	13	Feb	1893	10	Sept	1893	Robert H	Fannie	Dentinger				
B-1814	Zimmerman	Charles	Cleveland	10	Mar	1893	17	Sept	1893	Nathan	Harriet	Gerber				
B-1815	Hoffman	Mable	May	3	June	1893	1	Oct	1893	Charles	Annetta	Schaeffer	Lewis	Mantz	Polly	Zehner
B-1816	Snyder	Cleveland	-	-	-	1893	8	Oct	1893	Wallace O	Clara A J	Ebert				
B-1817	Andreas	Oliver	Charles	18	Nov	1893	24	Dec	1893	G E	Fianna	Rehrig				
B-1818	Albright	Ralph	Jacob	-	-	-	17	Jan	1894	John FH	Rosa A	Klotz				
B-1819	Ruch	Charles	Henry	30	Jan	1894	18	Feb	1894	Charles	Fianna Alevesta	Bowman	Susanna	Bowman		
B-1820	Gerber	Myrtle	Irene	19	Jan	1894	7	Mar	1894	Charles A	Mary Jane	Fether				
B-1821	McFarland	Elmer	Ulysses	6	Dec	1891	17	Apr	1894	John J	Fietta	Rex				
B-1822	McFarland	Vertie	Estella	4	Feb	1894	17	Apr	1894	John J	Fietta	Rex				
B-1823	Gerber	Williard	Emery	28	Feb	1894	21	Apr	1894	Franklin	Angie E	Eckert				
B-1824	Ginder	Warren	Calvin	12	Feb	1894	29	Apr	1894	John H	Hattie Annie	Eck				
B-1825	Semmel	Robert	Clayton	27	Apr	1894	27	May	1894	Granville Henry	Sallie Lovenah	Andrews				
B-1826	Schnella	Mollie	Grace	14	Dec	1893	13	June	1894	George A C	Cora	Johnson				
B-1827	Lorah	Mary	Matilda	26	July	1894	23	Aug	1894	Harrison	Kate	Guldner				
B-1828	Zimmerman	Ida	May	11	Aug	1894	29	Aug	1894	Nathan	Harriet	Gerber				
B-1829	Kerschner	Garrie	Alvin	10	Aug	1894	9	Sept	1894	Noah Albert	Henrietta Lucinda	Hontz				
B-1830	Fenner	Guy	Wilbur	8	Mar	1894	11	Sept	1894	Theodore F	Laura Anna	Miller				
B-1831	Mertz	Mable	Augusta	4	Aug	1894	15	Oct	1894	John R	Ellen L	Gombert				
B-1832	Solt	Girtie	Lydia Savannah	3	Mar	1894	15	Oct	1894	Jacob	Alice Savilla	Gombert				
B-1833	Gombert	Roy	Allen	30	Aug	1894	22	Oct	1894	Andrew J	Annie D	Long				
B-1834	Snyder	Howard	-	12	Oct	1894	4	Nov	1894	Charles	Sarah J	Freeby				
B-1835	Weaver	Meta	Augusta	15	Sept	1894	20	Dec	1894	Wilson August	Henrietta	Gombert				
B-1836	Gumbert	Bertha	Savannah	4	Dec	1894	20	Dec	1894	Frank	Caroline	Cunfer				
B-1837	Gumbert	Alvin	Henry	17	Oct	1894	1	Jan	1895	William P	Kate	Mertz	Henry	Gombert	Emaline	Hontz
B-1838	Cunfer	William	Lewis	5	Jan	1895	16	Feb	1895	Charles Lewis	Mena Amanda	Kuntz				
B-1839	Rehrig	Raymond	Augustus	5	Jan	1895	24	Feb	1895	Augustus	Ida E	Beltz				
B-1840	Flickinger	Raymond	George	29	Jan	1895	26	Feb	1895	George W	Messina	Frohnheiser				
B-1841	Lutz	Nathan	George	11	Dec	1894	3	Mar	1895	William	Mary A	Hoffman	Nathan	Hoffman	Lucy Anna	Fenstermacher
B-1842	Arnold	John	Jacob	12	Jan	1895	24	Mar	1895	Jacob J	Lizzie	Kunkle				
B-1843	Ginder	Pierce	Franklin	25	Feb	1878	3	Apr	1895	Alfred	Lydia	Lauchnor				
B-1844	Stahler	Calvin	James	8	Mar	1895	7	Apr	1895	William S	Clara L	Stoudt				
B-1845	Trumbore	Gussie	Leona	28	Jan	1895	18	Apr	1895	Edwin	July Ann	Klotz				
B-1846	Hough	Luella	Elizabeth	5	Feb	1895	28	Apr	1895	Martin	Mary	Miller				

Beyond the Blue Mountain, Vol. II

Births and Baptisms

Line #	Surname	Child Given	Middle	Birth Day	Mth	Year	Baptism Day	Mth	Year	Father Given	Mother Given	Nee	Witness Given	Surname	Witness Given	Surname
B-1847	Ginder	Minnie	Estella	21	Apr	1895	22	May	1895	Philip	Frances Isabella	Dreisbach				
B-1848	Fritzinger	Willie	Edgar	17	Feb	1895	9	June	1895	Edwin M	Emma F	Heffelfinger				
B-1849	Hendricks	Eva	May	14	Apr	1895	9	June	1895	R Jerome	Ida A	Weaver				
B-1850	Heintzelman	John	Clayton	7	May	1895	30	June	1895	Osvil M	Libbie A	Benninghoff				
B-1851	Schappel	Edna	May	8	July	1895	4	Aug	1895	Milton A	Sarah M	Rehrig				
B-1852	Lentz	Elmer	Stephen	13	June	1895	8	Aug	1895	Edwin J	Ida	Moyer				
B-1853	Gombert	Minerva	Tewilia	31	Mar	1895	12	Aug	1895	Elmer S	Alice Louisa	Beltz				
B-1854	David	William	Stanley	1	Aug	1895	28	Aug	1895	Albert	Rosa A	Rehrig	Emaline	David		
B-1855	Kemmerer	Blanchie	Estella	18	Aug	1895	7	Sept	1895	Henry Solomon	Lizzie	Bowman				
B-1856	Fritzinger	Helen	May	27	Aug	1895	4	Nov	1895		Jeanetta	Fritzinger				
B-1857	Gombert	Ruth	Alvenia	30	Sept	1895	1	Dec	1895	Andrew J	Annie D	Long				
B-1858	Riegel	Mabel	Luella	17	Feb	1895	22	Mar	1896	William E	Mary A	Steigerwalt				
B-1859	Semmel	Florence	Anna	6	Feb	1896	5	Apr	1896	Granville Henry	Sallie Lovenah	Andrews				
B-1860	Freeby	Darcy	May	29	Feb	1896	1	May	1896	Joseph	Jane Amanda	Frohnheiser				
B-1861	Freyman	Mabel	Esther	2	Mar	1896	7	May	1896	Albertis J	Harriet	Freeby				
B-1862	Schaefer	William	Daniel	12	Apr	1896	17	May	1896	William F	Josephine	Bourey	Daniel	Schaeffer	Sarah	Sendel
B-1863	Becker	Oscar	Franklin	7	May	1896	30	May	1896	William Henry	Carolina Savilla	Grow	Nathan	Grow	Sallie Ann	Hobbes
B-1864	Peter	Howard	Israel	15	Oct	1895	12	June	1896	Charles A	Margeret	Evert				
B-1865	Snyder	Robbie	-	18	Apr	1896	14	June	1896		Sarah J	Freeby				
B-1866	Bachman	Rayastor	-	3	May	1896	27	June	1896	Joseph E	Laura Jane	Freeby				
B-1867	Romig	Ervin	Victor	4	July	1896	26	July	1896	Victor James	Eva Agnes	Blose				
B-1868	Muthard	William	Leon	24	June	1896	17	Aug	1896	William H	Emma Elizabeth	David				
B-1869	Rickert	Raymond	Franklin	12	Apr	1896	25	Oct	1896	William L	Bessie	Ervin				
B-1870	Rehrig	Robert	Ralph	15	Sept	1896	23	nov	1896	Augustus	Ida E	Beltz				
B-1871	Keener	Floyd	William	3	Apr	1896	20	Dec	1896	Preston Calvin	Laura Ellen	Haintz	Adline	Haintz		
B-1872	Reichard	Minnie	Gertrude	21	Nov	1896	7	Jan	1897	James B	Clara Alice	Rehrig				
B-1873	Arnold	William	James	6	Mar	1897	16	Apr	1897	Jacob James	Lizzie	Kunkle				
B-1874	Moser	Raymond	Clare	14	Jan	1897	16	Apr	1897	Benjamin Franklii	Kitty Ann	Gombert				
B-1875	Weaver	Lula	Mable	2	Jan	1897	25	Apr	1897	Wilsor	Henrietta	Gombert				
B-1876	Sinyard	Pearl	Ruth	28	Dec	1896	8	May	1897	Mathew	Mary	Wertman				
B-1877	David	Helen	Sarah	12	May	1897	19	June	1897	Uriah	Jeanetta	Long				
B-1878	Gumbert	Oscar	Eugene	16	Feb	1897	25	June	1897	Frank	Caroline	Cunfer				
B-1879	David	Ella	May	3	June	1897	3	July	1897	Albert	Rosa A	Rehrig				
B-1880	George	Augustus	Franklin	5	July	1897	2	Aug	1897	Lewis	Ellamanda	Hahn				
B-1881	Ginder	Adam	Granville	6	July	1880	6	Aug	1897	Alfred	Lydia	Lauchnor				
B-1882	Klotz	Halena	Alda	31	May	1896	15	Aug	1897	Robert H	Fannie	Dentinger	Alda V	Marsh		
B-1883	Fritzinger	William	Adam	10	Aug	1897	25	Sept	1897	Francis	Mary Ann	Schott				
B-1884	Sherry	Virginia	Grace	10	Oct	1896	10	Oct	1897	Elwood H	Alice Louisa	Glace				
B-1885	Rex	Ruth	Helen	10	Sept	1897	17	Oct	1897	Elvin	Mary	Bechtel				
B-1886	Walters	Daisy	Orlean	3	Nov	1897	11	Dec	1897	Benjamin E	Dorah	Seeverson				
B-1887	Gombert	Helen	Sarah Medina	13	Aug	1897	9	Jan	1898	Elmer S	Alice Louisa	Beltz				
B-1888	Rehrig	Ida	Louisa	6	Oct	1897	8	Mar	1898	Aaron	Malinda	Fritzinger				

Beyond the Blue Mountain, Vol. II

Births and Baptisms

Line #	Surname	Child Given	Middle	Birth Day	Birth Mth	Birth Year	Baptism Day	Baptism Mth	Baptism Year	Father Given	Mother Given	Nee	Witness Given	Witness Surname	Witness Given	Witness Surname
B-1889	Andreas	Stanley	Jennings	3	Jan	1898	8	Apr	1898	James	Fietta	George				
B-1890	Frantz	Morgan	Irwin Owen	11	Feb	1898	24	Apr	1898	John H	Sophia	Heiser				
B-1891	Dreisbach	Margeret	Maria	1	Mar	1898	2	May	1898	Ervin	Ida Cecilia	Reichard				
B-1892	Rehrig	William	Francis	5	Apr	1898	1	June	1898	Noah	Anna Elizabe	Hollbach				
B-1893	Lentz	Minnie	Emma	17	July	1897	7	June	1898	Edwin J	Ida	Moyer				
B-1894	Riegel	Charlotte	Estella	4	May	1898	14	June	1898	William E	Mary A	Steigerwalt				
B-1895	Berger	Helen	Irene	17	June	1898	29	July	1898	John	Kate Alice	Stabelton				
B-1896	Fritzinger	Stanley	Dewey	26	July	1898	21	Aug	1898	Joseph H	Agnes	Ruch				
B-1897	Geiger	Wilbur	Allen	9	Sept	1897	15	Oct	1898	James A	Priscilla	Fritzinger				
B-1898	Cunfer	Irene	Gertrude	22	July	1898	23	Oct	1898	Charles Lewis	Mena Amanda	Kuntz				
B-1899	Ashner	George	Stanley	13	Aug	1898	31	Oct	1898	James F	Emma J	Schaeffer				
B-1900	Ohl	Edward	Joshua	10	Sept	1898	13	Nov	1898	George W	Cora Estella	Krum				
B-1901	Miller	Harry	Robert	28	Sept	1898	14	Nov	1898	Robert	Gussie E	Lentz				
B-1902	Rehrig	Mame	Alice	31	Oct	1898	26	Dec	1898	Augustus	Ida Irene	Beltz				
B-1903	Dreher	Clara	Estella	18	Oct	1898	27	Dec	1898	William	Elmira	Ginder	Antionetta	Ginder		
B-1904	Lazarus	Harry	Dewey	22	Aug	1898	19	Jan	1899	Harrison G	Sarah S	Sleider	Mary Ann	Sleider		
B-1905	Drumbore	Robert	William	21	Dec	1898	14	Mar	1899	Robert W	Irena	Houser				
B-1906	Arnold	Hattie	Pruella	23	Jan	1899	22	Mar	1899	Jacob James	Lizzie	Kunkle				
B-1907	Sinyard	Gertrude	Elda	3	Dec	1898	31	Mar	1899	John	Laura M	Sensinger				
B-1908	Sinyard	Jennie	Irene	2	Nov	1898	15	Apr	1899	Mathew	Mary	Wertman				
B-1909	Muthard	Nora	Jane	7	Nov	1898	17	Apr	1899	William H	Emma Elizabeth	David				
B-1910	Nothstein	Sadie	Julia Matilda	25	Jan	1898	22	Apr	1899	Milton	Emma J	Hoffman				
B-1911	Mertz	Hattie	May	11	July	1899	13	Aug	1899	Joseph	Alwilda	Lapp				
B-1912	Cunfer	Charles	John	22	July	1899	3	Sept	1899	Jacob	Emma Matilda	Freyman				
B-1913	Freeby	David	William	10	Aug	1899	3	Sept	1899	William J	Amanda E	Hartranft				
B-1914	Moulthrop	Cledous	Francis	11	Aug	1899	17	Sept	1899	Edgar Ulysses	Ella Jane	Campbell				
B-1915	Mertz	Harvey	Edgar	26	July	1899	14	Oct	1899	Samuel	Mantana	Stroup				
B-1916	Nothstein	Mande	Viola	3	Sept	1899	17	Nov	1899	Charles H	Ida Jane	Ebert				
B-1917	Ginder	Morris	Llewellyn	22	July	1899	24	Nov	1899	Philip	Francis Isabella	Dreisbach				
B-1918	Cunfer	Charles	Stephen	22	Nov	1899	15	Apr	1900	Charles Lewis	Mena Amanda	Kuntz				
B-1919	Hontz	Helena	Irene	7	Apr	1900	4	May	1900	Edwin	Ella Nora	Frantz				
B-1920	Freyman	Werner	Augusta	3	Feb	1900	10	May	1900	David	Mary A	Mertz				
B-1921	Freyman	Bertha	Lenora	9	Mar	1900	26	May	1900	Albertis J	Harriet	Freeby				
B-1922	Gumbert	Mable	Luella	30	Nov	1899	17	June	1900	Frank	Caroline	Cunfer				
B-1923	Rickert	William	Ervin	21	Sept	1899	22	July	1900	William L	Bessie	Ervin				
B-1924	Frantz	Marie	Amelia Margere	4	Feb	1900	12	Aug	1900	John H	Sophia E	Heiser	Amelia	Fruendt		
B-1925	Bachman	Gladys	Theadores	19	Mar	1899	2	Sept	1900	Francis E	Laura A	Weidaw				
B-1926	Muthard	Martha	Emaline	27	July	1900	5	Oct	1900	William H	Emma Elizabeth	David				
B-1927	Wertman	Mabel	Alline	8	Sept	1900	7	Oct	1900	Llewellyn Oscar	Minnie E	Reber				
B-1928	Krome	Raymond	Allen	11	Sept	1900	21	Oct	1900	Gust	Lillie	Semmel				
B-1929	Winter	Robert	Lewis	14	Aug	1900	22	Oct	1900	David A	Ivy M	Mohr				
B-1930	Sinyard	Russel	Walter	22	July	1900	13	Nov	1900	Mathew	Mary	Wertman				

Beyond the Blue Mountain, Vol. II

Births and Baptisms

Line #	Surname	Child Given	Middle	Birth Day	Birth Mth	Birth Year	Baptism Day	Baptism Mth	Baptism Year	Father Given	Mother Given	Nee	Witness Given	Witness Surname	Witness Given	Witness Surname
B-1931	Stamm	Elda	Elizabeth	13	May	1900	17	Nov	1900	William J	Mary J	Hill				
B-1932	Hawk	George	Franklin	26	Aug	1900	23	Nov	1900	Frank	Emma Elizabeth	Gombert				
B-1933	Funk	Charles	William	25	Oct	1900	2	Dec	1900	Samuel	Emma Elizabeth	Sendel				
B-1934	Andreas	Consuelo	Daisy	15	Oct	1900	16	Dec	1900	James	Fietta	George				
B-1935	Rehrig	Lula	Hulda	24	Nov	1900	27	Dec	1900	David	Anzonetta	Webb	Lizzie	Rehrig		
B-1936	Nothstein	Mary	Helen	24	Oct	1900	1	Jan	1901	Charles H	Ida Jane	Ebert	Emma S	Ebert		
B-1937	Rehrig	Helen	Esther	4	Nov	1900	8	Jan	1901	Augustus	Ida Irene	Beltz				
B-1938	Bachman	Mary	Ellen	24	Nov	1900	20	Jan	1901	Joseph E	Laura Jane	Freeby				
B-1939	Riegel	William	Edgar	25	Feb	1901	31	Mar	1901	William E	Mary A	Steigerwalt				
B-1940	Dreher	Russel	LeRoy	8	Dec	1900	14	Apr	1901	Clement	Adelia Elenora	Rehrig				
B-1941	Drumbore	Pauline	Margeret	15	Mar	1901	16	May	1901	Robert W	Irena	Houser				
B-1942	Ruch	Herald	Herbert	5	May	1901	30	May	1901	Ira	Ellemande Jane	Riegel				
B-1943	Frey	Hattie	Laneda	19	Mar	1901	3	June	1901	Jacob	Emma Louisa	Miller				
B-1944	Gombert	Masie	Mable	22	Oct	1900	3	July	1901	Elmer S	Alice Louisa	Beltz				
B-1945	Creitz	Mary	Catherine	11	July	1901	9	Sept	1901	Daniel A	Minnie	Smith				
B-1946	Graff	Maude	May	29	July	1901	19	Sept	1901	Jonathan W	Sallie V	Bachard	Emma	Frey		
B-1947	Cunfer	Clara	Elizabeth	2	Apr	1898	24	Oct	1901	John C	Mary L	David				
B-1948	Stemm	Jennie	Elizabeth	22	Oct	1901	23	Feb	1902	George E	Nora Irene	Hill				
B-1949	Freeby	Clifford	—	14	Feb	1902	22	Apr	1902	Joseph	Jane Amanda	Frohnheiser				
B-1950	Beltzner	Marion	Agnes	6	Apr	1902	24	May	1902	George	Minda	Wilbert	Charles W	Faust		
B-1951	Christman	Edna	Emma	26	Sept	1900	9	June	1902	Stewart	Emina	Bush				
B-1952	Salzman	Myrtle	Elizabeth	29	Apr	1902	14	June	1902	Edward H	Sarah Ellen	Frey	Emma	Frey		
B-1953	Gombert	Adam	Nathan	7	June	1902	27	July	1902	Elmer Sylvester	Alice Louisa	Beltz				
B-1954	Auge	Ella	Elizabeth	27	June	1902	14	Aug	1902	John A	Hattie	Grow	Ella	Hodge	Laura	Woolbert
B-1955	Kautzman	Bertha	Agnes	2	June	1902	31	Aug	1902	Oliver	Mary O	Heimbach				
B-1956	Kemerer	William	Henry	31	Dec	1901	1	Sept	1902	Rufus L	Ida	Nunamacher				
B-1957	Arnold	George	Jacob	26	May	1902	22	Nov	1902	Jacob J	Lizzie	Kunkle				
B-1958	Rehrig	Oliver	Gideon	18	Sept	1902	19	Dec	1902	Charles E	Carolina E	Fink				
B-1959	Webb	George	Henry	3	Feb	1902	28	Dec	1902	Victor Ellsworth	Mary Henrietta	Zindel				
B-1960	Nothstein	Warren	H	28	Feb	1902	14	Jan	1903	Charles H	Ida Jane	Ebert				
B-1961	Mertz	William	David	23	Dec	1902	27	Feb	1903	Samuel	Mantana	Straup				
B-1962	Cunfer	Hilda	Lauretta	9	Feb	1903	22	Mar	1903	Michael A	Lizzie Alice	Knepper	George	Follweiler	Amanda	Fenstermacher
B-1963	Hartranft	Robert	William	10	Jan	1903	6	May	1903	Jonathan	Sadie	Hoffman				
B-1964	Frantz	Paul	Owen	3	Apr	1903	16	May	1903	Lewis A	Ella E	Steigerwalt				
B-1965	Rehrig	Bessie	Grace	4	Apr	1903	31	Mar	1903	Augustus	Ida E	Beltz				
B-1966	Schofield	Marion	Amanda	4	May	1903	18	June	1903	William H	Ida Louisa	Fritzinger				
B-1967	Schlenker	Eva	Arlene	19	Mar	1903	21	June	1903	Albert M	Sallie Lovina	Freeby				
B-1968	Bachman	Daniel	Solomon	27	Apr	1903	21	June	1903	Joseph E	Laura Jane	Freeby				
B-1969	Andreas	Herbert	Valentine	14	Feb	1903	22	June	1903	James	Fietta	George				

Beyond the Blue Mountain: Vol. II Marriage Records

Bartholomew Marriages: "Copulatationen"   "ZEIT"   "Residenc"
April 13, 1862 to July 2, 1903

"Namen de Vierheiratheten"

Line	Groom Surname	Groom Given	Bride Surname	Bride Given	Day	Mth	Year	He from:	She from:
M-1	Hess	Thomas H	Nagel	Priscilla	13	Apr	1862	Nazareth, Nthptn	Nazareth, Nthptn
M-2	Bittenbender	Stephen	Fehnel	Hannah	7	Sept	1862	Moore Twp, Nthptn	Moore Twp, Nthptn
M-3	Schlitz	Levi	Bartholomew	Levina	30	Nov	1862	East Allen Twp, Nthptn	Moore Twp, Nthptn
M-4	Hoch	Stephen H	Heiny	Elizabeth Maria	15	Feb	1863	Bath, Nthptn	Beersville, Nthptn
M-5	Knauss	Mellen M	Lantee	Emma	26	Dec	1863	Plainfield Twp, Nthptn	Plainfield Twp, Nthptn
M-6	Gable	Mandes	Bartholomew	Sabina	28	Feb	1864	Cherryville, Nthptn	Dannersville, Nthptn
M-7	Dieter	William H	Mildenberger	Harriet	7	Aug	1864	Pennsville, Carbon	Moore Twp, Nthptn
M-8	Schlisler	Harrison	Leibenguth	Mary Ann	7	Aug	1864	Lehigh Twp, Nthptn	Lehigh Twp, Nthptn
M-9	Bartholomew	William	Bartholomew	Catherine	11	Aug	1864	Porter Twp, Clarion	Moore Twp, Nthptn
M-10	Bartholomew	David	Lubar	Mary	7	Oct	1864	Catasauqua, Lehigh	Stroudsburg, Monroe
M-11	Evans	William J	Bartholomew	Manda E	27	Oct	1864	Dannersville, Nthptn	Dannersville, Nthptn
M-12	Steinbrenner	Albrecht	Hontz	Lydia	21	Jan	1865	Lehighton, Carbon	Lehighton, Carbon
M-13	Foureider	Joseph	Snyder	Louisa Jane	14	Feb	1865	Mahoning Twp, Carbon	Mahoning Twp, Carbon
M-14	Heilman	Geo. Washingt	Kreitz	Susanna	19	Feb	1865	Lehighton, Carbon	East Penn Twp, Carbon
M-15	Otto	Joseph	Franciska	May	2	Mar	1865	Upper Towamensing, Carbon	Upper Towamensing, Carbon
M-16	Klotz	Jonathan	Scherer	Isabella	4	Mar	1865	Lower Towamensing Twp, Carbon	Lower Towamensing Twp, Carbon
M-17	Becker	Nicholas	Sandherr	Pauline	19	Mar	1865	Mauch Chunk, Carbon	Mauch Chunk, Carbon
M-18	Rehrig	John	Yenser	Rebecca	16	Apr	1865	East Penn Twp, Carbon	East Penn Twp, Carbon
M-19	Arner	William Harrisc	Snyder	Adeline Louisa	16	Apr	1865	Franklin Twp, Carbon	Franklin Twp, Carbon
M-20	Hawk	Amandus	Serfass	Rebecca	5	May	1865	Mottsville, Carbon	Albrightsville, Carbon
M-21	Anthony	Henry Tilghma	Gruber	Sarah	21	May	1865	Pennsville, Carbon	Pennsville, Carbon
M-22	Leibenguth	Franklin	Scheckler	Mary	27	May	1865	Lehighton, Carbon	Lehighton, Carbon
M-23	Farren	Charles	Hontz	Rebecca	4	June	1865	Lehighton, Carbon	Lehighton, Carbon
M-24	Bechtel	William	Rape	Elizabeth	11	June	1865	East Penn Twp, Carbon	East Mauch Chunk, Carbon
M-25	Bachman	Daniel	Balliet	Ellen	6	Aug	1865	East Penn Twp, Carbon	Heidelberg Twp, Lehigh
M-26	Moyer	Franklin	Bartholomew	Fyanna	15	Aug	1865	Lehighton, Carbon	Lehighton, Carbon
M-27	Zellner	Samuel	Rinerd	Ellen	20	Aug	1865	Lehighton, Carbon	Mauch Chunk, Carbon
M-28	Moulthrop	William HH	Trumbore	Priscilla	27	Aug	1865	South Lehighton, Carbon	South Lehighton, Carbon
M-29	Dengler	Isaac	Christman	Sarah	3	Oct	1865	East Penn Twp, Carbon	East Penn Twp, Carbon
M-30	Hontz	Moses	Graver	Sarah Ann	15	Oct	1865	Mahoning Twp, Carbon	Weissport, Carbon
M-31	Grow	William	Mertz	Anna Maria	7	Nov	1865	Mahoning Twp, Carbon	Mahoning Twp, Carbon
M-32	Sandherr	William	Armburster	Catherine	12	Nov	1865	Mauch Chunk, Carbon	Mauch Chunk, Carbon
M-33	Pettit	Robert	Rinker	Amanda	19	Nov	1865	Parryville, Carbon	Parryville, Carbon

Beyond the Blue Mountain: Vol. II

Marriage Records

Line	Groom Surname	Groom Given	Bride Surname	Bride Given	Day	Mth	Year	He from:	She from:
M-34	Graver	Martin	Moyer	Ellen	19	Nov	1865	Weissport, Carbon	Weissport, Carbon
M-35	Miller	Elias C	Zellner	Harriet	19	Nov	1865	West Penn Twp, Schuylkill	Mahoning Twp, Carbon
M-36	Stroup	Moses	Long	Caroline	20	Dec	1865	Lower Towamensing Twp, Carbon	Lynn Twp, Lehigh
M-37	Snyder	Washington	Schwartz	Sarah	5	Dec	1865	Lower Towamensing Twp, Carbon	Lower Towamensing Tw, Carbon
M-38	Levan	Hiram	Dreisbach	Maria	5	Dec	1865	Franklin Twp, Carbon	Franklin Twp, Carbon
M-39	Ziegenfuss	Levi	Anthony	Ellephina	16	Dec	1865	Lower Towamensing Twp, Carbon	Lehigh Twp, Nthptn
M-40	Kemery	Nathan	Patterson	Lucinda	19	Dec	1865	Lehighton, Carbon	Lehighton, Carbon
M-41	Blose	Peter	Buck	Mary	24	Dec	1865	Franklin Twp, Carbon	Lower Towamensing Tw, Carbon
M-42	Hawk	Linford S	Fritzinger	Elizabeth	25	Dec	1865	Allentown, Lehigh	Weissport, Carbon
M-43	Nunamacker	Frank. Washin;	Lower	Emalina	31	Dec	1865	Franklin Twp, Carbon	Lower Towamensing Tw, Carbon
M-44	Snyder	Aaron	Nothstein	Leannah	7	Jan	1866	Mahoning Twp, Carbon	Mahoning Twp, Carbon
M-45	Ziegenfuss	Charles	Strohl	Fayette	11	Feb	1866	Bethlehem, Lehigh	Lower Towamensing Tw, Carbon
M-46	Fuehree	William	Haupt	Susanna	11	Feb	1866	Lehighton, Carbon	Lehighton, Carbon
M-47	Trumbore	Joseph	Derr	Juliann	17	Feb	1866	Weatherly, Carbon	Weatherly, Carbon
M-48	Miller	Alexander	Haid	Mary	10	Mar	1866	Lehighton, Carbon	Penn Forest Twp, Carbon
M-49	Horn	Thomas J	Stroup	Refene	11	Mar	1866	Lehighton, Carbon	Franklin Twp, Carbon
M-50	Zellner	Henry	Adams	Catherine	1	Apr	1866	Mahoning Twp, Carbon	Lynn Twp, Lehigh
M-51	Knease	William	Gower	Maria	3	Apr	1866	West Penn Twp, Schuylkill	Lehighton, Carbon
M-52	Blose	Oliver	Boyer	Amanda	8	Apr	1866	Upper Towamensing, Carbon	Lower Towamensing Tw, Carbon
M-53	Rex	William R	Steigerwalt	Anjulina	23	Apr	1866	Lehighton, Carbon	East Penn Twp, Carbon
M-54	Farren	Daniel	O'Brian	Harriet	22	Apr	1866	Packerton, Carbon	Lehighton, Carbon
M-55	Sommet	Edwin Henry	Souers	Elmyra	13	May	1866	Packerton, Carbon	Weissport, Carbon
M-56	Shive	Alfred	Steigerwalt	Harriet	20	May	1866	Mahoning Twp, Carbon	East Penn Twp, Carbon
M-57	Miller	Marlon	Hollenbach	Alice	31	May	1866	Lehighton, Carbon	Lehighton, Carbon
M-58	Geggus	John	Haid	Louisa	2	June	1866	Lehighton, Carbon	Lehighton, Carbon
M-59	Mencke	Frederic	Hilden	Anna Francisca	3	June	1866	Lower Towamensing Twp, Carbon	Mahoning Twp, Carbon
M-60	Hough	Oliver	Kerschner	Bregitta	10	June	1866	Mahoning Twp, Carbon	Mahoning Twp, Carbon
M-61	Moyer	Daniel	Rex	Mary Elizabeth	14	June	1866	Lehighton, Carbon	Mahoning Twp, Carbon
M-62	Spoonheimer	Reuben	Kline	Lydia	23	June	1866	Lower Towamensing Twp, Carbon	Lower Towamensing Tw, Carbon
M-63	Yenser	James	Rehrig	Sarah	8	July	1866	East Penn Twp, Carbon	East Penn Twp, Carbon
M-64	Beidelman	Jacob H	Kantzman	Elizabeth	15	July	1866	Lower Towamensing Twp, Carbon	Lower Towamensing Tw, Carbon
M-65	Strohl	Adam	Gayler	Johanna	16	July	1866	Upper Towamensing, Carbon	Sugarloaf Twp, Luzerne
M-66	Serfass	Lewis	Getz	Elizabeth	19	July	1866	Penn Forest Twp, Carbon	Kidder Twp, Carbon
M-67	Lins	Joel	Rinker	Rebecca	21	July	1866	Tamaqua, Schuylkill	Tamaqua, Schuylkill
M-68	Ely	Frederic	Miller	Sarah	21	July	1866	Tamaqua, Schuylkill	Tamaqua, Schuylkill
M-69	Edinger	John N	Brutz	Mary	21	July	1866	White Haven, Luzerne	White Haven, Luzerne

Beyond the Blue Mountain: Vol. II

Marriage Records

Line	Groom Surname	Groom Given	Bride Surname	Bride Given	Day	Mth	Year	He from:	She from:
M-70	Lauchner	Edward	Simmon	Maria	27	July	1866	East Penn Twp, Carbon	Weatherly, Carbon
M-71	Weston	John	Foster	Mary	12	Aug	1866	Weissport, Carbon	Weissport, Carbon
M-72	Buck	James	Kuehner	Caroline	19	Aug	1866	Lower Towamensing Twp, Carbon	Lower Towamensing Twp, Carbon
M-73	Arner	Jacob M	Klinger	Anna	19	Aug	1866	Rahn Twp Schuylkill	West Penn Twp, Schuylkill
M-74	Snyder	David	Berkemeyer	Henrietta	19	Aug	1866	West Penn Twp, Schuylkill	Tamaqua, Schuylkill
M-75	Sherer	Edwin	Dreisbach	Ellemina	20	Aug	1866	Lower Towamensing Twp, Carbon	Lower Towamensing Twp, Carbon
M-76	Miller	John A	Brown	Mary A	26	Aug	1866	Lockport, Nthptn	Lower Towamensing Twp, Carbon
M-77	Rockel	Joseph	Miller	Mary Jane	27	Aug	1866	Eldred, Monroe	Weissport, Carbon
M-78	Strohl	Reuben	Hinger	Barbara	31	Aug	1866	Upper Towamensing, Carbon	Upper Towamensing, Carbon
M-79	Ruch	Elias	Sendal	Mary	2	Sept	1866	East Penn Twp, Carbon	East Penn Twp, Carbon
M-80	Beltz	Alexander	Miller	Amanda	2	Sept	1866	Mahoning Twp, Carbon	Mahoning Twp, Carbon
M-81	Walp	David	Schmehl	Sarah	3	Sept	1866	Upper Towamensing, Carbon	Polk Twp, Monroe
M-82	Berlin	Henry F	Arner	Anjulina	9	Sept	1866	Weissport, Carbon	Weissport, Carbon
M-83	Reynold	Noah	Miller	Mary Jane	13	Sept	1866	Weissport, Carbon	Weissport, Carbon
M-84	Shaw	Edward	Essex	Catherine Elizabeth	12	Sept	1866	Weissport, Carbon	Weissport, Carbon
M-85	Eberts	Peter	Miller	Mary	16	Sept	1866	Mahoning Twp, Carbon	Mahoning Twp, Carbon
M-86	Kromer	John	Sayer	Hannah	23	Sept	1866	Siegfried's Bridge, Nthptn	Moore Twp, Nthptn
M-87	Esrang	John	Sherer	Lucinda	30	Sept	1866	Lower Towamensing Twp, Carbon	Lower Towamensing Twp, Carbon
M-88	Hauck	Robert	Burger	Sarah Ann	1	Oct	1866	Kidder Twp, Monroe	Penn Forest Twp, Carbon
M-89	Kolb	John	Woolwert	Jane	6	Oct	1866	East Penn Twp, Carbon	East Penn Twp, Carbon
M-90	Dorwart	William	Shary	Harriet	6	Oct	1866	Lower Towamensing Twp, Carbon	Lower Towamensing Twp, Carbon
M-91	Behler	William	Blose	Matilda	7	Oct	1866	Lower Towamensing Twp, Carbon	Lower Towamensing Twp, Carbon
M-92	Rustay	Samuel	Gaidner	Mary	11	Oct	1866	East Mauch Chunk, Carbon	East Mauch Chunk, Carbon
M-93	Remaley	William	Kressley	Anna Louise	14	Oct	1866	Washington Twp, Lehigh	Heidelberg Twp, Lehigh
M-94	Lerch	Peter A	Romig	Mary Ann	16	Oct	1866	North Whitehall Twp, Lehigh	South Whitehall Twp, Lehigh
M-95	Mertz	Nathan	Freyman	Sarah Ann	15	Nov	1866	Mahoning Twp, Carbon	Mahoning Twp, Carbon
M-96	Koons	Willoughby	Kistler	Sarah	25	Nov	1866	Mahoning Twp, Carbon	Weisenberg, Lehigh
M-97	Miller	Charles	Otto	Caroline	2	Dec	1866	Weissport, Carbon	Weissport, Carbon
M-98	Bartholomew	Benjamin	Gamler	Anna	13	Dec	1866	Lehighton, Carbon	Allentown, Lehigh
M-99	Bartholomew	John	Serfass	Catherine	15	Dec	1866	Lehighton, Carbon	Lehighton, Carbon
M-100	Steigerwalt	Levi	Rex	Mary	16	Dec	1866	East Penn Twp, Carbon	West Penn Twp, Schuylkill
M-101	Rudolph	Jesse	Arner	Mary Ann	16	Dec	1866	Lower Towamensing Twp, Carbon	Lower Towamensing Twp, Carbon
M-102	Beers	Daniel	Kuehner	Luenda	23	Dec	1866	Mauch Chunk, Carbon	Lower Towamensing Twp, Carbon
M-103	Blose	Lewis	Brown	Isabella	25	Dec	1866	Lower Towamensing Twp, Carbon	Lower Towamensing Twp, Carbon
M-104	Zink	Tilghman	Schmoyer	Rebecca	25	Dec	1866	Franklin Twp, Carbon	Franklin Twp, Carbon
M-105	Bobst	Thomas	Roth	Edwilla	26	Dec	1866	East Mauch Chunk, Carbon	East Penn Twp, Carbon

Beyond the Blue Mountain: Vol. II

Marriage Records

Line	Groom Surname	Groom Given	Bride Surname	Bride Given	Day	Mth	Year	He from:	She from:
M-106	Eastman	Joseph	Weaver	Sarah	30	Dec	1866	Lower Towamensing Twp, Carbon	New Texas, Lehigh
M-107	Bachman	William	Miller	Sarah C	5	Jan	1867	East Penn Twp, Carbon	Mahoning Twp, Carbon
M-108	Sitler	Edward	Miller	Sarah	6	Jan	1867	Mahoning Twp, Carbon	Mahoning Twp, Carbon
M-109	Hahn	Edwin Henry	Dunlap	Elizabeth Jane	20	Jan	1867	Weissport, Carbon	Parryville, Carbon
M-110	Gottlob	George Christia	Hills	Lena	7	Feb	1867	Mauch Chunk, Carbon	Mauch Chunk, Carbon
M-111	Sandherr	William	Armbruster	Amelia	9	Feb	1867	Mauch Chunk, Carbon	Mauch Chunk, Carbon
M-112	Beer	Solomon	Dengler	Priscilla	11	Feb	1867	Berlinsville, Nthptn	East Penn Twp, Carbon
M-113	Field	Samuel F	Kern	Elvina	21	Feb	1867	Parryville, Carbon	Lower Towamensing Twp, Carbon
M-114	Fink	Thomas	Walk	Sarah Ann	24	Feb	1867	Lehighton, Carbon	Lower Towamensing Twp, Carbon
M-115	Ahner	Reuben	Hartman	Elizabeth	3	Mar	1867	Franklin Twp, Carbon	Franklin Twp, Carbon
M-116	Klinger	Lewis	Koch	Mary Elizabeth	23	Mar	1867	Butler Valley, Luzerne	Mahoning Twp, Carbon
M-117	Smith	Charles	Lentz	Amanda	31	Mar	1867	Mahoning Twp, Carbon	Lehighton, Carbon
M-118	Webb	Joseph S	Miller	Catherine	1	Apr	1867	Lehighton, Carbon	Lehighton, Carbon
M-119	Kolb	Jonas	Peter	Sarah	7	Apr	1867	East Penn Twp, Carbon	East Penn Twp, Carbon
M-120	Blose	Charles	Solt	Susanna	21	Apr	1867	Franklin Twp, Carbon	Lower Towamensing Twp, Carbon
M-121	Kressley	Daniel	Dilcher	Mary Ann	21	Apr	1867	Mahoning Twp, Carbon	Mahoning Twp, Carbon
M-122	Mantz	Lewis F	Wesner	Kitty Ann	27	Apr	1867	Lynn Twp, Lehigh	Lynn Twp, Lehigh
M-123	Walk	Augustus	Kunkle	Sabilla	5	May	1867	Franklin Twp, Carbon	Franklin Twp, Carbon
M-124	Pratt	John	Blackwell	Elizabeth	9	May	1867	Lehighton, Carbon	Lehighton, Carbon
M-125	Wirstein	Henry	Beltz	Elizabeth	12	May	1867	Mahoning Twp, Carbon	Franklin Twp, Carbon
M-126	Petri	William	Stroup	Esther	9	June	1867	Lower Towamensing Twp, Carbon	Franklin Twp, Carbon
M-127	Fenstermaker	Stephen	Snyder	Catherine	9	June	1867	Mahoning Twp, Carbon	West Penn Twp, Schuylkill
M-128	Rommel	Edwin	Flick	Anna Maria	9	June	1867	Allentown, Lehigh	Allentown, Lehigh
M-129	Semmel	David	Nothstein	Fyanna	16	June	1867	Mahoning Twp, Carbon	Mahoning Twp, Carbon
M-130	Kunkle	Enoch	Walker	Catherine	16	June	1867	Weissport, Carbon	Weissport, Carbon
M-131	Kuhns	David	Gilbert	Sarah	16	June	1867	Mahoning Twp, Carbon	Mahoning Twp, Carbon
M-132	Slight	Milton	Gower	Emma	22	June	1867	White Haven, Luzerne	White Haven, Luzerne
M-133	Bartholomew	Robert	Ritz	Anna Maria	22	June	1867	Lehighton, Carbon	Allentown, Lehigh
M-134	Olenwine	Charles	Kantzman	Caroline	22	June	1867	Franklin Twp, Carbon	Lower Towamensing Twp, Carbon
M-135	Zundle	Henry	Haines	Ellen	23	June	1867	East Mauch Chunk, Carbon	East Penn Twp, Carbon
M-136	Ginder	Alfred	Lauchnor	Lydia	30	June	1867	East Penn Twp, Carbon	Mahoning Twp, Carbon
M-137	Fritz	David	Bachman	Anna Maria	30	June	1867	Mahoning Twp, Carbon	Mahoning Twp, Carbon
M-138	Musselman	Thomas	Hunsicker	Emaline Elizabeth	30	June	1867	Mahoning Twp, Carbon	Mahoning Twp, Carbon
M-139	Webb	James	Shoemaker	Sarah Ann	8	July	1867	Lehighton, Carbon	Lehighton, Carbon
M-140	Shipe	Ephraim	Green	Amanda	16	July	1867	Lower Towamensing Twp, Carbon	Lower Towamensing Twp, Carbon
M-141	Rehrig	Martin R	Miller	Emma Susanna	18	July	1867	Mauch Chunk, Carbon	Mauch Chunk, Carbon

Beyond the Blue Mountain: Vol. II

Marriage Records

Line	Groom Surname	Given	Bride Surname	Given	Day	Mth	Year	He from:	She from:
M-142	Beltz	Thomas Benjai	Scheckler	Mary Jane	18	Aug	1867	Parryville, Carbon	Parryville, Carbon
M-143	Bowman	Wilson D	Arner	Caroline	25	Aug	1867	East Penn Twp, Carbon	West Penn Twp, Schuylkill
M-144	Sibbach	Philip Frederic	Campton	Anna Salinda	1	Sept	1867	East Mauch Chunk, Carbon	Mauch Chunk, Carbon
M-145	Weidaw	William	Strohm	Ellen	1	Sept	1867	Lehighton, Carbon	Lehighton, Carbon
M-146	Rothermel	Henry	Savage	Hannah	14	Sept	1867	Mahoning Twp, Carbon	East Penn Twp, Carbon
M-147	Hunsicker	Edwin	Esch	Eliza	15	Sept	1867	Lehighton, Carbon	Lehighton, Carbon
M-148	Wolf	William H	Ruger	Rhoda A	17	Sept	1867	White Haven, Luzerne	White Haven, Luzerne
M-149	Ruch	William	Arner	Louisa	6	Oct	1867	East Penn Twp, Carbon	West Penn Twp, Schuylkill
M-150	Boyer	Owen C	Kolb	Mary Jane	13	Oct	1867	Elldred, Monroe	East Penn Twp, Carbon
M-151	Millheim	William	Solt	Louisa	20	Oct	1867	Franklin Twp, Carbon	Franklin Twp, Carbon
M-152	Moyer	Lafayette	Rodger	Abigail	31	Oct	1867	Weissport, Carbon	Weissport, Carbon
M-153	Miller	Joseph R	Rex	Kitty Ann	9	Nov	1867	West Penn Twp, Schuylkill	West Penn Twp, Schuylkill
M-154	Meyer	Christian C H	Buckholtz	Caroline F J	28	Nov	1867	Mauch Chunk, Carbon	Mauch Chunk, Carbon
M-155	Kuhnsweiler	Catius	Lauth	Margaretha	8	Dec	1867	East Mauch Chunk, Carbon	East Mauch Chunk, Carbon
M-156	Stuckley	Jacob	DeFrehn	Hannah	15	Dec	1867	Lehighton, Carbon	Lehighton, Carbon
M-157	Ruch	Lewis	Mantz	Elizabeth	26	Dec	1867	East Penn Twp, Carbon	West Penn Twp, Schuylkill
M-158	Hahn	Enos	Smith	Catherine	4	Jan	1868	Lower Towamensing Twp, Carbon	Lower Towamensing Twp, Carbon
M-159	Millheim	Charles	Haines	Mary	11	Jan	1868	Parryville, Carbon	Parryville, Carbon
M-160	Kleintopp	James W	Walck	Amanda	11	Jan	1868	Lehighton, Carbon	Franklin Twp, Carbon
M-161	Shive	Edwin	Lauchnor	Abigail	12	Jan	1868	Mahoning Twp, Carbon	Mahoning Twp, Carbon
M-162	Strohl	William H	Grill	Mary Ann	2	Feb	1868	Lower Towamensing Twp, Carbon	Lower Towamensing Twp, Carbon
M-163	Heintzelman	Stephen	Kressley	Hannah Maria	8	Feb	1868	Slatington, Lehigh	Slatington, Lehigh
M-164	Peter	Cornelius	Rehrig	July Ann	11	Feb	1868	East Penn Twp, Carbon	East Penn Twp, Carbon
M-165	Fry	Samuel	Kemerer	Sabina	28	Mar	1868	Lehighton, Carbon	Lehighton, Carbon
M-166	May	Anthony	Goldberg	Wilhelmena	11	Apr	1868	Upper Towamensing, Carbon	Upper Towamensing, Carbon
M-167	Greasly	William F	Steigerwalt	Susanna	19	Apr	1868	East Penn Twp, Carbon	East Penn Twp, Carbon
M-168	Fritzinger	Charles H	Ziegler	Kitty Ann	19	Apr	1868	East Penn Twp, Carbon	West Penn Twp, Schuylkill
M-169	Graver	Owen	Solt	Fianna	5	May	1868	Weissport, Carbon	Franklin Twp, Carbon
M-170	Oplinger	Mifflin	Newhart	Elizabeth	9	May	1868	Cherryville, Nthptn	Mauch Chunk, Carbon
M-171	Donatt	David	Lieser	Hannah	10	May	1868	Lynn Twp, Lehigh	West Penn Twp, Schuylkill
M-172	Walck	David	Kunkle	Savannah	10	May	1868	Franklin Twp, Carbon	Franklin Twp, Carbon
M-173	Schwab	Edward	Buchman	Anjulina	14	May	1868	East Mauch Chunk, Carbon	East Mauch Chunk, Carbon
M-174	Broom	Charles	Mayer	Polly	15	May	1868	New York	Heidelberg Twp, Lehigh
M-175	Beer	Alexander	Mensing	Sarah Catherine	17	May	1868	Lower Towamensing Twp, Carbon	Lower Towamensing Twp, Carbon
M-176	Dunbar	James	Batman	Anna	30	May	1868	East Penn Twp, Carbon	East Penn Twp, Carbon
M-177	Strohl	Edwin	Serfass	Lydia Ann	31	May	1868	Upper Towamensing, Carbon	Upper Towamensing, Carbon

Beyond the Blue Mountain: Vol. II

Marriage Records

Line	Groom Surname	Groom Given	Bride Surname	Bride Given	Day	Mth	Year	He from:	She from:
M-178	Kuntz	John	Newhart	Lenah	2	June	1868	Cherryville, Nthptn	North Whitehall, Lehigh
M-179	Lentz	Edward	Mulhearn	Rosa Ann	7	June	1868	Lehighton, Carbon	Lehighton, Carbon
M-180	Eck	Nathan	Rex	Lydia	10	June	1868	East Penn Twp, Carbon	East Penn Twp, Carbon
M-181	Ramaly	Moses	Arner	Sarah M	14	June	1868	Lower Towamensing Twp, Carbon	Franklin Twp, Carbon
M-182	Eisenhower	Edwin	Flick	Mary Alice	14	June	1868	Lehighton, Carbon	Lehighton, Carbon
M-183	Fritzinger	Joseph M	Bartholomew	Sarah C	14	June	1868	Lehighton, Carbon	Weissport, Carbon
M-184	Grill	Samuel	McDaniel	Caroline	28	June	1868	Lower Towamensing Twp, Carbon	Lower Towamensing Twp, Carbon
M-185	Frantz	Godfrey	Rex	Anna Maria	28	June	1868	East Penn Twp, Carbon	Mahoning Twp, Carbon
M-186	Frank	George	Ram	Martha Elizabeth	28	June	1868	Hazelton, Luzerne	Hazelton, Luzerne
M-187	Dorwort	Francis	Walck	Abby Ann	12	July	1868	Franklin Twp, Carbon	Franklin Twp, Carbon
M-188	Xander	Charles Willian	Graver	Catherine Jane	26	July	1868	East Penn Twp, Carbon	East Mauch Chunk, Carbon
M-189	Klotz	William F	Henry	Lizzie B	1	Aug	1868	Weissport, Carbon	Weissport, Carbon
M-190	Zellner	Reuben Frankl	Blose	Mary Ann	16	Aug	1868	Heidelberg Twp, Lehigh	Lower Towamensing Twp, Carbon
M-191	Kolb	Nathan L B	Weidman	Anna	17	Aug	1868	East Penn Twp, Carbon	Philadelphia
M-192	Cain	John	Porter	Jane	10	Sept	1868	Parryville, Carbon	Parryville, Carbon
M-193	Clauss	Alfred	Horn	Zeniah	1	Oct	1868	Lehighton, Carbon	Lehighton, Carbon
M-194	Kolb	William	Clauss	Amanda	4	Oct	1868	East Penn Twp, Carbon	Mahoning Twp, Carbon
M-195	Serfass	Reuben	Britton	Carolina	7	Oct	1868	Tobehannna Twp, Monroe	Tobehanna Twp, Monroe
M-196	Mertz	William	Mertz	Joannah	13	Oct	1868	Mahoning Twp, Carbon	Mahoning Twp, Carbon
M-197	Snyder	Alexander	Shive	Rebecca	13	Oct	1868	Mahoning Twp, Carbon	Mahoning Twp, Carbon
M-198	Gangware	William	Bartholomew	Amanda	10	Nov	1868	Lehighton, Carbon	Lehighton, Carbon
M-199	Gommery	John	Horn	Anna M	19	Nov	1868	Mahoning Twp, Carbon	Mahoning Twp, Carbon
M-200	Koons	Jeremiah	Fenstermaker	Kitty	31	Nov	1868	Lehighton, Carbon	Heidelberg Twp, Lehigh
M-201	Wehr	Owen	Zimmerman	Ellen	13	Dec	1868	Mahoning Twp, Carbon	West Penn Twp, Schuylkill
M-202	Fenner	Oswald Hugo	Hills	Magdalena	14	Dec	1868	Mauch Chunk, Carbon	Mauch Chunk, Carbon
M-203	Miller	Charles	Scheirer	Babet	24	Dec	1868	Weissport, Carbon	Weissport, Carbon
M-204	Mantz	William H	Dilcher	Susanna	25	Dec	1868	Mahoning Twp, Carbon	Mahoning Twp, Carbon
M-205	Kunkle	Harrison	Dory	Amanda	25	Dec	1868	Kidder Twp, Monroe	Kidder Twp, Monroe
M-206	Remaly	William	Hontz	Sarah Jane	25	Dec	1868	Slatington, Lehigh	Mahoning Twp, Carbon
M-207	Snyder	Charles Edwar	Kinney	Mary Alice	25	Dec	1868	Rockport, Carbon	Rockport, Carbon
M-208	Bowman	Rodger	Jones	Sarah	25	Dec	1868	Lower Towamensing Twp, Carbon	East Penn Twp, Carbon
M-209	Fenstermacher	John	Weida	Rebecca	28	Dec	1868	Lower Towamensing Twp, Carbon	Lower Towamensing Twp, Carbon
M-210	Blose	Oliver	Stroup	Emma R	24	Jan	1869	Lower Towamensing Twp, Carbon	Lower Towamensing Twp, Carbon
M-211	McFarland	Edward	Rice	Ellenore	31	Jan	1869	Lower Towamensing Twp, Carbon	Upper Towamensing, Carbon
M-212	Schnell	Reuben	Dengler	Louisa	7	Feb	1869	Lower Towamensing Twp, Carbon	East Penn Twp, Carbon
M-213	Brown	Jacob	Green	Matilda	21	Feb	1869	Upper Towamensing, Carbon	Upper Towamensing, Carbon

Beyond the Blue Mountain: Vol. II

Marriage Records

Line	Groom Surname	Given	Bride Surname	Given	Day	Mth	Year	He from:	She from:
M-214	Mensing	Ammon	Shaefer	Jane L	21	Feb	1869	Lower Towamensing Twp, Carbon	Lower Towamensing Twp, Carbon
M-215	Rauch	Peter K	Miller	Polly	23	Feb	1869	Mahoning Twp, Carbon	Mahoning Twp, Carbon
M-216	Horn	Levi	Snyder	Martha	11	Mar	1869	Weissport, Carbon	Weissport, Carbon
M-217	Kistler	Jacob B P	Kern	Sarah A	21	Mar	1869	Allentown, Lehigh	Lower Towamensing Twp, Carbon
M-218	Bachman	Daniel	Dengler	Hannah	28	Mar	1869	Weatherly, Carbon	Mauch Chunk, Carbon
M-219	Trainer	John	Remely	Susan	11	Apr	1869	Lehighton, Carbon	Lehighton, Carbon
M-220	Heilman	Geo. Washingt	Frohnheiser	Mary	13	Apr	1869	Lehighton, Carbon	Lehighton, Carbon
M-221	Fritzinger	Francis	Bartholomew	Melinda	24	Apr	1869	Packerton, Carbon	Lehighton, Carbon
M-222	Walck	Philip	Larose	Mary	4	May	1869	Franklin Twp, Carbon	Franklin Twp, Carbon
M-223	Beck	Alfred	Moser	Amanda	16	May	1869	East Penn Twp, Carbon	Mahoning Twp, Carbon
M-224	Moyer	John	Whiteman	Maria	17	May	1869	Franklin Twp, Carbon	Franklin Twp, Carbon
M-225	Baumgarten	Anthony	Gilen	Sarah	22	May	1869	Parryville, Carbon	Parryville, Carbon
M-226	Arner	John H	Wehr	Mary	24	May	1869	Mahoning Twp, Carbon	Mahoning Twp, Carbon
M-227	O'Brian	Samuel	Kust	Anconetta	25	May	1869	Lehighton, Carbon	Weissport, Carbon
M-228	Trumbore	Nathan	Dreher	Ellen	6	June	1869	Lehighton, Carbon	Lehighton, Carbon
M-229	Weida	Aaron	Adams	Henrietta	13	June	1869	Lower Towamensing Twp, Carbon	Lower Towamensing Twp, Carbon
M-230	Leh	Alfred	Moyer	Clara	1	July	1869	Catasauqua, Lehigh	Franklin Twp, Carbon
M-231	Ramaly	Henry	Stroup	Willmine	18	July	1869	Lower Towamensing Twp, Carbon	Parryville, Carbon
M-232	Grill	John	Kuehner	Alice	1	Aug	1869	Lower Towamensing Twp, Carbon	Lower Towamensing Twp, Carbon
M-233	Walck	William	Selzer	Harriet	1	Aug	1869	Franklin Twp, Carbon	Franklin Twp, Carbon
M-234	Sleider	Edward	Beltz	Mary Ann	8	Aug	1869	Franklin Twp, Carbon	Franklin Twp, Carbon
M-235	Daring	Adolph	Boll	Emma	21	Aug	1869	East Mauch Chunk, Carbon	Mauch Chunk, Carbon
M-236	Ginder	Lewis	Walter	Maria	22	Aug	1869	East Penn Twp, Carbon	Heidelberg Twp, Lehigh
M-237	Smith	Franklin	Haid	Elizabeth	29	Aug	1869	Penn Forest Twp, Carbon	Penn Forest Twp, Carbon
M-238	Brown	Lewis	Cope	Mary Amanda	12	Sept	1869	Lower Towamensing Twp, Carbon	Upper Towamensing, Carbon
M-239	Evert	John	Fulton	Mary Jane	12	Sept	1869	Mahoning Twp, Carbon	Mahoning Twp, Carbon
M-240	Strassburger	Jacob	Moyer	Elphina	16	Sept	1869	Weissport, Carbon	Weissport, Carbon
M-241	Brong	Jacob	Graver	Anna Maria	28	Sept	1869	Weatherly, Carbon	Weissport, Carbon
M-242	Grim	Charles	Gerber	Mary	10	Oct	1869	West Penn Twp, Schuylkill	Lehighton, Carbon
M-243	George	Charles	McDaniel	Elamantina	10	Oct	1869	Eldred, Monroe	Lower Towamensing Twp, Carbon
M-244	Klotz	Benjamin Fran	Nothstein	Harriet	11	Oct	1869	Lehighton, Carbon	Mahoning Twp, Carbon
M-245	Seiler	Samuel	Graver	Elizabeth	14	Oct	1869	Packerton, Carbon	Lehighton, Carbon
M-246	Scherer	Martin	Scheible	Christiana	24	Oct	1869	Mahoning Twp, Carbon	Mauch Chunk, Carbon
M-247	Sendel	A. B.	Nesley	Hannah F	30	Oct	1869	Mauch Chunk, Carbon	Mauch Chunk, Carbon
M-248	Reihman	Herman	Armbruster	Minnie	7	Nov	1869	East Mauch Chunk, Carbon	East Mauch Chunk, Carbon
M-249	Grow	Henry	Cochran	Sally Ann	14	Nov	1869	Mahoning Twp, Carbon	Mahoning Twp, Carbon

Marriage Records

Line	Groom Surname	Groom Given	Bride Surname	Bride Given	Day	Mth	Year	He from:	She from:
M-250	Boyer	John F	Scherer	Anna	21	Nov	1869	Lower Towamensing Twp, Carbon	Lower Towamensing Twp, Carbon
M-251	Heintzelman	Levi	Fenstermacher	Sophia	5	Dec	1869	Lynn Twp, Lehigh	Lynn Twp, Lehigh
M-252	Steigerwalt	Reuben	David	Fianna	12	Dec	1869	East Penn Twp, Carbon	East Penn Twp, Carbon
M-253	Schoch	Daniel	Neff	Maria	12	Dec	1869	East Penn Twp, Carbon	East Penn Twp, Carbon
M-254	Dunbar	Samuel	Smoyer	Catherine Aquilla	14	Dec	1869	Parryville, Carbon	Parryville, Carbon
M-255	Schaefer	Charles	Stroup	Amelia	19	Dec	1869	Towamensing, Carbon	Lower Towamensing Twp, Carbon
M-256	Hundeshagen	Frederich	Klein	Wilhelmina	25	Dec	1869	Lehighton, Carbon	East Mauch Chunk, Carbon
M-257	Stermer	John	Wehr	Flora	26	Dec	1869	Mahoning Twp, Carbon	Heidelberg Twp, Lehigh
M-258	Frederic	William	Grow	Eliza	30	Dec	1869	Mahoning Twp, Carbon	Mahoning Twp, Carbon
M-259	Geggus	Lewis	Delp	Salome	8	Jan	1870	Lehighton, Carbon	New Britain, Bucks
M-260	Ziegenfuss	Nathan	Sensinger	Emaline	9	Jan	1870	Franklin Twp, Carbon	Heidelberg Twp, Lehigh
M-261	Beer	Alfred	Hagenbuch	Rosanna	9	Jan	1870	Lower Towamensing Twp, Carbon	Lower Towamensing Twp, Carbon
M-262	Esrang	John	Brown	Ellen	17	Jan	1870	Weissport, Carbon	Weissport, Carbon
M-263	Kemerer	W. E	Smith	Susanna	22	Jan	1870	Towamensing, Carbon	Towamensing, Carbon
M-264	Hahn	James William	Wagner	Elizabeth	3	Feb	1870	Plainfield Twp, Nthptn	Plainfield Twp, Nthptn
M-265	Markley	Tilghman	Dorwort	Elizabeth	10	Feb	1870	Mauch Chunk, Carbon	Franklin Twp, Carbon
M-266	Yohe	Alfred J	Krum	Elizabeth Jane	10	Feb	1870	Lehighton, Carbon	Weissport, Carbon
M-267	Schwartz	George	Bailey	Kate	13	Feb	1870	Bowmansville, Carbon	East Penn Twp, Carbon
M-268	Gombert	Nathan	Krum	Medina	26	Feb	1870	Mahoning Twp, Carbon	Mahoning Twp, Carbon
M-269	Rabenold	Tilghman	Frederic	Catherine	27	Feb	1870	Mahoning Twp, Carbon	Mahoning Twp, Carbon
M-270	Roth	John Tilghman	Bush	Mary Jane	27	Feb	1870	Weissport, Carbon	Lobachsville, Nthptn
M-271	Fritzinger	William	Blose	Lucy	1	Mar	1870	Franklin Twp, Carbon	Franklin Twp, Carbon
M-272	Frantz	Owen	Campsie	Margeret	13	Mar	1870	Mahoning Twp, Carbon	Mahoning Twp, Carbon
M-273	Weida	Thomas Alfred	Shirer	Priscilla	17	Mar	1870	Weissport, Carbon	Weissport, Carbon
M-274	Benninger	Wilson	Wher	Lucy	20	Mar	1870	Slatington, Lehigh	Mahoning Twp, Carbon
M-275	Remaly	Charles	Rabenold	Emma Elizabeth	26	Mar	1870	Mahoning Twp, Carbon	Mahoning Twp, Carbon
M-276	Andrew	Edwin	Boyer	Catherine	27	Mar	1870	Lower Towamensing Twp, Carbon	Lower Towamensing Twp, Carbon
M-277	Kelchner	Edward	Ramaley	Lydia	3	Apr	1870	Lower Towamensing Twp, Carbon	Lower Towamensing Twp, Carbon
M-278	Mencke	Friederich	Schmidt	Elizabeth	11	Apr	1870	Lower Towamensing Twp, Carbon	Lower Towamensing Twp, Carbon
M-279	Lauchnor	John	Trine	Harriet	16	Apr	1870	Mahoning Twp, Carbon	Mahoning Twp, Carbon
M-280	Nothstein	Alvin	Lauchnor	Susanna	17	Apr	1870	East Penn Twp, Carbon	Mahoning Twp, Carbon
M-281	Messinger	Frederic	Leukle	Elizabeth	1	May	1870	Franklin Twp, Carbon	Franklin Twp, Carbon
M-282	Kromer	Irwin	Hartman	Martha	1	May	1870	Franklin Twp, Carbon	Franklin Twp, Carbon
M-283	Peter	Wilson	Wells	Catherine	4	June	1870	Lehighton, Carbon	Lehighton, Carbon
M-284	Shoenberger	Benjamin Fran	Stroup	Eliza Jane	6	June	1870	Lower Towamensing Twp, Carbon	Lower Towamensing Twp, Carbon
M-285	Rex	William H	Kemerer	Catherine	9	June	1870	Lehighton, Carbon	Mahoning Twp, Carbon

Beyond the Blue Mountain: Vol. II

Marriage Records

Line	Groom Surname	Given	Bride Surname	Given	Day	Mth	Year	He from:	She from:
M-286	Youngkin	Robert J	Christman	Barbara	9	June	1870	Upper Towamensing, Carbon	Penn Forest Twp, Carbon
M-287	Zellner	Joseph	Vangilder	Minnie E	19	June	1870	East Mauch Chunk, Carbon	East Mauch Chunk, Carbon
M-288	Haintz	William F	Stuckley	Adline	21	June	1870	East Penn Twp, Carbon	Mahoning Twp, Carbon
M-289	Fritzinger	John	Kershner	Rebecca	2	July	1870	Lehighton, Carbon	Mahoning Twp, Carbon
M-290	Flickinger	Nathan	Kershner	Louisa	3	July	1870	Mahoning Twp, Carbon	Mahoning Twp, Carbon
M-291	Zeiser	Lorenz	Dreisbach	Harriet	6	July	1870	Lower Towamensing Twp, Carbon	Lower Towamensing Twp, Carbon
M-292	Rolfink	John	Rabe	Ellen	17	July	1870	East Mauch Chunk, Carbon	East Mauch Chunk, Carbon
M-293	Alspach	E. W.	Reed	Louisa	17	July	1870	Tamaqua, Schuylkill	Tamaqua, Schuylkill
M-294	Riffert	Andrew E	Deibert	Alwilda	21	July	1870	Lehighton, Carbon	Lehighton, Carbon
M-295	Schuyler	Hiram	Flickinger	Angeline	23	July	1870	Slatington, Lehigh	East Penn Twp, Carbon
M-296	Rapp	Joseph C	Miller	Sevilla	23	July	1870	Weissport, Carbon	Mahoning Twp, Carbon
M-297	Guldner	Henry	Rehrig	Sarah	30	July	1870	Tannery, Luzerne	Tannery, Luzerne
M-298	Wehr	Joseph	Balliet	Polly H	7	Aug	1870	West Penn Twp, Schuylkill	West Penn Twp, Schuylkill
M-299	Solt	Henry	Hahn	Amelia	20	Aug	1870	Franklin Twp, Carbon	Franklin Twp, Carbon
M-300	Hahn	Edwin	Weber	Emma	20	Aug	1870	Franklin Twp, Carbon	Franklin Twp, Carbon
M-301	Kester	Reuben J	Leibenguth	Matilda	21	Aug	1870	Lehigh Twp, Nthptn	Lehigh Gap, Carbon
M-302	Eisenhauer	Franklin	Bartholomew	Christianna	28	Aug	1870	Lehighton, Carbon	Weissport, Carbon
M-303	Holenbach	Elias F	Wells	Mary Ann	10	Sept	1870	Lehighton, Carbon	Lehighton, Carbon
M-304	Miller	James D	Osewalt	Rebecca	17	Sept	1870	Mahoning Twp, Carbon	West Penn Twp, Schuylkill
M-305	Miller	William F	Moyer	Mary Elizabeth	30	Sept	1870	Mahoning Twp, Carbon	Mahoning Twp, Carbon
M-306	Pettit	John F	Kepser	Helena	1	Oct	1870	Parryville, Carbon	Redington, Nthptn
M-307	Rohrbach	Abel	Green	Rebecca	12	Oct	1870	Catasauqua, Lehigh	Bowmansville, Carbon
M-308	Rimbey	John H	Koons	Angeline	16	Oct	1870	East Mauch Chunk, Carbon	East Mauch Chunk, Carbon
M-309	Bever	Alfred	Shadle	Rosa	16	Oct	1870	Weissport, Carbon	Lehighton, Carbon
M-310	Muschlitz	Wilson	Andrew	Emma	23	Oct	1870	Lower Towamensing Twp, Carbon	Lower Towamensing Twp, Carbon
M-311	Strong	James	Houseworth	Maggie	23	Oct	1870	Nockamisom Twp, Bucks	Nockamisom Twp, Bucks
M-312	Heilman	Nathan	Balliet	Amanda	25	Oct	1870	Lehighton, Carbon	Lehighton, Carbon
M-313	Reed	Aquilla E	Fritzinger	Maria L	30	Oct	1870	Weissport, Carbon	Parryville, Carbon
M-314	Reber	William Henry	Hettner	Kitty Ann	5	Nov	1870	Washington Twp, Lehigh	East Penn Twp, Carbon
M-315	Dreisbach	Aaron	Wher	Louisa	10	Dec	1870	Mahoning Twp, Carbon	Mahoning Twp, Carbon
M-316	Montz	Cassius	Rinker	Cassandra J	18	Dec	1870	Parryville, Carbon	Parryville, Carbon
M-317	Billheimer	Cornelius Cyru:	Krock	Lizzie	24	Dec	1870	Moore Twp, Nthptn	Moore Twp, Nthptn
M-318	Peter	Wallace I	Fritz	Hannah	24	Dec	1870	Lehighton, Carbon	Lehighton, Carbon
M-319	Trine	John	Peter	Polly	25	Dec	1870	Lehighton, Carbon	North Whitehall, Lehigh
M-320	Kemerer	Charles	Gilbert	Elizabeth	26	Dec	1870	Lehighton, Carbon	West Penn Twp, Schuylkill
M-321	Grow	Jonathan	Frederic	Elizabeth	29	Dec	1870	Mahoning Twp, Carbon	Mahoning Twp, Carbon

Beyond the Blue Mountain: Vol. II

Marriage Records

Line	Groom Surname	Groom Given	Bride Surname	Bride Given	Day	Mth	Year	He from:	She from:
M-322	Moser	Lewis	Miller	Kitty Ann	14	Jan	1871	Mahoning Twp, Carbon	Mahoning Twp, Carbon
M-323	Rabe	Michael	Rootman	Anna Maria Rebecca	20	Jan	1871	East Mauch Chunk, Carbon	East Mauch Chunk, Carbon
M-324	Trainer	Alfred	Gombert	Caroline	30	Jan	1871	Lehighton, Carbon	West Penn Twp, Schuylkill
M-325	Leimbach	John	Patterson	Mary Alice	4	Feb	1871	Lehighton, Carbon	Lehighton, Carbon
M-326	Rehrig	Reuben	Ruch	Emaline	5	Feb	1871	East Penn Twp, Carbon	East Penn Twp, Carbon
M-327	Fritzinger	John W	Kibbler	Lucy	11	Feb	1871	Packerton, Carbon	Lehighton, Carbon
M-328	Snyder	Nathan	George	Maria	12	Feb	1871	Lynn Twp, Lehigh	North Penn
M-329	Newhart	Michael	Simmon	Sarah	26	Feb	1871	Allen Twp, Nthptn	Allen Twp, Nthptn
M-330	Olenwine	Simeon	Whiteman	Mary Ann	1	Mar	1871	Lower Towamensing Twp, Carbon	East Penn Twp, Carbon
M-331	Grow	Nathan	Hobbes	Sarah	12	Mar	1871	Mahoning Twp, Carbon	Mahoning Twp, Carbon
M-332	Miller	William F	Fink	Flory Ann	16	Mar	1871	Heidelberg Twp, Lehigh	Heidelberg Twp, Lehigh
M-333	Rex	Alfred	Freyman	Sally Elmira	16	Mar	1871	Lehighton, Carbon	Mahoning Twp, Carbon
M-334	Beck	Charles A	Frantz	Sophia	18	Mar	1871	Lehighton, Carbon	Lehighton, Carbon
M-335	Haupt	Nathan	Klotz	Alavesta	28	Mar	1871	Lehighton, Carbon	Lehighton, Carbon
M-336	Hunsicker	Owen	Kistler	Sarah Catherine	3	Apr	1871	Mahoning Twp, Carbon	East Penn Twp, Carbon
M-337	Wartman	Daniel P	Shaffer	Eliza Jane	9	Apr	1871	West Penn Twp, Schuylkill	West Penn Twp, Schuylkill
M-338	Schwartz	Henry	Moser	Emaline	15	Apr	1871	Lehighton, Carbon	Mahoning Twp, Carbon
M-339	Beltz	Henry	Bock	Levina	30	Apr	1871	Lower Towamensing Twp, Carbon	Lower Towamensing Twp, Carbon
M-340	Schnell	Oliver	Rhoad	Priscilla	9	May	1871	Franklin Twp, Carbon	Franklin Twp, Carbon
M-341	Gilbert	Joseph	Reeser	Kate	28	May	1871	West Penn Twp, Schuylkill	West Penn Twp, Schuylkill
M-342	Boyer	Alexander	Remely	Elizabeth	4	June	1871	Lower Towamensing Twp, Carbon	Parryville, Carbon
M-343	Silfies	Jacob	Solt	Amanda	4	June	1871	Franklin Twp, Carbon	Franklin Twp, Carbon
M-344	Rehrig	Thomas	Frey	Alice N	6	June	1871	Mahoning Twp, Carbon	East Penn Twp, Carbon
M-345	Fritzinger	Tilghman	Goodheil	Anzonetta	13	June	1871	Heidelberg Twp, Lehigh	Lower Towamensing Twp, Carbon
M-346	Beltz	David	Koons	Mary Jane	15	June	1871	East Mauch Chunk, Carbon	East Mauch Chunk, Carbon
M-347	Gombert	James	Mertz	Ellen	25	June	1871	Mahoning Twp, Carbon	Mahoning Twp, Carbon
M-348	Boyer	L. W.	Ash	Amanda	16	July	1871	Millport, Carbon	Millport, Carbon
M-349	Reichard	Aaron	Nothstein	Ellen	27	Aug	1871	Weissport, Carbon	East Penn Twp, Carbon
M-350	Rute	Benjamin	Shive	Sarah	10	Sept	1871	East Mauch Chunk, Carbon	East Mauch Chunk, Carbon
M-351	Bruekres	George	Hills	Anna Maria	14	Sept	1871	Mauch Chunk, Carbon	Mauch Chunk, Carbon
M-352	Auge	John	Zahn	Susan	17	Sept	1871	Mahoning Twp, Carbon	Butler Valley, Luzerne
M-353	Remaley	Tilghman	Hankey	Anna Maria	24	Sept	1871	Franklin Twp, Carbon	North Whitehall, Lehigh
M-354	Schwab	Lewis Alfred	Barwick	Savilla	24	Sept	1871	East Mauch Chunk, Carbon	East Mauch Chunk, Carbon
M-355	Rehrig	Lewis H	Beidelman	Catherine Jane	1	Oct	1871	East Penn Twp, Carbon	Lower Towamensing Twp, Carbon
M-356	Raber	John	Eaches	Henrietta	5	Oct	1871	Franklin Twp, Carbon	Franklin Twp, Carbon
M-357	Blose	Samuel	Becker	Mary	5	Oct	1871	Parryville, Carbon	Parryville, Carbon

Beyond the Blue Mountain: Vol. II

Marriage Records

Line	Groom Surname	Groom Given	Bride Surname	Bride Given	Day	Mth	Year	He from:	She from:
M-358	Eckhart	Joseph	Shoneberger	Sabina	7	Oct	1871	Lower Towamensing Twp, Carbon	Lower Towamensing Twp, Carbon
M-359	German	Franklin H	Boyer	Priscilla	12	Oct	1871	Lehighton, Carbon	Weissport, Carbon
M-360	Reichard	Allen	Horn	Isabella	15	Oct	1871	East Penn Twp, Carbon	Mahoning Twp, Carbon
M-361	Schmieskors	Henry	Gower	Dianna	28	Oct	1871	Penn Haven, Carbon	Penn Haven, Carbon
M-362	Beer	Francis W	Blose	Wilmina	29	Oct	1871	Lower Towamensing Twp, Carbon	Lower Towamensing Twp, Carbon
M-363	Leukle	William	Walck	Priscilla	12	Nov	1871	Franklin Twp, Carbon	Franklin Twp, Carbon
M-364	Fritz	John	Wertman	Priscilla	26	Nov	1871	East Penn Twp, Carbon	West Penn Twp, Schuylkill
M-365	Fisher	Newton B	Rehrig	Mary A	2	Dec	1871	Tannery, Luzerne	Parryville, Carbon
M-366	Faust	Adam	Confer	Sarah	10	Dec	1871	Union Twp, Schuylkill	Mahoning Twp, Carbon
M-367	Guldner	Levi	Kressley	Sarah Amanda	24	Dec	1871	East Penn Twp, Carbon	East Penn Twp, Carbon
M-368	Riegel	John	Miller	Amanda	25	Dec	1871	Mahoning Twp, Carbon	Mahoning Twp, Carbon
M-369	Snyder	Stephen	Sherer	Susan	20	Jan	1872	Lehigh Twp, Nthptn	Lower Towamensing Twp, Carbon
M-370	Beer	Daniel	Walck	Rebecca	4	Feb	1872	White Haven, Luzerne	Lower Towamensing Twp, Carbon
M-371	Follweiler	J. B.	Schwartz	Josephine	5	Feb	1872	Slatington, Lehigh	Lehighton, Carbon
M-372	Heffelfinger	John	Beltz	Mary	11	Feb	1872	Franklin Twp, Carbon	Franklin Twp, Carbon
M-373	Schultz	William	Young	Mary E	12	Feb	1872	Weatherly, Carbon	Weatherly, Carbon
M-374	Moulthrop	John Francis	Shoemaker	Ellen	22	Feb	1872	Lehighton, Carbon	East Penn Twp, Carbon
M-375	Frohnheiser	Lewis	Miller	Anzonetta	24	Feb	1872	Lehighton, Carbon	Weissport, Carbon
M-376	Berger	Elias	Hunsicker	Emaline	25	Feb	1872	Mahoning Twp, Carbon	Mahoning Twp, Carbon
M-377	Lower	Tilghman	Reppert	Susanna	28	Feb	1872	Lower Towamensing Twp, Carbon	Lower Towamensing Twp, Carbon
M-378	Kostenbader	Samuel F	Boyer	Priscilla	2	Mar	1872	Lower Towamensing Twp, Carbon	Lower Towamensing Twp, Carbon
M-379	Noll	Aaron	Rehrig	Eliza	22	Mar	1872	East Penn Twp, Carbon	East Penn Twp, Carbon
M-380	Xander	Benjamin E	Mertz	Mary Ann	31	Mar	1872	East Penn Twp, Carbon	Mahoning Twp, Carbon
M-381	Rehrig	Alfred	Kolb	Emaline	28	Apr	1872	East Penn Twp, Carbon	East Penn Twp, Carbon
M-382	Kratzer	William Edwin	Sanborn	Amelia L	17	May	1872	Lower Towamensing Twp, Carbon	New Ark (Newark?), NJ
M-383	Wolf	Owen K	Billman	Mary Jane	18	May	1872	Lehighton, Carbon	East Penn Twp, Carbon
M-384	Walp	Robert	Andrew	Eliza	19	May	1872	Lower Towamensing Twp, Carbon	Lower Towamensing Twp, Carbon
M-385	Freyman	Lafayette	Steigerwalt	Rebecca	19	May	1872	East Penn Twp, Carbon	West Penn Twp, Schuylkill
M-386	Lower	George David	Krechel	Helena	21	May	1872	Lower Towamensing Twp, Carbon	Keesgueville, Monroe
M-387	Miller	Francis Dougla	Dinkey	Anna J	8	June	1872	Lehighton, Carbon	East Penn Twp, Carbon
M-388	Klotz	John F	Arner	Bregitta	9	June	1872	Lehighton, Carbon	Franklin Twp, Carbon
M-389	Reed	Franklin	Bartholomew	Ellemande	15	June	1872	Mauch Chunk, Carbon	Mauch Chunk, Carbon
M-390	Solt	Amos	Thomas	Alavesta Jane	16	June	1872	Franklin Twp, Carbon	Franklin Twp, Carbon
M-391	Quin	Monroe	Bowman	Alavesta A	20	June	1872	Lower Towamensing Twp, Carbon	Lower Towamensing Twp, Carbon
M-392	Diemer	John	Krug	Babette	26	June	1872	East Mauch Chunk, Carbon	East Mauch Chunk, Carbon
M-393	Sinyard	James	Frantz	Sarah Ann	3	July	1872	Mahoning Twp, Carbon	Mahoning Twp, Carbon

Beyond the Blue Mountain: Vol. II

Marriage Records

Line	Groom Surname	Groom Given	Bride Surname	Bride Given	Day	Mth	Year	He from:	She from:
M-394	Leukel	John	Miller	Catherine	7	July	1872	Lehighton, Carbon	Weissport, Carbon
M-395	Faist	Simon	Goldberg	Mary	13	July	1872	Lehighton, Carbon	Towamensing, Carbon
M-396	Serfass	Timothy	Sterner	Susanna	19	July	1872	Lower Towamensing Twp, Carbon	Polk Twp, Monroe
M-397	Arner	Charles	Solt	Ellen Jane	21	July	1872	Franklin Twp, Carbon	Franklin Twp, Carbon
M-398	Eddinger	Weldin	Reusch	Sophia	22	July	1872	East Mauch Chunk, Carbon	East Mauch Chunk, Carbon
M-399	Boyer	Franklin	Krill	Julia Ann	28	July	1872	Lower Towamensing Twp, Carbon	Lower Towamensing Twp, Carbon
M-400	Snyder	Paul	Keiser	Eliza Jane	4	Aug	1872	Lower Towamensing Twp, Carbon	Lower Towamensing Twp, Carbon
M-401	Stoudt	Zacharias	Shoenberger	Sarah A	4	Aug	1872	Franklin Twp, Carbon	Slatington, Lehigh
M-402	Bauer	Stephen	Houser	Sarah	10	Aug	1872	Rush Twp, Schuylkill	Rush Twp, Schuylkill
M-403	Drissell	Henry	Miller	Cecilia	20	Aug	1872	Lehighton, Carbon	Lehighton, Carbon
M-404	Schmidt	William	Lentz	Lydia	22	Aug	1872	Penn Haven, Carbon	Penn Haven, Carbon
M-405	Schultz	Edwin	Fritzinger	Savenna	25	Aug	1872	Lehighton, Carbon	Mahoning Twp, Carbon
M-406	Fisher	John Framklin	Kunkel	Elizabeth	31	Aug	1872	Franklin Twp, Carbon	Franklin Twp, Carbon
M-407	Arner	George	Scherer	Rosa Ann	1	Sept	1872	Franklin Twp, Carbon	Lower Towamensing Twp, Carbon
M-408	Long	Columbus	Fisher	Louisa	14	Sept	1872	Long Swamp, Berks	Franklin Twp, Carbon
M-409	Kuntz	David	Haintz	Mary Ann Elizabeth	15	Sept	1872	Walnutport, Nthptn	East Penn Twp, Carbon
M-410	Gombert	Joseph L	Fenstermacher	Sarah Ann	19	Sept	1872	West Penn Twp, Schuylkill	Low Hill Twp, Lehigh
M-411	Scherer	John	Moser	Rosa Ann	22	Sept	1872	Lower Towamensing Twp, Carbon	Mahoning Twp, Carbon
M-412	Long	Drake H	Gerber	Priscilla	1	Oct	1872	Lehighton, Carbon	Mahoning Twp, Carbon
M-413	Milheim	William	Bauer	Mary Ann	6	Oct	1872	Franklin Twp, Carbon	Franklin Twp, Carbon
M-414	Haupt	George Frederi	Donehue	Anna	6	Oct	1872	Mahoning Twp, Carbon	Mahoning Twp, Carbon
M-415	Rabe	Franklin	Traut	Catherine	13	Oct	1872	East Mauch Chunk, Carbon	East Mauch Chunk, Carbon
M-416	Miller	Jonathan	Kemmerer	Mary Ann	13	Oct	1872	West Penn Twp, Schuylkill	West Penn Twp, Schuylkill
M-417	Guardian	Joseph Frederi	Fisher	Henrietta	15	Oct	1872	WilkesBarre, Luzerne	East Mauch Chunk, Carbon
M-418	Stroup	Jacob B	Stroup	Catherine	19	Oct	1872	Franklin Twp, Carbon	Franklin Twp, Carbon
M-419	Fritzinger	Joseph	Scheckler	Selinda	27	Oct	1872	Franklin Twp, Carbon	Franklin Twp, Carbon
M-420	Meckes	Samuel L	Kleintopp	Anna F	1	Nov	1872	Penn Forest Twp, Carbon	Penn Forest Twp, Carbon
M-421	Ahner	Calvin	Strohl	Mary Jane	10	Nov	1872	Franklin Twp, Carbon	Upper Towamensing, Carbon
M-422	Haupt	Alfred	Houser	Anna Matilda	23	Nov	1872	Mahoning Twp, Carbon	Mahoning Twp, Carbon
M-423	Kemerer	Lewis	Cunfer	Emma	15	Dec	1872	Washington Twp, Lehigh	Mahoning Twp, Carbon
M-424	Webb	Thomas M	Lentz	Lucinda	15	Dec	1872	Lehighton, Carbon	Lehighton, Carbon
M-425	Krock	Daniel	Newhart	Miranda Louisa	21	Dec	1872	Lehighton, Carbon	Lehighton, Carbon
M-426	Wolf	Zacharias T	Anthony	Lucetta	22	Dec	1872	Lehighton, Carbon	Lehighton, Carbon
M-427	Kunkel	Dures	Walck	Susan	22	Dec	1872	Franklin Twp, Carbon	Franklin Twp, Carbon
M-428	Blose	David	Strassburger	Lucy Ann	24	Dec	1872	Lower Towamensing Twp, Carbon	Lower Towamensing Twp, Carbon
M-429	Horn	Charles T	Montz	Adaline	26	Dec	1872	Lehighton, Carbon	Mahoning Twp, Carbon

Beyond the Blue Mountain: Vol. II

Marriage Records

Line	Groom Surname	Groom Given	Bride Surname	Bride Given	Day	Mth	Year	He from:	She from:
M-430	Newhart	John	Kleppinger	Anna Maria Elizabeth	27	Dec	1872	Whitehall, Lehigh	Lehigh Twp, Nthptn
M-431	Koch	Franklin P	Fath	Mary Ann Susanna	27	Dec	1872	Upper Towamensing, Carbon	Franklin Twp, Carbon
M-432	Nothstein	Lewis F	Herring	Angeline Elizabeth	28	Dec	1872	Mahoning Twp, Carbon	Mahoning Twp, Carbon
M-433	Long	Abraham	Allis	Sarah	29	Dec	1872	Weissport, Carbon	Weissport, Carbon
M-434	Shoenberger	David H	Lindsey	Sarah	1	Jan	1873	Parryville, Carbon	Parryville, Carbon
M-435	Strohl	Amos	Schwab	Lydia Anna Maria	9	Jan	1873	Upper Towamensing, Carbon	Franklin Twp, Carbon
M-436	Brobst	Francis	Herring	Sarah Jane	11	Jan	1873	Franklin Twp, Carbon	Mahoning Twp, Carbon
M-437	Ownwalt	Samuel A	Knecht	Mary Ann	1	Feb	1873	Lower Towamensing Twp, Carbon	East Penn Twp, Carbon
M-438	Steigerwalt	John	Kistler	Caroline	1	Feb	1873	Lynn Twp, Lehigh	Lynn Twp, Lehigh
M-439	Serfass	John	Behrens	Helena	6	Mar	1873	Penn Forest Twp, Carbon	Penn Forest Twp, Carbon
M-440	Pettit	George	Ramely	Eliza	8	Mar	1873	Parryville, Carbon	Lower Towamensing Twp, Carbon
M-441	Kreamer	David S	Meyers	Ada	3	Apr	1873	Lehighton, Carbon	Fairmont, Luzerne
M-442	Seltzer	Henry	Moyer	Catherine	6	Apr	1873	Lower Towamensing Twp, Carbon	Upper Towamensing, Carbon
M-443	Mantz	Moses D	Steigerwalt	Levina	6	Apr	1873	Lynn Twp, Lehigh	East Penn Twp, Carbon
M-444	Long	Griffith D	Stroup	Elmira	13	Apr	1873	East Penn Twp, Carbon	Lower Towamensing Twp, Carbon
M-445	Strohl	Josiah	Zimmerman	Catherine Ellen	4	May	1873	Upper Towamensing, Carbon	Franklin Twp, Carbon
M-446	Trainer	Wilson	Haupt	Kate	8	May	1873	Lehighton, Carbon	Mahoning Twp, Carbon
M-447	Kemerer	George	Gilbert	Abby	1	June	1873	Lehighton, Carbon	Lehighton, Carbon
M-448	Scherer	Harvey	Snyder	Matilda	7	June	1873	Lower Towamensing Twp, Carbon	Lower Towamensing Twp, Carbon
M-449	Markley	William Frankli	Brown	Emma Louisa	12	June	1873	Franklin Twp, Carbon	Franklin Twp, Carbon
M-450	Shumaker	Owen	Hartranft	Mary Ellen	15	June	1873	Low Hill Twp, Lehigh	East Penn Twp, Carbon
M-451	Hiester	Joseph R	Frantz	Susanna	19	June	1873	Summit Hill, Carbon	Lehighton, Carbon
M-452	Rapp	Charles	Kemerer	Juliann	24	June	1873	WilkesBarre, Luzerne	Jamestown, Carbon
M-453	Kresge	C. A.	Frantz	Sarah	10	July	1873	Kresgeville, Monroe	Ross Twp, Monroe
M-454	Shive	William Harrisc Mertz		Ellen	13	July	1873	Mahoning Twp, Carbon	Mahoning Twp, Carbon
M-455	Rieger	Xavier	Saile	Balbine	20	July	1873	Packerton, Carbon	Packerton, Carbon
M-456	Schultz	James	Beck	Sarah Catherine	2	Aug	1873	East Penn Twp, Carbon	East Penn Twp, Carbon
M-457	Solt	Alfred	Heilman	Catherine Elizabeth	3	Aug	1873	Franklin Twp, Carbon	Franklin Twp, Carbon
M-458	Anders	Anthony	Hahn	Susanna	10	Aug	1873	Upper Towamensing, Carbon	Lower Towamensing Twp, Carbon
M-459	Sheckler	William L	Solt	Ellen	24	Aug	1873	Lehighton, Carbon	Weissport, Carbon
M-460	Horlacher	J	Smith	Sarah J	25	Aug	1873	Wescoesville, Lehigh	Lehighton, Carbon
M-461	Fawcett	John	Shafer	Rosa Ann	25	Aug	1873	Sugar Notch, Luzerne	Sugar Notch, Luzerne
M-462	Trenklin	Anthony	Mangold	Margeret	31	Aug	1873	Mauch Chunk, Carbon	Franklin Twp, Carbon
M-463	German	Peter	Weiss	Hannah	6	Sept	1873	Heidelberg Twp, Lehigh	Washington Twp, Lehigh
M-464	Dreisbach	Mandes	Silfies	Balinda	7	Sept	1873	Parryville, Carbon	Parryville, Carbon
M-465	Hahn	William	Klotz	Mary Rebecca	28	Sept	1873	Franklin Twp, Carbon	Franklin Twp, Carbon

Beyond the Blue Mountain: Vol. II

Marriage Records

Line	Groom Surname	Given	Bride Surname	Given	Day	Mth	Year	He from:	She from:
M-466	Straup	Wesley C	Henry	Catherine N	5	Oct	1873	Lower Towamensing Twp, Carbon	Lower Towamensing Twp, Carbon
M-467	Kolb	Reuben	Kern	Emaline	9	Oct	1873	South Easton, Nthptn	South Easton, Nhtptn
M-468	Smith	William Edwin	Anders	Catherine	10	Oct	1873	Upper Towamensing, Carbon	Lower Towamensing Twp, Carbon
M-469	Dorwort	James P	Weaver	Mary L	25	Oct	1873	Franklin Twp, Carbon	Franklin Twp, Carbon
M-470	Montz	Josiah	Gerhart	Sarah Catherine	26	Oct	1873	Weatherly, Carbon	Packer Twp, Carbon
M-471	Larash	Jacob J	Shoemaker	Mary Etta	4	Nov	1873	Allentown, Lehigh	Catasauqua, Lehigh
M-472	Reinerd	Daniel	Hobbes	Polly	9	Nov	1873	Mahoning Twp, Carbon	Mahoning Twp, Carbon
M-473	Hahn	Franklin	Hartman	Catherine	15	Nov	1873	Upper Towamensing, Carbon	Franklin Twp, Carbon
M-474	Zimmerman	Charles Alfred	Kunkle	Leah Vesta	23	Nov	1873	Franklin Twp, Carbon	Franklin Twp, Carbon
M-475	Sharer	Stephen L	Zellner	Mary Ann	30	Nov	1873	Lower Saucon, Nthptn	Mahoning Twp, Carbon
M-476	Bowman	Dallas	Noll	Emma	30	Nov	1873	East Penn Twp, Carbon	East Penn Twp, Carbon
M-477	Hildebrand	Peter	Long	Mary	8	Dec	1873	Lehighton, Carbon	Lehighton, Carbon
M-478	Krotzer	Walter V	Zimmerman	Sarah Rebecca	14	Dec	1873	Franklin Twp, Carbon	Franklin Twp, Carbon
M-479	Schappel	Milton T	Frohnheiser	Catherine	20	Dec	1873	East Penn Twp, Carbon	East Penn Twp, Carbon
M-480	Seeber	Charles	Kleheimer	Afra	10	Jan	1874	Penn Haven, Carbon	Penn Haven, Carbon
M-481	Fluck	Jacob	Miller	Emma Jane	10	Jan	1874	Lehighton, Carbon	Lehighton, Carbon
M-482	Riegel	William J	Correll	Sallena	17	Jan	1874	Easton, Nthptn	Kresgeville, Monroe
M-483	Gilbert	Dennis	Schweibens	Mary Ann	15	Feb	1874	Lehighton, Carbon	Lehighton, Carbon
M-484	Muhlbach	Charles Gustav	Beckendorf	Caroline Anna	15	Feb	1874	Easton, Nthptn	Lehighton, Carbon
M-485	McDaniel	Thomas	Brown	Melinda	22	Feb	1874	Upper Towamensing, Carbon	Lower Towamensing Twp, Carbon
M-486	Youse	Tobias	Schultz	Maria	28	Feb	1874	East Penn Twp, Carbon	East Penn Twp, Carbon
M-487	Widdoss	Richard B	Rehrig	Sallie	15	Mar	1874	Bath, Nthptn	East Penn Twp, Carbon
M-488	Ruckawuck	William	Kramer	Margeret Magdalene	20	Mar	1874	Parryville, Carbon	Franklin Twp, Carbon
M-489	Fenner	Ervin	Anthony	Edna B	5	Apr	1874	Weissport, Carbon	Weissport, Carbon
M-490	Conley	William J	Deibert	Violetta E	24	Apr	1874	Mauch Chunk, Carbon	Lehighton, Carbon
M-491	Dunbar	Calvin	Hartman	Mary Jane	30	Apr	1874	Parryville, Carbon	Parryville, Carbon
M-492	Clauss	Emanuel W	Esch	Ellen	7	May	1874	Lehighton, Carbon	Lehighton, Carbon
M-493	Eckstein	George A N	Bartholomew	Emma E	9	May	1874	Lehighton, Carbon	Lehighton, Carbon
M-494	Levan	Hiram P	Klotz	Catherine	19	May	1874	Weissport, Carbon	Weissport, Carbon
M-495	Wetzel	Daniel D	Goodheil	Caroline	23	May	1874	Packer Twp, Carbon	Lower Towamensing Twp, Carbon
M-496	Shoenberger	Charles O	Diehl	Matilda H	25	May	1874	Lower Towamensing Twp, Carbon	Franklin Twp, Carbon
M-497	Silfies	Chester P	Shive	Julian	28	May	1874	Mahoning Twp, Carbon	Mahoning Twp, Carbon
M-498	Horn	Alvin	Ross	Amanda Jane	7	June	1874	Lynn Twp, Lehigh	East Penn Twp, Carbon
M-499	Weaver	Wilson	Gombert	Henrietta	20	June	1874	Lehigh Twp, Nthptn	Mahoning Twp, Carbon
M-500	Ahner	Abraham	Remaley	Mary Ann	12	July	1874	Franklin Twp, Carbon	Mahoning Twp, Carbon
M-501	Scherer	Martin	Stickrath	Barbara	9	Aug	1874	Mahoning Twp, Carbon	Mahoning Twp, Carbon

Beyond the Blue Mountain: Vol. II

Marriage Records

Line	Groom Surname	Groom Given	Bride Surname	Bride Given	Day	Mth	Year	He from:	She from:
M-502	Green	Samuel J	Buchman	Caroline	15	Aug	1874	Upper Towamensing, Carbon	Lehighton, Carbon
M-503	Dunlap	Charles	Hahn	Mary Ann	30	Aug	1874	Franklin Twp, Carbon	Franklin Twp, Carbon
M-504	Fritzinger	Moses	Rehr	Emma	19	Sept	1874	Lehighton, Carbon	Mahoning Twp, Carbon
M-505	Hartman	Elias G	Fatzinger	Alice J	11	Oct	1874	Allentown, Lehigh	South Whitehall, Lehigh
M-506	Sensinger	Israel	Smith	Sarah E	12	Oct	1874	Washington Twp, Lehigh	North Whitehall, Lehigh
M-507	Rex	Joseph F	Koons	Elmira C	17	Oct	1874	Weissport, Carbon	Lehighton, Carbon
M-508	Schoenberger	George F	Kantz	Lenah	22	Oct	1874	Whitehall Twp, Lehigh	White Hall Twp. Lehigh
M-509	Fritz	Reuben L	Balliet	Kate D	24	Oct	1874	East Penn Twp, Carbon	Mahoning Twp, Carbon
M-510	Daniels	Jeremiah R	Kleintop	Mary Jane	24	Oct	1874	Lehighton, Carbon	Lehighton, Carbon
M-511	Bowman	Albert	Fritzinger	Isabella	27	Oct	1874	East Penn Twp, Carbon	Mahoning Twp, Carbon
M-512	Fisher	George Israel	Kunkel	Mary Etta	29	Oct	1874	Franklin Twp, Carbon	Franklin Twp, Carbon
M-513	Beer	Amos	Smith	Louisa Catherine	8	Nov	1874	Lower Towamensing Twp, Carbon	Lower Towamensing Twp, Carbon
M-514	Snyder	Samuel	Schafer	Kate	14	Nov	1874	Mahoning Twp, Carbon	West Penn Twp, Schuylkill
M-515	Reed	Lewis	Hettler	Sarah	21	Nov	1874	West Penn Twp, Schuylkill	East Penn Twp, Carbon
M-516	Bowman	Francis	Freyman	Amelia Isabella	6	Dec	1874	East Penn Twp, Carbon	Mahoning Twp, Carbon
M-517	Neff	Oscar A	Anthony	Tillie A	19	Dec	1874	Slatington, Lehigh	Slatington, Lehigh
M-518	Sandel	Jacob	Ruch	Caroline	25	Dec	1874	Mauch Chunk, Carbon	Mauch Chunk, Carbon
M-519	Ziegenfuss	Lewis	Wentz	Harriet	26	Dec	1874	Lower Towamensing Twp, Carbon	Franklin Twp, Carbon
M-520	Ziegenfuss	Martin	Anthony	Jane Amanda	26	Dec	1874	Lower Towamensing Twp, Carbon	Moore Twp, Nthptn
M-521	Reber	William Henry	Hettler	Mary Ann	31	Dec	1874	East Penn Twp, Carbon	East Penn Twp, Carbon
M-522	Dodendorf	John	Sherer	Sabina	1	Jan	1875	Lower Towamensing Twp, Carbon	Lower Towamensing Twp, Carbon
M-523	Reed	George	Bowers	Hetty	23	Jan	1875	Mauch Chunk, Carbon	Mauch Chunk, Carbon
M-524	Fritz	Charles D	Dilcher	Chrissilla	24	Jan	1875	Mahoning Twp, Carbon	Mahoning Twp, Carbon
M-525	Strohl	Franklin Thom:	Rice	Anna Tewilia	24	Jan	1875	Lower Towamensing, Carbon	Lower Towamensing Twp, Carbon
M-526	Ziegenfuss	Elias P	Strohl	Susanna	24	Jan	1875	Franklin Twp, Carbon	Lower Towamensing Twp, Carbon
M-527	Wolf	John S	Fritzinger	Selinda	13	Feb	1875	Lehighton, Carbon	Parryville, Carbon
M-528	Simpson	Robert	Getzinger	Ellen J	13	Feb	1875	East Mauch Chunk, Carbon	East Mauch Chunk, Carbon
M-529	Snyder	John	Ziegenfuss	Harriet	20	Feb	1875	Upper Towamensing, Carbon	Franklin Twp, Carbon
M-530	Barnes	Monroe Milton	Rehrig	Ruffina	21	Feb	1875	Bethlehem, Lehigh	Franklin Twp, Carbon
M-531	Rehrig	Dennis	Lentz	Julia Eliizabeth	6	Mar	1875	Mahoning Twp, Carbon	Mahoning Twp, Carbon
M-532	Grow	Reuben	Schwartz	Mary Magadalene	9	Mar	1875	Lehighton, Carbon	Lehighton, Carbon
M-533	Kreitz	George Henry	Miller	Harriet L	14	Mar	1875	Mahoning Twp, Carbon	Mahoning Twp, Carbon
M-534	Bartholomew	Philip	Rex	Maria	27	Mar	1875	Weissport, Carbon	Mahoning Twp, Carbon
M-535	Hontz	Granville	Sheckler	Susanna	10	Apr	1875	Lehighton, Carbon	Parryville, Carbon
M-536	Flickinger	Josiah	Hough	Clara	25	Apr	1875	Mahoning Twp, Carbon	Mahoning Twp, Carbon
M-537	Weiss	Neander	Strohl	Lucinda	1	May	1875	Upper Towamensing, Carbon	Upper Towamensing, Carbon

Beyond the Blue Mountain: Vol. II

Marriage Records

Line	Groom Surname	Groom Given	Bride Surname	Bride Given	Day	Mth	Year	He from:	She from:
M-538	Gearhard	David D	Gearhard	Anna M	4	May	1875	Packer Twp, Carbon	Packer Twp, Carbon
M-539	Kramer	W. C.	Muschlitz	Mary Ann	8	May	1875	Lower Towamensing Twp, Carbon	Lower Towamensing Twp, Carbon
M-540	Schwartz	John F	Hunsicker	Amelia	16	May	1875	Lehighton, Carbon	Berlinsville, Nthptn
M-541	Scherer	William	Reiner	Harriet	17	May	1875	Lower Towamensing Twp, Carbon	Lower Towamensing Twp, Carbon
M-542	Hartman	William H	Remaley	Lydia Ann	5	June	1875	Franklin Twp, Carbon	Franklin Twp, Carbon
M-543	Ahner	Reuben	Whiteman	Sarah	12	June	1875	Franklin Twp, Carbon	Franklin Twp, Carbon
M-544	Kostenbader	Peter L	Christman	Jane	3	July	1875	Lower Towamensing Twp, Carbon	Lower Towamensing Twp, Carbon
M-545	Serfass	Edward	Marcome	Anjuline Jane	3	July	1875	Lower Towamensing Twp, Carbon	Lower Towamensing Twp, Carbon
M-546	Sellars	John	Hill	Catherine Aurelio	3	July	1875	Franklin Twp, Carbon	Franklin Twp, Carbon
M-547	Gerhard	John H	Nothstein	Mary E	3	July	1875	Packer Twp, Carbon	Mahoning Twp, Carbon
M-548	Guth	Albert J	Hawk	Emma Jane	3	July	1875	Weissport, Carbon	Weissport, Carbon
M-549	Semmel	Joel	Kolb	Sabina	4	July	1875	Mahoning Twp, Carbon	East Penn Twp, Carbon
M-550	Krum	L. A	Hill	Sarah	31	July	1875	Lehighton, Carbon	West Penn Twp, Schuylkill
M-551	Emboddy	David	Gross	Lucetta Amelia	31	July	1875	East Penn Twp, Carbon	East Penn Twp, Carbon
M-552	Zellner	Charles	Wertman	Adaline Elizabeth	1	Aug	1875	Mahoning Twp, Carbon	West Penn Twp, Schuylkill
M-553	Gerber	Thomas	Frantz	Flora Ann	28	Aug	1875	Lehighton, Carbon	East Penn Twp, Carbon
M-554	Rhoads	Jeremiah J.	Miller	Matilda	28	Aug	1875	Lehighton, Carbon	Mahoning Twp, Carbon
M-555	Everitt	E.H.	Rex	Martha Julia Adline	4	Sep	1875	Weissport, Carbon	Lehighton, Carbon
M-556	Hess	Henry J.	Bartholomew	L.J.	11	Sep	1875	Weatherly, Carbon	Weatherly, Carbon
M-557	Miller	John Henry	Nothstein	Anna Jane	12	Sep	1875	Mahoning Twp, Carbon	East Penn Twp, Carbon
M-558	Ginder	Isaac	Reichard	Antionetta	26	Sep	1875	East Penn Twp, Carbon	East Penn Twp, Carbon
M-559	Lieser	William	Daubenspeck	Zeniah	3	Oct	1875	West Penn Twp, Schuylkill	West Penn Twp, Schuylkill
M-560	Balliet	Levi	Steckel	Susan E	13	Oct	1875	Easton, Nthptn	Easton, Nthptn
M-561	Mosteller	William H	Hahn	Harriet	14	Oct	1875	Franklin Twp, Carbon	Franklin Twp, Carbon
M-562	Markley	Benjamin	Dorwort	Ellen Jane	23	Oct	1875	Franklin Twp, Carbon	Franklin Twp, Carbon
M-563	Haberman	Jefferson	Walp	Lavina	31	Oct	1875	Mauch Chunk, Carbon	Hazardsville, Carbon
M-564	Peter	John A	Mantz	Emaline	2	Dec	1875	Lehighton, Carbon	Lehighton, Carbon
M-565	Hontz	William	Dilcher	Leila	5	Dec	1875	Mahoning Twp, Carbon	Mahoning Twp, Carbon
M-566	Schaeffer	F.W	Snyder	S.S.	12	Dec	1875	Schuylkill Twp, Schuylkill	West Penn Twp, Schuylkill
M-567	Knepper	William	Leiby	Caroline	25	Dec	1875	West Penn Twp, Schuylkill	West Penn Twp, Schuylkill
M-568	Rehrig	James H	Mulharen	Anna	25	Dec	1875	Lehighton, Carbon	Lehighton, Carbon
M-569	Kleintop	Joseph	Beer	Emaline	31	Dec	1875	Lower Towamensing Twp, Carbon	Lower Towamensing Twp, Carbon
M-570	Gombert	Henry	Hontz	Emaline	2	Jan	1876	Mahoning Twp, Carbon	Mahoning Twp, Carbon
M-571	Ginder	James W	Nothstein	Flora Ann	6	Feb	1876	East Penn Twp, Carbon	West Penn Twp, Schuylkill
M-572	Delong	James	Frantz	Emma	27	Feb	1876	East Penn Twp, Carbon	Mahoning Twp, Carbon
M-573	Boyer	Levi	Smith	Lydia Esther	27	Feb	1876	Lower Towamensing Twp, Carbon	Elldred, Monroe

Beyond the Blue Mountain: Vol. II

Marriage Records

Line	Groom Surname	Groom Given	Bride Surname	Bride Given	Day	Mth	Year	He from:	She from:
M-574	Moyer	Elias	Rex	Catherine	5	Mar	1876	Lynn Twp, Lehigh	Heidelberg Twp, Lehigh
M-575	Wetzel	David D	Gerhard	Lydia Ann	10	Mar	1876	Weatherly, Carbon	Packer Twp, Carbon
M-576	Hill	Abraham	Graver	E. L.	11	Mar	1876	Lower Towamensing Twp, Carbon	Franklin Twp, Carbon
M-577	Silfies	William	McFarland	Catherine	2	Apr	1876	Parryville, Carbon	East Penn Twp, Carbon
M-578	Kershner	Frank	Gombert	Elizabeth	8	Apr	1876	West Penn Twp, Schuylkill	West Penn Twp, Schuylkill
M-579	Gollus	Joseph	Gaumer	Urilla C	27	Apr	1876	Mauch Chunk, Carbon	Mauch Chunk, Carbon
M-580	Solt	Amandes W	Walck	Anna Maria	14	May	1876	Franklin Twp, Carbon	Franklin Twp, Carbon
M-581	Kistler	William Alfred	Handwerk	Hetty	3	June	1876	Heidelberg Twp, Lehigh	Heidelberg Twp, Lehigh
M-582	Benninghoff	William H	Hoffman	Adline	24	June	1876	Heidelberg Twp, Lehigh	East Penn Twp, Carbon
M-583	Scherer	Robert A	Blose	Eliza Ann	25	June	1876	Lower Towamensing Twp, Carbon	Lower Towamensing Twp, Carbon
M-584	Smith	John R	Schultz	Annie M	3	Aug	1876	Mauch Chunk, Carbon	Mauch Chunk, Carbon
M-585	Shipe	James Wilson	Bowman	Mary Jane	6	Aug	1876	Lower Towamensing Twp, Carbon	Lower Towamensing Twp, Carbon
M-586	Nesley	William	Boughner	Henrietta	10	Aug	1876	Summit Hill, Carbon	Tamanend, Schuylkill
M-587	Ohl	Henry	Gerber	Sabina	20	Aug	1876	West Penn Twp, Schuylkill	West Penn Twp, Schuylkill
M-588	Ruff	Joseph	Weiss	Catherine N	3	Sept	1876	Franklin Twp, Carbon	Franklin Twp, Carbon
M-589	Larose	William	Sensinger	Susanna	10	Sept	1876	Franklin Twp, Carbon	Franklin Twp, Carbon
M-590	Smawley	William A	Green	Francisca	10	Oct	1876	Lehighton, Carbon	Lehighton, Carbon
M-591	Horn	A. B.	Hunsicker	Sarah F	12	Oct	1876	Tamaqua, Schuylkill	Lehighton, Carbon
M-592	Bechtel	David	Eroh	Susan Elizabeth	12	Oct	1876	Delano, Schuylkill	Delano, Schuylkill
M-593	Hauser	Charles S.	Miller	Kate	15	Oct	1876	West Penn Twp, Schuylkill	Mahoning Twp, Carbon
M-594	Miner	Levi	Taney	Mary Ann	16	Oct	1876	Oxford, NJ	Oxford, NJ
M-595	Deppy	Lewis	Olewine	Susan Ann	22	Oct	1876	Franklin Twp, Carbon	Franklin Twp, Carbon
M-596	Haupt	Charles Martin	Rabenold	Henrietta	26	Oct	1876	Mahoning Twp, Carbon	Mahoning Twp, Carbon
M-597	Graver	Harron Oscar	Walck	Alice	3	Dec	1876	Franklin Twp, Carbon	Franklin Twp, Carbon
M-598	Moser	Benjamin Fran	Gombert	Kate	10	Dec	1876	Mahoning Twp, Carbon	Mahoning Twp, Carbon
M-599	Hill	Franklin	Gombert	Angeline Victoria	24	Dec	1876	West Penn Twp, Schuylkill	East Penn Twp, Carbon
M-600	Hollar	Ben G	Betz	Barbara Udella	27	Jan	1877	Rush Twp, Schuylkill	Rush Twp, Schuylkill
M-601	Wolf	George	Serfass	Lydia	1	Feb	1877	Mauch Chunk, Carbon	Mauch Chunk, Carbon
M-602	Fenstermacher	Lewis	Miller	Matilda	4	Feb	1877	West Penn Twp, Schuylkill	West Penn Twp, Schuylkill
M-603	Mangold	John M	Nennstiel	Caroline	11	Feb	1877	Franklin Twp, Carbon	Franklin Twp, Carbon
M-604	Scherer	Robert	Dreisbach	Fietta	16	Apr	1877	Lower Towamensing Twp, Carbon	Lower Towamensing Twp, Carbon
M-605	McDaniel	Reuben	Weiss	Sarah Alice	22	Apr	1877	Upper Towamensing, Carbon	Franklin Twp, Carbon
M-606	Reichard	Lafayette	Dreher	Emma	12	May	1877	Lehighton, Carbon	Lehighton, Carbon
M-607	Kolb	William	Steiner	Lizzie	20	May	1877	Weatherly, Carbon	Quakeuke Carbon (Schuylkill?)
M-608	Frohnheiser	James	Schappel	Emaline Elizabeth	9	June	1877	East Penn Twp, Carbon	East Penn Twp, Carbon
M-609	Heintzelman	Wilson W	Kistler	Elizabeth A	16	June	1877	Washington Twp, Lehigh	Heidelberg Twp, Lehigh

Beyond the Blue Mountain: Vol. II

Marriage Records

Line	Groom Surname	Groom Given	Bride Surname	Bride Given	Day	Mth	Year	He from:	She from:
M-610	Wertman	David A	Torrance	Elizabeth	16	July	1877	Lynn Twp, Lehigh	Mahoning Twp, Carbon
M-611	Zimmerman	Alfred	George	Kate	22	July	1877	West Penn Twp, Schuylkill	West Penn Twp, Schuylkill
M-612	Rustay	Frederic	Faeht	Mary	9	Aug	1877	East Mauch Chunk, Carbon	Franklin Twp, Carbon
M-613	Arner	Oscar	Anthony	Jane Elizabeth	19	Aug	1877	Weissport, Carbon	Slatington, Lehigh
M-614	Olenwine	Amandes	Koons	Amelia	19	Aug	1877	Lehighton, Carbon	Lehighton, Carbon
M-615	Rabenold	Charles B	O'Brian	Susan E	8	Sept	1877	Lehighton, Carbon	Mahoning Twp, Carbon
M-616	Peter	James F	Ruch	Kitty Ann	16	Sept	1877	East Penn Twp, Carbon	East Penn Twp, Carbon
M-617	McLean	John	Troxel	Emma	16	Sept	1877	Mahoning Twp, Carbon	West Penn Twp, Schuylkill
M-618	Zimmerman	Aaron	Sechler	Kate Elizabeth	11	Oct	1877	West Penn Twp, Schuylkill	West Penn Twp, Schuylkill
M-619	Sandherrs	George	Rehrig	Sarah Alice	11	Oct	1877	Packerton, Carbon	Mahoning Twp, Carbon
M-620	Ludwig	Franz	Sauers	Anna Eliza	13	Oct	1877	Mahoning Twp, Carbon	Lehighton, Carbon
M-621	Rinker	Albert A	Schnell	Susanna	28	Oct	1877	Franklin Twp, Carbon	Franklin Twp, Carbon
M-622	Reinhart	Joseph H	Christman	Amelia	13	Dec	1877	Parryville, Carbon	Lower Towamensing Twp, Carbon
M-623	Andreas	Levi	Gombert	Sarah	23	Dec	1877	East Penn Twp, Carbon	West Penn Twp, Schuylkill
M-624	Hoffman	Jerrane	Frohnheiser	Sally	30	Dec	1877	East Penn Twp, Carbon	East Penn Twp, Carbon
M-625	Stoneburner	W. A	Hawk	Sarah	16	Feb	1878	Danielsville, Nthptn	Kresgeville, Monroe
M-626	Leiby	Franklin	Stout	Sarah Ann Velare	24	Mar	1878	West Penn Twp, Schuylkill	West Penn Twp, Schuylkill
M-627	Maurer	Frank	Butz	Emma J	30	Mar	1878	East Penn Twp, Carbon	Snydersville, Monroe
M-628	Miller	Peter Richard	Ziegenfuss	Francisca Elizabeth	29	June	1878	Franklin Twp, Carbon	Franklin Twp, Carbon
M-629	Behler	Jeremiah	Haas	Amanda Jane	7	July	1878	East Brunswick, Schuylkill	West Penn Twp, Schuylkill
M-630	Schaeffer	A H	Godschall	Lilly Louisa	20	July	1878	Walker Twp, Schuylkill	East Brunswick, Schuylkill
M-631	Walter	George F	Houser	Rebecca	31	Aug	1878	Walker Twp, Schuylkill	Walker Twp, Schuylkill
M-632	Miller	James A	Krum	Louisa	1	Sept	1878	West Penn Twp, Schuylkill	West Penn Twp, Schuylkill
M-633	Zettelmoyer	John	Rehrig	Lydia	3	Sept	1878	West Penn Twp, Schuylkill	West Penn Twp, Schuylkill
M-634	Hunsicker	Edwin	Balliet	Susan	26	Sept	1878	Mahoning Twp, Carbon	Mahoning Twp, Carbon
M-635	Acker	Hiram V	Campbell	Eliza	10	Oct	1878	East Weissport, Carbon	East Weissport, Carbon
M-636	Frantz	John A B	Neff	Louisa S	14	Oct	1878	Slate Dale, Lehigh	Slate Dale, Lehigh
M-637	Houser	Amandes	Adams	Amanda Jane	21	Dec	1878	West Penn Twp, Schuylkill	West Penn Twp, Schuylkill
M-638	Blose	Alfred	Lynn	Ellen Jane	23	Dec	1878	Lower Towamensing Twp, Carbon	East Penn Twp, Carbon
M-639	Smith	James	Ruch	Alvena	5	Jan	1879	Steinsville, Lehigh	Mahoning Twp, Carbon
M-640	Nothstein	John Henry	Muffley	Sally A	18	Jan	1879	Mahoning Twp, Carbon	Kresgeville, Monroe
M-641	Whitaker	James Franklir	Ziegenfuss	Elemena	20	Jan	1879	Upper Towamensing, Carbon	Franklin Twp, Carbon
M-642	Brown	John C	Hartung	Mary	25	Jan	1879	McKeansburg, Schuylkill	West Penn Twp, Schuylkill
M-643	Hill	Thomas	Hardinger	Mary A	26	Jan	1879	West Penn Twp, Schuylkill	Albanay, Berks
M-644	Wher	Lewis A	Graver	Adline	30	Jan	1879	Lehighton, Carbon	Lehighton, Carbon
M-645	Kerschner	Noah Albert	Hontz	Henrietta Lucinda	2	Feb	1879	West Penn Twp, Schuylkill	West Penn Twp, Schuylkill

Beyond the Blue Mountain: Vol. II

Marriage Records

Line	Groom Surname	Groom Given	Bride Surname	Bride Given	Day	Mth	Year	He from:	She from:
M-646	Bowman	Aaron	Steigerwalt	Emaline	15	Feb	1879	East Penn Twp, Carbon	East Penn Twp, Carbon
M-647	Hill	Peter	Kerschner	Emma Jane	9	Mar	1879	West Penn Twp, Schuylkill	West Penn Twp, Schuylkill
M-648	Lechleitner	John H	Miller	Alice M	18	Mar	1879	West Penn Twp, Schuylkill	Mahoning Twp, Carbon
M-649	Strohl	John S	Keuhner	Amanda C	19	Mar	1879	Drakes Creek, Carbon	Drakes Creek, Carbon
M-650	Muthart	Edwin K	Nunnemacher	Sarah	20	Mar	1879	New Tripoli, Lehigh	Tamaqua, Schuylkill
M-651	Lapp	Franklin	Evert	Catherine	12	Apr	1879	Mahoning Twp, Carbon	Mahoning Twp, Carbon
M-652	Ruch	Horace Greely	Bachman	Hannah	13	Apr	1879	East Penn Twp, Carbon	East Penn Twp, Carbon
M-653	Gumbert	Elwin	Kuntzman	Rosa Mantana	13	Apr	1879	East Penn Twp, Carbon	Low Hill Twp, Lehigh
M-654	Williams	M.J.	Musselman	Elizabeth	1	May	1879	Tamaqua, Schuylkill	Mahoning Twp, Carbon
M-655	Ramaly	Daniel	Brown	Mary Jane	31	May	1879	Lower Towamensing Twp, Carbon	Lower Towamensing Twp, Carbon
M-656	Solt	Andrew	Schall	Venora	7	June	1879	Franklin Twp, Carbon	Lehighton, Carbon
M-657	Gerber	Isaac	Williams	Priscilla	14	June	1879	West Penn Twp, Schuylkill	Tamaqua, Schuylkill
M-658	Johnson	Claudious M	Rogers	Emma S	6	July	1879	Packerton, Carbon	Weissport, Carbon
M-659	Hunsicker	Joseph Jr	Reed	Kate A	12	July	1879	Mahoning Twp, Carbon	West Penn Twp, Schuylkill
M-660	Hontz	Dennis	Cunfer	Matilda	27	July	1879	Mahoning Twp, Carbon	Mahoning Twp, Carbon
M-661	Schwartz	George	Dotter	Anna	9	Aug	1879	Lehighton, Carbon	Lehighton, Carbon
M-662	Meitzler	Josiah Benjam	Kemerer	Ellen Jane	20	Sept	1879	Mahoning Twp, Carbon	Mahoning Twp, Carbon
M-663	Zimmerman	Nathan	Gerber	Harriet	9	Oct	1879	West Penn Twp, Schuylkill	West Penn Twp, Schuylkill
M-664	Semmel	Walter J	Patterson	Adline	23	Oct	1879	Lehighton, Carbon	Lehighton, Carbon
M-665	Bowman	John	Fritzinger	Matilda Fianna	9	Nov	1879	East Penn Twp, Carbon	East Penn Twp, Carbon
M-666	Alexander	Francis R	Kemerer	Harriet	10	Nov	1879	Philadelphia	Lehighton, Carbon
M-667	Yeager	John H	Webb	Emma	25	Dec	1879	Mauch Chunk, Carbon	Lehighton, Carbon
M-668	Petry	Richard	Hontz	Kitty Ann	26	Dec	1879	Rockport, Carbon	Mahoning Twp, Carbon
M-669	Ginder	Charles Harris	Gumbert	Mary Jane	28	Dec	1879	East Penn Twp, Carbon	Mahoning Twp, Carbon
M-670	Nuss	W.A.	Rehrig	Lizzie J	17	Jan	1880	Weatherly, Carbon	Mahoning Twp, Carbon
M-671	Zehner	Charles	Slough	Cornelia M	5	Feb	1880	Mauch Chunk, Carbon	Easton, Nthptn
M-672	Balliet	Tilghmam	Eberts	Kate Louisa	15	Feb	1880	West Penn Twp, Schuylkill	Mahoning Twp, Carbon
M-673	Taylor	Edward C	Eberts	Susanna	6	Mar	1880	Mahoning Twp, Carbon	Mahoning Twp, Carbon
M-674	Leaser	William F	Kolb	Maria	9	Mar	1880	Weisenberg, Lehigh	Easton, Nthptn
M-675	Hill	Sylvester	Houser	Emma Kate	15	Mar	1880	West Penn Twp, Schuylkill	West Penn Twp, Schuylkill
M-676	Kostenbader	Samuel D	Walck	Tillie	28	Mar	1880	Lehighton, Carbon	Lehighton, Carbon
M-677	Correll	John	Clouse	Mary Alice	15	May	1880	West Penn Twp, Schuylkill	West Penn Twp, Schuylkill
M-678	Rothermel	James H	Kern	Emma P	15	May	1880	Weissport, Carbon	Lower Towamensing Twp, Carbon
M-679	Wagner	Lewis H	Schwender	Lizzie	23	May	1880	West Penn Twp, Schuylkill	Brunswick, Schuylkill
M-680	Steigerwalt	A.F.	Bowman	Maria Elizabeth	12	June	1880	Mahoning Twp, Carbon	East Penn Twp, Carbon
M-681	Campbell	James A	Evert	Emaline	12	June	1880	Weissport, Carbon	Mahoning Twp, Carbon

Beyond the Blue Mountain: Vol. II

Marriage Records

Line	Groom Surname	Groom Given	Bride Surname	Bride Given	Day	Mth	Year	He from:	She from:
M-682	Olewine	William H	Ziegenfuss	Harriet	19	June	1880	Franklin Twp, Carbon	Franklin Twp, Carbon
M-683	Walck	George W	Rex	Mira Ann	10	July	1880	Lehighton, Carbon	Mahoning Twp, Carbon
M-684	Caffrey	John W	Raworth	Delilah	13	July	1880	Packerton, Carbon	Lehighton, Carbon
M-685	Markel	Charles W	Walck	Amelia Agnes	15	July	1880	Parryville, Carbon	Lehighton, Carbon
M-686	Beck	Charles O	Frantz	Amanda	24	July	1880	Lehighton, Carbon	Lehighton, Carbon
M-687	Rehrig	George	Knappenberger	Mary Ann	30	July	1880	East Penn Twp, Carbon	Lower Towamensing Twp, Carbon
M-688	Detrich	Allen	Hine	Mary E	31	July	1880	West Penn Twp, Schuylkill	Walker Twp, Schuylkill
M-689	Ohl	Owen	Steigerwalt	Rosa A	8	Aug	1880	West Penn Twp, Schuylkill	West Penn Twp, Schuylkill
M-690	Romig	Maurice A	Rehrig	Emaline	14	Aug	1880	East Penn Twp, Carbon	East Penn Twp, Carbon
M-691	Embody	Gideon	Kolb	Ellemina	14	Aug	1880	West Penn Twp, Schuylkill	East Penn Twp, Carbon
M-692	Yoxheimer	Amandus	Eckroth	Matilda	14	Aug	1880	West Penn Twp, Schuylkill	West Penn Twp, Schuylkill
M-693	Lebenberg	John	Cunfer	Lizzie	28	Aug	1880	Mahoning Twp, Carbon	Mahoning Twp, Carbon
M-694	Daubenspeck	Samuel F	Nunnamacher	Sarah R	29	Aug	1880	West Penn Twp, Schuylkill	Brunswick, Schuylkill
M-695	Balliet	Lewis Franklin	Bowman	Henrietta Louisa	5	Sept	1880	Bowmansville, Carbon	Bowmansville, Carbon
M-696	Schellhamer	Charles W	Fenstermaker	Eliza Jane	12	Sept	1880	West Penn Twp, Schuylkill	West Penn Twp, Schuylkill
M-697	Brink	William H	Hough	Ellen	30	Sept	1880	Lansford, Carbon	Bloomingdale, Carbon
M-698	Kershner	Nathan Alfred	Gerber	Caroline Jane	3	Oct	1880	West Penn Twp, Schuylkill	West Penn Twp, Schuylkill
M-699	Dreisbach	Moses	Rabenold	Emaline	3	Oct	1880	Mahoning Twp, Carbon	Mahoning Twp, Carbon
M-700	Hittinger	William Frederi	Kolb	Emaline	9	Oct	1880	Rockport, Carbon	East Penn Twp, Carbon
M-701	Guildner	William	Fink	Ellemina	9	Oct	1880	East Penn Twp, Carbon	Heidelberg Twp, Lehigh
M-702	Klinetop	John	Mehrkam	Sarah Jane	16	Oct	1880	Lower Towamensing Twp, Carbon	Lower Towamensing Twp, Carbon
M-703	Beer	Jonas C	Christman	Amanda Mary	23	Oct	1880	Trachsville, Carbon	Mauch Chunk, Carbon
M-704	Zimmerman	Allen S	Klingaman	Lizzie L	28	Oct	1880	West Penn Twp, Schuylkill	Steinsville, Lehigh
M-705	Rex	Alvin	Campbell	Annie	13	Nov	1880	East Penn Twp, Carbon	Mahoning Twp, Carbon
M-706	Mimm	Wilson F	Gerhart	Mary	25	Dec	1880	Mauch Chunk, Carbon	Mauch Chunk, Carbon
M-707	Stroh	William R	Yeager	Sophia L	25	Dec	1880	Weatherly, Carbon	Weatherly, Carbon
M-708	Ruff	Albert L	Sherar	Emma J	13	Jan	1881	Franklin Twp, Carbon	Franklin Twp, Carbon
M-709	Dreher	Charles	Kratzer	Anna M	22	Jan	1881	Lehighton, Carbon	Franklin Twp, Carbon
M-710	Rex	Jefferson	Frohnheiser	Lucinda Jane	23	Jan	1881	Mahoning Twp, Carbon	Mahoning Twp, Carbon
M-711	Berger	Adam	Ruch	Priscilla	6	Feb	1881	Mahoning Twp, Carbon	East Penn Twp, Carbon
M-712	Long	Geo. Washingt	Willman	Abby Lucinda	22	Feb	1881	Washington Twp, Lehigh	East Penn Twp, Carbon
M-713	Patterson	Pearce	Kidd	Alice Sarah	17	Mar	1881	Catasauqua, Lehigh	Catasauqua, Lehigh
M-714	Kemerer	Thomas	Shelly	Mary Jane	19	Mar	1881	Eckley, Luzerne	East Penn Twp, Carbon
M-715	Hough	Edwin	Horn	Mary Ann	19	Mar	1881	Mahoning Twp, Carbon	Mahoning Twp, Carbon
M-716	Brown	Albert	Freeby	Amanda L	20	Mar	1881	Bowmansville, Carbon	East Penn Twp, Carbon
M-717	Schwartz	Allen G	Blose	Henrietta S	3	Apr	1881	Parryville, Carbon	Lower Towamensing Twp, Carbon

Beyond the Blue Mountain: Vol. II

Marriage Records

Line	Groom Surname	Groom Given	Bride Surname	Bride Given	Day	Mth	Year	He from:	She from:
M-718	Lower	Darby J	Brown	Sarah R	14	Apr	1881	Parryville, Carbon	Parryville, Carbon
M-719	Correll	Charles	Gerber	Sarah Yetta	1	May	1881	West Penn Twp, Schuylkill	West Penn Twp, Schuylkill
M-720	Weaver	Wellington D	Andreas	Fianna	1	May	1881	East Brunswick, Schuylkill	West Penn Twp, Schuylkill
M-721	Ziegenfuss	David E	Christman	Amelia	7	May	1881	Lower Towamensing Twp, Carbon	Elldred, Monroe
M-722	Schabo	Peter	Mertz	Mary Ann	12	June	1881	Upper Towamensing, Carbon	Mahoning Twp, Carbon
M-723	King	William	Blose	Ellen M	15	June	1881	Lower Towamensing Twp, Carbon	Lower Towamensing Twp, Carbon
M-724	Knappenberger	William H	Gelay	Sarah A	19	June	1881	Lower Towamensing Twp, Carbon	Lower Towamensing Twp, Carbon
M-725	Reichard	James B	Rehrig	Clara Alice	25	June	1881	East Penn Twp, Carbon	Mahoning Twp, Carbon
M-726	Bowman	Henry James	Schoch	Mary Alice	25	June	1881	East Penn Twp, Carbon	East Penn Twp, Carbon
M-727	Kuntz	Cornelius	Young	Ellen Mina	2	July	1881	Lansford, Carbon	Lansford, Carbon
M-728	Daley	James	Rute	Rosa A	2	July	1881	Philadelphia	East Mauch Chunk, Carbon
M-729	Blose	Elwin	Rehrig	Mary L	17	July	1881	Lower Towamensing Twp, Carbon	Lower Towamensing Twp, Carbon
M-730	Muffley	Josiah	Strohl	Lydia Ann	23	July	1881	Trachsville, Carbon	Trachsville, Carbon
M-731	Rhoads	Thomas Henry	Brown	Clara Alice	23	July	1881	Lehighton, Carbon	Catasauqua, Lehigh
M-732	Armbruster	Henry F	Blose	Mary A	27	July	1881	Philipsburg, NJ	Lower Towamensing Twp, Carbon
M-733	Sheckler	Charles	Shive	Cordelia	28	Aug	1881	Lehighton, Carbon	Lehighton, Carbon
M-734	Rau	Lewis W F	Miller	Emma Alice	11	Sept	1881	Mahoning Twp, Carbon	Mahoning Twp, Carbon
M-735	Blose	Victor Oscar	Seyger	Agnes Jane	18	Sept	1881	Weissport, Carbon	Weissport, Carbon
M-736	Hamm	Andrew J	Leibensperger	Laura A	24	Sept	1881	Lynport, Lehigh	Wesnersville, Berks
M-737	Spohn	Samuel J	Stevelton	Jeanetta I	25	Sept	1881	Franklin Twp, Carbon	West Penn Twp, Schuylkill
M-738	Eck	Augustus	Kennel	Tevilia E	8	Oct	1881	East Penn Twp, Carbon	Schnecksville, Lehigh
M-739	Laury	Harvey E	Keiper	Ellen Amanda	9	Oct	1881	Weissport, Carbon	Weissport, Carbon
M-740	Balliet	John H	Miller	Sarah	13	Oct	1881	Mahoning Twp, Carbon	Mahoning Twp, Carbon
M-741	Behler	John Jackson	Bachman	Julia	15	Oct	1881	Millport, Carbon	East Penn Twp, Carbon
M-742	Schaeffer	Adam W	Campbell	Fannie M	29	oct	1881	Reynolds, Schuylkill	Tamaqua, Schuylkill
M-743	Ziegler	Jairus W	Gerber	Henrietta	5	Nov	1881	Friedensburg, Schuylkill	West Penn Twp, Schuylkill
M-744	Hunsicker	William Frankii	Correll	Kate	19	Nov	1881	Lynntown, Lehigh	West Penn Twp, Schuylkill
M-745	Houser	William	Knepper	Alice Jane	20	Nov	1881	Tamaqua, Schuylkill	West Penn Twp, Schuylkill
M-746	Peter	John J	Steigerwalt	Amanda	26	Nov	1881	Heidelberg, Lehigh	Heidelberg, Lehigh
M-747	Loch	Noah Albert	Stoudt	Mary Ann	18	Dec	1881	West Penn Twp, Schuylkill	West Penn Twp, Schuylkill
M-748	Lapp	Charles Henry	Evert	Adline	20	Dec	1881	Mahoning Twp, Carbon	Packerton, Carbon
M-749	Rehrig	Henry Harrison	Bowman	Catherine A	24	Dec	1881	East Penn Twp, Carbon	East Penn Twp, Carbon
M-750	Richards	Charles H	Daubenspeck	Emma E	25	Dec	1881	West Penn Twp, Schuylkill	West Penn Twp, Schuylkill
M-751	Krum	L.A.	Harpel	A.M.	14	Jan	1882	Lehighton, Carbon	Lehighton, Carbon
M-752	Reppert	John	Dieter	Susan Isabella	16	Jan	1882	Lower Towamensing Twp, Carbon	Lower Towamensing Twp, Carbon
M-753	Cunfer	John E	David	Mary L	19	Jan	1882	Mahoning Twp, Carbon	Mahoning Twp, Carbon

Beyond the Blue Mountain: Vol. II

Marriage Records

Line	Groom Surname	Given	Bride Surname	Given	Day	Mth	Year	He from:	She from:
M-754	Warg	Robert	Fagan	Katie J	4	Feb	1882	Weatherly, Carbon	Weatherly, Carbon
M-755	Miller	Albright Mahlo	Green	Amanda Isabella	5	Feb	1882	Mahoning Twp, Carbon	Stemlersville, Carbon
M-756	Neumayer	John	Mantz	Emaline	12	Feb	1882	Mahoning Twp, Carbon	Mahoning Twp, Carbon
M-757	Brown	W. H.	Daubenspeck	Fianna	5	Mar	1882	West Penn Twp, Schuylkill	West Penn Twp, Schuylkill
M-758	Nothstein	Nelson Thomas	Fenstermaker	Julia Louisa	11	Mar	1882	Mahoning Twp, Carbon	Weatherly, Carbon
M-759	Frantz	Willoughby	Moser	Alavesta K	19	Mar	1882	East Penn Twp, Carbon	Mahoning Twp, Carbon
M-760	Beltz	Robert F	Blose	Anna D	19	Mar	1882	Parryville, Carbon	Lower Towamensing Twp, Carbon
M-761	Mertz	Edwin	Rex	Mary Alice	2	Apr	1882	Mahoning Twp, Carbon	Mahoning Twp, Carbon
M-762	Savitz	Wilson	Blose	Ellen Priscilla	11	Apr	1882	Lower Towamensing Twp, Carbon	Lower Towamensing Twp, Carbon
M-763	Stout	Edwin Thomas	Hill	Mary Louisa	15	Apr	1882	North Weissport, Carbon	Franklin Twp, Carbon
M-764	Markley	Jonah J	Beaver	Sarah J	16	Apr	1882	Franklin Twp, Carbon	Franklin Twp, Carbon
M-765	Morrison	James L	Snyder	Catherine	13	May	1882	Mauch Chunk, Carbon	Packerton, Carbon
M-766	Gregg	David	Strausburger	Sarah Ellen	14	May	1882	Hockendaugua, Lehigh	Upper Towamensing, Carbon
M-767	Knepper	Frank	Eberts	Matilda	16	May	1882	West Penn Twp, Schuylkill	New Mahoning, Carbon
M-768	Freeby	George Edwin	Shipe	Mary Ann	28	May	1882	East Penn Twp, Carbon	East Penn Twp, Carbon
M-769	Behler	Robert F	Gerber	Alvenia M	24	June	1882	Millport, Carbon	West Penn Twp, Schuylkill
M-770	Cunfer	Josiah	Shoemaker	Fyetta J	1	July	1882	Mahoning Twp, Carbon	Mahoning Twp, Carbon
M-771	Troxel	William	Miller	Mary	2	July	1882	West Penn Twp, Schuylkill	West Penn Twp, Schuylkill
M-772	Rehrig	Charles G	Romig	Catherine Susanna	4	July	1882	East Penn Twp, Carbon	East Penn Twp, Carbon
M-773	Loch	Joseph	Lutz	Sarah	14	Aug	1882	West Penn Twp, Schuylkill	West Penn Twp, Schuylkill
M-774	Shuck	George D	Hankey	Ellen J	19	Aug	1882	Lehigh Gap, Carbon	Lehigh Gap, Carbon
M-775	Andreas	James Irvin	George	Fietta	19	Aug	1882	East Penn Twp, Carbon	East Penn Twp, Carbon
M-776	Green	Nathaniel	Field	Susan Catherine	20	Aug	1882	Parryville, Carbon	Parryville, Carbon
M-777	Wentz	Addison	Belford	Sarah Emma	20	Aug	1882	Parryville, Carbon	Parryville, Carbon
M-778	Eaches	Adam	Spangler	Susanna	1	Sept	1882	Franklin Twp, Carbon	Franklin Twp, Carbon
M-779	Knepper	Alfred	Cole	Sarah Ann	17	Sept	1882	West Penn Twp, Schuylkill	West Penn Twp, Schuylkill
M-780	Strohl	Joseph	Fenner	Effie Jane	5	Oct	1882	Weissport, Carbon	Weissport, Carbon
M-781	Reinhart	Elias B	Osenbach	Ida Rebecca	22	Oct	1882	West Penn Twp, Schuylkill	West Penn Twp, Schuylkill
M-782	Hill	David K	Peter	Amelia Elizabeth	22	Oct	1882	West Penn Twp, Schuylkill	Lynn Twp, Lehigh
M-783	Nicholas	Amandes	Hartley	Mary Alice	9	Nov	1882	Packerton, Carbon	Packerton, Carbon
M-784	Schwartz	John	Modder	Lucetta	11	Nov	1882	Lehighton, Carbon	Low Hill Twp, Lehigh
M-785	Haldeman	Albert	Balliet	Emma E	19	Nov	1882	West Penn Twp, Schuylkill	West Penn Twp, Schuylkill
M-786	Gerber	Gideon	Zehner	Ellen Jane	7	Dec	1882	West Penn Twp, Schuylkill	Mahoning Twp, Carbon
M-787	Hamm	Franklin B	Dreisbach	Polly	20	Dec	1882	West Penn Twp, Schuylkill	West Penn Twp, Schuylkill
M-788	Lentz	Edwin J	Moyer	Ida	8	Jan	1883	Mahoning Twp, Carbon	Mahoning Twp, Carbon
M-789	Hoffman	Griffith	Hartung	Susanna	13	Jan	1883	West Penn Twp, Schuylkill	West Penn Twp, Schuylkill

Beyond the Blue Mountain: Vol. II

Marriage Records

Line	Groom Surname	Groom Given	Bride Surname	Bride Given	Day	Mth	Year	He from:	She from:
M-790	Kresge	John William	Kunkle	Sarah	11	Feb	1883	Weissport, Carbon	Packerton, Carbon
M-791	Bachman	John	Mclean	Emaline	17	Feb	1883	West Penn Twp, Schuylkill	East Brunswick, Schuylkill
M-792	Eck	William F	Kolb	Matilda	3	Mar	1883	East Penn Twp, Carbon	East Penn Twp, Carbon
M-793	Steigerwalt	T. W.	Fink	Mary Ann	5	Mar	1883	East Penn Twp, Carbon	Lehighton, Carbon
M-794	Winter	Daniel	Geiger	Annetta	1	Apr	1883	West Penn Twp, Schuylkill	West Penn Twp, Schuylkill
M-795	Mertz	Granville	Freyman	Emaline	10	Apr	1883	Mahoning Twp, Carbon	Mahoning Twp, Carbon
M-796	Flickinger	Thomas	Beltz	Sarah Alice	15	Apr	1883	Weatherly, Carbon	Mahoning Twp, Carbon
M-797	Fritz	William A	Bowman	Susanna V	21	April	1883	East Penn Twp, Carbon	East Penn Twp, Carbon
M-798	Moyer	Cornelius Phac Rex		Eva Jane	1	May	1883	Lynn Twp, Lehigh	Lynn Twp, Lehigh
M-799	Engelman	Charles Joseph	Tracy	Mary Elizabeth	3	May	1883	East Mauch Chunk, Carbon	East Mauch Chunk, Carbon
M-800	Liser	Joseph S	Bolich	Susanna	15	May	1883	West Penn Twp, Schuylkill	West Penn Twp, Schuylkill
M-801	Gerber	David Allen	Rex	Fianna	20	May	1883	West Penn Twp, Schuylkill	West Penn Twp, Schuylkill
M-802	Clauss	Aaron	Wentz	Anna E	20	May	1883	West Penn Twp, Schuylkill	Parryville, Carbon
M-803	Augle	William M	Smith	Lucretia V	11	June	1883	Dingmans Ferry, Pike	Packerton, Carbon
M-804	Hamm	Jonas Albert	Fenstermaker	Molly	15	July	1883	West Penn Twp, Schuylkill	West Penn Twp, Schuylkill
M-805	Schertzinger	Saffron	Zimmerman	Emma	29	July	1883	West Penn Twp, Schuylkill	West Penn Twp, Schuylkill
M-806	Moyer	Jonas Isaac	Hoffman	Anna Maria Susanna	15	Sept	1883	Mahoning Twp, Carbon	Weissport, Carbon
M-807	Lower	Tilghman	Reed	Mary Amanda	22	Sept	1883	Lower Towamensing Twp, Carbon	Lower Towamensing Twp, Carbon
M-808	Graver	Lafayette	Hofford	Emma	29	Sept	1883	Lehighton, Carbon	Lehighton, Carbon
M-809	Deppe	Allen C	Serfass	Hulda R	4	Oct	1883	Albrightsville, Carbon	Albrightsville, Carbon
M-810	Frantz	Alvin	Breiner	Kate	11	Nov	1883	New Mahoning, Carbon	West Penn Twp, Schuylkill
M-811	Andreas	William Henry	Ruch	Susanna Elizabeth	11	Nov	1883	East Penn Twp, Carbon	East Penn Twp, Carbon
M-812	Zimmerman	Franklin E	Hill	Mary J	7	Dec	1883	West Penn Twp, Schuylkill	West Penn Twp, Schuylkill
M-813	Troxel	Pierce J	Longacre	Emaline	11	Dec	1883	West Penn Twp, Schuylkill	New Mahoning, Carbon
M-814	Behm	John H	Benner	Eurilla Ida	13	Dec	1883	Lehighton, Carbon	Jamestown, Carbon
M-815	Kistler	John W	Gerber	Savina	25	Dec	1883	West Penn Twp, Schuylkill	West Penn Twp, Schuylkill
M-816	Smith	John	Ruch	Ellen Manda	6	Jan	1884	East Penn Twp, Carbon	East Penn Twp, Carbon
M-817	Hartung	Amandus	Stahler	Mary Jane	15	Jan	1884	West Penn Twp, Schuylkill	West Penn Twp, Schuylkill
M-818	Stemler	Oliver A	Beer	Emma J	26	Jan	1884	Towamensing, Carbon	Towamensing, Carbon
M-819	Hoffman	William E	Oldt	Emma I	27	Jan	1884	West Penn Twp, Schuylkill	West Penn Twp, Schuylkill
M-820	Gombert	Andrew J	Long	Annie D	2	Feb	1884	Mahoning Twp, Carbon	Mahoning Twp, Carbon
M-821	Isaac	William	Gallagher	Maggie	6	Feb	1884	Mauch Chunk, Carbon	Mauch Chunk, Carbon
M-822	Weiss	William	Bartholomew	Anna Maria	10	Feb	1884	Lehighton, Carbon	Lehighton, Carbon
M-823	Spengler	James A	Hofford	Ella May	11	Feb	1884	Lehighton, Carbon	Lehighton, Carbon
M-824	Bowman	Wilson D	Blose	Jane A	23	Feb	1884	East Penn Twp, Carbon	Lehigh Twp, Nthptn
M-825	Weidner	Jefferson	Kaiser	Ida Priscilla	7	Mar	1884	Lehighton, Carbon	Lehighton, Carbon

Beyond the Blue Mountain: Vol. II

Marriage Records

Line	Groom Surname	Groom Given	Bride Surname	Bride Given	Day	Mth	Year	He from:	She from:
M-826	Schelhamer	Thomas F	Miller	Sarah Amanda	15	Mar	1884	West Penn Twp, Schuylkill	West Penn Twp, Schuylkill
M-827	Ashner	James Franklin	Shafer	Emma Jane	22	Mar	1884	Mahoning Twp, Carbon	Mahoning Twp, Carbon
M-828	Fenstermacher	Nelson F	Smith	Rosa Alice	17	Apr	1884	East Penn Twp, Carbon	East Penn Twp, Carbon
M-829	Weaver	Jacob O	Haberman	Sarah Jane	4	May	1884	East Brunswick, Schuylkill	East Penn Twp, Carbon
M-830	Geiger	George	Lutz	Sarah Jane	10	May	1884	West Penn Twp, Schuylkill	West Penn Twp, Schuylkill
M-831	Xander	C. E.	Frantz	Alice	11	May	1884	Mahoning Twp, Carbon	East Penn Twp, Carbon
M-832	Loch	Daniel	Stoudt	Fianna R	11	May	1884	West Penn Twp, Schuylkill	West Penn Twp, Schuylkill
M-833	Schmidt	Herman	Schnell	Louisa	17	May	1884	Franklin Twp, Carbon	Franklin Twp, Carbon
M-834	Eberts	Frank	Sittler	Agnes V	1	June	1884	Mahoning Twp, Carbon	Mahoning Twp, Carbon
M-835	Zahn	Lewis Aaron	Rehrig	Mattie E	14	June	1884	Lehighton, Carbon	Slatington, Lehigh
M-836	Rex	Elvin	Bechtel	Mary Ellen	3	July	1884	Lehighton, Carbon	Mahoning Twp, Carbon
M-837	Hohnchen	Edwin W	Rex	Emma J	12	July	1884	Lehighton, Carbon	Lehighton, Carbon
M-838	Fritzinger	Elanius P	Bowman	Mary Amanda	19	July	1884	East Penn Twp, Carbon	East Penn Twp, Carbon
M-839	Ohl	Jefferson	Rex	Malissa Catherine	3	Aug	1884	West Penn Twp, Schuylkill	Mahoning Twp, Carbon
M-840	Borhor	Lewis	Wetzel	Sevilla	9	Aug	1884	Hudsondale, Carbon	Hudsondale, Carbon
M-841	Borger	Aaron	Rex	Lucy Ann	16	Aug	1884	Elldred, Monroe	Mahoning Twp, Carbon
M-842	Guldner	Owen	Fink	Lydia	17	Aug	1884	Lansford, Carbon	Heidelberg, Lehigh
M-843	Moyer	David	Semmel	Louisa Jane	27	Aug	1884	Mauch Chunk, Carbon	East Penn Twp, Carbon
M-844	Searfass	H. W.	Christman	E. C.	6	Sept	1884	Penn Forest Twp, Carbon	Albrightsville, Carbon
M-845	Kuntz	William C	Ramaly	Mary	18	Oct	1884	Franklin Twp, Carbon	Lehighton, Carbon
M-846	Philips	Joseph	Ronemus	Mary Eva	21	Oct	1884	Lansford, Carbon	Mahoning Twp, Carbon
M-847	Gollus	Charles C	Brandon	Emma B	27	Nov	1884	Mauch Chunk, Carbon	Mauch Chunk, Carbon
M-848	Meyers	George R	Krum	Isabella A. M.	29	Nov	1884	Mauch Chunk, Carbon	Lehighton, Carbon
M-849	Highland	Charles W	Graver	Emma E	1	Dec	1884	Parryville, Carbon	Mahoning Twp, Carbon
M-850	Heintzelman	Osville	Benninghoff	Libbie	7	Dec	1884	East Penn Twp, Carbon	Mahoning Twp, Carbon
M-851	Bretney	Granville A	Peters	Ella R	14	Dec	1884	Lehighton, Carbon	Lehighton, Carbon
M-852	Ruch	Sylvester	Kugler	Kate A	25	Dec	1884	East Penn Twp, Carbon	Mahoning Twp, Carbon
M-853	Thomas	Thomas D	Graver	Emma	25	Dec	1884	Lehighton, Carbon	Lehighton, Carbon
M-854	Krumm	William W	Fenkner	Susanna	1	Jan	1885	West Penn Twp, Schuylkill	West Penn Twp, Schuylkill
M-855	Nothstein	James M	Newhart	Rosa L	10	Jan	1885	Lehighton, Carbon	Lehighton, Carbon
M-856	Schaeffer	John C	Haydt	Elmira	17	Jan	1885	Mahoning Twp, Carbon	Trachsville, Carbon
M-857	Morgan	Frederick James	Shirey	Catherine	20	Jan	1885	Mauch Chunk, Carbon	Mauch Chunk, Carbon
M-858	Stoudt	Hiram H	Houser	Mary E	31	Jan	1885	West Penn Twp, Schuylkill	West Penn Twp, Schuylkill
M-859	Bamford	Robert G	Pettitt	Clara H	5	Feb	1885	Parryville, Carbon	Parryville, Carbon
M-860	Hagenbuch	James M	Scherer	Ellen Jane	5	Feb	1885	Hazard, Carbon	Bowmansville, Carbon
M-861	Balliet	Tilghman G	Herring	Lavina	8	Mar	1885	West Penn Twp, Schuylkill	New Mahoning, Carbon

Beyond the Blue Mountain: Vol. II

Marriage Records

Line	Groom Surname	Groom Given	Bride Surname	Bride Given	Day	Mth	Year	He from:	She from:
M-862	Bachman	Lewis	Mclean	Mary Jane	21	Mar	1885	West Penn Twp, Schuylkill	East Brunswick, Schuylkill
M-863	Green	Alvin Harrison	Schafer	Lillie Clendora	4	Apr	1885	Franklin Twp, Carbon	Franklin Twp, Carbon
M-864	Fisher	Samuel	Begel	Arminta	4	May	1885	Franklin Twp, Carbon	Franklin Twp, Carbon
M-865	Hesin	Lewis F	Beltz	Amanda	16	May	1885	West Penn Twp, Schuylkill	West Penn Twp, Schuylkill
M-866	Shoemaker	Lanies A	Hontz	Emma Jane	16	May	1885	Mahoning Twp, Carbon	Lehighton, Carbon
M-867	Knepper	Thomas	Gerber	Emma	23	May	1885	Weatherly, Carbon	West Penn Twp, Schuylkill
M-868	Rehrig	Augustus	Beltz	Ida E	23	May	1885	Bowmansville, Carbon	Hazard, Carbon
M-869	Reinsmith	Granville	Frantz	Ida Louise	24	May	1885	Mahoning Twp, Carbon	Mahoning Twp, Carbon
M-870	Kishbaugh	Wilson	Buchman	Emma L	26	May	1885	East Mauch Chunk, Carbon	East Mauch Chunk, Carbon
M-871	Gallagher	John	Haney	Lizzie	27	May	1885	Lehighton, Carbon	Lehighton, Carbon
M-872	Mummer	Milton	Bogle	Bid	4	June	1885	East Mauch Chunk, Carbon	East Mauch Chunk, Carbon
M-873	Young	Asa B	Frohnheiser	Rosa E	13	June	1885	Stenton, Nthptn	East Penn Twp, Carbon
M-874	Houser	Jacob M	Zehner	Polly A	22	Aug	1885	Brunswick, Schuylkill	West Penn Twp, Schuylkill
M-875	Bartholomew	Calvin E	Anthony	Ella L	27	Aug	1885	Lehighton, Carbon	Siegfried's Bridge, Nthptn
M-876	Klotz	Reuben Milton	Freeby	Polly Ann	6	Sept	1885	Lehighton, Carbon	East Penn Twp, Carbon
M-877	Miller	Henry Franklin	Hamilton	Eliza Jane	7	Sept	1885	Mahoning Twp, Carbon	Summit Hill, Carbon
M-878	German	Edwin F	Zimmerman	Viola	12	Sept	1885	West Penn Twp, Schuylkill	East Penn Twp, Carbon
M-879	Brown	Wesley H	Bowman	Mary A	19	Sept	1885	Bowmansville, Carbon	Parryville, Carbon
M-880	Reinheimer	William H	Reiner	Elizabeth A	19	Sept	1885	Easton, Nthptn	West Penn Twp, Schuylkill
M-881	Freyman	William H	Loch	Kate M	20	Sept	1885	Mahoning Twp, Carbon	Franklin Twp, Carbon
M-882	Weber	Thomas D	Hartman	Ella Amanda	26	Sept	1885	Heidelberg Twp, Lehigh	East Penn Twp, Carbon
M-883	Steigerwalt	William	Freeby	Ida Elizabeth	26	Sept	1885	Mahoning Twp, Carbon	West Penn Twp, Schuylkill
M-884	Snyder	David	Lieser	Saunia	8	Oct	1885	West Penn Twp, Schuylkill	Lower Towamensing Twp, Carbon
M-885	Minnich	John	Blose	Emma	26	Nov	1885	Weatherly, Carbon	Weissport, Carbon
M-886	Arner	Daniel	O'Brien	Hattie	7	Dec	1885	Weissport, Carbon	East Penn Twp, Carbon
M-887	Ginder	Charles A	Eck	Mary	26	Dec	1885	East Penn Twp, Carbon	Bowmansville, Carbon
M-888	Musselman	John H	Weidaw	Elmira	2	Jan	1886	Weissport, Carbon	West Penn Twp, Schuylkill
M-889	Kistler	David Amandu	Zimmerman	Alvena	16	Jan	1886	Mahoning Twp, Carbon	Mahoning Twp, Carbon
M-890	Nothstein	John F	Nichlas	Comilla	30	Jan	1886	Lehighton, Carbon	Penn Forest Twp, Carbon
M-891	Benninger	J. M.	Christman	Sallie A	23	Feb	1886	Walnutport, Nthptn	Mahoning Twp, Carbon
M-892	Ebberts	Amandus A	Sitler	Emma E	14	Mar	1886	Mahoning Twp, Carbon	New Philadelphia, Schuylkill
M-893	Houser	Alfred	Correll	Alice	21	Mar	1886	West Penn Twp, Schuylkill	East Penn Twp, Carbon
M-894	Youse	Milton A	Beltz	Celesta	24	Mar	1886	East Penn Twp, Carbon	Mahoning Twp, Carbon
M-895	Zellner	Moses	Hoffman	Alice	11	Apr	1886	Mahoning Twp, Carbon	Broadheadsville, Monroe
M-896	Wentz	Tobias	Hufsmith	Etna	24	April	1886	Parryville, Carbon	West Penn Twp, Schuylkill
M-897	Houser	Roland	Correll	Mary	12	June	1886	West Penn Twp, Schuylkill	

Beyond the Blue Mountain: Vol. II

Marriage Records

Line	Groom Surname	Groom Given	Bride Surname	Bride Given	Day	Mth	Year	He from:	She from:
M-898	Willman	James	Miller	Elmira	29	June	1886	East Penn Twp, Carbon	Quakake, Schuylkill
M-899	Bachman	James M	Rehrig	Angelina	31	July	1886	East Penn Twp, Carbon	East Penn Twp, Carbon
M-900	Boyer	Frank P	Gumbert	Emma	15	Aug	1886	Parryville, Carbon	East Penn Twp, Carbon
M-901	Serfass	Charles	Fritzinger	Ellen Almira	22	Aug	1886	Lehighton, Carbon	East Penn Twp, Carbon
M-902	Hill	Alfred	Steigerwalt	Hettie	5	Sept	1886	West Penn Twp, Schuylkill	East Penn Twp, Carbon
M-903	Nothstein	Milton	Hoffman	Emma J	5	Sept	1886	Mahoning Twp, Carbon	Mahoning Twp, Carbon
M-904	Ohl	Nathan	Reed	Mary A	3	Oct	1886	West Penn Twp, Schuylkill	West Penn Twp, Schuylkill
M-905	Haas	Edwin Albert	Miller	Jane	9	Oct	1886	West Penn Twp, Schuylkill	Mahoning Twp, Carbon
M-906	Eckert	Harry	Smith	Cora J	28	Oct	1886	Lehighton, Carbon	Pennsville, Carbon
M-907	Troxel	Frank A	Schock	Agnes M	7	Nov	1886	West Penn Twp, Schuylkill	Walker Twp, Schuylkill
M-908	Greenogle	Ferdinand	Fether	Louisa	9	Nov	1886	Tamaqua, Schuylkill	Walker Twp, Schuylkill
M-909	Beltz	David	Troxall	Catherine	6	Feb	1887	West Penn Twp, Schuylkill	West Penn Twp, Schuylkill
M-910	Steigerwalt	Willoughby Ric	Moyer	Emma	12	Feb	1887	Mahoning Twp, Carbon	Mahoning Twp, Carbon
M-911	Guldner	Lewis	Schwartz	Lucetta Camille	19	Feb	1887	Bowmanstown, Carbon	Bowmanstown, Carbon
M-912	Frederick	Jefferson	Gombert	Sarah Jane	10	Mar	1887	Mahoning Twp, Carbon	Mahoning Twp, Carbon
M-913	Beltz	Thomas D	Miller	Susannah	13	Mar	1887	West Penn Twp, Schuylkill	West Penn Twp, Schuylkill
M-914	Mantz	J. F.	Schaefer	E. L.	20	Mar	1887	West Penn Twp, Schuylkill	West Penn Twp, Schuylkill
M-915	Sendel	Richard	Long	Mary	9	Apr	1887	Mahoning Twp, Carbon	Mahoning Twp, Carbon
M-916	Arner	Thomas Jeffers	Mertz	Cora Alice	10	Apr	1887	Mahoning Twp, Carbon	East Penn Twp, Carbon
M-917	Boyer	Milton C	Fenstermaker	Sarah	5	May	1887	Lehighton, Carbon	Walnutport, Nthptn
M-918	Wehr	Tilghman	Mantz	Lizzie	28	May	1887	West Penn Twp, Schuylkill	West Penn Twp, Schuylkill
M-919	Ziegler	Amandus A	Klingeman	Louisa	29	May	1887	Quakake, Schuylkill	Steinsville, Lehigh
M-920	Miller	Hebron	Hess	Louisa I	29	May	1887	Mahoning Twp, Carbon	Lynn Twp, Lehigh
M-921	Hamm	Noah A	Becker	Sarah A	19	June	1887	West Penn Twp, Schuylkill	Mahoning Twp, Carbon
M-922	Heintzelman	Oscar S	Keiper	Clara	4	July	1887	Upper Lehigh, Luzerne	Upper Lehigh, Luzerne
M-923	Meitzler	John Calvin	Gerber	Emaline Jane	31	July	1887	Mahoning Twp, Carbon	Mahoning Twp, Carbon
M-924	Ziegler	Elias	Henry	Sallie	20	Aug	1887	Quakake, Schuylkill	Weatherly, Carbon
M-925	Ebberts	Charles A	Cunfer	Tillie M	28	Aug	1887	Mahoning Twp, Carbon	Mahoning Twp, Carbon
M-926	Lorah	Harrison	Guldner	Kate	23	Aug	1887	West Penn Twp, Schuylkill	East Penn Twp, Carbon
M-927	Schleicher	Charles Frankl	Moyer	Emma Catherine	6	Nov	1887	East Penn Twp, Carbon	East Penn Twp, Carbon
M-928	Andreas	Thomas Frankl	Hunt	Emma Louisa	6	Nov	1887	East Penn Twp, Carbon	East Penn Twp, Carbon
M-929	Heydt	Jacob	Kibbler	Annie	30	Nov	1887	Wild Creek, Carbon	Albrightsville, Carbon
M-930	Ruch	Charles	Bowman	Fianna Alavesta	24	Dec	1887	East Penn Twp, Carbon	East Penn Twp, Carbon
M-931	Smith	Henry	Steigerwalt	Harriet	25	Dec	1887	Mahoning Twp, Carbon	East Penn Twp, Carbon
M-932	Fink	Joseph W	Fritzinger	Sarah Catherine	27	Dec	1887	Weissport, Carbon	Lehighton, Carbon
M-933	Moser	David M	Holtzer	Sallie C	1	Jan	1888	Mahoning Twp, Carbon	Mahoning Twp, Carbon

Beyond the Blue Mountain: Vol. II

Marriage Records

Line	Groom Surname	Given	Bride Surname	Given	Day	Mth	Year	He from:	She from:
M-934	Smith	J.P	Swartz	Emma L	1	Jan	1888	Lehighton, Carbon	Lehighton, Carbon
M-935	Cunfer	George Benjan	Ebberts	Minerva	22	Jan	1888	Mahoning Twp, Carbon	Mahoning Twp, Carbon
M-936	Freyman	John	Kramer	Lottie	30	Jan	1888	Mahoning Twp, Carbon	Beaver Run, Carbon
M-937	Trainer	Robert Milton	Rehrig	Ida	11	Feb	1888	Lehighton, Carbon	Lehighton, Carbon
M-938	Smith	James O	Boyer	Amelia Ann	17	Mar	1888	Lower Towamensing Twp, Carbon	Lower Towamensing Twp, Carbon
M-939	Hill	Edwin	Andreas	Louisa A	18	Mar	1888	West Penn Twp, Schuylkill	West Penn Twp, Schuylkill
M-940	Roth	Charles F	Arner	Ellen K	18	Mar	1888	Mahoning Twp, Carbon	Mahoning Twp, Carbon
M-941	Boyer	Abel	Bowman	Maggie	31	Mar	1888	Lower Towamensing Twp, Carbon	Lower Towamensing Twp, Carbon
M-942	Neifert	George Albert	Mengel	Emma	31	Mar	1888	West Penn Twp, Schuylkill	East Penn Twp, Carbon
M-943	Rex	Nathan L	Moser	Alvenia	14	Apr	1888	Mahoning Twp, Carbon	Mahoning Twp, Carbon
M-944	Schoch	George Frankli	Bierman	Angelina	22	Apr	1888	East Penn Twp, Carbon	Mahoning Twp, Carbon
M-945	Smith	Adam A	Smoyer	Emma M	1	May	1888	Parryville, Carbon	Parryville, Carbon
M-946	Schaeffer	Alexander O	Haymam	Emma	20	May	1888	Mahoning Twp, Carbon	Reynolds, Schuylkill
M-947	Fink	Henry	Mertz	Emma	20	May	1888	East Penn Twp, Carbon	East Penn Twp, Carbon
M-948	Mantz	Milton C	Klingaman	Rosa A	26	May	1888	West Penn Twp, Schuylkill	Steinsville, Lehigh
M-949	Koons	Alvin R	Rex	S. Elizabeth	21	May	1888	Mahoning Twp, Carbon	Mahoning Twp, Carbon
M-950	Markell	William H	Best	Lizzie J	29	May	1888	Lehigh Gap, Carbon	Lehigh Gap, Carbon
M-951	Scheirer	Christian	Mangold	Sarah	2	June	1888	Mauch Chunk, Carbon	Franklin Twp, Carbon
M-952	Snyder	Sylvester L (Pro	Albright	Amanda L	2	June	1888	Franklin Twp, Carbon	Weissport, Carbon
M-953	Hough	Martin A	Miller	Mary	23	June	1888	Weissport, Carbon	Lehighton, Carbon
M-954	Remaley	Wilson	Hunsicker	Polly	24	June	1888	Mahoning Twp, Carbon	Mahoning Twp, Carbon
M-955	Wisler	Frank	Henry	Louisa R	14	July	1888	Bowmanstown, Carbon	Weatherly, Carbon
M-956	Heintzelman	James G	Berger	Ellen	22	July	1888	East Penn Twp, Carbon	East Penn Twp, Carbon
M-957	Hamm	Charles	Balliet	Anna E	4	Aug	1888	West Penn Twp, Schuylkill	West Penn Twp, Schuylkill
M-958	Bartholomew	Eugene U	Schuler	Emaline	6	Aug	1888	Lehighton, Carbon	Lehighton, Carbon
M-959	Hausman	John A	Everitt	Emma	11	Aug	1888	Weissport, Carbon	Weissport, Carbon
M-960	Mertz	Thomas	Lentz	Lillie R	19	Aug	1888	Mahoning Twp, Carbon	Mahoning Twp, Carbon
M-961	Steigerwalt	William	Billman	Lizzie	1	Sept	1888	West Penn Twp, Schuylkill	West Penn Twp, Schuylkill
M-962	Hoffman	Nathan	Fenstermacher	Lucy Anna Amanda	8	Oct	1888	East Penn Twp, Carbon	East Penn Twp, Carbon
M-963	Fenstermacher	John H	Smith	Rosa	8	Oct	1888	Packerton, Carbon	Packerton, Carbon
M-964	Bowman	John	Leaser	Maria	11	Nov	1888	East Penn Twp, Carbon	East Penn Twp, Carbon
M-965	Hilliard	Charles	Hill	Emma	12	Nov	1888	Jackson Twp, Monroe	Franklin Twp, Carbon
M-966	Andreas	Owen A	Steigerwalt	Louisa	16	Dec	1888	West Penn Twp, Schuylkill	East Penn Twp, Carbon
M-967	Rubrecht	W. A.	Freyman	Lucy A	22	Dec	1888	West Penn Twp, Schuylkill	Mahoning Twp, Carbon
M-968	Gumbert	Frank	Cunfer	Caroline	22	Dec	1888	Mahoning Twp, Carbon	Mahoning Twp, Carbon
M-969	Geiger	James A	Fritzinger	Priscilla	25	Dec	1888	Lehighton, Carbon	East Penn Twp, Carbon

Beyond the Blue Mountain: Vol. II

Marriage Records

Line	Groom Surname	Groom Given	Bride Surname	Bride Given	Day	Mth	Year	He from:	She from:
M-970	Daubenspeck	John	Hill	Mary A	13	Jan	1889	West Penn Twp, Schuylkill	West Penn Twp, Schuylkill
M-971	Weiss	John O	Reber	Emma L	13	Jan	1889	Franklin Twp, Carbon	Franklin Twp, Carbon
M-972	Cunfer	Charles L	Kuntz	Mena Amanda	14	Feb	1889	Mahoning Twp, Carbon	Mahoning Twp, Carbon
M-973	Steigerwalt	Alfred A	Ohl	Mary J	17	Feb	1889	West Penn Twp, Schuylkill	West Penn Twp, Schuylkill
M-974	Mertz	Frank	Drumbore	Clara	15	Mar	1889	Mahoning Twp, Carbon	Mahoning Twp, Carbon
M-975	Gumbert	William	Mertz	Kate	16	Mar	1889	Mahoning Twp, Carbon	Mahoning Twp, Carbon
M-976	Pryor	Elmer H	Graver	Minnie A	23	Mar	1889	Mountain Top, Luzerne	Weissport, Carbon
M-977	Bailey	James S	Neff	Amanda Jane	14	Apr	1889	East Penn Twp, Carbon	East Penn Twp, Carbon
M-978	Graver	John F	Handwerk	Magdella M	20	Apr	1889	Weissport, Carbon	Parryville, Carbon
M-979	Siglin	George E	Arner	Jennetta	18	May	1889	Lycoming County	Mahoning Twp, Carbon
M-980	Fritzinger	Francis H	Schott	Mary N	8	June	1889	Lynn Twp, Lehigh	Lynn Twp, Lehigh
M-981	Brown	Albert G A	Sandel	Clara Eva Jane	29	June	1889	Mahoning Twp, Carbon	Mahoning Twp, Carbon
M-982	Day	John E	Andrew	Ella	3	July	1889	Penn Forest Twp, Carbon	Penn Forest Twp, Carbon
M-983	Fritzinger	Edwin M	Heffelfinger	Emma Jane	13	July	1889	East Penn Twp, Carbon	Danielsville, Nmptn
M-984	Gerber	Edwin F	Schminke	Annie	20	July	1889	West Penn Twp, Schuylkill	Mahanoy City, Schuylkill
M-985	Yenser	Thomas	Romig	Diana M	21	July	1889	Bowmanstown, Carbon	East Penn Twp, Carbon
M-986	Albright	Harvey K	Knauss	Emma	27	July	1889	Weissport, Carbon	Weissport, Carbon
M-987	Funk	Samuel	Sendel	Emma E	7	Sept	1889	Lehighton, Carbon	Mahoning Twp, Carbon
M-988	Mertz	John R	Gombert	Ellen L	28	Sept	1889	Mahoning Twp, Carbon	Mahoning Twp, Carbon
M-989	Gombert	John G	Mertz	Sarah E	4	Oct	1889	Mahoning Twp, Carbon	Mahoning Twp, Carbon
M-990	Bast	Edward D	Rinker	Ella	5	Oct	1889	Bethlehem, Lehigh	Parryville, Carbon
M-991	Becker	William Henry	Grow	Carolina Savilla	6	Oct	1889	Mahoning Twp, Carbon	Mahoning Twp, Carbon
M-992	Sendel	Nelson Ellswor	Sheckler	Lydia A S	3	Nov	1889	Mahoning Twp, Carbon	East Weissport, Carbon
M-993	Remmel	Ezra Jerome	Andreas	Mary Agnes	29	Nov	1889	Penn Forest Twp, Carbon	Penn Forest Twp, Carbon
M-994	Strohm	Oscar J	Raddatz	Amelia A	30	Dec	1889	Lehighton, Carbon	Hokendaugua, Lehigh
M-995	Fritzinger	J. H.	Schoch	Agnes	4	Jan	1890	East Penn Twp, Carbon	East Penn Twp, Carbon
M-996	Andreas	Rodger Elmer	Sensinger	Louisa	9	Mar	1890	East Penn Twp, Carbon	Heidelberg, Lehigh
M-997	Troxell	Elias A	Merkel	Zeriah	6	Apr	1890	West Penn Twp, Schuylkill	Lewistown, Schuylkill
M-998	Miller	Edward	Geggins	Alice	26	Apr	1890	Lehighton, Carbon	Lehighton, Carbon
M-999	Hartranft	Francis C	Shidely	Anna	24	May	1890	East Penn Twp, Carbon	East Penn Twp, Carbon
M-1000	Biebelheimer	Jeremiah	Wehr	Emma	25	May	1890	West Penn Twp, Schuylkill	West Penn Twp, Schuylkill
M-1001	Loch	Alfred B	Kemerer	Annie M	25	May	1890	West Penn Twp, Schuylkill	East Penn Twp, Carbon
M-1002	Eberts	Oliver O	Hunsicker	Ellen T	28	June	1890	Mahoning Twp, Carbon	West Penn Twp, Schuylkill
M-1003	Gerber	Moses A	Arndt	Ida E	5	July	1890	West Penn Twp, Schuylkill	West Penn Twp, Schuylkill
M-1004	Reber	Francis O	Sittler	Lucetta	26	July	1890	Mahoning Twp, Carbon	Mahoning Twp, Carbon
M-1005	Steigerwalt	Elias	Arndt	Mantana	30	Aug	1890	West Penn Twp, Schuylkill	West Penn Twp, Schuylkill

Beyond the Blue Mountain: Vol. II

Marriage Records

Line	Groom Surname	Groom Given	Bride Surname	Bride Given	Day	Mth	Year	He from:	She from:
M-1006	Rehrig	John A	Schleicher	Lillie J	30	Aug	1890	East Penn Twp, Carbon	East Penn Twp, Carbon
M-1007	Schwab	William A	Dracy	Minnie	25	Sept	1890	East Mauch Chunk, Carbon	East Mauch Chunk, Carbon
M-1008	Yehl	Robert Allen	Klotz	Laura Tana	11	Oct	1890	Lehighton, Carbon	Lehighton, Carbon
M-1009	Hoffman	Alvin	Smith	Sarah	13	Oct	1890	East Penn Twp, Carbon	East Penn Twp, Carbon
M-1010	Steinmetz	Robert S	Fritzinger	Alavesta	18	Oct	1890	Allentown, Lehigh	East Penn Twp, Carbon
M-1011	Hafer	Jared M	Hoppes	Rosa R	21	Dec	1890	East Brunswick, Schuylkill	West Penn Twp, Schuylkill
M-1012	McDaniel	James Erwin	Miller	Alice Cora	25	Dec	1890	Mahoning Twp, Carbon	Summit Hill, Carbon
M-1013	Romig	Daniel F	Schultz	Sallie Ann	25	Dec	1890	East Penn Twp, Carbon	Lehighton, Carbon
M-1014	Horn	Oscar E	Ziegenfuss	Alice Louise	25	Dec	1890	Mahoning Twp, Carbon	Franklin Twp, Carbon
M-1015	Solt	Jacob	Gumbert	Alice S	3	Jan	1891	Jamestown, Carbon	Mahoning Twp, Carbon
M-1016	Frohnheiser	Nathan Henry	Bachman	Mary Ellen	18	Jan	1891	East Penn Twp, Carbon	East Penn Twp, Carbon
M-1017	Schoch	Francis Oliver	Bauer	Elizabeth Jane	24	Jan	1891	East Penn Twp, Carbon	East Penn Twp, Carbon
M-1018	Miller	Oliver D	Frank	Dora H	1	Feb	1891	West Penn Twp, Schuylkill	Rush Twp, Schuylkill
M-1019	Guldner	Charles L	Bauer	Sarah Ann	17	Feb	1891	East Penn Twp, Carbon	East Penn Twp, Carbon
M-1020	Mumbower	Elmer	McDaniel	Emma Martha	22	Feb	1891	Mauch Chunk, Carbon	Mahoning Twp, Carbon
M-1021	Leeser	Thomas	Longacre	Jennie	21	Mar	1891	West Penn Twp, Schuylkill	West Penn Twp, Schuylkill
M-1022	Oldt	A. F.	Hunsicker	Lizzie J	29	Mar	1891	Mahoning Twp, Carbon	Mahoning Twp, Carbon
M-1023	David	Vester	Frohnheiser	Sarah Agnes	9	Apr	1891	Lehighton, Carbon	Lehighton, Carbon
M-1024	Quick	William Henry	Rubrecht	Emma Seniah	30	Apr	1891	Philadelphia	West Penn Twp, Schuylkill
M-1025	Campbell	Daniel H	Hartman	Elmira	14	May	1891	Weissport, Carbon	Weissport, Carbon
M-1026	Battenfield	Severinus	Schwartz	Meda	16	May	1891	Whitehall Twp, Lehigh	Whitehall Twp, Lehigh
M-1027	Frantz	Moses G	Balliet	Sarah	17	May	1891	Mahoning Twp, Carbon	West Penn Twp, Schuylkill
M-1028	Miller	Charles O	Wehr	Lizzie A	17	May	1891	West Penn Twp, Schuylkill	West Penn Twp, Schuylkill
M-1029	Dreibelbies	George A	Wehr	Amanda	24	May	1891	West Penn Twp, Schuylkill	West Penn Twp, Schuylkill
M-1030	Semmel	Granville Henry	Andrews	Sallie Loveneh	31	May	1891	East Penn Twp, Carbon	East Penn Twp, Carbon
M-1031	Campbell	Martin	Solt	Isabella	13	June	1891	Weissport, Carbon	Weissport, Carbon
M-1032	Blose	Oscar	Gumbert	Lesta	5	July	1891	Parryville, Carbon	East Penn Twp, Carbon
M-1033	Koch	Henry	Miller	Lizzie	10	July	1891	Franklin Twp, Carbon	Franklin Twp, Carbon
M-1034	Maidenwald	Henry M	Boyer	Lizzie	16	July	1891	Bowmans, Carbon	Bowmans, Carbon
M-1035	Schelly	James	Hoffman	Fietta	18	Sept	1891	East Penn Twp, Carbon	East Penn Twp, Carbon
M-1036	Gerber	Charles A	Fether	Mary Jane	19	Sept	1891	West Penn Twp, Schuylkill	Walker Twp, Schuylkill
M-1037	Braerman	L H	Strohl	Josephine	19	Sept	1891	Bath, Nthptn	Towamensing, Carbon
M-1038	Stahler	William S	Stoudt	Clara L	24	Sept	1891	West Penn Twp, Schuylkill	West Penn Twp, Schuylkill
M-1039	Woods	John B	Kostenbader	Sue	31	Oct	1891	Reading, Berks	Reading, Berks
M-1040	Heiser	Erwin D	Snyder	Emma S	28	Nov	1891	Mahoning Twp, Carbon	Mahoning Twp, Carbon
M-1041	Rehrig	Harrison O	Gaumer	Nora L	5	Dec	1891	East Mauch Chunk, Carbon	East Mauch Chunk, Carbon

Beyond the Blue Mountain: Vol. II

Marriage Records

Line	Groom Surname	Groom Given	Bride Surname	Bride Given	Day	Mth	Year	He from:	She from:
M-1042	Oswald	John	Hartung	Laura	12	Dec	1891	East Brunswick, Schuylkill	West Penn Twp, Schuylkill
M-1043	Schultz	Athabay	Sowers	Sitney F	24	Dec	1891	Lehighton, Carbon	Lehighton, Carbon
M-1044	Young	Levi A	Bachman	Emma	25	Dec	1891	East Penn Twp, Carbon	East Penn Twp, Carbon
M-1045	Schappel	Milton A	Rehrig	Sarah M	28	Dec	1891	East Penn Twp, Carbon	East Penn Twp, Carbon
M-1046	Ginder	John Henry	Eck	Hattie Anna	3	Jan	1892	East Penn Twp, Carbon	East Penn Twp, Carbon
M-1047	Snyder	Wallace O	Ebert	Clara A. J.	9	Feb	1892	West Penn Twp, Schuylkill	Heidelberg Twp, Lehigh
M-1048	Bauer	J DeHaven	Miller	Sallie Ann	17	Feb	1892	Lehighton, Carbon	Lehighton, Carbon
M-1049	Lentz	James O	Meitzler	Elamanda P.T.	20	Feb	1892	Towamensing, Carbon	Kresgeville, Monroe
M-1050	Rex	William Penn	Fritzinger	Mary J	13	Mar	1892	West Penn Twp, Schuylkill	East Penn Twp, Carbon
M-1051	Lapp	Edward	Baumholtzer	Mary Ann	9	Apr	1892	Lehighton, Carbon	Lehighton, Carbon
M-1052	Schnella	George A.C.	Johnson	Cora	19	May	1892	Lehighton, Carbon	Packerton, Carbon
M-1053	Jones	Edwin M	Searfass	Lucinda	24	May	1892	Lehighton, Carbon	Lehighton, Carbon
M-1054	Ziegler	Lewis A	Haas	Elmira L	19	June	1892	West Penn Twp, Schuylkill	West Penn Twp, Schuylkill
M-1055	Diehl	Morris	Hontz	Annie S	10	July	1892	Allentown, Lehigh	Allentown, Lehigh
M-1056	Bowman	Charles P	Bowman	Ella	31	Aug	1892	East Penn Twp, Carbon	East Penn Twp, Carbon
M-1057	Ohl	William F	Brown	Josephine	11	Sept	1892	West Penn Twp, Schuylkill	Weissport, Carbon
M-1058	Goldburg	Martin	Getz	Augusta	22	Sept	1892	Lehighton, Carbon	Lehighton, Carbon
M-1059	Grant	Arnold D.	Laurish	Emma L	1	Oct	1892	Packerton, Carbon	Packerton, Carbon
M-1060	Wolfskeil	Conrad	Hill	Emma J	20	Oct	1892	Hazelton, Luzerne	Hazelton, Luzerne
M-1061	Arner	Joseph D	Briner	Agnes E	31	Dec	1892	Mahoning Twp, Carbon	West Penn Twp, Schuylkill
M-1062	Kemmerer	C. D.	Steigerwalt	Mantana	14	Jan	1893	East Penn Twp, Carbon	West Penn Twp, Schuylkill
M-1063	Wehr	Lewis Oscar	Reichard	Sally Ann	1	Apr	1893	East Penn Twp, Carbon	East Penn Twp, Carbon
M-1064	Mertz	Samuel	Stroup	Mantana L	1	Apr	1893	Mahoning Twp, Carbon	Mahoning Twp, Carbon
M-1065	Kluger	William T	Morgan	Catherine	1	Apr	1893	Mauch Chunk, Carbon	Mauch Chunk, Carbon
M-1066	Hartranft	Elias	Cooper	Sarah Ann	9	May	1893	Lansford, Carbon	Mahoning Twp, Carbon
M-1067	Arner	Emanuel	Snyder	Percy May	20	May	1893	Parryville, Carbon	Parryville, Carbon
M-1068	Pettit	Harry R	Stemler	Emma L	30	May	1893	Pottsville, Schuylkill	Stemlersville, Carbon
M-1069	Snyder	Lewis	Kline	Catherine	15	June	1893	East Mauch Chunk, Carbon	East Mauch Chunk, Carbon
M-1070	Graver	George Benjan Klotz	Huntzinger	Sarah Irene Carrie	8	July	1893	Franklin Twp, Carbon	Franklin Twp, Carbon
M-1071	Beltz	Harrison	Huntzinger	Emma	13	July	1893	Mauch Chunk, Carbon	Mauch Chunk, Carbon
M-1072	Snyder	Samuel Phaon	Hollenbach	Kate	16	July	1893	East Penn Twp, Carbon	Lansford, Carbon
M-1073	Andreas	G. E.	Rehrig	Fianna	22	July	1893	East Penn Twp, Carbon	East Penn Twp, Carbon
M-1074	Evans	John W	Spoonheimer	Mary J	6	Aug	1893	Slatington, Lehigh	Slatington, Lehigh
M-1075	Gerber	Austin B	George	Alice P	26	Aug	1893	West Penn Twp, Schuylkill	West Penn Twp, Schuylkill
M-1076	Rehrig	Lester B	Ulrich	Carrie I	8	Sept	1893	Lehighton, Carbon	Lehighton, Carbon
M-1077	Walter	Lewis A	Heintzelman	Mantana I	23	Sept	1893	Tripoli, Lehigh	Tripoli, Lehigh

Beyond the Blue Mountain: Vol. II

Marriage Records

Line	Groom Surname	Groom Given	Bride Surname	Bride Given	Day	Mth	Year	He from:	She from:
M-1078	Brown	Albert J	Snyder	Annie E	14	Oct	1893	Towamensing, Carbon	Towamensing, Carbon
M-1079	Miller	William H	Mantz	Valeria A	14	Oct	1893	West Penn Twp, Schuylkill	West Penn Twp, Schuylkill
M-1080	Wehr	Alvin Adam	Creitz	Cora E	2	Nov	1893	Mahoning Twp, Carbon	Mahoning Twp, Carbon
M-1081	Muthard	David M	Moyer	Katie Ann R	18	Nov	1893	Mahoning Twp, Carbon	Mahoning Twp, Carbon
M-1082	McDaniel	Thomas	Strohl	Mary	29	Dec	1893	Towamensing, Carbon	Towamensing, Carbon
M-1083	Ervin	John	Kressley	Emma L	28	Jan	1894	Mahoning Twp, Carbon	Mahoning Twp, Carbon
M-1084	Bachman	John R	Youse	Emma E	28	Jan	1894	East Penn Twp, Carbon	East Penn Twp, Carbon
M-1085	Snyder	T. B.	Billig	Elmira E	17	Feb	1894	West Penn Twp, Schuylkill	West Penn Twp, Schuylkill
M-1086	Snyder	Charles	Freeby	Sarah J	8	Apr	1894	Bowmans, Carbon	East Penn Twp, Carbon
M-1087	Larasch	Edwin H	Blose	Dianna	13	Apr	1894	Packerton, Carbon	Towamensing, Carbon
M-1088	Hill	Franklin	Shelhamer	Josephine	14	Apr	1894	West Penn Twp, Schuylkill	West Penn Twp, Schuylkill
M-1089	Arnold	Jacob J	Kunkle	Lizzie	13	May	1894	Mahoning Twp, Carbon	Mahoning Twp, Carbon
M-1090	Campbell	Frank Pierce	Reed	Ella B	15	July	1894	Lehighton, Carbon	Lehighton, Carbon
M-1091	Beltzner	Charles	Heiser	Bertha	15	July	1894	East Mauch Chunk, Carbon	Beaver Run, Carbon
M-1092	Fether	Daniel Amandt	Swank	Clara M	25	Aug	1894	Walker Twp, Schuylkill	Muncy Twp, Lycoming
M-1093	Ziegler	Amandus C	Berger	Katie	4	Nov	1894	West Penn Twp, Schuylkill	East Penn Twp, Carbon
M-1094	Lutz	Willliam J	Hoffman	Mary A	10	Nov	1894	East Penn Twp, Carbon	East Penn Twp, Carbon
M-1095	George	Lewis	Hahn	Ellemanda	22	Dec	1894	East Penn Twp, Carbon	Long Run, Carbon
M-1096	Evans	William A	Oswald	Mary J	25	Dec	1894	Slatington, Lehigh	Jacksonville, Lehigh
M-1097	Berger	John	Stabelton	Kate Alice	5	Jan	1895	East Penn Twp, Carbon	West Penn Twp, Schuylkill
M-1098	Kemmerer	Henry Solomor	Bowman	Lizzie E	2	Feb	1895	East Penn Twp, Carbon	East Penn Twp, Carbon
M-1099	David	Albert	Rehrig	Rosa A	3	Mar	1895	Mahoning Twp, Carbon	Mahoning Twp, Carbon
M-1100	Riegel	William E	Steigerwalt	Mary A	16	Mar	1895	East Penn Twp, Carbon	East Penn Twp, Carbon
M-1101	Peters	Charles A	Evert	Margeret M	13	Apr	1895	Lehighton, Carbon	Jamestown, Carbon
M-1102	Berlin	William O	Gilbert	Kate A	13	Apr	1895	Lehighton, Carbon	Lehighton, Carbon
M-1103	Freyman	Granville P	Smith	Malinda E	14	Apr	1895	Mahoning Twp, Carbon	Towamensing, Carbon
M-1104	Raudenbush	Grant	Wertman	Lillie Ida	2	June	1895	Mahanoy City, Schuylkill	West Penn Twp, Schuylkill
M-1105	Ouldt	Franklin J	Haas	Emma T	8	June	1895	West Penn Twp, Schuylkill	West Penn Twp, Schuylkill
M-1106	Romig	Victor James	Blose	Eva Agnes	16	June	1895	East Penn Twp, Carbon	Hazard, Carbon
M-1107	Fritzinger	Peter M	Fritzinger	Anna M	13	July	1895	Lehighton, Carbon	Lehighton, Carbon
M-1108	Wagner	Charles Nathai	Houser	Laura Ida	27	July	1895	Tamaqua, Schuylkill	Reynolds, Schuylkill
M-1109	Dreisbach	Ervin	Reichard	Ida Cecilia	10	Aug	1895	Mahoning Twp, Carbon	Mahoning Twp, Carbon
M-1110	Keener	Preston C	Haintz	Laura Ellen J	17	Aug	1895	Jamestown, Carbon	Jamestown, Carbon
M-1111	Schilbach	Henry	Beaver	Clara J	28	Sept	1895	Weissport, Carbon	Weissport, Carbon
M-1112	Rickert	William L	Ervin	Bessie	20	Oct	1895	Summit Hill, Carbon	Mahoning Twp, Carbon
M-1113	Daubenspeck	D. W.	Wentz	Laura A	27	Oct	1895	West Penn Twp, Schuylkill	Parryville, Carbon

Beyond the Blue Mountain: Vol. II

Marriage Records

Line	Groom Surname	Given	Bride Surname	Given	Day	Mth	Year	He from:	She from:
M-1114	Strohm	George	Kromer	Stella Y	2	Nov	1895	Lehighton, Carbon	Weissport, Carbon
M-1115	Bachman	Joseph E	Freeby	Laura Jane	15	Dec	1895	East Penn Twp, Carbon	East Penn Twp, Carbon
M-1116	Frantz	John H	Heiser	Sophia E	25	Dec	1895	Mahoning Twp, Carbon	Mauch Chunk, Carbon
M-1117	Haas	Charles A	Hartman	Louisa	28	Dec	1895	West Penn Twp, Schuylkill	West Penn Twp, Schuylkill
M-1118	Horn	W. H.	Boyer	Minnie	7	Mar	1896	Mahoning Twp, Carbon	Parryville, Carbon
M-1119	Arner	Clinton A	Fritzinger	Kate A	14	Mar	1896	Bowmanstown, Carbon	Bowmanstown, Carbon
M-1120	Noll	Ambrose E	Pettit	Beulah M	4	Apr	1896	Bowmanstown, Carbon	Towamensing, Carbon
M-1121	Rex	Oscar E	Fenstermaker	Minie	11	Apr	1896	Mahoning Twp, Carbon	Mahoning Twp, Carbon
M-1122	Smith	Alfred A	Mclean	Lillie	21	May	1896	Mahoning Twp, Carbon	Mahoning Twp, Carbon
M-1123	Kolb	Pierce	Riegel	Hattie V	21	June	1896	East Penn Twp, Carbon	East Penn Twp, Carbon
M-1124	Stahler	James G	Strohl	Carrie A	27	June	1896	Mauch Chunk, Carbon	Nesquehoning, Carbon
M-1125	Frantz	Charles A	Ziegenfuss	Lillie A	8	Aug	1896	East Penn Twp, Carbon	Franklin Twp, Carbon
M-1126	Neff	George Henry	Rehrig	Maggie J	8	Aug	1896	East Penn Twp, Carbon	East Penn Twp, Carbon
M-1127	Heiselmoyer	George A	Beaver	Lillie M	31	Oct	1896	Allentown, Lehigh	Weissport, Carbon
M-1128	Goldberg	Joseph N	Markley	Clara	14	Nov	1896	Franklin Twp, Carbon	Franklin Twp, Carbon
M-1129	Freeby	William J	Hartranft	Amanda E	29	Nov	1896	East Penn Twp, Carbon	East Penn Twp, Carbon
M-1130	Rush	John A	Snyder	Lydia E	19	Dec	1896	Mahoning Twp, Carbon	Packerton, Carbon
M-1131	Young	Frank	Blose	Ilerda	15	Feb	1897	Franklin Twp, Carbon	Franklin Twp, Carbon
M-1132	Cunfer	Jacob	Freyman	Emma	20	Mar	1897	Mahoning Twp, Carbon	Mahoning Twp, Carbon
M-1133	Davidson	Irvin	Balliet	Kate	22	Apr	1897	New Mahoning, Carbon	West Penn Twp, Schuylkill
M-1134	Zellner	James	Davidson	Rosa	6	May	1897	Mahoning Twp, Carbon	Mahoning Twp, Carbon
M-1135	Miller	Levi A	Frantz	Safena	15	May	1897	East Penn Twp, Carbon	Bloomingdale, Carbon
M-1136	Greenzweig	Charles S.	Grow	Mary S	15	May	1897	Packerton, Carbon	Packerton, Carbon
M-1137	Drumbore	Robert W	Houser	Irena	31	July	1897	Lehighton, Carbon	West Penn Twp, Schuylkill
M-1138	Gerber	Amandus F	Wagaman	Lilly A S	3	Oct	1897	West Penn Twp, Schuylkill	Mahoning Twp, Carbon
M-1139	Schappel	Assipa J	Treichler	Mary A	27	Nov	1897	Weisenberg, Lehigh	Weisenberg, Lehigh
M-1140	Ohl	George W	Krum	Cora Estella	25	Dec	1897	Lehighton, Carbon	Lehighton, Carbon
M-1141	Snyder	Charles Edwin	Fenstermaker	Katie Louisa	9	Jan	1898	East Penn Twp, Carbon	West Penn Twp, Schuylkill
M-1142	Gombert	William F	Brown	Lizzie Viola	23	Apr	1898	West Penn Twp, Schuylkill	West Penn Twp, Schuylkill
M-1143	Grim	Charles M	Williams	Ida Priscilla	9	June	1898	West Penn Twp, Schuylkill	Lehighton, Carbon
M-1144	Feist	William	Blose	Barbara I	18	June	1898	Lehighton, Carbon	Lehighton, Carbon
M-1145	McDaniel	James E	Semmel	Emma L	21	June	1898	Weissport, Carbon	Lehighton, Carbon
M-1146	Kemerer	Thomas C	Mantz	Lizzie E	30	July	1898	East Penn Twp, Carbon	West Penn Twp, Schuylkill
M-1147	Brinker	Edward C Jr	Sprigel	Flora M	19	Oct	1898	Easton, Nthptn	Easton, Nthptn
M-1148	Hontz	Walter N	Friend	Elnora	29	Oct	1898	Lehighton, Carbon	Lehighton, Carbon
M-1149	Xander	Uriah	Ginder	Lizzie Jane	27	Nov	1898	Mahoning Twp, Carbon	Mahoning Twp, Carbon

Beyond the Blue Mountain: Vol. II

Marriage Records

Line	Groom Surname	Groom Given	Bride Surname	Bride Given	Day	Mth	Year	He from:	She from:
M-1150	Mantz	Oliver L	Ohl	Harriet	19	Mar	1899	West Penn Twp, Schuylkill	West Penn Twp, Schuylkill
M-1151	Smith	Henry A	Frantz	Lizzie M	22	Apr	1899	Mahoning Twp, Carbon	Mahoning Twp, Carbon
M-1152	Paetzel	Edward I J	Llewellyn	Mary	25	May	1899	Mauch Chunk, Carbon	Mauch Chunk, Carbon
M-1153	Miller	Calvin A	Berger	Maggie E	27	May	1899	Franklin Twp, Carbon	Franklin Twp, Carbon
M-1154	Kressley	Assaby	Reed	Rachel	27	May	1899	Lehighton, Carbon	Lehighton, Carbon
M-1155	Frantz	Lewis A	Steigerwalt	Ella E	8	July	1899	East Penn Twp, Carbon	East Penn Twp, Carbon
M-1156	Creitz	Charles M	Hunsicker	Hattie S	9	Sept	1899	Bloomingdale, Carbon	West Penn Twp, Schuylkill
M-1157	Hough	Daniel J	Creitz	Laura M	9	Seot	1899	Bloomingdale, Carbon	Mahoning Twp, Carbon
M-1158	Bartholomew	Edward	Llewellyn	Sallie	28	Sept	1899	Mauch Chunk, Carbon	Summit Hill, Carbon
M-1159	Zellner	James Oliver	Wehr	Ellen Jane	25	Nov	1899	Lehighton, Carbon	Mahoning Twp, Carbon
M-1160	Yale	William D	Ebsen	Sallie Ann	25	Nov	1899	Lehighton, Carbon	Philadelphia
M-1161	Newhart	John M	Lerch	Hannah	12	Dec	1899	Cementon, Lehigh	Siegfried's Bridge, Nthptn
M-1162	Freyman	David	Mertz	Mary A	14	Dec	1899	Mahoning Twp, Carbon	Mahoning Twp, Carbon
M-1163	Solt	Sylvester	Gombert	Cora E	7	Jan	1900	Parryville, Carbon	Mahoning Twp, Carbon
M-1164	Lora	Elias	Eckroid	Maud C A	25	Feb	1900	Summit Hill, Carbon	Summit Hill, Carbon
M-1165	Hartranft	Jonathan	Hoffman	Sadddie	23	Mar	1900	East Penn Twp, Carbon	East Penn Twp, Carbon
M-1166	Whiteman	Oliver	Hoffman	Mary	23	Mar	1900	Bowmanstown, Carbon	East Penn Twp, Carbon
M-1167	Krome	Gust	Semmel	Lillie	21	Apr	1900	Lehighton, Carbon	Lehighton, Carbon
M-1168	Gaston	Ira C	Schrayer	Elisa	4	Aug	1900	West Penn Twp, Schuylkill	East Penn Twp, Carbon
M-1169	Creitz	Daniel	Smith	Minnie	24	Dec	1900	Mahoning Twp, Carbon	Mahoning Twp, Carbon
M-1170	Beltzner	George	Wilbert	Minda	21	Feb	1901	Mauch Chunk, Carbon	Weissport, Carbon
M-1171	Searfass	Elmer A	Snyder	Susan T	16	Mar	1901	Lehighton, Carbon	Lehighton, Carbon
M-1172	Auge	John A Jr	Grow	Hattie	17	Mar	1901	Lehighton, Carbon	Lehighton, Carbon
M-1173	Bowman	Assipa M	Peters	Sura	27	May	1901	Bowmanstown, Carbon	East Penn Twp, Carbon
M-1174	Neff	Oscar A	Rehrig	Cora Rebecca	30	May	1901	East Penn Twp, Carbon	East Penn Twp, Carbon
M-1175	Faust	Charles W	Woolbert	Laura S	24	Aug	1901	Lehighton, Carbon	Lehighton, Carbon
M-1176	Freeby	Amandus E	Ruch	Ida	14	Sept	1901	East Penn Twp, Carbon	East Penn Twp, Carbon
M-1177	Webb	Victor E	Zindel	Mary H	26	Sept	1901	Lehighton, Carbon	Lehighton, Carbon
M-1178	Smith	O F	Morder	Annie	23	Nov	1901	Mahoning Twp, Carbon	Mahoning Twp, Carbon
M-1179	Dreyer	Anthony	Beerman	Lydia	12	Oct	1901	Mahoning Twp, Carbon	East Weissport, Carbon
M-1180	Kuntz	George H	Beever	Ella L	23	Nov	1901	Lehighton, Carbon	Lehighton, Carbon
M-1181	Schofield	William H	Fritzinger	Ida Louisa	14	June	1902	Weissport, Carbon	East Penn Twp, Carbon
M-1182	Rehrig	Charles E	Fink	Carolina E	19	Dec	1902	East Penn Twp, Carbon	East Penn Twp, Carbon
M-1183	Romig	Calvin A	Balliet	Emma S	15	Jan	1903	East Penn Twp, Carbon	Mahoning Twp, Carbon
M-1184	Snyder	Willliam	Gombert	Hattie	18	Jan	1903	Mahoning Twp, Carbon	East Penn Twp, Carbon
M-1185	Reber	Holmes	Guldner	Mary	7	Feb	1903	East Penn Twp, Carbon	East Penn Twp, Carbon

Beyond the Blue Mountain: Vol. II

Marriage Records

Line	Groom Surname	Groom Given	Bride Surname	Bride Given	Day	Mth	Year	He from:	She from:
M-1186	Stevens	Charles	Snyder	Mary J	21	Feb	1903	Philadelphia	Lehighton, Carbon
M-1187	Gombert	James H	Miller	Mamie V	28	Feb	1903	Lehighton, Carbon	East Penn Twp, Carbon
M-1188	Bittner	John H	Hodge	Ella	25	Apr	1903	Hazelton, Luzerne	Lehighton, Carbon
M-1189	Grow	Robert E	Kirschbaum	Margeret A	29	Apr	1903	Lehighton, Carbon	Lehighton, Carbon
M-1190	Drumbore	Milton E	Hetter	Ellen A	3	June	1903	Lehighton, Carbon	Lehighton, Carbon
M-1191	Kipp	Edward	Freeman	Marie Ada	2	July	1903	Lehighton, Carbon	Lehighton, Carbon

Bartholomew Deaths

Namen der Verstorbenen *Wann Gestorben* *Alter*

June 1861 - April 1895

Line #	Surname	Person Given Name	Middle	Day	Mth	Year	Years	Mths.	Days
D-1	Spengler	Ellemanda		9	June	1861			21
D-2	Barral	George	Washington	15	Oct	1861	1	8	23
D-3	Weiss	Michael		14	Jan	1862	73	3	2
D-4	Louts	Logan		3	Apr	1862	1	1	9
D-5	Schlabach	Catherine	E.	27	April	1862	24	5	10
D-6	Johnson	Oliver	Amandus	27	Aug	1860	1	3	7
D-7	Johnson	John	Edwin	22	July	1863	22	5	23
D-8	Arner	Anna	Maria	19	Dec	1863	72	10	11
D-9	Larasch	William	Elmer	22	Feb	1864	1	11	21
D-10	Ebert	John	Cavinough	23	June	1861	1	2	13
D-11	Whitehead	Jacob		3	Nov	1861	90		
D-12	Walck	(s/o Simon and Sabrina (Stout))		18	Nov	1864			1.5
D-13	Kuntz	David		9	Jan	1865	68	1	2
D-14	Rheinschmidt	John		11	Jan	1865	64	11	5
D-15	Fischer	Christina		16	Jan	1865	78	9	29
D-16	Dunlap	Iola		22	Jan	1865	4	6	25
D-17	Buss	(s/o Jacob & Josephine (Hills))		12	Mar	1865			12
D-18	Bowman	Anna	Barbara	24	Mar	1865	71	7	7
D-19	Flickinger	Maria	Anna	31	Mar	1865	39	11	23
D-20	Klotz	Jonathan		28	Mar	1865	24	9	20
D-21	Shive	Juliana		2	Apr	1865	67	6	11
D-22	Hinger	William	Henry	6	Apr	1865		5	7
D-23	Horn	James	Madison	11	Feb	1865	21	11	24
D-24	Heilman	Anna	Maria	11	May	1865	76	6	2
D-25	Gilbreth	John		6	May	1865	33		
D-26	Hontz	Susanna	Amanda	12	May	1865	2	6	12
D-27	Diehl	Josephina	Barbara	10	June	1865	8	3	23
D-28	Moser	Anderson		11	June	1865		1	2
D-29	Esch	Sarah	Elizabeth	12	June	1865	18	11	12
D-30	Hontz	Elmer	Augustus	14	June	1865	1		5
D-31	Kocher	Juliann				1865		1	25
D-32	Blose	Lafayette		15	July	1865	24	10	
D-33	Row	George	Milton	19	July	1865	8	10	5
D-34	Asch	Samuel		26	July	1865	64		2
D-35	Kaiser	Henry		26	July	1865	36	10	8
D-36	Strohl	James		26	July	1865	32	10	16
D-37	Bechtel	Cephallen	Elsworth	26	July	1865		1	19
D-38	Klotz	Hannah	E	27	July	1865	74	10	18
D-39	Sherer	Henrietta		2	Aug	1865	5	11	15
D-40	Arner	Mary	Janetta	3	Aug	1865	8	1	22
D-41	Arner	Emma	Elizabeth	12	Aug	1865	2	5	4
D-42	Arner	Samuel	Elijah	13	Aug	1865	5		5
D-43	Arner	Hannah	Louisa	16	Aug	1865	9	11	13
D-44	Straub	William	Henry	18	Aug	1865	17	10	10
D-45	Lower	James	Henry	30	Aug	1865	1	3	18
D-46	O'Brian	John	C	30	Aug	1865	1	5	14
D-47	Schwartz	Wilhelmenia	Adolphina	5	Sept	1865	4	5	29
D-48	Hontz	Mary	Elizabeth	9	Sept	1865		3	18
D-49	Rinker	Sarah	Susanna	10	Sept	1865	1	3	25
D-50	Nothstein	Peter		16	Sept	1865	51	5	21
D-51	Laubach	Charles		7	Oct	1865	49	1	

Deaths

Line #	Surname	Person Given Name	Middle	Death Date Day	Mth	Year	Age Years	Mths.	Days
D-52	Behler	Samuel		17	Oct	1865	76	8	2
D-53	Snyder	Howard	Monroe	18	Oct	1865		1	12
D-54	Flickinger	Lewis		29	Oct	1865	11	1	14
D-55	Klein	Ellen	K	2	Nov	1865	1	8	15
D-56	Fogel	Philibina		13	Nov	1865	82	5	11
D-57	Aschner	Melchior		17	Nov	1865	32	2	1
D-58	Asch	Charles		17	Nov	1865	51	7	2
D-59	Palmer	Francis		1	Dec	1865	27		1
D-60	Rehrig	Mary	Elizabeth	16	Dec	1865		4	25
D-61	Levan	Henry		13	Dec	1865	20	1	8
D-62	Ruepcha	Amanda		27	Dec	1865	18	10	9
D-63	O'Brian	Emma	Laura	13	Jan	1866		10	28
D-64	Bachman	Sarah	Adilla	21	Jan	1866	4		13
D-65	Faust	Catherine		22	Jan	1866	67	7	25
D-66	Kelchner	George	William	10	Feb	1866	24		24
D-67	Moyer	Emma	Elizabeth	18	Feb	1866	2	3	5
D-68	Ahner	Mary	Eva	20	Feb	1866	80	7	18
D-69	Brown	Levina	MJ	23	Feb	1866		11	6
D-70	Thomas	Henry	Evan	9	Mar	1866	4	1	28
D-71	Hagenbuch	Thomas	J	11	Mar	1866	20		21
D-72	Stedtler	Mary	Jane	12	Mar	1866	9		27
D-73	Serfass	Josiah	Elmer	17	Mar	1866		1	21
D-74	Hahn	Maria	Alice	21	Mar	1866	3	5	14
D-75	Gutheil	Margmeretha		31	Mar	1866	78	9	3
D-76	Hoffman	Eliza	Catherine	31	Mar	1866		8	29
D-77	Schabach	(d/o John & Eva)		1	Apr	1866			30
D-78	Klientopp	Edwin	Charles	3	Apr	1866	18	8	29
D-79	Haintz	Robert	Henry	9	Apr	1866	1	5	6
D-80	Schnell	Susanna		13	Apr	1866	44	4	18
D-81	Straussburger	Lydia	Anna	13	Apr	1866	4		3
D-82	Snyder	Henry		1	May	1866	22	10	
D-83	Metzger	Daniel	Jacob	1	May	1866	24		27
D-84	Stenner	Emma	Luzetta	9	May	1866	2	9	12
D-85	Williams	(d/o Edward & Mary (Evans))		29	May	1866	1	6	25
D-86	Muschlitz	Elizabeth		29	May	1866		8	4
D-87	Brinkman	Elwin		31	May	1866	5	6	11
D-88	Burkart	Catherine		8	June	1866	2	1	29
D-89	Leinbach	John		12	June	1866	55	11	15
D-90	Stroup	Mary	Magdelena	20	June	1866	60	3	1
D-91	Bachman	Jonas		11	July	1866	64	4	9
D-92	Trimm	Henry		15	July	1866	1	11	6
D-93	Lichtenwalter	Anna	Laura	18	July	1866		3	2
D-94	Stein	Catherine		23	July	1866	51	3	15
D-95	Kiebler	Oliver	Franklin	24	July	1866		6	6
D-96	Dreisbach	Thomas		28	July	1866	49	3	9
D-97	Rustay	Rebecca		29	July	1866	41	4	26
D-98	Miller	William	Oscar	30	July	1866	1	3	21
D-99	Ruepcha	Maximilian	Henry	9	Aug	1866		7	26
D-100	Hausman	Maria	Sarah Ann	12	Aug	1866		6	3
D-101	Graver	Laura		15	Aug	1866		9	17
D-102	Bobst	Salome		15	Aug	1866	42	6	
D-103	Snyder	Welles	Jackson	18	Aug	1866		10	
D-104	Hontz	Mary Ann	Rebecca	31	Aug	1866	1	10	23
D-105	Beltz	Alice	Louisa	5	Sep	1866	1		1
D-106	Ahner	Nathan		13	Sep	1866		1	19
D-107	Sandherr	Catherine		1	Oct	1866	28	10	4

Beyond the Blue Mountain, Vol. II   Deaths

Line #	Surname	Person Given Name	Middle	Death Date Day	Mth	Year	Age Years	Mths.	Days
D-108	Shive	Sarah		4	Oct	1866	39		1
D-109	Schwab	Emaline		13	Oct	1866	23		13
D-110	Miller	William	George	15	Oct	1866	2		29
D-111	Roth	Elizabeth		21	Oct	1866	70		13
D-112	Hontz	Robison	Edgar	2	Nov	1866		2	2
D-113	Ziegenfuss	Catherine		10	Nov	1866	75	11	2
D-114	Schleicher	Amelia		11	Nov	1866	1	3	23
D-115	Schleicher	Awilda		12	Nov	1866	4	1	27
D-116	Stout	William		18	Nov	1866	1	3	21
D-117	Mangold	(d/o Frederick & Frederica (Ehley))		18	Nov	1866		5	10
D-118	Brown	Cassenta		19	Nov	1866	7	4	14
D-119	Buck	George		11	Dec	1866	29	4	12
D-120	Snyder	George	Washington	12	Dec	1866	2	7	16
D-121	Knappenberger	Abraham		25	Dec	1866	2	8	7
D-122	Stout	Adda	Ann	27	Dec	1866			9
D-123	Kleintopp	Ellen		17	Jan	1867	2	4	19
D-124	Behler	Matilda	Catherine	26	Jan	1867	1	11	17
D-125	Scherer	Henry		2	Feb	1867	15	9	27
D-126	Miller	Sarah		3	Feb	1867		11	29
D-127	Beltz	Elizabeth		7	Feb	1867	105	1	23
D-128	Kaiser	Amanda	Ellen	10	Feb	1867	10	5	7
D-129	Balliet	Matilda		15	Feb	1867	6	10	14
D-130	Moyer	Elizabeth		19	Feb	1867	68	11	
D-131	Sauer	Sarah	Emma	23	Feb	1867	14	8	13
D-132	Kaiser	Henry	Reuben	4	Mar	1867		11	5
D-133	Miller	John		17	Mar	1867	22	11	27
D-134	Bowman	Catherine		21	Mar	1867	35	10	16
D-135	O'Brian	Henry	Edwin	26	Mar	1867	1	9	11
D-136	Miller	Anna		28	Mar	1867	37	5	3
D-137	Buck	James		30	Mar	1867	31	3	16
D-138	Vogel	Joel	Elwin	30	Mar	1867		2	25
D-139	Campbell	Isabella		7	Apr	1867		3	8
D-140	Musselman	Harriet		9	Apr	1867	20	9	23
D-141	Kirby	Hannah		23	Apr	1867	36	9	3
D-142	Bauer	William	Wilson	28	Apr	1867	1	2	2
D-143	Rockel	Charles	Henry	11	May	1867		2	8
D-144	Bauer	Albert	Elmer	11	May	1867	1	11	21
D-145	George	William		28	May	1867	41	3	4
D-146	Hauck	Clarissa		30	May	1867	4	4	23
D-147	Hauck	Alexander		6	June	1867	1	6	15
D-148	Nunamacker	Mary	Alice	11	June	1867		11	27
D-149	Markley	Elwin	Lazarus	12	June	1867	5	5	25
D-150	Winkler	Barbara		13	June	1867	1	4	3
D-151	Peter	Gideon		16	June	1867	18	10	20
D-152	Scheckler	Thomas	Jefferson	23	June	1867	5	7	11
D-153	Miller	Sarah	Agnes	17	July	1867	1		8
D-154	Geigel	John		22	July	1867		8	21
D-155	Hisky	Eva		25	July	1867	74	11	15
D-156	Schwartz	Valentine		26	July	1867		5	23
D-157	Moyer	Charles	William	29	July	1867	3	7	28
D-158	Waterbor	August	Otto	29	July	1867		10	26
D-159	Hontz	Caroline	Elizabeth	31	July	1867	11		17
D-160	Wuersten	(d/o John and Mary)		7	Aug	1867		3	28
D-161	Eck	Jonas		7	Aug	1867	37	10	23
D-162	Roth	Alavesta	Savana	9	Aug	1867	1		17
D-163	Trumbore	Thomas		16	Aug	1867	58		

Beyond the Blue Mountain, Vol. II — Deaths

Line #	Surname	Person Given Name	Middle	Death Date Day	Mth	Year	Age Years	Mths.	Days
D-164	Rex	Amelia		17	Aug	1867		10	10
D-165	Clauss	James	Henry	18	Aug	1867		4	9
D-166	Shoneberger	Margaret		23	Aug	1867	61	8	23
D-167	Miller	Alwin	Oscar	23	Aug	1867		9	9
D-168	Hess	William	Calvin	25	Aug	1867	1	4	4
D-169	Beer	Elizabeth		31	Aug	1867	1	4	21
D-170	Stout	James	Franklin	1	Sept	1867	1	9	9
D-171	Beltz	Dannis	Alfred	4	Sept	1867	12	10	7
D-172	Schnell	Caroline		17	Sept	1867	23	10	25
D-173	Siefried	Andrew		17	Sept	1867	74	8	12
D-174	Bachman	Henry		24	Sept	1867	39	2	
D-175	Silfies	Jonas	Franklin	26	Sept	1867	5	1	24
D-176	Kemerer	Emma	Louisa	26	Sept	1867	1	8	22
D-177	Millheim	John		7	Oct	1867	59	10	7
D-178	Dorwart	Emma	Jane	13	Oct	1867		2	15
D-179	Mertz	Jonathan	Joseph	12	Oct	1867	18	3	9
D-180	Peter	Ellen	Jane	27	Oct	1867	1	10	21
D-181	Solt	Reuben		28	Oct	1867		6	1
D-182	Green	George		18	Nov	1867	43	6	17
D-183	Stein	George	Balzar	1	Dec	1867		3	29
D-184	Reber	John	Alfred	18	Dec	1867	1	2	3
D-185	Blose	Elizabeth		23	Dec	1867	29		23
D-186	Blose	Daniel		26	Dec	1867	72		
D-187	Gumbert	Josiah		28	Jan	1868	23	7	29
D-188	Peter	Jonas		10	Jan	1868	63	4	17
D-189	Wierstein	Frederica	Mary	15	Jan	1868	19		24
D-190	Zellner	Alwina		17	Jan	1868	1	1	6
D-191	Weiss	Elias		26	Jan	1868	46	2	14
D-192	Schaboch	Anna	Maria	31	Jan	1868	15		21
D-193	Esrang	Lucinda		6	Feb	1868	18	2	25
D-194	Musselman	Magdalena		9	Feb	1868	59	6	8
D-195	Levan	Isaac		8	Feb	1868	64	4	4
D-196	Hoffman	Jefferson	Franklin	15	Feb	1868	1	3	7
D-197	Bauer	John	Frederic	18	Feb	1868	29	2	22
D-198	Cyrus	Joseph	Jefferson	22	Feb	1868		10	2
D-199	Shive	Thomas	Edwin	24	Feb	1868		1	28
D-200	Rammer	Horace	Sherman	28	Feb	1868	3		19
D-201	Getz	Alwilda	Amelia	11	Mar	1868	3	9	23
D-202	Esrang	Adda	Priscilla	20	Mar	1868	1	1	3
D-203	Ferber	Mary	Ann	5	Apr	1868	10	3	8
D-204	Fichweiler	Catherine	Minamina	2	May	1868	1	7	7
D-205	Schaefer	Alavesta		9	May	1868			7
D-206	Ackerschauser	Cresincia		13	May	1868	47	3	12
D-207	Moyer	Morris	Edgar	18	May	1868	1	10	2
D-208	Heilman	Susanna		29	May	1868	24	5	24
D-209	Miller	Caroline		4	June	1868	22	7	3
D-210	Strassburger	Edwin	Henry	9	June	1868		4	16
D-211	Anthony	Anna	Maria	19	June	1868	40		6
D-212	Blose	Thomas		22	June	1868	56	4	
D-213	Beidelman	(s/o Elias & Sarah)		11	July	1868		1	10
D-214	Strassburger	William		15	July	1868	18	2	29
D-215	Graver	Henry	George	15	July	1868	10	10	16
D-216	Coffin	Emma		16	July	1868		8	9
D-217	Bowman	Mary	Alice	22	July	1868	2	4	15
D-218	Wemmer	Bernhard		24	July	1868		3	9
D-219	Brown	James	Elmer	25	July	1868	1	6	2

Beyond the Blue Mountain, Vol. II Deaths

Line #	Surname	Given Name	Middle	Day	Mth	Year	Years	Mths.	Days
D-220	Graver	John		29	July	1868	64	4	10
D-221	Kratzer	Catherine	Amelia	29	July	1868		4	20
D-222	Schwab	(s/o Charles and Matilda)		29	July	1868		4	7
D-223	Kern	Maria	Margaret	4	Aug	1868		1	7
D-224	Hestman	Elizabeth		12	Aug	1868		3	11
D-225	Reed	Charles	Winfield	17	Aug	1868		8	22
D-226	Trumbore	Eliz	Agnes	20	Aug	1868		6	29
D-227	Beltz	Thomas	Jefferson	23	Aug	1868		2	
D-228	Frey	William	Edgar	28	Aug	1868		2	
D-229	Semmel	Joseph	Peter	28	Aug	1868	2	6	1
D-230	Seip	Reuben		30	Aug	1868	32	2	19
D-231	Moyer	Salome		30	Aug	1868	78	8	14
D-232	Taylor	Mary	Elizabeth	31	Aug	1868	16	9	24
D-233	Schwab	Elias	Thomas	2	Sept	1868		6	28
D-234	Hahn	Savannah	Matilida	4	Sept	1868	10	1	21
D-235	Kiebler	Paul		9	Sept	1868	34	5	12
D-236	Taylor	Mary	Elizabeth	10	Sept	1868		1	1
D-237	Greenewalt	Martha	Aquilla	11	Sept	1868	1	6	13
D-238	Beltz	Lewis	William	13	Sept	1868	20	6	8
D-239	Beltz	Thomas	Benjamin	13	Sept	1868	23	7	10
D-240	Webb	William	A	14	Sept	1868		11	29
D-241	Frantz	Harry		16	Sept	1868			6
D-242	Koons	George	David	17	Sept	1868	1	9	28
D-243	Confer	Elizabeth		17	Sept	1868	77	2	21
D-244	Raph	Sarah	Jane	19	Sept	1868	4	7	13
D-245	Fuss	Kanz	John	21	Sept	1868	16	5	21
D-246	Lower	Sophronia	Jane	23	Sept	1868	2	6	26
D-247	Behler	William	Wilson	24	Sept	1868	1	7	6
D-248	Wentz	Lewis	Phillip	25	Sept	1868		8	10
D-249	Rex	William	Willard	2	Oct	1868		6	11
D-250	Markley	Caroline		3	Oct	1868	20	6	16
D-251	Markley	Dennis	Milton	7	Oct	1868	11	1	
D-252	Reiner	Solomon	Peter	8	Oct	1868	3	4	28
D-253	Gamer	Sophia		8	Oct	1868	8	3	11
D-254	Kemerer	David		9	Oct	1868	14	4	15
D-255	Nesley	Agnes	Lewilia	17	Oct	1868		3	18
D-256	Enders	Adolph		20	Oct	1868	23	7	4
D-257	Spoonheimer	Thomas	Franklin	21	Oct	1868	1	1	18
D-258	Eschbach	George	Albert	22	Oct	1868	1	2	26
D-259	Faust	John	George	13	Nov	1868	73	1	18
D-260	Beltz	Sabina		13	Nov	1868	14		16
D-261	Pehle	Lily	Augusta	27	Nov	1868	6	8	16
D-262	Kern	Elizabeth		4	Dec	1868	79	9	3
D-263	Schwartz	Sarah	Emma	10	Dec	1868	4	5	24
D-264	Walton	Justus		17	Dec	1868	39	4	4
D-265	Nise	William	Henry	21	Dec	1868			16
D-266	Bartholomew	Charlette	Jane	5	Jan	1869		6	17
D-267	Flickinger	John		7	Jan	1869	25	11	3
D-268	Fartwengler	Anna		9	Jan	1869	27	8	29
D-269	Ruch	Rebecca		23	Jan	1869	45	4	
D-270	Snyder	Emma	Irena	30	Jan	1869	1	4	17
D-271	Walck	John	Austin	4	Feb	1869		1	24
D-272	Kuehner	(d/o Levi & Mary)		8	Feb	1869		3	24
D-273	Beltz	Charles	Oscar	9	Feb	1869	1	9	4
D-274	Fenstermacher	Mary	Alice	12	Feb	1869	3	3	20
D-275	Webb	John	Franklin	13	Feb	1869	13	5	20

Line #	Surname	Person Given Name	Middle	Death Date Day	Mth	Year	Age Years	Mths.	Days
D-276	Mencke	Anna	Francisca	17	Feb	1869	52		
D-277	Walck	Savannah		7	Mar	1869	21	9	7
D-278	Goodheil	Nelson		12	Mar	1869		3	4
D-279	Heiny	Agnes	Rebecca	18	Mar	1869	1		6
D-280	Becker	Amelia		20	Mar	1869	24	9	8
D-281	Harron	William	Charles	22	Mar	1869	2	7	6
D-282	Romig	Robert		22	Mar	1869		4	27
D-283	Bast	Mary	Jane	23	Mar	1869	2		
D-284	Moser	Henry	Sylvester	29	Mar	1869	4	5	15
D-285	Hunsicker	Sarah	Ann	31	Mar	1869	17	5	26
D-286	Shipe	Sarah	Louisa	9	Apr	1869			11
D-287	Ackerschauser	Emma		23	Apr	1869	5	11	
D-288	Frederic	Amanda	Susanna	23	Apr	1869	1	6	18
D-289	Kuntz	Jeremiah	James	29	Apr	1869	3	4	5
D-290	Eberts	Emma	Elizabeth	3	May	1869		7	24
D-291	Buss	Jacob		12	May	1869		11	10
D-292	Ketrich	Anna	Sophia	20	May	1869	6		6
D-293	Lower	Elizabeth		24	May	1869	76	4	20
D-294	Moser	Leanna		27	May	1869	16	8	25
D-295	Brown	Isabella	Anconetta	3	June	1869		1	9
D-296	Rule	Celius	Henry	5	June	1869	3	9	11
D-297	Flickinger	Hannah		15	June	1869	42	7	29
D-298	Behler	Joseph	Daniel	27	June	1869		11	11
D-299	Miller	Alexandra	Alois	29	June	1869			29
D-300	Fritzinger	Ellenora		9	July	1869		1	5
D-301	Macke	Rebecca		10	July	1869	68	4	9
D-302	Allender	Maria		10	July	1869	50	8	1
D-303	Wher	Emma		15	July	1869		10	1
D-304	Snyder	Jacob		18	July	1869	32	11	2
D-305	Graver	Rulvin	Amandus	4	Aug	1869	2	6	10
D-306	Ziegenfuss	Harry	Edgar	5	Aug	1869	1	3	25
D-307	Remaly	William	Edgar	10	Aug	1869		8	27
D-308	Coffin	Hazard	P	12	Aug	1869		1	27
D-309	Stout	Celestia	Elizabeth	20	Aug	1869	1	3	20
D-310	Webb	Daniel	Webster	21	Aug	1869		3	26
D-311	Holzer	Andrew		27	Aug	1869	41	6	29
D-312	Bechtel	Jane	Elizabeth	27	Aug	1869		5	29
D-313	Musselman	Oliver	Franklin	29	Aug	1869		1	14
D-314	Schaefer	Dennis	Alfredo	12	Sept	1869	1	3	15
D-315	Klotz	Edwin	Morris	19	Sept	1869		5	27
D-316	Reed	Franklin		27	Sept	1869	48	11	8
D-317	Volke	Reuben		28	Sept	1869	15	3	6
D-318	Blose	William	Thomas	29	Sept	1869	1		13
D-319	Beidelman	Emma	Susan	14	Oct	1869		1	3
D-320	Fisher	Jacob		24	Oct	1869	53	4	9
D-321	Graver	Vererva	Catherine	30	Oct	1869		10	6
D-322	Leibenguth	Edward	Franklin	21	Nov	1869		2	4
D-323	Zahn	Otilla	Johannah	19	Dec	1869	5		1
D-324	Pettit	Oliver	George	30	Dec	1869	2	4	15
D-325	Steinhauser	Henry	Franklin	3	Jan	1870	1	10	10
D-326	Boyer	John	Austin	8	Jan	1870	2		27
D-327	Schoneberger	Milton	Henry	13	Jan	1870		3	25
D-328	Zahn	Amelia	Johannah	17	Jan	1870	2	10	2
D-329	Beer	Francisca	Louisa	17	Jan	1870	6	11	
D-330	Beer	Lydia	Jane	20	Jan	1870	4	4	24
D-331	Schwartz	Ida	Arabella	21	Jan	1870		1	21

Line #	Surname	Person Given Name	Middle	Day	Mth	Year	Years	Mths.	Days
D-332	Kauffman	William	Henry	26	Jan	1870		1	7
D-333	Kistler	Allen	Levi	29	Jan	1870		8	3
D-334	Balliet	Sarah	Jeanetta	3	Feb	1870			16
D-335	Hartman	Daniel		16	Feb	1870	49	6	24
D-336	Marccom	Catherine		19	Feb	1870	78	9	14
D-337	Leibenguth	Philip		23	Feb	1870	86	11	3
D-338	Blose	Adelina		6	Mar	1870	3	11	29
D-339	Guth	Henry	Milton	6	Mar	1870	5	5	10
D-340	Reiner	Lydia	Amelia	9	Mar	1870		11	26
D-341	Kunkle	Enoch		11	Mar	1870	50	5	11
D-342	Kern	Jacob	Milton	12	Mar	1870		3	3
D-343	Guth	Franklin	Oscar	14	Mar	1870	3	6	11
D-344	Hagenbuch	Eugene		15	Mar	1870	1	4	
D-345	Lentz	Daniel		20	Mar	1870	74	1	10
D-346	Meinhart	Elizabeth	Catherine	28	Mar	1870	9	9	15
D-347	Arner	Harrison		29	Mar	1870	32	7	17
D-348	Ziegenfuss	Ida		30	Mar	1870			4
D-349	Guth	John	Edgar	3	Apr	1870		9	13
D-350	Dunbar	Benjamin	Daniel	3	Apr	1870	5	10	
D-351	Leibenguth	Daniel		12	Apr	1870	83	8	2
D-352	Serfass	Priscilla	Jane	19	Apr	1870		4	29
D-353	Stein	William		22	Apr	1870	6	10	2
D-354	Ziegenfuss	Mary	Catherine	25	Apr	1870		9	26
D-355	Strohl	William		8	May	1870	45	10	11
D-356	Weber	Mary	Elizabeth	17	May	1870	1	5	17
D-357	Milheim	Robert	Edwin	5	June	1870		4	25
D-358	Frederic	Anna	Sevilla	8	June	1870		2	8
D-359	Dunbar	Catherine		11	June	1870	56	5	13
D-360	Teschiaschky	Anna	Wilheminia	11	June	1870	2	4	20
D-361	Breifogel	Anna	Elizabeth	23	June	1870	72	5	9
D-362	Weiss	Harry	Grant	5	July	1870	5	2	2
D-363	Kauffman	William		14	July	1870	19	3	7
D-364	Larose	Jane		16	July	1870	6	3	9
D-365	Nanstiel	John	Adolph	24	July	1870		8	23
D-366	Raber	Edward	Robert	8	Aug	1870	4	9	23
D-367	Lentz	Aaron	J	23	Aug	1870	23	5	9
D-368	Bartholomew	John	Henry	25	Aug	1870		4	5
D-369	Krumm	Selinda		26	Aug	1870	19	11	7
D-370	Heim	Catherine	Elizabeth	29	Aug	1870	13	4	12
D-371	Sterling	Clara	Isabella	2	Sept	1870		1	16
D-372	Heim	John	Franklin	5	Sept	1870	5	6	28
D-373	Solt	Sarah	Ann	6	Sept	1870	66	5	
D-374	Heim	Amanda		8	Sept	1870	33	5	10
D-375	Brinkman	Daniel	David	8	Sept	1870	2	1	2
D-376	Kolb	George	Mcclellan	17	Sept	1870	8	6	19
D-377	Hertman	Emma	Levina	21	Sept	1870	3	10	23
D-378	Wuchter	Hannah	Margaret	23	Sept	1870	1	1	25
D-379	Frederic	Elizabeth	Catherine	24	Sept	1870	4	9	1
D-380	Romig	Clarissa	Irma	24	Sept	1870		6	19
D-381	Solt	Sarah		28	Sept	1870	40	8	5
D-382	Weida	Nelson		9	Oct	1870	1	2	24
D-383	Weida	Harrison		10	Oct	1870	2	10	1
D-384	Serfass	Eliza		10	Oct	1870	20	9	23
D-385	Krumm	Peter		11	Oct	1870	80	8	10
D-386	Moyer	Thomas	William	23	Oct	1870	2	1	28
D-387	Sensinger	Emaline		1	Nov	1870		1	15

Line #	Surname	Given Name	Middle	Day	Mth	Year	Years	Mths.	Days
D-388	Buss	William		4	Nov	1870	4	1	25
D-389	Hahne	Sophia	Charlotte	12	Nov	1870	69		29
D-390	Levan	Maria		17	Nov	1870	29	9	25
D-391	Stenner	Martha	Edilla	25	Nov	1870			13
D-392	Dorwart	Sidney		27	Nov	1870	1	11	1
D-393	Stenner	Dianna	Elizabeth	2	Dec	1870	5	7	13
D-394	Mertz	Sally	Ann	11	Dec	1870	39	7	8
D-395	Barwick	Emma		14	Dec	1870	3	9	10
D-396	Geggus	Ida		15	Dec	1870	2	2	10
D-397	Ziegenfuss	Carolina		16	Dec	1870	17	4	25
D-398	Bolsgrofe	Laura	Agnes	18	Dec	1870	2	3	7
D-399	Beltz	James	Dennis	20	Dec	1870	2	10	
D-400	Walck	Emma	Louisa	22	Dec	1870	6	6	11
D-401	Adams	Elizabeth		22	Dec	1870	6	9	16
D-402	Schinke	Maria		24	Dec	1870	55	8	12
D-403	Ziegenfuss	Sally	Ann	7	Jan	1871	1	3	17
D-404	Stroup	Thomas		10	Jan	1871	61	1	27
D-405	Strohl	Lydia	Jane	16	Jan	1871		3	21
D-406	Stroup	Anna	Elizabeth	18	Jan	1871	21		26
D-407	Peter	Anna	Elizabeth	20	Jan	1871	1	5	9
D-408	McFarland	Ellenora	Catherine	25	Jan	1871	17	9	7
D-409	Webb	Ida		2	Feb	1871		4	8
D-410	Sleider	John		13	Feb	1871	54	8	28
D-411	Horn	Refene		26	Feb	1871	31	2	13
D-412	Kratzer	(s/o Charles and Sarah)		7	Mar	1871			24
D-413	Held	Clemens	David	12	Mar	1871		9	
D-414	Serfass	Adam	Missouri	11	Mar	1871		8	7
D-415	Wehr	Peter		13	Mar	1871	68	2	19
D-416	Bartholomew	Minnie	Nora	14	Mar	1871	3		24
D-417	Dunbar	Sarah	Elizabeth	20	Mar	1871	1	8	3
D-418	Hartranft	James	Wesly	20	Mar	1871	8		27
D-419	Rapp	William	Christian	22	Mar	1871	3	3	19
D-420	Riegel	Milton		26	Mar	1871	1	11	17
D-421	Horn	Ida	L	31	Mar	1871	4	6	25
D-422	Hahn	James	Albert	1	Apr	1871	3	4	25
D-423	Lower	Elmira	R	12	Apr	1871	3		17
D-424	Kramer	Ellen	J. C.	17	Apr	1871		3	14
D-425	Zellner	Reuben		23	Apr	1871	54	2	18
D-426	Row	Magdalena		25	Apr	1871	82	11	15
D-427	Miller	Lena		1	May	1871	29	6	7
D-428	Deuchler	Susanna	Catherine	11	May	1871	48	3	4
D-429	Bauer	Clara	Victoria	12	May	1871	3	6	11
D-430	Walck	Sarah	Amanda	19	May	1871	4	7	17
D-431	Rabe	Charles	Jonas	1	June	1871	5		25
D-432	Schaefer	Thomas	Benjamin	9	July	1871	4	8	20
D-433	Bachman	Franklin	Eugene	25	July	1871	4	5	13
D-434	Metzger	Sophia		30	July	1871	1		20
D-435	Schaefer	Susanna		31	July	1871	7	6	17
D-436	Bolsgrofe	Kate	Irena	31	July	1871		6	6
D-437	Schnell	Sarah		1	Aug	1871	19	9	28
D-438	Schmoyer	Charles	Irael	3	Aug	1871	8	7	5
D-439	Genshart	Charles	William	3	Aug	1871	11	8	27
D-440	Flickinger	Milton	Albert	6	Aug	1871			16
D-441	Stein	John		19	Aug	1871	66	1	17
D-442	Sibbach	George	William	22	Aug	1871		10	16
D-443	Graver	Alfred		22	Aug	1871	17	10	5

Beyond the Blue Mountain, Vol. II   Deaths

Line #	Surname	Person Given Name	Middle	Day	Mth	Year	Years	Mths.	Days
D-444	Grill	(s/o John and Alice)		28	Aug	1871		2	3
D-445	Armbruster	Hugo	Valentine	6	Sept	1871	4	9	21
D-446	Schoch	Pearcy	Franklin	14	Sept	1871		1	7
D-447	Brotzman	Jacob		24	Sept	1871	78	3	3
D-448	Hofacker	William		24	Sept	1871	4	11	24
D-449	Schafer	Wilson	Lewis	3	Oct	1871		8	27
D-450	Beck	Leanna	Martina	4	Oct	1871		4	9
D-451	Rabe	Michael		4	Oct	1871	24	7	9
D-452	Millheim	Louisa		10	Nov	1871	21	4	9
D-453	Zahn	Rosa	Louisa	17	Nov	1871			15
D-454	Fenstermacher	John		19	Oct	1871	35	10	10
D-455	Andreas	William		3	Dec	1871	80	5	3
D-456	Stemler	Daniel		15	Dec	1871	66	11	2
D-457	Solt	Catherine		16	Dec	1871	52	8	26
D-458	Brown	Matilda		29	Dec	1871	43		29
D-459	Arner	Pearcie		8	Feb	1872	6	4	20
D-460	Arner	Nelson	Ellsworth	12	Feb	1872	4	4	3
D-461	Brown	Palmer	Jacob	20	Feb	1872		4	3
D-462	Mertz	Joseph		5	Mar	1872	50	5	13
D-463	Beck	Charles	William	5	Mar	1872	2	7	12
D-464	Lower	Ansonetta		9	Mar	1872		5	23
D-465	Blose	Sally	Ann	15	Mar	1872	1	4	24
D-466	Schinke	Reinhart		17	Mar	1872	7	2	11
D-467	Fogel	Lafenns		24	Mar	1872		9	11
D-468	Fogel	Catherine		29	Mar	1872	3	9	11
D-469	Schinke	Frederick		2	Apr	1872	4	11	
D-470	Boyer	Henry		7	Apr	1872	10	9	
D-471	Miller	Maria		13	Apr	1872	38	1	16
D-472	Fisher	John		20	Apr	1872	51	7	8
D-473	Strassburger	David	Mathias	21	Apr	1872		1	22
D-474	Olewine	John		28	Apr	1872	53	3	6
D-475	Quillman	Adam		30	Apr	1872	88	6	19
D-476	Schmieskors	Dianna		9	May	1872	22	10	20
D-477	Dorwart	Harrie	Ellsworth	11	May	1872		4	22
D-478	Larasch	Alfred	Peter	25	May	1872	37	4	12
D-479	Snyder	Samuel		4	June	1872	62	11	
D-480	Dorwart	Sarah Anna	Elizabeth	18	June	1872	18	8	14
D-481	Kemerer	Reuben		25	June	1872	20	4	19
D-482	Zink	Jacob		26	June	1872	63	10	20
D-483	Kuhn	Frederic		8	July	1872	1	2	29
D-484	Boyer	John	Frederic	8	July	1872	91	8	4
D-485	Nothstein	Leah		11	July	1872			2
D-486	Knerr	Milton	Edward	11	July	1872	1		4
D-487	Gombert	Stephen		19	July	1872	48		29
D-488	Sittler	Minnie	Melissa	21	July	1872		7	20
D-489	Miller	George		6	July	1872	10	11	20
D-490	Miller	Christianna		12	June	1872	16	7	17
D-491	Rehrig	Mary	Alice	27	June	1872	17	2	26
D-492	Wehr	Polly	Louisa	27	July	1872		6	1
D-493	Greenewalt	Edwin	Sperrie	27	July	1872	4	4	7
D-494	Miller	Jacob	F	5	Aug	1872		4	4
D-495	Gombert	Ira	Irena	7	Aug	1872		5	1
D-496	Brown	Mary	Jane	9	Aug	1872		2	
D-497	Reiner	John	H	10	Aug	1872	9	5	21
D-498	Zellner	William	F	14	Aug	1872		6	3
D-499	Shive	Alice	Mary	14	Aug	1872	1	4	4

Line #	Surname	Person Given Name	Middle	Death Date Day	Mth	Year	Age Years	Mths.	Days
D-500	Held	Martin	Ambrose	16	Aug	1872		8	26
D-501	Wolf	Augustus		22	Aug	1872	39		11
D-502	Schleicher	Ellemina		28	Aug	1872			18
D-503	Rehrig	Charles	Henry	1	Sept	1872	1	2	13
D-504	Stenner	Charles	Adam	2	Sept	1872		5	24
D-505	Bartholomew	St	Edward	6	Sept	1872		8	22
D-506	Ripprit	Anna	L	8	Sept	1872	3	11	21
D-507	Fisher	Clara	Ellen	12	Sept	1872		2	14
D-508	Bowman	Victor	Calvin	15	Sept	1872	3	10	23
D-509	Faust	Mary	Ellen	16	Sept	1872		4	4
D-510	Dorwart	Calvin		12	Sept	1872	1	5	15
D-511	Boyer	Susanna		7	Oct	1872	68	3	2
D-512	Strohl	Catherine		18	Oct	1872	36	7	27
D-513	Stettler	Harrison	A	21	Oct	1872		7	18
D-514	Boyer	Edith	Elizabeth	25	Oct	1872	4	10	13
D-515	Evert	George	Philip	25	Oct	1872	77	11	10
D-516	Hough	Wilson		28	Nov	1872	69	3	22
D-517	Kleintopp	Emma	Elmira	28	Nov	1872		11	14
D-518	Bachman	John	Peter	3	Dec	1872	76	3	6
D-519	Weiss	Anna	Maria	14	Dec	1872	18	4	10
D-520	Galey	William		15	Dec	1872	76	7	9
D-521	Geggus	Mary	Etta	11	Jan	1873		5	11
D-522	Geggus	Anna	Elizabeth	13	Jan	1873		5	13
D-523	Strauss	Catherine		14	Jan	1873	68	9	14
D-524	Maurer	Caroline		17	Jan	1873	46	1	
D-525	Fenstermacher	Jacob	D	19	Jan	1873		2	8
D-526	Remert	Joseph		18	Jan	1873	59	5	
D-527	Hahn	Joseph		22	Jan	1873	13	4	29
D-528	Webb	Abraham		1	Feb	1873	3	9	6
D-529	Moyer	Agnes	Marcetta	3	Feb	1873	6	4	1
D-530	Hontz	Kitty Ann	Minerva	7	Feb	1873		6	
D-531	Remaly	William		10	Feb	1873	33	7	1
D-532	Blose	Tilghman		14	Feb	1873	19	4	22
D-533	Fritzinger	Henry	Wilson	14	Feb	1873	1	6	21
D-534	Heiney	Flora	Alice	16	Feb	1873	9	5	17
D-535	Krum	Daniel		19	Feb	1873	54		14
D-536	Snyder	(d/o of Alexander and Rebecca)		20	Feb	1873		2	19
D-537	Brong	Charles	Andrew	22	Feb	1873		6	25
D-538	Werth	Rosa	Alvenia	26	Feb	1873	1	2	28
D-539	Rehrig	(s/o John & Rebecca)		28	Feb	1873		7	2
D-540	Roberts	Luella		5	Mar	1873		11	4
D-541	Flickinger	Catherine		10	Mar	1873	42	4	27
D-542	Schafer	Susanna	Isabella	13	Mar	1873	1	5	3
D-543	Hough	Charles	William	8	Feb	1873	4	9	12
D-544	Knecht	Freddie	Anderson	8	April	1873		1	15
D-545	Muschlitz	Elizabeth	Levina	25	April	1873	2	4	27
D-546	Balliet	George		27	April	1873	54	10	29
D-547	Albright	John		27	April	1873	57	11	3
D-548	O'Brian	Mary	Elizabeth	29	April	1873		1	
D-549	Meckes	William	Oscar	1	May	1873	1		15
D-550	Hartman	John	V	3	May	1873	20	8	19
D-551	Kershner	Gideon		5	May	1873	59	5	26
D-552	Sterling	Tobias	Ambrose	28	May	1873	1		19
D-553	Weiss	Lilie	Louisa	12	May	1873	1	8	26
D-554	Larash	Elmira		21	June	1873	14	5	17
D-555	Webb	Rosa	Ann	31	July	1873	1	9	

Beyond the Blue Mountain, Vol. II Deaths

Line #	Surname	Person Given Name	Middle	Death Date Day	Mth	Year	Age Years	Mths.	Days
D-556	Kichler	Charles	Ludwig Gustav	6	Aug	1873		5	22
D-557	Hontz	Lewis	Elmer	7	Aug	1873	1	8	29
D-558	Dreher	Minnie	May	9	Aug	1873		6	7
D-559	Walbert	Oscar	Daniel	10	Aug	1873	1	3	20
D-560	Rabenold	Sevilla	Isabella	10	Aug	1873		5	26
D-561	Markley	Lewis	Theodore	13	Aug	1873	1	9	9
D-562	Spoonheimer	Catherine		14	Aug	1873	71	4	12
D-563	Milheim	Harrison	Eugene	17	Aug	1873		2	10
D-564	Fisher	(s/o William & Emaline)		17	Aug	1873		1	8
D-565	Youngkin	Charles		24	Aug	1873	1	2	11
D-566	Haupt	Joshua		2	Sept	1873	63	8	27
D-567	Bowman	Ellen	Korah	3	Sept	1873		5	20
D-568	Maurer	Emma	Elizabeth	4	Sept	1873		7	4
D-569	Grow	Caroline	Sevilla	20	Sept	1873		10	25
D-570	Walck	Elwin	Jacob	18	Sept	1873		2	24
D-571	Walck	Maria		21	Sept	1873	34		4
D-572	Dreisbach	Elwin	Henry	26	Sept	1873		8	25
D-573	Fritzinger	Emma	Jane	1	Oct	1873	2	8	10
D-574	Muschlitz	Abel	Robert	4	Oct	1873	12	10	29
D-575	Galey	Latitia		13	Oct	1873	73	8	24
D-576	Solt	Daniel		14	Oct	1873	74	8	16
D-577	Esch	George		18	Oct	1873	52	4	8
D-578	Saile	Catherine	Louisa	24	Oct	1873	39	4	23
D-579	Thomas	Maria	Anna	30	Oct	1873	41	4	7
D-580	Waterboer	Henrietta		7	Nov	1873	40	10	21
D-581	Fenstermaker	Ellenora	May	7	Dec	1873			21
D-582	Moulthrop	Elizabeth		13	Dec	1873	63	2	17
D-583	Ahner	Abraham		17	Dec	1873	82	6	6
D-584	Frohnheiser	Lydia		23	Dec	1873	75	11	15
D-585	Walck	Susanna	Sophia	9	Jan	1874		8	24
D-586	Campbell	Joseph	Daniel	15	Jan	1874	17	9	12
D-587	Schabo	(d/o Peter & Mary (Distler))		21	Jan	1874		2	4
D-588	Walbert	Eliza	Edna	23	Jan	1874	3	2	24
D-589	Britton	Elizabeth		18	Feb	1874	78	1	23
D-590	Klotz	Charles	Daniel	14	Mar	1874	1	2	9
D-591	Wehr	Ellen	Jane	18	Mar	1874		9	8
D-592	Montz	Carrie	Elizabeth	22	Mar	1874		1	9
D-593	Harron	Franklin	Rossville	1	Apr	1874		2	13
D-594	Scherer	Christianna		7	Apr	1874	53	5	17
D-595	Rhoads	Tilghman	Llwellynn	15	Apr	1874	4		3
D-596	McDaniel	Edna	Lucinda	17	Apr	1874			26
D-597	Kauffman	Milton	Oliver	22	Apr	1874	1	1	2
D-598	Solt	Ellen		5	May	1874	33	7	27
D-599	Hiskey	Angeline		16	May	1874	44		4
D-600	Kaiser	Johannah	FH	18	May	1874	77	5	24
D-601	Shoemaker	William	Oscar	3	June	1874			19
D-602	Moyer	Owen		4	June	1874	50	10	5
D-603	Boyer	Irwin		6	June	1874	1	5	12
D-604	Strohl	William	Henry	8	June	1874	12	8	17
D-605	Shive	Elias		13	June	1874	58	6	7
D-606	Riegel	George	Washington	23	June	1874		4	1
D-607	Strohl	Maria		28	June	1874	88	3	8
D-608	Beidelman	John	Harrison	14	July	1874	1	6	4
D-609	Hiskey	Conrad	Floyd	30	July	1874	1	9	17
D-610	Moser	John	Anderson	6	Aug	1874		1	15
D-611	Miller	Catherine		9	Aug	1874	73		27

Line #	Surname	Person Given Name	Middle	Day	Mth	Year	Years	Mths.	Days
D-612	Auer	Christian		19	Aug	1874	54		
D-613	Sharer	Elmer	Elias	11	Sept	1874		1	27
D-614	Zahn	Mamie	Clara	18	Sept	1874	1	7	15
D-615	O'Brian	Samuel		23	Sept	1874	24		19
D-616	Kleintopp	George	Walter	30	Sept	1874		5	4
D-617	Guth	John	Benjamin	2	Oct	1874	41	9	12
D-618	Moser	Estella	Esther	10	Oct	1874	5	2	9
D-619	Peter	William		26	Oct	1874	30	2	5
D-620	Shive	James	Monroe	27	Oct	1874	21		18
D-621	Beltz	Catherine		7	Nov	1874	76	3	7
D-622	Rabenold	Sarah		8	Nov	1874		2	5
D-623	Hills	George	Curtin	17	Nov	1874		4	6
D-624	Peter	Christiana		17	Nov	1874	75	6	2
D-625	Ferber	Ellen	Amelia	23	Nov	1874		11	23
D-626	Kunsman	Alfred		3	Dec	1874		2	14
D-627	Montz	Joseph		3	Dec	1874	61	8	1
D-628	Otto	William		7	Dec	1874	45		
D-629	Fenstermacher	Lucetta		7	Dec	1874	39		
D-630	Jordan	John		—	Dec	1874	47		
D-631	Krock	Howard	Milan	12	Jan	1874	1	3	9
D-632	Remely	James		15	Jan	1875	60	2	3
D-633	Trach	Anna		17	Jan	1875	73		9
D-634	Sherer	Henry	Alwin	27	Jan	1875	5	7	18
D-635	Berger	Franklin		28	Jan	1875		3	9
D-636	Ahner	Elizabeth		1	Feb	1875	27	10	29
D-637	Rehrig	Charles		6	Feb	1875	61	9	2
D-638	Sherer	Robert	Edwin	10	Feb	1875	1	6	22
D-639	Bechtel	George	Washington	13	Feb	1875			29
D-640	Esch	Charles		13	Feb	1875	1		26
D-641	Moyer	Charles		15	Feb	1875	5	2	15
D-642	Blose	Henry	Edwin	23	Feb	1875	1	7	11
D-643	Weiss	Louisa	Martha	27	Feb	1875		9	7
D-644	Rhoads	Hattie	Jane	2	Mar	1875		5	7
D-645	German	Charles		8	Mar	1875	2	11	12
D-646	Palmer	Frantz		12	Mar	1875	62	3	9
D-647	Maurer	Charles	William	15	Mar	1875		9	10
D-648	Arner	Daniel		15	Mar	1875	58	3	28
D-649	Olenwine	Elizabeth		18	Mar	1875	78		
D-650	Hauser	Emaline		29	Mar	1875	17	8	15
D-651	Solt	Harvey	O	23	Apr	1875		1	16
D-652	Osenbach	Sarah		23	Apr	1875	40	5	4
D-653	Youse	Magdalene		23	Apr	1875	73	5	28
D-654	Rabenold	Catherine		24	Apr	1875	30	3	15
D-655	Walck	George	Ammon	26	Apr	1875	3	7	5
D-656	Shellhammer	Francis	Oliver	28	Apr	1875	3	9	22
D-657	Levan	Pearcy	Daniel	27	Apr	1875	1	7	5
D-658	Remaley	Henry		6	May	1875	75	5	
D-659	Sittler	Lucretia	Amanda	9	May	1875		6	8
D-660	Reicheldorfer	Samuel		24	May	1875	27	11	10
D-661	Bowman	(s/o Francis and Amelia)		27	May	1875			21
D-662	Bowman	Susanna		29	May	1875	86	10	24
D-663	Blose	Ellen	Rebecca	29	May	1875	1	6	13
D-664	Graver	Harry	Elmer	22	June	1875		5	27
D-665	Michael	George		24	June	1875	64		12
D-666	Dunbar	Matilda	Elizabeth	8	July	1875		3	26
D-667	Hartzell	Elizabeth		12	July	1875	62	3	23

Beyond the Blue Mountain, Vol. II — Deaths

Line #	Surname	Person Given Name	Middle	Death Date Day	Mth	Year	Age Years	Mths.	Days
D-668	Schnell	Charles		15	July	1875	29	10	15
D-669	Gerber	Daniel		19	July	1875	75	1	20
D-670	Rolfink	William	Henry	21	July	1875	1	6	23
D-671	Schultz	Sarah	Catherine	24	Mar	1875	18	3	3
D-672	Schultz	Nathan	Alwin	26	Mar	1875		3	25
D-673	Rieger	Emma	Alevenia	25	July	1875		1	22
D-674	Miller	(d/o Alexander S. & Mary E.)		4	Aug	1875			18
D-675	Dorwort	Ida		4	Aug	1875		4	10
D-676	Riegel	James	Daniel	11	Aug	1875		4	19
D-677	Reed	Aquilla	E	13	Aug	1875	25	7	4
D-678	Kern	Elsie	May	15	Aug	1875			17
D-679	Kershner	George		14	Aug	1875	53	5	27
D-680	Kunsman	Emma	Catherine	17	Aug	1875	2	5	3
D-681	Moser	Adaline	Elizabeth	19	Aug	1875			15
D-682	Ruch	Maymie	Estella	30	Aug	1875			18
D-683	Feuner	Joseph		1	Sept	1875	61		7
D-684	Evert	Sarah	Jane	4	Sept	1875		6	11
D-685	Ahner	James	Daniel	8	Sept	1875	1	3	7
D-686	Friederich	Purietta		9	Sept	1875	1		
D-687	Boyer	Edwin		12	Sept	1875		10	18
D-688	Gogel	Hattie	Minerva	14	Sept	1875	1	1	5
D-689	Kratzer	Anna		14	Sept	1875	54	11	5
D-690	Mantz	Jacob		19	Sept	1875	68	4	25
D-691	Wehr	Jacob		12	Oct	1875	74	6	1
D-692	Mantz	Josiah		16	Nov	1875	23	4	19
D-693	Koons	George	Henry	2	Dec	1875	2	7	22
D-694	Sittler	Edilia	Jeannetta	6	Dec	1875	2	5	17
D-695	Brobst	Charles		12	Dec	1875	45	6	28
D-696	Faeht	Anthony		21	Jan	1876	65	9	13
D-697	Remer	Elizabeth	Christianna	28	Jan	1876	3	7	
D-698	Weiss	Lillie	May	28	Jan	1876			27
D-699	Hartinger	Minnie	Anna	31	Jan	1876		2	12
D-700	Dreisbach	Albert	Harrison	5	Feb	1876		1	28
D-701	Zimmerman	John		3	Feb	1876	21	11	21
D-702	Eck	Manuel	Edward	15	Feb	1876		5	19
D-703	Schellhamer	Anna		5	Mar	1876	60	10	20
D-704	Schaefer	Oscar	Douglas	8	Mar	1876	3	3	9
D-705	Krotzer	Sarah	Amelia	22	Mar	1876	47	8	5
D-706	Hontz	Jonas		2	Apr	1876	78	4	20
D-707	Focht	Charles	Harrison	4	Apr	1876		3	8
D-708	Schriver	Maria	Matilda	9	Apr	1876	46	5	2
D-709	Rex	Mary	Willmina	14	Apr	1876	2	2	17
D-710	Hill	Prestie	Monroe	17	Apr	1876		8	5
D-711	Maurer	Alice	Mantena	18	Apr	1876	22	8	17
D-712	Fenstermacker	Ellemanda	Sovira	23	Apr	1876		9	9
D-713	Geiger	Caroline	Arabella	3	May	1876		7	17
D-714	Stenner	Henry	Joseph	20	May	1876	58	2	8
D-715	Sleider	William	Henry	26	May	1876	2	2	25
D-716	Schaefer	David	James	9	June	1876	2		27
D-717	Strohl	Elizabeth		12	June	1876	76	8	
D-718	Hill	George		29	June	1876	75		14
D-719	Weidaw	Alwin		5	July	1876	1	7	16
D-720	Solt	Maria		6	July	1876	74		25
D-721	Hill	Harry	Ector	9	July	1876	6	10	
D-722	Kunkle	Mary	Elizabeth	23	July	1876		6	29
D-723	Fink	Rosina		26	July	1876	55	5	8

Beyond the Blue Mountain, Vol. II — Deaths

Line #	Surname	Person Given Name	Middle	Death Date Day	Mth	Year	Age Years	Mths.	Days
D-724	Kuntz	Samuel		29	July	1876	75		
D-725	Scherer	Mary	Ellen	2	Aug	1876		10	27
D-726	Maurer	George	Adam	4	Aug	1876		3	17
D-727	Kunkel	Mary	Ann	8	Aug	1876	54	1	21
D-728	Rhoads	Korah	Jannie	13	Aug	1876		2	10
D-729	Queen	Alavista	Agnes	15	Aug	1876	20	6	7
D-730	Kemerer	Mary	Jane	18	Aug	1876		6	7
D-731	Quin	Alavista		16	Sept	1876		1	7
D-732	Houser	Maria		29	Sept	1876	87	9	12
D-733	Hess	Emma	Catherine	29	Sept	1876	14	3	2
D-734	Beck	Edgar	Samuel	5	Oct	1876	3	3	
D-735	Scherer	Alice	Laura	8	Oct	1876	3	5	23
D-736	Brown	Thomas		20	Oct	1876	62		2
D-737	Laub	John	Enos	29	Dec	1876			1
D-738	Schantz	Esram	S	4	Jan	1877	29	7	
D-739	Leiby	Maria		9	Jan	1877	46	4	11
D-740	Fenstermacher	Pearce	Franklin	13	Jan	1877	6	8	3
D-741	Sachs	Elizabeth		22	Jan	1877	73	5	19
D-742	Kressley	Mary	Adella	8	Mar	1877	1	9	
D-743	McLean	Memphis	Adella	12	Mar	1877	5		10
D-744	Roth	Sarah		27	Mar	1877	60	1	14
D-745	Balliet	Henry	Milton	28	Mar	1877	9	2	17
D-746	Christman	George	Jacob	7	Apr	1877	4	1	17
D-747	Bretney	Emma	Minerva	11	Apr	1877	2		1
D-748	Andrews	Owen		20	Apr	1877	36	5	18
D-749	Kolb	Daniel		23	Apr	1877	61		17
D-750	Becker	Oliver		13	May	1877	2	8	4
D-751	Snyder	Jacob		16	May	1877	85	7	18
D-752	Shive	Mary	Alice	3	June	1877	6	7	6
D-753	McLean	Jennie		6	June	1877		9	10
D-754	Shive	Harriet	Isabella	7	June	1877	2		9
D-755	Gerber	Anna		9	June	1877	41	11	14
D-756	Gerber	Elizabeth		29	June	1877	59		16
D-757	Ruch	Sarah	Ann	29	July	1877	25	1	3
D-758	Gerber	Anna	Rebecca	12	Aug	1877		2	3
D-759	Mantz	Francis	Joel	12	Aug	1877		5	2
D-760	Kemerer	Sarah	Minerva	18	Aug	1877	2	1	5
D-761	Yenser	Minnie	Elmira	24	Aug	1877	2	2	17
D-762	Schumacher	Rosa	Cassilia	22	Sept	1877	6		15
D-763	Hauser	Esther	Rebecca	29	Sept	1877	11		13
D-764	Bear	Mary	Alloway	15	Apr	1877	3		22
D-765	Britton	Elizabeth		27	Oct	1877	78		9
D-766	Moyer	Isaac		8	Nov	1877	62	9	1
D-767	Hettinger	William		6	Jan	1865	35	9	22
D-768	Hettinger	Aaron		18	Aug	1877	21	4	21
D-769	Frantz	George		2	Dec	1877	56	1	19
D-770	Eberts	Birtie	Eurene	3	Dec	1877	5	5	10
D-771	Benigoff	Nathan	Jonas	17	Dec	1877		7	25
D-772	Hauser	Gideon		19	Dec	1877	31	3	3
D-773	Wehr	William	Alfred	21	Dec	1877	9	1	16
D-774	Shellhammer	Daniel		21	Dec	1877	91	10	10
D-775	Kocher	Mary		28	Dec	1877	28		
D-776	Haberman	Elmira		4	Jan	1878		11	20
D-777	Hill	Alavesta		15	Jan	1878		3	11
D-778	Zeiser	Harriet		19	Jan	1878	25	11	14
D-779	Greasley	William	Franklin	9	Mar	1878	30	5	19

Line #	Surname	Given Name	Middle	Day	Mth	Year	Years	Mths.	Days
D-780	Kocher	Sophia		10	Mar	1878	71	8	16
D-781	Bruekres	Charles	Frederick	25	Mar	1878	3	1	13
D-782	Leibenguth	Robert	Jacob	4	Apr	1878		7	28
D-783	Evert	(s/o Lyman & Aquilla)		16	Apr	1878			18
D-784	Gildner	John		20	Apr	1878	14	10	14
D-785	Moser	Austin	Vincent	7	May	1878	1	1	15
D-786	Gerber	Carrie	Alvinia	9	May	1878	3	4	20
D-787	Hartranft	Charles	William	22	May	1878	18	4	3
D-788	Trumbore	Ellen	Jane	7	June	1878	21	6	6
D-789	Hauser	John		20	June	1878	75	6	18
D-790	Winterholder	Charles		24	June	1878	59		
D-791	Bachman	Peter		1	July	1878	78	4	3
D-792	Gombert	Salome		12	July	1878	83	9	1
D-793	Schelhammer	Jacob		25	July	1878	72	4	12
D-794	Wher	William	Henry	31	July	1878		6	13
D-795	Herter	Tileila		9	Aug	1878	52	5	18
D-796	Snyder	Thomas	Monroe	21	Aug	1878	2	6	18
D-797	Hoffman	Nathan	Granville	11	Sept	1878		7	18
D-798	Lutz	Jerras		13	Sept	1878	3	4	2
D-799	Fenstermacher	William	Oscar	19	Sept	1878		7	2
D-800	Guldner	William	Henry	24	Sept	1878	1		4
D-801	Snyder	Elmer	Reuben	28	Sept	1878	4	3	11
D-802	Schaefer	William	Franklin	13	Oct	1878		11	25
D-803	Hoffman	James	Milton	16	Oct	1878	1		14
D-804	Schray	Gostwen		24	Oct	1878	7	2	14
D-805	Snyder	William	Tilden	25	Oct	1878	2	1	4
D-806	Hoffman	Sally	Ann	30	Dec	1878	6		16
D-807	Hoffman	Emaline		31	Dec	1878	7	11	5
D-808	Hoffman	Estella	May	5	Jan	1879	4	1	11
D-809	Nester	Alfred		15	Jan	1879	4		15
D-810	Nester	Rosa		19	Jan	1879	3		3
D-811	Boyer	John	A	2	Feb	1879	72	10	2
D-812	Lutz	John	Jacob	2	Mar	1879	27	5	17
D-813	Noll	Oliver	George	18	Mar	1879	2	10	23
D-814	Neff	Charles		21	Mar	1879		5	8
D-815	Smith	George		2	Apr	1879	79		11
D-816	Bechtel	Aaron	Franklin	11	Apr	1879	3	1	20
D-817	Krum	Charles	Edmund	11	Apr	1879	3	11	11
D-818	Freyman	Harvey	Franklin	9	Apr	1879	5	10	25
D-819	Freyman	Lillie	Mantana	12	Apr	1879	4	8	11
D-820	Geiger	Mary	Rebecca	16	Apr	1879	7	3	12
D-821	Gombert	Mary	Alice	16	Apr	1879	7	3	12
D-822	Farren	Willie	Henry	20	Apr	1879	12	1	23
D-823	Scherer	William	Edgar	23	Apr	1879		1	9
D-824	Beltz	Lydia		11	May	1879	65	4	21
D-825	Kuehner	July	Ann	21	May	1879	70		6
D-826	Schoupe	Kitty	Ann	25	May	1879	30	6	2
D-827	Schlegel	Ellsworth	Earthkin	29	May	1879		6	26
D-828	Wert	Alice	Isabella	30	May	1879	2	11	25
D-829	Mertz	Eva	Estella	11	June	1879		2	21
D-830	Balliet	Alice	Elmira	11	June	1879	19	10	21
D-831	Sassaman	Frederic		20	June	1879	74	6	26
D-832	Romig	William	Henry	28	June	1879	13	8	13
D-833	Schumacher	Minnie	Catherine	13	July	1879	2	5	1
D-834	Rheinsmith	Willie	Franklin	6	Aug	1879	1	9	12
D-835	Rehrig	Edgar	Milton	27	Aug	1879		6	2

Line #	Surname	Person Given Name	Middle	Death Date Day	Mth	Year	Age Years	Mths.	Days
D-836	Berwick	Lewis		12	Sept	1879	24	5	21
D-837	Andreas	William		14	Sept	1879	14	4	3
D-838	Reinhart	Wallace	Edwin	14	Sept	1879	1	8	13
D-839	Rabe	William	Michael	29	Sept	1879	8	6	11
D-840	Frantz	Charles	Franklin	9	Oct	1879	8		28
D-841	George	Monroe		9	Oct	1879	27	10	10
D-842	Kocher	Catherine		11	Oct	1879	79	5	5
D-843	Lieser	William		18	Oct	1879	29	11	14
D-844	Kreiner	Hannah		30	Oct	1879	36		6
D-845	Blose	Catherine		3	Nov	1879	62	6	20
D-846	Freeby	Christian		3	Nov	1879	101	10	8
D-847	Kistler	Rosa	Kitty Ann	1	Dec	1879	2	11	28
D-848	Gombert	John	Philip	3	Jan	1880	87	11	27
D-849	Scherer	Eli		21	Jan	1880	48		20
D-850	Eck	Enos		27	Jan	1880	24	11	17
D-851	Stahler	Samuel	Mandes	28	Jan	1880	9	4	4
D-852	Miller	Daniel	S	3	Feb	1880	73	2	
D-853	Stahler	Allen	Hughe	7	Feb	1880	7	3	22
D-854	Hontz	Matilda	Elmira	9	Feb	1880	1	8	6
D-855	Remaley	Annie	Zeniah	10	Feb	1880		2	25
D-856	Stahler	Lauretta	Agnes	14	Feb	1880	5	2	2
D-857	Stahler	Emma	Henrietta	16	Feb	1880		10	6
D-858	Stahler	Isaac	Henry	17	Feb	1880	3	7	5
D-859	Remaley	Jacob		23	Feb	1880	78	5	20
D-860	Hauser	Daniel		4	Mar	1880	71		29
D-861	Smith	Ellen		16	Nar	1880	3		26
D-862	Steigerwalt	Rachel		20	Mar	1880	75	7	16
D-863	Balliet	Joseph		23	Mar	1880	87	11	16
D-864	Hollenbach	Horace	Lee	29	Mar	1880	2		9
D-865	Snyder	Jacob	C	13	Apr	1880	36	10	5
D-866	Steigerwalt	Emma Eulena	Alavesta	23	Apr	1880	2	5	6
D-867	Steigerwalt	Annie	Jeannetta	28	Apr	1880	8	4	
D-868	Wehr	Rachel		30	Apr	1880	73	3	15
D-869	Steigerwalt	Tilghman	Elmore	11	May	1880	10	11	23
D-870	Sittler	Samuel		24	May	1880	77	1	16
D-871	Snyder	George	Washington	27	May	1880		6	27
D-872	Patterson	Charles		2	July	1880	78	8	11
D-873	Burger	Lillie	Celesta	3	July	1880	4		26
D-874	Leiby	Luretta	Agnes	4	July	1880			29
D-875	Shellhamer	Lafenus	Victor	24	July	1880		9	22
D-876	Gerber	Jonathan		31	July	1880	84	10	25
D-877	Hill	Robbie	Elias	1	Aug	1880		6	29
D-878	Romig	Irwin	Sylvester	7	Aug	1880		7	25
D-879	Frehn	Gertie	Irena	7	Aug	1880		11	9
D-880	Frehn	David		10	Aug	1880	55	10	13
D-881	Moser	Minnie	Elizabeth	18	Aug	1880	3	10	16
D-882	Eberts	Charles	Albert	22	Aug	1880		3	7
D-883	Zimmerman	Maria	Sarah	24	Aug	1880	77	6	12
D-884	Schellhamer	Catherine		28	Aug	1880	75	5	25
D-885	Houser	Albert		29	Aug	1880		3	4
D-886	Knapp	Frederic	A	31	Aug	1880	74	4	22
D-887	Sassaman	Katie	Mantana	26	Sept	1880		11	2
D-888	Hartzel	Harrie		16	Oct	1880		4	15
D-889	Hoffman	John	Franklin	18	Oct	1880		3	3
D-890	Grim	Hattie	Mantana	27	Oct	1880	4	10	22
D-891	Leiby	Susanna		27	Oct	1880	80	7	

Beyond the Blue Mountain, Vol. II Deaths

Line #	Surname	Given Name	Middle	Day	Mth	Year	Years	Mths.	Days
D-892	Rex	Katie		31	Oct	1880	57	6	24
D-893	Albright	Katie	Eveline	12	Nov	1880		1	14
D-894	Borhor	Leah		17	Nov	1880	29	1	23
D-895	Reinert	Elizabeth		5	Dec	1880	79	10	
D-896	Neff	Salome		12	Dec	1880	76	3	12
D-897	Kratzer	Charles	Franklin	22	Dec	1880	1	11	4
D-898	Barral	Cassie	Ann	14	Jan	1880	9		18
D-899	Stoudt	John	Franklin	17	Jan	1881	13	2	25
D-900	Balliet	Manda	Maria	1	Feb	1881	15	8	9
D-901	Hobbes	David		9	Feb	1881	85		10
D-902	Guldner	Susanna		20	Feb	1881	80	8	19
D-903	Marks	Ida	Jane	26	March	1881	5	10	11
D-904	Fritzinger	Oscar	Monroe	28	March	1881	21		22
D-905	Smith	James		3	Apr	1881	20	10	17
D-906	Steigerwalt	Fannie	C	11	Apr	1881	37	4	9
D-907	Houser	Henry		14	Apr	1881	69	7	21
D-908	Dreyer	George	Edgar	18	Apr	1881	1	0	8
D-909	Hill	Barton		28	Apr	1881		4	18
D-910	Wehrstein	Henry		2	May	1881	42	6	8
D-911	Price	America		5	May	1881	74	4	3
D-912	Nunnemacher	James		13	May	1881	76	2	26
D-913	Zellner	Charles		26	May	1881	25	8	15
D-914	Hauser	Conrad		1	June	1881	78	1	4
D-915	Reinhard	John		4	June	1881	49	8	
D-916	Godshall	Daniel		13	June	1881	54		10
D-917	Kuhns	Granville	Ambrosius	14	June	1881	8	6	
D-918	Klinetop	David	Henry	15	June	1881	13	6	18
D-919	Schellhamer	Charles		15	June	1881	44	11	26
D-920	Moyer	John		30	June	1881	73	11	15
D-921	Kreitz	John		9	July	1881	70	3	21
D-922	Bretney	Henry		12	July	1881	78	3	
D-923	Sassaman	John	Jost	25	July	1881	82	10	16
D-924	Gerber	Daniel	Gerber	29	July	1881	53	2	4
D-925	Taylor	Emma	Elizabeth	30	July	1881	1	4	14
D-926	Dilcher	Gabriel		3	Aug	1881	65	4	1
D-927	McClean	Mary		6	Aug	1881	74	8	21
D-928	Beck	Abigail		8	Aug	1881	64	3	7
D-929	Grasely	Louisa	Jane	9	Aug	1881		1	6
D-930	Ginder	Flora	Ann	12	Aug	1881	21	7	20
D-931	Knepper	Alberehina		22	Aug	1881	62	10	10
D-932	Fenkner	Amelia	Sevilla	27	Aug	1881		2	27
D-933	Lieser	David		28	Aug	1881	75	1	26
D-934	Hill	Clara	Sevilla	31	Aug	1881	3	2	9
D-935	Hester	Hester		6	Sept	1881	12		17
D-936	Steigerwalt	George	Washington	14	Sept	1881		5	21
D-937	Rehrig	William	Harrison	7	Oct	1881		6	7
D-938	Shelhamer	Abigail		18	Oct	1881	61	5	27
D-939	Leiby	Mary	Jeannetta	18	Oct	1881			24
D-940	Gommery	Louisa	Anna	23	Oct	1881	62	4	28
D-941	Hartzel	Korah		2	Dec	1881		2	20
D-942	Miller	Nathan	Daniel	21	Dec	1881		2	12
D-943	Hill	Ellemanda		23	Jan	1882	10	5	6
D-944	Freeby	Catherine		2	Feb	1882	47	7	24
D-945	Beck	Jonathan		19	Feb	1882	63	11	16
D-946	Houser	Catherine		24	Feb	1882	77		7
D-947	Lower	Sarah	Rebecca	1	Mar	1882	17	2	17

Beyond the Blue Mountain, Vol. II — Deaths

Line #	Surname	Person Given Name	Middle	Death Date Day	Mth	Year	Age Years	Mths.	Days
D-948	Scheiry	Henry		20	Mar	1882	80	11	14
D-949	Frantz	Wilson	Tilghman	22	Mar	1882		1	6
D-950	Knapp	Catherine		23	Mar	1882	86	4	28
D-951	Arndt	Susanna		27	Mar	1882	70	9	
D-952	Lynn	Benjamin		14	Apr	1882	83		12
D-953	Torrance	Jonathan		28	Apr	1882	55		
D-954	Freyman	Jacob		30	Apr	1882	75	11	4
D-955	Houser	Priscilla		2	May	1882	31		24
D-956	McClean	Thomson		17	May	1882	85	9	17
D-957	Sittler	Milo	John	4	June	1882	3	1	29
D-958	Maurer	Ida	Mantana	25	June	1882	6	1	2
D-959	Kistler	Sarah		29	June	1882	81	10	25
D-960	Beltz	Milton	Albert	14	July	1882	15	11	11
D-961	Zimmerman	Maria		28	July	1882	47	3	27
D-962	Hunsicker	Jacob		27	July	1882	70	6	26
D-963	Eckroth	Ida	Gertrude	12	Aug	1882		3	29
D-964	Steigerwalt	Emmaline		24	Aug	1882	12	10	14
D-965	Correll	Clara	Olivia	27	Aug	1882			23
D-966	Rehrig	Lillie	Mable	31	Aug	1882		4	22
D-967	Fridirici	Matilda		31	Aug	1882	41	4	29
D-968	Miller	Reuben		1	Sept	1882	73	9	18
D-969	Rex	Gertrade	May	13	Sept	1882		8	2
D-970	Mclaughlin	Reuben (s/o Edwin & Kate)		20	Oct	1882	1	6	28
D-971	Ohl	Joseph		16	Nov	1882	65	1	9
D-972	Peter	Oliver	Stanley	26	Nov	1882	1	2	17
D-973	Nunnemacher	Mary	Catherine	4	Dec	1882	8	10	5
D-974	Gerber	Catherine		31	Dec	1882	84	2	2
D-975	Mertz	Charles	Sylvester	10	Jan	1883	3	1	29
D-976	Correll	John	Franklin	10	Jan	1883		9	21
D-977	Markley	Zeniah		18	Jan	1883	36	11	19
D-978	Derrick	Maria	Jane	24	Jan	1883	17	3	20
D-979	Nunnemacher	Harriet	Annie Emaline	16	Feb	1883		6	23
D-980	Schumacher	William	Franklin	25	Feb	1883	7	11	27
D-981	Koons	Mary	Alice	28	Mar	1883	8	4	8
D-982	Fritzinger	Leon		31	Mar	1883	1	11	18
D-983	Bechtel	Fransie	Elizabeth	30	Mar	1883	13	4	26
D-984	Dreisbach	Peter		1	Apr	1883	75	4	9
D-985	Kershner	William	Wilson	21	Apr	1883	33	8	25
D-986	Miller	Katie		22	Apr	1883		4	3
D-987	Youse	Gideon		23	Apr	1883	77		
D-988	Peter	Gideon		28	Apr	1883	59	4	21
D-989	Eckroth	Lewis	Granville	2	May	1883	5	4	12
D-990	Weiss	Levi		5	May	1883	71	4	19
D-991	Lohra	Jacob		6	May	1883	79	3	9
D-992	Beltz	Lydia		28	May	1883	78	9	15
D-993	Rheinsmith	Timothy		1	June	1883	26	2	15
D-994	Gerber	Amos		6	June	1883	58	6	25
D-995	Dengler	Sarah		23	June	1883	73	7	6
D-996	Reichard	George		26	June	1883	75	4	17
D-997	Gerber	Anna	Maria	26	July	1883	1	11	22
D-998	Berg	Kitty	Ann	26	July	1883	38		19
D-999	Hartranft	David		29	July	1883	51		28
D-1000	Smith	Hudson	James	31	July	1883	1	2	25
D-1001	Balliet	Maria	Anna	6	Aug	1883	62	6	20
D-1002	Hobbes	Elizabeth		4	Sept	1883	67		21
D-1003	Houser	John	Burton	2	Sept	1883	1	5	17

Beyond the Blue Mountain, Vol. II   Deaths

Line #	Surname	Given Name	Middle	Day	Mth	Year	Years	Mths.	Days
D-1004	Schelhamer	Henry	Simon	11	Sept	1883	5		16
D-1005	Hamm	Lewis	Franklin	6	Oct	1883		2	29
D-1006	Hill	Caroline		31	Oct	1883	45	2	30
D-1007	Koons	Willoughby		6	Nov	1883	42	7	6
D-1008	Berg	Mary	Ann	11	Nov	1883	7	9	8
D-1009	Schumacher	James	Albert	18	Nov	1883		7	27
D-1010	Schabo	Charles	Franklin	30	Dec	1883		3	
D-1011	Kemerer	Maria		24	Jan	1884	75		22
D-1012	Bear	John		29	Jan	1884	47	6	17
D-1013	Lentz	Marie	Minerva	5	Feb	1884	5	2	22
D-1014	Hartung	Lizzie	Jeanetta	7	Feb	1884	10	2	21
D-1015	Shuck	Theresa		17	Mar	1884	59	9	11
D-1016	Peter	Henry		19	Mar	1884	85	3	21
D-1017	Remaly	Nicholas		24	Mar	1884	72	8	20
D-1018	Musselman	Charles		2	Apr	1884	82	10	4
D-1019	Balliet	Bertha	May	11	Apr	1884	3	1	22
D-1020	Wehr	Elizabeth		14	Apr	1884	73		13
D-1021	Stocker	Francis		18	Apr	1884	63	9	7
D-1022	Schumacher	Mary	Ellen	21	Apr	1884	26	6	13
D-1023	Kreitz	Samuel	Edward	21	Apr	1884	18	6	13
D-1024	Fritzinger	Leah	Amanda	27	Apr	1884	52	10	6
D-1025	Miller	Eliza		30	Apr	1884	51	9	7
D-1026	Trine	Maria	Anna	5	May	1884	71	8	20
D-1027	Houser	Isaac		5	June	1884	80	5	2
D-1028	Koons	Henry	Oscar	30	June	1884	5	7	25
D-1029	Hill	Harvey	Willie	19	July	1884	9	11	20
D-1030	German	Elias	James	2	Aug	1884	14	1	19
D-1031	Lapp	Scott	Winfield	6	Aug	1884	2		19
D-1032	Rex	Eva	Magdalene	18	Aug	1884		10	28
D-1033	Borhor	Sabastian		21	Aug	1884	68	8	14
D-1034	Graver	Martin	B	22	Aug	1884	39	9	11
D-1035	Hess	Lillie	Alice	28	Aug	1884		2	23
D-1036	Lapp	Lizzie	Jane	10	Sept	1884	2	8	11
D-1037	Andreas	Susanna		16	Sept	1884	80	6	20
D-1038	Lauchnor	Martha	Victoria	27	Sept	1884	1	10	19
D-1039	Schwartz	Jennie	May	12	Oct	1884		1	29
D-1040	Albright	Jacob	H	14	Oct	1884	45	10	26
D-1041	Weaver	Calvin	Daniel	28	Oct	1884			5
D-1042	Hoffman	Clyde	Sylvester	29	Oct	1884	1	2	19
D-1043	Dauber	Isaac		13	Nov	1884	51	10	3
D-1044	Montz	Mary	Susanna	17	Nov	1884	1	10	12
D-1045	Hartung	Abigail		17	Nov	1884	70	1	24
D-1046	Balliet	Anna	Maria	25	Nov	1884	87	7	27
D-1047	Arner	Henry		10	Dec	1884	89	6	12
D-1048	Beck	Torrance	C	4	Jan	1885		7	11
D-1049	Weidaw	Amanda		20	Jan	1885	6	4	17
D-1050	Schelhamer	Phenus	Clorius	3	Feb	1885	33	3	10
D-1051	Hough	William	Wilson	12	Feb	1885		10	8
D-1052	Mantz	Clara	Agnes	20	Feb	1885		4	1
D-1053	Knepper	John		24	Feb	1885	71	11	29
D-1054	Follweiler	Clinton	William	27	Feb	1885		1	27
D-1055	Ziegler	William	Jacob	9	Mar	1885		6	16
D-1056	Nothstein	Emma	Susanna	17	Mar	1885		4	15
D-1057	Hill	Lillie	Jeanetta	19	Mar	1885	9	1	26
D-1058	Haas	Robbie	Ambrose	23	Mar	1885		1	9
D-1059	Kemerer	Levi		26	Mar	1885	37	5	10

Line #	Surname	Person Given Name	Middle	Death Date Day	Mth	Year	Age Years	Mths.	Days
D-1060	Hillman	Rebecca		27	Mar	1885	45	6	12
D-1061	Lessman	Bilig	August	29	Mar	1885	55	10	5
D-1062	Kolb	Henry		4	Apr	1885	71	6	20
D-1063	Wahl	John		8	Apr	1885	51	1	24
D-1064	Fritzinger	John	Jacob	13	Apr	1885	86	4	6
D-1065	Willman	Louisa	Sibilla	20	Apr	1885	17	1	8
D-1066	Baer	John		20	Apr	1885	68	3	3
D-1067	Kolb	Margeret		21	Apr	1885	71	7	16
D-1068	Evert	Ira	Sylvester	27	Apr	1885		10	9
D-1069	Fenstermacher	Anna	Maria	28	Apr	1885	78	3	4
D-1070	Hiester	Joseph		17	May	1885	88	5	29
D-1071	Steigerwalt	Solomon		27	May	1885	57	9	13
D-1072	Wertman	Catherine		7	June	1885	83	3	18
D-1073	Hill	Granville		29	June	1885	11	11	6
D-1074	Xander	Catherine		1	July	1885	73	8	17
D-1075	Correll	Catherine		20	July	1885	61	7	1
D-1076	Barral	Cora	Estella	24	Aug	1885		2	18
D-1077	Remaly	Nathan		4	Sept	1885	68	11	
D-1078	Miller	Maria	Elizabeth	6	Oct	1885	41	3	14
D-1079	Andreas	Jonas		9	Oct	1885	83	6	8
D-1080	Levan	Maria		12	Oct	1885	78	6	9
D-1081	Kershner	Jane	Sevilla	22	Oct	1885		11	23
D-1082	Mertz	Emaline		3	Nov	1885	22		23
D-1083	Mertz	Henry	Milton	16	Nov	1885			15
D-1084	Reed	Daniel		25	Nov	1885	70	2	13
D-1085	Fenstermaker	Nelson	F	2	Dec	1885	24		13
D-1086	Nunemaker	Lewis	James	7	Dec	1885	53	2	14
D-1087	Sittler	Elizabeth		17	Jan	1886	79	7	4
D-1088	Correll	Mary	Ann	21	Jan	1886	52	6	23
D-1089	Knell	Rebecca		3	Feb	1886	69	10	18
D-1090	Wehr	Lafayette		8	Feb	1886	11	5	16
D-1091	Reichard	Lydia		9	Feb	1886	57	11	27
D-1092	Forreider	Samuel		6	Mar	1886	80		
D-1093	Billman	Samuel		20	Mar	1886	88	10	12
D-1094	Kemerer	Katie	Rebecca	26	Mar	1886	2		16
D-1095	Rehrig	Sarah		1	Mar	1886	79	2	22
D-1096	Adams	Charles		24	Apr	1886	80	5	2
D-1097	Balliet	Sallie	Leah	6	May	1886	13	5	15
D-1098	Zimmerman	Jacob		11	May	1886	58	8	9
D-1099	Miller	Joel		30	May	1886	72	9	23
D-1100	Wagner	Levi	Albert	19	June	1886	25	1	13
D-1101	Wagner	Charles	Andrew	22	June	1886		5	3
D-1102	Behm	Catherine	Elizabeth	30	June	1886	63	8	12
D-1103	Miller	Cora	Estella	7	July	1886		1	10
D-1104	Balliet	Henry		10	July	1886	70	8	1
D-1105	Lapp	Carrie	May	30	July	1886	2	1	8
D-1106	Koons	Anna	Sevilla	7	Aug	1886	6	2	21
D-1107	Hough	Caroline		10	Aug	1886	71	7	14
D-1108	Hartranft	Matilda		12	Aug	1886	44		20
D-1109	Gerber	Michael		26	Aug	1886	81	3	2
D-1110	Eck	John		5	Sept	1886	72		
D-1111	Miller	Susanna		9	Sept	1886	53	3	9
D-1112	Knapp	Maria		10	Sept	1886	58	10	29
D-1113	Neumayer	Harry	Oliver Franklin	17	Sept	1886	1	7	27
D-1114	Miller	John	Franklin	19	Sept	1886		7	18
D-1115	Womer	Lucy		25	Sept	1886	46	6	9

Beyond the Blue Mountain, Vol. II — Deaths

Line #	Surname	Person Given Name	Middle	Death Date Day	Mth	Year	Age Years	Mths.	Days
D-1116	Bachman	Elizabeth		26	Sept	1886	79	8	16
D-1117	Balliet	Estella	Louisa	26	Sept	1886		5	11
D-1118	Cunfer	Emma	Luzetta	31	Oct	1886	1	1	23
D-1119	Miller	Mary	Martha	1	Nov	1886	7	8	10
D-1120	Gerber	David		3	Nov	1886	75	9	20
D-1121	Behler	Elizabeth		16	Nov	1886	67	10	21
D-1122	Reinsmith	John	Orlando	27	Nov	1886	17	11	20
D-1123	Romig	Elmer	James	11	Dec	1886	2	10	12
D-1124	Romig	Daniel		25	Dec	1886	84	9	2
D-1125	Shelhamer	Estella	Agnes	6	Jan	1887		9	15
D-1126	Frantz	Homes	Webster	4	Jan	1887	13	8	25
D-1127	Riegel	Alexander	George	11	Jan	1887		3	9
D-1128	Maurer	George		15	Jan	1887	69	4	9
D-1129	Youse	Carrie	Adella	17	Jan	1887		4	25
D-1130	Mantz	Ida	Estella	22	Jan	1887		9	18
D-1131	Ohl	Harry		27	Jan	1887		6	4
D-1132	Kolb	Elizabeth	Catherine	3	Feb	1887	3	5	24
D-1133	Frederic	Renades		4	Feb	1887	81	4	4
D-1134	Ginder	Irwin	Daniel	12	Feb	1887		5	16
D-1135	Nothstein	Raymond	Ulysses	15	Feb	1887		4	27
D-1136	Bowman	Robert	William	22	Feb	1887		2	7
D-1137	Heintzelman	Esther	Zenobia	21	Feb	1887	4	2	9
D-1138	Kolb	George	Emanuel	6	Mar	1887	2		14
D-1139	Bowman	Matilda	Fianna	10	Mar	1887	23	2	14
D-1140	Schaefer	Samuel		17	Mar	1887	64	10	5
D-1141	Schaeffer	Sarah Ann	Elizabeth	9	Apr	1887		1	
D-1142	Leiby	Jenny	Lillie	18	Apr	1887	2	2	9
D-1143	Koenig	Annie	Ester	19	Apr	1887	5		1
D-1144	Koenig	Harvey	Isaac	20	Apr	1887	1	8	
D-1145	Shires	Christopher		17	May	1887	90	5	1
D-1146	Stoudt	Charles	William	28	May	1887	16	3	22
D-1147	Bachman	(c/o Daniel)						6	20
D-1148	Sassaman	John		3	Apr	1888	59	4	23
D-1149	Houser	Peter		28	Apr	1888	73	4	27
D-1150	Stoudt	Alexander		1	May	1888	53		29
D-1151	Emery	Charlie	Robert	7	May	1888	2		7
D-1152	Hoffman	Catherine	Anna	1	June	1888	35	4	12
D-1153	Nothstein	Calvin	Walter	15	July	1888	1	4	26
D-1154	Kocher	Benjamin		15	July	1888	67	3	12
D-1155	O'Brian	Lydia		4	Aug	1888	73	5	18
D-1156	Zellner	Abigail		15	Aug	1888	68		2
D-1157	Rehrig	Angeline		15	Aug	1888	59	2	7
D-1158	McLean	Thomas		11	Sept	1888	62	4	3
D-1159	Schleicher	George	Daniel	13	Sept	1888		4	19
D-1160	Fenstermacher	Emma	Jane	15	Sept	1888		1	18
D-1161	Balliet	Katie	Fietta	17	Sept	1888		1	14
D-1162	Kistler	Oris	David	26	Sept	1888		1	13
D-1163	Wertman	(s/o william D & Kate)		28	Sept	1888			4
D-1164	Ginder	James	W	27	Sept	1888	35	3	24
D-1165	Serfass	Howard	Clayton	27	Sept	1888		8	6
D-1166	Zehner	Francis	Harvey	1	Oct	1888	2	3	11
D-1167	Kolb	Magdalene		13	Oct	1888	73	9	21
D-1168	Hunsicker	John		17	Oct	1888	79	9	2
D-1169	Hoffman	Kate	Henrietta	6	Nov	1888		2	28
D-1170	Nunnemacher	Catharine		6	Nov	1888	77	10	15
D-1171	Krumm	Naunie		10	Nov	1888	66	7	11

Line #	Surname	Given Name	Middle	Day	Mth	Year	Years	Mths.	Days
D-1172	Lorah	s/o Henry & Kate		16	Nov	1888			20
D-1173	Dreisbach	Hannah	Louisa	5	Dec	1888	36	8	25
D-1174	Embody	Emma	Caroline	8	Dec	1888		4	4
D-1175	Klotz	Lydia		7	Dec	1888	79	4	28
D-1176	Schappell	Jacob		25	Dec	1888	67	1	2
D-1177	Krotzer	Charles		1	Jan	1889	65		20
D-1178	Balliet	Sarah		2	Jan	1889	40	7	28
D-1179	Krum	Joshua		2	Jan	1889	69	4	27
D-1180	Fritz	Emma	Estella	10	Jan	1889		8	22
D-1181	Miller	Levi	R	2	Feb	1889	58	10	29
D-1182	Zehner	Polly		5	Feb	1889	57	5	13
D-1183	Frantz	Freddie	Howard	11	Mar	1889	3	8	29
D-1184	Dreisbach	(s/o Tilghman- St Peters)				1889			
D-1185	Dreisbach	(s/o Tilghman- St Peters)				1889			
D-1186	Bacher	Mary	Ann	28	Apr	1889	48	3	6
D-1187	Embodie	Jeremia		6	May	1889	70	6	21
D-1188	Schweibens	Hattie	G	2	July	1889	3		23
D-1189	Gilbert	Sarah	Elizabeth	10	July	1889	29		19
D-1190	Bachman	Rosa	Tillie	3	Aug	1889		4	18
D-1191	Folk	Henry		17	Aug	1889	61	10	16
D-1192	Boyer	Emma		19	Aug	1889	21	3	19
D-1193	Geiger	Clyde	Eugene	26	Aug	1889		3	18
D-1194	Schaeffer	Roy	Harrison	6	Sept	1889		8	20
D-1195	Remaley	Wilson		8	Oct	1889	48	2	14
D-1196	Ohl	Elizabeth		7	Oct	1889	95		3
D-1197	Fritz	Henry	Harrison	17	Oct	1889	41		15
D-1198	Moyer	David		7	Nov	1889	32	5	4
D-1199	Remaley	Emalina		23	Nov	1889	36	2	24
D-1200	Troxel	William		28	Nov	1889	78	7	18
D-1201	Hamm	Emma	Elizabeth	20	Dec	1889		7	7
D-1202	Zimmerman	Sarah		14	Jan	1890	65	1	7
D-1203	Youse	Jennie	Estella	23	Jan	1890		4	25
D-1204	Gerber	Reuben		30	Jan	1890	86	7	15
D-1205	Hill	Harriet		2	Feb	1890	51	11	29
D-1206	Heilman	Maria	Anna	14	Mar	1890	78	7	8
D-1207	Kuntz	Elias		3	Apr	1890	67	11	29
D-1208	Sachs	John		4	Apr	1890	91	7	3
D-1209	Serfass	Preston	Erwin	12	May	1890		7	20
D-1210	Beltz	Abilona		15	May	1890	73	10	4
D-1211	Rex	Levi		21	May	1890	61	11	8
D-1212	Gilbert	Magdalene		8	June	1890	74	7	19
D-1213	Freyman	Catherine		13	June	1890	79	9	3
D-1214	Ginder	Isaac		28	June	1890	73	7	15
D-1215	Mengel	Ida		2	July	1890	20	2	4
D-1216	Wehr	Harrison	William	16	July	1890		6	24
D-1217	Flickinger	Catherine		1	Aug	1890	69	5	4
D-1218	Siglin	Jennie	Alice	3	Aug	1890		4	26
D-1219	Baer	Jacob		5	Aug	1890	85	11	3
D-1220	Bachman	Angeline		6	Aug	1890	21	9	5
D-1221	Bachman	Daniel	Richard	7	Aug	1890	3	7	27
D-1222	Miller	Absalom		18	Aug	1890	75	2	10
D-1223	Beltz	Lizzie	Savilla	6	Sept	1890	1	10	12
D-1224	Eck	Albert		13	Sept	1890		9	21
D-1225	Homm	Lydia		16	Sept	1890	55	9	11
D-1226	Kerschner	Ida Katie	Ann	17	Sept	1890	1		13
D-1227	Lauchnor	Annetta		21	Sept	1890	25	5	24

Beyond the Blue Mountain, Vol. II Deaths

Line #	Surname	Person Given Name	Middle	Death Date Day	Mth	Year	Age Years	Mths.	Days
D-1228	Turner	Hesikiel		2	Oct	1890	66	6	1
D-1229	Snyder	Sarah	Susanna	25	Oct	1890	40	4	24
D-1230	Freyman	Mary	Ann	16	Nov	1890	53	3	24
D-1231	Hill	Sarah	Louisa	17	Nov	1890		2	11
D-1232	Arner	David		1	Dec	1890	78	1	14
D-1233	Siegfried	Catherine		10	Dec	1890	78	5	25
D-1234	Schaeffer	Mary	Ann	10	Dec	1890	75	11	15
D-1235	Rubrecht	Polly		28	Dec	1890	59	6	9
D-1236	Smith	(d/o Andrew & Amanda)		2	Jan	1891		1	3
D-1237	Leiby	Lydia		8	Jan	1891	75	5	15
D-1238	Hill	Mable	Florence	14	Jan	1891		2	4
D-1239	Smith	Cora		21	Jan	1891	8		23
D-1240	Frantz	Ellen		7	Feb	1891			12
D-1241	Daubenspeck	John	William	8	Feb	1891		4	18
D-1242	Grasely	George	Henry	16	Feb	1891	1	5	12
D-1243	Smith	Charles		21	Feb	1891	22		15
D-1244	Smith	Albert	Martin	7	Mar	1891			23
D-1245	Trine	Jonathan		7	Mar	1891	83		24
D-1246	Gerber	Flossie	Albertha	11	Apr	1891		5	3
D-1247	Larasch	Irwin	Wilbert	16	Apr	1891	22	8	8
D-1248	Smith	Mamie	Sallie	18	Apr	1891	1	6	15
D-1249	Smith	Lizzie	Jane	19	Apr	1891	6	7	13
D-1250	Smith	Annie	Estella	20	Apr	1891	5	1	12
D-1251	Smith	Ida	Luella	20	Apr	1891	2	10	2
D-1252	Smith	Martha		27	Apr	1891	3	6	11
D-1253	Reber	Ada		6	May	1891	4	2	11
D-1254	Heiser	Susanna		9	May	1891	66	7	17
D-1255	Hunsicker	Lewis	Franklin	14	May	1891	6	1	19
D-1256	Brown	Ephearin		30	May	1891	71	4	26
D-1257	Fritzinger	Catherine		15	June	1891	89	5	23
D-1258	Sassaman	Catherine		17	June	1891	53	6	7
D-1259	Breisch	Catherine		28	June	1891	83	5	8
D-1260	Reber	Harvey	Franklin	2	July	1891	10	1	23
D-1261	Young	Esther		3	Sept	1891	20	4	22
D-1262	Gombert	Lydia		7	Sept	1891	64	10	25
D-1263	Youse	Clara	Atlas	22	Sept	1891	1	3	3
D-1264	Rehrig	William	Lewis	12	Oct	1891	25	4	1
D-1265	Mantz	John	Raymond	19	Oct	1891		2	5
D-1266	Hill	Peter	Noah	21	Oct	1891	33	9	18
D-1267	Ginder	Bertha	May	15	Nov	1891	1	8	19
D-1268	Schraer	William		20	Nov	1891	45	10	28
D-1269	Adams	Magdalene		28	Nov	1891	82	1	6
D-1270	Wiltsie	Ruth	Alvesta	3	Dec	1891		7	26
D-1271	Krum	Odillin	Muffley	10	Dec	1891	3	5	24
D-1272	Peter	Anna	Elizabeth	11	Dec	1891	20	4	8
D-1273	Troxell	Charles		22	Dec	1891	68	11	7
D-1274	McLean	Elsie		26	Dec	1891		10	2
D-1275	Gerber	David		29	Dec	1891	52	2	7
D-1276	Correll	Simon	A	10	Jan	1892	18	7	6
D-1277	Hill	Angeline	Victoria	13	Jan	1892	33	6	5
D-1278	Loch	Samuel		16	Jan	1892	57		
D-1279	Neumayer	Charles	David	22	Jan	1892		1	17
D-1280	Hoffman	Emanuel		23	Jan	1892	65	5	27
D-1281	Zehner	Maria		29	Jan	1892	76	7	18
D-1282	Reed	Margeret		29	Jan	1892	74	2	18
D-1283	Remaley	John	Charles	31	Jan	1892	83	7	22

Beyond the Blue Mountain, Vol. II Deaths

Line #	Surname	Person Given Name	Middle	Death Date Day	Mth	Year	Age Years	Mths.	Days
D-1284	Miller	Gabriel		31	Jan	1892	13	2	14
D-1285	Kemerer	Rebecca		26	Feb	1892	73	10	12
D-1286	Lechleitner	Jonas		29	Feb	1892	65	8	17
D-1287	Cooper	William	Henry	23	Apr	1892	42	6	23
D-1288	Gumbert	Fietta		27	Apr	1892	44	8	12
D-1289	Kerschner	Catherine		12	May	1892	65	9	11
D-1290	Moser	Catherine		1	June	1892	67	6	27
D-1291	Levan	Lydia	Janetta	19	June	1892	22	3	4
D-1292	Hill	Daniel	M	29	June	1892	56	7	11
D-1293	Reeser	Mary		3	July	1892	73		
D-1294	Gerber	Emma		9	July	1892			17
D-1295	Miller	Catherine		10	July	1892	79	4	22
D-1296	Billman	Anna	Magdalene	22	July	1892	1	6	14
D-1297	Wertman	Reuben		29	July	1892	53		20
D-1298	Weidaw	Herby	Alvin	13	Aug	1892			13
D-1299	Houser	Maria		11	Aug	1892	60	6	7
D-1300	Gommerry	Erwin	Albert	17	Aug	1892		2	4
D-1301	Gerber	Wallace		8	Sept	1892	3	6	29
D-1302	Troxel	Elias		18	Sept	1892	76	10	16
D-1303	Remaley	Tilghman	Amandes	26	Sept	1892			13
D-1304	Wehr	William	Henry	4	Oct	1892	44		5
D-1305	Williams	Arbean	Margaretta	23	Oct	1892		9	1
D-1306	Mclean	John		7	Nov	1892	58	10	14
D-1307	Lorah	Henry		11	Oct	1892	67	9	8
D-1308	Reichard	Samuel		5	Dec	1892	60	6	11
D-1309	Liston	Fatima	May	14	Jan	1893	4	11	25
D-1310	Houser	George		15	Jan	1893	80	6	8
D-1311	Loch	Edwin		3	Feb	1893	52	5	5
D-1312	Hill	Joshua		13	Feb	1893	77	10	16
D-1313	Oldt	Benjamin		14	Feb	1893	69	9	26
D-1314	Harter	Catherine		12	Mar	1893	83	2	28
D-1315	Zimmerman	Charles	Milton	28	Mar	1893		10	25
D-1316	Dreisbach	Annie		7	May	1893			27
D-1317	Bowman	Peter		8	May	1893	63	3	5
D-1318	Leaser	George	Samuel	18	May	1893	9	7	18
D-1319	Dengler	Isaac		18	June	1893	76	10	8
D-1320	Hoffman	George		26	June	1893	92	2	28
D-1321	Britton	Israel		7	July	1893	53	5	11
D-1322	Britton	William	Howard	13	July	1893	10	1	6
D-1323	Dreisbach	Mame		23	July	1893			3
D-1324	Osenbach	Albert	Raymond	7	Aug	1893		6	9
D-1325	Gumbert	Sophia		14	Aug	1893		9	20
D-1326	Rex	John	George	18	Aug	1893	76	4	23
D-1327	Fetter	Joseph		21	Aug	1893	56	2	14
D-1328	Hess	Pierce	Robert	20	Aug	1893	6		8
D-1329	Herring	Elizabeth		1	Sept	1893	75	3	6
D-1330	Kemerer	Elizabeth		3	Sept	1893	86	8	7
D-1331	Kistler	Beulah	Polly	11	Sept	1893		4	28
D-1332	Houser	Elizabeth	Sophia	26	Sept	1893	42	2	24
D-1333	Gombert	Cecilia	May	3	Oct	1893		7	6
D-1334	Mantz	Mary	Alvenia	18	Oct	1893	12	9	20
D-1335	Beck	Anna		6	Dec	1893	63	8	5
D-1336	Fritzinger	John		14	Dec	1893	58	8	22
D-1337	Maurer	Elizabeth		23	Jan	1894	74	10	12
D-1338	Embody	Beulah	Mable	28	Jan	1894	1	2	18
D-1339	Rex	David		24	Feb	1894	76	6	25

Line #	Surname	Given Name	Middle	Day	Mth	Year	Years	Mths.	Days
D-1340	Steigerwalt	Maria		6	Mar	1894	79	7	27
D-1341	Heintzelman	Mable	Glendora	13	Mar	1894		3	3
D-1342	Serfass	Flossie	Eva	16	Apr	1894		3	26
D-1343	Mantz	Nathan		1	May	1894	79	4	5
D-1344	Dreisbach	Elias		16	May	1894			25
D-1345	Hill	Ida	Jeanetta	19	May	1894		8	7
D-1346	Krainer	Michael		31	May	1894	84	8	2
D-1347	Boyer	Mary	Elizabeth	6	June	1894		10	27
D-1348	Hoffman	Estella	Ida May	10	June	1894	8	2	2
D-1349	Correll	Daniel		14	June	1894	74	8	13
D-1350	Ginder	Hannah	Meta	21	June	1894	2		28
D-1351	Balliet	Rebecca		15	Sept	1894	68	6	6
D-1352	George	Howard	Elias	21	Oct	1894	3	7	24
D-1353	Dreisbach	George		26	Oct	1894	85	11	27
D-1354	Keiser	Hulda	May	19	Mar	1895	15		5
D-1355	Ginder	Alice	Malara	23	Mar	1895	12	1	5
D-1356	Fink	Reuben		27	Mar	1895	77	3	13
D-1357	Smith	William	Albert	3	Apr	1895		2	
D-1358	Lutz	Nathan	George	5	Apr	1895		3	21
D-1359	Arnold	John	Jacob	15	Apr	1895		3	3
D-1360	Frantz	Charles		9	Sept	1895	75	9	11

Combined Index

Births; Baptisms; Marriages; Deaths

Line #	Surname	Given Name
B-29	(Anewalt)	Eliza
B-410	(Anewalt)	Sarah
B-31	(Arner)	Eliza_
B-381	(Arner)	Harriet
B-1201	(Beckendorf)	Maria
B-685	(Beer)	July Ann
B-528	(Beer)	July Ann
B-171	(Behler)	Christianna
B-522	(Behler)	Christianna
B-469	(Behler)	Matilda
B-169	(Beltz)	Lydia
B-282	(Blose)	Isabella
B-125	(Blose)	Wilhelmina
B-29	(Bower)	Lydia
B-344	(Boyer)	Elizabeth
B-1627	(Breiner)	Janetta
B-433	(Brown)	Catherine
B-30	(Brown)	Matilda
B-282	(Brown)	Rebecca
B-273	(Buck)	Catherine
B-246	(Chirstman)	Catherine
B-1626	(Fink)	Burga
B-281	(Fogel)	Catherine
B-297	(Gottshall)	Eliza
B-249	(Gower)	Susanna
B-196	(Green)	Catherine
B-40	(Green)	Mary
B-247	(Green)	Mary
B-119	(Grill)	Carolina
B-508	(Grill)	Elizabeth
B-751	(Grill)	Elizabeth
B-197	(Hartman)	Matilida
B-329	(Heffelfinger)	Eliza
B-1748	(Hill)	Angelina
B-223	(Klotz)	Rebecca
B-287	(Kuehner)	Christianna
B-223	(Kunkle)	Elizabeth
B-158	(Kunkle)	Sarah
B-40	(Lichtenwalter)	Sally Ann
B-1109	(Long)	Maryetta
B-235	(Markley)	Zeniah
B-119	(McDaniel)	Elizabeth
B-130	(McFarland)	Rebecca
B-867	(Mehrcam)	Fayette
B-585	(Mertz)	Joannah
B-898	(Meyer)	Maria
B-495	(Montz)	Leah
B-510	(Moyer)	Catherine
B-418	(Petzel)	Sarah
B-689	(Rabenold)	Mary
B-310	(Rapp)	Hannah
B-485	(Rex)	Sarah
B-1178	Ackerman	Hannah
B-31	(Schaefer)	Sally Ann
B-305	(Schafer)	Catherine
B-435	(Schinke)	Maria Anna
B-1203	(Schumaker)	Lewina
B-470	(Schwartz)	Eliza
B-505	(Schweibens)	Louisa
B-373	(Sensinger)	Caroline
B-280	(Sleider)	Alvena
B-203	(Smith)	Catherine
B-598	(Smith)	Catherine
B-874	(Smith)	Emma Jane
B-865	(Solt)	Catherine
B-529	(Solt)	Eliza
B-434	(Souders)	Mary Ann
B-492	(Stemler)	Louisa
B-874	(Stemmler)	Lucy
B-118	(Strohl)	Eva
B-131	(Strohl)	Eva
B-560	(Strohl)	Eva
B-131	(Strohl)	Sarah
B-171	(Strohl)	Susanna
B-968	(Stroup)	Amelia
B-1055	(Swartz)	Emaline
B-67	(Walck)	Elizabeth
B-234	(Walck)	Elizabeth
B-67	(Walck)	Mary
B-626	(Walck)	Mary
B-801	(Walck)	Mary
B-897	(Walck)	Mary
B-626	(Walck)	Salinda
B-452	(Weida)	Elizabeth
B-373	(Ziegenfuss)	Amanda
B-873	(Ziegenfuss)	Ellamanda
B-873	(Ziegenfuss)	Emma
B-281	(Ziegenfuss)	Lucetta
B-287	(Ziegenfuss)	Lucetta
B-688	(Ziegenfuss)	Luzetta
B-246	(Ziegenfuss)	Mary
B-103	Acker	Celestia Jane
B-182	Acker	Ellen
M-635	Acker	Hiram V
B-182	Acker	Howard
B-182	Acker	John
B-764	Acker	Manassas
B-155	Acker	Manasseh
B-206	Acker	Mary
B-103	Acker	Mary Ann
B-517	Ackerman	Catherine
B-1081	Ackerman	David
B-464	Ackerman	Elizabeth
B-454	Ackerman	Hannah
B-868	Ackerman	Hannah
M-433	Allis	Sarah

Line #	Surname	Given Name	Line #	Surname	Given Name
B-577	Ackerman	Kate	M-293	Alspach	E. W.
B-839	Ackerman	Kitty	B-570	Anders	Adam
B-1147	Ackerman	Kitty	M-458	Anders	Anthony
D-206	Ackerschauser	Cresincia	M-468	Anders	Catherine
D-287	Ackerschauser	Emma	B-1073	Anders	Charles
M-637	Adams	Amanda Jane	B-1347	Anders	Ida
M-50	Adams	Catherine	B-1073	Anders	Josiah
D-1096	Adams	Charles	B-1347	Anders	Josiah
D-401	Adams	Elizabeth	B-934	Andrea	Emma
B-963	Adams	Emaline	B-934	Andrea	Joseph
B-1236	Adams	Emaline	B-745	Andrea	Joseph
B-55	Adams	Emma	B-1441	Andreas	Adam
B-121	Adams	Henrietta	B-1701	Andreas	Adam
B-336	Adams	Henrietta	B-1400	Andreas	Addie
B-692	Adams	Henrietta	B-1735	Andreas	Calvin
B-923	Adams	Henrietta	B-1723	Andreas	Clara
M-229	Adams	Henrietta	B-1934	Andreas	Consuelo
D-1269	Adams	Magdalene	B-473	Andreas	Ellen
B-1379	Addams	Emaline	B-468	Andreas	Eva
D-583	Ahner	Abraham	B-1441	Andreas	Fiana
B-1311	Ahner	Abraham	M-720	Andreas	Fianna
M-500	Ahner	Abraham	B-1817	Andreas	G E
M-421	Ahner	Calvin	M-1073	Andreas	G. E.
D-636	Ahner	Elizabeth	B-1712	Andreas	Hannah
B-52	Ahner	Emma	B-1969	Andreas	Herbert
B-1311	Ahner	Ida	B-1889	Andreas	James
D-685	Ahner	James	B-1934	Andreas	James
D-68	Ahner	Mary	B-1969	Andreas	James
D-106	Ahner	Nathan	M-775	Andreas	James Irvin
B-52	Ahner	Reuben	B-1635	Andreas	James Irwin
M-115	Ahner	Reuben	D-1079	Andreas	Jonas
M-543	Ahner	Reuben	B-473	Andreas	Josiah
B-1247	Albright	Allen	B-1787	Andreas	Katie
M-952	Albright	Amanda L	B-1400	Andreas	Levi
B-1302	Albright	Emma	B-1723	Andreas	Levi
B-372	Albright	Enos	M-623	Andreas	Levi
B-670	Albright	Enos B	B-1701	Andreas	Louisa
B-1247	Albright	Enos B	M-939	Andreas	Louisa A
B-1651	Albright	George	M-993	Andreas	Mary Agnes
M-986	Albright	Harvey K	B-1817	Andreas	Oliver
D-1040	Albright	Jacob	M-966	Andreas	Owen A
D-547	Albright	John	B-1635	Andreas	Robert
B-1367	Albright	John F H	B-1735	Andreas	Rodger Elmer
B-1651	Albright	John F H	M-996	Andreas	Rodger Elmer
B-1302	Albright	John FH	B-892	Andreas	Salinda
B-1818	Albright	John FH	B-1125	Andreas	Selinda
D-893	Albright	Katie	B-1889	Andreas	Stanley
B-1367	Albright	Katie	D-1037	Andreas	Susanna
B-670	Albright	Lizzie	B-1712	Andreas	Thomas Franklin
B-1818	Albright	Ralph	M-928	Andreas	Thomas Franklin
B-518	Albright	Sophia	B-892	Andreas	Tilghman
B-1241	Albright	Sophia	D-455	Andreas	William
B-372	Albright		D-837	Andreas	William
M-666	Alexander	Francis R	B-1787	Andreas	William Henry
D-302	Allender	Maria	M-811	Andreas	William Henry
M-276	Andrew	Edwin	M-732	Armbruster	Henry F
M-384	Andrew	Eliza	D-445	Armbruster	Hugo
M-982	Andrew	Ella	B-399	Armbruster	Mary

Line #	Surname	Given Name	Line #	Surname	Given Name
B-992	Andrew	Ellen	B-178	Armbruster	Mary Ann
M-310	Andrew	Emma	M-248	Armbruster	Minnie
B-992	Andrew	Levi	B-376	Armbruster	Selinda
B-398	Andrews	Elizabeth	B-399	Armbruster	Selinda
D-748	Andrews	Owen	M-32	Armburster	Catherine
B-338	Andrews	Sabina	M-1003	Arndt	Ida E
B-1762	Andrews	Sallie Lovenah	B-1018	Arndt	Lennius
B-1825	Andrews	Sallie Lovenah	B-1018	Arndt	Levi
B-1859	Andrews	Sallie Lovenah	M-1005	Arndt	Mantana
M-1030	Andrews	Sallie Loveneh	D-951	Arndt	Susanna
B-338	Andrews	Selinda	B-57	Arner	Ammon
B-166	Anewalt	Amanda	M-82	Arner	Anjulina
B-29	Anewalt	Elias	B-430	Arner	Anjuline
B-104	Anewalt	Elias	D-8	Arner	Anna
B-167	Anewalt	Elias	M-388	Arner	Bregitta
B-582	Anewalt	Elias	B-15	Arner	Calvin
B-880	Anewalt	Eliza	B-628	Arner	Calvin
B-1217	Anewalt	Ellen	B-175	Arner	Carolina
B-526	Anewalt	Eva	B-605	Arner	Caroline
B-882	Anewalt	John	M-143	Arner	Caroline
B-526	Anewalt	Lewis	B-628	Arner	Charles
B-882	Anewalt	Lewis	B-808	Arner	Charles
B-166	Anewalt	Lewis	B-431	Arner	Charles
B-410	Anewalt	Lewis	M-397	Arner	Charles
B-882	Anewalt	Lizzie	M-1119	Arner	Clinton A
B-582	Anewalt	Manda	D-648	Arner	Daniel
B-1217	Anewalt	Samuel	B-142	Arner	Daniel
D-211	Anthony	Anna	B-162	Arner	Daniel
B-155	Anthony	Catherine	B-349	Arner	Daniel
B-764	Anthony	Catherine	M-886	Arner	Daniel
B-995	Anthony	Edna B	D-1232	Arner	David
M-489	Anthony	Edna B	B-945	Arner	Edwin
B-1586	Anthony	Ella L	B-431	Arner	Eliza
B-1731	Anthony	Ella L	B-1730	Arner	Ellen K
M-875	Anthony	Ella L	M-940	Arner	Ellen K
M-39	Anthony	Ellephina	B-339	Arner	Emanuel
B-126	Anthony	Elmira	M-1067	Arner	Emanuel
B-1136	Anthony	Helenah	D-41	Arner	Emma
M-21	Anthony	Henry Tilghman	B-57	Arner	Emma
M-520	Anthony	Jane Amanda	B-1287	Arner	Franklin
B-1227	Anthony	Jane Elizabeth	B-808	Arner	George
B-1287	Anthony	Jane Elizabeth	B-738	Arner	George
M-613	Anthony	Jane Elizabeth	B-430	Arner	George
B-126	Anthony	John	M-407	Arner	George
B-1206	Anthony	Lucetta	D-43	Arner	Hannah
M-426	Anthony	Lucetta	D-347	Arner	Harrison
B-638	Anthony	Lucette	D-1047	Arner	Henry
B-746	Anthony	Mary	B-1695	Arner	Henry
M-517	Anthony	Tillie A	B-381	Arner	Henry
B-1155	Anthony	William	B-713	Arner	Henry
B-1155	Anthony	William H	B-1227	Arner	Howard
M-111	Armbruster	Amelia	M-73	Arner	Jacob M
B-178	Armbruster	Charles	M-979	Arner	Jennetta
B-295	Arner	John	B-1899	Ashner	George
B-339	Arner	John	B-1899	Ashner	James F
B-15	Arner	John H	B-1699	Ashner	James Franklin
B-191	Arner	John H	B-1804	Ashner	James Franklin
M-226	Arner	John H	M-827	Ashner	James Franklin

Line #	Surname	Given Name	Line #	Surname	Given Name
B-713	Arner	Joseph	B-1804	Ashner	William
M-1061	Arner	Joseph D	D-612	Auer	Christian
B-404	Arner	Laura	B-1525	Auge	Allen
B-738	Arner	Laura	B-1414	Auge	Anna
B-870	Arner	Lizzie	B-438	Auge	David
B-575	Arner	Louisa	B-836	Auge	David
B-1476	Arner	Louisa	B-1263	Auge	David
B-1611	Arner	Louisa	B-1414	Auge	David
M-149	Arner	Louisa	B-1525	Auge	David
D-40	Arner	Mary	B-277	Auge	David
M-101	Arner	Mary Ann	B-836	Auge	Edgar
B-1218	Arner	Matilda	B-1954	Auge	Ella
B-191	Arner	Minnie	B-1263	Auge	Harvey
B-945	Arner	Moses	M-352	Auge	John
D-460	Arner	Nelson	B-1954	Auge	John A
B-870	Arner	Oscar	M-1172	Auge	John A Jr
B-1227	Arner	Oscar	B-438	Auge	William
B-1287	Arner	Oscar	M-803	Augle	William M
M-613	Arner	Oscar	B-1946	Bachard	Sallie V
D-459	Arner	Pearcie	D-1186	Bacher	Mary
B-31	Arner	Quintin	B-1226	Bacherd	Priscilla
D-42	Arner	Samuel	B-1660	Bachert	Catherine
B-58	Arner	Sarah	D-1147	Bachman	(c/o Daniel)
B-662	Arner	Sarah	D-1220	Bachman	Angeline
B-349	Arner	Sarah Amanda	B-132	Bachman	Anna Maria
M-181	Arner	Sarah M	B-239	Bachman	Anna Maria
B-1019	Arner	Sarah Manda	B-765	Bachman	Anna Maria
B-31	Arner	Thomas	B-965	Bachman	Anna Maria
B-1695	Arner	Thomas J	B-1329	Bachman	Anna Maria
M-916	Arner	Thomas Jefferson	M-137	Bachman	Anna Maria
B-295	Arner	William	D-1221	Bachman	Daniel
B-381	Arner	William	B-1968	Bachman	Daniel
B-404	Arner	William Harrison	B-86	Bachman	Daniel
M-19	Arner	William Harrison	B-695	Bachman	Daniel
B-1957	Arnold	George	M-25	Bachman	Daniel
B-1906	Arnold	Hattie	M-218	Bachman	Daniel
B-1811	Arnold	Jacob	B-186	Bachman	Edgar
B-1842	Arnold	Jacob J	D-1116	Bachman	Elizabeth
B-1957	Arnold	Jacob J	B-86	Bachman	Emaline
M-1089	Arnold	Jacob J	B-418	Bachman	Emma
B-1873	Arnold	Jacob James	B-1750	Bachman	Emma
B-1906	Arnold	Jacob James	M-1044	Bachman	Emma
D-1359	Arnold	John	B-1779	Bachman	Emma Rebecca
B-1842	Arnold	John	B-1925	Bachman	Francis E
B-1873	Arnold	William	D-433	Bachman	Franklin
D-58	Asch	Charles	B-1670	Bachman	George James
D-34	Asch	Samuel	B-1925	Bachman	Gladys
D-57	Aschner	Melchior	B-1567	Bachman	Hannah
B-727	Ash	Amanda	M-652	Bachman	Hannah
M-348	Ash	Amanda	D-174	Bachman	Henry
B-1699	Ashner	Birdie	M-899	Bachman	James M
B-1659	Bachman	Jane	B-1241	Balliet	James
D-518	Bachman	John	B-518	Balliet	James D
M-791	Bachman	John	B-604	Balliet	John
M-1084	Bachman	John R	B-1109	Balliet	John
B-695	Bachman	Johnnie	B-1306	Balliet	John
D-91	Bachman	Jonas	M-740	Balliet	John H
B-418	Bachman	Joseph	D-863	Balliet	Joseph

Line #	Surname	Given Name
B-1866	Bachman	Joseph E
B-1938	Bachman	Joseph E
B-1968	Bachman	Joseph E
M-1115	Bachman	Joseph E
M-741	Bachman	Julia
M-862	Bachman	Lewis
B-1938	Bachman	Mary
M-1016	Bachman	Mary Ellen
D-791	Bachman	Peter
B-1149	Bachman	Peter
B-1866	Bachman	Rayastor
B-1670	Bachman	Robbie
D-1190	Bachman	Rosa
D-64	Bachman	Sarah
B-186	Bachman	William
M-107	Bachman	William
D-1219	Baer	Jacob
D-1066	Baer	John
B-1072	Baer	Mary
B-1072	Baer	Reuben
B-1794	Bailey	James S
M-977	Bailey	James S
M-267	Bailey	Kate
B-1794	Bailey	Raymond
B-1208	Bailey	Sally
D-830	Balliet	Alice
B-290	Balliet	Amanda
M-312	Balliet	Amanda
D-1046	Balliet	Anna
M-957	Balliet	Anna E
B-604	Balliet	Benjamin
B-1465	Balliet	Benjamin
D-1019	Balliet	Bertha
B-817	Balliet	Calvin
B-1494	Balliet	Carrie
M-25	Balliet	Ellen
B-86	Balliet	Ellen
M-785	Balliet	Emma E
M-1183	Balliet	Emma S
D-1117	Balliet	Estella
B-1595	Balliet	Estella
B-1402	Balliet	Eva
D-546	Balliet	George
B-1306	Balliet	Harry
B-1694	Balliet	Harvey
D-745	Balliet	Henry
D-1104	Balliet	Henry
B-550	Balliet	Isabella
B-1241	Balliet	James
B-1521	Barry	George
B-1519	Barry	Manda
B-1521	Barry	Theodore
B-114	Barta	Paulina
B-143	Barta	Paulina
B-78	Barta	Pauline
B-211	Barthholomew	Elias
B-211	Barthholomew	Ida
B-194	Barthholomew	Melinda
B-1108	Balliet	Kate
B-1360	Balliet	Kate
B-1504	Balliet	Kate
M-1133	Balliet	Kate
M-509	Balliet	Kate D
D-1161	Balliet	Katie
B-1681	Balliet	Katie
M-560	Balliet	Levi
B-1465	Balliet	Lewis
B-1595	Balliet	Lewis Franklin
B-1734	Balliet	Lewis Franklin
M-695	Balliet	Lewis Franklin
B-1046	Balliet	Lizzie
D-900	Balliet	Manda
D-1001	Balliet	Maria
B-1109	Balliet	Martha
B-1230	Balliet	Mary Ann
D-129	Balliet	Matilda
B-34	Balliet	Nathan
B-817	Balliet	Nathan
M-298	Balliet	Polly H
B-1734	Balliet	Raymond
D-1351	Balliet	Rebecca
D-1097	Balliet	Sallie
B-1264	Balliet	Samuel
D-334	Balliet	Sarah
D-1178	Balliet	Sarah
B-34	Balliet	Sarah
B-518	Balliet	Sarah
M-1027	Balliet	Sarah
B-1490	Balliet	Savilla
B-1046	Balliet	Stephen
B-1490	Balliet	Stephen
B-1694	Balliet	Stephen
M-634	Balliet	Susan
M-672	Balliet	Tilghmam
B-1402	Balliet	Tilghman
B-1494	Balliet	Tilghman
B-1681	Balliet	Tilghman G
M-861	Balliet	Tilghman G
B-1784	Bamford	Laura Matilda
M-859	Bamford	Robert G
M-530	Barnes	Monroe Milton
D-898	Barral	Cassie
D-1076	Barral	Cora
D-2	Barral	George
B-547	Barrel	Catherine
B-999	Barrick	Joel
B-999	Barrick	Mary
M-556	Bartholomew	L.J.
B-364	Bartholomew	Lenah
M-3	Bartholomew	Levina
B-1586	Bartholomew	Lloyd
M-11	Bartholomew	Manda E
B-1401	Bartholomew	Maria
B-320	Bartholomew	Mary
B-860	Bartholomew	Melinda
B-1111	Bartholomew	Melinda

Line #	Surname	Given Name
B-1086	Barthold	Ellen
B-569	Bartholomew	Abraham
B-569	Bartholomew	Albert
B-617	Bartholomew	Amand
B-970	Bartholomew	Amanda
M-198	Bartholomew	Amanda
B-1566	Bartholomew	Amanda Eliza
B-715	Bartholomew	Anna
M-822	Bartholomew	Anna Maria
M-98	Bartholomew	Benjamin
B-1586	Bartholomew	Calvin E
B-1731	Bartholomew	Calvin E
M-875	Bartholomew	Calvin E
B-1770	Bartholomew	Carrie
B-1277	Bartholomew	Carrie
B-934	Bartholomew	Catherine
M-9	Bartholomew	Catherine
D-266	Bartholomew	Charlette
B-900	Bartholomew	Christianna
M-302	Bartholomew	Christianna
M-10	Bartholomew	David
M-1158	Bartholomew	Edward
B-680	Bartholomew	Elias
B-948	Bartholomew	Elias
B-567	Bartholomew	Ellemanda
M-389	Bartholomew	Ellemande
B-1103	Bartholomew	Ellen
B-1233	Bartholomew	Ellen
B-900	Bartholomew	Ellen
B-11	Bartholomew	Ellen
B-682	Bartholomew	Ellen
M-493	Bartholomew	Emma E
M-958	Bartholomew	Eugene U
B-1770	Bartholomew	Eugene M
B-11	Bartholomew	Fianna
M-26	Bartholomew	Fyanna
B-1731	Bartholomew	Grace
B-680	Bartholomew	Harrie
B-1110	Bartholomew	Harry
B-69	Bartholomew	Henry
D-368	Bartholomew	John
B-278	Bartholomew	John
B-715	Bartholomew	John
B-1110	Bartholomew	John
B-1277	Bartholomew	John
M-99	Bartholomew	John
B-745	Bartholomew	Kate
B-467	Baumgartner	Sarah
M-1051	Baumholtzer	Mary Ann
D-1012	Bear	John
D-764	Bear	Mary
B-1226	Bear	Nathan
M-1111	Beaver	Clara J
M-1127	Beaver	Lillie M
M-764	Beaver	Sarah J
D-816	Bechtel	Aaron
B-982	Bechtel	Aaron
B-16	Bechtel	Aaron

Line #	Surname	Given Name
B-617	Bartholomew	Melinda
M-221	Bartholomew	Melinda
B-69	Bartholomew	Minerva
D-416	Bartholomew	Minnie
M-534	Bartholomew	Philip
B-278	Bartholomew	Robert
B-721	Bartholomew	Robert
B-776	Bartholomew	Robert
M-133	Bartholomew	Robert
B-259	Bartholomew	Sabina
B-775	Bartholomew	Sabina
M-6	Bartholomew	Sabina
B-558	Bartholomew	Sarah
M-183	Bartholomew	Sarah C
D-505	Bartholomew	St
B-278	Bartholomew	William
B-948	Bartholomew	William
M-9	Bartholomew	William
D-395	Barwick	Emma
B-390	Barwick	Hester
B-733	Barwick	Hetty
B-397	Barwick	Martin
M-354	Barwick	Savilla
B-397	Barwick	Sevilla
B-717	Barwick	Susan
B-389	Barwick	Susanna
B-390	Barwick	Susanna
B-391	Barwick	Susanna
M-990	Bast	Edward D
D-283	Bast	Mary
M-176	Batman	Anna
B-339	Batman	Jane
M-1026	Battenfield	Severinus
D-144	Bauer	Albert
D-429	Bauer	Clara
M-1017	Bauer	Elizabeth Jane
M-1048	Bauer	J DeHaven
D-197	Bauer	John
B-293	Bauer	Lucy ann
M-413	Bauer	Mary Ann
M-1019	Bauer	Sarah Ann
M-402	Bauer	Stephen
D-142	Bauer	William
B-117	Baumgarten	Anthony
M-225	Baumgarten	Anthony
B-117	Baumgarten	Mary
B-467	Baumgartner	Anthony
B-1549	Beck	Torence
D-1048	Beck	Torrance
B-407	Beck	William
M-484	Beckendorf	Caroline Anna
B-1201	Beckendorf	Henry
D-280	Becker	Amelia
B-1807	Becker	Cassie
B-374	Becker	Edward
B-111	Becker	Edwin
B-111	Becker	Edwin
B-221	Becker	Emma

Line #	Surname	Given Name	Line #	Surname	Given Name
B-694	Bechtel	Aaron	B-821	Becker	Jacob
B-694	Bechtel	Anna	M-357	Becker	Mary
D-37	Bechtel	Cephallen	M-17	Becker	Nicholas
M-592	Bechtel	David	D-750	Becker	Oliver
B-447	Bechtel	Ellen	B-804	Becker	Oliver
B-16	Bechtel	Francis	B-1863	Becker	Oscar
D-983	Bechtel	Fransie	B-221	Becker	Peter
D-639	Bechtel	George	B-804	Becker	Peter
B-828	Bechtel	George	B-1807	Becker	Peter
D-312	Bechtel	Jane	B-821	Becker	Samuel
B-1885	Bechtel	Mary	B-374	Becker	Sarah
B-1563	Bechtel	Mary Ann	M-921	Becker	Sarah A
M-836	Bechtel	Mary Ellen	B-821	Becker	William
B-447	Bechtel	William	B-1807	Becker	William Henry
B-828	Bechtel	William	B-1863	Becker	William Henry
B-982	Bechtel	William	M-991	Becker	William Henry
M-24	Bechtel	William	B-1680	Beer	Adam
D-928	Beck	Abigail	B-794	Beer	Adam
B-220	Beck	Alfred	B-1064	Beer	Alexander
B-629	Beck	Alfred	B-1065	Beer	Alexander
M-223	Beck	Alfred	M-175	Beer	Alexander
D-1335	Beck	Anna	B-93	Beer	Alfred
D-463	Beck	Charles	B-551	Beer	Alfred
B-407	Beck	Charles A	M-261	Beer	Alfred
B-714	Beck	Charles A	B-996	Beer	Amos
B-977	Beck	Charles A	M-513	Beer	Amos
B-320	Beck	Charles A	B-794	Beer	Belinda
M-334	Beck	Charles A	B-374	Beer	Cassenda
M-686	Beck	Charles O	B-111	Beer	Cassenta
D-734	Beck	Edgar	B-1079	Beer	Christiana
B-629	Beck	Edgar	B-439	Beer	Christianna
B-220	Beck	Emma	B-461	Beer	Daniel
D-945	Beck	Jonathan	B-35	Beer	Daniel
D-450	Beck	Leanna	M-370	Beer	Daniel
B-577	Beck	Lucinda	D-169	Beer	Elizabeth
B-977	Beck	Mary	B-1355	Beer	Ellen
B-714	Beck	Osville	B-1432	Beer	Ellen
B-657	Beck	Salome	M-569	Beer	Emaline
B-713	Beck	Salome	B-461	Beer	Emma
B-1583	Beck	Sarah	B-1530	Beer	Emma J
B-839	Beck	Sarah	M-818	Beer	Emma J
M-456	Beck	Sarah Catherine	B-367	Beer	Francis
B-16	Beck	Susan	B-831	Beer	Francis
B-1583	Beck	Thom. Washington	M-362	Beer	Francis W
B-1549	Beck	Thomas J	D-329	Beer	Francisca
B-831	Beer	Grant	D-213	Beidelman	(s/o Elias & Sarah)
B-1065	Beer	Hattie	B-826	Beidelman	Catherine
B-367	Beer	Henry	B-1256	Beidelman	Catherine
B-98	Beer	Isaiah	B-1791	Beidelman	Catherine Jane
B-1680	Beer	John	M-355	Beidelman	Catherine Jane
M-703	Beer	Jonas C	B-260	Beidelman	Elias
B-996	Beer	Leander	D-319	Beidelman	Emma
D-330	Beer	Lydia	B-574	Beidelman	Jacob H
B-528	Beer	Lynford	M-64	Beidelman	Jacob H
B-685	Beer	Lynnford	D-608	Beidelman	John
B-98	Beer	Mary Jane	B-574	Beidelman	John
B-1064	Beer	Milton	B-260	Beidelman	Theodosia
B-1298	Beer	Priscilla	B-87	Beinemman	Henry

Line #	Surname	Given Name	Line #	Surname	Given Name
B-1374	Beer	Priscilla	B-544	Beitelman	Catherine
B-1443	Beer	Priscilla	B-1493	Beitelman	Catherine
B-1513	Beer	Priscilla	B-471	Beitelman	Catherine
B-1574	Beer	Priscilla	B-1437	Belford	Rachel
B-93	Beer	Rosanna	B-1474	Belford	Rachel
B-551	Beer	Sally	M-777	Belford	Sarah Emma
B-685	Beer	Sarah	D-1210	Beltz	Abilona
M-112	Beer	Solomon	M-80	Beltz	Alexander
M-1179	Beerman	Lydia	D-105	Beltz	Alice
M-102	Beers	Daniel	B-1801	Beltz	Alice Louisa
M-1180	Beever	Ella L	B-1853	Beltz	Alice Louisa
M-864	Begel	Arminta	B-1887	Beltz	Alice Louisa
B-1550	Behen	Clara	B-1944	Beltz	Alice Louisa
B-1550	Behen	John H	B-1953	Beltz	Alice Louisa
B-161	Behler	Christianna	B-1650	Beltz	Amanda
B-788	Behler	Christianna	M-865	Beltz	Amanda
B-171	Behler	Daniel	B-57	Beltz	Anna
B-522	Behler	Daniel	B-543	Beltz	Anna
D-1121	Behler	Elizabeth	B-133	Beltz	Aquilla
B-125	Behler	Harry	D-621	Beltz	Catherine
B-469	Behler	Henry	B-747	Beltz	Catherine
B-338	Behler	Jacob	B-1130	Beltz	Catherine
M-629	Behler	Jeremiah	B-1609	Beltz	Celesta
B-215	Behler	John	B-1684	Beltz	Celesta
B-1033	Behler	John	M-894	Beltz	Celesta
M-741	Behler	John Jackson	D-273	Beltz	Charles
D-298	Behler	Joseph	B-625	Beltz	Daniel
B-24	Behler	Levi	D-171	Beltz	Dannis
B-215	Behler	Levi	B-133	Beltz	David
D-124	Behler	Matilda	B-730	Beltz	David
B-1033	Behler	Rebecca	B-492	Beltz	David
M-769	Behler	Robert F	B-1355	Beltz	David
D-52	Behler	Samuel	M-346	Beltz	David
B-1104	Behler	Sarah	M-909	Beltz	David
D-247	Behler	William	B-1452	Beltz	Elias
B-125	Behler	William	D-127	Beltz	Elizabeth
B-469	Behler	William	B-587	Beltz	Elizabeth
B-655	Behler	William	B-768	Beltz	Elizabeth
M-91	Behler	William	B-1130	Beltz	Elizabeth
B-24	Behler	Wilson	M-125	Beltz	Elizabeth
D-1102	Behm	Catherine	B-1683	Beltz	Elmer Ellsworth
M-814	Behm	John H	B-4	Beltz	Estella
M-439	Behrens	Helena	B-1452	Beltz	Franklin
B-1452	Beltz	Franklin	B-369	Beltz	Sarah Jane
B-7	Beltz	Harrison	D-227	Beltz	Thomas
B-741	Beltz	Harrison	D-239	Beltz	Thomas
M-1071	Beltz	Harrison	B-273	Beltz	Thomas
B-1293	Beltz	Harry	B-1334	Beltz	Thomas
B-1293	Beltz	Harry	B-1432	Beltz	Thomas
B-273	Beltz	Henry	M-142	Beltz	Thomas Benjamin
B-673	Beltz	Henry	B-1690	Beltz	Thomas D
M-339	Beltz	Henry	M-913	Beltz	Thomas D
B-1632	Beltz	Ida E	B-741	Beltz	William
B-1711	Beltz	Ida E	M-1091	Beltzner	Charles
B-1766	Beltz	Ida E	B-1950	Beltzner	George
B-1839	Beltz	Ida E	M-1170	Beltzner	George
B-1870	Beltz	Ida E	B-1950	Beltzner	Marion
B-1965	Beltz	Ida E	D-771	Benigoff	Nathan

Line #	Surname	Given Name	Line #	Surname	Given Name
M-868	Beltz	Ida E	B-51	Beninger	Adam
B-1902	Beltz	Ida Irene	B-370	Beninger	Clara
B-1937	Beltz	Ida Irene	B-51	Beninger	James
B-4	Beltz	Isaac	B-370	Beninger	Wilson
B-254	Beltz	Isaac	M-814	Benner	Eurilla Ida
B-542	Beltz	Isaac	B-42	Bennett	Rebecca
D-399	Beltz	James	B-668	Bennett	Rebecca
B-213	Beltz	James E	B-224	Benninger	Isola Anna
B-216	Beltz	James E	M-891	Benninger	J. M.
B-878	Beltz	John	B-224	Benninger	Wilson
B-41	Beltz	John	M-274	Benninger	Wilson
B-77	Beltz	John	M-850	Benninghoff	Libbie
B-169	Beltz	Joseph	B-1569	Benninghoff	Libbie A
B-169	Beltz	Joseph	B-1639	Benninghoff	Libbie A
B-476	Beltz	Joseph	B-1850	Benninghoff	Libbie A
B-1366	Beltz	Kate	B-1481	Benninghoff	Victor
B-476	Beltz	Korah	B-1481	Benninghoff	William H
B-7	Beltz	Laura	M-582	Benninghoff	William H
D-238	Beltz	Lewis	B-1223	Bennygoff	George
D-1223	Beltz	Lizzie	B-1223	Bennygoff	Phaon
B-1690	Beltz	Lizzie	B-1104	Bennygouph	Gideon
B-1683	Beltz	Lottie	B-1147	Bennygouph	Nathan
D-824	Beltz	Lydia	B-1104	Bennygouph	William
D-992	Beltz	Lydia	B-1147	Bennygouph	William
B-537	Beltz	Lydia	B-88	Bennyhoof	Alvina
B-117	Beltz	Lydia	B-89	Bennyhoof	Emaline
B-747	Beltz	Lydia	B-54	Bennyhoof	John
B-216	Beltz	Lydia Ann	B-54	Bennyhoof	John
B-673	Beltz	Manda	B-89	Bennyhoof	Jonas
B-213	Beltz	Mary	B-310	Berg	Charles
M-372	Beltz	Mary	B-1181	Berg	John
B-537	Beltz	Mary Ann	D-998	Berg	Kitty
B-771	Beltz	Mary Ann	D-1008	Berg	Mary
M-234	Beltz	Mary Ann	B-310	Berg	Peter
D-960	Beltz	Milton	B-1483	Berger	Adam
B-730	Beltz	Minnie	M-711	Berger	Adam
B-538	Beltz	Rebecca	B-252	Berger	Alwin
M-760	Beltz	Robert F	B-493	Berger	Elias
D-260	Beltz	Sabina	B-766	Berger	Elias
B-878	Beltz	Sarah	B-1088	Berger	Elias
M-796	Beltz	Sarah Alice	B-1336	Berger	Elias
M-376	Berger	Elias	B-1581	Billman	Charles Benjamin
M-956	Berger	Ellen	B-1047	Billman	Eli
D-635	Berger	Franklin	B-1231	Billman	Elias
B-822	Berger	Franklin	B-1573	Billman	Emma A
B-253	Berger	Frederic	B-1581	Billman	George
B-1336	Berger	George	B-1416	Billman	Gideon
B-1483	Berger	George	B-1047	Billman	Harriet
B-230	Berger	George	B-1231	Billman	Harry
B-822	Berger	George	B-1533	Billman	Harry
B-1895	Berger	Helen	B-531	Billman	Henrietta
B-493	Berger	Ida	B-1533	Billman	James W
B-1088	Berger	Ira	B-1317	Billman	Levina
B-230	Berger	John	M-961	Billman	Lizzie
B-1895	Berger	John	B-1511	Billman	Mary
M-1097	Berger	John	M-383	Billman	Mary Jane
M-1093	Berger	Katie	B-1185	Billman	Rebecca
B-766	Berger	Laura	B-1305	Billman	Rebecca

Line #	Surname	Given Name
M-1153	Berger	Maggie E
B-53	Berger	Mary
B-253	Berger	Matilda
B-53	Berger	William
B-253	Berger (?)	Emmanuel
B-252	Berger (?)	Frederic
B-252	Berger (?)	
B-253	Berger (?)	
B-43	Bergy	Sarah
B-44	Bergy	Sarah
B-45	Bergy	Sarah
B-46	Bergy	Sarah
B-185	Berkemeyer	Henrietta
M-74	Berkemeyer	Henrietta
B-56	Berkemeyer	Louisa
B-430	Berlin	Henry F
M-82	Berlin	Henry F
B-430	Berlin	William
M-1102	Berlin	William O
B-294	Berthol	Elizabeth
D-836	Berwick	Lewis
M-950	Best	Lizzie J
M-600	Betz	Barbara Udella
B-1550	Beuner	Eurilla
M-309	Bever	Alfred
M-1000	Biebelheimer	Jeremiah
B-421	Biek	Cresencia
B-1738	Bierman	Angelina
M-944	Bierman	Angelina
M-317	Billheimer	Cornelius Cyrus
M-1085	Billig	Elmira E
B-1107	Billig	Polly
D-1296	Billman	Anna
B-1531	Billman	Caroline
B-1473	Billman	Charles
B-1511	Billman	Charles
B-1533	Billman	Charles
B-1573	Billman	Charles
B-1511	Billman	Charles B
M-885	Blose	Emma
B-1867	Blose	Eva Agnes
M-1106	Blose	Eva Agnes
B-1348	Blose	Geiden
M-717	Blose	Henrietta S
D-642	Blose	Henry
B-631	Blose	Henry
M-1131	Blose	Ilerda
B-1007	Blose	Isabella
B-165	Blose	Jacob
B-165	Blose	Jacob
B-831	Blose	Jacob
M-824	Blose	Jane A
D-32	Blose	Lafayette
B-282	Blose	Lewis
B-696	Blose	Lewis
B-1007	Blose	Lewis
M-103	Blose	Lewis
B-124	Blose	Louisa
D-1093	Billman	Samuel
B-1047	Billman	William
B-952	Billmer	Elias
B-311	Billy	Helena
B-311	Billy	James
M-2	Bittenbender	Stephen
B-1549	Bittner	Christiana
M-1188	Bittner	John H
M-124	Blackwell	Elizabeth
D-338	Blose	Adelina
B-1422	Blose	Afred
B-282	Blose	Albert
B-1348	Blose	Alfred
M-638	Blose	Alfred
M-760	Blose	Anna D
M-1144	Blose	Barbara I
B-1009	Blose	Carrie
D-845	Blose	Catherine
B-654	Blose	Charles
B-834	Blose	Charles
M-120	Blose	Charles
B-1422	Blose	Daisie
D-186	Blose	Daniel
B-631	Blose	David
M-428	Blose	David
B-35	Blose	Dianna
M-1087	Blose	Dianna
B-894	Blose	Eliza
M-583	Blose	Eliza Ann
D-185	Blose	Elizabeth
B-929	Blose	Ellemina
D-663	Blose	Ellen
B-696	Blose	Ellen
B-894	Blose	Ellen Jane
B-696	Blose	Ellen Jane
M-723	Blose	Ellen M
M-762	Blose	Ellen Priscilla
B-654	Blose	Elmira
M-729	Blose	Elwin
B-167	Blose	Thomas
D-532	Blose	Tilghman
M-735	Blose	Victor Oscar
D-318	Blose	William
B-367	Blose	Wilmina
B-831	Blose	Wilmina
M-362	Blose	Wilmina
D-102	Bobst	Salome
M-105	Bobst	Thomas
B-1464	Bochard	Ellen
B-1583	Bochard	Ellen
M-339	Bock	Levina
B-313	Boehmler	Daniel
B-313	Boehmler	Frederich
M-872	Bogle	Bid
M-800	Bolich	Susanna
B-5	Boll	Emma
M-235	Boll	Emma
B-412	Bollsgrofe	Charles

Line #	Surname	Given Name	Line #	Surname	Given Name
B-1561	Blose	Louisa	B-907	Bollsgrofe	Charles
B-77	Blose	Lovina	B-262	Bollsgrofe	Elizabeth
B-621	Blose	Lucy	B-907	Bollsgrofe	Frankie
B-802	Blose	Lucy	B-412	Bollsgrofe	Hattie
M-271	Blose	Lucy	B-263	Bollsgrofe	Sarah
B-107	Blose	Mary	B-784	Bolsgrafe	Charles
M-732	Blose	Mary A	B-199	Bolsgrofe	Charles Jacob
B-201	Blose	Mary Ann	B-784	Bolsgrofe	Eliza
B-353	Blose	Mary Ann	D-436	Bolsgrofe	Kate
B-665	Blose	Mary Ann	B-199	Bolsgrofe	Kate
B-910	Blose	Mary Ann	D-398	Bolsgrofe	Laura
B-482	Blose	Mary Ann	M-841	Borger	Aaron
B-780	Blose	Mary Ann	B-711	Borhor	Ada
B-929	Blose	Mary Ann	B-540	Borhor	Elmira
M-190	Blose	Mary Ann	D-894	Borhor	Leah
B-125	Blose	Matilda	B-163	Borhor	Lewis
B-655	Blose	Matilda	B-540	Borhor	Lewis
M-91	Blose	Matilda	B-711	Borhor	Lewis
B-39	Blose	Minnie	M-840	Borhor	Lewis
B-572	Blose	Oliver	B-163	Borhor	Mary
B-654	Blose	Oliver	D-1033	Borhor	Sabastian
M-52	Blose	Oliver	M-586	Boughner	Henrietta
M-210	Blose	Oliver	B-1862	Bourey	Josephine
B-469	Blose	Oliwer	B-1804	Bourey	Sophia
M-1032	Blose	Oscar	B-29	Bower	John
B-77	Blose	Peter	B-29	Bower	Louisa
M-41	Blose	Peter	B-1233	Bowers	Hetty
B-35	Blose	Rebecca	M-523	Bowers	Hetty
B-1009	Blose	Robert	D-661	Bowman	(s/o Francis and Amelia)
D-465	Blose	Sally	M-646	Bowman	Aaron
B-167	Blose	Sally	B-175	Bowman	Abbey
M-357	Blose	Samuel	B-847	Bowman	Abby
B-635	Blose	Sarah	B-1058	Bowman	Alavesta
B-201	Blose	Simeon	M-391	Bowman	Alavesta A
B-35	Blose	Simon	B-847	Bowman	Albert
B-367	Blose	Simon	B-1132	Bowman	Albert
D-212	Blose	Thomas	M-511	Bowman	Albert
B-56	Bowman	Alton	M-838	Bowman	Mary Amanda
B-1337	Bowman	Alwin	M-585	Bowman	Mary Jane
D-18	Bowman	Anna	D-1139	Bowman	Matilda
B-1132	Bowman	Asapa	D-1317	Bowman	Peter
M-1173	Bowman	Assipa M	D-1136	Bowman	Robert
B-1156	Bowman	Berthie	B-1527	Bowman	Robert
B-174	Bowman	Carolina	B-12	Bowman	Rodger
D-134	Bowman	Catherine	M-208	Bowman	Rodger
B-1439	Bowman	Catherine	B-1427	Bowman	Sarah Louisa
M-749	Bowman	Catherine A	D-662	Bowman	Susanna
M-1056	Bowman	Charles P	B-1673	Bowman	Susanna
B-1766	Bowman	Clara Ann	B-1337	Bowman	Susanna
B-1156	Bowman	Dallas	B-1644	Bowman	Susanna
M-476	Bowman	Dallas	B-1819	Bowman	Susanna
M-1056	Bowman	Ella	B-1725	Bowman	Susanna V
D-567	Bowman	Ellen	M-797	Bowman	Susanna V
B-605	Bowman	Ellen	D-508	Bowman	Victor
B-175	Bowman	Emma	B-550	Bowman	Victor
B-1644	Bowman	Emma	B-175	Bowman	Wilson
B-1722	Bowman	Fianna	B-605	Bowman	Wilson D
B-1774	Bowman	Fianna	M-143	Bowman	Wilson D

Line #	Surname	Given Name
B-1819	Bowman	Fianna Alavesta
M-930	Bowman	Fianna Alavesta
B-1159	Bowman	Francis
B-1411	Bowman	Francis
B-1527	Bowman	Francis
M-516	Bowman	Francis
B-1738	Bowman	George
B-550	Bowman	Glyde
B-1644	Bowman	Harry James
B-1411	Bowman	Harvey
B-1465	Bowman	Henrietta
B-1595	Bowman	Henrietta
B-1734	Bowman	Henrietta
M-695	Bowman	Henrietta Louisa
B-12	Bowman	Henry
B-550	Bowman	Henry
B-1738	Bowman	Henry James
M-726	Bowman	Henry James
B-1745	Bowman	James
B-1337	Bowman	John
B-1745	Bowman	John
M-665	Bowman	John
M-964	Bowman	John
B-56	Bowman	Josiah
B-12	Bowman	Lee
B-1855	Bowman	Lizzie
M-1098	Bowman	Lizzie E
M-941	Bowman	Maggie
B-1378	Bowman	Maria
B-1775	Bowman	Maria E
M-680	Bowman	Maria Elizabeth
B-1725	Bowman	Marie E
D-217	Bowman	Mary
B-1159	Bowman	Mary
M-879	Bowman	Mary A
B-947	Boyer	Lavina
M-573	Boyer	Levi
B-727	Boyer	Levi W
B-179	Boyer	Levina
M-1034	Boyer	Lizzie
B-139	Boyer	Lora
B-654	Boyer	Manda
D-1347	Boyer	Mary
B-572	Boyer	Mary
B-142	Boyer	Mary
B-528	Boyer	Mary
B-210	Boyer	Mary
B-773	Boyer	Mary
B-953	Boyer	Mary
B-866	Boyer	Mary Ann
B-1760	Boyer	Milton C
B-1761	Boyer	Milton C
M-917	Boyer	Milton C
M-1118	Boyer	Minnie
B-508	Boyer	Oscar
M-150	Boyer	Owen C
B-137	Boyer	Owen H
B-137	Boyer	Pearce
M-824	Bowman	Wilson D
M-941	Boyer	Abel
B-572	Boyer	Alexander
B-819	Boyer	Alexander
B-820	Boyer	Alexander
M-342	Boyer	Alexander
M-52	Boyer	Amanda
M-938	Boyer	Amelia Ann
M-276	Boyer	Catherine
B-434	Boyer	Christiana
B-332	Boyer	Christianna
D-514	Boyer	Edith
B-866	Boyer	Edward
D-687	Boyer	Edwin
B-819	Boyer	Edwin
D-1192	Boyer	Emma
B-1761	Boyer	Ermie
B-1760	Boyer	Florence
M-900	Boyer	Frank P
B-508	Boyer	Franklin
M-399	Boyer	Franklin
B-891	Boyer	Hattie
D-470	Boyer	Henry
B-866	Boyer	Ida
D-603	Boyer	Irwin
D-326	Boyer	John
D-484	Boyer	John
D-811	Boyer	John
B-61	Boyer	John A
B-94	Boyer	John A
B-344	Boyer	John A
B-139	Boyer	John F
B-744	Boyer	John F
M-250	Boyer	John F
M-348	Boyer	L.. W.
B-1375	Briner	Henrietta
M-697	Brink	William H
M-1147	Brinker	Edward C Jr
D-375	Brinkman	Daniel
D-87	Brinkman	Elwin
B-712	Britton	Benoville
M-195	Britton	Carolina
D-589	Britton	Elizabeth
D-765	Britton	Elizabeth
B-1200	Britton	Elizabeth
D-1321	Britton	Israel
B-712	Britton	Manda
D-1322	Britton	William
B-1693	Brobst	Bessie
D-695	Brobst	Charles
M-436	Brobst	Francis
B-1693	Brobst	James S
D-537	Brong	Charles
B-488	Brong	Charles
B-901	Brong	Harry
B-160	Brong	Jacob
B-488	Brong	Jacob
B-901	Brong	Jacob

Line #	Surname	Given Name	Line #	Surname	Given Name
M-359	Boyer	Priscilla	M-241	Brong	Jacob
M-378	Boyer	Priscilla	B-160	Brong	William
B-744	Boyer	Purcy	M-174	Broom	Charles
B-1590	Boyer	Rebecca	B-332	Brotzman	Charles
B-727	Boyer	Robert	B-434	Brotzman	Charles
B-891	Boyer	Samuel	D-447	Brotzman	Jacob
B-36	Boyer	Susan	B-30	Brotzman	Jane
D-511	Boyer	Susanna	B-203	Brotzman	Jane
B-32	Boyer	Susanna	B-570	Brotzman	Jane
B-834	Boyer	Susanna	B-332	Brotzman	Stewart
M-1037	Braerman	L H	B-64	Brotzman	Susanna Amanda
M-847	Brandon	Emma B	B-966	Brotzman	Susanna Amanda
D-361	Breifogel	Anna	B-1652	Brown	Albert
B-19	Breifogel	Catharine	M-716	Brown	Albert
B-1470	Breifogel	Ellen	M-981	Brown	Albert G A
B-821	Breifogel	Lydia	M-1078	Brown	Albert J
B-1627	Breiner	Benjamin Franklin	D-118	Brown	Cassenta
B-1627	Breiner	Elmer	B-1357	Brown	Clara
M-810	Breiner	Kate	M-731	Brown	Clara Alice
B-1341	Breiner	Lydia	M-262	Brown	Ellen
D-1259	Breisch	Catherine	B-14	Brown	Ellen
B-657	Bretney	Clemen	B-1008	Brown	Emaline
D-747	Bretney	Emma	B-881	Brown	Emma
B-857	Bretney	Emma	M-449	Brown	Emma Louisa
M-851	Bretney	Granville A	D-1256	Brown	Ephearin
D-922	Bretney	Henry	B-751	Brown	Franklin
B-657	Bretney	Henry	D-295	Brown	Isabella
B-713	Bretney	Henry	B-696	Brown	Isabella
B-657	Bretney	Thomas J	B-1007	Brown	Isabella
B-857	Bretney	Thomas J	M-103	Brown	Isabella
B-1656	Breyfogel	Ellen	B-314	Brown	Jacob
B-272	Bridelman	Jane	B-30	Brown	Jacob
M-1061	Briner	Agnes E	M-213	Brown	Jacob
D-219	Brown	James	B-1170	Bucks	George
B-615	Brown	James	B-1170	Bucks	Rosa
B-881	Brown	James	B-385	Buhl	Caroline
B-1357	Brown	John C	B-91	Bundly	Matilda
B-1423	Brown	John C	D-873	Burger	Lillie
M-642	Brown	John C	M-88	Burger	Sarah Ann
M-1057	Brown	Josephine	D-88	Burkart	Catherine
B-8	Brown	Lafayette	B-1951	Bush	Emina
B-881	Brown	Lafayette	M-270	Bush	Mary Jane
B-433	Brown	Levi	D-17	Buss	(s/o Jacob & Josephine (Hills))
B-751	Brown	Levi	B-986	Buss	Amelia
D-69	Brown	Levina	B-1239	Buss	Eva
B-14	Brown	Lewis	D-291	Buss	Jacob
M-238	Brown	Lewis	B-127	Buss	Jacob
B-1423	Brown	Lizzie	B-985	Buss	Jacob
D-496	Brown	Mary	B-986	Buss	Jacob
B-433	Brown	Mary	B-1239	Buss	Jacob
M-76	Brown	Mary A	B-91	Buss	John Tobias
M-655	Brown	Mary Jane	B-985	Buss	Josephena
D-458	Brown	Matilda	B-884	Buss	Korah
B-984	Brown	Melinda	B-1239	Buss	Martha
M-485	Brown	Melinda	B-127	Buss	Mary
D-461	Brown	Palmer	B-91	Buss	Matilida
B-314	Brown	Palmer	B-884	Buss	Solomon
M-718	Brown	Sarah R	D-388	Buss	William

Line #	Surname	Given Name
B-743	Brown	Simeon
B-433	Brown	Simon
D-736	Brown	Thomas
B-615	Brown	Thomas
B-282	Brown	Thomas
M-757	Brown	W. H.
M-879	Brown	Wesley H
M-1142	Brown	Lizzie Viola
D-781	Bruekres	Charles
M-351	Bruekres	George
M-69	Brutz	Mary
M-173	Buchman	Anjulina
M-502	Buchman	Caroline
M-870	Buchman	Emma L
B-1670	Buck	Carrie
B-688	Buck	Eliza
D-119	Buck	George
D-137	Buck	James
M-72	Buck	James
B-688	Buck	John
B-273	Buck	Jonas
B-812	Buck	Jonas
B-273	Buck	Lavina
B-673	Buck	Levina
B-1670	Buck	Louisa
B-77	Buck	Lovina
B-77	Buck	Mary
B-465	Buck	Mary
M-41	Buck	Mary
B-14	Buck	P.
M-154	Buckholtz	Caroline F J
B-630	Christman	Barbara
B-1151	Christman	Barbara
M-286	Christman	Barbara
M-844	Christman	E. C.
B-1951	Christman	Edna
B-649	Christman	Elizabeth
B-61	Christman	Elizabeth
B-94	Christman	Elizabeth
D-746	Christman	George
B-581	Christman	George
M-544	Christman	Jane
B-581	Christman	Joel
B-204	Christman	Mary Ann
M-891	Christman	Sallie A
B-394	Christman	Sarah
M-29	Christman	Sarah
B-1951	Christman	Stewart
B-604	Clause	Elizabeth
M-802	Clauss	Aaron
M-193	Clauss	Alfred
M-194	Clauss	Amanda
B-886	Clauss	Emanuel W
M-492	Clauss	Emanuel W
B-886	Clauss	George
D-165	Clauss	James
B-515	Clauss	Polly
B-380	Cleaver	Rebecca

Line #	Surname	Given Name
M-627	Butz	Emma J
B-1564	Buzzard	George
B-1564	Buzzard	Miles
M-684	Caffrey	John W
M-192	Cain	John
B-1433	Campbell	Annie
M-705	Campbell	Annie
B-238	Campbell	Archibald
B-1342	Campbell	Charles
M-1025	Campbell	Daniel H
M-635	Campbell	Eliza
B-1914	Campbell	Ella Jane
M-742	Campbell	Fannie M
M-1090	Campbell	Frank Pierce
D-139	Campbell	Isabella
B-1342	Campbell	James
M-681	Campbell	James A
D-586	Campbell	Joseph
B-238	Campbell	Martin
M-1031	Campbell	Martin
M-272	Campsie	Margeret
B-177	Campton	Anna S
B-403	Campton	Anna Salinda
M-144	Campton	Anna Salinda
B-1120	Chamberlain	Mary
B-334	Chardon	Daniel
B-334	Chardon	Emma
B-246	Chirstman	Samuel
M-703	Christman	Amanda Mary
M-622	Christman	Amelia
M-721	Christman	Amelia
B-858	Confer	Sarah
M-366	Confer	Sarah
M-490	Conley	William J
B-958	Connor	Elizabeth
M-1066	Cooper	Sarah Ann
D-1287	Cooper	William
B-14	Cope	Mary Amanda
M-238	Cope	Mary Amanda
M-893	Correll	Alice
D-1075	Correll	Catherine
M-719	Correll	Charles
D-965	Correll	Clara
D-1349	Correll	Daniel
B-1707	Correll	Emma
B-200	Correll	Florando
D-976	Correll	John
M-677	Correll	John
M-744	Correll	Kate
B-854	Correll	Laura
B-854	Correll	Lewis
B-1186	Correll	Lydia
D-1088	Correll	Mary
B-705	Correll	Mary
M-897	Correll	Mary
B-1083	Correll	Rebecca
B-1295	Correll	Rebecca
M-482	Correll	Sallena

Line #	Surname	Given Name	Line #	Surname	Given Name
B-1211	Clewell	Ellen	D-1276	Correll	Simon
B-1027	Clewell	Franklin	M-1156	Creitz	Charles M
B-723	Clewell	George	M-1080	Creitz	Cora E
B-1027	Clewell	George	M-1169	Creitz	Daniel
B-1211	Clewell	George	B-1945	Creitz	Daniel A
B-1401	Clewell	George	M-1157	Creitz	Laura M
B-723	Clewell	Martha	B-1945	Creitz	Mary
B-1401	Clewell	Mary	B-1675	Cunfer	Alvena
M-677	Clouse	Mary Alice	B-1726	Cunfer	Alvena
B-157	Cochran	Sally Ann	B-1450	Cunfer	Alvenia
B-503	Cochran	Sally Ann	B-1754	Cunfer	Caroline
B-221	Cochran	Sally Ann	B-1798	Cunfer	Caroline
B-666	Cochran	Sally Ann	B-1836	Cunfer	Caroline
M-249	Cochran	Sally Ann	B-1878	Cunfer	Caroline
D-216	Coffin	Emma	B-1922	Cunfer	Caroline
D-308	Coffin	Hazard	M-968	Cunfer	Caroline
M-779	Cole	Sarah Ann	B-1912	Cunfer	Charles
B-794	Collins	Eugene	B-1918	Cunfer	Charles
B-794	Collins	John Henry	M-972	Cunfer	Charles L
B-858	Confer	Anna	B-1838	Cunfer	Charles Lewis
D-243	Confer	Elizabeth	B-1898	Cunfer	Charles Lewis
B-699	Confer	Ella	B-1918	Cunfer	Charles Lewis
B-809	Confer	Emma	B-1947	Cunfer	Clara
B-677	Confer	Emma	D-1118	Cunfer	Emma
B-226	Confer	John	M-423	Cunfer	Emma
B-115	Confer	John	B-1667	Cunfer	George Benjamin
B-420	Confer	Sarah	M-935	Cunfer	George Benjamin
B-443	Confer	Sarah	B-1962	Cunfer	Hilda
B-677	Confer	Sarah	B-1898	Cunfer	Irene
B-810	Cunfer	Jacob	B-1926	David	Emma Elizabeth
B-1912	Cunfer	Jacob	M-252	David	Fianna
M-1132	Cunfer	Jacob	B-1877	David	Helen
B-1094	Cunfer	John	B-1692	David	Mary L
B-1692	Cunfer	John C	B-1947	David	Mary L
B-1947	Cunfer	John C	M-753	David	Mary L
M-753	Cunfer	John E	B-1877	David	Uriah
B-1501	Cunfer	Josiah	M-1023	David	Vester
M-770	Cunfer	Josiah	B-1854	David	William
B-1667	Cunfer	Lilia	M-1133	Davidson	Irvin
M-693	Cunfer	Lizzie	M-1134	Davidson	Rosa
B-1692	Cunfer	Mandes	M-982	Day	John E
B-1094	Cunfer	Matilda	B-793	Day	Mary
B-1331	Cunfer	Matilda	M-156	DeFrehn	Hannah
B-1430	Cunfer	Matilda	M-294	Deibert	Alwilda
M-660	Cunfer	Matilda	B-644	Deibert	Mary
B-810	Cunfer	Michael	M-490	Deibert	Violetta E
B-1962	Cunfer	Michael A	B-1314	DeLong	Harry
B-1501	Cunfer	Robert	B-1124	DeLong	James
B-303	Cunfer	Sarah	B-1314	DeLong	James
B-1331	Cunfer	Sarah Ann	B-1417	Delong	James
M-925	Cunfer	Tillie M	B-1487	Delong	James
B-1838	Cunfer	William	M-572	Delong	James
D-198	Cyrus	Joseph	B-1124	DeLong	William
M-728	Daley	James	B-164	Delp	Salome
B-959	Danber	Kate	B-457	Delp	Salome
B-935	Daniels	Jeremiah R	B-855	Delp	Salome
M-510	Daniels	Jeremiah R	B-1166	Delp	Salome
B-935	Daniels	Robert	M-259	Delp	Salome

Line #	Surname	Given Name
M-235	Daring	Adolph
B-5	Daring	Amelia
B-5	Darring	Adolph
M-1113	Daubenspeck	D. W.
M-750	Daubenspeck	Emma E
M-757	Daubenspeck	Fianna
D-1241	Daubenspeck	John
M-970	Daubenspeck	John
B-1128	Daubenspeck	Kate
B-1316	Daubenspeck	Kate
B-1365	Daubenspeck	Mary
B-1431	Daubenspeck	Mary
M-694	Daubenspeck	Samuel F
M-559	Daubenspeck	Zeniah
D-1043	Dauber	Isaac
B-1082	Dauber	Isaac
B-719	Dauber	Kate
B-1082	Dauber	Sarah
B-152	David	Albert
B-1854	David	Albert
B-1879	David	Albert
M-1099	David	Albert
B-152	David	Charles
B-1879	David	Ella
B-1854	David	Emaline
B-1868	David	Emma Elizabeth
B-1909	David	Emma Elizabeth
B-1551	Diehl	Esther
B-1551	Diehl	Frank P
B-1358	Diehl	Isabella
D-27	Diehl	Josephina
B-1084	Diehl	Matilda
M-496	Diehl	Matilda H
M-1055	Diehl	Morris
M-392	Diemer	John
B-433	Dieter	Belinda
B-751	Dieter	Belinda
M-752	Dieter	Susan Isabella
M-7	Dieter	William H
B-592	Dieterlein	Amelia
B-592	Dieterlein	Timothy
B-1005	Dieterline	Harry
B-267	Dieterline	Sarah
B-1005	Dieterline	Timothy
M-524	Dilcher	Chrissilla
D-926	Dilcher	Gabriel
M-565	Dilcher	Leila
B-1161	Dilcher	Mary
B-678	Dilcher	Mary Ann
B-1300	Dilcher	Mary Ann
M-121	Dilcher	Mary Ann
M-204	Dilcher	Susanna
M-387	Dinkey	Anna J
B-1294	Ditcher	Maria
M-522	Dodendorf	John
M-171	Donatt	David
B-648	Donehue	Anna
M-414	Donehue	Anna

Line #	Surname	Given Name
B-408	Dengler	Eliza Amanda
B-695	Dengler	Hannah
M-218	Dengler	Hannah
D-1319	Dengler	Isaac
B-394	Dengler	Isaac
M-29	Dengler	Isaac
B-13	Dengler	Louisa
B-300	Dengler	Louisa
M-212	Dengler	Louisa
B-1116	Dengler	Lydia
M-112	Dengler	Priscilla
D-995	Dengler	Sarah
B-1720	Dentinger	Fannie
B-1813	Dentinger	Fannie
B-1882	Dentinger	Fannie
M-809	Deppe	Allen C
M-595	Deppy	Lewis
B-244	Derr	Julia
M-47	Derr	Juliann
D-978	Derrick	Maria
M-688	Detrich	Allen
D-428	Deuchler	Susanna
B-1646	Dewerth	Charles William
B-1646	Dewerth	Norma
B-568	Diehl	Alavesta
B-568	Diehl	Alwin
B-800	Diehl	Amandus
M-469	Dorwort	James P
B-170	Dorwort	Jannie
B-1052	Dorwort	Sarah
B-588	Dorwort	Thomas
B-1020	Dorwort	Thomas
B-170	Dorwort	William
M-205	Dory	Amanda
B-1410	Dotter	Amelia
M-661	Dotter	Anna
B-1184	Dotter	Catherine
B-333	Dotter	Harry
B-20	Dotter	Irwin
B-20	Dotter	Lazarus
B-333	Dotter	Lewis
B-745	Dotter	Manda
B-615	Dotterer	Cassenda
B-881	Dotterer	Catherine
B-461	Dotterer	Mary
B-62	Dottery	Mary
M-1007	Dracy	Minnie
B-1214	Dreher	Agnes
B-622	Dreher	Benoville
B-888	Dreher	Benoville
B-1385	Dreher	Benoville
B-1515	Dreher	Benoville
B-1617	Dreher	Benoville
B-1449	Dreher	Charles
B-1555	Dreher	Charles
B-1697	Dreher	Charles
M-709	Dreher	Charles
B-1903	Dreher	Clara

Line #	Surname	Given Name	Line #	Surname	Given Name
D-510	Dorwart	Calvin	B-1940	Dreher	Clement
D-178	Dorwart	Emma	B-71	Dreher	Ellen
B-588	Dorwart	Emma	B-1438	Dreher	Ellen
B-588	Dorwart	Francis	M-228	Dreher	Ellen
D-477	Dorwart	Harrie	M-606	Dreher	Emma
D-480	Dorwart	Sarah Anna	B-888	Dreher	Franklin
D-392	Dorwart	Sidney	B-802	Dreher	Frederic
B-251	Dorwart	Thomas	B-621	Dreher	Frederic
M-90	Dorwart	William	B-802	Dreher	Frederic
B-640	Dorword	Girdy	B-1617	Dreher	George
B-640	Dorword	William	B-622	Dreher	Harrie
B-1020	Dorwort	Bertha	B-1697	Dreher	Ida
B-251	Dorwort	Elizabeth	B-1386	Dreher	Ida
B-658	Dorwort	Elizabeth	B-1516	Dreher	Ida
M-265	Dorwort	Elizabeth	B-1608	Dreher	Ida
B-1021	Dorwort	Ellen	B-1515	Dreher	Katie
M-562	Dorwort	Ellen Jane	B-1555	Dreher	Laura
B-1052	Dorwort	Estella	B-109	Dreher	Mary
B-126	Dorwort	Esther	B-291	Dreher	Mary
B-885	Dorwort	Francis	B-652	Dreher	Mary
B-1052	Dorwort	Francis	B-1385	Dreher	Milton
M-187	Dorwort	Francis	D-558	Dreher	Minnie
D-675	Dorwort	Ida	B-621	Dreher	Minnie
B-885	Dorwort	Ida	B-1449	Dreher	Robert
B-1020	Dorwort	James	B-1940	Dreher	Russel
B-1903	Dreher	William	B-37	Dreisbach	Matilda
M-1029	Dreibelbies	George A	B-625	Dreisbach	Matilda
D-1184	Dreisbach	(s/o Tilghman- St Peters)	B-1051	Dreisbach	Matilda
D-1185	Dreisbach	(s/o Tilghman- St Peters)	B-1162	Dreisbach	Minnie
B-479	Dreisbach	Aaron	M-699	Dreisbach	Moses
B-954	Dreisbach	Aaron	D-984	Dreisbach	Peter
B-1162	Dreisbach	Aaron	M-787	Dreisbach	Polly
B-1320	Dreisbach	Aaron	B-299	Dreisbach	Sarah
B-1415	Dreisbach	Aaron	B-1349	Dreisbach	Susanna
B-1503	Dreisbach	Aaron	B-1503	Dreisbach	Theresa
M-315	Dreisbach	Aaron	D-96	Dreisbach	Thomas
D-700	Dreisbach	Albert	B-479	Dreisbach	Valera
B-616	Dreisbach	Alexander	B-763	Dreisbach	William
B-902	Dreisbach	Alexander	B-795	Dressel	Maria
B-134	Dreisbach	Alwena	M-1179	Dreyer	Anthony
B-902	Dreisbach	Anna	D-908	Dreyer	George
D-1316	Dreisbach	Annie	B-1202	Drier	Charles Francis
B-1415	Dreisbach	Carrie	B-1202	Drier	Clemens
B-381	Dreisbach	Catherine	M-403	Drissell	Henry
B-134	Dreisbach	Dennis	B-1145	Druckenmiller	Rosa
B-299	Dreisbach	Dennis	B-1438	Drumbore	Charlie
B-555	Dreisbach	Dennis	M-974	Drumbore	Clara
B-757	Dreisbach	Dennis	M-1190	Drumbore	Milton E
D-1344	Dreisbach	Elias	B-1438	Drumbore	Nathan
B-625	Dreisbach	Elizabeth	B-1941	Drumbore	Pauline
M-75	Dreisbach	Ellemina	B-1905	Drumbore	Robert
B-679	Dreisbach	Elmina	B-1905	Drumbore	Robert W
D-572	Dreisbach	Elwin	B-1941	Drumbore	Robert W
B-555	Dreisbach	Elwin	M-1137	Drumbore	Robert W
B-1891	Dreisbach	Ervin	D-350	Dunbar	Benjamin
M-1109	Dreisbach	Ervin	B-862	Dunbar	Calvin
B-954	Dreisbach	Eva	M-491	Dunbar	Calvin
B-902	Dreisbach	Fayette	D-359	Dunbar	Catherine

Line #	Surname	Given Name	Line #	Surname	Given Name
M-604	Dreisbach	Fietta	M-176	Dunbar	James
B-1847	Dreisbach	Frances Isabella	D-666	Dunbar	Matilda
B-1576	Dreisbach	Francis	B-862	Dunbar	Matilda
B-1721	Dreisbach	Francis	B-8	Dunbar	Robert
B-1917	Dreisbach	Francis Isabella	B-261	Dunbar	Robert
B-1614	Dreisbach	Francisca	M-254	Dunbar	Samuel
D-1353	Dreisbach	George	D-417	Dunbar	Sarah
D-1173	Dreisbach	Hannah	B-8	Dunbar	Sarah
B-679	Dreisbach	Harriet	B-941	Dunlap	Charles
B-1007	Dreisbach	Harriet	M-503	Dunlap	Charles
M-291	Dreisbach	Harriet	B-50	Dunlap	Elizabeth Jane
B-384	Dreisbach	Louisa	M-109	Dunlap	Elizabeth Jane
B-555	Dreisbach	Louisa	B-941	Dunlap	Ellen
B-1232	Dreisbach	Lydia	D-16	Dunlap	Iola
D-1323	Dreisbach	Mame	B-941	Dunlap	Samuel
B-616	Dreisbach	Mandes	B-1416	Dunn	Charles
B-763	Dreisbach	Mandes	B-1416	Dunn	James H
M-464	Dreisbach	Mandes	B-1607	Dutcher	Mary Martha
B-1891	Dreisbach	Margeret	B-1709	Dutcher	Mary Martha
B-101	Dreisbach	Maria	B-1755	Dutcher	Mary Martha
M-38	Dreisbach	Maria	B-1638	Dutcher	Mary Martha
B-1320	Dreisbach	Martha	B-1687	Dutcher	Mary Martha
B-757	Dreisbach	Mary	M-778	Eaches	Adam
B-1589	Eaches	Catherine	B-1487	Eck	Augustus
B-746	Eaches	Henrietta	B-1604	Eck	Augustus
M-356	Eaches	Henrietta	M-738	Eck	Augustus
B-1589	Eaches	John	B-1772	Eck	Calvin
M-106	Eastman	Joseph	B-1519	Eck	Cassia
B-1628	Ebberts	Amandus A	B-1520	Eck	Cassia
M-892	Ebberts	Amandus A	B-1521	Eck	Cassia
M-925	Ebberts	Charles A	B-1604	Eck	Charles
B-1667	Ebberts	Minerva	B-1604	Eck	Clara
M-935	Ebberts	Minerva	B-1487	Eck	Emma
B-1050	Ebberts	Nathan	D-850	Eck	Enos
B-1628	Ebberts	Walace	B-1652	Eck	Flossie
B-193	Ebert	Carolina	B-1069	Eck	Franklin
B-102	Ebert	Carolina	B-1824	Eck	Hattie Annie
B-4	Ebert	Caroline	D-1110	Eck	John
B-1352	Ebert	Charles	B-458	Eck	John
B-1816	Ebert	Clara A J	B-1069	Eck	John
M-1047	Ebert	Clara A. J.	D-161	Eck	Jonas
B-1936	Ebert	Emma S	B-474	Eck	Manda
B-1916	Ebert	Ida Jane	D-702	Eck	Manuel
B-1936	Ebert	Ida Jane	B-701	Eck	Mary
B-1960	Ebert	Ida Jane	B-975	Eck	Mary
D-10	Ebert	John	B-1642	Eck	Mary
B-1351	Ebert	Lewis	B-1778	Eck	Mary
B-1177	Ebert	Owen	M-887	Eck	Mary
B-1351	Ebert	Owen	B-358	Eck	Mary Cassia
B-1352	Ebert	Owen	B-1157	Eck	Mary Cassia
B-1177	Ebert	William	M-180	Eck	Nathan
D-770	Eberts	Birtie	B-458	Eck	Oliver
B-1050	Eberts	Caroline	B-1605	Eck	William
D-882	Eberts	Charles	B-1652	Eck	William
D-290	Eberts	Emma	B-1772	Eck	William
B-190	Eberts	Emma	M-792	Eck	William F
B-275	Eberts	Emma	M-1046	Eck	Hattie Anna
M-834	Eberts	Frank	B-821	Eckern	Sussanna

Line #	Surname	Given Name	Line #	Surname	Given Name
B-1341	Eberts	John	B-1823	Eckert	Angie E
B-1494	Eberts	Kate Louisa	M-906	Eckert	Harry
M-672	Eberts	Kate Louisa	B-1087	Eckhart	Christianna
B-1402	Eberts	Louisa	B-745	Eckhart	Daniel
B-1777	Eberts	Lydia	B-745	Eckhart	Emery
B-1395	Eberts	Mary	B-14	Eckhart	Eva Ann
B-1485	Eberts	Matilda	M-358	Eckhart	Joseph
M-767	Eberts	Matilda	B-180	Eckhart	Mary
B-190	Eberts	Nathan	B-932	Eckhart	Mary
B-1117	Eberts	Nathan	B-507	Eckhart	Mary Ann
M-1002	Eberts	Oliver O	B-777	Eckhart	Mary Ann
B-275	Eberts	Owen	B-673	Eckhart	Polly
M-85	Eberts	Peter	B-97	Eckhart	Sarah
B-1341	Eberts	Susanna	M-1164	Eckroid	Maud C A
B-1381	Eberts	Susanna	D-963	Eckroth	Ida
M-673	Eberts	Susanna	D-989	Eckroth	Lewis
B-1777	Eberts	William	B-854	Eckroth	Matilda
B-1777	Eberts	William	M-692	Eckroth	Matilda
M-1160	Ebsen	Sallie Ann	M-493	Eckstein	George A N
D-1224	Eck	Albert	M-398	Eddinger	Weldin
B-1605	Eck	Alice	M-69	Edinger	John N
B-322	Ehle	Kitty	B-263	Evans	James
M-302	Eisenhauer	Franklin	M-1074	Evans	John W
B-301	Eisenhower	Edwin	B-970	Evans	William J
B-718	Eisenhower	Edwin	B-1566	Evans	William J
M-182	Eisenhower	Edwin	M-11	Evans	William J
B-301	Eisenhower	Eugene	M-1096	Evans	William A
B-900	Eisenhower	Franklin	M-555	Everitt	E.H.
B-900	Eisenhower	Herbert	B-1086	Everitt	Ellen
B-718	Eisenhower	Lillie	M-959	Everitt	Emma
M-68	Ely	Frederic	B-1086	Everitt	Lyman
M-551	Emboddy	David	D-783	Fvert	(s/o Lyman & Aquilla)
D-1187	Embodle	Jeremia	B-1458	Evert	Adline
D-1338	Embody	Beulah	B-1536	Evert	Adline
D-1174	Embody	Emma	M-748	Evert	Adline
B-1579	Embody	Gideon	B-1140	Evert	Amos
M-691	Embody	Gideon	B-1506	Evert	Beula
B-1579	Embody	Lizzie	M-651	Evert	Catherine
B-875	Emert	William	B-1538	Evert	Charles
B-875	Emert	William	B-498	Evert	Ellen
D-1151	Emery	Charlie	B-1342	Evert	Emaline
D-256	Enders	Adolph	M-681	Evert	Emaline
M-799	Engelman	Charles Joseph	D-515	Evert	George
B-512	Engelman	George	B-1281	Evert	Gertrude
B-511	Engelman	Julius	B-1017	Evert	Ida
B-511	Engelman	Sylvester	D-1068	Evert	Ira
B-512	Engelman	Sylvester	B-1538	Evert	Ires
B-726	Enzian	George	B-481	Evert	John
B-726	Enzian	Henry	B-1067	Evert	John
B-451	Ernst	Louisa	B-1281	Evert	John
M-592	Eroh	Susan Elizabeth	B-1506	Evert	John
B-1869	Ervin	Bessie	B-1600	Evert	John
B-1923	Ervin	Bessie	B-1705	Evert	John
M-1112	Ervin	Bessie	B-698	Evert	John
M-1083	Ervin	John	B-849	Evert	John
B-189	Erwin	William A	M-239	Evert	John
D-640	Esch	Charles	B-1705	Evert	Lizzie
B-92	Esch	Eliza	B-849	Evert	Lyman

Line #	Surname	Given Name	Line #	Surname	Given Name
B-312	Esch	Eliza	B-1017	Evert	Lyman
M-147	Esch	Eliza	B-1140	Evert	Lyman
B-886	Esch	Ellen	B-1291	Evert	Lyman
M-492	Esch	Ellen	B-1600	Evert	Mamie
D-577	Esch	George	B-1864	Evert	Margeret
B-411	Esch	John	M-1101	Evert	Margeret M
D-29	Esch	Sarah	B-482	Evert	Mary Ann
D-258	Eschbach	George	B-1101	Evert	Mary Ann
B-451	Eslinger	Henry	B-1269	Evert	Mary Ann
B-451	Eslinger	John	B-1562	Evert	Mary Ann
D-202	Esrang	Adda	B-1067	Evert	Minnie
M-87	Esrang	John	B-498	Evert	Nathan
M-262	Esrang	John	B-1291	Evert	Robert
D-193	Esrang	Lucinda	B-697	Evert	Samuel
M-84	Essex	Catherine Elizabeth	D-684	Evert	Sarah
B-339	Evans	Elizabeth	B-849	Evert	Sarah
B-1566	Evans	Flossy	B-481	Evert	Silas
B-970	Evans	George	B-1318	Everts	Catherine
B-263	Evans	Henry	B-697	Everts	Mary Ann
B-698	Everts	Mary Ann	M-854	Fenkner	Susanna
D-696	Faeht	Anthony	B-995	Fenner	Adella
M-612	Faeht	Mary	M-780	Fenner	Effie Jane
M-754	Fagan	Katie J	M-489	Fenner	Ervin
B-899	Faht	Mary Ann	B-995	Fenner	Erwin
M-395	Faist	Simon	B-1830	Fenner	Guy
B-917	Farrel	Rebecca	M-202	Fenner	Oswald Hugo
B-1060	Farren	Bertha	B-1830	Fenner	Theodore F
M-23	Farren	Charles	B-1963	Fenstermacher	Amanda
B-63	Farren	Daniel	D-1069	Fenstermacher	Anna
B-386	Farren	Daniel	B-1539	Fenstermacher	Calvin
B-1060	Farren	Daniel	B-903	Fenstermacher	Ellemanda
B-1257	Farren	Daniel	B-676	Fenstermacher	Ellenora
M-54	Farren	Daniel	D-1160	Fenstermacher	Emma
B-386	Farren	Hattie	B-155	Fenstermacher	Emma
B-1257	Farren	Kate	B-1462	Fenstermacher	Franklin S
B-63	Farren	Thomas	B-1539	Fenstermacher	Franklin S
D-822	Farren	Willie	B-1580	Fenstermacher	Franklin S
D-268	Fartwengler	Anna	B-1688	Fenstermacher	Franklin S
B-340	Fath	Mary Ann	B-1629	Fenstermacher	Herman
M-431	Fath	Mary Ann Susanna	B-1580	Fenstermacher	Ida
M-505	Fatzinger	Alice J	B-636	Fenstermacher	Irena
B-420	Faust	Adam	D-525	Fenstermacher	Jacob
B-677	Faust	Adam	B-1688	Fenstermacher	Jenneva
B-858	Faust	Adam	D-454	Fenstermacher	John
B-303	Faust	Adam	B-155	Fenstermacher	John
M-366	Faust	Adam	B-676	Fenstermacher	John
D-65	Faust	Catherine	B-903	Fenstermacher	John
B-858	Faust	Charles	M-209	Fenstermacher	John
B-1811	Faust	Charles	M-963	Fenstermacher	John H
B-1950	Faust	Charles W	B-1391	Fenstermacher	Kate
M-1175	Faust	Charles W	B-393	Fenstermacher	Kitty
B-1811	Faust	Emma	M-602	Fenstermacher	Lewis
B-1094	Faust	Ida	B-1462	Fenstermacher	Lizzie
B-1094	Faust	Jesse W	D-629	Fenstermacher	Lucetta
D-259	Faust	John	B-1841	Fenstermacher	Lucy Anna
D-509	Faust	Mary	M-962	Fenstermacher	Lucy Anna Amanda
B-420	Faust	Mary	D-274	Fenstermacher	Mary
B-677	Faust	Sevilla	B-989	Fenstermacher	Mary Ann

Line #	Surname	Given Name	Line #	Surname	Given Name
M-461	Fawcett	John	B-1334	Fenstermacher	Minnie
M-2	Fehnel	Hannah	M-828	Fenstermacher	Nelson F
B-1567	Fehnel	Manda	D-740	Fenstermacher	Pearce
B-710	Fehr	Ellevena	B-636	Fenstermacher	Rueben
B-1057	Fehr	Emma	B-675	Fenstermacher	Sally Ann
B-728	Feierich	Amelia	B-1078	Fenstermacher	Sarah
B-728	Feierich	Henry	B-1760	Fenstermacher	Sarah A
B-879	Feist	Addie	B-1761	Fenstermacher	Sarah A
B-683	Feist	Andrew	B-1303	Fenstermacher	Sarah Ann
B-487	Feist	Joseph	B-1534	Fenstermacher	Sarah Ann
B-683	Feist	Joseph	B-1593	Fenstermacher	Sarah Ann
B-879	Feist	Joseph	M-410	Fenstermacher	Sarah Ann
B-160	Feist	Joseph	M-251	Fenstermacher	Sophia
B-487	Feist	Laura	B-1080	Fenstermacher	Stephen
M-1144	Feist	William	B-1080	Fenstermacher	Stephen
B-421	Felker	Barbara	B-1334	Fenstermacher	Stephen
D-932	Fenkner	Amelia	B-1629	Fenstermacher	Stephen
B-1689	Fenstermacher	Stephen	M-842	Fink	Lydia
B-1689	Fenstermacher	Walter	B-534	Fink	Mary Ann
D-799	Fenstermacher	William	M-793	Fink	Mary Ann
D-712	Fenstermacker	Ellemanda	B-1626	Fink	Myrtle
B-646	Fenstermaker	Albert	D-1356	Fink	Reuben
B-1740	Fenstermaker	Daisie	B-1741	Fink	Robert
M-696	Fenstermaker	Eliza Jane	D-723	Fink	Rosina
D-581	Fenstermaker	Ellenora	B-1579	Fink	Rueben
B-1740	Fenstermaker	Franklin S	B-181	Fink	Thomas
B-515	Fenstermaker	Jacob	M-114	Fink	Thomas
B-515	Fenstermaker	John	B-20	Fink	Thomas
M-758	Fenstermaker	Julia Louisa	B-1626	Fink	William
M-1141	Fenstermaker	Katie Louisa	B-1687	Fink	Willie
B-129	Fenstermaker	Kitty	B-325	Finkler	Charles
M-200	Fenstermaker	Kitty	D-598	Finkler	Flory
M-1121	Fenstermaker	Minie	B-325	Finkler	Peter
M-804	Fenstermaker	Molly	B-598	Finkler	Peter
D-1085	Fenstermaker	Nelson	B-614	Finkler	Peter
M-917	Fenstermaker	Sarah	D-15	Fischer	Christina
B-597	Fenstermaker	Sarah Amelia	D-564	Fisher	(s/o William & Emaline)
B-722	Fenstermaker	Sarah Amelia	B-348	Fisher	Adam
B-646	Fenstermaker	Stephen	B-53	Fisher	Amanda
M-127	Fenstermaker	Stephen	B-471	Fisher	Charles
D-625	Ferber	Ellen	D-507	Fisher	Clara
B-693	Ferber	Ellen	B-448	Fisher	Clara
B-274	Ferber	Ida	M-512	Fisher	George Israel
B-968	Ferber	Lillie	B-875	Fisher	Harriet
D-203	Ferber	Mary	B-261	Fisher	Henrietta
B-274	Ferber	Reuben	B-556	Fisher	Henrietta
B-693	Ferber	Reuben	B-865	Fisher	Henrietta
B-968	Ferber	Reuben	M-417	Fisher	Henrietta
M-1092	Fether	Daniel Amandus	D-320	Fisher	Jacob
M-908	Fether	Louisa	B-1010	Fisher	Jennie
B-1820	Fether	Mary Jane	D-472	Fisher	John
M-1036	Fether	Mary Jane	B-348	Fisher	John
D-1327	Fetter	Joseph	B-958	Fisher	John
D-683	Feuner	Joseph	M-406	Fisher	John Framklin
D-204	Fichweiler	Catherine	B-958	Fisher	Joseph
B-90	Fickweiler	Anna Margeret	B-115	Fisher	Katelei
B-90	Fickweiler	Christian	B-592	Fisher	Lewis
B-90	Fickweiler	John	B-1040	Fisher	Louisa

Line #	Surname	Given Name	Line #	Surname	Given Name
B-38	Field	Samuel F	B-559	Fisher	Louisa
M-113	Field	Samuel F	M-408	Fisher	Louisa
M-776	Field	Susan Catherine	B-1274	Fisher	Mary Etta
B-38	Field	William	B-471	Fisher	Newton B
B-388	Fillhower	Magdalene	M-365	Fisher	Newton B
B-1958	Fink	Carolina E	B-256	Fisher	Pauline
M-1182	Fink	Carolina E	B-559	Fisher	Pauline
M-701	Fink	Ellemina	B-863	Fisher	Pauline
M-332	Fink	Flory Ann	M-864	Fisher	Samuel
M-947	Fink	Henry	B-265	Fisher	Sarah
B-1687	Fink	Joseph W	B-115	Fisher	Thomas
B-1741	Fink	Joseph W	B-448	Fisher	William
B-1803	Fink	Joseph W	B-1010	Fisher	William
M-932	Fink	Joseph W	B-911	Flexer	Sarah
B-1803	Fink	Lulu	B-1186	Flexer	Sarah
M-128	Flick	Anna Maria	D-1054	Follweiler	Clinton
B-271	Flick	Emaline	B-1963	Follweiler	George
B-220	Flick	Emaline	B-998	Follweiler	George W
B-406	Flick	Emaline	M-371	Follweiler	J. B.
B-723	Flick	Emaline	B-470	Follweiler	J.B.
B-1075	Flick	Emaline	B-1096	Follweiler	Maria
B-1173	Flick	Emaline	B-1175	Follweiler	Maria
B-301	Flick	Mary Alice	B-470	Follweiler	Oliver W
B-718	Flick	Mary Alice	B-1325	Follweiler	Rebecca
M-182	Flick	Mary Alice	B-998	Follweiler	Willoughby
B-449	Flickinger	Angeline	B-833	Forreider	Caroline
M-295	Flickinger	Angeline	D-1092	Forreider	Samuel
B-1354	Flickinger	Carrie	B-144	Foster	Adam
D-541	Flickinger	Catherine	B-348	Foster	Adam
D-1217	Flickinger	Catherine	B-594	Foster	Adam
B-564	Flickinger	Elias	B-1167	Foster	Adam
B-564	Flickinger	Elizabeth	B-895	Foster	Manda
B-565	Flickinger	Elwina Jane	M-71	Foster	Mary
B-949	Flickinger	George	B-144	Foster	Sophia
B-1354	Flickinger	George	M-13	Foureider	Joseph
B-1442	Flickinger	George	M-15	Franciska	May
B-1769	Flickinger	George W	M-186	Frank	George
B-1840	Flickinger	George W	M-1018	Frank	Dora H
D-297	Flickinger	Hannah	B-1685	Frantz	_____
B-1445	Flickinger	Hannah	B-1524	Frantz	Adella
D-267	Flickinger	John	M-831	Frantz	Alice
B-1363	Flickinger	Josiah	M-810	Frantz	Alvin
B-1445	Flickinger	Josiah	M-686	Frantz	Amanda
M-536	Flickinger	Josiah	B-1148	Frantz	Calvin
D-54	Flickinger	Lewis	D-840	Frantz	Charles
B-1769	Flickinger	Lillie	D-1360	Frantz	Charles
D-19	Flickinger	Maria	B-150	Frantz	Charles
D-440	Flickinger	Milton	M-1125	Frantz	Charles A
B-254	Flickinger	Milton	B-1919	Frantz	Ella Nora
B-1363	Flickinger	Moses	D-1240	Frantz	Ellen
B-254	Flickinger	Nathan	B-1575	Frantz	Ellenora
M-290	Flickinger	Nathan	B-1314	Frantz	Emaline
B-564	Flickinger	Peter	B-1124	Frantz	Emma
B-1840	Flickinger	Raymond	B-1417	Frantz	Emma
B-1442	Flickinger	Sarah	B-1487	Frantz	Emma
M-796	Flickinger	Thomas	M-572	Frantz	Emma
B-949	Flickinger	Tillie	B-1011	Frantz	Flora Ann
M-481	Fluck	Jacob	B-1238	Frantz	Flora Ann

Line #	Surname	Given Name	Line #	Surname	Given Name
D-707	Focht	Charles	M-553	Frantz	Flora Ann
B-889	Fogel	Abraham	B-961	Frantz	Francis F
B-59	Fogel	Alavesta	D-1183	Frantz	Freddie
D-468	Fogel	Catherine	D-769	Frantz	George
B-59	Fogel	Christian	B-150	Frantz	Godfrey
B-94	Fogel	John	B-483	Frantz	Godfrey
D-467	Fogel	Lafenns	B-933	Frantz	Godfrey
B-281	Fogel	Lafenns	B-1148	Frantz	Godfrey
D-56	Fogel	Philibina	B-983	Frantz	Godfrey
B-94	Fogel	Stephen	B-1199	Frantz	Godfrey
B-281	Fogel	Stephen	B-1637	Frantz	Godfrey
B-889	Fogel	Stephen	B-1641	Frantz	Godfrey
D-1191	Folk	Henry	M-185	Frantz	Godfrey
D-241	Frantz	Harry	D-358	Frederic	Anna
B-150	Frantz	Hetty	B-292	Frederic	Calvin
D-1126	Frantz	Homes	B-292	Frederic	Catharine
B-961	Frantz	Ida	B-554	Frederic	Catherine
M-869	Frantz	Ida Louise	B-779	Frederic	Catherine
B-1051	Frantz	Jacob	B-371	Frederic	Catherine
B-1314	Frantz	Jacob	B-441	Frederic	Catherine
B-16	Frantz	Jarrusa	M-269	Frederic	Catherine
B-694	Frantz	Jarrusa	B-633	Frederic	Charlie
M-636	Frantz	John A B	D-379	Frederic	Elizabeth
B-1890	Frantz	John H	B-303	Frederic	Elizabeth
B-1924	Frantz	John H	B-699	Frederic	Elizabeth
M-1116	Frantz	John H	B-1090	Frederic	Elizabeth
B-636	Frantz	Levina	B-1253	Frederic	Elizabeth
B-919	Frantz	Lewis	M-321	Frederic	Lewis
B-919	Frantz	Lewis	B-633	Frederic	Oscar
B-1964	Frantz	Lewis A	B-596	Frederic	Puryetta
M-1155	Frantz	Lewis A	B-820	Frederic	Renades
B-1180	Frantz	Lizzie	D-1133	Frederic	Stephen
M-1151	Frantz	Lizzie M	B-446	Frederic	Stephen
B-1924	Frantz	Marie	B-820	Frederic	Stephen
B-1389	Frantz	Mary	B-446	Frederic	Steven
B-592	Frantz	Mary	B-292	Frederic	William
B-483	Frantz	Minnie	B-596	Frederic	William
B-1890	Frantz	Morgan	B-157	Frederic	William
M-1027	Frantz	Moses G	M-258	Frederic	William
B-1223	Frantz	Nathan	B-161	Frederici	Charles
M-272	Frantz	Owen	B-1308	Frederici	Jeannetta
B-1964	Frantz	Paul	B-161	Frederici	W.C.
B-1790	Frantz	Priscilla	B-788	Frederici	W.C.
B-1702	Frantz	Raymond	B-788	Frederici	Willie
M-1135	Frantz	Safena	B-95	Frederick	Anna
B-592	Frantz	Sally Ann	M-912	Frederick	Jefferson
B-643	Frantz	Sarah	B-1356	Frederick	Lean
B-1005	Frantz	Sarah	B-1356	Frederick	Walter
M-453	Frantz	Sarah	B-95	Frederick	Wm. Frederick
B-937	Frantz	Sarah Ann	B-1652	Freeby	Amanda
B-1174	Frantz	Sarah Ann	M-716	Freeby	Amanda L
M-393	Frantz	Sarah Ann	M-1176	Freeby	Amandus E
B-407	Frantz	Sophia	D-944	Freeby	Catherine
B-714	Frantz	Sophia	D-846	Freeby	Christian
B-977	Frantz	Sophia	B-1949	Freeby	Clifford
B-320	Frantz	Sophia	B-1860	Freeby	Darcy
M-334	Frantz	Sophia	B-1913	Freeby	David
M-451	Frantz	Susanna	B-1255	Freeby	Ellen

Line #	Surname	Given Name
B-933	Frantz	William
B-1389	Frantz	William H
B-1180	Frantz	William H
B-1524	Frantz	Willoughby
B-1575	Frantz	Willoughby
M-759	Frantz	Willoughby
D-949	Frantz	Wilson
B-1702	Frantz	Wilson
B-21	Franz	Henry
B-82	Frederic	____
D-288	Frederic	Amanda
B-1860	Freeby	Joseph
B-1949	Freeby	Joseph
B-1866	Freeby	Laura Jane
B-1938	Freeby	Laura Jane
B-1968	Freeby	Laura Jane
M-1115	Freeby	Laura Jane
B-1372	Freeby	Mandes
M-876	Freeby	Polly Ann
B-1967	Freeby	Sallie Lovina
B-1477	Freeby	Sally
B-1834	Freeby	Sarah J
B-1865	Freeby	Sarah J
M-1086	Freeby	Sarah J
B-1030	Freeby	William
B-1913	Freeby	William J
M-1129	Freeby	William J
M-1191	Freeman	Marie Ada
B-565	Frehley	Charles
D-880	Frehn	David
D-879	Frehn	Gertie
M-344	Frey	Alice N
B-356	Frey	Dianna
B-343	Frey	Emma
B-1946	Frey	Emma
B-1952	Frey	Emma
B-1943	Frey	Hattie
B-1943	Frey	Jacob
B-343	Frey	Samuel
B-1952	Frey	Sarah Ellen
D-228	Frey	William
B-1810	Freyman	Albertis J
B-1861	Freyman	Albertis J
B-1921	Freyman	Albertis J
B-1411	Freyman	Amelia
B-1527	Freyman	Amelia
B-1159	Freyman	Amelia Isabella
M-516	Freyman	Amelia Isabella
B-1921	Freyman	Bertha
D-1213	Freyman	Catherine
B-833	Freyman	Daniel
B-1920	Freyman	David
M-1162	Freyman	David
M-795	Freyman	Emaline
B-1528	Freyman	Emma
M-1132	Freyman	Emma
B-833	Freyman	Emma
B-1912	Freyman	Emma Matilda
B-1739	Freeby	George
B-1739	Freeby	George E
B-1477	Freeby	George Edwin
M-768	Freeby	George Edwin
B-1810	Freeby	Harriet
B-1861	Freeby	Harriet
B-1921	Freeby	Harriet
M-883	Freeby	Ida Elizabeth
B-1030	Freeby	Joseph
B-1255	Freeby	Joseph
B-1372	Freeby	Joseph
B-509	Freyman	Kitty
B-478	Freyman	Kitty
B-496	Freyman	Kitty Ann
B-806	Freyman	Kitty Ann
B-833	Freyman	Kitty Ann
B-1105	Freyman	Kitty Ann
B-1317	Freyman	Kitty Ann
B-503	Freyman	KittyAnn
M-385	Freyman	Lafayette
D-819	Freyman	Lillie
M-967	Freyman	Lucy A
B-1861	Freyman	Mabel
D-1230	Freyman	Mary
B-354	Freyman	Mary Ann
B-355	Freyman	Mary Ann
B-1637	Freyman	Masie
B-1713	Freyman	Meta
B-768	Freyman	Sally
B-82	Freyman	Sally Ann
B-371	Freyman	Sally Ann
B-1105	Freyman	Sally Ann
B-1301	Freyman	Sally Ann
B-352	Freyman	Sally Elmira
B-1228	Freyman	Sally Elmira
B-453	Freyman	Sally Elmira
B-1433	Freyman	Sally Elmira
M-333	Freyman	Sally Elmira
B-1421	Freyman	Sally Elmira
B-409	Freyman	Sarah Ann
B-813	Freyman	Sarah Ann
M-95	Freyman	Sarah Ann
B-509	Freyman	Thomas
B-1920	Freyman	Werner
B-1637	Freyman	William H
B-1713	Freyman	William H
B-1765	Freyman	William H
M-881	Freyman	William H
D-967	Fridirici	Matilda
D-686	Friederich	Purietta
M-1148	Friend	Elnora
B-1509	Fritz	Allen
B-484	Fritz	Anna
B-1230	Fritz	Catherine
M-524	Fritz	Charles D
B-1509	Fritz	Clarence
M-137	Fritz	David
D-1180	Fritz	Emma

Line #	Surname	Given Name
B-1810	Freyman	Girtie
M-1103	Freyman	Granville P
D-818	Freyman	Harvey
B-1765	Freyman	Herbert
D-954	Freyman	Jacob
M-936	Freyman	John
B-221	Freyman	July Ann
B-804	Freyman	July Ann
B-1807	Freyman	July Ann
D-1197	Fritz	Henry
M-364	Fritz	John
B-1725	Fritz	Laura
B-1732	Fritz	Mary
M-509	Fritz	Reuben L
B-1725	Fritz	Wiliiam Amandes
B-1673	Fritz	William A
M-797	Fritz	William A
M-1010	Fritzinger	Alavesta
B-1607	Fritzinger	Allie
M-1107	Fritzinger	Anna M
B-556	Fritzinger	Anna Maria
D-1257	Fritzinger	Catherine
B-1755	Fritzinger	Charles
B-1736	Fritzinger	Charles H
M-168	Fritzinger	Charles H
B-286	Fritzinger	Clara
B-1709	Fritzinger	Curtie
B-782	Fritzinger	Edgar
B-1848	Fritzinger	Edwin M
M-983	Fritzinger	Edwin M
M-838	Fritzinger	Elanius P
M-42	Fritzinger	Elizabeth
B-556	Fritzinger	Ellen
M-901	Fritzinger	Ellen Almira
D-300	Fritzinger	Ellenora
D-573	Fritzinger	Emma
B-194	Fritzinger	Emma
B-1111	Fritzinger	Eva
B-1337	Fritzinger	Fianna
B-860	Fritzinger	Francis
B-194	Fritzinger	Francis
B-860	Fritzinger	Francis
B-1111	Fritzinger	Francis
B-1883	Fritzinger	Francis
B-617	Fritzinger	Francis
M-221	Fritzinger	Francis
B-1759	Fritzinger	Francis H
M-980	Fritzinger	Francis H
B-1229	Fritzinger	George
B-659	Fritzinger	Harrison
B-1856	Fritzinger	Helen
D-533	Fritzinger	Henry
B-270	Fritzinger	Henry
B-815	Fritzinger	Ida
B-1966	Fritzinger	Ida Louisa
M-1181	Fritzinger	Ida Louisa
B-847	Fritzinger	Isabella
B-1132	Fritzinger	Isabella
B-1673	Fritz	Emma
B-248	Fritz	Hannah
B-562	Fritz	Hannah
B-1146	Fritz	Hannah
B-1289	Fritz	Hannah
B-1426	Fritz	Hannah
B-1560	Fritz	Hannah
B-1602	Fritz	Hannah
M-318	Fritz	Hannah
B-261	Fritzinger	John
B-556	Fritzinger	John
B-865	Fritzinger	John
M-289	Fritzinger	John
M-327	Fritzinger	John W
B-286	Fritzinger	John W.
B-659	Fritzinger	Joseph
M-419	Fritzinger	Joseph
B-1896	Fritzinger	Joseph H
B-558	Fritzinger	Joseph M
M-183	Fritzinger	Joseph M
M-1119	Fritzinger	Kate A
B-1012	Fritzinger	Korah
D-1024	Fritzinger	Leah
B-1229	Fritzinger	Lennius
D-982	Fritzinger	Leon
B-815	Fritzinger	Levi
B-1888	Fritzinger	Malinda
B-227	Fritzinger	Maria L
B-524	Fritzinger	Maria L
B-942	Fritzinger	Maria L
M-313	Fritzinger	Maria L
B-558	Fritzinger	Mary
M-1050	Fritzinger	Mary J
M-665	Fritzinger	Matilda Fianna
M-504	Fritzinger	Moses
D-904	Fritzinger	Oscar
B-1607	Fritzinger	Oscar
B-1709	Fritzinger	Oscar
B-1755	Fritzinger	Oscar
B-1638	Fritzinger	Oscar
B-1687	Fritzinger	Oscar
M-1107	Fritzinger	Peter M
B-1737	Fritzinger	Priscilla
B-1808	Fritzinger	Priscilla
B-1897	Fritzinger	Priscilla
M-969	Fritzinger	Priscilla
B-261	Fritzinger	Robert
B-1736	Fritzinger	Sally Ann
B-8	Fritzinger	Sarah
B-1687	Fritzinger	Sarah
B-1803	Fritzinger	Sarah
B-261	Fritzinger	Sarah
B-1741	Fritzinger	Sarah Catherine
M-932	Fritzinger	Sarah Catherine
B-847	Fritzinger	Savenna
M-405	Fritzinger	Savenna
M-527	Fritzinger	Selinda
B-1896	Fritzinger	Stanley

Line #	Surname	Given Name	Line #	Surname	Given Name
M-511	Fritzinger	Isabella	B-194	Fritzinger	Stephen
M-995	Fritzinger	J. H.	B-556	Fritzinger	Stephen H
B-1856	Fritzinger	Jeanetta	B-270	Fritzinger	Tilghman
D-1064	Fritzinger	John	B-782	Fritzinger	Tilghman
D-1336	Fritzinger	John	B-1012	Fritzinger	Tilghman
B-865	Fritzinger	John	M-345	Fritzinger	Tilghman
B-1759	Fritzinger	John	B-1883	Fritzinger	William
M-271	Fritzinger	William	B-849	Fulton	Mary Jane
B-1848	Fritzinger	Willie	M-239	Fulton	Mary Jane
B-925	Fritzinger	Zeniah	B-1933	Funk	Charles
B-1856	Fritzinger		B-1933	Funk	Samuel
B-870	Frohnheiser	Benjamin	M-987	Funk	Samuel
B-949	Frohnheiser	Benjamin	B-762	Fuss	Charles
B-870	Frohnheiser	Caroline	D-245	Fuss	Kanz
B-545	Frohnheiser	Catherine	B-762	Fuss	Mary
B-774	Frohnheiser	Catherine	B-259	Gable	Irwin
B-1322	Frohnheiser	Catherine	B-259	Gable	Mandes
M-479	Frohnheiser	Catherine	B-775	Gable	Mandes
B-1307	Frohnheiser	Charles	M-6	Gable	Mandes
B-858	Frohnheiser	Charles	B-775	Gable	Meta
B-501	Frohnheiser	Harry	M-92	Gaidner	Mary
B-1307	Frohnheiser	James	B-83	Gale	Levinia
B-1457	Frohnheiser	James	D-575	Galey	Latitia
M-608	Frohnheiser	James	D-520	Galey	William
B-1030	Frohnheiser	Jane Amanda	M-871	Gallagher	John
B-1255	Frohnheiser	Jane Amanda	M-821	Gallagher	Maggie
B-1372	Frohnheiser	Jane Amanda	D-253	Gamer	Sophia
B-1860	Frohnheiser	Jane Amanda	M-98	Gamler	Anna
B-1949	Frohnheiser	Jane Amanda	B-617	Gangware	Eliza
B-501	Frohnheiser	Lewis	B-617	Gangware	William
M-375	Frohnheiser	Lewis	M-198	Gangware	William
M-710	Frohnheiser	Lucinda Jane	M-1168	Gaston	Ira C
D-584	Frohnheiser	Lydia	B-55	Gaumer	Elizabeth
M-220	Frohnheiser	Mary	M-1041	Gaumer	Nora L
B-418	Frohnheiser	Messina	M-579	Gaumer	Urilla C
B-949	Frohnheiser	Messina	M-65	Gayler	Johanna
B-1354	Frohnheiser	Messina	M-538	Gearhard	Anna M
B-1442	Frohnheiser	Messina	M-538	Gearhard	David D
B-1769	Frohnheiser	Messina	M-998	Geggins	Alice
B-1840	Frohnheiser	Messina	D-522	Geggus	Anna
M-1016	Frohnheiser	Nathan Henry	B-456	Geggus	Anna
M-873	Frohnheiser	Rosa E	B-1166	Geggus	Anna
B-1359	Frohnheiser	Sallie	B-457	Geggus	Clara
B-1568	Frohnheiser	Sallie	B-670	Geggus	Emma
B-1623	Frohnheiser	Sallie	B-1247	Geggus	Emma
M-624	Frohnheiser	Sally	B-855	Geggus	Harrison
B-1457	Frohnheiser	Sarah	B-778	Geggus	Hattie
B-238	Frohnheiser	Sarah	D-396	Geggus	Ida
M-1023	Frohnheiser	Sarah Agnes	B-455	Geggus	John
B-1924	Fruendt	Amelia	B-456	Geggus	John
M-165	Fry	Samuel	B-778	Geggus	John
M-46	Fuehree	William	M-58	Geggus	John
B-445	Fuehrer	Emma	B-164	Geggus	Lewis
B-445	Fuehrer	William	B-457	Geggus	Lewis
B-19	Fulmer	Carrie	B-855	Geggus	Lewis
B-19	Fulmer	Edwin	B-1166	Geggus	Lewis
B-182	Fulmer	George W	M-259	Geggus	Lewis
B-1506	Fulton	Mary	D-521	Geggus	Mary

Line #	Surname	Given Name	Line #	Surname	Given Name
B-1281	Fulton	Mary Ann	B-164	Geggus	Mary
B-481	Fulton	Mary Jane	B-455	Geggus	Mary
B-1067	Fulton	Mary Jane	B-1013	Gehl	Ellen J
B-1600	Fulton	Mary Jane	D-154	Geigel	John
B-1705	Fulton	Mary Jane	B-1748	Geiger	Annetta
M-794	Geiger	Annetta	M-769	Gerber	Alvenia M
D-713	Geiger	Caroline	B-1180	Gerber	Amanda
B-946	Geiger	Caroline	B-1389	Gerber	Amanda
B-209	Geiger	Caroline	M-1138	Gerber	Amandus F
B-627	Geiger	Caroline	D-994	Gerber	Amos
B-845	Geiger	Caroline	D-755	Gerber	Anna
D-1193	Geiger	Clyde	D-758	Gerber	Anna
B-590	Geiger	David	D-997	Gerber	Anna
B-1808	Geiger	Earl	B-1149	Gerber	Anna
B-1136	Geiger	George	M-1075	Gerber	Austin B
M-830	Geiger	George	M-698	Gerber	Caroline Jane
B-1737	Geiger	James A	D-786	Gerber	Carrie
B-1808	Geiger	James A	D-974	Gerber	Catherine
B-1897	Geiger	James A	B-963	Gerber	Charles
M-969	Geiger	James A	B-1820	Gerber	Charles A
B-362	Geiger	Jane	M-1036	Gerber	Charles A
B-1541	Geiger	Jennie	B-1011	Gerber	Clinton
B-362	Geiger	Joseph	D-669	Gerber	Daniel
B-611	Geiger	Joseph	D-924	Gerber	Daniel
B-776	Geiger	Joseph	B-963	Gerber	Daniel
B-946	Geiger	Joseph	B-1236	Gerber	Daniel
B-419	Geiger	Joseph	B-1379	Gerber	Daniel
B-1541	Geiger	Joseph	D-1120	Gerber	David
B-1136	Geiger	Joseph	D-1275	Gerber	David
B-590	Geiger	Korah	B-1231	Gerber	David
B-1541	Geiger	Levi L	B-1655	Gerber	David
D-820	Geiger	Mary	M-801	Gerber	David Allen
B-776	Geiger	Mary	B-928	Gerber	Edwin
B-1737	Geiger	Raymond	M-984	Gerber	Edwin F
B-611	Geiger	Susanna	D-756	Gerber	Elizabeth
B-1897	Geiger	Wilbur	B-1312	Gerber	Elizabeth
M-724	Gelay	Sarah A	B-1677	Gerber	Emaline Jane
D-439	Genshart	Charles	M-923	Gerber	Emaline Jane
M-1075	George	Alice P	D-1294	Gerber	Emma
B-1880	George	Augustus	M-867	Gerber	Emma
M-243	George	Charles	D-1246	Gerber	Flossie
B-1440	George	Charlie	B-1823	Gerber	Franklin
B-339	George	Elias	M-786	Gerber	Gideon
B-1635	George	Fietta	B-927	Gerber	H. A.
B-1889	George	Fietta	B-1424	Gerber	Harriet
B-1934	George	Fietta	B-1505	Gerber	Harriet
B-1969	George	Fietta	B-1570	Gerber	Harriet
M-775	George	Fietta	B-1645	Gerber	Harriet
D-1352	George	Howard	B-1710	Gerber	Harriet
B-1220	George	Kate	B-1814	Gerber	Harriet
M-611	George	Kate	B-1828	Gerber	Harriet
B-1880	George	Lewis	M-663	Gerber	Harriet
M-1095	George	Lewis	M-743	Gerber	Henrietta
M-328	George	Maria	B-1245	Gerber	Henry A
B-1229	George	Mary Ann	B-1149	Gerber	Isaac
D-841	George	Monroe	B-927	Gerber	Isaac
B-1440	George	Penrose	M-657	Gerber	Isaac
B-444	George	Polly	B-1245	Gerber	Jennie

Line #	Surname	Given Name
B-1226	George	Sophia
D-145	George	William
B-1203	Gerber	Alice
B-1490	Gerber	Kate
B-1694	Gerber	Kate
B-1238	Gerber	Martha
B-1379	Gerber	Mary
B-962	Gerber	Mary
M-242	Gerber	Mary
B-1209	Gerber	Mary Ann
B-1343	Gerber	Mary Ann
B-1235	Gerber	Matilda
D-1109	Gerber	Michael
B-927	Gerber	Morris
M-1003	Gerber	Moses A
B-1820	Gerber	Myrtle
B-1268	Gerber	Nathan
M-412	Gerber	Priscilla
B-1416	Gerber	Rebecca
D-1204	Gerber	Reuben
B-1115	Gerber	Sabina
B-1625	Gerber	Sabina
M-587	Gerber	Sabina
B-1236	Gerber	Sarah
B-1339	Gerber	Sarah Ann
M-719	Gerber	Sarah Yetta
M-815	Gerber	Savina
B-1011	Gerber	Thomas
B-1238	Gerber	Thomas
M-553	Gerber	Thomas
D-1301	Gerber	Wallace
B-1823	Gerber	Williard
M-547	Gerhard	John H
M-575	Gerhard	Lydia Ann
M-706	Gerhart	Mary
M-470	Gerhart	Sarah Catherine
B-1137	German	Amanda
B-426	German	Amanda Elizabeth
B-682	German	Anna Maria
B-780	German	Benjamin F
B-665	German	Benjamin F
D-645	German	Charles
M-878	German	Edwin F
D-1030	German	Elias
M-359	German	Franklin H
B-783	German	Lewina
B-646	German	Manda
B-780	German	Mary
M-463	German	Peter
B-515	German	Phillip
B-11	German	Wilson
B-682	German	Wilson
D-201	Getz	Alwilda
M-1058	Getz	Augusta
M-66	Getz	Elizabeth
M-528	Getzinger	Ellen J
B-309	Giggle	Alwies
B-309	Giggle	Alwies

Line #	Surname	Given Name
D-876	Gerber	Jonathan
B-1203	Gerber	Josiah
B-1046	Gerber	Kate
B-147	Giggle	William
M-447	Gilbert	Abby
B-832	Gilbert	Anna
M-483	Gilbert	Dennis
B-533	Gilbert	Elizabeth
M-320	Gilbert	Elizabeth
M-341	Gilbert	Joseph
M-1102	Gilbert	Kate A
D-1212	Gilbert	Magdalene
D-1189	Gilbert	Sarah
B-145	Gilbert	Sarah
B-1172	Gilbert	Sarah
B-1183	Gilbert	Sarah
B-1362	Gilbert	Sarah
B-1461	Gilbert	Sarah
B-1102	Gilbert	Sarah
M-131	Gilbert	Sarah
B-755	Gilbert	Susanna
B-922	Gilbert	Susanna
B-1102	Gilbert	Susanna
D-25	Gilbreth	John
D-784	Gildner	John
M-225	Gilen	Sarah
B-1881	Ginder	Adam
B-950	Ginder	Alfred
B-951	Ginder	Alfred
B-1843	Ginder	Alfred
B-1881	Ginder	Alfred
M-136	Ginder	Alfred
D-1355	Ginder	Alice
B-950	Ginder	Amandes
B-1903	Ginder	Antionetta
B-951	Ginder	Asaba
B-1642	Ginder	Benjamin
D-1267	Ginder	Bertha
B-1193	Ginder	Charles
B-1642	Ginder	Charles A
B-1778	Ginder	Charles A
M-887	Ginder	Charles A
B-1636	Ginder	Charles Harrison
M-669	Ginder	Charles Harrison
B-1576	Ginder	Clayton
B-1903	Ginder	Elmira
D-930	Ginder	Flora
D-1350	Ginder	Hannah
B-1778	Ginder	Hannah
D-1134	Ginder	Irwin
B-1606	Ginder	Irwin
D-1214	Ginder	Isaac
B-707	Ginder	Isaac
B-1237	Ginder	Isaac
M-558	Ginder	Isaac
B-651	Ginder	Isabella
D-1164	Ginder	James
B-1606	Ginder	James

Line #	Surname	Given Name	Line #	Surname	Given Name
B-147	Giggle	Oliver	B-1001	Ginder	James W
B-1193	Ginder	James W	B-835	Gombert	Aaron
B-1444	Ginder	James W	B-1953	Gombert	Adam
B-1653	Ginder	James W	B-595	Gombert	Addie
M-571	Ginder	James W	B-383	Gombert	Alice
B-1444	Ginder	John	B-1785	Gombert	Alice Savilla
B-1824	Ginder	John H	B-1832	Gombert	Alice Savilla
M-1046	Ginder	John Henry	B-1556	Gombert	Andrew J
B-650	Ginder	Lewis	B-1640	Gombert	Andrew J
B-651	Ginder	Lewis	B-1708	Gombert	Andrew J
M-236	Ginder	Lewis	B-1727	Gombert	Andrew J
B-1466	Ginder	Lewis	B-1763	Gombert	Andrew J
B-1467	Ginder	Lewis	B-1799	Gombert	Andrew J
B-1468	Ginder	Lewis	B-1833	Gombert	Andrew J
B-1469	Ginder	Lewis Franklin	B-1857	Gombert	Andrew J
M-1149	Ginder	Lizzie Jane	M-820	Gombert	Andrew J
B-1237	Ginder	Mary	M-599	Gombert	Angeline Victoria
B-1409	Ginder	Mary	B-1326	Gombert	Annie
B-1674	Ginder	Mary Ann	B-1640	Gombert	Bertha
B-1353	Ginder	Mary Susanna	B-1118	Gombert	Bertie
B-1847	Ginder	Minnie	M-324	Gombert	Caroline
B-1917	Ginder	Morris	B-1534	Gombert	Carrie
B-1636	Ginder	Oscar	B-1223	Gombert	Catherine
B-707	Ginder	Philip	D-1333	Gombert	Cecilia
B-1576	Ginder	Philip	B-1799	Gombert	Cecilia
B-1614	Ginder	Philip	M-1163	Gombert	Cora E
B-1721	Ginder	Philip	M-578	Gombert	Elizabeth
B-1847	Ginder	Philip	B-1593	Gombert	Ellanora
B-1917	Ginder	Philip	B-81	Gombert	Ellen
B-1843	Ginder	Pierce	B-1718	Gombert	Ellen
B-650	Ginder	Robert	B-1831	Gombert	Ellen L
B-1614	Ginder	Rowlands	M 988	Gombert	Ellen L
B-1468	Ginder	Sally Ann	B-586	Gombert	Elmer
B-1466	Ginder	Thomas	B-1853	Gombert	Elmer S
B-1653	Ginder	Urias	B-1887	Gombert	Elmer S
B-1467	Ginder	Wallace	B-1944	Gombert	Elmer S
B-1824	Ginder	Warren	B-1953	Gombert	Elmer Sylvester
B-1721	Ginder	Wesley	B-1649	Gombert	Emma
B-1001	Ginder	William	B-1932	Gombert	Emma Elizabeth
B-1469	Ginder	William	B-1727	Gombert	George
B-1634	Glace	Alice	B-675	Gombert	Harvey
B-1517	Glace	Alice Louisa	M-1184	Gombert	Hattie
B-1753	Glace	Alice Louisa	B-1782	Gombert	Hattie Estell
B-1884	Glace	Alice Louisa	B-1887	Gombert	Helen
B-1398	Glace	Alice Louise	B-835	Gombert	Henrietta
B-1703	Glace	Alice Louise	B-1268	Gombert	Henrietta
M-630	Godschall	Lilly Louisa	B-1479	Gombert	Henrietta
D-916	Godshall	Daniel	B-1749	Gombert	Henrietta
B-1571	Godshall	Lilly Louisa	B-1793	Gombert	Henrietta
D-688	Gogel	Hattie	B-1835	Gombert	Henrietta
M-1128	Goldberg	Joseph N	B-1875	Gombert	Henrietta
M-395	Goldberg	Mary	M-499	Gombert	Henrietta
M-166	Goldberg	Wilhelmena	B-1206	Gombert	Henry
M-1058	Goldburg	Martin	B-480	Gombert	Henry
M-847	Gollus	Charles C	B-1837	Gombert	Henry
M-579	Gollus	Joseph	M-570	Gombert	Henry
B-732	Gombert	—	B-806	Gombert	Ida
B-1541	Gombert	Ida A	B-1400	Gombert	Sarah

Line #	Surname	Given Name	Line #	Surname	Given Name
D-495	Gombert	Ira	B-1723	Gombert	Sarah
B-382	Gombert	Ira	M-623	Gombert	Sarah
B-872	Gombert	James	M-912	Gombert	Sarah Jane
B-595	Gombert	James	D-487	Gombert	Stephen
B-872	Gombert	James	B-383	Gombert	Stephen
B-1118	Gombert	James	B-1727	Gombert	Tillie
B-176	Gombert	James	M-1142	Gombert	William F
M-347	Gombert	James	B-1206	Gombert	Zacharis
M-1187	Gombert	James H	D-1300	Gommerry	Erwin
D-848	Gombert	John	B-18	Gommery	Harrison
M-989	Gombert	John G	B-356	Gommery	John
B-541	Gombert	Jonas	B-356	Gommery	John
B-869	Gombert	Jonas	B-198	Gommery	John
B-81	Gombert	Jonathan	M-199	Gommery	John
B-382	Gombert	Jonathan	D-940	Gommery	Louisa
B-806	Gombert	Jonathan	B-18	Gommery	William
B-1188	Gombert	Jonathan	B-110	Gommery	William
B-675	Gombert	Joseph	B-154	Goodheil	Amelia
B-382	Gombert	Joseph	B-270	Goodheil	Anzonetta
B-1078	Gombert	Joseph L	B-782	Goodheil	Anzonetta
B-1303	Gombert	Joseph L	B-1012	Goodheil	Anzonetta
B-1534	Gombert	Joseph L	M-345	Goodheil	Anzonetta
B-1593	Gombert	Joseph L	M-495	Goodheil	Caroline
M-410	Gombert	Joseph L	B-154	Goodheil	John
B-1141	Gombert	Kate	B-93	Goodheil	John
M-598	Gombert	Kate	B-125	Goodheil	John
B-1113	Gombert	Kitty Ann	D-278	Goodheil	Nelson
B-1261	Gombert	Kitty Ann	B-972	Gorde	Maria
B-1484	Gombert	Kitty Ann	B-1191	Gordon	Maria
B-1874	Gombert	Kitty Ann	M-110	Gottlob	George Christian
B-1188	Gombert	Kitty Ann	B-297	Gottshall	Jacob
B-1078	Gombert	Lillie	B-1383	Gottshall	Mary Ann
B-1303	Gombert	Lindney	B-1384	Gottshall	Mary Ann
D-1262	Gombert	Lydia	B-769	Gould	Hattie
B-1708	Gombert	Mamie	B-769	Gould	Jacob
D-821	Gombert	Mary	M-361	Gower	Dianna
B-102	Gombert	Mary	B-1262	Gower	Elmira
B-276	Gombert	Mary	M-132	Gower	Emma
B-193	Gombert	Mary Ann	B-249	Gower	Frederic
B-1944	Gombert	Masie	B-249	Gower	George
B-1188	Gombert	Meta	B-1262	Gower	Joseph
B-1763	Gombert	Meta	M-51	Gower	Maria
B-1853	Gombert	Minerva	B-694	Graf	Zacilia
B-586	Gombert	Nathan	B-1946	Graff	Jonathan W
B-1326	Gombert	Nathan	B-1946	Graff	Maude
B-1649	Gombert	Nathan	M-1059	Grant	Arnold D.
B-81	Gombert	Nathan	B-1237	Grasely	Asapa
B-302	Gombert	Nathan	B-642	Grasely	Catherine
M-268	Gombert	Nathan	B-1237	Grasely	Charles
B-1556	Gombert	Pearlie	B-1409	Grasely	Charles
B-541	Gombert	Polly	D-1242	Grasely	George
B-1833	Gombert	Roy	D-929	Grasely	Louisa
B-1857	Gombert	Ruth	B-1409	Grasely	Louisa
B-1509	Gombert	Sabina	B-497	Graver	Adam Monroe
D-792	Gombert	Salome	B-1315	Graver	Adline
B-1647	Graver	Adline	M-976	Graver	Minnie A
M-644	Graver	Adline	B-105	Graver	Molly
B-1054	Graver	Alburtis	B-417	Graver	Molly

Line #	Surname	Given Name
D-443	Graver	Alfred
B-148	Graver	Andrew
B-488	Graver	Andrew
B-978	Graver	Andrew
B-609	Graver	Andrew (Sr)
B-488	Graver	Anna
B-901	Graver	Anna
B-160	Graver	Anna Maria
M-241	Graver	Anna Maria
B-218	Graver	Caroline
B-516	Graver	Carrie
B-1344	Graver	Catherime
B-988	Graver	Catherine
B-1216	Graver	Catherine
B-70	Graver	Catherine
M-188	Graver	Catherine Jane
B-1526	Graver	David
M-576	Graver	E. L.
B-66	Graver	Elizabeth
M-245	Graver	Elizabeth
B-686	Graver	Emma
B-1657	Graver	Emma
M-853	Graver	Emma
B-1624	Graver	Emma E
M-849	Graver	Emma E
B-1330	Graver	Emma V
M-1070	Graver	George Benjamin F
B-120	Graver	Hannah
B-843	Graver	Harrie
M-597	Graver	Harron Oscar
D-664	Graver	Harry
B-219	Graver	Harvey
D-215	Graver	Henry
B-978	Graver	Ida
B-289	Graver	Jennie
D-220	Graver	John
M-978	Graver	John F
B-218	Graver	Joshua
B-219	Graver	Joshua
M-808	Graver	Lafayette
D-101	Graver	Laura
B-66	Graver	Lewis
B-901	Graver	Lewis
B-1054	Graver	Lewis
B-669	Graver	Lillie
B-148	Graver	Luelue
D-1034	Graver	Martin
B-1561	Graver	Martin
M-34	Graver	Martin
B-843	Graver	Martin B
B-1054	Graver	Martin B
B-1526	Graver	Martin B
B-1561	Graver	Martin B
M-776	Green	Nathaniel
B-475	Green	Rebecca
M-307	Green	Rebecca
B-247	Green	Reuben
B-40	Green	Reuben

Line #	Surname	Given Name
B-1154	Graver	Molly Ann
B-289	Graver	Owen
B-669	Graver	Owen
B-978	Graver	Owen
M-169	Graver	Owen
D-305	Graver	Rulvin
B-120	Graver	Samuel
B-497	Graver	Sarah
B-879	Graver	Sarah
B-487	Graver	Sarah Ann
B-683	Graver	Sarah Ann
B-160	Graver	Sarah Ann
M-30	Graver	Sarah Ann
D-321	Graver	Vererva
B-516	Graver	William A
B-1126	Greasley	Mantana
D-779	Greasley	William
B-1126	Greasley	William F
M-167	Greasly	William F
B-9	Green	Aaron
B-368	Green	Aaron
M-863	Green	Alvin Harrison
B-314	Green	Amanda
M-140	Green	Amanda
B-1472	Green	Amanda Isabella
M-755	Green	Amanda Isabella
B-984	Green	Elizabeth
B-761	Green	Elizabeth
B-204	Green	Emma
B-368	Green	Emma
B-956	Green	Emmaretha
B-344	Green	Eva Ann
B-992	Green	Eva Ann
B-956	Green	Eve Ann
M-590	Green	Francisca
B-1168	Green	Francisco
B-1259	Green	Francisco
D-182	Green	George
B-1638	Green	Isabella
B-9	Green	James
B-992	Green	Jane
B-180	Green	John
B-956	Green	John
B-807	Green	Laura
B-956	Green	Lewis W
B-112	Green	Lucy
B-279	Green	Lucy
B-1659	Green	Mary
B-1660	Green	Mary
B-247	Green	Mary Amanda
B-314	Green	Matilda
M-213	Green	Matilda
B-196	Green	Nathan
B-376	Gross	Theresa
B-82	Grow	___
B-699	Grow	Albert
B-503	Grow	Carolina
B-666	Grow	Carolina

Line #	Surname	Given Name
B-198	Green	Rosa
B-807	Green	Samuel
M-502	Green	Samuel J
B-204	Green	Thomas
B-180	Green	William
B-298	Greenewalt	Abraham
B-369	Greenewalt	Daniel
D-493	Greenewalt	Edwin
B-369	Greenewalt	Ida
D-237	Greenewalt	Martha
M-908	Greenogle	Ferdinand
B-743	Greenzweig	Catherine
M-1136	Greenzweig	Charles S.
B-867	Greenzweig	Eva
B-62	Greenzweig	Eva Ann
B-653	Greenzweig	Eva Ann
B-507	Greenzweig	James
B-777	Greenzweig	Thomas
B-32	Greenzweig	Tobias
B-507	Greenzweig	William
B-777	Greenzweig	William
M-766	Gregg	David
B-1087	Gregory	James
B-1087	Gregory	Nathan Gregory
B-1087	Gregory	William
D-444	Grill	(s/o John and Alice)
B-119	Grill	Elmira
M-232	Grill	John
B-508	Grill	July Ann
B-499	Grill	Mary Ann
M-162	Grill	Mary Ann
B-508	Grill	Nicholas
B-751	Grill	Nicholas
B-119	Grill	Samuel
M-184	Grill	Samuel
B-962	Grim	Charles
M-242	Grim	Charles
B-1209	Grim	Charles Alfred
B-1343	Grim	Charles Alfred
M-1143	Grim	Charles M
D-890	Grim	Hattie
B-962	Grim	Hattie
B-1343	Grim	Josephene
B-1209	Grim	Mary Ann
B-1022	Groman	Manda
B-758	Gromen	Manda
B-146	Gross	Anna Elizabeth
B-69	Gross	Euphenia
B-376	Gross	Henry
B-399	Gross	Henry
M-551	Gross	Lucetta Amelia
B-115	Guldner	Elizabeth
B-226	Guldner	Elizabeth
B-1094	Guldner	Elizabeth
B-465	Guldner	Henry
M-297	Guldner	Henry
B-1827	Guldner	Kate
M-926	Guldner	Kate
B-1863	Grow	Carolina Savilla
M-991	Grow	Carolina Savilla
B-1807	Grow	Carolina Sevilla
D-569	Grow	Caroline
B-95	Grow	Eliza
B-292	Grow	Eliza
B-596	Grow	Eliza
B-157	Grow	Eliza
M-258	Grow	Eliza
B-157	Grow	Emma
B-1954	Grow	Hattie
M-1172	Grow	Hattie
B-157	Grow	Henry
B-503	Grow	Henry
B-221	Grow	Henry
B-666	Grow	Henry
M-249	Grow	Henry
B-699	Grow	John
B-1090	Grow	John
B-1253	Grow	John
B-303	Grow	Jonathan
M-321	Grow	Jonathan
B-1090	Grow	Korah
B-1686	Grow	Lulu
B-1253	Grow	Mary
M-1136	Grow	Mary S
B-1160	Grow	Minnie
B-666	Grow	Nathan
B-1507	Grow	Nathan
B-1863	Grow	Nathan
M-331	Grow	Nathan
B-1160	Grow	Reuben
B-1292	Grow	Reuben
B-1686	Grow	Reuben
M-532	Grow	Reuben
B-1292	Grow	Robbie
M-1189	Grow	Robert E
B-1507	Grow	Sarah
B-303	Grow	Surie
B-95	Grow	William
B-596	Grow	William
M-31	Grow	William
B-402	Gruber	Henry
B-402	Gruber	Hester
B-476	Gruber	Lydia
B-882	Gruber	Mary
M-21	Gruber	Sarah
M-417	Guardian	Joseph Frederick
M-701	Guildner	William
B-465	Guldner	Charles
M-1019	Guldner	Charles L
D-339	Guth	Henry
D-349	Guth	John
D-617	Guth	John
B-997	Guth	Laura
B-184	Guth	Paul
B-619	Guth	Paul
B-912	Guth	Paul

Line #	Surname	Given Name	Line #	Surname	Given Name
M-367	Guldner	Levi	B-619	Guth	Percy
M-911	Guldner	Lewis	B-912	Guth	Susan
B-1226	Guldner	Lewis H	D-75	Gutheil	Margmeretha
B-1226	Guldner	Mantana	M-629	Haas	Amanda Jane
B-254	Guldner	Maria	M-1117	Haas	Charles A
B-542	Guldner	Maria	M-905	Haas	Edwin Albert
M-1185	Guldner	Mary	M-1054	Haas	Elmira L
M-842	Guldner	Owen	M-1105	Haas	Emma T
D-902	Guldner	Susanna	D-1058	Haas	Robbie
D-800	Guldner	William	D-776	Haberman	Elmira
M-1015	Gumbert	Alice S	M-563	Haberman	Jefferson
B-1837	Gumbert	Alvin	B-1545	Haberman	Joseph
B-1601	Gumbert	Andrew J	B-1545	Haberman	Sarah Jane
B-1836	Gumbert	Bertha	M-829	Haberman	Sarah Jane
B-1801	Gumbert	Daisie	B-1032	Haefer	Jared
B-1801	Gumbert	Elmer	B-1032	Haefer	Moses
M-653	Gumbert	Elwin	B-853	Hafer	Frederick
M-900	Gumbert	Emma	M-1011	Hafer	Jared M
D-1288	Gumbert	Fietta	B-853	Hafer	Jarret
B-1754	Gumbert	Flossie	D-344	Hagenbuch	Eugene
B-1754	Gumbert	Frank	M-860	Hagenbuch	James M
B-1798	Gumbert	Frank	B-104	Hagenbuch	John
B-1836	Gumbert	Frank	B-104	Hagenbuch	John
B-1878	Gumbert	Frank	B-494	Hagenbuch	John
B-1922	Gumbert	Frank	B-605	Hagenbuch	John
M-968	Gumbert	Frank	B-494	Hagenbuch	Malton
B-350	Gumbert	James	B-93	Hagenbuch	Rosanna
D-187	Gumbert	Josiah	B-551	Hagenbuch	Rosanna
B-1074	Gumbert	Korah	M-261	Hagenbuch	Rosanna
M-1032	Gumbert	Lesta	D-71	Hagenbuch	Thomas
B-1922	Gumbert	Mable	B-243	Hahn	Amelia
B-350	Gumbert	Mary	B-527	Hahn	Amelia
B-350	Gumbert	Mary	B-142	Hahn	Amelia
B-1636	Gumbert	Mary Jane	B-162	Hahn	Amelia
M-669	Gumbert	Mary Jane	B-349	Hahn	Amelia
B-1451	Gumbert	Matilda	M-299	Hahn	Amelia
B-1601	Gumbert	Mattie	B-664	Hahn	Edwin
B-1074	Gumbert	Nathan	M-300	Hahn	Edwin
B-1878	Gumbert	Oscar	B-50	Hahn	Edwin H
D-1325	Gumbert	Sophia	M-109	Hahn	Edwin Henry
B-1798	Gumbert	Sophia	B-1880	Hahn	Ellamanda
B-1797	Gumbert	Welles	M-1095	Hahn	Ellemanda
M-975	Gumbert	William	B-50	Hahn	Elmira
B-1797	Gumbert	William P	M-158	Hahn	Enos
B-1837	Gumbert	William P	B-895	Hahn	Franklin
B-997	Guth	Albert J	B-702	Hahn	Franklin
M-548	Guth	Albert J	M-473	Hahn	Franklin
B-184	Guth	Emma	M-561	Hahn	Harriet
D-343	Guth	Franklin	D-422	Hahn	James
M-264	Hahn	James William	B-1435	Hamm	Andrew J
B-735	Hahn	Jannie	M-736	Hamm	Andrew J
D-527	Hahn	Joseph	M-957	Hamm	Charles
D-74	Hahn	Maria	D-1201	Hamm	Emma
B-895	Hahn	Mary	M-787	Hamm	Franklin B
B-387	Hahn	Mary	M-804	Hamm	Jonas Albert
B-448	Hahn	Mary	B-1435	Hamm	Lenah
B-1010	Hahn	Mary	D-1005	Hamm	Lewis
B-23	Hahn	Mary	M-921	Hamm	Noah A

Line #	Surname	Given Name	Line #	Surname	Given Name
B-941	Hahn	Mary Ann	B-50	Hand	Lucinda
M-503	Hahn	Mary Ann	B-162	Hand	Selinda
D-234	Hahn	Savannah	B-1181	Handrisks	Emma
M-458	Hahn	Susanna	B-1025	Handwerk	Caroline
B-210	Hahn	Thomas	M-581	Handwerk	Hetty
B-773	Hahn	Thomas	M-978	Handwerk	Magdella M
B-953	Hahn	Thomas	M-871	Haney	Lizzie
B-664	Hahn	William	B-604	Hankee	Hiram
B-735	Hahn	William	M-353	Hankey	Anna Maria
M-465	Hahn	William	M-774	Hankey	Ellen J
D-389	Hahne	Sophia	B-437	Hankey	Emma
B-141	Haid	Elizabeth	B-892	Harder	Polly
B-502	Haid	Elizabeth	M-643	Hardinger	Mary A
B-1119	Haid	Elizabeth	B-811	Harleman	Abraham
B-1243	Haid	Elizabeth	B-889	Harleman	Abraham
M-237	Haid	Elizabeth	B-724	Harleman	Priscilla
B-52	Haid	Kate	B-257	Haron	Edwin
B-232	Haid	Lizzie	B-257	Haron	Jonathan
B-571	Haid	Lizzie	M-751	Harpel	A.M.
B-455	Haid	Louisa	B-1455	Harpel	Meme
B-456	Haid	Louisa	B-420	Harris	Mary
M-58	Haid	Louisa	B-740	Harron	Frankie
B-778	Haid	Lucy	D-593	Harron	Franklin
B-432	Haid	Mary	B-740	Harron	John
M-48	Haid	Mary	D-281	Harron	William
B-53	Haid	Sally	D-1314	Harter	Catherine
M-135	Haines	Ellen	B-1584	Harter	Eva Elizabeth
M-159	Haines	Mary	B-1213	Harter	John
B-834	Haint	Selinda	B-1478	Harter	John
B-1871	Haintz	Adline	B-1482	Harter	Lewina
B-644	Haintz	Bowman	B-1213	Harter	Martha
B-672	Haintz	Charles	B-1478	Harter	Oliver
B-174	Haintz	Harry	B-1108	Hartinger	Aggie
B-173	Haintz	Henry	B-980	Hartinger	Christian
B-174	Haintz	Henry	B-1108	Hartinger	David
B-672	Haintz	Henry D	B-1200	Hartinger	Jeannetta
B-1871	Haintz	Laura Ellen	B-980	Hartinger	Letta
M-1110	Haintz	Laura Ellen J	B-1296	Hartinger	Mary
B-173	Haintz	Luther	B-980	Hartinger	Mary
M-409	Haintz	Mary Ann Elizabeth	D-699	Hartinger	Minnie
B-173	Haintz	Rachel	B-1200	Hartinger	Thomas
D-79	Haintz	Robert	M-783	Hartley	Mary Alice
B-644	Haintz	William F	B-895	Hartman	Catherine
M-288	Haintz	William F	B-702	Hartman	Catherine
M-785	Haldeman	Albert	M-473	Hartman	Catherine
M-877	Hamilton	Eliza Jane	B-100	Hartman	Charles
B-694	Hamm	Andrea	B-197	Hartman	Charles
B-378	Hartman	Charles	M-999	Hartranft	Francis C
B-862	Hartman	Charles	D-418	Hartranft	James
D-335	Hartman	Daniel	B-1963	Hartranft	Jonathan
B-911	Hartman	Daniel H	M-1165	Hartranft	Jonathan
M-505	Hartman	Elias G	B-316	Hartranft	Maria
B-52	Hartman	Elizabeth	B-722	Hartranft	Maria
B-151	Hartman	Elizabeth	B-1036	Hartranft	Maria
M-115	Hartman	Elizabeth	B-1127	Hartranft	Mary
B-256	Hartman	Elizabeth	B-1267	Hartranft	Mary
M-882	Hartman	Ella Amanda	B-1392	Hartranft	Mary
B-256	Hartman	Elmira	B-1495	Hartranft	Mary

Line #	Surname	Given Name	Line #	Surname	Given Name
M-1025	Hartman	Elmira	B-844	Hartranft	Mary Ellen
B-528	Hartman	Elwin	M-450	Hartranft	Mary Ellen
B-378	Hartman	Hannah	D-1108	Hartranft	Matilda
B-632	Hartman	Hannah	B-1963	Hartranft	Robert
B-863	Hartman	James	B-1406	Hartranft	Sally
D-550	Hartman	John	D-1045	Hartung	Abigail
B-256	Hartman	Joseph	M-817	Hartung	Amandus
B-559	Hartman	Joseph	B-1471	Hartung	Christian
B-863	Hartman	Joseph	B-1207	Hartung	Christian
B-142	Hartman	Lewis	B-1360	Hartung	David
B-528	Hartman	Lewis	B-1504	Hartung	David
M-1117	Hartman	Louisa	B-1360	Hartung	Della
B-151	Hartman	Martha	B-1207	Hartung	Ellen
B-466	Hartman	Martha	B-1504	Hartung	Hattie
B-702	Hartman	Martha	B-1207	Hartung	John
M-282	Hartman	Martha	M-1042	Hartung	Laura
B-953	Hartman	Martha Ann	D-1014	Hartung	Lizzie
B-1167	Hartman	Martha Ann	B-1357	Hartung	Mary
B-1274	Hartman	Martha Ann	B-1423	Hartung	Mary
B-994	Hartman	Mary	M-642	Hartung	Mary
B-613	Hartman	Mary Ann	B-1471	Hartung	Robbie
B-994	Hartman	Mary Ann	M-789	Hartung	Susanna
B-862	Hartman	Mary Jane	D-888	Hartzel	Harrie
M-491	Hartman	Mary Jane	D-941	Hartzel	Korah
B-559	Hartman	Milton	B-1249	Hartzell	Allie
B-597	Hartman	Philip	D-667	Hartzell	Elizabeth
B-458	Hartman	Polly	B-1249	Hartzell	Henry
B-491	Hartman	Polly	B-399	Hassel	Jacob
B-142	Hartman	Samuel	B-399	Hassel	Lewis
B-100	Hartman	Sarah	D-147	Hauck	Alexander
B-400	Hartman	Sarah	B-326	Hauck	Carolina
B-1533	Hartman	Sarah Ann	B-639	Hauck	Caroline
D-1403	Hartman	William	B-178	Hauck	Charles
M-542	Hartman	William H	D-146	Hauck	Clarissa
B-994	Hartman	William H	B-178	Hauck	John
B-1212	Hartranft	Amanda	M-88	Hauck	Robert
B-1913	Hartranft	Amanda E	B-1144	Haupt	Alfred
M-1129	Hartranft	Amanda E	B-539	Haupt	Alfred
D-787	Hartranft	Charles	M-422	Haupt	Alfred
D-999	Hartranft	David	B-1027	Haupt	Alvesta
B-491	Hartranft	David	B-1144	Haupt	Charles
B-1212	Hartranft	David	M-596	Haupt	Charles Martin
B-1406	Hartranft	David	B-585	Haupt	Frederic
B-491	Hartranft	Edwin	B-585	Haupt	George
M-1066	Hartranft	Elias	B-648	Haupt	George Frederick
M-414	Haupt	George Frederick	M-983	Heffelfinger	Emma Jane
D-566	Haupt	Joshua	B-329	Heffelfinger	Freeman
M-446	Haupt	Kate	B-265	Heffelfinger	John
B-648	Haupt	Mary	M-372	Heffelfinger	John
B-1708	Haupt	Mary	B-1244	Heil	Kate
B-406	Haupt	Nathan	B-116	Heiland	Catherine
M-335	Haupt	Nathan	B-116	Heiland	Maria
B-827	Haupt	Sarah	D-24	Heilman	Anna
B-1017	Haupt	Sarah	B-341	Heilman	Anna
B-827	Haupt	Sarah	B-416	Heilman	Catherine E
B-445	Haupt	Susanna	M-457	Heilman	Catherine Elizabeth
M-46	Haupt	Susanna	B-652	Heilman	Clara
B-406	Haupt	Thomas	B-877	Heilman	Elmer

Line #	Surname	Given Name
B-1096	Hauser	Aaron
B-1175	Hauser	Aaron
B-1144	Hauser	Anna
B-1103	Hauser	Caroline
B-1265	Hauser	Charles S
M-593	Hauser	Charles S.
B-1265	Hauser	Claudius
D-914	Hauser	Conrad
D-860	Hauser	Daniel
B-1183	Hauser	Daniel
B-1102	Hauser	Daniel
B-1095	Hauser	Denah
B-987	Hauser	Elizabeth
D-650	Hauser	Emaline
D-763	Hauser	Esther
B-1175	Hauser	Franklin
D-772	Hauser	Gideon
B-1183	Hauser	Harry
D-789	Hauser	John
B-511	Hauser	Mary
B-512	Hauser	Mary
B-1175	Hauser	William
M-959	Hausman	John A
D-100	Hausman	Maria
M-20	Hawk	Amandus
B-997	Hawk	Emma
M-548	Hawk	Emma Jane
B-1932	Hawk	Frank
B-1932	Hawk	George
M-42	Hawk	Linford S
B-712	Hawk	Mary
M-625	Hawk	Sarah
B-1419	Haydt	Elizabeth
M-856	Haydt	Elmira
M-946	Haymam	Emma
B-1699	Hayman	Emma
B-360	Heberling	John
B-360	Heberling	Samuel G
B-329	Heffelfinger	Alwin
B-265	Heffelfinger	Catherine
B-327	Heffelfinger	Eliza
B-704	Heffelfinger	Elizabeth
B-1848	Heffelfinger	Emma F
B-1117	Heintzelman	Lydia
B-190	Heintzelman	Lydia Ann
D-1341	Heintzelman	Mable
M-1077	Heintzelman	Mantana I
B-1639	Heintzelman	Minnie
M-922	Heintzelman	Oscar S
B-1569	Heintzelman	Osvil M
B-1850	Heintzelman	Osvil M
M-850	Heintzelman	Osville
B-1639	Heintzelman	Osville M
B-275	Heintzelman	Polly
B-1177	Heintzelman	Polly
B-1351	Heintzelman	Polly
B-1352	Heintzelman	Polly
M-163	Heintzelman	Stephen
B-1454	Heilman	Elsie
B-1335	Heilman	Emma
B-109	Heilman	Geo. Washington
M-14	Heilman	Geo. Washington
M-220	Heilman	Geo. Washington
B-291	Heilman	George W
B-652	Heilman	George W
B-291	Heilman	Ida
B-877	Heilman	John
B-1039	Heilman	John
B-1153	Heilman	John
B-1276	Heilman	John
B-1335	Heilman	John
B-1454	Heilman	John
D-1206	Heilman	Maria
B-1039	Heilman	Mary
B-290	Heilman	Nathan
M-312	Heilman	Nathan
B-1276	Heilman	Orlando
B-290	Heilman	Oscar
B-109	Heilman	Pearcy
D-208	Heilman	Susanna
B-1153	Heilman	Wilson
D-374	Heim	Amanda
D-370	Heim	Catherine
B-1650	Heim	Charles
D-372	Heim	John
B-1650	Heim	Lewis F
B-1955	Heimbach	Mary O
B-1251	Heinbach	Ellenora
B-1251	Heinbach	Solomon
D-534	Heiney	Flora
B-1781	Heintzelman	Alvin
B-190	Heintzelman	Daniel
B-1177	Heintzelman	Daniel
B-444	Heintzelman	E. S.
B-1569	Heintzelman	Estella
D-1137	Heintzelman	Esther
B-1781	Heintzelman	Gideon
M-956	Heintzelman	James G
B-1850	Heintzelman	John
M-251	Heintzelman	Levi
B-1050	Heintzelman	Lydia
B-713	Henny	Harriet
B-148	Henry	Catherine
M-466	Henry	Catherine N
B-149	Henry	Lizzie B
M-189	Henry	Lizzie B
M-955	Henry	Louisa R
B-211	Henry	Rebecca
B-680	Henry	Rebecca
B-948	Henry	Rebecca
M-924	Henry	Sallie
B-148	Henry	Sarah
B-1452	Heor	Ida
B-215	Herb	Kate
B-1123	Herder	Lewina
B-197	Herman	Amelia

Line #	Surname	Given Name
M-609	Heintzelman	Wilson W
D-279	Heiny	Agnes
B-60	Heiny	Catherine
M-4	Heiny	Elizabeth Maria
B-43	Heiny	Franklin
B-43	Heiny	Levi
B-44	Heiny	Levi
B-45	Heiny	Levi
B-46	Heiny	Levi
B-44	Heiny	Louisa
B-46	Heiny	Mary
B-45	Heiny	Minnie
M-1127	Heiselmoyer	George A
M-1091	Heiser	Bertha
B-1245	Heiser	Emma
B-927	Heiser	Emma E
M-1040	Heiser	Erwin D
B-883	Heiser	Joshua
B-690	Heiser	Mary
B-690	Heiser	Monroe
B-1890	Heiser	Sophia
B-1924	Heiser	Sophia E
M-1116	Heiser	Sophia E
D-1254	Heiser	Susanna
B-883	Heiser	William
B-143	Held	Alwin
D-413	Held	Clemens
B-143	Held	Franklin
B-618	Held	Llewellynn
D-500	Held	Martin
B-618	Held	Wilmer
B-8	Helder	Mary Ann
B-979	Heller	William
B-979	Heller	Wilson
B-565	Helmers	Charles
B-565	Helmers	Charles
B-297	Hemler	Mary
B-1849	Hendricks	Eva
B-1849	Hendricks	R Jerome
B-1312	Henninger	Charles
B-1312	Henninger	Matilda
D-1070	Hiester	Joseph
M-451	Hiester	Joseph R
B-1624	Highland	Charles W
M-849	Highland	Charles W
B-1624	Highland	William
B-756	Hildebrand	Laura
B-756	Hildebrand	Peter
M-477	Hildebrand	Peter
M-59	Hilden	Anna Francisca
B-1204	Hill	Aaron
B-271	Hill	Abby
B-364	Hill	Abraham
M-576	Hill	Abraham
B-1659	Hill	Adam
B-1660	Hill	Adam
D-777	Hill	Alavesta
B-1204	Hill	Alavesta

Line #	Surname	Given Name
B-522	Herman	Amelia
B-743	Herman	Amelia
B-195	Herman	Amelia
B-218	Herman	Catherine
B-219	Herman	Catherine
B-100	Herman	Matilda
B-378	Herman	Matilda
B-862	Herman	Matilda
B-1117	Herring	Angeline
B-1260	Herring	Angeline
B-408	Herring	Angeline
B-1594	Herring	Angeline Eliz
M-432	Herring	Angeline Elizabeth
D-1329	Herring	Elizabeth
B-1681	Herring	Lavina
M-861	Herring	Lavina
M-436	Herring	Sarah Jane
D-795	Herter	Tileila
D-377	Hertman	Emma
M-865	Hesin	Lewis F
D-733	Hess	Emma
M-556	Hess	Henry J.
B-1107	Hess	Jane A B
D-1035	Hess	Lillie
M-920	Hess	Louisa I
D-1328	Hess	Pierce
B-1107	Hess	Thomas
M-1	Hess	Thomas H
D-168	Hess	William
D-935	Hester	Hester
D-224	Hestman	Elizabeth
M-1190	Hetter	Ellen A
D-768	Hettinger	Aaron
D-767	Hettinger	William
M-521	Hettler	Mary Ann
M-515	Hettler	Sarah
M-314	Hettner	Kitty Ann
M-929	Heydt	Jacob
B-1782	Heyser	Beuhla
B-1782	Heyser	Erwin
B-823	Heyser	Monroe
D-1238	Hill	Mable
B-128	Hill	Magdalena
B-1185	Hill	Manda
B-127	Hill	Maria
B-1208	Hill	Mary
M-970	Hill	Mary A
B-1092	Hill	Mary Ann
B-1931	Hill	Mary J
M-812	Hill	Mary J
M-763	Hill	Mary Louisa
B-1002	Hill	Melinda
B-1573	Hill	Milton
B-1948	Hill	Nora Irene
D-1266	Hill	Peter
M-647	Hill	Peter
B-1092	Hill	Polly
B-1204	Hill	Polly

Line #	Surname	Given Name	Line #	Surname	Given Name
M-902	Hill	Alfred	D-710	Hill	Prestie
D-1277	Hill	Angeline	D-877	Hill	Robbie
D-909	Hill	Barton	B-1323	Hill	Robbie
B-1116	Hill	Calvin	D-1231	Hill	Sarah
D-1006	Hill	Caroline	M-550	Hill	Sarah
M-546	Hill	Catherine Aurelio	B-1388	Hill	Sylvester
D-934	Hill	Clara	M-675	Hill	Sylvester
B-1305	Hill	Clara	B-1296	Hill	Thomas
D-1292	Hill	Daniel	M-643	Hill	Thomas
B-1091	Hill	Daniel	B-1573	Hill	William
B-1748	Hill	Daniel	B-1660	Hill	Willie
B-1091	Hill	Daniel M	B-715	Hiller	Anna
M-782	Hill	David K	M-965	Hilliard	Charles
B-1701	Hill	Edwin	D-1060	Hillman	Rebecca
M-939	Hill	Edwin	B-796	Hills	Abraham
D-943	Hill	Ellemanda	M-351	Hills	Anna Maria
B-364	Hill	Emma	D-623	Hills	George
M-965	Hill	Emma	B-796	Hills	George
M-1060	Hill	Emma J	B-985	Hills	Josephena
B-1701	Hill	Estella	B-986	Hills	Josephena
B-1659	Hill	Flossie	B-1239	Hills	Josephena
M-599	Hill	Franklin	M-110	Hills	Lena
M-1088	Hill	Franklin	M-202	Hills	Magdalena
D-718	Hill	George	M-688	Hine	Mary E
D-1073	Hill	Granville	M-78	Hinger	Barbara
B-1388	Hill	Gurdie	D-22	Hinger	William
D-1205	Hill	Harriet	D-599	Hiskey	Angeline
D-721	Hill	Harry	B-742	Hiskey	Caroline
D-1029	Hill	Harvey	B-519	Hiskey	Carrie
D-1345	Hill	Ida	D-609	Hiskey	Conrad
B-1296	Hill	Ida	B-519	Hiskey	Henry
B-1185	Hill	Jonas	D-155	Hisky	Eva
B-1323	Hill	Jonas	M-700	Hittinger	William Frederick
B-1305	Hill	Jonas K	B-852	Hobbes	Albert
B-127	Hill	Josephina	D-901	Hobbes	David
D-1312	Hill	Joshua	B-852	Hobbes	Elias
B-1116	Hill	Levi	D-1002	Hobbes	Elizabeth
D-1057	Hill	Lillie	B-1672	Hobbes	Freddie
B-1776	Hill	Lydia	B-426	Hobbes	Leah
B-1137	Hobbes	Lydia	B-1272	Hoffman	Jacob D
B-1729	Hobbes	Mamie	D-803	Hoffman	James
B-427	Hobbes	Polly	D-196	Hoffman	Jefferson
B-1675	Hobbes	Polly	B-1359	Hoffman	Jerrane
M-472	Hobbes	Polly	B-1568	Hoffman	Jerrane
B-1863	Hobbes	Sallie Ann	B-1623	Hoffman	Jerrane
B-666	Hobbes	Sally Ann	M-624	Hoffman	Jerrane
B-1507	Hobbes	Sarah	D-889	Hoffman	John
M-331	Hobbes	Sarah	B-351	Hoffman	Juliann
B-1672	Hobbes	Solomon	D-1169	Hoffman	Kate
B-1729	Hobbes	Solomon D	B-1272	Hoffman	Katie
B-509	Hobbes	Susanna	B-1815	Hoffman	Mable
M-4	Hoch	Stephen H	M-1166	Hoffman	Mary
B-1954	Hodge	Ella	B-1841	Hoffman	Mary A
M-1188	Hodge	Ella	M-1094	Hoffman	Mary A
D-448	Hofacker	William	D-797	Hoffman	Nathan
B-1147	Hoffman	Adline	B-517	Hoffman	Nathan
B-1481	Hoffman	Adline	B-577	Hoffman	Nathan
M-582	Hoffman	Adline	B-839	Hoffman	Nathan

Line #	Surname	Given Name	Line #	Surname	Given Name
M-895	Hoffman	Alice	B-1147	Hoffman	Nathan
B-1613	Hoffman	Alice Ellen	B-1841	Hoffman	Nathan
B-1744	Hoffman	Alice Ellen	M-962	Hoffman	Nathan
M-1009	Hoffman	Alvin	M-1165	Hoffman	Sadddie
B-952	Hoffman	Amanda	B-1963	Hoffman	Sadie
B-22	Hoffman	Anna Christianna	D-806	Hoffman	Sally
B-283	Hoffman	Anna Cristianna	B-517	Hoffman	Sally
B-726	Hoffman	Anna Elizabeth	B-1047	Hoffman	Solomon
B-1558	Hoffman	Anna Maria	B-531	Hoffman	Solomon D
M-806	Hoffman	Anna Maria Susanna	B-576	Hoffman	Susanna
D-1152	Hoffman	Catherine	M-819	Hoffman	William E
B-1795	Hoffman	Catherine	B-1553	Hofford	Ella
B-1815	Hoffman	Charles	B-1596	Hofford	Ella May
B-1568	Hoffman	Clendora	M-823	Hofford	Ella May
D-1042	Hoffman	Clyde	M-808	Hofford	Emma
B-110	Hoffman	David	M-837	Hohnchen	Edwin W
B-351	Hoffman	David	M-303	Holenbach	Elias F
D-76	Hoffman	Eliza	M-600	Hollar	Ben G
B-531	Hoffman	Elmira	B-1892	Hollbach	Anna Elizabe
D-807	Hoffman	Emaline	B-207	Hollenbach	Alice
D-1280	Hoffman	Emanuel	M-57	Hollenbach	Alice
B-110	Hoffman	Emma	B-642	Hollenbach	Franklin
B-1623	Hoffman	Emma	D-864	Hollenbach	Horace
B-1666	Hoffman	Emma	B-642	Hollenbach	Ida
B-1620	Hoffman	Emma J	M-1072	Hollenbach	Kate
B-1780	Hoffman	Emma J	B-1733	Holtzer	Sallie C
B-1910	Hoffman	Emma J	M-933	Holtzer	Sallie C
M-903	Hoffman	Emma J	D-311	Holzer	Andrew
D-808	Hoffman	Estella	B-1262	Holzer	Elmira Jane
D-1348	Hoffman	Estella	B-1407	Hom	Lilla
M-1035	Hoffman	Fietta	B-1407	Hom	Zacharis H
D-1320	Hoffman	George	D-1225	Homm	Lydia
M-789	Hoffman	Griffith	B-1377	Hontz	Agnes
B-1359	Hoffman	Ida	B-1195	Hontz	Alavesta
B-952	Hoffman	Jacob	B-47	Hontz	Amanda
B-1218	Hoffman	Jacob	B-304	Hontz	Amanda
B-531	Hoffman	Jacob D	B-1304	Hontz	Amanda
B-322	Hontz	Ammon	D-48	Hontz	Mary
B-1665	Hontz	Ammon	D-104	Hontz	Mary Ann
B-81	Hontz	Anna	D-854	Hontz	Matilda
B-382	Hontz	Anna	B-1248	Hontz	Matilda
B-806	Hontz	Anna	B-480	Hontz	Moses
B-1188	Hontz	Anna	B-1248	Hontz	Moses
M-1055	Hontz	Annie S	B-1377	Hontz	Moses
B-1665	Hontz	baby	B-1496	Hontz	Moses
B-322	Hontz	Boaz	B-1682	Hontz	Moses
B-1496	Hontz	Carolina	B-1724	Hontz	Moses
D-159	Hontz	Caroline	M-30	Hontz	Moses
B-733	Hontz	Delilah	B-138	Hontz	Nathan
B-1331	Hontz	Dennis	B-939	Hontz	Nathan
B-1430	Hontz	Dennis	B-1194	Hontz	Nathan
M-660	Hontz	Dennis	B-1331	Hontz	Pearcy
B-1919	Hontz	Edwin	B-233	Hontz	Polly
B-396	Hontz	Elizabeth	B-1724	Hontz	Raymond
D-30	Hontz	Elmer	M-23	Hontz	Rebecca
B-1206	Hontz	Emaline	D-112	Hontz	Robison
B-480	Hontz	Emaline	B-939	Hontz	Sarah
B-1837	Hontz	Emaline	B-1051	Hontz	Sarah

Line #	Surname	Given Name	Line #	Surname	Given Name
M-570	Hontz	Emaline	B-960	Hontz	Sarah
M-866	Hontz	Emma Jane	M-206	Hontz	Sarah Jane
M-535	Hontz	Granville	B-396	Hontz	Silbie
B-1919	Hontz	Helena	D-26	Hontz	Susanna
B-990	Hontz	Henrietta	B-428	Hontz	Thomas
B-1829	Hontz	Henrietta Lucinda	B-1194	Hontz	Valentine
M-645	Hontz	Henrietta Lucinda	M-1148	Hontz	Walter N
B-138	Hontz	Henry	B-1430	Hontz	William
B-625	Hontz	Ida	M-565	Hontz	William
B-322	Hontz	Ira	B-428	Hontz	Wilson
B-37	Hontz	John	B-1195	Hontz	Wilson
B-37	Hontz	John	B-1788	Hoppes	Minnie
B-625	Hontz	John	M-1011	Hoppes	Rosa R
B-1051	Hontz	John	B-1788	Hoppes	Solomon D
D-706	Hontz	Jonas	M-460	Horlacher	J
B-396	Hontz	Josiah	M-591	Horn	A. B.
B-733	Hontz	Josiah	B-534	Horn	Alfie P
B-480	Hontz	Kitty	M-498	Horn	Alvin
D-530	Hontz	Kitty Ann	B-783	Horn	Alwin
M-668	Hontz	Kitty Ann	B-1025	Horn	Alwin
D-557	Hontz	Lewis	B-295	Horn	Amanda
B-1777	Hontz	Lillie Missouri	B-876	Horn	Amanda
B-1682	Hontz	Lizzie	B-356	Horn	Anna
B-122	Hontz	Louisa	B-198	Horn	Anna M
B-440	Hontz	Louisa	M-199	Horn	Anna M
B-770	Hontz	Louisa	B-1025	Horn	Benjamin
B-976	Hontz	Louisa	B-830	Horn	Benjamin
B-616	Hontz	Louisa	B-1025	Horn	Benjamin
B-1242	Hontz	Lucy Ann	M-429	Horn	Charles T
B-740	Hontz	Lucy Ann	B-1758	Horn	Clyde
B-835	Hontz	Lucy Ann	B-534	Horn	Elmira
B-383	Hontz	Lydia	B-1224	Horn	Garrett
M-12	Hontz	Lydia	B-120	Horn	Hannah
B-940	Hontz	Manda	B-269	Horn	Hermena
B-1521	Hontz	Manda	B-641	Horn	Hermena
B-842	Horn	Hermena	D-946	Houser	Catherine
B-1176	Horn	Hermena	B-1122	Houser	Charles S
D-421	Horn	Ida	B-1658	Houser	Charles S
B-783	Horn	Ida	B-1122	Houser	Clara
M-360	Horn	Isabella	B-709	Houser	Diana
D-23	Horn	James	B-392	Houser	Dianna
M-216	Horn	Levi	B-1150	Houser	Dianna
B-1535	Horn	Mary Ann	D-1332	Houser	Elizabeth
M-715	Horn	Mary Ann	B-1364	Houser	Emma
B-123	Horn	Oscar	B-1388	Houser	Emma Kate
B-1758	Horn	Oscar E	M-675	Houser	Emma Kate
B-1802	Horn	Oscar E	D-1310	Houser	George
M-1014	Horn	Oscar E	B-1324	Houser	Gideon
B-1802	Horn	Raymond	D-907	Houser	Henry
D-411	Horn	Refene	B-1905	Houser	Irena
B-830	Horn	Sallie	B-1941	Houser	Irena
B-120	Horn	Susan	M-1137	Houser	Irena
B-356	Horn	Thomas	D-1027	Houser	Isaac
B-123	Horn	Thomas J	M-874	Houser	Jacob M
M-49	Horn	Thomas J	B-1171	Houser	Jefferson
M-1118	Horn	W. H.	D-1003	Houser	John
B-1224	Horn	Zacharias H	B-413	Houser	Jonas
M-193	Horn	Zeniah	B-294	Houser	Joseph T

Line #	Surname	Given Name	Line #	Surname	Given Name
B-302	Hough	Carolina	B-298	Houser	Josephina
D-1107	Hough	Caroline	M-1108	Houser	Laura Ida
D-543	Hough	Charles	B-1138	Houser	Lewis
B-1363	Hough	Clara	D-732	Houser	Maria
B-1445	Hough	Clara	D-1299	Houser	Maria
M-536	Hough	Clara	M-858	Houser	Mary E
M-1157	Hough	Daniel J	B-1658	Houser	Meinnie
B-896	Hough	Edith	B-1138	Houser	Minnie
B-1535	Hough	Edwin	B-413	Houser	Oscar
M-715	Hough	Edwin	D-1149	Houser	Peter
M-697	Hough	Ellen	D-955	Houser	Priscilla
B-1214	Hough	Franklin	B-1356	Houser	Rebecca
B-1771	Hough	John	M-631	Houser	Rebecca
B-1846	Hough	Luella	M-897	Houser	Roland
B-1846	Hough	Martin	B-928	Houser	Sarah
B-1771	Hough	Martin A	M-402	Houser	Sarah
M-953	Hough	Martin A	B-1324	Houser	Sarah Ann
B-323	Hough	Moses	B-1325	Houser	Sarah Ann
B-302	Hough	Oliver	M-745	Houser	William
B-896	Hough	Oliver	M-311	Houseworth	Maggie
M-60	Hough	Oliver	B-359	Houseworth	Margaret
B-1214	Hough	Oscar	M-896	Hufsmith	Etna
D-1051	Hough	William	M-256	Hundeshagen	Frederick
B-1535	Hough	William	B-72	Hundshammer	Agata
D-516	Hough	Wilson	B-73	Hundshammer	Agata
D-885	Houser	Albert	B-293	Hunsicker	Alfred
M-893	Houser	Alfred	B-911	Hunsicker	Alfred
B-1171	Houser	Alwenia	B-1043	Hunsicker	Amelia
M-637	Houser	Amandes	B-1160	Hunsicker	Amelia
B-294	Houser	Amelia	M-540	Hunsicker	Amelia
M-422	Houser	Anna Matilda	B-1186	Hunsicker	Charles
B-539	Houser	Anna Matilda	B-312	Hunsicker	Clara
B-1664	Houser	Caroline	B-312	Hunsicker	Edwin
M-147	Hunsicker	Edwin	B-1396	Johnson	Anna
M-634	Hunsicker	Edwin	B-1396	Johnson	Claudious M
B-1450	Hunsicker	Elizabeth	M-658	Johnson	Claudious M
M-1002	Hunsicker	Ellen T	B-1826	Johnson	Cora
B-493	Hunsicker	Emaline	M-1052	Johnson	Cora
B-766	Hunsicker	Emaline	D-7	Johnson	John
B-1088	Hunsicker	Emaline	B-392	Johnson	Korah
B-1336	Hunsicker	Emaline	B-392	Johnson	M. L
M-376	Hunsicker	Emaline	B-1150	Johnson	M.L.
B-1428	Hunsicker	Emaline E	D-6	Johnson	Oliver
M-138	Hunsicker	Emaline Elizabeth	B-709	Johnston	Laura
B-1425	Hunsicker	Harriet	B-709	Johnston	M. L
B-1499	Hunsicker	Harriet	M-1053	Jones	Edwin M
B-1726	Hunsicker	Harry	B-401	Jones	Elmira
M-1156	Hunsicker	Hattie S	B-946	Jones	Maria
D-962	Hunsicker	Jacob	B-12	Jones	Sarah
B-1675	Hunsicker	Jacob	M-208	Jones	Sarah
B-1450	Hunsicker	Jacob	D-630	Jordan	John
B-1675	Hunsicker	Jacob	B-754	Kahn	Charles
B-1726	Hunsicker	Jacob	B-754	Kahn	Magdaline
B-991	Hunsicker	Jane	D-128	Kaiser	Amanda
B-911	Hunsicker	Jeremiah D	B-614	Kaiser	Eliza
B-1186	Hunsicker	Jeremiah D	B-781	Kaiser	Hannah
D-1168	Hunsicker	John	B-74	Kaiser	Henrietta
B-1582	Hunsicker	John	B-315	Kaiser	Henrietta

Line #	Surname	Given Name
B-1450	Hunsicker	John
B-1103	Hunsicker	Joseph
B-1664	Hunsicker	Joseph
M-659	Hunsicker	Joseph Jr
B-989	Hunsicker	Leah
D-1255	Hunsicker	Lewis
B-1757	Hunsicker	Lizzie
M-1022	Hunsicker	Lizzie J
B-1164	Hunsicker	Louisa
B-1582	Hunsicker	Mary
B-567	Hunsicker	Owen
B-1093	Hunsicker	Owen
B-1234	Hunsicker	Owen
M-336	Hunsicker	Owen
B-991	Hunsicker	Owen A
B-1664	Hunsicker	Polly
M-954	Hunsicker	Polly
B-293	Hunsicker	Reuben
D-285	Hunsicker	Sarah
M-591	Hunsicker	Sarah F
M-744	Hunsicker	William Franklin
B-1712	Hunt	Emma Louisa
M-928	Hunt	Emma Louisa
B-1069	Huntzberger	Mary
M-1071	Huntzinger	Emma
M-821	Isaac	William
B-178	Islem	Sarah
B-958	Jackaway	Joseph
B-396	Jenkins	Sarah
B-733	Jenkins	Sarah
B-1150	Johnson	Alwin
B-23	Kauffman	William
B-23	Kauffman	William
B-97	Kauffman	Charles
B-97	Kauffman	Emma
B-1955	Kautzman	Bertha
B-1955	Kautzman	Oliver
B-1584	Keegan	Irwin
B-1584	Keegan	Irwin
B-1871	Keener	Floyd
M-1110	Keener	Preston C
B-1871	Keener	Preston Calvin
B-504	Keiffly	Adam
B-504	Keiffly	Sabilla
B-638	Keiner	Mary
M-922	Keiper	Clara
M-739	Keiper	Ellen Amanda
M-400	Keiser	Eliza Jane
D-1354	Keiser	Hulda
B-1590	Keiser	Ida Priscilla
B-245	Kelchner	Edward
B-600	Kelchner	Edward
B-1041	Kelchner	Edward
M-277	Kelchner	Edward
B-245	Kelchner	Ellen
D-66	Kelchner	George
B-600	Kelchner	Lilie
B-1041	Kelchner	Mame
D-35	Kaiser	Henry
D-132	Kaiser	Henry
M-825	Kaiser	Ida Priscilla
D-600	Kaiser	Johannah
B-17	Kaiser	Johannah
B-296	Kaiser	Johannah
B-536	Kaiser	Johannah
B-74	Kaiser	Johannah
B-147	Kaiser	Margaretha
B-309	Kaiser	Margeret
B-781	Kaiser	William
B-574	Kansman	Elizabeth
B-1380	Kantz	Elias
M-508	Kantz	Lenah
M-134	Kantzman	Caroline
M-64	Kantzman	Elizabeth
B-189	Kast	Anzonetta
B-189	Kast	Ellamantina
B-199	Kast	Sarah
B-351	Kast	Sarah
B-1024	Kauffman	Charles
B-288	Kauffman	Charles
B-573	Kauffman	Charles
B-748	Kauffman	Charles
B-1024	Kauffman	Charles
D-597	Kauffman	Milton
B-573	Kauffman	Milton
B-288	Kauffman	Robert
B-748	Kauffman	Sabina
D-332	Kauffman	William
D-363	Kauffman	William
M-452	Kemerer	Juliann
D-1094	Kemerer	Katie
B-163	Kemerer	Leah
B-540	Kemerer	Leah
B-711	Kemerer	Leah
D-1059	Kemerer	Levi
B-809	Kemerer	Lewis
B-677	Kemerer	Lewis
M-423	Kemerer	Lewis
D-1011	Kemerer	Maria
D-730	Kemerer	Mary
B-1044	Kemerer	Nathan
D-1285	Kemerer	Rebecca
D-481	Kemerer	Reuben
B-1956	Kemerer	Rufus L
M-165	Kemerer	Sabina
B-343	Kemerer	Sabrina
B-961	Kemerer	Sally Ann
D-760	Kemerer	Sarah
B-1280	Kemerer	Thomas
M-714	Kemerer	Thomas
M-1146	Kemerer	Thomas C
M-263	Kemerer	W. E
B-1956	Kemerer	William
B-75	Kemery	Kate
B-75	Kemery	Nathan
B-375	Kemery	Nathan

Line #	Surname	Given Name
B-76	Kelchner	Susan
B-1175	Keller	Elizabeth
B-411	Keller	Fietta
B-1554	Kemerer	Alice
M-1001	Kemerer	Annie M
B-1044	Kemerer	Arthur
B-352	Kemerer	Catharine
B-230	Kemerer	Catherine
B-822	Kemerer	Catherine
B-264	Kemerer	Catherine
M-285	Kemerer	Catherine
B-832	Kemerer	Charles
M-320	Kemerer	Charles
D-254	Kemerer	David
B-1280	Kemerer	David
D-1330	Kemerer	Elizabeth
B-1001	Kemerer	Elizabeth
B-1333	Kemerer	Ellen Jane
M-662	Kemerer	Ellen Jane
B-1097	Kemerer	Emaline
D-176	Kemerer	Emma
B-240	Kemerer	Emma
B-674	Kemerer	Emma
B-1546	Kemerer	Esther
M-447	Kemerer	George
B-1546	Kemerer	George H
B-832	Kemerer	Harrie
M-666	Kemerer	Harriet
B-809	Kemerer	Ida
D-342	Kern	Jacob
B-30	Kern	Jacob
B-1006	Kern	Jeremiah
B-1006	Kern	Korah
B-917	Kern	Lafayette A
D-223	Kern	Maria
B-38	Kern	Nathan
B-30	Kern	Peter
B-203	Kern	Peter
B-570	Kern	Peter
B-212	Kern	Sally Ann
M-217	Kern	Sarah A
B-570	Kern	William
B-313	Kerner	Carolina
B-313	Kerner	Fransisca
M-60	Kerschner	Bregitta
D-1289	Kerschner	Catherine
M-647	Kerschner	Emma Jane
B-1829	Kerschner	Garrie
D-1226	Kerschner	Ida Katie
B-254	Kerschner	Louisa
B-496	Kerschner	Messina
B-1332	Kerschner	Messina
B-1610	Kerschner	Messina
B-1829	Kerschner	Noah Albert
M-645	Kerschner	Noah Albert
B-896	Kershner	Bregitta
M-578	Kershner	Frank
D-679	Kershner	George
M-40	Kemery	Nathan
B-375	Kemery	Urilla
B-1855	Kemmerer	Blanchie
M-1062	Kemmerer	C. D.
B-533	Kemmerer	Charles
B-1855	Kemmerer	Henry Solomon
M-1098	Kemmerer	Henry Solomon
B-533	Kemmerer	Katie
M-416	Kemmerer	Mary Ann
B-1487	Kennel	Tevilia
M-738	Kennel	Tevilia E
B-1604	Kennel	Tewilia
B-1170	Kepner	Catherine
B-1246	Kepner	Catherine
M-306	Kepser	Helena
B-561	Kern	Alice
B-749	Kern	Alice
B-1004	Kern	Alice
B-655	Kern	Anna
B-1251	Kern	Catherine
D-262	Kern	Elizabeth
D-678	Kern	Elsie
B-917	Kern	Elsie
B-38	Kern	Elvina
M-113	Kern	Elvina
M-467	Kern	Emaline
M-678	Kern	Emma P
B-655	Kern	Francis
B-203	Kern	Henry
B-302	Kirschner	Bregitta
M-870	Kishbaugh	Wilson
D-333	Kistler	Allen
D-1331	Kistler	Beulah
B-1800	Kistler	Bula
M-438	Kistler	Caroline
B-1082	Kistler	Catherine
B-1747	Kistler	Clifford
B-1137	Kistler	David H
B-1618	Kistler	David Amandes
B-1678	Kistler	David Amandes
B-1747	Kistler	David Amandes
B-1800	Kistler	David Amandes
M-889	Kistler	David Amandus
B-1258	Kistler	Elizabeth
B-1397	Kistler	Elizabeth
B-852	Kistler	Elizabeth
M-609	Kistler	Elizabeth A
B-1138	Kistler	Elmia
B-1137	Kistler	Estella
M-217	Kistler	Jacob B P
M-815	Kistler	John W
B-1669	Kistler	Jonathan
B-233	Kistler	Joseph
B-1669	Kistler	Mary
D-1162	Kistler	Oris
B-1678	Kistler	Oris
B-1618	Kistler	Oscar
D-847	Kistler	Rosa

Line #	Surname	Given Name
D-551	Kershner	Gideon
D-1081	Kershner	Jane
M-290	Kershner	Louisa
M-698	Kershner	Nathan Alfred
M-289	Kershner	Rebecca
D-985	Kershner	William
B-85	Kessler	Anna
M-301	Kester	Reuben J
D-292	Ketrich	Anna
M-649	Keuhner	Amanda C
M-929	Kibbler	Annie
M-327	Kibbler	Lucy
D-556	Kichler	Charles
M-713	Kidd	Alice Sarah
D-95	Kiebler	Oliver
D-235	Kiebler	Paul
B-76	Kiefer	Mary Ann
B-958	Kifley	Louisa
B-36	Kindt	Francis
B-36	Kindt	Howard
M-723	King	William
M-207	Kinney	Mary Alice
B-1294	Kinsel	Charles
B-1294	Kinsel	Lenah
M-1191	Kipp	Edward
D-141	Kirby	Hannah
M-1189	Kirschbaum	Margeret A
B-99	Kleintopp	Charles
B-377	Kleintopp	David
B-761	Kleintopp	David
D-123	Kleintopp	Ellen
D-517	Kleintopp	Emma
B-377	Kleintopp	Emma
B-460	Kleintopp	Fayetta
D-616	Kleintopp	George
B-761	Kleintopp	George
B-647	Kleintopp	James
B-691	Kleintopp	James
B-181	Kleintopp	James W
B-425	Kleintopp	James W
M-160	Kleintopp	James W
B-181	Kleintopp	Lily
B-935	Kleintopp	Mary Jane
B-1221	Kleintopp	Susanna
B-769	Kleppinger	Anna Catherine
M-430	Kleppinger	Anna Maria Elizabeth
B-363	Kliefer	Eva
D-78	Klientopp	Edwin
M-1069	Kline	Catherine
B-761	Kline	Emaline
B-1015	Kline	Emaline
B-225	Kline	Lydia
M-62	Kline	Lydia
B-696	Kline	William
D-918	Klinetop	David
M-702	Klinetop	John
B-1514	Klingaman	Lizzie
B-1663	Klingaman	Lizzie
D-959	Kistler	Sarah
B-233	Kistler	Sarah
B-587	Kistler	Sarah
B-824	Kistler	Sarah
B-1234	Kistler	Sarah
B-1093	Kistler	Sarah
M-96	Kistler	Sarah
B-1234	Kistler	Sarah Catherine
M-336	Kistler	Sarah Catherine
B-567	Kistler	Sarah E
M-581	Kistler	William Alfred
M-480	Kleheimer	Afra
D-55	Klein	Ellen
B-377	Klein	Emaline
M-256	Klein	Wilhelmina
B-1015	Kleintop	Charlie
B-1015	Kleintop	David
B-1532	Kleintop	James W
M-569	Kleintop	Joseph
B-1532	Kleintop	Laura
B-1680	Kleintop	Lucinda
M-510	Kleintop	Mary Jane
B-321	Kleintopp	Anna F
M-420	Kleintopp	Anna F
B-750	Kleintopp	Anna Fayetta
B-321	Kleintopp	Annetta
B-99	Kleintopp	Charles
D-38	Klotz	Hannah
B-423	Klotz	John F
M-388	Klotz	John F
D-20	Klotz	Jonathan
M-16	Klotz	Jonathan
B-864	Klotz	Joseph
B-223	Klotz	Josiah
B-538	Klotz	Josiah
B-1173	Klotz	July Ann
B-1544	Klotz	July Ann
B-1698	Klotz	July Ann
B-1845	Klotz	July Ann
B-271	Klotz	Laura
B-1698	Klotz	Laura
M-1008	Klotz	Laura Tana
B-416	Klotz	Leanna
D-1175	Klotz	Lydia
B-735	Klotz	Mary
M-465	Klotz	Mary Rebecca
B-271	Klotz	Owen
B-220	Klotz	Owen
B-406	Klotz	Owen
B-723	Klotz	Owen
B-1075	Klotz	Owen
B-1173	Klotz	Owen
M-876	Klotz	Reuben Milton
B-1720	Klotz	Robert H
B-1813	Klotz	Robert H
B-1882	Klotz	Robert H
B-1367	Klotz	Rosa
B-1302	Klotz	Rosa A

Line #	Surname	Given Name	Line #	Surname	Given Name
M-704	Klingaman	Lizzie L	B-1651	Klotz	Rosa A
M-948	Klingaman	Rosa A	B-1818	Klotz	Rosa A
B-852	Klingeman	Jacob	B-734	Klotz	Sarah
M-919	Klingeman	Louisa	B-723	Klotz	Sarah
B-852	Klingemen	Maria	B-1027	Klotz	Sarah
M-73	Klinger	Anna	B-1211	Klotz	Sarah
M-116	Klinger	Lewis	B-1401	Klotz	Sarah
B-623	Klose	Augustin	M-1070	Klotz	Sarah Irene Carrie
B-703	Klotz	Adline	B-423	Klotz	Sylvester
B-943	Klotz	Adline	B-149	Klotz	William F
B-1219	Klotz	Adline	M-189	Klotz	William F
B-223	Klotz	Agnes	M-1065	Kluger	William T
B-406	Klotz	Alavesta	D-950	Knapp	Catherine
M-335	Klotz	Alavesta	D-886	Knapp	Frederic
M-244	Klotz	Benjamin Franklin	D-1112	Knapp	Maria
M-494	Klotz	Catherine	D-121	Knappenberger	Abraham
D-590	Klotz	Charles	B-410	Knappenberger	Catherine
B-149	Klotz	Charles	B-838	Knappenberger	Catherine
B-538	Klotz	Charles	B-446	Knappenberger	Catherine
B-1720	Klotz	Dora	B-368	Knappenberger	Lucy
D-315	Klotz	Edwin	B-9	Knappenberger	Lucy Ann
B-1813	Klotz	Emma	B-1439	Knappenberger	Mary
B-416	Klotz	Franklin	M-687	Knappenberger	Mary Ann
B-734	Klotz	Franklin	B-260	Knappenberger	Sarah
B-1882	Klotz	Halena	M-724	Knappenberger	William H
M-986	Knauss	Emma	B-803	Koda	Mary
B-431	Knauss	Lewis	D-1143	Koenig	Annie
M-5	Knauss	Mellen M	B-928	Koenig	Elizabeth
B-431	Knauss	William	D-1144	Koenig	Harvey
M-51	Knease	William	B-928	Koenig	Solomon
B-1063	Knecht	Edgar	B-1292	Kohl	Hannah
B-357	Knecht	Elizabeth	B-907	Kolb	Anna
B-620	Knecht	Elizabeth	B-199	Kolb	Anna Maria
B-814	Knecht	Elizabeth	B-784	Kolb	Anna Maria
B-55	Knecht	Francis	B-412	Kolb	Anna Marie
D-544	Knecht	Freddie	D-749	Kolb	Daniel
B-563	Knecht	Freddie	B-458	Kolb	Daniel
B-800	Knecht	George	B-491	Kolb	Daniel
B-1242	Knecht	James	D-1132	Kolb	Elizabeth
B-906	Knecht	Mary	M-691	Kolb	Ellemina
B-1217	Knecht	Mary	M-381	Kolb	Emaline
M-437	Knecht	Mary Ann	M-700	Kolb	Emaline
B-563	Knecht	Reuben	D-376	Kolb	George
B-800	Knecht	Reuben	D-1138	Kolb	George
B-1063	Knecht	Reuben	B-818	Kolb	George
B-414	Knecht	Samuel	B-971	Kolb	Harrison
B-414	Knecht	Susan	B-1252	Kolb	Harvey
B-55	Knecht	William	D-1062	Kolb	Henry
B-1242	Knecht	William	M-89	Kolb	John
B-1207	Kneese	Catherine	B-705	Kolb	Jonas
B-68	Kneff	Caroline	B-1059	Kolb	Jonas
B-908	Kneily	Pauline	M-119	Kolb	Jonas
D-1089	Knell	Rebecca	B-1059	Kolb	Kitty
D-931	Knepper	Alberehina	B-1404	Kolb	Leon
M-779	Knepper	Alfred	B-1579	Kolb	Levina
M-745	Knepper	Alice Jane	D-1167	Kolb	Magdalene
B-1095	Knepper	Alwenia	D-1067	Kolb	Margeret
B-1339	Knepper	Charles	B-1338	Kolb	Maria

Line #	Surname	Given Name	Line #	Surname	Given Name
B-1339	Knepper	Emma	B-1745	Kolb	Maria
B-1485	Knepper	Frank	M-674	Kolb	Maria
M-767	Knepper	Frank	B-79	Kolb	Mary Ann
D-1053	Knepper	John	B-137	Kolb	Mary Jane
B-1095	Knepper	Jonas	M-150	Kolb	Mary Jane
B-1962	Knepper	Lizzie Alice	B-1212	Kolb	Matilda
B-1485	Knepper	Odilla	B-1406	Kolb	Matilda
M-867	Knepper	Thomas	B-1605	Kolb	Matilda
B-1068	Knepper	William	B-1652	Kolb	Matilda
M-567	Knepper	William	B-1772	Kolb	Matilda
D-486	Knerr	Milton	M-792	Kolb	Matilda
B-298	Knerr	Milton	B-491	Kolb	Matilida
B-298	Knerr	William	B-818	Kolb	Nathan
B-899	Koch	Emma	B-1252	Kolb	Nathan
M-431	Koch	Franklin P	B-1404	Kolb	Nathan B
B-899	Koch	Franklin T	B-971	Kolb	Nathan L B
M-1033	Koch	Henry	M-191	Kolb	Nathan L B
M-116	Koch	Mary Elizabeth	M-1123	Kolb	Pierce
D-1154	Kocher	Benjamin	B-705	Kolb	Reuben
D-842	Kocher	Catherine	M-467	Kolb	Reuben
D-31	Kocher	Juliann	B-880	Kolb	Sabina
D-775	Kocher	Mary	B-1750	Kolb	Sabina
D-780	Kocher	Sophia	M-549	Kolb	Sabina
M-194	Kolb	William	M-539	Kramer	W. C.
M-607	Kolb	William	B-938	Kranich	Catherine
M-949	Koons	Alvin R	B-99	Kratz	Harriet
M-614	Koons	Amelia	D-412	Kratzer	(s/o Charles and Sarah)
M-308	Koons	Angeline	D-689	Kratzer	Anna
D-1106	Koons	Anna	B-1697	Kratzer	Anna
B-829	Koons	Annetta	B-1449	Kratzer	Anna M
B-1053	Koons	Annetta	M-709	Kratzer	Anna M
B-1572	Koons	Charles	D-221	Kratzer	Catherine
B-1572	Koons	Cornelius	D-897	Kratzer	Charles
B-1362	Koons	David	B-916	Kratzer	Jane
B-1461	Koons	David	B-462	Kratzer	Mary Jane
M-507	Koons	Elmira C	B-463	Kratzer	Mary Jane
B-347	Koons	Emma	M-382	Kratzer	William Edwin
B-1461	Koons	Emma	B-1671	Krauc	Edward
D-242	Koons	George	B-1671	Krauc	Odillon
D-693	Koons	George	B-947	Kreamer	Charles
B-587	Koons	George	M-441	Kreamer	David S
D-1028	Koons	Henry	B-947	Kreamer	W.C.
B-393	Koons	Jeremiah	M-386	Krechel	Helena
B-129	Koons	Jeremiah	B-635	Krechel	Helenah
B-393	Koons	Jeremiah	D-844	Kreiner	Hannah
M-200	Koons	Jeremiah	B-114	Kreiser	Amelia
B-1234	Koons	Lillie	B-114	Kreiser	Jacob
D-981	Koons	Mary	B-1340	Kreitz	Charles
B-824	Koons	Mary	B-1093	Kreitz	Emaline
B-824	Koons	Mary	B-1280	Kreitz	Emaline
M-346	Koons	Mary Jane	B-1444	Kreitz	George
B-233	Koons	Minnie	B-1081	Kreitz	George Henry
B-347	Koons	Richard	B-1340	Kreitz	George Henry
B-1362	Koons	Savilla	B-1492	Kreitz	George Henry
D-1007	Koons	Willoughby	M-533	Kreitz	George Henry
B-233	Koons	Willoughby	B-351	Kreitz	Harriet
B-587	Koons	Willoughby	B-110	Kreitz	Harriet
B-824	Koons	Willoughby	D-921	Kreitz	John

Line #	Surname	Given Name
B-1234	Koons	Willoughby
M-96	Koons	Willoughby
B-129	Koons	Zacharias
B-539	Kop	Matilda
B-1592	Kostenbader	Bulah
B-61	Kostenbader	Calvin
B-1055	Kostenbader	Josiah
B-61	Kostenbader	Josiah
B-345	Kostenbader	Josiah
B-1055	Kostenbader	Josiah
B-345	Kostenbader	Mary Ann
M-544	Kostenbader	Peter L
B-1592	Kostenbader	Samuel D
M-676	Kostenbader	Samuel D
M-378	Kostenbader	Samuel F
M-1039	Kostenbader	Sue
D-1346	Krainer	Michael
D-424	Kramer	Ellen
M-936	Kramer	Lottie
M-488	Kramer	Margeret Magdalene
B-400	Kramer	Susanna
B-1353	Kressley	Charles
B-1674	Kressley	Charles
B-678	Kressley	Daniel
B-1161	Kressley	Daniel
B-1300	Kressley	Daniel
M-121	Kressley	Daniel
M-1083	Kressley	Emma L
M-163	Kressley	Hannah Maria
B-1674	Kressley	John
B-678	Kressley	Korah
D-742	Kressley	Mary
M-367	Kressley	Sarah Amanda
B-1161	Kressley	Thomas
M-399	Krill	Julia Ann
B-812	Krill	Mary
B-663	Krock	Daniel
B-1057	Krock	Daniel
M-425	Krock	Daniel
D-631	Krock	Howard
B-663	Krock	Howard
M-317	Krock	Lizzie
B-1928	Krome	Gust
M-1167	Krome	Gust
B-1928	Krome	Raymond
B-241	Kromer	Alfred
B-266	Kromer	Alfred
B-864	Kromer	Alfred
B-10	Kromer	Alfred
B-702	Kromer	Catherine
B-1167	Kromer	Charles
B-864	Kromer	Estella
B-466	Kromer	George
B-953	Kromer	Irvin
B-151	Kromer	Irwin
B-466	Kromer	Irwin
B-702	Kromer	Irwin
B-1167	Kromer	Irwin

Line #	Surname	Given Name
B-1081	Kreitz	John
B-110	Kreitz	Mary
B-18	Kreitz	Mary Ann
D-1023	Kreitz	Samuel
M-14	Kreitz	Susanna
B-1492	Kreitz	William
B-1796	Kremer	Essie
B-1062	Kremer	Henry
B-1062	Kremer	Lenah
B-1796	Kremer	Tilghman
M-453	Kresge	C. A.
B-279	Kresge	Ida
M-790	Kresge	John William
B-279	Kresge	Paul
B-1026	Kresge	Paul
B-687	Kresgy	Charles
B-687	Kresgy	Paul
B-1353	Kressley	Andrew
M-93	Kressley	Anna Louise
M-1154	Kressley	Assaby
B-1300	Kressley	Bessie
B-1085	Krotzer	Sarah
B-1085	Krotzer	Walter V
B-1500	Krotzer	Walter V
M-478	Krotzer	Walter V
M-392	Krug	Babette
D-817	Krum	Charles
B-1900	Krum	Cora Estella
M-1140	Krum	Cora Estella
D-535	Krum	Daniel
B-54	Krum	Elizabeth
B-708	Krum	Elizabeth
B-1768	Krum	Elizabeth
M-266	Krum	Elizabeth Jane
B-1768	Krum	Emma
M-848	Krum	Isabella A. M.
D-1179	Krum	Joshua
B-1455	Krum	Katie
M-550	Krum	L. A
M-751	Krum	L. A.
B-237	Krum	Levi
B-1455	Krum	Lewis
B-237	Krum	Louisa
B-1264	Krum	Louisa
M-632	Krum	Louisa
B-586	Krum	Medina
B-1074	Krum	Medina
B-1326	Krum	Medina
B-1649	Krum	Medina
B-81	Krum	Medina
B-302	Krum	Medina
M-268	Krum	Medina
D-1271	Krum	Odillin
B-991	Krum	Rebecca
B-1106	Krum	Rebecca
B-275	Krumm	Carolina
B-1152	Krumm	Caroline
B-856	Krumm	Levi

Line #	Surname	Given Name	Line #	Surname	Given Name
B-1274	Kromer	Irwin	B-856	Krumm	Lillie
M-282	Kromer	Irwin	D-1171	Krumm	Naunie
B-10	Kromer	John	D-385	Krumm	Peter
M-86	Kromer	John	D-369	Krumm	Selinda
B-1274	Kromer	Joseph	M-854	Krumm	William W
B-864	Kromer	Lydia	B-682	Krumn	John
B-284	Kromer	Mandaleine	B-682	Krumn	Nathan
B-241	Kromer	Martha	B-124	Kuebler	Aaron
B-10	Kromer	Martin	B-124	Kuebler	Henry
B-151	Kromer	Mary	B-124	Kuebler	Henry
B-953	Kromer	Savennah	B-286	Kuebler	Lucy
M-1114	Kromer	Stella Y	B-285	Kuebler	Rebecca
B-266	Kromer	William	B-1056	Kuebler	Rebecca
B-1555	Krotzer	Anna Maria	B-1327	Kuebler	Rebecca
D-1177	Krotzer	Charles	B-286	Kuebler	Rebecca
B-909	Krotzer	Eliza	B-1369	Kuebler	Rebecca
B-909	Krotzer	Ephraim W	B-816	Kuebler	Rebecca
B-1500	Krotzer	Laura	D-272	Kuehner	(d/o Levi & Mary)
D-705	Krotzer	Sarah	M-232	Kuehner	Alice
B-287	Kuehner	August	B-1957	Kunkle	Lizzie
B-325	Kuehner	Carolina	M-1089	Kunkle	Lizzie
B-598	Kuehner	Caroline	B-144	Kunkle	Manda
B-614	Kuehner	Caroline	D-722	Kunkle	Mary
M-72	Kuehner	Caroline	B-158	Kunkle	Mary
B-287	Kuehner	Ellen	B-210	Kunkle	Mary
B-793	Kuehner	Jemima	B-890	Kunkle	Quinton
D-825	Kuehner	July	B-594	Kunkle	Sabilla
B-793	Kuehner	Levi	M-123	Kunkle	Sabilla
M-102	Kuehner	Luenda	M-790	Kunkle	Sarah
B-589	Kuehner	Luzetta	M-172	Kunkle	Savannah
B-811	Kuehner	Suanna	B-209	Kunkle	Sebilla
B-889	Kuehner	Susanna	D-626	Kunsman	Alfred
M-852	Kugler	Kate A	B-790	Kunsman	Alfred
D-483	Kuhn	Frederic	B-889	Kunsman	Catherine
B-145	Kuhns	David	D-680	Kunsman	Emma
M-131	Kuhns	David	B-601	Kunsman	Emma
D-917	Kuhns	Granville	B-39	Kunsman	Jacob
B-145	Kuhns	Louisa	B-307	Kunsman	Jacob
M-155	Kuhnsweiler	Catius	B-601	Kunsman	Jacob
M-427	Kunkel	Dures	B-790	Kunsman	Jacob
M-406	Kunkel	Elizabeth	B-307	Kunsman	Mary
B-530	Kunkel	Hilorus	B-39	Kunsman	Oliver
B-743	Kunkel	Joseph	B-308	Kuntz	Abigail
B-743	Kunkel	Laura	B-477	Kuntz	Annetta
B-504	Kunkel	Manda	B-1172	Kuntz	Annie
B-1167	Kunkel	Martha Ann	B-811	Kuntz	Catherine
D-727	Kunkel	Mary	B-1633	Kuntz	Cornelius
M-512	Kunkel	Mary Etta	M-727	Kuntz	Cornelius
B-530	Kunkel	Paul	B-1221	Kuntz	Daisy
B-801	Kunkel	Sabilla	D-13	Kuntz	David
B-973	Kunkel	Sabilla	B-1172	Kuntz	David
B-223	Kunkle	Albert	M-409	Kuntz	David
B-348	Kunkle	Amanda	D-1207	Kuntz	Elias
B-594	Kunkle	Amanda	B-785	Kuntz	Eliza
B-1270	Kunkle	Dures	B-106	Kuntz	Francis
B-348	Kunkle	Elizabeth	M-1180	Kuntz	George H
B-522	Kunkle	Ellen	D-289	Kuntz	Jeremiah
B-1270	Kunkle	Emma	M-178	Kuntz	John

Line #	Surname	Given Name
D-341	Kunkle	Enoch
M-130	Kunkle	Enoch
B-32	Kunkle	Eugene
B-158	Kunkle	George
M-205	Kunkle	Harrison
B-890	Kunkle	Hiloras
B-210	Kunkle	Hilovius
B-32	Kunkle	Joel
B-197	Kunkle	Joseph
B-522	Kunkle	Joseph
B-195	Kunkle	Joseph
B-197	Kunkle	Korah
M-474	Kunkle	Leah Vesta
B-1811	Kunkle	Lizzie
B-1842	Kunkle	Lizzie
B-1873	Kunkle	Lizzie
B-1906	Kunkle	Lizzie
B-908	Kupfer	John
M-227	Kust	Anconetta
B-96	Lackawuck	Frederic
B-96	Lackawuck	Mary
B-184	Lambes	Mary
B-619	Lambes	Mary
B-912	Lambes	Mary
M-5	Lantee	Emma
B-1394	Lapp	Alwilda
B-1475	Lapp	Alwilda
B-1543	Lapp	Alwilda
B-1911	Lapp	Alwilda
D-1105	Lapp	Carrie
B-1536	Lapp	Carrie
B-1458	Lapp	Charles Henry
B-1536	Lapp	Charles Henry
M-748	Lapp	Charles Henry
M-1051	Lapp	Edward
B-543	Lapp	Emma
B-1318	Lapp	Franklin
M-651	Lapp	Franklin
B-543	Lapp	John
D-1036	Lapp	Lizzie
B-1318	Lapp	Mary Ann
D-1031	Lapp	Scott
B-1458	Lapp	Scott
D-478	Larasch	Alfred
M-1087	Larasch	Edwin H
D-1247	Larasch	Irwin
D-9	Larasch	William
D-554	Larash	Elmira
M-471	Larash	Jacob J
D-364	Larose	Jane
M-222	Larose	Mary
B-1037	Larose	William
M-589	Larose	William
B-720	Laub	Aaron
B-1098	Laub	Aaron
B-1198	Laub	Aaron
B-1031	Laub	Aaron
D-737	Laub	John
B-1633	Kuntz	Mary
B-730	Kuntz	Mary
B-1838	Kuntz	Mena Amanda
B-1898	Kuntz	Mena Amanda
B-1918	Kuntz	Mena Amanda
M-972	Kuntz	Mena Amanda
B-106	Kuntz	Richard
B-553	Kuntz	Richard
B-785	Kuntz	Richard
D-724	Kuntz	Samuel
B-553	Kuntz	William
B-1221	Kuntz	William
M-845	Kuntz	William C
B-94	Kuntzman	Catherine
B-589	Kuntzman	Catherine
M-653	Kuntzman	Rosa Mantana
B-908	Kupfer	Emma
B-901	Lauchnor	Leah
B-1661	Lauchnor	Lewis
B-950	Lauchnor	Lydia
B-951	Lauchnor	Lydia
B-1843	Lauchnor	Lydia
B-1881	Lauchnor	Lydia
M-136	Lauchnor	Lydia
D-1038	Lauchnor	Martha
B-228	Lauchnor	Susanna
B-557	Lauchnor	Susanna
B-1460	Lauchnor	Susanna
M-280	Lauchnor	Susanna
M-1059	Laurish	Emma L
M-739	Laury	Harvey E
M 155	Lauth	Margaretha
B-608	Laux	Amour
B-606	Laux	Benjamin
B-607	Laux	Edwin
B-606	Laux	Maehlon B
B-607	Laux	Maehlon B
B-608	Laux	Maehlon B
B-609	Laux	Maehlon B
B-609	Laux	Robert
B-1904	Lazarus	Harrison G
B-1904	Lazarus	Harry
B-1338	Leaser	Franklin
D-1318	Leaser	George
M-964	Leaser	Maria
B-1338	Leaser	William F
M-674	Leaser	William F
M-693	Lebenberg	John
B-1420	Lecheitner	Sarah
B-382	Lechleiter	Catherine
B-1314	Lechleiter	Christiana
B-1051	Lechleitner	Denah
B-1196	Lechleitner	Edward
B-1196	Lechleitner	John
M-648	Lechleitner	John H
D-1286	Lechleitner	Jonas
B-1616	Lechleitner	Sarah
B-429	Lechliter	John

Line #	Surname	Given Name
B-1098	Laub	John
B-1198	Laub	Lizzie
B-720	Laub	Minerva
D-51	Laubach	Charles
B-1552	Laubach	Emma
B-26	Lauber	Catherine
B-27	Lauber	Catherine
B-379	Lauber	Catherine
M-70	Lauchner	Edward
M-161	Lauchnor	Abigail
D-1227	Lauchnor	Annetta
B-1661	Lauchnor	Clinton
M-279	Lauchnor	John
B-66	Lauchnor	Leah
B-1054	Lauchnor	Leah
B-395	Leffler	William
M-230	Leh	Alfred
B-655	Lehr	Amanda
B-183	Leibenguth	Bessie
D-351	Leibenguth	Daniel
D-322	Leibenguth	Edward
B-6	Leibenguth	Edward
B-6	Leibenguth	Franklin
B-183	Leibenguth	Franklin
M-22	Leibenguth	Franklin
M-8	Leibenguth	Mary Ann
M-301	Leibenguth	Matilda
D-337	Leibenguth	Philip
D-782	Leibenguth	Robert
B-1435	Leibensperger	Laura A
M-736	Leibensperger	Laura A
B-1068	Leiby	Caroline
M-567	Leiby	Caroline
B-1254	Leiby	Clara
B-1232	Leiby	Clinton Ell
B-1732	Leiby	Daniel
B-362	Leiby	Elizabeth
B-725	Leiby	Elizabeth
B-129	Leiby	Elizabeth
B-1349	Leiby	Emaline
B-1232	Leiby	Franklin
B-1350	Leiby	Franklin
M-626	Leiby	Franklin
B-1235	Leiby	Jacob
D-1142	Leiby	Jenny
D-874	Leiby	Luretta
B-1350	Leiby	Luretta
D-1237	Leiby	Lydia
D-739	Leiby	Maria
D-939	Leiby	Mary
B-760	Leiby	Mary
B-1254	Leiby	Nathan
B-1096	Leiby	Rebecca
B-841	Leiby	Rebecca
B-1232	Leiby	Reuben F
B-318	Leiby	Sarah
B-729	Leiby	Sarah
B-1068	Leiby	Sarah S
B-429	Lechliter	John
B-1646	Leeds	Elmira
M-1021	Leeser	Thomas
B-87	Leffler	Aaron
B-277	Leffler	Aaron
B-88	Leffler	Aaron
B-1768	Leffler	Augustus
B-108	Leffler	Edward
B-87	Leffler	Ellen
B-1768	Leffler	Fred A
B-277	Leffler	George
B-195	Leffler	Jacob
B-195	Leffler	Joseph
B-108	Leffler	Nathan
B-395	Leffler	Nathan
B-1512	Lentz	Anna
B-1219	Lentz	Charles
D-345	Lentz	Daniel
B-890	Lentz	Edward
M-179	Lentz	Edward
B-1512	Lentz	Edwin J
B-1557	Lentz	Edwin J
B-1679	Lentz	Edwin J
B-1717	Lentz	Edwin J
B-1756	Lentz	Edwin J
B-1809	Lentz	Edwin J
B-1852	Lentz	Edwin J
B-1893	Lentz	Edwin J
M-788	Lentz	Edwin J
B-1852	Lentz	Elmer
B-599	Lentz	Elmira
B-1717	Lentz	Estella
B-1901	Lentz	Gussie E
M-1049	Lentz	James O
B-1131	Lentz	Julia
B-1328	Lentz	Julia
B-955	Lentz	Julia Elizabeth
B-1743	Lentz	Julia Elizabeth
M-531	Lentz	Julia Elizabeth
B-422	Lentz	Juliann
B-918	Lentz	July Ann
B-1557	Lentz	Lillie Ann
M-960	Lentz	Lillie R
B-591	Lentz	Lucinda
M-424	Lentz	Lucinda
M-404	Lentz	Lydia
B-584	Lentz	Manda
D-1013	Lentz	Marie
B-298	Lentz	Mary
B-1809	Lentz	Maud
B-1893	Lentz	Minnie
B-1756	Lentz	Robert
B-1679	Lentz	Sadie
B-268	Lentz	Sophia
B-599	Lentz	Stephen
B-589	Lerch	Charles
B-811	Lerch	Ellen
M-1161	Lerch	Hannah

Line #	Surname	Given Name	Line #	Surname	Given Name
D-891	Leiby	Susanna	B-25	Lerch	Morris
B-1767	Leiby	Susanna	B-589	Lerch	Owen
B-1732	Leiby	William	B-811	Lerch	Owen
B-359	Leichliter	Maehlon	B-25	Lerch	Peter A
M-325	Leimbach	John	M-94	Lerch	Peter A
D-89	Leinbach	John	D-1061	Lessman	Bilig
B-1181	Leininger	Anna Katella	M-394	Leukel	John
B-999	Leininger	Elmina	B-323	Leukle	Charles
B-999	Leininger	Maria	M-281	Leukle	Elizabeth
D-367	Lentz	Aaron	B-323	Leukle	William
B-1219	Lentz	Alfred	B-1040	Leukle	William
B-1315	Lentz	Alvenia	M-363	Leukle	William
M-117	Lentz	Amanda	B-384	Levan	Ameda
B-101	Levan	Elmer	B-1048	Loch	Polly
B-1776	Levan	Frank	B-1578	Loch	Polly
D-61	Levan	Henry	B-1352	Loch	Polly
B-101	Levan	Hiram	D-1278	Loch	Samuel
M-38	Levan	Hiram	D-991	Lohra	Jacob
M-494	Levan	Hiram P	M-433	Long	Abraham
D-195	Levan	Isaac	B-1556	Long	Annie
B-384	Levan	Isaac	B-1727	Long	Annie
B-555	Levan	Isaac	B-1601	Long	Annie D
D-1291	Levan	Lydia	B-1640	Long	Annie D
D-390	Levan	Maria	B-1708	Long	Annie D
D-1080	Levan	Maria	B-1763	Long	Annie D
D-657	Levan	Pearcy	B-1799	Long	Annie D
B-1776	Levan	William	B-1833	Long	Annie D
B-1386	Levers	Anna	B-1857	Long	Annie D
B-1386	Levers	Espen	M-820	Long	Annie D
B-1608	Levers	Espen	B-306	Long	Carloline
B-1516	Levers	Espin	M-36	Long	Caroline
B 1516	Lcvcrs	Harry	B-1040	Long	Columbus
B-1608	Levers	Mary	B-559	Long	Columbus
B-436	Lewis	Mary	M-408	Long	Columbus
B-728	Lichtenberger	Catherine	B-1109	Long	David D
B-40	Lichtenwalder	Anna	B-1165	Long	David D
B-40	Lichtenwalder	Daniel	M-412	Long	Drake H
B-724	Lichtenwalter	Albert	M-712	Long	Geo. Washington
D-93	Lichtenwalter	Anna	M-444	Long	Griffith D
B-969	Lichtenwalter	Daisy	B-827	Long	Henry
B-969	Lichtenwalter	Edwin	B-1014	Long	Jacob
B-724	Lichtenwalter	Osville	B-1877	Long	Jeanetta
D-933	Lieser	David	B-1014	Long	Katie
M-171	Lieser	Hannah	B-756	Long	Mary
M-884	Lieser	Saunia	M-477	Long	Mary
D-843	Lieser	William	M-915	Long	Mary
M-559	Lieser	William	B-827	Long	Sarah
M-434	Lindsey	Sarah	B-1165	Long	Villiera
M-67	Lins	Joel	B-1040	Long	William
B-703	Lintz	Charles	M-813	Longacre	Emaline
B-943	Lintz	Charles	M-1021	Longacre	Jennie
B-579	Lintz	Elizabeth	B-719	Longacre	Sarah
B-580	Lintz	Elizabeth	B-848	Longacre	Sarah
B-943	Lintz	John	B-1135	Longacre	Sarah
B-703	Lintz	Nora	B-1390	Longacre	Sarah
M-800	Liser	Joseph S	B-1489	Longacre	Sarah
D-1309	Liston	Fatima	B-1597	Longacre	Sarah
M-1152	Llewellyn	Mary	B-427	Longaker	David

Line #	Surname	Given Name
M-1158	Llewellyn	Sallie
M-1001	Loch	Alfred B
M-832	Loch	Daniel
D-1311	Loch	Edwin
B-1134	Loch	Fianna
M-773	Loch	Joseph
B-1637	Loch	Kate M
B-1713	Loch	Kate M
B-1765	Loch	Kate M
M-881	Loch	Kate M
M-747	Loch	Noah Albert
M-718	Lower	Darby J
D-293	Lower	Elizabeth
B-446	Lower	Elizabeth
B-820	Lower	Elizabeth
B-582	Lower	Ellen
D-423	Lower	Elmira
M-43	Lower	Emalina
B-42	Lower	Emaline
B-635	Lower	Emma
B-166	Lower	Eva
B-635	Lower	George D
M-386	Lower	George David
D-45	Lower	James
B-1399	Lower	Mary
B-583	Lower	Sally
D-947	Lower	Sarah
B-167	Lower	Sarah
B-28	Lower	Sarah
B-762	Lower	Sarah
D-246	Lower	Sophronia
B-583	Lower	Tilghman
M-377	Lower	Tilghman
M-807	Lower	Tilghman
B-166	Lower	William
B-582	Lower	William
M-10	Lubar	Mary
B-17	Ludwig	Franz
M-620	Ludwig	Franz
B-1767	Lutz	Andrew D
B-321	Lutz	Christianna
B-1189	Lutz	Elmer
B-1418	Lutz	Irwin
B-321	Lutz	Isaac B
B-1189	Lutz	Jacob
B-1418	Lutz	Jacob
D-798	Lutz	Jerras
D-812	Lutz	John
B-1767	Lutz	Maud
D-1358	Lutz	Nathan
B-1841	Lutz	Nathan
M-773	Lutz	Sarah
M-830	Lutz	Sarah Jane
B-1841	Lutz	William
M-1094	Lutz	Willliam J
B-945	Lutz	Wilmina
D-952	Lynn	Benjamin
B-1035	Lynn	Daniel

Line #	Surname	Given Name
B-427	Longaker	Sarah
M-1164	Lora	Elias
B-1091	Lorah	Angeline
B-1827	Lorah	Harrison
M-926	Lorah	Harrison
D-1307	Lorah	Henry
B-1827	Lorah	Mary
D-1172	Lorah	s/o Henry & Kate
D-4	Louts	Logan
B-196	Lower	Anna
D-464	Lower	Ansonetta
B-759	Lynn	Simon
B-1192	Lynn	Simon
D-301	Macke	Rebecca
M-1034	Maidenwald	Henry M
B-132	Malhearn	Rosa Ann
D-117	Mangold	(d/o Frederick & Frederica (Ehley))
B-205	Mangold	Amelia
B-593	Mangold	Caroline
B-1023	Mangold	Charles
B-593	Mangold	Frederic
B-898	Mangold	Frederick
B-767	Mangold	Frederick
B-205	Mangold	Friederick
B-1023	Mangold	John
B-593	Mangold	John
M-603	Mangold	John M
B-530	Mangold	Leah
M-462	Mangold	Margeret
B-898	Mangold	Mary
M-951	Mangold	Sarah
B-1452	Mantz	Abbey
B-1669	Mantz	Alvena
B-1597	Mantz	Bula
B-719	Mantz	Carrie
B-1128	Mantz	Carrie
B-1316	Mantz	Charles
D-1052	Mantz	Clara
B-1676	Mantz	Edna
B-1616	Mantz	Elias
B-1420	Mantz	Elias
B-1616	Mantz	Elias
B-1319	Mantz	Elizabeth
M-157	Mantz	Elizabeth
M-564	Mantz	Emaline
M-756	Mantz	Emaline
B-990	Mantz	Emma
B-1655	Mantz	Estella
B-1489	Mantz	Eugene
D-759	Mantz	Francis
B-1135	Mantz	Francis
B-719	Mantz	Francis
B-1135	Mantz	Francis G
B-1390	Mantz	Francis G
B-1489	Mantz	Francis G
B-1597	Mantz	Francis G
B-1375	Mantz	Harrie
D-1130	Mantz	Ida

Line #	Surname	Given Name	Line #	Surname	Given Name
B-1285	Lynn	Daniel	B-1676	Mantz	J F
B-1422	Lynn	Ellen	M-914	Mantz	J. F.
B-1348	Lynn	Ellen Jane	D-690	Mantz	Jacob
M-638	Lynn	Ellen Jane	B-1375	Mantz	Jacob
B-1035	Lynn	Harrison	B-990	Mantz	James
B-1374	Lynn	Judith	B-1391	Mantz	James
B-759	Lynn	Korah	D-1265	Mantz	John
B-1285	Lynn	Mary	D-692	Mantz	Josiah
B-1192	Lynn	Sarah	B-959	Mantz	Lewis
B-959	Mantz	Lewis	B-561	Maurer	Emma
B-1128	Mantz	Lewis	M-627	Maurer	Frank
B-1316	Mantz	Lewis	B-561	Maurer	Franklin
B-1655	Mantz	Lewis	B-749	Maurer	Franklin
B-719	Mantz	Lewis	B-1004	Maurer	Franklin
B-1815	Mantz	Lewis	D-726	Maurer	George
M-122	Mantz	Lewis F	D-1128	Maurer	George
M-918	Mantz	Lizzie	B-1004	Maurer	George
D-1334	Mantz	Mary	D-958	Maurer	Ida
B-1391	Mantz	Mary	B-1028	Maurer	Ida
B-155	Mantz	Mary Ann	B-280	Maury	Carolina
M-948	Mantz	Milton C	B-771	Maury	Ellemena
B-1420	Mantz	Minnie	B-668	Maury	Elmina
M-443	Mantz	Moses D	B-1210	Maury	Fanny C
D-1343	Mantz	Nathan	B-91	Maute	Eva
M-1150	Mantz	Oliver L	M-166	May	Anthony
B-1387	Mantz	Polly Jane	B-3	May	Charles
B-1390	Mantz	Sabina	M-174	Mayer	Polly
M-1079	Mantz	Valeria A	B-1417	McClean	Amacin
M-204	Mantz	William H	D-927	McClean	Mary
M-1146	Mantz	Lizzie E	B-1417	McClean	Robert
D-336	Marccom	Catherine	D-956	McClean	Thomson
M-545	Marcomc	Anjuline Jane	M-184	McDaniel	Caroline
B-49	Marecome	Eliza	D-596	McDaniel	Edna
B-1376	Markel	Charles F	M-243	McDaniel	Elamantina
M-685	Markel	Charles W	B-1764	McDaniel	Ella
B-1376	Markel	Emma	B-276	McDaniel	Emma
M-950	Markell	William H	B-1746	McDaniel	Emma Martha
M-562	Markley	Benjamin	M-1020	McDaniel	Emma Martha
D-250	Markley	Caroline	M-1145	McDaniel	James E
M-1128	Markley	Clara	B-1764	McDaniel	James Erwin
D-251	Markley	Dennis	M-1012	McDaniel	James Erwin
B-235	Markley	Elmer	B-276	McDaniel	John Thomson
D-149	Markley	Elwin	B-870	McDaniel	Lucinda
B-658	Markley	Eugene	B-949	McDaniel	Lucinda
B-251	Markley	Hattie	B-984	McDaniel	Puriette
M-764	Markley	Jonah J	M-605	McDaniel	Reuben
D-561	Markley	Lewis	B-119	McDaniel	Robert
B-60	Markley	Sarah	B-377	McDaniel	Robert
B-235	Markley	Stephen	B-761	McDaniel	Robert
B-251	Markley	Tilghman	B-984	McDaniel	Robert
B-658	Markley	Tilghman	B-984	McDaniel	Thomas
M-265	Markley	Tilghman	M-485	McDaniel	Thomas
M-449	Markley	William Franklin	M-1082	McDaniel	Thomas
D-977	Markley	Zeniah	B-1641	McFarland	Amanda E
D-903	Marks	Ida	B-1751	McFarland	Amanda Eliza
B-1882	Marsh	Alda V	B-1806	McFarland	Amanda Eliza
B-1345	Martz	Mary Ann	M-577	McFarland	Catherine
B-257	Math	Sarah	M-211	McFarland	Edward

Line #	Surname	Given Name
D-711	Maurer	Alice
D-524	Maurer	Caroline
D-647	Maurer	Charles
B-749	Maurer	Charles
B-1028	Maurer	Edwin
D-1337	Maurer	Elizabeth
D-568	Maurer	Emma
B-1728	McFarland	John J
B-1821	McFarland	John J
B-1822	McFarland	John J
B-297	McFarland	Joseph
B-1728	McFarland	Rachel
B-1822	McFarland	Vertie
B-130	McFarland	Wesley
B-172	McGinlay	Henry
B-172	McGinlay	Robert
D-970	Mclaughlin	Reuben (s/o Edwin & Kate)
D-1274	McLean	Elsie
M-791	Mclean	Emaline
B-1811	Mclean	Emma
D-753	McLean	Jennie
D-1306	Mclean	John
M-617	McLean	John
B-1685	McLean	Lettie
M-1122	Mclean	Lillie
M-862	Mclean	Mary Jane
D-743	McLean	Memphis
B-1685	McLean	Robert
D-1158	McLean	Thomas
B-1321	McWilliams	M.J.
B-1321	McWilliams	Thomas
B-1706	Mearhoff	Eliza
B-1792	Mearhoff	Eliza
B-460	Meckes	Annetta
B-459	Meckes	Henry
B-459	Meckes	Joseph
B-460	Meckes	Joseph
B-321	Meckes	Samuel
B-460	Meckes	Samuel
B-750	Meckes	Samuel L
M-420	Meckes	Samuel L
B-750	Meckes	Tillie
D-549	Meckes	William
B-1066	Meensing	Ammon
B-1064	Meensing	Charles
B-1065	Meensing	Charles
B-1064	Meensing	Sarah Catherine
B-1065	Meensing	Sarah Catherine
B-1066	Meensing	William
B-807	Mehrcam	Peter
B-867	Mehrcam	Peter
B-1598	Mehrhoff	Eliza
M-702	Mehrkam	Sarah Jane
B-3	Meinhard	Charles
B-3	Meinhard	Charles
B-421	Meinhart	Charles
B-421	Meinhart	Conrad
D-346	Meinhart	Elizabeth

Line #	Surname	Given Name
D-408	McFarland	Ellenora
B-1821	McFarland	Elmer
B-297	McFarland	Emma
B-634	McFarland	Frank
B-130	McFarland	Henry
B-634	McFarland	Henry
B-499	Mcfarland	Henry
M-923	Meitzler	John Calvin
B-1333	Meitzler	Josiah Benjamin
M-662	Meitzler	Josiah Benjamin
B-1677	Meitzler	Minnie
D-276	Mencke	Anna
M-59	Mencke	Frederic
B-188	Mencke	Friederich
M-278	Mencke	Friederich
B-188	Mencke	Louisa
M-942	Mengel	Emma
D-1215	Mengel	Ida
B-1693	Mengel	Regina
B-1158	Mengel	Sarah
M-214	Mensing	Ammon
M-175	Mensing	Sarah Catherine
B-337	Merkel	Lewis
B-337	Merkel	Theodore
M-997	Merkel	Zeriah
B-1021	Merkley	Benjamin
B-767	Merkley	Frederick
B-1021	Merkley	Homer
B-1021	Merkley	Jonas
B-217	Merkley	Martha
B-767	Merkley	Stephen
B-217	Merkley	Thomas
B-1562	Mertz	Adam
B-371	Mertz	Agnew
B-482	Mertz	Alfred
B-697	Mertz	Alfred
B-698	Mertz	Alfred
B-1101	Mertz	Alfred
B-1269	Mertz	Alfred
B-1395	Mertz	Alfred
B-1562	Mertz	Alfred
B-542	Mertz	Alwin
B-1301	Mertz	Amanda
B-1475	Mertz	Anna
B-176	Mertz	Anna
B-95	Mertz	Anna Maria
B-596	Mertz	Anna Maria
M-31	Mertz	Anna Maria
B-1718	Mertz	Arthur
D-975	Mertz	Charles
B-1695	Mertz	Cora Alice
M-916	Mertz	Cora Alice
B-1528	Mertz	Edwin
B-1459	Mertz	Edwin
B-1547	Mertz	Edwin
M-761	Mertz	Edwin
B-334	Mertz	Ella
B-82	Mertz	Ellamanda

Line #	Surname	Given Name
B-34	Meinhart	Sarah Ann
B-817	Meinhart	Sarah Ann
M-1049	Meitzler	Elamanda P.T.
B-1333	Meitzler	Jacob
B-1677	Meitzler	John Calvin
M-454	Mertz	Ellen
D-1082	Mertz	Emaline
B-1105	Mertz	Emma
B-1269	Mertz	Emma
M-947	Mertz	Emma
D-829	Mertz	Eva
M-974	Mertz	Frank
B-1394	Mertz	George
B-1528	Mertz	Granville
M-795	Mertz	Granville
B-1395	Mertz	Harrie
B-482	Mertz	Harrieta
B-1915	Mertz	Harvey
B-1911	Mertz	Hattie
D-1083	Mertz	Henry
B-896	Mertz	Ida
B-1459	Mertz	Ida
B-176	Mertz	Irwin
B-768	Mertz	Jefferson
B-176	Mertz	Joannah
B-542	Mertz	Joannah
M-196	Mertz	Joannah
B-859	Mertz	Johannah
B-1718	Mertz	John R
B-1831	Mertz	John R
M-988	Mertz	John R
D-179	Mertz	Jonathan
D-462	Mertz	Joseph
B-1394	Mertz	Joseph
B-1475	Mertz	Joseph
B-1543	Mertz	Joseph
B-1911	Mertz	Joseph
B-1797	Mertz	Kate
B-1837	Mertz	Kate
M-975	Mertz	Kate
B-1543	Mertz	Lillie
B-1547	Mertz	Lillie
B-1831	Mertz	Mable
B-1101	Mertz	Magdalene
B-859	Mertz	Mary
B-1463	Mertz	Mary
B-1518	Mertz	Mary
B-1920	Mertz	Mary A
M-1162	Mertz	Mary A
B-585	Mertz	Mary Ann
B-1630	Mertz	Mary Ann
B-1714	Mertz	Mary Ann
M-380	Mertz	Mary Ann
M-722	Mertz	Mary Ann
B-804	Mertz	Mary Ann
B-1301	Mertz	Nathan
B-82	Mertz	Nathan
B-371	Mertz	Nathan
B-350	Mertz	Ellen
B-595	Mertz	Ellen
B-872	Mertz	Ellen
B-1118	Mertz	Ellen
M-347	Mertz	Ellen
M-95	Mertz	Nathan
B-698	Mertz	Robert
D-394	Mertz	Sally
B-1915	Mertz	Samuel
B-1961	Mertz	Samuel
M-1064	Mertz	Samuel
M-989	Mertz	Sarah E
B-697	Mertz	Scottie
M-960	Mertz	Thomas
B-896	Mertz	Wilford
B-1961	Mertz	William
B-176	Mertz	William
B-542	Mertz	William
B-859	Mertz	William
B-585	Mertz	William
M-196	Mertz	William
M-281	Messinger	Frederic
B-704	Metzger	Christoph
B-327	Metzger	Christopher
D-83	Metzger	Daniel
B-327	Metzger	Ellemanda
B-704	Metzger	Francis
D-434	Metzger	Sophia
M-154	Meyer	Christian C H
B-972	Meyer	Frederich
B-972	Meyer	Frederick
B-972	Meyer	Frederick Wilhelm
B-898	Meyer	Jacob
M-441	Meyers	Ada
B-913	Meyers	Fanny
B-914	Meyers	Fanny
B-915	Meyers	Fanny
M-848	Meyers	George R
D-665	Michael	George
M-7	Mildenberger	Harriet
D-563	Milheim	Harrison
D-357	Milheim	Robert
B-994	Milheim	William
M-413	Milheim	William
B-613	Milherin	Harrison
B-41	Milherin	Robert
B-41	Milherin	William
B-613	Milherin	William
D-674	Miller	(d/o Alexander S. & Mary E.)
B-1308	Miller	Aaron
D-1222	Miller	Absalom
B-1638	Miller	Albright M
B-1472	Miller	Albright Mahlon
M-755	Miller	Albright Mahlon
B-432	Miller	Alexander
M-48	Miller	Alexander
D-299	Miller	Alexandra
B-792	Miller	Alice

Line #	Surname	Given Name	Line #	Surname	Given Name
B-768	Mertz	Nathan	B-1112	Miller	Alice
B-1105	Mertz	Nathan	B-1764	Miller	Alice Cora
B-1301	Mertz	Nathan	M-1012	Miller	Alice Cora
M-648	Miller	Alice M	B-255	Miller	Frederic
D-167	Miller	Alwin	B-317	Miller	Frederic
B-1155	Miller	Amanda	B-851	Miller	Frederick
M-80	Miller	Amanda	D-1284	Miller	Gabriel
M-368	Miller	Amanda	D-489	Miller	George
B-381	Miller	Amos	B-758	Miller	George
B-1235	Miller	Amos R	B-1523	Miller	George
D-136	Miller	Anna	B-376	Miller	George
B-255	Miller	Anna	B-1189	Miller	Hannah
B-1149	Miller	Anna	B-1418	Miller	Hannah
B-927	Miller	Anna	B-311	Miller	Hannah
B-501	Miller	Anzonetta	B-1340	Miller	Harriet
M-375	Miller	Anzonetta	B-1444	Miller	Harriet
M-1153	Miller	Calvin A	B-1081	Miller	Harriet L
D-209	Miller	Caroline	B-1492	Miller	Harriet L
B-207	Miller	Caroline	M-533	Miller	Harriet L
B-1264	Miller	Carrie	B-1901	Miller	Harry
B-1472	Miller	Carrie	B-1208	Miller	Harvey
B-1643	Miller	Carrie	B-1719	Miller	Hattie
D-611	Miller	Catherine	M-920	Miller	Hebron
D-1295	Miller	Catherine	B-758	Miller	Henry
B-490	Miller	Catherine	B-1022	Miller	Henry
B-797	Miller	Catherine	B-1283	Miller	Henry
B-1035	Miller	Catherine	M-877	Miller	Henry Franklin
B-1171	Miller	Catherine	D-494	Miller	Jacob
M-118	Miller	Catherine	B-432	Miller	Jacob
M-394	Miller	Catherine	B-1264	Miller	James A
M-403	Miller	Cecilia	M-632	Miller	James A
B-379	Miller	Charles	M-304	Miller	James D
M-97	Miller	Charles	M-905	Miller	Jane
M-203	Miller	Charles	D-1099	Miller	Joel
B-26	Miller	Charles	D-133	Miller	John
M-1028	Miller	Charles O	D-1114	Miller	John
D-490	Miller	Christianna	B-450	Miller	John
D-1103	Miller	Cora	M-76	Miller	John A
D-852	Miller	Daniel	M-557	Miller	John Henry
B-1412	Miller	David	M-416	Miller	Jonathan
B-1523	Miller	David	M-153	Miller	Joseph R
B-1643	Miller	David	B-699	Miller	Josiah
B-1719	Miller	David	B-1301	Miller	Josiah
M-998	Miller	Edward	B-383	Miller	July Ann
B-1366	Miller	Edwin	B-1122	Miller	Kate
B-1456	Miller	Eli	B-1265	Miller	Kate
M-35	Miller	Elias C	B-1658	Miller	Kate
D-1025	Miller	Eliza	M-593	Miller	Kate
B-856	Miller	Elizabeth	D-986	Miller	Katie
B-237	Miller	Elizabeth	B-1285	Miller	Kitty Ann
B-1638	Miller	Ella	M-322	Miller	Kitty Ann
M-898	Miller	Elmira	B-1830	Miller	Laura Anna
B-1789	Miller	Elmira	B-815	Miller	Leah
B-1434	Miller	Emma Alice	D-427	Miller	Lena
M-734	Miller	Emma Alice	D-1181	Miller	Levi
M-481	Miller	Emma Jane	M-1135	Miller	Levi A
B-1943	Miller	Emma Louisa	B-805	Miller	Lewis A
M-141	Miller	Emma Susanna	B-1092	Miller	Livie

Line #	Surname	Given Name	Line #	Surname	Given Name
M-387	Miller	Francis Douglas	B-805	Miller	Lizzie
M-1033	Miller	Lizzie	M-826	Miller	Sarah Amanda
B-58	Miller	Lydia	B-186	Miller	Sarah C
B-600	Miller	Lydia	M-107	Miller	Sarah C
B-207	Miller	Mahlon	B-1028	Miller	Sarah Jane
B-490	Miller	Malvenia	M-296	Miller	Sevilla
B-1412	Miller	Mamie	B-1092	Miller	Solomon
M-1187	Miller	Mamie V	B-1208	Miller	Solomon
B-869	Miller	Manda	D-1111	Miller	Susanna
D-471	Miller	Maria	B-1690	Miller	Susanna
D-1078	Miller	Maria	B-1786	Miller	Susanna Alvaretta
B-1299	Miller	Maria	M-913	Miller	Susannah
B-415	Miller	Maria	B-1308	Miller	Ulalia
B-1081	Miller	Maria	D-98	Miller	William
B-1149	Miller	Maria	D-110	Miller	William
M-57	Miller	Marlon	B-1022	Miller	William
D-1119	Miller	Mary	B-1235	Miller	William
B-1279	Miller	Mary	B-450	Miller	William
B-780	Miller	Mary	B-1279	Miller	William
B-1412	Miller	Mary	M-305	Miller	William F
B-1643	Miller	Mary	M-332	Miller	William F
B-1719	Miller	Mary	M-1079	Miller	William H
B-1846	Miller	Mary	M-159	Millheim	Charles
B-665	Miller	Mary	D-177	Millheim	John
B-1716	Miller	Mary	D-452	Millheim	Louisa
M-85	Miller	Mary	M-151	Millheim	William
M-771	Miller	Mary	B-1310	Millhouse	Amanda
B-931	Miller	Mary	B-1662	Millhouse	Amanda
M-953	Miller	Mary	B-444	Mimm	Katie
B-1771	Miller	Mary A	B-444	Mimm	Levi
B-1523	Miller	Mary Ann	M-706	Mimm	Wilson F
M-77	Miller	Mary Jane	M-594	Miner	Levi
M-83	Miller	Mary Jane	B-1044	Miner	Mary Ann
B-1049	Miller	Matilda	M-885	Minnich	John
B-1361	Miller	Matilda	B-565	Minnich	Matilida
M-554	Miller	Matilda	M-784	Modder	Lucetta
M-602	Miller	Matilda	B-1929	Mohr	Ivy M
D-942	Miller	Nathan	M-429	Montz	Adaline
B-1366	Miller	Nathan	B-495	Montz	Alwenia
M-1018	Miller	Oliver D	D-592	Montz	Carrie
M-628	Miller	Peter Richard	B-235	Montz	Cassanta
B-514	Miller	Polly	B-495	Montz	Cassius
M-215	Miller	Polly	B-235	Montz	Cassius
B-1171	Miller	Rebecca	M-316	Montz	Cassius
B-514	Miller	Rebecca	B-322	Montz	Elizabeth
B-760	Miller	Rebecca	B-1034	Montz	Emaline
D-968	Miller	Reuben	B-848	Montz	Francis
B-931	Miller	Richard	B-495	Montz	Jacob
B-1901	Miller	Robert	D-627	Montz	Joseph
B-1283	Miller	Rosa	M-470	Montz	Josiah
M-1048	Miller	Sallie Ann	B-236	Montz	Maria
B-442	Miller	Sally Ann	B-647	Montz	Maria
D-126	Miller	Sarah	B-217	Montz	Maria
D-153	Miller	Sarah	D-1044	Montz	Mary
M-68	Miller	Sarah	B-903	Montz	Mary
M-108	Miller	Sarah	B-515	Montz	Mary Ann
M-740	Miller	Sarah	B-676	Montz	Mary Ann
B-848	Montz	Sarah	B-578	Moser	Rosa Ann

Line #	Surname	Given Name	Line #	Surname	Given Name
B-767	Montz	Zeniah	M-411	Moser	Rosa Ann
B-784	Moran	Frank	B-51	Moser	Sally
B-262	Moran	Mary	B-717	Moser	Sophia
B-262	Moran	William	B-1537	Moser	Susan E
B-784	Moran	William	B-893	Moser	Susanna
M-1178	Morder	Annie	B-391	Moser	William
B-1182	Morey	Dora	B-1448	Moser	Wilson
B-1288	Morey	Dora	M-561	Mosteller	William H
M-1065	Morgan	Catherine	B-660	Moulthrop	Aniza
M-857	Morgan	Frederick James	B-1205	Moulthrop	Annetta
M-765	Morrison	James L	B-1914	Moulthrop	Cledous
D-681	Moser	Adaline	B-453	Moulthrop	Edgar
B-922	Moser	Adaline	B-1914	Moulthrop	Edgar Ulysses
B-1524	Moser	Alavesta	D-582	Moulthrop	Elizabeth
B-1575	Moser	Alavesta	B-222	Moulthrop	Henry
M-759	Moser	Alavesta K	B-453	Moulthrop	John F
B-1447	Moser	Albert David	B-739	Moulthrop	John Francis
B-1448	Moser	Albert David	B-964	Moulthrop	John Francis
M-943	Moser	Alvenia	B-1199	Moulthrop	John Francis
B-220	Moser	Amanda	M-374	Moulthrop	John Francis
M-223	Moser	Amanda	B-1199	Moulthrop	Lambert
D-28	Moser	Anderson	B-964	Moulthrop	Lillie
D-785	Moser	Austin	B-739	Moulthrop	Minnie
B-1141	Moser	Austin	B-222	Moulthrop	William H
B-1141	Moser	Benjamin F	B-660	Moulthrop	William H H
B-1874	Moser	Benjamin Franklin	B-1205	Moulthrop	William H H
M-598	Moser	Benjamin Franklin	M-28	Moulthrop	William HH
D-1290	Moser	Catherine	B-1704	Moyer	_____
B-1733	Moser	David M	B-546	Moyer	Abraham
M-933	Moser	David M	B-957	Moyer	Abraham
B-389	Moser	Edward	D-529	Moyer	Agnes
B-1447	Moser	Edward	B-1558	Moyer	Agnes
B-1473	Moser	Emaline	B-772	Moyer	Amelia
M-338	Moser	Emaline	B-510	Moyer	B J
B-602	Moser	Emma	B-1033	Moyer	Caroline
D-618	Moser	Estella	B-563	Moyer	Catherine
D-284	Moser	Henry	B-731	Moyer	Catherine
B-390	Moser	Hester	B-800	Moyer	Catherine
B-755	Moser	Jacob	B-967	Moyer	Catherine
B-922	Moser	Jacob	M-442	Moyer	Catherine
B-1102	Moser	Jacob	D-157	Moyer	Charles
D-610	Moser	John	D-641	Moyer	Charles
B-755	Moser	John	B-11	Moyer	Charles
B-717	Moser	Joseph	B-308	Moyer	Clara
B-389	Moser	Joseph David	M-230	Moyer	Clara
B-390	Moser	Joseph David	M-798	Moyer	Cornelius Phaon
B-391	Moser	Joseph David	B-546	Moyer	Daniel
D-294	Moser	Leanna	M-61	Moyer	Daniel
M-322	Moser	Lewis	D-1198	Moyer	David
B-1733	Moser	Luellen	B-957	Moyer	David
B-629	Moser	Manda	M-843	Moyer	David
D-881	Moser	Minnie	M-574	Moyer	Elias
B-1102	Moser	Minnie	D-130	Moyer	Elizabeth
B-1874	Moser	Raymond	B-124	Moyer	Elizabeth
B-135	Moser	Rosa Ann	B-1033	Moyer	Elizabeth
M-34	Moyer	Ellen	D-386	Moyer	Thomas
B-525	Moyer	Elphina	B-803	Moyer	William
M-240	Moyer	Elphina	M-730	Muffley	Josiah

Line #	Surname	Given Name	Line #	Surname	Given Name
D-67	Moyer	Emma	B-1429	Muffley	Sallie A
B-310	Moyer	Emma	M-640	Muffley	Sally A
B-1648	Moyer	Emma	B-1671	Muffly	Lizzie
B-1704	Moyer	Emma	M-484	Muhlbach	Charles Gustav
M-910	Moyer	Emma	B-1114	Mulharen	Anna
B-1654	Moyer	Emma Cather	B-1286	Mulharen	Anna
M-927	Moyer	Emma Catherine	M-568	Mulharen	Anna
B-510	Moyer	Erastes	B-1622	Mulharen	Anna
B-11	Moyer	Franklin	B-965	Mulharen	Edward
M-26	Moyer	Franklin	B-965	Mulharen	Mary
B-803	Moyer	Frederic	B-132	Mulhearn	Charles
B-1191	Moyer	Frederic	B-132	Mulhearn	Edward
B-1191	Moyer	Frederic W	B-239	Mulhearn	Edward
B-1704	Moyer	Harrison	B-765	Mulhearn	Edward
B-1512	Moyer	Ida	B-1329	Mulhearn	Edward F
B-1557	Moyer	Ida	B-1329	Mulhearn	Ida
B-1679	Moyer	Ida	B-239	Mulhearn	Lilie
B-1717	Moyer	Ida	B-890	Mulhearn	Rosa Ann
B-1756	Moyer	Ida	M-179	Mulhearn	Rosa Ann
B-1809	Moyer	Ida	B-765	Mulhearn	Rosalee
B-1852	Moyer	Ida	B-1746	Mumbower	Elmer
B-1893	Moyer	Ida	M-1020	Mumbower	Elmer
M-788	Moyer	Ida	B-1746	Mumbower	Harry
D-766	Moyer	Isaac	M-872	Mummer	Milton
B-129	Moyer	Isaac	D-574	Muschlitz	Abel
B-362	Moyer	Isaac	D-86	Muschlitz	Elizabeth
B-725	Moyer	Isaac	D-545	Muschlitz	Elizabeth
B-1033	Moyer	Jacob	B-179	Muschlitz	Elizabeth
D-920	Moyer	John	B-947	Muschlitz	Mary Ann
B-401	Moyer	John	M-539	Muschlitz	Mary Ann
B-772	Moyer	John	B-966	Muschlitz	Robert
D-773	Moyer	John	B-179	Muschlitz	Robert
M-224	Moyer	John	B-947	Muschlitz	Robert
B-1558	Moyer	Jonas Isaac	B-599	Muschlitz	Sarah
M-806	Moyer	Jonas Isaac	B-64	Muschlitz	Sylvester
B-1063	Moyer	Kate	B-64	Muschlitz	William
M-1081	Moyer	Katie Ann R	B-966	Muschlitz	William
B-308	Moyer	Lafayette	M-310	Muschlitz	Wilson
M-152	Moyer	Lafayette	D-1018	Musselman	Charles
B-1191	Moyer	Maria	B-1321	Musselman	Elizabeth
B-401	Moyer	Mary	M-654	Musselman	Elizabeth
B-773	Moyer	Mary	D-140	Musselman	Harriet
B-1416	Moyer	Mary	B-85	Musselman	Harrison
B-311	Moyer	Mary Ann	B-85	Musselman	Ida
M-305	Moyer	Mary Elizabeth	M-888	Musselman	John H
D-207	Moyer	Morris	B-581	Musselman	Lizzie
D-602	Moyer	Owen	B-1428	Musselman	Mable
D-231	Moyer	Salome	D-194	Musselman	Magdalena
B-498	Moyer	Sarah	D-313	Musselman	Oliver
B-928	Moyer	Sarah	B-148	Musselman	Reuben
B-192	Moyer	Sarah Amanda	B-1428	Musselman	Thomas
B-505	Moyer	Sarah Amanda	M-138	Musselman	Thomas
B-1240	Moyer	Susanna	B-740	Muth	Sarah
M-1081	Muthard	David M	B-1702	Neumayer	Mary Ann
B-1926	Muthard	Martha	B-593	Neunstiel	Caroline
B-1909	Muthard	Nora	B-65	Newhard	Allen
B-1868	Muthard	William	B-65	Newhard	John
B-1868	Muthard	William H	B-887	Newhart	Derias William

Line #	Surname	Given Name	Line #	Surname	Given Name
B-1909	Muthard	William H	M-170	Newhart	Elizabeth
B-1926	Muthard	William H	M-430	Newhart	John
B-1145	Muthart	Daniel	M-1161	Newhart	John M
M-650	Muthart	Edwin K	M-178	Newhart	Lenah
B-1473	Muthart	Katie	M-329	Newhart	Michael
B-1473	Muthart	Levi	B-887	Newhart	Minnie
B-1145	Muthart	Willie	B-1057	Newhart	Miranda
B-602	Muthhart	Levi	B-663	Newhart	Miranda Louisa
B-602	Muthhart	William	M-425	Newhart	Miranda Louisa
B-686	Nace	Benjamin	M-855	Newhart	Rosa L
B-686	Nace	Quincy	B-569	Newhart	Sarah
M-1	Nagel	Priscilla	B-251	Newhart	Sarah
B-283	Nanstiel	Edward	B-588	Newhart	Sarah
B-283	Nanstiel	Henry	B-1020	Newhart	Sarah
D-365	Nanstiel	John	M-890	Nichlas	Comilla
B-22	Nanstiel	John	M-783	Nicholas	Amandes
B-22	Nanstiel	John A	B-60	Nicholous	Benjamin
B-1794	Neff	Amanda	B-60	Nicholous	Irwin
M-977	Neff	Amanda Jane	D-265	Nise	William
B-656	Neff	Caroline	B-143	Nitche	Amelia
B-772	Neff	Caroline	B-143	Nitche	William
D-814	Neff	Charles	B-78	Nitsche	Pauline Barta
M-1126	Neff	George Henry	B-78	Nitsche	William
B-1222	Neff	Harry	B-114	Nitschie	William
B-880	Neff	Henry	B-452	Noll	Aaron
B-1222	Neff	John	B-671	Noll	Aaron
B-1750	Neff	Lewis	B-1290	Noll	Aaron
M-636	Neff	Louisa S	B-1766	Noll	Aaron
B-798	Neff	Maria	M-379	Noll	Aaron
M-253	Neff	Maria	B-105	Noll	Alvin
M-517	Neff	Oscar A	B-1656	Noll	Alvin
M-1174	Neff	Oscar A	B-1470	Noll	Alvin Henry
B-880	Neff	Paul	B-547	Noll	Ambrose
B-1750	Neff	Paul	M-1120	Noll	Ambrose E
D-896	Neff	Salome	B-671	Noll	Angeline
B-361	Neier	George	B-547	Noll	Augustus
B-361	Neier	Isaac	B-1154	Noll	Bessie
M-942	Neifert	George Albert	B-417	Noll	Charles
B-7	Neitzel	Emma	B-1156	Noll	Emma
B-741	Neitzel	Emma	M-476	Noll	Emma
B-1293	Neitzel	Emma	B-452	Noll	Harrison
B-7	Neitzel	Rebecca	B-1656	Noll	Harvey
M-603	Nennstiel	Caroline	B-1470	Noll	Minerva
D-255	Nesley	Agnes	D-813	Noll	Oliver
M-247	Nesley	Hannah F	B-1290	Noll	Sally
M-586	Nesley	William	B-105	Noll	William
D-809	Nester	Alfred	B-417	Noll	William
D-810	Nester	Rosa	B-1154	Noll	William
D-1279	Neumayer	Charles	B-1542	Norwood	Maria
D-1113	Neumayer	Harry	B-1460	Nothstein	Alvin
M-756	Neumayer	John	M-280	Nothstein	Alvin
B-228	Nothstein	Alwin	B-1429	Nothstein	John Henry
B-557	Nothstein	Alwin	M-640	Nothstein	John Henry
B-135	Nothstein	Ammon	B-1001	Nothstein	Jonas
M-557	Nothstein	Anna Jane	B-271	Nothstein	Joseph
B-1093	Nothstein	Benjamin	B-1594	Nothstein	Josiah
B-1280	Nothstein	Benjamin	B-509	Nothstein	Kitty Ann
D-1153	Nothstein	Calvin	B-1093	Nothstein	Laura

Line #	Surname	Given Name
B-1620	Nothstein	Calvin
B-478	Nothstein	Charles
B-823	Nothstein	Charles
B-1916	Nothstein	Charles H
B-1936	Nothstein	Charles H
B-1960	Nothstein	Charles H
B-1429	Nothstein	Claudius
B-464	Nothstein	Conrad H
B-341	Nothstein	Daniel
B-989	Nothstein	David
B-426	Nothstein	Dennis
B-646	Nothstein	Dennis
B-1137	Nothstein	Dennis
B-426	Nothstein	Elias
B-341	Nothstein	Ellen
B-1077	Nothstein	Ellen
B-483	Nothstein	Ellen
M-349	Nothstein	Ellen
B-152	Nothstein	Emaline
D-1056	Nothstein	Emma
B-823	Nothstein	Emma
B-1092	Nothstein	Ephraim
B-1780	Nothstein	Etta
B-1666	Nothstein	Eva
B-1193	Nothstein	Flora
B-1653	Nothstein	Flora
B-1001	Nothstein	Flora Ann
B-1444	Nothstein	Flora Ann
B-1606	Nothstein	Flora Ann
M-571	Nothstein	Flora Ann
M-129	Nothstein	Fyanna
B-1786	Nothstein	George
B-37	Nothstein	Gideon
M-244	Nothstein	Harriet
B-135	Nothstein	Henry
B-1786	Nothstein	Henry Adam
B-1218	Nothstein	Jacob
B-989	Nothstein	James H
M-855	Nothstein	James M
B-478	Nothstein	John
B-496	Nothstein	John
B-503	Nothstein	John
B-509	Nothstein	John
B-833	Nothstein	John
B-1105	Nothstein	John
B-1317	Nothstein	John
B-806	Nothstein	John
B-1248	Nothstein	John H
M-890	Nothstein	John F
D-973	Nunnemacher	Mary
M-650	Nunnemacher	Sarah
M-670	Nuss	W.A.
B-342	O Brian	David O
B-342	O Brian	Scott
B-198	O'Brian	Benjamin
B-1119	O'Brian	Charles
B-198	O'Brian	David
B-189	O'Brian	Ellen

Line #	Surname	Given Name
D-485	Nothstein	Leah
B-426	Nothstein	Leah
M-44	Nothstein	Leannah
B-408	Nothstein	Lewis
B-1117	Nothstein	Lewis F
B-1260	Nothstein	Lewis F
B-1594	Nothstein	Lewis F
M-432	Nothstein	Lewis F
B-408	Nothstein	Maehlon
B-1916	Nothstein	Mande
B-228	Nothstein	Mary
B-1117	Nothstein	Mary
B-1936	Nothstein	Mary
M-547	Nothstein	Mary E
B-1620	Nothstein	Milton
B-1666	Nothstein	Milton
B-1780	Nothstein	Milton
B-1910	Nothstein	Milton
M-903	Nothstein	Milton
B-478	Nothstein	Nathan
M-758	Nothstein	Nelson Thomas
B-1460	Nothstein	Pearce
D-50	Nothstein	Peter
D-1135	Nothstein	Raymond
B-1910	Nothstein	Sadie
B-1364	Nothstein	Sally
B-989	Nothstein	Sarah
B-1193	Nothstein	Sophia
B-408	Nothstein	Wallace
B-1960	Nothstein	Warren
B-464	Nothstein	William
B-557	Nothstein	William
B-1218	Nothstein	William
B-1260	Nothstein	William
B-1956	Nunamacher	Ida
M-43	Nunamacker	Frank. Washington
D-148	Nunamacker	Mary
D-1086	Nunemaker	Lewis
B-1197	Nunemaker	Priscilla
B-1383	Nunnamacher	Abraham
B-1384	Nunnamacher	Abraham
B-1383	Nunnamacher	Alice
B-1384	Nunnamacher	Kora
M-694	Nunnamacher	Sarah R
D-1170	Nunnemacher	Catharine
B-1531	Nunnemacher	George
D-979	Nunnemacher	Harriet
D-912	Nunnemacher	James
B-1531	Nunnemacher	Lewis
M-839	Ohl	Jefferson
B-1104	Ohl	John
D-971	Ohl	Joseph
B-1661	Ohl	Louisa
B-1364	Ohl	Manda
B-1625	Ohl	Mary
M-973	Ohl	Mary J
B-1368	Ohl	Milton
M-904	Ohl	Nathan

Line #	Surname	Given Name	Line #	Surname	Given Name
D-63	O'Brian	Emma	B-1431	Ohl	Oliver
B-232	O'Brian	Franklin	B-1368	Ohl	Owen
B-63	O'Brian	Harriet	B-1486	Ohl	Owen
B-386	O'Brian	Harriet	B-1615	Ohl	Owen
B-1060	O'Brian	Harriet	M-689	Ohl	Owen
B-1257	O'Brian	Harriet	B-1364	Ohl	William
M-54	O'Brian	Harriet	M-1057	Ohl	William F
B-893	O'Brian	Harriet	B-1757	Oldt	A F
D-135	O'Brian	Henry	M-1022	Oldt	A. F.
D-46	O'Brian	John	D-1313	Oldt	Benjamin
B-232	O'Brian	Joseph	B-1757	Oldt	Carrie
B-571	O'Brian	Joseph	M-819	Oldt	Emma I
B-1119	O'Brian	Joseph	M-614	Olenwine	Amandes
B-1243	O'Brian	Joseph	B-98	Olenwine	Catherine
D-1155	O'Brian	Lydia	M-134	Olenwine	Charles
D-548	O'Brian	Mary	D-649	Olenwine	Elizabeth
B-571	O'Brian	Mary	B-633	Olenwine	Sarah Ann
B-1243	O'Brian	Minnie	M-330	Olenwine	Simeon
D-615	O'Brian	Samuel	D-474	Olewine	John
B-189	O'Brian	Samuel	M-595	Olewine	Susan Ann
B-893	O'Brian	Samuel	M-682	Olewine	William H
M-227	O'Brian	Samuel	B-237	O'Niel	Lilie
M-615	O'Brian	Susan E	B-237	O'Niel	William
M-886	O'Brien	Hattie	B-906	Onwalt	Adam
B-1006	Odenwelder	Mary C	B-906	Onwalt	Samuel
B-1121	Ohl	Albert	M-170	Oplinger	Mifflin
B-1115	Ohl	Alwenia	D-1324	Osenbach	Albert
B-1104	Ohl	Christianna	M-781	Osenbach	Ida Rebecca
B-1365	Ohl	Daniel	B-853	Osenbach	Kitty
B-1431	Ohl	Daniel	B-1032	Osenbach	Kitty
B-1900	Ohl	Edward	D-652	Osenbach	Sarah
B-1121	Ohl	Elias	M-304	Osewalt	Rebecca
B-1431	Ohl	Elias	M-1042	Oswald	John
D-1196	Ohl	Elizabeth	M-1096	Oswald	Mary J
B-1900	Ohl	George W	M-97	Otto	Caroline
M-1140	Ohl	George W	B-421	Otto	John
B-990	Ohl	Harriet	M-15	Otto	Joseph
B-1368	Ohl	Harriet	D-628	Otto	William
M-1150	Ohl	Harriet	M-1105	Ouldt	Franklin J
B-1812	Ohl	Harrison	M-437	Ownwalt	Samuel A
D-1131	Ohl	Harry	M-1152	Paetzel	Edward I J
B-1115	Ohl	Henry	D-59	Palmer	Francis
B-1625	Ohl	Henry	D-646	Palmer	Frantz
M-587	Ohl	Henry	B-1002	Pasch	Jacob
B-1615	Ohl	Ida	B-1002	Pasch	Jacob
B-1486	Ohl	James	M-664	Patterson	Adline
B-1812	Ohl	Jefferson	D-872	Patterson	Charles
B-267	Patterson	Charles A	B-1497	Peter	Lula
B-1120	Patterson	George	B-39	Peter	Mary
B-375	Patterson	John	B-307	Peter	Mary
B-267	Patterson	Levi	B-601	Peter	Mary
B-1120	Patterson	Lizzie	B-790	Peter	Mary
B-75	Patterson	Lucinda	B-24	Peter	Matilda
B-375	Patterson	Lucinda	B-215	Peter	Matilda
B-1044	Patterson	Lucinda	B-214	Peter	Matilida
M-40	Patterson	Lucinda	B-1289	Peter	Norton
B-75	Patterson	Maria	D-972	Peter	Oliver
B-1097	Patterson	Maria	B-1426	Peter	Oliver

Line #	Surname	Given Name	Line #	Surname	Given Name
M-325	Patterson	Mary Alice	B-264	Peter	Polly
M-713	Patterson	Pearce	B-535	Peter	Polly
B-436	Paul	John	B-799	Peter	Polly
B-436	Paul	Mary	M-319	Peter	Polly
B-337	Pehle	Amelia	B-1013	Peter	Robert
D-261	Pehle	Lily	B-1215	Peter	Rosa Ann
B-789	Peter	Abby	B-1059	Peter	Sarah
B-248	Peter	Ambrose	M-119	Peter	Sarah
B-603	Peter	Amelia	B-568	Peter	Sarah C
M-782	Peter	Amelia Elizabeth	B-165	Peter	Selinda
D-407	Peter	Anna	B-831	Peter	Selinda
D-1272	Peter	Anna	B-248	Peter	Wallace
B-1184	Peter	Anna	B-1289	Peter	Wallace
B-562	Peter	Charles	B-1426	Peter	Wallace
B-1864	Peter	Charles A	B-562	Peter	Wallace I
D-624	Peter	Christiana	B-1146	Peter	Wallace I
B-1591	Peter	Cora	B-1560	Peter	Wallace I
B-1602	Peter	Cora	B-1602	Peter	Wallace I
M-164	Peter	Cornelius	M-318	Peter	Wallace I
B-1163	Peter	Edwin	B-1560	Peter	Wilbur
B-1184	Peter	Edwin	D-619	Peter	William
B-1275	Peter	Edwin	B-214	Peter	William
B-1591	Peter	Edwin C	B-486	Peter	William
D-180	Peter	Ellen	B-789	Peter	William
B-1034	Peter	Emma	B-24	Peter	William
B-1275	Peter	Emma	B-380	Peter	Wilson
D-151	Peter	Gideon	M-283	Peter	Wilson
D-988	Peter	Gideon	M-1101	Peters	Charles A
B-1148	Peter	Gideon	M-851	Peters	Ella R
B-1163	Peter	Gideon	M-1173	Peters	Sura
B-1146	Peter	Harrison	B-501	Pethsel	Edward
D-1016	Peter	Henry	B-501	Pethsel	Sarah
B-1864	Peter	Howard	M-126	Petri	William
B-486	Peter	Ida	M-668	Petry	Richard
B-1497	Peter	James F	M-1120	Pettit	Beulah M
M-616	Peter	James F	B-1042	Pettit	Buhla
B-1034	Peter	John A	B-661	Pettit	Emma
M-564	Peter	John A	B-661	Pettit	George
M-746	Peter	John J	B-1042	Pettit	George
D-188	Peter	Jonas	M-440	Pettit	George
B-12	Peter	Lewina	M-1068	Pettit	Harry R
B-550	Peter	Lewina	M-306	Pettit	John F
B-1013	Peter	Lewis H	D-324	Pettit	Oliver
B-1163	Peter	Lillie	B-28	Pettit	Robert
B-590	Peter	Louisa	B-28	Pettit	Robert
M-33	Pettit	Robert	B-478	Rabenold	Catherine
M-859	Pettitt	Clara H	B-823	Rabenold	Catherine
B-418	Petzel	Edward	B-1537	Rabenold	Charles B
B-931	Pfahl	Justina	M-615	Rabenold	Charles B
B-328	Pfeifer	Mary	B-689	Rabenold	Eliza
B-33	Pfleider	Sophia	B-690	Rabenold	Eliza
B-905	Pfleiderer	Sophia	M-699	Rabenold	Emaline
B-484	Philhower	John	B-441	Rabenold	Emma
B-484	Philhower	Maria	B-752	Rabenold	Emma E
B-1577	Philips	Joanna	B-1403	Rabenold	Emma E
B-1577	Philips	Joseph	B-1508	Rabenold	Emma Eliza
M-846	Philips	Joseph	B-974	Rabenold	Emma Elizabeth
B-706	Platt	Lena	B-554	Rabenold	Emma Elizabeth

Line #	Surname	Given Name	Line #	Surname	Given Name
B-330	Platt	Lenah	M-275	Rabenold	Emma Elizabeth
B-506	Platt	Lenah	B-226	Rabenold	Emma Elizabth
B-1313	Platt	Lenah	B-115	Rabenold	Hannah
B-80	Polsgrafe	Lucy Ann	M-596	Rabenold	Henrietta
B-80	Polsgrafe	Mary Ann	B-689	Rabenold	Nathan
B-79	Polsgrofe	Mary Ann	B-974	Rabenold	Nathan
B-229	Polsgrove	Mary Ann	B-779	Rabenold	Nathan
M-192	Porter	Jane	D-622	Rabenold	Sarah
M-124	Pratt	John	B-700	Rabenold	Sarah
D-911	Price	America	D-560	Rabenold	Sevilla
M-976	Pryor	Elmer H	B-554	Rabenold	Sevilla
D-729	Queen	Alavista	B-554	Rabenold	Tilghman
M-1024	Quick	William Henry	B-779	Rabenold	Tilghman
D-475	Quillman	Adam	B-292	Rabenold	Tilghman
B-1058	Quin	Alavesta	B-371	Rabenold	Tilghman
D-731	Quin	Alavista	B-441	Rabenold	Tilghman
B-1058	Quin	Eliza	M-269	Rabenold	Tilghman
B-688	Quin	Mary Ann	B-1537	Rabenold	Zacharias
B-1058	Quin	Monroe	B-779	Rabenold	Zurah
M-391	Quin	Monroe	D-366	Raber	Edward
D-431	Rabe	Charles	B-746	Raber	John
B-447	Rabe	Elizabeth	M-356	Raber	John
B-828	Rabe	Elizabeth	B-746	Raber	Mary
B-982	Rabe	Elizabeth	B-1062	Rackawack	Amelia
B-716	Rabe	Ellen	B-335	Rackawack	Anna
B-981	Rabe	Ellen	B-335	Rackawack	Frederic
M-292	Rabe	Ellen	B-334	Rackawack	Sarah
B-637	Rabe	Emma	B-1062	Rackawack	William
B-637	Rabe	Franklin	B-1598	Radcliff	Justus
B-716	Rabe	Franklin	B-1598	Radcliff	Matilda
M-415	Rabe	Franklin	M-994	Raddatz	Amelia A
B-881	Rabe	Mary	B-1075	Raeder	Sibilla
D-451	Rabe	Michael	M-186	Ram	Martha Elizabeth
B-398	Rabe	Michael	M-277	Ramaley	Lydia
M-323	Rabe	Michael	M-655	Ramaly	Daniel
B-402	Rabe	Rachel	B-58	Ramaly	Ellen
B-402	Rabe	Rebecca	B-58	Ramaly	Henry
D-839	Rabe	William	M-231	Ramaly	Henry
B-398	Rabe	William	M-845	Ramaly	Mary
B-810	Rabenold	Carolina	B-58	Ramaly	Moses
B-690	Rabenold	Caroline	M-181	Ramaly	Moses
B-823	Rabenold	Caroline	M-440	Ramely	Eliza
D-654	Rabenold	Catherine	B-662	Ramely	Moses
B-662	Ramely	Sallie	B-1588	Reed	Edwin
D-200	Rammer	Horace	M-1090	Reed	Ella B
M-24	Rape	Elizabeth	B-1070	Reed	Ellen
B-21	Rape	Harry	B-524	Reed	Elmer
B-21	Rape	Jonas	B-1103	Reed	Frank
D-244	Raph	Sarah	B-1233	Reed	Frank
M-452	Rapp	Charles	D-316	Reed	Franklin
B-379	Rapp	Christian C	B-567	Reed	Franklin
B-310	Rapp	George	M-389	Reed	Franklin
B-393	Rapp	Hannah	B-1233	Reed	George
M-296	Rapp	Joseph C	B-1233	Reed	George
D-419	Rapp	William	M-523	Reed	George
B-379	Rapp	William	M-659	Reed	Kate A
B-26	Rappe	Christian	B-1588	Reed	Lewis
B-27	Rappe	Christian	M-515	Reed	Lewis

Line #	Surname	Given Name	Line #	Surname	Given Name
B-26	Rappe	George	M-293	Reed	Louisa
B-27	Rappe	William	D-1282	Reed	Margeret
B-1706	Ratcliff	Elmer	M-904	Reed	Mary A
B-1706	Ratcliff	Justus	M-807	Reed	Mary Amanda
B-1792	Ratcliff	Justus	M-1154	Reed	Rachel
B-1792	Ratcliff	Myrtle	B-1588	Reed	Sarah N
B-1434	Rau	Lewis W F	B-567	Reed	Willie
M-734	Rau	Lewis W F	B-1095	Reedy	Alice
B-1434	Rau	Mary	B-1095	Reedy	Harrison
B-514	Rauch	Osville	B-1235	Reeser	Kate
B-514	Rauch	Peter	M-341	Reeser	Kate
M-215	Rauch	Peter K	D-1293	Reeser	Mary
M-1104	Raudenbush	Grant	B-991	Reeser	Sarah A
M-684	Raworth	Delilah	B-33	Reger	Ida
D-1253	Reber	Ada	B-33	Reger	William E
B-1427	Reber	Charles	B-1299	Rehr	David
B-746	Reber	Edward	M-504	Rehr	Emma
M-971	Reber	Emma L	B-1299	Rehr	John
M-1004	Reber	Francis O	B-1299	Rehr	Mary
D-1260	Reber	Harvey	D-539	Rehrig	(s/o John & Rebecca)
M-1185	Reber	Holmes	B-1711	Rehrig	Aaron
D-184	Reber	John	B-1888	Rehrig	Aaron
B-1165	Reber	Margetta	B-1358	Rehrig	Adam
B-1927	Reber	Minnie E	B-1940	Rehrig	Adelia Elenora
B-1330	Reber	Oliver	B-1358	Rehrig	Alexander
B-1330	Reber	W. W. (Dr)	B-798	Rehrig	Alfred
B-1427	Reber	W.W	M-381	Rehrig	Alfred
M-314	Reber	William Henry	B-1559	Rehrig	Alice
M-521	Reber	William Henry	B-1565	Rehrig	Alice
B-979	Redditz	Lina	B-604	Rehrig	Amanda
B-942	Reed	Acquilla	B-1109	Rehrig	Amanda
B-942	Reed	Acquilla E	B-1306	Rehrig	Amanda
B-227	Reed	Aquila E	M-899	Rehrig	Angelina
D-677	Reed	Aquilla	D-1157	Rehrig	Angeline
B-524	Reed	Aquilla E	B-965	Rehrig	Anna
M-313	Reed	Aquilla E	B-1632	Rehrig	Augustus
B-1103	Reed	Caroline	B-1711	Rehrig	Augustus
B-227	Reed	Carrie	B-1766	Rehrig	Augustus
D-225	Reed	Charles	B-1839	Rehrig	Augustus
D-1084	Reed	Daniel	B-1870	Rehrig	Augustus
B-1070	Reed	Daniel	B-1902	Rehrig	Augustus
B-1937	Rehrig	Augustus	M-687	Rehrig	George
B-1965	Rehrig	Augustus	B-1240	Rehrig	Gideon
M-868	Rehrig	Augustus	B-1371	Rehrig	Harrie
B-1743	Rehrig	Bertha	B-1163	Rehrig	Harriet
B-1965	Rehrig	Bessie	B-1275	Rehrig	Harriet
B-1791	Rehrig	Catherine	B-1591	Rehrig	Harriet
B-1791	Rehrig	Catherine	M-1041	Rehrig	Harrison O
D-503	Rehrig	Charles	B-1937	Rehrig	Helen
D-637	Rehrig	Charles	B-1439	Rehrig	Henry
B-1131	Rehrig	Charles	B-1439	Rehrig	Henry
B-206	Rehrig	Charles	M-749	Rehrig	Henry Harrison
B-465	Rehrig	Charles	B-1529	Rehrig	Herbert
B-272	Rehrig	Charles	B-1888	Rehrig	Ida
B-1278	Rehrig	Charles E	M-937	Rehrig	Ida
B-1370	Rehrig	Charles E	B-1114	Rehrig	James H
B-1958	Rehrig	Charles E	B-1286	Rehrig	James H
M-1182	Rehrig	Charles E	B-1622	Rehrig	James H

Line #	Surname	Given Name	Line #	Surname	Given Name
B-1491	Rehrig	Charles G	M-568	Rehrig	James H
B-1529	Rehrig	Charles G	M-18	Rehrig	John
M-772	Rehrig	Charles G	M-1006	Rehrig	John A
B-1619	Rehrig	Clara Alice	B-1048	Rehrig	Jonas
B-1872	Rehrig	Clara Alice	B-1578	Rehrig	Jonas
M-725	Rehrig	Clara Alice	B-705	Rehrig	Jonas
B-1585	Rehrig	Clinton	B-1352	Rehrig	Jonas
M-1174	Rehrig	Cora Rebecca	M-164	Rehrig	July Ann
B-1632	Rehrig	Daisie	B-1187	Rehrig	Lambert
B-1805	Rehrig	David	B-1237	Rehrig	Leah
B-1935	Rehrig	David	B-87	Rehrig	Leanna
B-999	Rehrig	David	B-277	Rehrig	Leanna
B-955	Rehrig	Dennis	B-88	Rehrig	Leanna
B-1131	Rehrig	Dennis	B-424	Rehrig	Lester
B-1328	Rehrig	Dennis	M-1076	Rehrig	Lester B
B-1743	Rehrig	Dennis	B-544	Rehrig	Lewis
M-531	Rehrig	Dennis	B-826	Rehrig	Lewis
D-835	Rehrig	Edgar	B-1256	Rehrig	Lewis
B-1273	Rehrig	Edgar	B-471	Rehrig	Lewis
B-1766	Rehrig	Eliza	B-1493	Rehrig	Lewis F
B-452	Rehrig	Eliza	B-272	Rehrig	Lewis H
B-671	Rehrig	Eliza	M-355	Rehrig	Lewis H
B-1290	Rehrig	Eliza	B-1791	Rehrig	Lewis Henry
M-379	Rehrig	Eliza	D-966	Rehrig	Lillie
B-1328	Rehrig	Ellen	B-206	Rehrig	Lillie
B-1437	Rehrig	Ellen	B-1446	Rehrig	Lillie
B-1578	Rehrig	Ellen	B-1278	Rehrig	Lizzie
B-1192	Rehrig	Emaline	B-1935	Rehrig	Lizzie
B-1691	Rehrig	Emaline	M-670	Rehrig	Lizzie J
B-1742	Rehrig	Emaline	B-552	Rehrig	Lucy Ann
M-690	Rehrig	Emaline	B-846	Rehrig	Lucy Ann
B-759	Rehrig	Emeline	B-1603	Rehrig	Luella
B-1370	Rehrig	Emma	B-1935	Rehrig	Lula
B-383	Rehrig	Ephraim	M-633	Rehrig	Lydia
B-1491	Rehrig	Estella	B-1805	Rehrig	Mable
B-1817	Rehrig	Fianna	B-544	Rehrig	Maggie
M-1073	Rehrig	Fianna	B-798	Rehrig	Maggie
B-1256	Rehrig	George	M-1126	Rehrig	Maggie J
B-1439	Rehrig	George	B-1902	Rehrig	Mame
B-603	Rehrig	Mandes	D-937	Rehrig	William
M-141	Rehrig	Martin R	D-1264	Rehrig	William
D-60	Rehrig	Mary	B-1622	Rehrig	William
D-491	Rehrig	Mary	B-603	Rehrig	William B
B-1114	Rehrig	Mary	B-1892	Rehrig	Willliam
B-182	Rehrig	Mary	B-341	Reichard	Aaron
B-1240	Rehrig	Mary	B-1077	Reichard	Aaron
M-365	Rehrig	Mary A	B-483	Reichard	Aaron
B-424	Rehrig	Mary Ann	M-349	Reichard	Aaron
B-471	Rehrig	Mary Ann	M-360	Reichard	Allen
M-729	Rehrig	Mary L	M-558	Reichard	Antionetta
M-835	Rehrig	Mattie E	B-1559	Reichard	Carrie
B-1286	Rehrig	Maude	B-846	Reichard	Charles
B-1474	Rehrig	Maurice	B-582	Reichard	Eliza
B-1774	Rehrig	Messina	B-1077	Reichard	Emma
B-1493	Rehrig	Newton	B-1619	Reichard	Emma
B-1892	Rehrig	Noah	D-996	Reichard	George
B-1958	Rehrig	Oliver	B-1891	Reichard	Ida Cecilia
B-424	Rehrig	Owen	M-1109	Reichard	Ida Cecilia

Line #	Surname	Given Name
B-955	Rehrig	Pearcy
B-532	Rehrig	Priscilla
B-1839	Rehrig	Raymond
B-532	Rehrig	Reuben
B-1585	Rehrig	Reuben
M-326	Rehrig	Reuben
B-1870	Rehrig	Robert
B-1048	Rehrig	Rosa
B-1854	Rehrig	Rosa A
B-1879	Rehrig	Rosa A
M-1099	Rehrig	Rosa A
M-530	Rehrig	Ruffina
M-487	Rehrig	Sallie
D-1095	Rehrig	Sarah
B-465	Rehrig	Sarah
B-836	Rehrig	Sarah
B-1225	Rehrig	Sarah
B-277	Rehrig	Sarah
M-63	Rehrig	Sarah
M-297	Rehrig	Sarah
M-619	Rehrig	Sarah Alice
B-1263	Rehrig	Sarah Ann
B-1414	Rehrig	Sarah Ann
B-1525	Rehrig	Sarah Ann
B-1773	Rehrig	Sarah M
B-1851	Rehrig	Sarah M
M-1045	Rehrig	Sarah M
B-438	Rehrig	Sarah Susanna
B-1187	Rehrig	Thomas
B-1273	Rehrig	Thomas
B-1371	Rehrig	Thomas
M-344	Rehrig	Thomas
B-1446	Rehrig	Thomas A
B-1603	Rehrig	Thomas A
B-1437	Rehrig	Thomas J
B-1474	Rehrig	Thomas J
B-826	Rehrig	Victor
B-1079	Reinerd	Simon
D-895	Reinert	Elizabeth
D-915	Reinhard	John
B-1181	Reinhard	Katie
B-1181	Reinhard	W. H
M-781	Reinhart	Elias B
B-1272	Reinhart	George
M-622	Reinhart	Joseph H
B-1201	Reinhart	Maria
D-838	Reinhart	Wallace
B-1076	Reinheimer	Albert
B-1421	Reinheimer	George
B-1228	Reinheimer	Harry
B-850	Reinheimer	Irwin
B-415	Reinheimer	John
B-850	Reinheimer	John
B-1076	Reinheimer	John
B-1433	Reinheimer	Joseph
B-1228	Reinheimer	Joseph A
B-1421	Reinheimer	Joseph A
B-415	Reinheimer	Sarah
B-1559	Reichard	James
B-1619	Reichard	James
B-1872	Reichard	James B
M-725	Reichard	James B
M-606	Reichard	Lafayette
D-1091	Reichard	Lydia
B-552	Reichard	Maehlon
B-552	Reichard	Maehlon
B-846	Reichard	Maehlon
B-1872	Reichard	Minnie
M-1063	Reichard	Sally Ann
D-1308	Reichard	Samuel
B-1134	Reichard	Samuel S
B-341	Reichard	Sulie
B-1134	Reichard	William
B-1244	Reichelderfer	Rowland
B-1244	Reichelderfer	William
D-660	Reicheldorfer	Samuel
B-104	Reichert	Eliza
B-167	Reichert	Eliza
M-248	Reihman	Herman
B-764	Reiley	Susanna
B-1190	Reimold	Anna
B-419	Reinard	Susan
B-837	Reinard	Susan
B-439	Reiner	Elizabeth
M-880	Reiner	Elizabeth A
M-541	Reiner	Harriet
D-497	Reiner	John
D-340	Reiner	Lydia
B-439	Reiner	Simon
D-252	Relner	Solomon
B-611	Reiner	Susanna
B-1079	Reinerd	Adam
B-196	Reinerd	Anna
M-472	Reinerd	Daniel
B-196	Reinerd	Peter
M-542	Remaley	Lydia Ann
M-500	Remaley	Mary Ann
B-752	Remaley	Matilda
B-1311	Remaley	Matilda
B-1019	Remaley	Moses
B-1508	Remaley	Nathan
B-1650	Remaley	Polly
B-441	Remaley	Sarah
B-1280	Remaley	Sarah Ann
B-752	Remaley	Sevilla
B-1675	Remaley	Thomas
D-1303	Remaley	Tilghman
M-353	Remaley	Tilghman
B-1403	Remaley	William
B-960	Remaley	William
M-93	Remaley	William
D-1195	Remaley	Wilson
B-1664	Remaley	Wilson
M-954	Remaley	Wilson
B-1052	Remaly	Benjamin
B-615	Remaly	Catherine

Line #	Surname	Given Name	Line #	Surname	Given Name
M-880	Reinheimer	William H	B-974	Remaly	Charles
M-869	Reinsmith	Granville	M-275	Remaly	Charles
D-1122	Reinsmith	John	B-661	Remaly	Eliza
B-496	Reinsmith	Lister	B-245	Remaly	Eliza
B-1610	Reinsmith	Mable	B-572	Remaly	Elizabeth
B-1332	Reinsmith	Meta	B-1323	Remaly	Harriet
B-496	Reinsmith	Nathan	B-213	Remaly	Julia
B-1332	Reinsmith	Nathan	B-245	Remaly	Lydia
B-1610	Reinsmith	Nathan	B-600	Remaly	Lydia
B-91	Reiser	Enos	B-974	Remaly	Mary
B-226	Remaley	Albert	B-1311	Remaly	Mary
D-855	Remaley	Annie	D-1077	Remaly	Nathan
B-659	Remaley	Catherine	D-1017	Remaly	Nicholas
B-960	Remaley	Charles	D-307	Remaly	William
B-226	Remaley	Charles	D-531	Remaly	William
B-441	Remaley	Charles	B-39	Remaly	William
B-752	Remaley	Charles	M-206	Remaly	William
B-1403	Remaley	Charles	B-437	Remely	Almer
B-1508	Remaley	Charles	B-349	Remely	Amelia
B-554	Remaley	Charles	M-342	Remely	Elizabeth
B-1019	Remaley	Daniel	D-632	Remely	James
B-1042	Remaley	Eliza	B-349	Remely	Moses
B-444	Remaley	Elizabeth	B-413	Remely	Susan
B-819	Remaley	Elizabeth	M-219	Remely	Susan
B-820	Remaley	Elizabeth	B-437	Remely	Tilghman
D-1199	Remaley	Emalina	D-697	Remer	Elizabeth
B-635	Remaley	George	D-526	Remert	Joseph
B-1664	Remaley	Hattie	M-993	Remmel	Ezra Jerome
D-658	Remaley	Henry	B-59	Reppert	Cassian
B-600	Remaley	Henry	M-752	Reppert	John
D-859	Remaley	Jacob	B-583	Reppert	Rebecca
D-1283	Remaley	John	B-583	Reppert	Susanna
B-1041	Remaley	Lydia	M-377	Reppert	Susanna
B-1042	Remaley	Lydia	M-398	Reusch	Sophia
B-994	Remaley	Lydia Ann	B-1522	Rex	Agnes
B-352	Rex	Alfred	M-710	Rex	Jefferson
B-453	Rex	Alfred	D-1326	Rex	John
M-333	Rex	Alfred	B-1519	Rex	John
B-1433	Rex	Alvin	B-1488	Rex	John G
M-705	Rex	Alvin	D-892	Rex	Katie
B-983	Rex	Amanda	M-153	Rex	Kitty Ann
D-164	Rex	Amelia	B-840	Rex	Lafayette
B-150	Rex	Anna	B-1282	Rex	Lafayette
B-483	Rex	Anna	B-1373	Rex	Lafayette
B-933	Rex	Anna	B-485	Rex	Layfayette
B-1148	Rex	Anna Maria	D-1211	Rex	Levi
B-983	Rex	Anna Maria	B-1522	Rex	Lewis
B-1199	Rex	Anna Maria	B-560	Rex	Lewis A
B-1637	Rex	Anna Maria	B-1349	Rex	Lillie
M-185	Rex	Anna Maria	M-841	Rex	Lucy Ann
B-701	Rex	Asabey	M-180	Rex	Lydia
M-574	Rex	Catherine	B-840	Rex	Mahlon
B-352	Rex	Charles	B-1812	Rex	Malissa
B-358	Rex	Charles	M-839	Rex	Malissa Catherine
B-409	Rex	Charles	B-1579	Rex	Maria
B-1520	Rex	Clara	B-1641	Rex	Maria
D-1339	Rex	David	M-534	Rex	Maria
B-1282	Rex	David	M-555	Rex	Martha Julia Adline

Line #	Surname	Given Name	Line #	Surname	Given Name
B-1083	Rex	David	B-1373	Rex	Martin
B-1768	Rex	Dennis	D-709	Rex	Mary
B-450	Rex	Elizabeth	B-1279	Rex	Mary
B-1405	Rex	Ellen C	B-1459	Rex	Mary
B-1488	Rex	Ellen C	B-1547	Rex	Mary
B-1133	Rex	Ellenora	M-100	Rex	Mary
B-1563	Rex	Elvin	M-761	Rex	Mary Alice
B-1885	Rex	Elvin	B-1177	Rex	Mary Ann
M-836	Rex	Elvin	M-61	Rex	Mary Elizabeth
B-925	Rex	Emanuel	B-1369	Rex	Mira Ann
B-1349	Rex	Emanuel	B-1480	Rex	Mira Ann
M-837	Rex	Emma J	B-1248	Rex	Mira Ann
D-1032	Rex	Eva	M-683	Rex	Mira Ann
M-798	Rex	Eva Jane	B-409	Rex	Moses
M-801	Rex	Fianna	B-813	Rex	Moses
B-1728	Rex	Fietta	M-943	Rex	Nathan L
B-1821	Rex	Fietta	M-1121	Rex	Oscar E
B-1822	Rex	Fietta	B-1885	Rex	Ruth
B-1157	Rex	George	M-949	Rex	S. Elizabeth
B-1451	Rex	George	B-38	Rex	Sally
B-1727	Rex	George	B-840	Rex	Sarah
D-969	Rex	Gertrade	B-1282	Rex	Sarah
B-1433	Rex	Gertrude	B-1373	Rex	Sarah
B-925	Rex	Gideon	B-919	Rex	Sarah Ann
B-485	Rex	Harriet	B-1349	Rex	Tilghman
B-813	Rex	Harriet	B-1790	Rex	Tilghman F
B-1451	Rex	Harry	B-1133	Rex	Tilghman R
B-1563	Rex	Ida Anna	B-560	Rex	Tuwitta
B-1783	Rex	Ida E	D-249	Rex	William
B-975	Rex	James	B-358	Rex	William
B-1790	Rex	James	B-701	Rex	William
B-1224	Rex	Jane Amanda	B-975	Rex	William
B-1407	Rex	Jane Amanda	B-1157	Rex	William
B-1519	Rex	William	B-1923	Rickert	William L
B-1520	Rex	William	M-1112	Rickert	William L
B-1521	Rex	William	D-1127	Riegel	Alexander
B-264	Rex	William H	B-842	Riegel	Anna
B-352	Rex	William H	B-1894	Riegel	Charlotte
M-285	Rex	William H	B-269	Riegel	Clemen
M-1050	Rex	William Penn	B-1942	Riegel	Ellemande Jane
M-53	Rex	William R	B-1176	Riegel	Ellen
B-480	Rex	Zeniah	D-606	Riegel	George
B-1248	Rex	Zeniah	B-729	Riegel	George
B-1377	Rex	Zeniah	M-1123	Riegel	Hattie V
B-1496	Rex	Zeniah	D-676	Riegel	James
B-1682	Rex	Zeniah	B-869	Riegel	James
B-1724	Rex	Zeniah	B-318	Riegel	John
M-507	Rex	Joseph F	B-869	Riegel	John
M-83	Reynold	Noah	M-368	Riegel	John
D-14	Rheinschmidt	John	B-269	Riegel	Joseph
B-172	Rheinsmith	Abby	B-641	Riegel	Joseph
B-276	Rheinsmith	Lucy Ann	B-842	Riegel	Joseph
D-993	Rheinsmith	Timothy	B-1176	Riegel	Joseph
D-834	Rheinsmith	Willie	B-318	Riegel	Joshua
B-742	Rhoad	Martha	B-729	Riegel	Joshua
B-340	Rhoad	Priscilla	B-1858	Riegel	Mabel
B-645	Rhoad	Priscilla	B-641	Riegel	Mary
B-944	Rhoad	Priscilla	D-420	Riegel	Milton

Line #	Surname	Given Name
B-1284	Rhoad	Priscilla
M-340	Rhoad	Priscilla
B-742	Rhoad	Reuben
B-1281	Rhoads	Annetta
D-644	Rhoads	Hattie
B-829	Rhoads	Hattie
B-477	Rhoads	Ida
B-497	Rhoads	Isabella
B-1049	Rhoads	Jeremiah J
B-1361	Rhoads	Jeremiah J
M-554	Rhoads	Jeremiah J.
D-728	Rhoads	Korah
B-1049	Rhoads	Korah
M-731	Rhoads	Thomas Henry
D-595	Rhoads	Tilghman
B-1361	Rhoads	Tilghman
B-1053	Rhoads	William
B-477	Rhoads	William
B-829	Rhoads	William
B-1053	Rhoads	William
B-986	Rice	Amelia
B-825	Rice	Anna Tewilia
M-525	Rice	Anna Tewilia
M-211	Rice	Ellenore
B-500	Rice	Etna
B-1047	Rice	Polly
B-500	Rice	Tilghman
M-750	Richards	Charles H
B-1869	Rickert	Raymond
B-1923	Rickert	William
B-1869	Rickert	William L
B-776	Ritz	Anna
B-278	Ritz	Anna Maria
B-721	Ritz	Anna Maria
M-133	Ritz	Anna Maria
B-1031	Ritz	George
B-721	Ritz	James
B-1031	Ritz	James
B-236	Robert	Joseph
B-425	Roberts	J M
D-540	Roberts	Luella
B-425	Roberts	Luella
B-1589	Robinson	Ida
D-143	Rockel	Charles
M-77	Rockel	Joseph
M-152	Rodger	Abigail
B-876	Roeder	Alfred
B-876	Roeder	Herman A
B-876	Roeder	Sabilla
B-921	Roeder	Sybilla
B-1396	Rogers	Emma
M-658	Rogers	Emma S
B-48	Rohrbach	Abel
B-475	Rohrbach	Abel
M-307	Rohrbach	Abel
B-475	Rohrbach	Harriet
B-48	Rohrbach	William
B-981	Rolfink	John
B-541	Riegel	Sarah
B-869	Riegel	Sarah
B-1939	Riegel	William
B-1858	Riegel	William E
B-1894	Riegel	William E
B-1939	Riegel	William E
M-1100	Riegel	William E
M-482	Riegel	William J
D-673	Rieger	Emma
B-905	Rieger	Emma
B-905	Rieger	William
M-455	Rieger	Xavier
M-294	Riffert	Andrew E
B-800	Right	Jeanetta
B-952	Right	Polly
B-1447	Riling	Anna Elizabeth
B-1448	Riling	Anna Elizabeth
M-308	Rimbey	John H
M-27	Rinerd	Ellen
M-621	Rinker	Albert A
B-28	Rinker	Amanda
M-33	Rinker	Amanda
B-495	Rinker	Cassanda
M-316	Rinker	Cassandra J
M-990	Rinker	Ella
M-67	Rinker	Rebecca
D-49	Rinker	Sarah
B-28	Rinker	William
B-762	Rinker	William
D-506	Ripprit	Anna
B-721	Ritz	Adlina
M-94	Romig	Mary Ann
B-1691	Romig	Maurice A
B-1742	Romig	Maurice A
M-690	Romig	Maurice A
D-282	Romig	Robert
B-1867	Romig	Victor James
M-1106	Romig	Victor James
D-832	Romig	William
M-128	Rommel	Edwin
B-1621	Ronamus	Harriet
B-1510	Ronamus	Robert
B-1510	Ronamus	William
B-1621	Ronamus	William
B-1542	Ronemus	James S
B-1577	Ronemus	Mary Eva
M-846	Ronemus	Mary Eva
B-1542	Ronemus	Robert
B-1380	Ronemus	Samuel
B-1587	Ronemus	Sarah
B-1380	Ronemus	William
B-1587	Ronemus	William
B-1577	Ronemus	William
B-397	Root	Esther
B-398	Rootman	Anna Maria
M-323	Rootman	Anna Maria Rebecca
B-398	Rootman	Peter
B-973	Rose	Mary

Line #	Surname	Given Name	Line #	Surname	Given Name
B-716	Rolfink	John	M-498	Ross	Amanda Jane
B-981	Rolfink	John	B-783	Ross	Jane Amanda
M-292	Rolfink	John	B-1025	Ross	Manda
D-670	Rolfink	William	B-783	Ross	William
B-716	Rolfink	William	D-162	Roth	Alavesta
M-1183	Romig	Calvin A	B-1730	Roth	Charles F
B-1491	Romig	Catherine	M-940	Roth	Charles F
B-1529	Romig	Catherine	M-105	Roth	Edwilla
B-1427	Romig	Catherine	D-111	Roth	Elizabeth
M-772	Romig	Catherine Susanna	B-32	Roth	Elizabeth
B-229	Romig	Charles	B-516	Roth	Isabella Jane
B-80	Romig	Clara	M-270	Roth	John Tilghman
D-380	Romig	Clarissa	B-10	Roth	Priscilla
D-1124	Romig	Daniel	D-744	Roth	Sarah
B-1795	Romig	Daniel F	B-1730	Roth	Willie
M-1013	Romig	Daniel F	M-146	Rothermel	Henry
B-1795	Romig	Daniel L	M-678	Rothermel	James H
M-985	Romig	Diana M	D-33	Row	George
D-1123	Romig	Elmer	D-426	Row	Magdalena
B-1691	Romig	Emma	B-754	Ruben	Christiana
B-79	Romig	Ephraim	M-1024	Rubrecht	Emma Seniah
B-80	Romig	Ephraim	B-1582	Rubrecht	Mary Ann
B-229	Romig	Ephraim	B-1450	Rubrecht	Mary Jane
B-1867	Romig	Ervin	D-1235	Rubrecht	Polly
B-1742	Romig	Hattie	M-967	Rubrecht	W. A.
D-878	Romig	Irwin	B-1476	Ruch	Adda
B-1795	Romig	Isabella	B-1896	Ruch	Agnes
B-79	Romig	Lucy	B-1346	Ruch	Alvena
B-25	Romig	Mary Ann	M-639	Ruch	Alvena
B-360	Ruch	Angeline	B-1139	Ruch	Richard
M-518	Ruch	Caroline	D-757	Ruch	Sarah
B-575	Ruch	Catherine	M-811	Ruch	Susanna Elizabeth
B-575	Ruch	Charles	B-1787	Ruch	Sussanna Elizabeth
B-1819	Ruch	Charles	M-852	Ruch	Sylvester
B-1722	Ruch	Charles	B-1567	Ruch	William
B-1774	Ruch	Charles	B-575	Ruch	William
B-1819	Ruch	Charles	B-1476	Ruch	William
M-930	Ruch	Charles	B-1611	Ruch	William
B-5	Ruch	Christopher	M-149	Ruch	William
B-1611	Ruch	Clinton	M-488	Ruckawuck	William
B-319	Ruch	Elias	M-101	Rudolph	Jesse
B-610	Ruch	Elias	D-62	Ruepcha	Amanda
B-926	Ruch	Elias	D-99	Ruepcha	Maximilian
B-1139	Ruch	Elias	M-708	Ruff	Albert L
M-79	Ruch	Elias	B-1284	Ruff	Catherine
B-1715	Ruch	Ellen	M-588	Ruff	Joseph
B-1668	Ruch	Ellen Manda	B-944	Ruff	Waldburg
M-816	Ruch	Ellen Manda	M-148	Ruger	Rhoda A
B-1502	Ruch	Elmira	D-296	Rule	Celius
B-532	Ruch	Emaline	B-689	Rumble	Gordon
B-1585	Ruch	Emaline	B-689	Rumble	Rudolph
M-326	Ruch	Emaline	B-420	Rumble	Rudolph
B-5	Ruch	Emma	B-690	Rumble	Rudolph
B-468	Ruch	Francis	B-1324	Rumple	Hannah
B-1783	Ruch	Freddie	M-1130	Rush	John A
B-1148	Ruch	Hannah	M-612	Rustay	Frederic
B-1163	Ruch	Hannah	D-97	Rustay	Rebecca
B-319	Ruch	Harry	M-92	Rustay	Samuel

Line #	Surname	Given Name	Line #	Surname	Given Name
B-1783	Ruch	Harvey A	M-350	Rute	Benjamin
B-468	Ruch	Henry	M-728	Rute	Rosa A
B-1942	Ruch	Herald	B-850	Ruth	Rachael
B-1567	Ruch	Horace Greely	B-21	Ruth	Rachel
M-652	Ruch	Horace Greely	B-415	Ruth	Rachel
B-1045	Ruch	Ida	B-1076	Ruth	Rachel
M-1176	Ruch	Ida	B-177	Sabbach	George
B-786	Ruch	Ira	B-177	Sabbach	Philip Frederich
B-1942	Ruch	Ira	D-741	Sachs	Elizabeth
B-786	Ruch	Jacob	D-1208	Sachs	John
B-1045	Ruch	Jacob	B-1170	Sachs	Lucy Ann
B-364	Ruch	John	B-10	Saeger	Hannah
B-933	Ruch	Joseph	M-455	Saile	Balbine
B-1497	Ruch	Kitty Ann	D-578	Saile	Catherine
M-616	Ruch	Kitty Ann	B-1952	Salzman	Edward H
B-1319	Ruch	Lewis	B-1952	Salzman	Myrtle
M-157	Ruch	Lewis	M-382	Sanborn	Amelia L
B-1774	Ruch	Lillie	M-981	Sandel	Clara Eva Jane
B-1319	Ruch	Lizzie	M-518	Sandel	Jacob
B-1722	Ruch	Lizzie	D-107	Sandherr	Catherine
B-331	Ruch	Lucy Ann	B-128	Sandherr	Charles
B-926	Ruch	Mamie	B-128	Sandherr	Christian
D-682	Ruch	Maymie	B-127	Sandherr	Christian
B-610	Ruch	Moulton	B-1565	Sandherr	Estella
B-1483	Ruch	Priscilla	B-128	Sandherr	Frederica
M-711	Ruch	Priscilla	B-1565	Sandherr	George
D-269	Ruch	Rebecca	M-17	Sandherr	Pauline
M-32	Sandherr	William	B-1387	Schaefer	Mary
M-111	Sandherr	William	B-657	Schaefer	Mary Alice
M-619	Sandherrs	George	B-459	Schaefer	Mary Ann
B-1225	Sandhers	Charles	B-460	Schaefer	Mary Ann
B-1225	Sandhers	George	D-704	Schaefer	Oscar
D-1258	Sassaman	Catherine	B-116	Schaefer	Peter
D-831	Sassaman	Frederic	B-1587	Schaefer	Rebecca
D-923	Sassaman	John	B-1577	Schaefer	Rebecca
D-1148	Sassaman	John	D-1140	Schaefer	Samuel
D-887	Sassaman	Katie	B-117	Schaefer	Sarah
B-1246	Sassaman	Louisa	B-518	Schaefer	Sarah Ann
B-1170	Sassaman	William	B-747	Schaefer	Solomon
B-1246	Sassaman	Wm	B-1130	Schaefer	Solomon
D-131	Sauer	Sarah	D-435	Schaefer	Susanna
M-620	Sauers	Anna Eliza	D-432	Schaefer	Thomas
M-146	Savage	Hannah	B-116	Schaefer	Thomas
B-217	Savitz	Elizabeth	B-192	Schaefer	Thomas
B-807	Savitz	Sally Ann	D-802	Schaefer	William
M-762	Savitz	Wilson	B-1862	Schaefer	William
M-86	Sayer	Hannah	B-710	Schaefer	William
B-1776	Saylor	Codilla	B-644	Schaefer	William
D-77	Schabach	(d/o John & Eva)	B-1862	Schaefer	William F
D-587	Schabo	(d/o Peter & Mary (Distler))	B-192	Schaefer	Wilson
B-1714	Schabo	Agnes	B-1571	Schaeffer	A H
D-1010	Schabo	Charles	M-630	Schaeffer	A H
B-1518	Schabo	Charles	M-742	Schaeffer	Adam W
B-1630	Schabo	Minnie	B-1699	Schaeffer	Alexander
B-1463	Schabo	Peter	M-946	Schaeffer	Alexander O
B-1518	Schabo	Peter	B-1815	Schaeffer	Annetta
B-1630	Schabo	Peter	B-1571	Schaeffer	Charles
B-1714	Schabo	Peter	B-1862	Schaeffer	Daniel

Line #	Surname	Given Name	Line #	Surname	Given Name
M-722	Schabo	Peter	B-103	Schaeffer	David
B-1463	Schabo	William	B-1899	Schaeffer	Emma J
D-192	Schaboch	Anna	B-1699	Schaeffer	Emma Jane
D-205	Schaefer	Alavesta	B-1804	Schaeffer	Emma Jane
B-1190	Schaefer	Anna	M-566	Schaeffer	F.W
B-1130	Schaefer	Calvin	M-856	Schaeffer	John C
B-212	Schaefer	Charles	B-505	Schaeffer	Lizzie
B-1026	Schaefer	Charles	D-1234	Schaeffer	Mary
B-920	Schaefer	Charles	B-103	Schaeffer	Mary
M-255	Schaefer	Charles	B-705	Schaeffer	Rebecca
B-1387	Schaefer	Daniel	B-1510	Schaeffer	Rebecca
D-716	Schaefer	David	B-1621	Schaeffer	Rebecca
B-747	Schaefer	David	D-1194	Schaeffer	Roy
B-31	Schaefer	David	D-1141	Schaeffer	Sarah Ann
B-212	Schaefer	David	B-505	Schaeffer	Thomas
D-314	Schaefer	Dennis	B-1804	Schaeffer	William
B-1676	Schaefer	E L	B-479	Schafer	Daniel
M-914	Schaefer	E. L.	B-1087	Schafer	Elizabeth
B-65	Schaefer	Elizabeth Ann	B-1066	Schafer	Jane L
B-212	Schaefer	Elmira	M-514	Schafer	Kate
B-710	Schaefer	Herbert	M-863	Schafer	Lillie Clendora
B-1026	Schaefer	Howard	B-305	Schafer	Solomon
B-1190	Schaefer	Justus	D-542	Schafer	Susanna
B-871	Schaefer	Kate	B-305	Schafer	William
B-1089	Schaefer	Kate	D-449	Schafer	Wilson
M-656	Schall	Venora	M-1035	Schelly	James
B-1107	Schantz	Arabella	D-735	Scherer	Alice
D-738	Schantz	Esram	B-578	Scherer	Alice
B-1107	Schantz	Esram S	B-744	Scherer	Anna
B-1773	Schappel	—	M-250	Scherer	Anna
B-774	Schappel	Asaba	B-139	Scherer	Anny
M-1139	Schappel	Assipa J	D-594	Scherer	Christianna
B-1851	Schappel	Edna	B-679	Scherer	Edwin
M-608	Schappel	Emaline Elizabeth	D-849	Scherer	Eli
B-1773	Schappel	Milton A	M-860	Scherer	Ellen Jane
B-1851	Schappel	Milton A	B-1456	Scherer	Emma
M-1045	Schappel	Milton A	B-170	Scherer	Harriet
B-774	Schappel	Milton T	B-1029	Scherer	Harvey
B-1322	Schappel	Milton T	B-240	Scherer	Harvey
M-479	Schappel	Milton T	B-241	Scherer	Harvey
B-1322	Schappel	Oliver	M-448	Scherer	Harvey
B-1457	Schappell	Emma	D-125	Scherer	Henry
B-1307	Schappell	Emma E	M-16	Scherer	Isabella
D-1176	Schappell	Jacob	B-76	Scherer	Jacob
B-1309	Schappell	Sally Ann	B-100	Scherer	Jacob
B-128	Schatzlein	John	B-578	Scherer	John
B-1552	Scheckler	Daniel	B-150	Scherer	John
B-216	Scheckler	Lydia	M-411	Scherer	John
B-6	Scheckler	Mary	M-246	Scherer	Martin
B-183	Scheckler	Mary	M-501	Scherer	Martin
M-22	Scheckler	Mary	D-725	Scherer	Mary
M-142	Scheckler	Mary Jane	B-1029	Scherer	Mary
B-1552	Scheckler	Robert	B-679	Scherer	Robert
B-887	Scheckler	Sarah	M-604	Scherer	Robert
B-216	Scheckler	Selinda	M-583	Scherer	Robert A
M-419	Scheckler	Selinda	B-738	Scherer	Rosa Ann
D-152	Scheckler	Thomas	M-407	Scherer	Rosa Ann
B-216	Scheckler	William	B-1456	Scherer	Stephen

Line #	Surname	Given Name	Line #	Surname	Given Name
B-615	Scheekler	Jacob	B-521	Scherer	Susan
B-659	Scheekler	Jacob	D-823	Scherer	William
B-566	Scheekler	Levina	M-541	Scherer	William
B-659	Scheekler	Salinda	M-805	Schertzinger	Saffron
M-246	Scheible	Christiana	M-1111	Schilbach	Henry
B-379	Scheirer	Babet	B-201	Schindler	Christian
M-203	Scheirer	Babet	B-201	Schindler	Ida
M-951	Scheirer	Christian	D-469	Schinke	Frederick
D-948	Scheiry	Henry	D-402	Schinke	Maria
D-1004	Schelhamer	Henry	B-435	Schinke	Paulina
D-1050	Schelhamer	Phenus	D-466	Schinke	Reinhart
M-826	Schelhamer	Thomas F	B-435	Schinke	Wentzel
D-793	Schelhammer	Jacob	D-5	Schlabach	Catherine
D-703	Schellhamer	Anna	B-1288	Schlegel	Addie
D-884	Schellhamer	Catherine	D-827	Schlegel	Ellsworth
D-919	Schellhamer	Charles	B-1182	Schlegel	Henry
M-696	Schellhamer	Charles W	B-1182	Schlegel	Tilghman
B-1246	Schellhammer	Carrie	B-1288	Schlegel	Tilghman
B-1324	Schellhammer	Franklin B	D-114	Schleicher	Amelia
B-1325	Schellhammer	Franklin B	D-115	Schleicher	Awilda
B-1324	Schellhammer	James	B-96	Schleicher	Catherine
B-1246	Schellhammer	Monroe	B-335	Schleicher	Catherine
B-1325	Schellhammer	Polly	B-1654	Schleicher	Charles Franklin
M-927	Schleicher	Charles Franklin	B-340	Schnell	Oliver
D-502	Schleicher	Ellemina	B-645	Schnell	Oliver
B-454	Schleicher	Ellemina	B-944	Schnell	Oliver
B-868	Schleicher	Emma	B-1284	Schnell	Oliver
D-1159	Schleicher	George	M-340	Schnell	Oliver
B-1654	Schleicher	George	B-13	Schnell	Reuben
M-1006	Schleicher	Lillie J	B-300	Schnell	Reuben
B-1178	Schleicher	Milton	M-212	Schnell	Reuben
B-454	Schleicher	Paul	D-437	Schnell	Sarah
B-868	Schleicher	Paul	D-80	Schnell	Susanna
B-1178	Schleicher	Paul	M-621	Schnell	Susanna
B-1202	Schleicher	Tewilia	B-340	Schnell	Tilghman
B-1967	Schlenker	Albert M	B-340	Schnell	Tilghman
B-1967	Schlenker	Eva	B-1826	Schnella	George A C
M-8	Schlisler	Harrison	M-1052	Schnella	George A.C.
M-3	Schlitz	Levi	B-1826	Schnella	Mollie
M-81	Schmehl	Sarah	M-995	Schoch	Agnes
B-375	Schmehl	Susan	M-253	Schoch	Daniel
B-188	Schmidt	Anna Eliza	B-1070	Schoch	Elizabeth
M-278	Schmidt	Elizabeth	M-1017	Schoch	Francis Oliver
B-141	Schmidt	Franklin	M-944	Schoch	George Franklin
B-1548	Schmidt	Herman	M-726	Schoch	Mary Alice
M-833	Schmidt	Herman	D-446	Schoch	Pearcy
B-1548	Schmidt	Lillie	B-1631	Schock	Agnes M
B-112	Schmidt	Louisa	B-1716	Schock	Agnes M
B-187	Schmidt	Lucinda	M-907	Schock	Agnes M
B-141	Schmidt	Maehlon	B-1738	Schock	Alice
B-202	Schmidt	Maria	B-577	Schock	Ellen
B-936	Schmidt	Maria	B-436	Schock	Frederic
B-892	Schmidt	Owen	B-1738	Schock	George
B-446	Schmidt	William	B-436	Schock	Jarrettie
M-404	Schmidt	William	B-577	Schock	John
B-892	Schmidt	Wilson	B-1644	Schock	Mary Alice
D-476	Schmieskors	Dianna	M-508	Schoenberger	George F
M-361	Schmieskors	Henry	B-1201	Schoepe	Albert

Line #	Surname	Given Name	Line #	Surname	Given Name
M-984	Schminke	Annie	B-1201	Schoepe	Harry
B-265	Schmitt	Susanna	B-1966	Schofield	Marion
D-438	Schmoyer	Charles	B-1966	Schofield	William H
M-104	Schmoyer	Rebecca	M-1181	Schofield	William H
B-882	Schneck	Sarah	D-327	Schoneberger	Milton
B-166	Schneck	Sarah	B-1883	Schott	Mary Ann
B-526	Schneck	Sarah Ann	B-1759	Schott	Mary N
B-154	Schneider	Mary Ann	M-980	Schott	Mary N
B-656	Schnell	Aaron	D-826	Schoupe	Kitty
B-656	Schnell	Alwin	D-1268	Schraer	William
B-300	Schnell	Ambrose	B-1292	Schray	Adam
B-423	Schnell	Bregitta	D-804	Schray	Gostwen
D-172	Schnell	Caroline	M-1168	Schrayer	Elisa
D-668	Schnell	Charles	D-708	Schriver	Maria
B-645	Schnell	Charles	B-324	Schuck	Charles
B-944	Schnell	Eliza	B-268	Schuck	Charles
B-13	Schnell	Emma	B-324	Schuck	George
B-1284	Schnell	Emma	B-204	Schuck	George
B-1548	Schnell	Louisa	B-268	Schuck	Pearcy
M-833	Schnell	Louisa	M-958	Schuler	Emaline
B-645	Schnell	Lydia	B-1770	Schuler	Emma
M-584	Schultz	Annie M	M-173	Schwab	Edward
B-576	Schultz	Asaba	D-233	Schwab	Elias
M-1043	Schultz	Athabay	D-109	Schwab	Emaline
B-847	Schultz	Edwin	B-548	Schwab	George
M-405	Schultz	Edwin	B-1498	Schwab	Harrison
B-576	Schultz	Henry	B-397	Schwab	Ida
B-839	Schultz	James	B-265	Schwab	John
M-456	Schultz	James	B-904	Schwab	Lewis
B-1061	Schultz	Maria	B-397	Schwab	Lewis
B-1297	Schultz	Maria	B-396	Schwab	Lewis
M-486	Schultz	Maria	M-354	Schwab	Lewis Alfred
B-526	Schultz	Mary	M-435	Schwab	Lydia Anna Maria
D-672	Schultz	Nathan	B-1038	Schwab	Sabina
B-839	Schultz	Nathan	B-717	Schwab	Suvilla
M-1013	Schultz	Sallie Ann	B-136	Schwab	William
B-1795	Schultz	Sally Ann	M-1007	Schwab	William A
D-671	Schultz	Sarah	B-328	Schwartwood	Carolina
B-414	Schultz	Sarah	B-549	Schwartwood	Caroline
B-449	Schultz	William	B-549	Schwartwood	Sarah
M-373	Schultz	William	M-717	Schwartz	Allen G
B-1017	Schumacher	Acquilla	B-104	Schwartz	Eliza
B-1291	Schumacher	Aquila	B-605	Schwartz	Eliza
B-849	Schumacher	Aquilla	B-494	Schwartz	Eliza____
B-1392	Schumacher	Charlie	B-1546	Schwartz	Ella Priscilla
B-1267	Schumacher	Cyrus	B-1540	Schwartz	Elmasia
D-1009	Schumacher	James	B-388	Schwartz	Franklin
B-1495	Schumacher	James	M-267	Schwartz	George
B-90	Schumacher	John	M-661	Schwartz	George
B-983	Schumacher	Levi	B-1043	Schwartz	Harvey
D-1022	Schumacher	Mary	B-752	Schwartz	Henry
D-833	Schumacher	Minnie	B-1311	Schwartz	Henry
B-983	Schumacher	Minnie	M-338	Schwartz	Henry
B-1127	Schumacher	Minnie	D-331	Schwartz	Ida
B-844	Schumacher	Owen	D-1039	Schwartz	Jennie
B-1127	Schumacher	Owen	B-1540	Schwartz	Jennie
B-1267	Schumacher	Owen	B-388	Schwartz	John
B-1392	Schumacher	Owen	M-784	Schwartz	John

Line #	Surname	Given Name	Line #	Surname	Given Name
B-1495	Schumacher	Owen	B-1043	Schwartz	John F
D-762	Schumacher	Rosa	B-1160	Schwartz	John F
D-980	Schumacher	William	M-540	Schwartz	John F
B-844	Schumacher	William	B-470	Schwartz	Josephine
B-1140	Schumaker	Aquila	M-371	Schwartz	Josephine
B-742	Schumaker	Augusta	M-911	Schwartz	Lucetta Camille
B-1203	Schumaker	Gideon	B-484	Schwartz	Maria Magdalene
B-1142	Schumaker	Sarah	B-1160	Schwartz	Mary
B-1121	Schuman	Lydia	B-1686	Schwartz	Mary
B-449	Schuyler	Hiram	B-173	Schwartz	Mary Ann
M-295	Schuyler	Hiram	B-174	Schwartz	Mary Ann
B-449	Schuyler	Mary	B-672	Schwartz	Mary Ann
D-222	Schwab	(s/o Charles and Matilda)	M-532	Schwartz	Mary Magadalene
B-736	Schwab	Anna Maria	B-1292	Schwartz	Mary Magdalene
B-136	Schwab	Charles H	M-1026	Schwartz	Meda
B-548	Schwab	Charles H	D-263	Schwartz	Sarah
B-904	Schwab	Charles H	M-37	Schwartz	Sarah
B-1498	Schwab	Charles H	B-411	Schwartz	Sarah Ann
B-1038	Schwab	Charles W	B-106	Schwartz	Selinda
B-347	Schwartz	Selinda	M-549	Semmel	Joel
B-553	Schwartz	Selinda	D-229	Semmel	Joseph
B-785	Schwartz	Selinda	B-1928	Semmel	Lillie
B-1540	Schwartz	Thomas A	M-1167	Semmel	Lillie
D-156	Schwartz	Valentine	M-843	Semmel	Louisa Jane
B-470	Schwartz	Wendel	B-1193	Semmel	Nathan
D-47	Schwartz	Wilhelmenia	B-1825	Semmel	Robert
D-1188	Schweibens	Hattie	M-664	Semmel	Walter J
M-483	Schweibens	Mary Ann	M-79	Sendal	Mary
B-530	Schweibens	Paul	M-247	Sendel	A. B.
B-505	Schweibens	William	B-443	Sendel	Clara
M-679	Schwender	Lizzie	M-987	Sendel	Emma E
B-400	Schwenk	Henry	B-1933	Sendel	Emma Elizabeth
B-400	Schwenk	John	B-319	Sendel	Mary
B-206	Seaboldt	Susan	B-610	Sendel	Mary
B-120	Seaboldt	William	B-926	Sendel	Mary Ann
M-1171	Searfass	Elmer A	B-1139	Sendel	Mary Ann
M-844	Searfass	H. W.	M-992	Sendel	Nelson Ellsworth
M-1053	Searfass	Lucinda	M-915	Sendel	Richard
M-618	Sechler	Kate Elizabeth	B-479	Sendel	Sarah
M-480	Seeber	Charles	B-857	Sendel	Sarah
B-1886	Seeverson	Dorah	B-1862	Sendel	Sarah
B-1440	Seibert	Anna	B-443	Sendel	William
B-681	Seidel	Carrie	B-1331	Sendel	William
B-1268	Seidel	Maria	B-792	Sensinger	Alfred
B-1554	Seila	Charles	B-1112	Sensinger	Alfred
B-1554	Seila	Maple	B-1758	Sensinger	Alice Louisa
B-66	Seiler	Emma	B-1802	Sensinger	Alice Louisa
B-66	Seiler	Samuel	B-1003	Sensinger	Bertha
M-245	Seiler	Samuel	B-792	Sensinger	Calvin
B-266	Seiley	Lydia	B-194	Sensinger	Catherine
B-864	Seily	Lydia Ann	B-68	Sensinger	Daniel
D-230	Seip	Reuben	B-373	Sensinger	Daniel
B-48	Seitz	Rebecca	B-656	Sensinger	Daniel
M-546	Sellars	John	B-772	Sensinger	Daniel
B-606	Seller	Kate	B-209	Sensinger	Edwin
B-607	Seller	Kate	B-627	Sensinger	Edwin
B-608	Seller	Kate	B-845	Sensinger	Edwin
B-609	Seller	Kate	B-627	Sensinger	Ellemanda

Line #	Surname	Given Name	Line #	Surname	Given Name
B-967	Seltzer	Henry	D-387	Sensinger	Emaline
M-442	Seltzer	Henry	B-208	Sensinger	Emaline
B-967	Seltzer	Milton	B-612	Sensinger	Emaline
B-113	Selzer	Harriet	B-791	Sensinger	Emaline
B-472	Selzer	Harriet	M-260	Sensinger	Emaline
M-233	Selzer	Harriet	B-68	Sensinger	Emmaline
B-731	Selzer	Henry	M-506	Sensinger	Israel
B-113	Selzer	Henry	B-1112	Sensinger	Laura
B-731	Selzer	William	B-1907	Sensinger	Laura M
M-129	Semmel	David	B-1735	Sensinger	Louisa
M-1145	Semmel	Emma L	M-996	Sensinger	Louisa
B-1859	Semmel	Florence	B-489	Sensinger	Mary
B-1762	Semmel	Granville Henry	B-1538	Sensinger	Mary
B-1825	Semmel	Granville Henry	B-612	Sensinger	Sally Ann
B-1859	Semmel	Granville Henry	B-930	Sensinger	Sarah Ann
M-1030	Semmel	Granville Henry	B-656	Sensinger	Seniah
B-1762	Semmel	Irwin	B-791	Sensinger	Susanna
M-589	Sensinger	Susanna	M-992	Sheckler	Lydia A S
B-489	Sensinger	William F	M-535	Sheckler	Susanna
B-1003	Sensinger	William F	B-725	Sheckler	William L
B-1191	Sepman	Maria	M-459	Sheckler	William L
D-414	Serfass	Adam	B-284	Sheiry	Catherine
B-936	Serfass	Amandus	B-284	Sheiry	George
B-278	Serfass	Catherine	D-938	Shelhamer	Abigail
B-715	Serfass	Catherine	D-1125	Shelhamer	Estella
B-1110	Serfass	Catherine	M-1088	Shelhamer	Josephine
B-1277	Serfass	Catherine	B-361	Shell	Harriet
M-99	Serfass	Catherine	D-875	Shellhamer	Lafenus
M-901	Serfass	Charles	B-1203	Shellhammer	Amanda
M-545	Serfass	Edward	D-774	Shellhammer	Daniel
D-384	Serfass	Eliza	D-656	Shellhammer	Francis
D-1342	Serfass	Flossie	M-714	Shelly	Mary Jane
D-1165	Serfass	Howard	M-708	Sherar	Emma J
M-809	Serfass	Hulda R	B-642	Sherer	Angeline
M-439	Serfass	John	M-75	Sherer	Edwin
B-202	Serfass	Joseph	D-39	Sherer	Henrietta
D-73	Serfass	Josiah	D-634	Sherer	Henry
B-49	Serfass	Josiah	M-87	Sherer	Lucinda
M-66	Serfass	Lewis	D-638	Sherer	Robert
B-1169	Serfass	Lydia	M-522	Sherer	Sabina
M-601	Serfass	Lydia	M-369	Sherer	Susan
M-177	Serfass	Lydia Ann	B-1204	Sherry	Alice
B-202	Serfass	Mandes	B-1753	Sherry	Cora
B-1413	Serfass	Mandes	B-1517	Sherry	Ellwood
B-1413	Serfass	Owen	B-1517	Sherry	Ellwood
D-1209	Serfass	Preston	B-1753	Sherry	Ellwood
D-352	Serfass	Priscilla	B-1634	Sherry	Ellwood H
B-49	Serfass	Priscilla	B-1703	Sherry	Ellwood H
M-20	Serfass	Rebecca	B-1398	Sherry	Elwood
M-195	Serfass	Reuben	B-1884	Sherry	Elwood H
B-936	Serfass	Sarah	B-1520	Sherry	Harvey
M-396	Serfass	Timothy	B-1703	Sherry	Ida
B-570	Settenfeld	Maria	B-1398	Sherry	Lillie
M-735	Seyger	Agnes Jane	B-1634	Sherry	Mabel
B-545	Shabel	Milton	B-1884	Sherry	Virginia
B-545	Shabel	Milton T	M-999	Shidely	Anna
M-309	Shadle	Rosa	B-1197	Shindler	James
B-467	Shaefer	Catherine	B-1197	Shindler	William

Line #	Surname	Given Name	Line #	Surname	Given Name
M-214	Shaefer	Jane L	M-140	Shipe	Ephraim
B-857	Shaefer	Mary Alice	M-585	Shipe	James Wilson
B-1380	Shaefer	Rebecca	M-768	Shipe	Mary Ann
B-467	Shaefer	Sarah	D-286	Shipe	Sarah
B-857	Shaeffer	Daniel	B-334	Shipe	William
M-827	Shafer	Emma Jane	B-1403	Shirer	Matilda
M-461	Shafer	Rosa Ann	M-273	Shirer	Priscilla
M-337	Shaffer	Eliza Jane	D-1145	Shires	Christopher
D-613	Sharer	Elmer	M-857	Shirey	Catherine
M-475	Sharer	Stephen L	B-760	Shive	Alexander
B-640	Shary	Harriet	B-231	Shive	Alfred
M-90	Shary	Harriet	M-56	Shive	Alfred
M-84	Shaw	Edward	D-499	Shive	Alice
M-733	Sheckler	Charles	B-760	Shive	Charles
B-725	Sheckler	Lillie	M-733	Shive	Cordelia
M-161	Shive	Edwin	M-401	Shoenberger	Sarah A
D-605	Shive	Elias	D-166	Shoneberger	Margaret
B-664	Shive	Ella	M-358	Shoneberger	Sabina
B-247	Shive	Emma	B-993	Shuck	George D
B-247	Shive	Ephraim	M-774	Shuck	George D
B-314	Shive	Ephraim	B-993	Shuck	Pearl
D-754	Shive	Harriet	D-1015	Shuck	Theresa
D-620	Shive	James	B-1399	Shultz	James
B-1099	Shive	Julia A	B-1399	Shultz	William
B-1100	Shive	Julia A	B-623	Shumacher	Ellen
M-497	Shive	Julian	B-623	Shumacher	John
D-21	Shive	Juliana	M-450	Shumaker	Owen
D-752	Shive	Mary	B-403	Sibbach	Anna
B-231	Shive	Mary	D-442	Sibbach	George
B-405	Shive	Mary Ann	M-144	Sibbach	Philip Frederic
B-1477	Shive	Mary Ann	B-403	Sibbach	Philip Frederich
B-1739	Shive	Mary Ann	D-173	Siefried	Andrew
B-1143	Shive	Rebecca	D-1233	Siegfried	Catherine
M-197	Shive	Rebecca	M-979	Siglin	George E
B-753	Shive	Rebecca	D-1218	Siglin	Jennie
D-108	Shive	Sarah	B-763	Silfies	Balinda
B-805	Shive	Sarah	M-464	Silfies	Balinda
M-350	Shive	Sarah	B-1099	Silfies	Chester
D-199	Shive	Thomas	B-1100	Silfies	Chester
M-454	Shive	William Harrison	M-497	Silfies	Chester P
B-1299	Shively	Franklin	B-1522	Silfies	Ellamanda
B-941	Shively	Salena	B-1100	Silfies	Estella
B-1641	Shoemaker	Charles M	B-667	Silfies	Jacob
B-1751	Shoemaker	Charles M	B-861	Silfies	Jacob
B-1806	Shoemaker	Charles M	M-343	Silfies	Jacob
B-1751	Shoemaker	Clendora	D-175	Silfies	Jonas
B-453	Shoemaker	Ellen	B-861	Silfies	Laura
B-739	Shoemaker	Ellen	B-667	Silfies	Lillie
B-964	Shoemaker	Ellen	B-187	Silfies	Mary
B-1199	Shoemaker	Ellen	B-1099	Silfies	Namie
M-374	Shoemaker	Ellen	B-187	Silfies	Reuben
B-1501	Shoemaker	Fietta	M-577	Silfies	William
M-770	Shoemaker	Fyetta J	M-70	Simmon	Maria
B-1806	Shoemaker	Girtie	M-329	Simmon	Sarah
B-1502	Shoemaker	Granville Addison	B-597	Simon	Harrison
M-866	Shoemaker	Lanies A	B-597	Simon	Michael
B-1502	Shoemaker	Marvin	B-894	Simpson	Emma
M-471	Shoemaker	Mary Etta	B-894	Simpson	John

Line #	Surname	Given Name	Line #	Surname	Given Name
B-156	Shoemaker	Sarah	M-528	Simpson	Robert
B-317	Shoemaker	Sarah	B-1174	Sinyard	Addie
B-591	Shoemaker	Sarah Ann	B-1907	Sinyard	Gertrude
B-851	Shoemaker	Sarah Ann	B-643	Sinyard	James
M-139	Shoemaker	Sarah Ann	B-937	Sinyard	James
B-1641	Shoemaker	Victor	B-1174	Sinyard	James
D-601	Shoemaker	William	M-393	Sinyard	James
M-284	Shoenberger	Benjamin Franklin	B-1908	Sinyard	Jennie
B-1084	Shoenberger	Charles O	B-1907	Sinyard	John
M-496	Shoenberger	Charles O	B-643	Sinyard	Jonathan
M-434	Shoenberger	David H	B-1876	Sinyard	Mathew
B-1084	Shoenberger	Harrison	B-1908	Sinyard	Mathew
B-691	Shoenberger	Sarah	B-1930	Sinyard	Mathew
B-937	Sinyard	Matthew	B-1453	Smith	Alvin
B-1876	Sinyard	Pearl	D-1250	Smith	Annie
B-1930	Sinyard	Russel	B-878	Smith	Catherine
M-108	Sitler	Edward	M-158	Smith	Catherine
B-1628	Sitler	Emma E	D-1243	Smith	Charles
M-892	Sitler	Emma E	B-874	Smith	Charles
M-834	Sittler	Agnes V	B-584	Smith	Charles
B-1499	Sittler	Birdie	B-1464	Smith	Charles
B-681	Sittler	Clairessa	M-117	Smith	Charles
D-694	Sittler	Edilia	B-762	Smith	Christianna
D-1087	Sittler	Elizabeth	D-1239	Smith	Cora
B-1777	Sittler	Frank	M-906	Smith	Cora J
B-1164	Sittler	George	B-795	Smith	Edward
B-681	Sittler	John	B-1123	Smith	Elias
M-1004	Sittler	Lucetta	B-1482	Smith	Elias
D-659	Sittler	Lucretia	B-795	Smith	Eliza
D-957	Sittler	Milo	D-861	Smith	Ellen
D-488	Sittler	Minnie	B-1123	Smith	Ellen
D-870	Sittler	Samuel	B-539	Smith	Emil
B-1164	Sittler	Tilghman E	B-502	Smith	Emma
B-1425	Sittler	Wallace	B-502	Smith	Franklin
B-1499	Sittler	Wallace A	B-1419	Smith	Franklin
B-1425	Sittler	Wallace Ambrose	B-1707	Smith	Franklin
B-195	Sleicher	Catherine	D-815	Smith	George
B-280	Sleider	Anna	B-1346	Smith	George
B-537	Sleider	Edward	B-1511	Smith	Harriet
B-771	Sleider	Edward	B-1581	Smith	Harriet Adora
M-234	Sleider	Edward	B-874	Smith	Harrison
B-213	Sleider	Edwin	B-1700	Smith	Henry
B-668	Sleider	Ida	B-203	Smith	Henry
D-410	Sleider	John	B-598	Smith	Henry
B-213	Sleider	John	M-931	Smith	Henry
B-305	Sleider	Mary	M-1151	Smith	Henry A
B-537	Sleider	Mary	D-1000	Smith	Hudson
B-1904	Sleider	Mary Ann	D-1251	Smith	Ida
B-1904	Sleider	Sarah S	B-1668	Smith	Ida
D-715	Sleider	William	B-649	Smith	Irwin
B-771	Sleider	William	B-1464	Smith	Irwin
B-280	Sleider	William	M-934	Smith	J.P
B-668	Sleider	William Dennis	D-905	Smith	James
B-771	Sleider	William H	B-1410	Smith	James
M-132	Slight	Milton	M-639	Smith	James
M-671	Slough	Cornelia M	B-1346	Smith	James O
B-1168	Smawley	Ida	M-938	Smith	James O
B-1259	Smawley	William	B-838	Smith	John

Line #	Surname	Given Name	Line #	Surname	Given Name
M-590	Smawley	William A	B-1668	Smith	John
B-1168	Smawley	Wilson A	B-1715	Smith	John
B-1259	Smawley	Wilson A	M-816	Smith	John
B-877	Smethers	Angeline	M-584	Smith	John R
B-1700	Smith	—	B-1419	Smith	Korah
D-1236	Smith	(d/o Andrew & Amanda)	B-1482	Smith	Korah
B-1707	Smith	Adam	B-878	Smith	Leanda
M-945	Smith	Adam A	B-584	Smith	Lesta
D-1244	Smith	Albert	D-1249	Smith	Lizzie
B-338	Smith	Alfred	B-539	Smith	Lizzie
M-1122	Smith	Alfred A	B-996	Smith	Louisa Cather
M-513	Smith	Louisa Catherine	M-19	Snyder	Adeline Louisa
M-803	Smith	Lucretia V	B-753	Snyder	Alexander
B-622	Smith	Lucy	B-1143	Snyder	Alexander
B-888	Smith	Lucy	M-197	Snyder	Alexander
B-920	Smith	Lucy	B-1143	Snyder	Andrew
B-1515	Smith	Lucy	M-1078	Snyder	Annie E
B-1617	Smith	Lucy	B-646	Snyder	Catherine
B-1385	Smith	Lucy	B-1080	Snyder	Catherine
M-573	Smith	Lydia Esther	B-1334	Snyder	Catherine
M-1103	Smith	Malinda E	M-127	Snyder	Catherine
B-1715	Smith	Mame	M-765	Snyder	Catherine
D-1248	Smith	Mamie	B-240	Snyder	Charles
B-1413	Smith	Maria	B-1834	Snyder	Charles
B-266	Smith	Maria	B-1865	Snyder	Charles
B-267	Smith	Maria M	M-1086	Snyder	Charles
D-1252	Smith	Martha	M-207	Snyder	Charles Edward
B-83	Smith	Mary	M-1141	Snyder	Charles Edwin
B-1945	Smith	Minnie	B-84	Snyder	Christianna
M-1169	Smith	Minnie	B-1816	Snyder	Cleveland
M-1178	Smith	O F	B-185	Snyder	David
B-1125	Smith	Owen	M-74	Snyder	David
B-338	Smith	Owen	M-884	Snyder	David
B-1125	Smith	Owen	B-474	Snyder	Elias
B-410	Smith	Quinton	B-1068	Snyder	Ellemanda
B-1410	Smith	Richard	D-801	Snyder	Elmer
M-963	Smith	Rosa	D-270	Snyder	Emma
M-828	Smith	Rosa Alice	B-324	Snyder	Emma
B-83	Smith	Samuel	B-993	Snyder	Emma
B-1213	Smith	Sarah	B-204	Snyder	Emma
B-1478	Smith	Sarah	M-1040	Snyder	Emma S
M-1009	Smith	Sarah	B-411	Snyder	Eugene
M-506	Smith	Sarah E	B-807	Snyder	Fayetta
M-460	Smith	Sarah J	B-1250	Snyder	Franklin
M-263	Smith	Susanna	D-120	Snyder	George
B-649	Smith	Theodore	D-871	Snyder	George
D-1357	Smith	William	B-674	Snyder	George
B-410	Smith	William	B-1317	Snyder	George
B-838	Smith	William	B-804	Snyder	George H
B-1453	Smith	William	D-82	Snyder	Henry
M-468	Smith	William Edwin	D-53	Snyder	Howard
M-237	Smith	Franklin	B-1834	Snyder	Howard
M-254	Smoyer	Catherine Aquilla	D-304	Snyder	Jacob
M-945	Smoyer	Emma M	D-751	Snyder	Jacob
B-929	Smoyer	James	D-865	Snyder	Jacob
B-929	Smoyer	Sarah	B-1662	Snyder	James
B-1039	Smutters	Angeline	B-933	Snyder	Jane Amanda
B-1153	Smutters	Angeline	B-185	Snyder	Jefferson

Line #	Surname	Given Name	Line #	Surname	Given Name
B-1276	Smutters	Angeline	B-521	Snyder	Jennie
B-1335	Smutters	Angeline	B-1355	Snyder	John
B-1454	Smutters	Angeline	B-921	Snyder	John
D-536	Snyder	(d/o of Alexander and Rebecca)	B-1096	Snyder	John
M-44	Snyder	Aaron	B-841	Snyder	John
B-1097	Snyder	Abraham	M-529	Snyder	John
B-1355	Snyder	Adam	B-1629	Snyder	Kate
B-1432	Snyder	Adam	B-1689	Snyder	Kate
B-404	Snyder	Adeline Louisa	B-1089	Snyder	Katie
B-474	Snyder	Laura	B-1370	Snyder	Viletta
M-1069	Snyder	Lewis	B-1816	Snyder	Wallace O
B-133	Snyder	Louisa	M-1047	Snyder	Wallace O
B-492	Snyder	Louisa	B-411	Snyder	Washington
B-1355	Snyder	Louisa	M-37	Snyder	Washington
M-13	Snyder	Louisa Jane	D-103	Snyder	Welles
B-1250	Snyder	Luzetta	D-805	Snyder	William
B-871	Snyder	Lydia	B-1096	Snyder	William
M-1130	Snyder	Lydia E	B-1310	Snyder	William
B-1662	Snyder	M R	B-1432	Snyder	William
M-216	Snyder	Martha	M-1184	Snyder	Willliam
B-1057	Snyder	Mary	B-1	Solomon	Anna
B-841	Snyder	Mary	B-1	Solomon	George
M-1186	Snyder	Mary J	B-2	Solomon	George
B-1029	Snyder	Matilda	B-2	Solomon	John
B-1520	Snyder	Matilda	B-78	Solt	Agnes
M-448	Snyder	Matilda	M-457	Solt	Alfred
B-1310	Snyder	Matthew R	B-861	Solt	Amanda
M-328	Snyder	Nathan	M-343	Solt	Amanda
B-614	Snyder	Paul	M-580	Solt	Amandes W
M-400	Snyder	Paul	B-734	Solt	Amelia
M-1067	Snyder	Percy May	B-529	Solt	Amos
B-1057	Snyder	Peter	B-845	Solt	Amos
B-240	Snyder	Phaon	B-875	Solt	Amos
B-674	Snyder	Phaon	M-390	Solt	Amos
B-1097	Snyder	Phaon	M-656	Solt	Andrew
B-520	Snyder	Polly	B-1785	Solt	Arthur
B-787	Snyder	Polly	D-457	Solt	Catherine
B-911	Snyder	Polly	D-576	Solt	Daniel
B-687	Snyder	Rebecca	D-598	Solt	Ellen
B-1080	Snyder	Rebecca	B-725	Solt	Ellen
B-1865	Snyder	Robbie	B-431	Solt	Ellen
B-753	Snyder	Robert	B-1038	Solt	Ellen
M-566	Snyder	S.S.	M-459	Solt	Ellen
D-479	Snyder	Samuel	B-808	Solt	Ellen
B-871	Snyder	Samuel	B-628	Solt	Ellen Jane
B-1089	Snyder	Samuel	M-397	Solt	Ellen Jane
B-1317	Snyder	Samuel	B-243	Solt	Elva
M-514	Snyder	Samuel	B-918	Solt	Emaline
M-1072	Snyder	Samuel Phaon	B-84	Solt	Emma
D-1229	Snyder	Sarah	B-289	Solt	Fianna
B-1071	Snyder	Sarah	B-669	Solt	Fianna
B-1271	Snyder	Sarah	B-978	Solt	Fianna
B-430	Snyder	Sarah	M-169	Solt	Fianna
B-1334	Snyder	Sarah	B-1832	Solt	Girtie
B-1432	Snyder	Sarah	D-651	Solt	Harvey
B-921	Snyder	Sitna	B-243	Solt	Henry
B-521	Snyder	Stephen	B-527	Solt	Henry
M-369	Snyder	Stephen	M-299	Solt	Henry

Line #	Surname	Given Name	Line #	Surname	Given Name
M-1171	Snyder	Susan T	B-422	Solt	Isabella
M-952	Snyder	Sylvester L (Prof.)	M-1031	Solt	Isabella
M-1085	Snyder	T. B.	B-168	Solt	Isaiah
D-796	Snyder	Thomas	B-1785	Solt	Jacob
B-614	Snyder	Thomas	B-1832	Solt	Jacob
B-1068	Snyder	Tilghman	M-1015	Solt	Jacob
B-1278	Snyder	Viletta	B-168	Solt	James
B-84	Solt	Josiah	B-225	Spoonheimer	Martha
B-41	Solt	Louisa	B-47	Spoonheimer	Mary
M-151	Solt	Louisa	M-1074	Spoonheimer	Mary J
B-735	Solt	Lucy Ann	B-225	Spoonheimer	Reuben
B-41	Solt	Manda	M-62	Spoonheimer	Reuben
D-720	Solt	Maria	D-257	Spoonheimer	Thomas
B-78	Solt	Paul	B-47	Spoonheimer	William H
D-181	Solt	Reuben	M-1147	Sprigel	Flora M
B-422	Solt	Reuben	B-1895	Stabelton	Kate Alice
B-918	Solt	Reuben	M-1097	Stabelton	Kate Alice
B-529	Solt	Reuben	B-1014	Stahl	Molly
B-1037	Solt	Salinda	D-853	Stahler	Allen
D-373	Solt	Sarah	B-1844	Stahler	Calvin
D-381	Solt	Sarah	B-1083	Stahler	Charles
B-527	Solt	Sarah	B-1295	Stahler	Charles
B-845	Solt	Sarah	D-857	Stahler	Emma
B-416	Solt	Sarah	B-1295	Stahler	Emma
B-734	Solt	Sarah	D-858	Stahler	Isaac
B-1023	Solt	Sarah	B-1083	Stahler	Isaac
B-234	Solt	Selinda	M-1124	Stahler	James G
B-134	Solt	Selinda	D-856	Stahler	Lauretta
B-529	Solt	Sitna	M-817	Stahler	Mary Jane
B-92	Solt	Solomon	B-1083	Stahler	Priscilla
B-654	Solt	Susanna	D-851	Stahler	Samuel
M-120	Solt	Susanna	B-1000	Stahler	Stephen
M-1163	Solt	Sylvester	B-1000	Stahler	Victorion
B-865	Solt	Thomas	B-1844	Stahler	William S
B-92	Solt	William	M-1038	Stahler	William S
M-55	Sommet	Edwin Henry	B-1931	Stamm	Elda
B-76	Souders	Charles	B-1931	Stamm	William J
B-434	Souders	David	B-419	Stansberry	Edward
B-76	Souders	Joseph	B-611	Stansberry	L. S.
B-434	Souders	Joseph	B-419	Stansberry	Lorence
M-55	Souers	Elmyra	B-837	Stansberry	Lorence
M-1043	Sowers	Sitney F	B-837	Stansberry	Wilmer
M-778	Spangler	Susanna	B-938	Stark	Henry
D-1	Spengler	Ellemanda	B-938	Stark	Maria
B-1553	Spengler	Estella	M-560	Steckel	Susan E
B-1596	Spengler	Harrison	D-72	Stedtler	Mary
B-1553	Spengler	James A	B-1378	Steigerwalt	A F
B-1596	Spengler	James A	B-1775	Steigerwalt	A F
M-823	Spengler	James A	B-1725	Steigerwalt	A F
B-1222	Spengler	Polly	M-680	Steigerwalt	A.F.
B-1580	Spengler	Viletta	M-973	Steigerwalt	Alfred A
B-1688	Spengler	Vinetta C	M-746	Steigerwalt	Amanda
B-1539	Spengler	Vionetta	M-53	Steigerwalt	Anjulina
B-1462	Spengler	Vionetta C	D-867	Steigerwalt	Annie
B-1740	Spengler	Vionetta C	B-1298	Steigerwalt	Benjamin
M-737	Spohn	Samuel J	B-1374	Steigerwalt	Benjamin F
D-562	Spoonheimer	Catherine	B-1443	Steigerwalt	Benjamin F
B-1304	Spoonheimer	Charles	B-1513	Steigerwalt	Benjamin F

Line #	Surname	Given Name
B-304	Spoonheimer	Edward
B-304	Spoonheimer	Henry
B-940	Spoonheimer	Henry
B-1304	Spoonheimer	Henry
B-940	Spoonheimer	Lillie
B-1371	Steigerwalt	Codilia
B-1603	Steigerwalt	Codilia
B-1446	Steigerwalt	Cordelia
B-1129	Steigerwalt	Denah
B-1266	Steigerwalt	Denah
B-1179	Steigerwalt	Edgar
M-1005	Steigerwalt	Elias
B-1964	Steigerwalt	Ella E
M-1155	Steigerwalt	Ella E
B-1106	Steigerwalt	Elmira J
M-646	Steigerwalt	Emaline
B-1210	Steigerwalt	Emma
B-1574	Steigerwalt	Emma
B-1775	Steigerwalt	Emma
D-866	Steigerwalt	Emma Eulena
D-964	Steigerwalt	Emmaline
B-1443	Steigerwalt	Ensebius
D-906	Steigerwalt	Fannie
B-1701	Steigerwalt	Flora Ann
B-990	Steigerwalt	Franklin
B-1368	Steigerwalt	Franklin
D-936	Steigerwalt	George
B-919	Steigerwalt	Hannah
B-231	Steigerwalt	Harriet
B-1700	Steigerwalt	Harriet
M-56	Steigerwalt	Harriet
M-931	Steigerwalt	Harriet
M-902	Steigerwalt	Hettie
M-438	Steigerwalt	John
B-1223	Steigerwalt	Leah
B-37	Steigerwalt	Leah
M-100	Steigerwalt	Levi
M-443	Steigerwalt	Levina
B-1179	Steigerwalt	Lewis
B-1513	Steigerwalt	Llewellyn
M-966	Steigerwalt	Louisa
B-1126	Steigerwalt	Lusanna
B-786	Steigerwalt	Lydia
B-1045	Steigerwalt	Lydia
M-1062	Steigerwalt	Mantana
D-1340	Steigerwalt	Maria
B-1378	Steigerwalt	Mary
B-1441	Steigerwalt	Mary
B-1858	Steigerwalt	Mary A
B-1894	Steigerwalt	Mary A
B-1939	Steigerwalt	Mary A
M-1100	Steigerwalt	Mary A
B-991	Steigerwalt	Nathan
B-1106	Steigerwalt	Nathan
B-1648	Steigerwalt	Oliver
D-862	Steigerwalt	Rachel
M-385	Steigerwalt	Rebecca
M-252	Steigerwalt	Reuben
B-1574	Steigerwalt	Benjamin F
B-1374	Steigerwalt	Buhla
B-564	Steigerwalt	Catherine
B-1273	Steigerwalt	Codelia
B-1187	Steigerwalt	Codilia
M-689	Steigerwalt	Rosa A
B-684	Steigerwalt	Rosina
B-1298	Steigerwalt	Sallie
D-1071	Steigerwalt	Solomon
B-1374	Steigerwalt	Solomon
M-167	Steigerwalt	Susanna
B-1210	Steigerwalt	T W
M-793	Steigerwalt	T. W.
D-869	Steigerwalt	Tilghman
M-883	Steigerwalt	William
M-961	Steigerwalt	William
B-1648	Steigerwalt	Willoughby
M-910	Steigerwalt	Willoughby Richard
D-94	Stein	Catherine
B-326	Stein	Emma
D-183	Stein	George
B-326	Stein	George
B-639	Stein	George
B-639	Stein	Harry
D-441	Stein	John
B-1009	Stein	Lizzie
D-353	Stein	William
M-12	Steinbrenner	Albrecht
M-607	Steiner	Lizzie
B-89	Steiner	Nelson David
B-89	Steiner	William
D-325	Steinhauser	Henry
B-153	Steinheiser	Charles
B-639	Steinheiser	Charles
B-153	Steinheiser	Thomas
B-93	Steinheisser	Mary
B-884	Steinmetz	Mary
M-1010	Steinmetz	Robert S
B-908	Steitly	Pauline
B-1530	Stemler	Claude
D-456	Stemler	Daniel
B-920	Stemler	Elmira
M-1068	Stemler	Emma L
B-1026	Stemler	Mary
B-687	Stemler	Mary Ann
B-687	Stemler	Nathan
B-1080	Stemler	Nathan
B-1530	Stemler	Oliver A
M-818	Stemler	Oliver A
B-492	Stemler	Reuben
B-920	Stemler	Reuben
B-492	Stemler	Wilson
B-1948	Stemm	George E
B-1948	Stemm	Jennie
B-279	Stemmler	Mary Ann
B-112	Stemmler	Quinton
B-112	Stemmler	Reuben
B-112	Stemmler	Solomon

Line #	Surname	Given Name	Line #	Surname	Given Name
B-1368	Steigerwalt	Rosa	B-279	Stemmler	Solomon
B-1486	Steigerwalt	Rosa	B-874	Stemmler	Solomon
B-1615	Steigerwalt	Rosa A	B-969	Stenner	Amanda
D-504	Stenner	Charles	D-170	Stout	James
B-387	Stenner	Charles	B-1071	Stout	John
D-393	Stenner	Dianna	B-1271	Stout	John
D-84	Stenner	Emma	B-1405	Stout	Mary
D-714	Stenner	Henry	B-691	Stout	Milton
B-387	Stenner	Henry	B-1488	Stout	Morris
D-391	Stenner	Martha	B-1405	Stout	Morris Lessly
B-969	Stenner	Mary Ann	B-1488	Stout	Morris Lessly
D-371	Sterling	Clara	B-1350	Stout	Sarah Ann
D-552	Sterling	Tobias	B-1232	Stout	Sarah Ann Velare
B-23	Stermer	Henry	M-626	Stout	Sarah Ann Velare
M-257	Stermer	John	D-116	Stout	William
B-23	Stermer	Louisa Sarah	B-691	Stout	Zacharias
M-396	Sterner	Susanna	B-974	Stoyer	Mary
B-519	Stettler	Angeline	B-779	Stoyer	Mary
D-513	Stettler	Harrison	B-843	Strassberger	Regina
M-737	Stevelton	Jeanetta I	B-1054	Strassberger	Regina E
M-1186	Stevens	Charles	D-473	Strassburger	David
M-501	Stickrath	Barbara	B-378	Strassburger	David
B-266	Stiles	W. Lee	D-210	Strassburger	Edwin
B-267	Stiles	W. Lee	B-632	Strassburger	Hannah
D-1021	Stocker	Francis	B-525	Strassburger	Jacob
B-385	Stolle	Albien	M-240	Strassburger	Jacob
B-385	Stolle	Anna	B-100	Strassburger	Lucy
B-385	Stolle	Elizabeth	B-631	Strassburger	Lucy Ann
B-73	Stolmacher	Helga	M-428	Strassburger	Lucy Ann
B-72	Stolmacher	John	B-632	Strassburger	Mathias
B-73	Stolmacher	John	B-378	Strassburger	Matthias
B-72	Stolmacher	Mary	B-525	Strassburger	Warren
M-625	Stoneburner	W. A	D-214	Strassburger	William
D-1150	Stoudt	Alexander	D-44	Straub	William
D-1146	Stoudt	Charles	B-1961	Straup	Mantana
B-1844	Stoudt	Clara L	M-466	Straup	Wesley C
M-1038	Stoudt	Clara L	M-766	Strausburger	Sarah Ellen
M-832	Stoudt	Fianna R	D-523	Strauss	Catherine
M-858	Stoudt	Hiram H	D-81	Straussburger	Lydia
D-899	Stoudt	John	B-1526	Straussburger	Regina
M-747	Stoudt	Mary Ann	B-1561	Straussburger	Regina
M-401	Stoudt	Zacharias	M-707	Stroh	William R
B-1136	Stout	Abraham L	B-118	Strohl	Aaron
D-122	Stout	Adda	B-131	Strohl	Aaron
B-1271	Stout	Alwin	B-560	Strohl	Aaron
B-913	Stout	Amelia	B-825	Strohl	Aaron
B-159	Stout	Araminda	M-65	Strohl	Adam
D-309	Stout	Celestia	B-736	Strohl	Amos
B-913	Stout	Charles	M-435	Strohl	Amos
B-914	Stout	Charles	M-1124	Strohl	Carrie A
B-915	Stout	Charles	B-118	Strohl	Carry
B-159	Stout	David	D-512	Strohl	Catherine
B-885	Stout	David	B-737	Strohl	Christianna
B-1405	Stout	David	B-200	Strohl	Conrad
M-763	Stout	Edwin Thomas	M-177	Strohl	Edwin
B-1071	Stout	Elmira	D-717	Strohl	Elizabeth
B-1488	Stout	Eva Etta	B-171	Strohl	Elmira
B-915	Stout	Ida	B-825	Strohl	Eve

Line #	Surname	Given Name	Line #	Surname	Given Name
B-914	Stout	Isaac	M-45	Strohl	Fayette
M-525	Strohl	Franklin Thomas	B-359	Strong	James C
B-131	Strohl	Harrison	B-429	Strong	Liberia
B-764	Strohl	Ida	B-359	Strong	Willmer
D-36	Strohl	James	B-212	Stroup	Amelia
M-649	Strohl	John S	B-1026	Stroup	Amelia
B-274	Strohl	Joseph	B-920	Stroup	Amelia
M-780	Strohl	Joseph	M-255	Stroup	Amelia
B-825	Strohl	Josephine	D-406	Stroup	Anna
M-1037	Strohl	Josephine	B-123	Stroup	Anna Eliza
B-737	Strohl	Josiah	B-789	Stroup	Catherine
M-445	Strohl	Josiah	M-418	Stroup	Catherine
B-274	Strohl	Kate	M-284	Stroup	Eliza Jane
B-171	Strohl	Levi	M-444	Stroup	Elmira
B-764	Strohl	Levi	B-572	Stroup	Emma
M-537	Strohl	Lucinda	M-210	Stroup	Emma R
D-405	Strohl	Lydia	B-469	Stroup	Emma Rebecca
M-730	Strohl	Lydia Ann	B-214	Stroup	Esther
B-794	Strohl	Margaret	B-486	Stroup	Esther
D-607	Strohl	Maria	B-789	Stroup	Esther
B-131	Strohl	Mary	M-126	Stroup	Esther
M-1082	Strohl	Mary	B-520	Stroup	Fayetta
B-118	Strohl	Mary Ann	B-968	Stroup	Harriet
M-421	Strohl	Mary Jane	B-24	Stroup	Harriet
B-473	Strohl	Matilda	B-968	Stroup	Harrison
B-1073	Strohl	Matilda	B-274	Stroup	Henrietta
B-1347	Strohl	Matilda	B-693	Stroup	Henrietta
B-200	Strohl	Purey	B-789	Stroup	Jacob
B-736	Strohl	Quinton	B-123	Stroup	Jacob B
B-634	Strohl	Rebecca	M-418	Stroup	Jacob B
B-499	Strohl	Rebecca	B 520	Stroup	Josiah
M-78	Strohl	Reuben	B-787	Stroup	Josiah
B-560	Strohl	Sarah	B-1915	Stroup	Mantana
B-500	Strohl	Savenna	M-1064	Stroup	Mantana L
M-526	Strohl	Susanna	D-90	Stroup	Mary
B-825	Strohl	Thomas Franklin	B-787	Stroup	Matilda
B-499	Strohl	Ulysses	B-306	Stroup	Messina
B-812	Strohl	Vinnie	B-306	Stroup	Moses
D-355	Strohl	William	M-36	Stroup	Moses
D-604	Strohl	William	B-190	Stroup	Polly
B-118	Strohl	William H	B-123	Stroup	Refena
B-499	Strohl	William H	M-49	Stroup	Refene
M-162	Strohl	William H	B-618	Stroup	Sabina
B-812	Strohl	William H	D-404	Stroup	Thomas
B-1683	Strohm	Bel Lucretia	M-231	Stroup	Willmine
B-140	Strohm	Ellen	M-288	Stuckley	Adline
B-250	Strohm	Ellen	M-156	Stuckley	Jacob
B-624	Strohm	Ellen	B-644	Stuckly	Adline
B-924	Strohm	Ellen	M-1092	Swank	Clara M
M-145	Strohm	Ellen	M-934	Swartz	Emma L
B-566	Strohm	George	B-1055	Swartz	Jacob
M-1114	Strohm	George	B-1	Taglehner	Anna Eliza
B-566	Strohm	Joseph	B-2	Taglehner	Anna Eliza
B-1196	Strohm	Liberia	M-594	Taney	Mary Ann
M-994	Strohm	Oscar J	B-1341	Taylor	Edward C
B-1551	Strohrm	Mary	B-1381	Taylor	Edward C
M-311	Strong	James	M-673	Taylor	Edward C
D-925	Taylor	Emma	B-1716	Troxel	Amanda

Line #	Surname	Given Name	Line #	Surname	Given Name
B-1341	Taylor	Emma	B-1129	Troxel	Amelia
D-232	Taylor	Mary	B-1129	Troxel	Charles
D-236	Taylor	Mary	D-1302	Troxel	Elias
B-1381	Taylor	William	M-617	Troxel	Emma
B-435	Techiaschky	Frederich	B-1716	Troxel	Frank A
B-435	Techiaschky	Gustav	M-907	Troxel	Frank A
D-360	Teschiaschky	Anna	B-531	Troxel	July Ann
B-1062	Thoma	Margeret	B-1218	Troxel	July Ann
B-529	Thomas	Alavesta	M-813	Troxel	Pierce J
B-845	Thomas	Alavesta	D-1200	Troxel	William
B-3	Thomas	Alavesta	B-1716	Troxel	William
B-875	Thomas	Alavesta	M-771	Troxel	William
M-390	Thomas	Alavesta Jane	D-1273	Troxell	Charles
D-70	Thomas	Henry	B-1266	Troxell	Charles
D-579	Thomas	Maria	B-1266	Troxell	Charles
B-1657	Thomas	Ruth	M-997	Troxell	Elias A
B-1657	Thomas	Thomas D	B-1631	Troxell	Frank Albert
M-853	Thomas	Thomas D	B-1631	Troxell	Harvey
B-700	Thomas	Zacharias	B-952	Troxell	July Ann
B-700	Thomas	Zacharias	B-1272	Troxell	July Ann
B-88	Tinny	Harry	B-1272	Troxell	Sally Ann
B-88	Tinny	Newton H	B-1545	Troxell	Sarah
M-610	Torrance	Elizabeth	B-579	Trumbore	Alfred
D-953	Torrance	Jonathan	B-580	Trumbore	Alfred
D-633	Trach	Anna	B-1544	Trumbore	Edwin
M-799	Tracy	Mary Elizabeth	B-1845	Trumbore	Edwin
M-324	Trainer	Alfred	D-226	Trumbore	Eliz
B-330	Trainer	Charles	D-788	Trumbore	Ellen
B-506	Trainer	Charles	B-71	Trumbore	Elsie
B-706	Trainer	Charles	B-1173	Trumbore	Elwin
B-1313	Trainer	Charles	B-1544	Trumbore	Elwin
B-330	Trainer	Ellen	B-1698	Trumbore	Elwin
M-219	Trainer	John	B-380	Trumbore	Eugene
B-1313	Trainer	Martha	B-1845	Trumbore	Gussie
M-937	Trainer	Robert Milton	B-380	Trumbore	Henry
B-706	Trainer	Sarah	B-580	Trumbore	John
B-506	Trainer	Thomas	B-244	Trumbore	Joseph
M-446	Trainer	Wilson	M-47	Trumbore	Joseph
B-637	Traut	Catherine	B-244	Trumbore	Laura
M-415	Traut	Catherine	B-1698	Trumbore	Laura
M-1139	Treichler	Mary A	B-71	Trumbore	Nathan
M-462	Trenklin	Anthony	M-228	Trumbore	Nathan
D-92	Trimm	Henry	B-222	Trumbore	Priscilla
B-799	Trine	Elmer	B-660	Trumbore	Priscilla
M-279	Trine	Harriet	B-1205	Trumbore	Priscilla
B-264	Trine	John	M-28	Trumbore	Priscilla
B-535	Trine	John	B-1173	Trumbore	Robert
B-799	Trine	John	D-163	Trumbore	Thomas
M-319	Trine	John	B-579	Trumbore	William
D-1245	Trine	Jonathan	B-405	Tucker	Henry
D-1026	Trine	Maria	B-405	Tucker	May
B-535	Trine	Meta	B-1382	Turner	Clara
B-264	Trine	William	D-1228	Turner	Hesikiel
B-716	Trout	Catherine	B-1382	Turner	William
M-909	Troxall	Catherine	M-1076	Ulrich	Carrie I
B-394	Unangst	Henry	B-234	Walck	David
B-394	Unangst	Henry	B-1037	Walck	David
M-287	Vangilder	Minnie E	B-134	Walck	David

Line #	Surname	Given Name	Line #	Surname	Given Name
B-90	Voegel	Anna Margeret	B-626	Walck	David
B-3	Voelker	Elizabeth B	M-172	Walck	David
D-138	Vogel	Joel	B-236	Walck	Edward
B-841	Vogt	Lenius	B-647	Walck	Edward
B-979	Vogt	Mary Ann	B-217	Walck	Edward
B-841	Vogt	Sarah	B-647	Walck	Ellemanda
D-317	Volke	Reuben	B-816	Walck	Elmira
M-1138	Wagaman	Lilly A S	D-570	Walck	Elwin
B-1696	Wageman	Hannah	B-647	Walck	Elwin
B-1612	Wageman	Minnie	D-400	Walck	Emma
B-1436	Wageman	Nathan	B-1056	Walck	Emma
B-1612	Wageman	Nathan	B-285	Walck	Eugene
B-1696	Wageman	Nathan	B-61	Walck	Fayetta
B-1436	Wageman	Pearce	B-1055	Walck	Fayetta
D-1101	Wagner	Charles	B-345	Walck	Fayette
M-1108	Wagner	Charles Nathan	D-655	Walck	George
B-1382	Wagner	Elizabeth	B-344	Walck	George
M-264	Wagner	Elizabeth	B-1369	Walck	George
B-201	Wagner	Harriet	B-62	Walck	George
B-35	Wagner	Harrietta	B-461	Walck	George
B-367	Wagner	Herinetta	B-1369	Walck	George W
D-1100	Wagner	Levi	B-1480	Walck	George W
M-679	Wagner	Lewis H	M-683	Walck	George W
D-1063	Wahl	John	B-1037	Walck	Granville
B-97	Walb	David	B-113	Walck	Henry
B-97	Walb	Maria	B-973	Walck	Herby
B-1075	Walbert	Alfred A	D-271	Walck	John
B-876	Walbert	Alfred A	B-344	Walck	John
B-921	Walbert	Alfred A	B-451	Walck	John
D-588	Walbert	Eliza	B-62	Walck	John E
B-1075	Walbert	Osbon	B-653	Walck	John E
D-559	Walbert	Oscar	B-867	Walck	John E
D-12	Walck	(s/o Simon and Sabrina (Stout))	B-956	Walck	John E
B-588	Walck	Abby Ann	B-992	Walck	John E
B-885	Walck	Abby Ann	B-364	Walck	July Ann
B-1052	Walck	Abby Ann	B-796	Walck	July Ann
M-187	Walck	Abby Ann	B-867	Walck	Lewis
B-67	Walck	Alice	B-285	Walck	Lewis
B-1037	Walck	Alice	B-816	Walck	Lewis
M-597	Walck	Alice	B-1056	Walck	Lewis
B-181	Walck	Amanda	B-1327	Walck	Lewis
B-1532	Walck	Amanda	B-286	Walck	Lewis
B-691	Walck	Amanda	B-1369	Walck	Lewis
M-160	Walck	Amanda	B-236	Walck	Lilie
B-1376	Walck	Amelia Agnes	B-472	Walck	Loretta
B-323	Walck	Anna Maria	B-890	Walck	Louisa
M-580	Walck	Anna Maria	B-210	Walck	Lucy
B-209	Walck	Augustus	B-530	Walck	Lucy
B-594	Walck	Augustus	B-1194	Walck	Lucy
B-504	Walck	Augustus	B-138	Walck	Lucy Ann
B-973	Walck	Augustus	B-939	Walck	Lucy Ann
B-801	Walck	Augustus A	B-425	Walck	Manda
B-1021	Walck	Catherine	D-571	Walck	Maria
B-113	Walck	Maria	B-288	Walp	Maria
B-62	Walck	Mary	B-573	Walp	Maria
B-801	Walck	Mary	B-748	Walp	Maria
B-428	Walck	Mary	B-1024	Walp	Maria Anna
B-1195	Walck	Mary	B-245	Walp	Robert

Line #	Surname	Given Name	Line #	Surname	Given Name
B-885	Walck	Mary	M-384	Walp	Robert
B-1405	Walck	Mary	B-153	Walter	Anna Maria
B-159	Walck	Mary Ann	B-1179	Walter	Emma
B-1592	Walck	Matilda	M-631	Walter	George F
B-1327	Walck	Minnie	M-1077	Walter	Lewis A
B-626	Walck	Nelson	B-650	Walter	Maria
B-67	Walck	Philip	B-651	Walter	Maria
B-626	Walck	Philip	M-236	Walter	Maria
B-973	Walck	Philip	B-1466	Walter	Sarah Maria
B-801	Walck	Philip	B-1467	Walter	Sarah Maria
B-897	Walck	Philip	B-1468	Walter	Sarah Maria
M-222	Walck	Philip	B-1469	Walter	Sarah Maria
B-323	Walck	Priscilla	B-1886	Walters	Benjamin E
B-1040	Walck	Priscilla	B-1886	Walters	Daisy
M-363	Walck	Priscilla	D-264	Walton	Justus
B-461	Walck	Rebecca	B-42	Wanamacher	Charles
M-370	Walck	Rebecca	B-42	Wanamacher	Franklin W
B-1480	Walck	Robert	B-1250	Wanemacher	Anna
B-504	Walck	Sabilla	M-754	Warg	Robert
D-430	Walck	Sarah	B-785	Warley	Mary
B-653	Walck	Sarah	B-785	Warley	Monroe
B-134	Walck	Sarah	M-337	Wartman	Daniel P
B-299	Walck	Sarah	B-89	Wasem	Elizabeth
B-425	Walck	Sarah	B-523	Washbon	Charles
B-555	Walck	Sarah	B-523	Washbon	John Joseph
B-757	Walck	Sarah	B-1781	Washburn	Ellen
B-236	Walck	Sarah	B-74	Waterbaer	Emma
B-20	Walck	Sarah Ann	B-315	Waterbaer	Franklin
B-181	Walck	Sarah Ann	B-74	Waterbaer	William
D-277	Walck	Savannah	B-315	Waterbaer	William
B-472	Walck	Simon	D-580	Waterboer	Henrietta
B-67	Walck	Solomon	D-158	Waterbor	August
B-234	Walck	Solomon	B-365	Waters	Mary Ann
B-594	Walck	Susan	B-366	Waters	Mary Ann
B-1270	Walck	Susan	D-1041	Weaver	Calvin
M-427	Walck	Susan	B-1545	Weaver	Clinton
D-585	Walck	Susanna	B-1849	Weaver	Ida A
B-209	Walck	Sylvester	B-1545	Weaver	Jacob
M-676	Walck	Tillie	M-829	Weaver	Jacob O
B-113	Walck	William	B-1875	Weaver	Lula
B-472	Walck	William	M-469	Weaver	Mary L
M-233	Walck	William	B-1835	Weaver	Meta
B-234	Walck	Wilson	B-1793	Weaver	Minnie
M-685	Walck	Amelia Agnes	B-835	Weaver	Oscar
M-123	Walk	Augustus	B-1749	Weaver	Sadie
M-114	Walk	Sarah Ann	M-106	Weaver	Sarah
B-639	Walker	Anna Maria	B-1441	Weaver	Wellington D
B-342	Walker	Catherine	M-720	Weaver	Wellington D
M-130	Walker	Catherine	B-1441	Weaver	William
M-81	Walp	David	B-835	Weaver	Wilson
M-563	Walp	Lavina	B-1875	Weaver	Wilson
M-499	Weaver	Wilson	B-1268	Weber	Wilson
B-1749	Weaver	Wilson August	B-1479	Weber	Wilson
B-1793	Weaver	Wilson August	B-664	Webes	Solomon
B-1835	Weaver	Wilson August	B-102	Wehr	Alvin
D-528	Webb	Abraham	M-1080	Wehr	Alvin Adam
B-1805	Webb	Anconetta	M-1029	Wehr	Amanda
B-1935	Webb	Anzonetta	B-1230	Wehr	Cyrus

Line #	Surname	Given Name	Line #	Surname	Given Name
D-310	Webb	Daniel	B-102	Wehr	David
B-1142	Webb	Ellen	D-1020	Wehr	Elizabeth
B-255	Webb	Ellen	B-781	Wehr	Elizabeth
B-317	Webb	Ellen	D-591	Wehr	Ellen
B-851	Webb	Ellen	B-258	Wehr	Emma
B-1408	Webb	Emma	M-1000	Wehr	Emma
M-667	Webb	Emma	M-257	Wehr	Flora
B-1959	Webb	George	D-1216	Wehr	Harrison
D-409	Webb	Ida	D-691	Wehr	Jacob
B-156	Webb	Ida	M-298	Wehr	Joseph
B-156	Webb	James	D-1090	Wehr	Lafayette
B-317	Webb	James	M-1063	Wehr	Lewis Oscar
B-591	Webb	James	M-1028	Wehr	Lizzie A
B-851	Webb	James	B-1415	Wehr	Louisa
M-139	Webb	James	B-1503	Wehr	Louisa
B-1142	Webb	James A	B-370	Wehr	Lucy
D-275	Webb	John	B-15	Wehr	Mary
B-797	Webb	Joseph	M-226	Wehr	Mary
B-490	Webb	Joseph S	B-102	Wehr	Nathan
B-797	Webb	Joseph S	B-276	Wehr	Nathan
M-118	Webb	Joseph S	B-258	Wehr	Owen
B-490	Webb	Lizzie	M-201	Wehr	Owen
B-255	Webb	Mary	D-415	Wehr	Peter
B-107	Webb	Mary	D-492	Wehr	Polly
B-1142	Webb	Mary Ann	D-868	Wehr	Rachel
B-107	Webb	Nathan	B-1230	Wehr	Savilla
B-851	Webb	Oliver	B-1230	Wehr	Thomas
D-555	Webb	Rosa	M-918	Wehr	Tilghman
B-317	Webb	Rosanna	D-773	Wehr	William
B-107	Webb	Samuel	D-1304	Wehr	William
B-591	Webb	Thomas	M-1159	Wehr	Ellen Jane
B-591	Webb	Thomas M	D-910	Wehrstein	Henry
M-424	Webb	Thomas M	B-768	Wehrstein	Henry
M-1177	Webb	Victor E	B-121	Weida	Aaron
B-1959	Webb	Victor Ellsworth	B-336	Weida	Aaron
D-240	Webb	William	B-692	Weida	Aaron
B-721	Weber	Alavesta	B-923	Weida	Aaron
B-1031	Weber	Alavesta	M-229	Weida	Aaron
B-1268	Weber	Emma	B-814	Weida	Alwin
B-664	Weber	Emma	B-357	Weida	Benjamin
M-300	Weber	Emma	B-620	Weida	Benjamin
B-1479	Weber	Ida	B-814	Weida	Benjamin
B-720	Weber	Lucinda	B-452	Weida	Benjamin
B-1098	Weber	Lucinda	B-336	Weida	Charles
B-1198	Weber	Lucinda	D-383	Weida	Harrison
D-356	Weber	Mary	B-692	Weida	Harrison
B-1020	Weber	Mary	B-924	Weida	Irena
B-1000	Weber	Sally Ann	B-620	Weida	James
M-882	Weber	Thomas D	B-250	Weida	Laura
B-331	Weida	Lily	D-643	Weiss	Louisa
D-382	Weida	Nelson	B-770	Weiss	Louisa
B-140	Weida	Nelson	B-257	Weiss	Matilda
B-923	Weida	Peter	D-3	Weiss	Michael
B-331	Weida	Peter	M-537	Weiss	Neander
B-357	Weida	Priscilla	B-122	Weiss	Nero
B-563	Weida	Priscilla	B-440	Weiss	Nero
M-209	Weida	Rebecca	B-770	Weiss	Nero
M-273	Weida	Thomas Alfred	B-976	Weiss	Nero

Line #	Surname	Given Name	Line #	Surname	Given Name
B-121	Weida	William	B-616	Weiss	Nero
B-140	Weida	William	B-333	Weiss	Sally Ann
B-250	Weida	William	B-1008	Weiss	Samuel
B-624	Weida	William	M-605	Weiss	Sarah Alice
B-924	Weida	William	B-1008	Weiss	Stewart
B-624	Weida	Wilson	B-684	Weiss	William
B-1309	Weidaw	Aaron	M-822	Weiss	William
B-1309	Weidaw	Alice	B-205	Weisset	Frederica
D-719	Weidaw	Alwin	B-380	Wells	Catherine
D-1049	Weidaw	Amanda	M-283	Wells	Catherine
M-888	Weidaw	Elmira	M-303	Wells	Mary Ann
D-1298	Weidaw	Herby	D-218	Wemmer	Bernhard
B-1784	Weidaw	Herby	M-777	Wentz	Addison
B-1925	Weidaw	Laura A	M-802	Wentz	Anna E
B-1784	Weidaw	Samuel	B-162	Wentz	Clara
M-145	Weidaw	William	B-932	Wentz	Harriet
M-191	Weidman	Anna	M-519	Wentz	Harriet
M-825	Weidner	Jefferson	B-162	Wentz	Harrison
B-898	Weisch	Frederica	B-834	Wentz	Harrison
B-767	Weiser	Frederica	M-1113	Wentz	Laura A
D-519	Weiss	Anna	D-248	Wentz	Lewis
B-240	Weiss	Anna Maria	B-834	Wentz	Samuel
B-241	Weiss	Anna Maria	M-896	Wentz	Tobias
B-684	Weiss	Carrie	B-1283	Werly	Sarah
M-588	Weiss	Catherine N	B-830	Werner	Mary Ann
B-902	Weiss	Charles A	B-587	Werstein	Henry
B-363	Weiss	Charles August	B-1130	Werstein	Henry
D-191	Weiss	Elias	D-828	Wert	Alice
B-108	Weiss	Ellen	B-1036	Wert	Alice
B-395	Weiss	Ellen	B-722	Wert	Ida
B-241	Weiss	Ellen Jane	B-316	Wert	Rosa
B-616	Weiss	Ellen Jane	B-316	Wert	Willoughby
B-902	Weiss	Ellen Jane	B-722	Wert	Willoughby
B-523	Weiss	Emma Louisa	B-1036	Wert	Willoughby
B-122	Weiss	George	B-597	Werth	Maria
M-463	Weiss	Hannah	D-538	Werth	Rosa
D-362	Weiss	Harry	B-1215	Wertmam	Owen Alfred
B-108	Weiss	Henrietta	B-1215	Wertmam	Thura
B-363	Weiss	John	D-1163	Wertman	(s/o william D & Kate)
B-440	Weiss	John	B-1152	Wertman	Adaline
M-971	Weiss	John O	M-552	Wertman	Adaline Elizabeth
D-990	Weiss	Levi	B-1573	Wertman	Carolina
B-514	Weiss	Levi	B-1473	Wertman	Caroline
B-760	Weiss	Levi	B-1533	Wertman	Caroline
D-553	Weiss	Lilie	D-1072	Wertman	Catherine
D-698	Weiss	Lillie	B-1186	Wertman	David
B-976	Weiss	Lilly	M-610	Wertman	David A
B-442	Wertman	Eli	B-1320	Wher	Louisa
B-1531	Wertman	Hetty	M-315	Wher	Louisa
B-980	Wertman	Kate	B-224	Wher	Lucy
B-1254	Wertman	Kate	M-274	Wher	Lucy
B-1471	Wertman	Kate	B-1315	Wher	Mapel
B-1207	Wertman	Kate	B-191	Wher	Mary
M-1104	Wertman	Lillie Ida	B-193	Wher	Nathan
B-1927	Wertman	Llewellyn Oscar	B-350	Wher	Nathan
B-1927	Wertman	Mabel	B-513	Wher	Owen
B-1511	Wertman	Magdaline	B-1016	Wher	Owen
B-1200	Wertman	Mary	D-794	Wher	William

Line #	Surname	Given Name	Line #	Surname	Given Name
B-1876	Wertman	Mary	B-1647	Wher	William
B-1908	Wertman	Mary	B-1752	Whitaker	Irwin
B-1930	Wertman	Mary	B-1393	Whitaker	James Franklin
B-1264	Wertman	Mary	B-1752	Whitaker	James Franklin
B-722	Wertman	Philip	M-641	Whitaker	James Franklin
B-837	Wertman	Philip	B-1393	Whitaker	William
M-364	Wertman	Priscilla	B-488	Whitehead	Elizabeth
B-362	Wertman	Rebecca	B-609	Whitehead	Elizabeth
B-546	Wertman	Rebecca	B-978	Whitehead	Elizabeth
B-611	Wertman	Rebecca	D-11	Whitehead	Jacob
B-776	Wertman	Rebecca	B-328	Whiteman	Abraham
B-946	Wertman	Rebecca	B-818	Whiteman	Anna
B-957	Wertman	Rebecca	B-1252	Whiteman	Anna
B-1136	Wertman	Rebecca	B-971	Whiteman	Anna Maria
B-419	Wertman	Rebecca	B-1404	Whiteman	Anna Maria
B-1541	Wertman	Rebecca	B-328	Whiteman	Daniel
D-1297	Wertman	Reuben	B-549	Whiteman	Daniel
B-919	Wertman	Reuben	B-772	Whiteman	Maria
B-1200	Wertman	Reuben	B-773	Whiteman	Maria
B-442	Wertman	Samuel	M-224	Whiteman	Maria
B-1436	Wertman	Sophia	B-458	Whiteman	Mary Ann
B-1612	Wertman	Sophia	M-330	Whiteman	Mary Ann
B-1696	Wertman	Sophia	M-1166	Whiteman	Oliver
B-275	Wertman	William	M-543	Whiteman	Sarah
B-1152	Wertman	William	B-549	Whiteman	Thomas
B-526	Wertz	Harrison	B-1590	Whiteneck	Ellemanda
M-122	Wesner	Kitty Ann	B-1590	Whiteneck	Jefferson
B-1308	Westen	John F	B-548	Whitmer	Lucy
M-71	Weston	John	M-487	Widdoss	Richard B
M-495	Wetzel	Daniel D	D-189	Wierstein	Frederica
M-575	Wetzel	David D	B-593	Wieser	Fredrica
M-840	Wetzel	Sevilla	B-1950	Wilbert	Minda
B-1050	Wher	Charles	M-1170	Wilbert	Minda
B-193	Wher	David	B-136	Wilkraut	Matilda
B-1050	Wher	David	B-548	Wilkraut	Matilda
D-303	Wher	Emma	B-1038	William	Charles
B-193	Wher	Emma	B-1038	William	Jacob
B-513	Wher	Ida	D-85	Williams	(d/o Edward & Mary (Evans))
B-1315	Wher	Lewis A	D-1305	Williams	Arbean
B-1647	Wher	Lewis A	M-1143	Williams	Ida Priscilla
M-644	Wher	Lewis A	B-1113	Williams	James
B-1016	Wher	Lillie	B-1261	Williams	James
B-479	Wher	Louisa	B-1484	Williams	James
B-954	Wher	Louisa	B-1188	Williams	James
B-1162	Wher	Louisa	B-1484	Williams	Katie
B-1261	Williams	Lovetta	M-1175	Woolbert	Laura S
M-654	Williams	M.J.	M-89	Woolwert	Jane
B-1113	Williams	Norah	B-1231	Wright	Polly
M-657	Williams	Priscilla	D-378	Wuchter	Hannah
B-732	Williamson	Ida	D-160	Wuersten	(d/o John and Mary)
B-732	Williamson	James	B-346	Wuerstler	Anna
B-904	Willkraut	Matilda	B-1345	Xander	Benjamin
B-1498	Willkraut	Matilda	M-380	Xander	Benjamin E
M-712	Willman	Abby Lucinda	M-831	Xander	C. E.
B-451	Willman	Amelia	D-1074	Xander	Catherine
B-1789	Willman	Howard	B-988	Xander	Charles W
M-898	Willman	James	B-1216	Xander	Charles W
B-1789	Willman	James Henry	B-1344	Xander	Charles W

Line #	Surname	Given Name	Line #	Surname	Given Name
D-1065	Willman	Louisa	M-188	Xander	Charles William
D-1270	Wiltsie	Ruth	B-70	Xander	Charles Wm.
D-150	Winkler	Barbara	B-1345	Xander	Clifford
B-740	Winsland	Franklin	B-988	Xander	Helenah
B-1748	Winter	Daniel	B-1344	Xander	James
M-794	Winter	Daniel	B-1216	Xander	John
B-1929	Winter	David A	B-1564	Xander	Mary Anna
B-1748	Winter	Harry	M-1149	Xander	Uriah
B-1929	Winter	Robert	B-70	Xander	Wilson
D-790	Winterholder	Charles	M-1160	Yale	William D
B-114	Wirkley	Catherine	B-1408	Yeager	John H
M-125	Wirstein	Henry	M-667	Yeager	John H
M-955	Wisler	Frank	B-1408	Yeager	Josephine
B-146	Wissner	Catherine	M-707	Yeager	Sophia L
B-146	Wissner	John	M-1008	Yehl	Robert Allen
B-916	Wolf	Annie	B-320	Yenser	Charles
D-501	Wolf	Augustus	B-320	Yenser	Charles
B-1169	Wolf	Carrie	M-63	Yenser	James
B-463	Wolf	Frank	B-1380	Yenser	Mary
B-1169	Wolf	George	D-761	Yenser	Minnie
M-601	Wolf	George	B-1158	Yenser	Minnie
B-242	Wolf	Henry	M-18	Yenser	Rebecca
B-638	Wolf	Henry	B-394	Yenser	Sarah
B-242	Wolf	John	M-985	Yenser	Thomas
M-527	Wolf	John S	B-1158	Yenser	Wilson
B-462	Wolf	Lillie	B-708	Yohe	Alfred J
B-638	Wolf	Owen	M-266	Yohe	Alfred J
M-383	Wolf	Owen K	B-708	Yohe	Charles
B-463	Wolf	William	B-1204	Yostheimer	Ephraim
M-148	Wolf	William H	M-873	Young	Asa B
B-462	Wolf	William M	B-1572	Young	Ellen
B-916	Wolf	William M	B-1633	Young	Ellen
B-638	Wolf	Zacharias T	M-727	Young	Ellen Mina
M-426	Wolf	Zacharias T	B-1779	Young	Elsie
B-1206	Wolf	Zacharis	B-355	Young	Esta
B-897	Wolff	John	D-1261	Young	Esther
B-897	Wolff	Philip	M-1131	Young	Frank
M-1060	Wolfskeil	Conrad	B-354	Young	George
B-346	Wolkermuth	Emma	B-354	Young	James
B-346	Wolkermuth	Otto	B-355	Young	James
D-1115	Womer	Lucy	B-1779	Young	Levi A
M-1039	Woods	John B	M-1044	Young	Levi A
B-1950	Woolbert	Laura	B-449	Young	Mary
M-373	Young	Mary E	B-679	Zeiser	Lorenz
B-1568	Young	Rosa E	M-291	Zeiser	Lorenz
B-1151	Youngkin	Allen	D-1156	Zellner	Abigail
D-565	Youngkin	Charles	B-1152	Zellner	Albert
B-630	Youngkin	Charlie	D-190	Zellner	Alwina
B-630	Youngkin	Robert J	B-667	Zellner	Amanda
B-1151	Youngkin	Robert J	D-913	Zellner	Charles
M-286	Youngkin	Robert J	B-1152	Zellner	Charles
D-1129	Youse	Carrie	M-552	Zellner	Charles
B-1609	Youse	Carrie	B-1613	Zellner	Emma
D-1263	Youse	Clara	B-665	Zellner	F Reuben
B-1453	Youse	Ellen Lovina	B-353	Zellner	Franklin
B-1061	Youse	Emma	B-482	Zellner	Franklin
M-1084	Youse	Emma E	B-1456	Zellner	Harriet
B-1453	Youse	Fianna	M-35	Zellner	Harriet

Line #	Surname	Given Name	Line #	Surname	Given Name
D-987	Youse	Gideon	M-50	Zellner	Henry
D-1203	Youse	Jennie	B-910	Zellner	Ida
D-653	Youse	Magdalene	M-1134	Zellner	James
B-1609	Youse	Milton A	M-1159	Zellner	James Oliver
B-1684	Youse	Milton A	M-287	Zellner	Joseph
M-894	Youse	Milton A	B-998	Zellner	Louisa
B-1684	Youse	Robert	B-1456	Zellner	Mary
B-1061	Youse	Tobias	M-475	Zellner	Mary Ann
B-1297	Youse	Tobias	B-1014	Zellner	Mary Jane
M-486	Youse	Tobias	B-1744	Zellner	Moses
B-1297	Youse	William	B-1613	Zellner	Moses
M-692	Yoxheimer	Amandus	B-1744	Zellner	Moses
D-328	Zahn	Amelia	M-895	Zellner	Moses
B-781	Zahn	Hannah	D-425	Zellner	Reuben
B-536	Zahn	Joseph	B-780	Zellner	Reuben
M-835	Zahn	Lewis Aaron	B-910	Zellner	Reuben F
D-614	Zahn	Mamie	B-929	Zellner	Reuben Franklin
B-536	Zahn	Minnie	M-190	Zellner	Reuben Franklin
D-323	Zahn	Otilla	M-27	Zellner	Samuel
D-453	Zahn	Rosa	B-665	Zellner	Tilghman
M-352	Zahn	Susan	D-498	Zellner	William
B-1258	Zehner	Benjamin	B-353	Zellner	William
M-671	Zehner	Charles	B-1014	Zellner	William
B-1397	Zehner	Ellemanda	B-1018	Zettelmoyer	Ellen
B-1655	Zehner	Ellemanda	B-1121	Zettelmoyer	John
M-786	Zehner	Ellen Jane	M-633	Zettelmoyer	John
D-1166	Zehner	Francis	B-1672	Zettelmoyer	Levina
B-987	Zehner	Jane	B-1729	Zettelmoyer	Levina
B-987	Zehner	Levi	B-1788	Zettelmoyer	Lovina
B-1231	Zehner	Manda	B-1121	Zettelmoyer	Lydia
D-1281	Zehner	Maria	B 1431	Zettelmoyer	Lydia
B-1796	Zehner	Mary	B-1133	Zettelmoyer	Maria
D-1182	Zehner	Polly	B-883	Zettelmoyer	Polly
B-1655	Zehner	Polly	B-1249	Zettelmoyer	Sarah
B-1815	Zehner	Polly	B-812	Ziegenfus	Kate
M-874	Zehner	Polly A	B-891	Ziegenfuss	Adelaide
B-1365	Zehner	Susanna	M-1014	Ziegenfuss	Alice Louise
B-1258	Zehner	Timothy	B-20	Ziegenfuss	Angelina
B-1397	Zehner	Timothy	D-397	Ziegenfuss	Carolina
D-778	Zeiser	Harriet	D-113	Ziegenfuss	Catherine
B-1007	Zeiser	Lorentz	M-45	Ziegenfuss	Charles
B-930	Ziegenfuss	Daniel	M-743	Ziegler	Jairus W
M-721	Ziegenfuss	David E	B-1736	Ziegler	Kitty Ann
B-627	Ziegenfuss	Edwin	M-168	Ziegler	Kitty Ann
B-932	Ziegenfuss	Edwin	M-1054	Ziegler	Lewis A
B-1393	Ziegenfuss	Elemena	B-1364	Ziegler	Nathan
B-1752	Ziegenfuss	Elemena	B-1365	Ziegler	Oliver
M-641	Ziegenfuss	Elemena	B-1106	Ziegler	Ross
M-526	Ziegenfuss	Elias P	D-1055	Ziegler	William
B-931	Ziegenfuss	Elizabeth	M-618	Zimmerman	Aaron
B-873	Ziegenfuss	Emma	B-1220	Zimmerman	Alfred
M-628	Ziegenfuss	Francisca Elizabeth	M-611	Zimmerman	Alfred
B-921	Ziegenfuss	Harriet	B-1514	Zimmerman	Allen S
M-529	Ziegenfuss	Harriet	B-1663	Zimmerman	Allen S
M-682	Ziegenfuss	Harriet	M-704	Zimmerman	Allen S
D-306	Ziegenfuss	Harry	B-1618	Zimmerman	Alvena
D-348	Ziegenfuss	Ida	B-1678	Zimmerman	Alvena
B-68	Ziegenfuss	Ida	B-1747	Zimmerman	Alvena

Line #	Surname	Given Name	Line #	Surname	Given Name
B-373	Ziegenfuss	Ida	B-1800	Zimmerman	Alvena
B-208	Ziegenfuss	Irwin	M-889	Zimmerman	Alvena
B-246	Ziegenfuss	James	B-1505	Zimmerman	Alwin
B-673	Ziegenfuss	James	B-366	Zimmerman	Catherine
B-932	Ziegenfuss	James	B-737	Zimmerman	Catherine Ellen
B-281	Ziegenfuss	Joel	M-445	Zimmerman	Catherine Ellen
B-287	Ziegenfuss	Joel	D-1315	Zimmerman	Charles
B-589	Ziegenfuss	Joel	B-1814	Zimmerman	Charles
B-688	Ziegenfuss	Joel	M-474	Zimmerman	Charles Alfred
B-612	Ziegenfuss	Korah	B-1424	Zimmerman	Effie
M-39	Ziegenfuss	Levi	B-258	Zimmerman	Ellen
B-932	Ziegenfuss	Lewis	B-513	Zimmerman	Ellen
M-519	Ziegenfuss	Lewis	B-1016	Zimmerman	Ellen
M-1125	Ziegenfuss	Lillie A	M-201	Zimmerman	Ellen
B-373	Ziegenfuss	Lyman	M-805	Zimmerman	Emma
B-627	Ziegenfuss	Lyman	M-812	Zimmerman	Franklin E
B-873	Ziegenfuss	Lyman	B-365	Zimmerman	Gideon
M-520	Ziegenfuss	Martin	B-366	Zimmerman	Gideon
D-354	Ziegenfuss	Mary	B-1645	Zimmerman	Harvey
B-1003	Ziegenfuss	Mary	B-1828	Zimmerman	Ida
B-489	Ziegenfuss	Mary Maria	B-1663	Zimmerman	Ira
B-68	Ziegenfuss	Nathan	D-1098	Zimmerman	Jacob
B-208	Ziegenfuss	Nathan	D-701	Zimmerman	John
B-612	Ziegenfuss	Nathan	B-791	Zimmerman	John
B-791	Ziegenfuss	Nathan	B-1220	Zimmerman	Korah
B-873	Ziegenfuss	Nathan	B-168	Zimmerman	Lucy Ann
M-260	Ziegenfuss	Nathan	B-1570	Zimmerman	Mame
B-242	Ziegenfuss	Rebecca	D-883	Zimmerman	Maria
B-897	Ziegenfuss	Rebecca	D-961	Zimmerman	Maria
D-403	Ziegenfuss	Sally	B-791	Zimmerman	Nathan
B-246	Ziegenfuss	Samuel	B-1424	Zimmerman	Nathan
B-52	Ziegenfuss	William	B-1505	Zimmerman	Nathan
B-612	Ziegenfuss	William A	B-1570	Zimmerman	Nathan
B-930	Ziegenfuss	Wlliam A	B-1645	Zimmerman	Nathan
M-919	Ziegler	Amandus A	B-1710	Zimmerman	Nathan
M-1093	Ziegler	Amandus C	B-1814	Zimmerman	Nathan
B-1106	Ziegler	Clara	B-1828	Zimmerman	Nathan
M-924	Ziegler	Elias	M-663	Zimmerman	Nathan
B-1365	Ziegler	Henry	D-1202	Zimmerman	Sarah
B-1500	Zimmerman	Sarah	B-1959	Zindel	Mary Henrietta
B-1085	Zimmerman	Sarah R	D-482	Zink	Jacob
B-909	Zimmerman	Sarah Rebecca	M-104	Zink	Tilghman
M-478	Zimmerman	Sarah Rebecca	B-17	Zone	Charles
B-1072	Zimmerman	Susanna	B-17	Zone	Joseph
M-878	Zimmerman	Viola	B-296	Zone	Joseph
B-1710	Zimmerman	Warren	B-296	Zone	Rosa
B-365	Zimmerman	William	M-135	Zundle	Henry
B-1514	Zimmerman	Willmore	B-87	Zundle	Margaret
M-1177	Zindel	Mary H			

www.ingramcontent.com/pod-product-compliance
Lightning Source LLC
Chambersburg PA
CBHW082038230426
43670CB00016B/2704